THE PSYCHODYNAMICS
OF PATIENT CARE

Hospitalization
148-171

Dignity
Assist in grooming (image)
Privacy
Rt to know (info)

34

THE PSYCHODYNAMICS OF PATIENT CARE

Lawrence H. Schwartz, M.D.
Clinical Associate Professor
Department of Psychiatry
University of Washington

Jane Linker Schwartz, R.N., M.S.W.

PRENTICE-HALL, INC., Englewood Cliffs, N.J.

© 1972 by
PRENTICE-HALL, INC.
Englewood Cliffs, New Jersey

All rights reserved. No part of this book may be reproduced in any way or by any means without permission in writing from the publisher.

10 9 8 7 6 5 4 3 2 1

ISBN: 0-13-732578-9 (P)
 0-13-732586-X (C)

Library of Congress Catalog Card Number: 75-38245
Printed in the United States of America

PRENTICE-HALL INTERNATIONAL, INC., *London*
PRENTICE-HALL OF AUSTRALIA, PTY. LTD., *Sydney*
PRENTICE-HALL OF CANADA, LTD., *Toronto*
PRENTICE-HALL OF INDIA PRIVATE LIMITED, *New Delhi*
PRENTICE-HALL OF JAPAN, INC., *Tokyo*

For our parents,
and our children,
Karen, Joel, and David

ACKNOWLEDGMENTS

We would like to express our appreciation to the faculty of the University of Washington School of Nursing for their cooperation in helping to bring this book to completion. The nurse-author, who is doing graduate work to further her research in patient care, owes a special debt of gratitude to her faculty advisor, Dr. Katherine Hoffman. Dean Madeleine Leininger and Dr. Jacqueline Holt Vandeman have been most generous with their suggestions and encouragement.

The discussion of psychoanalytic aspects of children and youth owes much to the insightful contributions offered by Dr. Edith Buxbaum, who shared with us her wide range of knowledge and experience as a psychoanalyst and educator.

We are most grateful to Mrs. Arthur Bestor for her editing and for preparation of the Index. Her suggestions regarding content and form, as well as her tact and good humor, have helped much to make this book possible. Mrs. Leonard Lang also gave invaluable editing assistance in organizing and proofreading this manuscript.

Dr. Dorothy White, Visiting Professor at the University of Washington School of Nursing, and Dr. and Mrs. George Bluestone have encouraged us from the outset and we wish to express our appreciation for their continued interest.

We would also like to acknowledge the cooperation of Dr. Roy Wahle and Mrs. George Douglas, Director of the Bellevue Community College School of Nursing, for allowing us to work with students in their nursing program, and to students with whom we shared this material.

Mr. Thomas Robert Stevenson, Mrs. Leonard Banos, and Miss Barbara

Bloome, students at the University of Washington, were most helpful as part-time assistants in our research. Mrs. David Barnes, our secretary, has been especially devoted to our task of preparing the manuscript. Her loyal assistance and patience during the many months of this project is most appreciated.

Throughout our work on this book, we have received unfailing support and kindness from Albert K. Belskie, Science Editor of Prentice-Hall.

The final selection of readings for inclusion in our book was especially difficult because of the large number of excellent articles which were generously made available to us by publishers and authors alike. Space limitations compelled us to omit many fine publications. Some of these have been referred to in the text while others are mentioned in the bibliographies.

Our thanks are extended to the authors and publishers who generously granted us permission to reprint articles from the following journals: *Nursing Forum, American Journal of Nursing, Nursing Outlook, Nursing Clinics of North America, Bulletin of the Menninger Clinic, Medical Insight, Psychosomatics, Hospital Progress, New England Journal of Medicine, Annals of Internal Medicine, The American Journal of Psychiatry, Psychiatry Digest,* and *R.N.*

We also want to express our gratitude to the American Psychiatric Association for permission to publish excerpts from their Glossary, as well as to the publishers Lea and Febiger for allowing us to reprint "Developmental Schema Charts" by Dr. Milton J. E. Senn and Dr. Albert J. Solnit from their book *Problems in Child Behavior and Development.*

Finally, our deep appreciation and love go to our children who shared with us the variety of experiences we encountered while this manuscript was in process.

CONTENTS

Foreword   xi

Preface   xiii

1. The Nurse and Her Patient   1

Introduction, 1
Transference Elements in the Nurse-Patient Relationship, 9
Suggested Readings, 16
Discussion of Selected Readings, 19
   To Nurse and to Nurture, Bruno Bettelheim, 20
   Listening with any Ear at All, Hedi Freund, 29
   The Invisible Patient, Edward T. Auer, 36

2. Introduction to Psychoanalytic Concepts   42

Preconscious and Unconscious States of Mind, 47
The Divisions of the Mind, 48
Suggested Readings on the Life of Sigmund Freud, 52
Suggested Readings on Psychoanalysis, 52

3. Infancy   54

Early Infancy, 54
Later Infancy, 77
Suggested Readings on Infancy, 86
Discussion of Selected Readings, 89
Developmental Schema Chart, Milton J. E. Senn, Albert J. Solnit, 90
   Maria, the Hungry Baby, Thelma Ingles, 93
   Working with Mothers and Babies Who Fail to Thrive,
     Julina P. Rhymes, 99

4. Pre-School Children   111

The Toddler Stage, 111
The Toddler in the Hospital, 127
The Child from 3–6, 135
Oedipal Stage, 136
Suggested Readings on the Pre-School Child, 141
Discussion of Selected Readings, 145
Developmental Schema Chart, Milton J. E. Senn and Albert J. Solnit, 146
   Reactions of Children to Hospital Experience, Florence Erickson, 148
   The Hospitalized Child—His Emotional Needs, Edward A. Mason, 157

5. Middle Childhood   175

School Adjustment Problems, 176
Preparing for Adult Roles, 177
Repression in Middle Childhood, 180
Discussion of Selected Readings, 183
Developmental Schema Chart, Milton J. E. Senn, Albert J. Solnit, 183
   Responses of Three Girls to Burn Injuries and Hospitalization,
     Carolyn P. Stoll, 186

6. Adolescence   196

Suggested Readings, 205
Discussion of Selected Readings, 210
Developmental Schema Chart, Milton J. E. Senn, Albert J. Solnit, 211
   The Hospitalized Adolescent, Mary Lou Byers, 214
   Predictable Problems of Hospitalized Adolescents, Herbert L. Meyer, 219

7. Adult Stage — 226

Reactions to Illness, 227
Psychosomatic Medicine, 243
Suggested Readings on the Adult and Illness, 250
Discussion of Readings, 254
  The Impact of Mastectomy, Jeanne C. Quint, 256
  A Life Setting Conducive to Illness: The Giving-Up–Given Up Complex, George L. Engel, 266
  The Irony of the ICU, Howard P. Rome, 275
  Defenses Against Anxiety in the Nurse–Patient Relationship, Margaret Aasterud, 279
  Cancer, Emotions, and Nurses, Samuel C. Klagsbrun, 294

8. Middle Age — 305

Suggested Readings, 310
Discussion of Selected Readings, 311
  Emotional Problems (During Middle Age), Francis J. Braceland, 312
  The Crisis of Middle Age, Judd Marmor, 318

9. Old Age — 322

Aging in Other Cultures, 322
General Needs of the Aging Person, 323
The Family and the Aged, 324
Chronic Illness and Aging, 326
Abnormal Psychological Reactions to Aging, 329
Care for the Aged Mentally Ill Patient, 332
Emotional Health and Physical Functioning, 333
Need for Hospitalization, 334
Psychodynamics of Old Age, 335
The Nurse, the Doctor, and the Aged Patient, 336
Planning for the Aged Patient, 337
Suggested Reading, 338
Discussion of Selected Readings, 341
  Of Time and the Woman, Marya Mannes, 342
  The Loneliness of Old Age, Mary Louise Conti, 348

10. Death, Grief, and Mourning — 354

Communication with the Dying Patient, 356
Impending Death, 356
Support and Awareness: The Nurse's Role with Dying Patients, 358
Impact of Death on the Family, 360
Grief and the Work of Mourning, 364
Normal Grief, 365
Usefulness of Ritual, 366
Pathological Grief, 369
The Bereaved Child, 369
Grief Reactions in Later Life, 371
Suggested Readings, 371
   Grief and Grieving, George L. Engel, 376
   A Time to Die, Wilma R. Lewis, 388

Epilogue — 401

Glossary — 403

Index — 413

FOREWORD

Within our American culture, the strong desire to understand man's behavior from a humanistic and scientific perspective continues to pervade the thoughts of many students, scholars, therapists, and researchers of human behavior. Among the groups desiring such a comprehensive understanding of human behavior is the professional nurse, who has been privileged through time to have a direct personal relationship to people who suffer a variety of life-threatening illnesses. The nurse recognizes this privilege and the concomitant responsibilities. She continues to find ways to understand the many intrapsychic and extrapsychic forces that influence the patients' behavior so that her nursing will be effective.

One of the schools of behavioral thought that continues to offer rich insights into human behavior is the psychoanalytic school. Psychoanalytic and psychodynamic concepts of behavior have challenged the student and practitioners' modes of thinking, feeling, and action. This frame of reference has been used by the authors of this book as an important means to examine nurse-patient relationships. The authors, a professional nurse and a psychiatrist, have sensitively and comprehensively presented to their readers a number of psychoanalytical concepts relevant to the dynamics of human development, nurse-patient relationships, and dynamic nursing care practices. These concepts are presented in a direct, practical, and interesting manner so that the nurse can understand them without difficulty. Special effort has been made to correlate theoretical concepts with practical nursing solutions. For example, the basic defense mechanisms that protect, guide, and serve man are presented clearly and applied to patient situations from birth to old age. Psychodynamic concepts that explain the development of man's behavior are closely related to common nursing problems. This content should be exceedingly valuable to the nurse and offers important guidelines for determining appropriate nursing interventions.

Throughout the book, the authors descriptively present the nurses' reaction to common patient behavior and provide psychodynamic explanations of the behavior. The authors' warm sensitivity to patient behavior is combined with a deep appreciation of the significant role of the nurse in helping patients. Most importantly, the book offers some practical and straightforward explanations of human behavior according to age and health problems. These concepts reveal the artistic skill of the authors in making psychodynamic concepts of human behavior come alive for the reader. It is evident that the authors' past professional and life experience and systematic observations of human behavior have contributed greatly to the professional richness and substance of this book.

Another important feature of this book is the absence of major language hurdles and highly theoretical concepts. The authors have made a deliberate effort to simplify all psychoanalytical concepts and to relate them to practical clinical situations. Moreover, the highly relevant articles help further to clarify and extend the readers' knowledge about the psychodynamics of human behavior.

With the current trend in nursing to have the nurse become a significant therapeutic figure in the patient's life so that she can deal with behavior in an effective way, this book should prove to be exceedingly useful as a reference book for undergraduate students. Nursing students in diploma, associate, and baccalaureate degree programs will undoubtedly recognize that this book provides a clear picture of the dynamics of human behavior. Undoubtedly, the users of this book will be able to give to others because they have gained a deep and meaningful understanding of man's behavior under stress throughout the life cycle.

MADELEINE LEININGER, Ph.D., R.N.
Professor of Nursing and Lecturer
of Anthropology
Dean, School of Nursing
University of Washington
Seattle, Washington

PREFACE

The nurse–patient relationship is one of the most essential ingredients of nursing care. For many patients, illness and hospitalization represent stressful or critical life experiences. The nurse is frequently with the patient when he is in deep trouble, burdened by some personal crisis. He expects the nurse, as a "helping person," to accept and understand his feelings and reactions. One of our objectives is to increase the nurse's knowledge of psychological factors affecting the patient's equilibrium so that she can manage her relationship with patients.

Certain theoretical formulations regarding human behavior can clarify the nurse's reactions, as well as those of her patients. Mental health professionals have strongly supported findings indicating that a psychodynamic approach can be of crucial importance in contributing to our understanding of individuals and social institutions. Erik Erikson's studies in the field of identity have extensive implications for helping us understand the individual in a mass society.[1]

Historically, the first concepts one could call "psychodynamic"—that is, dealing with the development and interaction of conscious and unconscious mental factors—grew out of certain discoveries of psychoanalysis. Many of these concepts have been accepted in our culture and are now thought of as "common sense." Our purpose is to discuss with nurses some of the discoveries and contributions of psychoanalytic psychology; moreover, since we believe that psychodynamic knowledge offers a sound foundation for

[1] Erik H. Erikson. *Childhood and Society.* New York: W. W. Norton & Company, Inc., 1963.

studying and understanding human behavior, we are attempting here to apply some of these concepts to general nursing care. This approach can provide the nurse with a scientific and humanistic point of view in her theoretical and clinical work.

Today, the medical profession and the general public recognize psychoanalysis as one form of psychotherapy. Fewer people are familiar with it as a research method for the study of mental life. In addition, psychoanalysis refers to a substantial body of observations, inferences, and theoretical concepts pertaining to the mental processes. Our focus, in this text, is not on the therapeutic implications of psychoanalysis but on its contributions to our knowledge of human growth and development, as well as of normal and abnormal behavior.

Psychoanalytic concepts have significantly influenced modern psychiatry and medicine. "Dynamic psychiatry" is the outgrowth of the impact of psychoanalysis upon the field of psychiatry.[2] The specialty of psychiatric nursing first introduced these theories into the nursing field. Psychiatric nursing textbooks are frequently psychodynamically oriented, and articles in nursing journals on anxiety, separation, regression, autonomy, loneliness depression and so forth, often reflect familiar concepts originating from psychoanalytic psychology.[3] Crisis theory is also indebted to psychoanalysis as a basis for understanding human problems.[4]

The psychoanalytic trend in anthropology has led to a cross-fertilization of ideas within psychiatry referred to as social psychiatry. Psychoanalytic contributions to psychosomatic medicine has given an added dimension to our understanding of physical responses of the human organism to emotional problems and societal stresses.

[2] Franz Alexander and Helen Ross (eds.). *Dynamic Psychiatry*. Chicago: University of Chicago Press, 1952.

[3] Margaret Aasterud. "Defenses Against Anxiety in the Nurse–Patient Relationship." *Nursing Forum*. Summer, 1962. Pp. 35–39.

Florence Blake. "In Quest of Hope and Autonomy." *Nursing Forum*. Winter, 1961–1962. Pp. 9–32.

Charles K. Hofling, Madeline M. Leininger, and Elizabeth A. Bregg. *Basic Psychiatric Concepts in Nursing*. New York: J. B. Lippincott Company, 1967.

Marion E. Kalkman. *Introduction to Psychiatric Nursing*. New York: McGraw-Hill Book Company, 1950.

Ruth V. Matheney and Mary Topalis. *Psychiatric Nursing*. St. Louis: The C. V. Mosby Co., 1965.

Dorothy Mereness. *Psychiatric Nursing—A Book of Readings*. Vols. 1, 2. Dubuque, Iowa: William C. Brown Company, Publishers, 1966.

Jeanette Nehren and Naomi Gilliam. "Separation Anxiety." *American Journal of Nursing*. January, 1965. Pp. 109–12.

Hildegard Peplau. *Interpersonal Relations in Nursing*. New York: G. P. Putnam's Sons, 1952.

[4] Howard J. Parad (ed.). *Crisis Intervention: Selected Readings*. New York: Family Service Association of America, 1965.

For over one hundred years, the intention of nursing education has been to produce a practitioner with something more than mere technical skills. Today, in our fast-paced and highly mechanized society, the nurse can easily and unintentionally relinquish her human compassion to scientific and technical knowledge. Technology has increasingly intruded into the nurse-patient relationship. The psychodynamic approach offers a way to restore and emphasize the human dimension to nursing care and to refocus the nurse's attention on patients' needs and emotional reactions.

Over the past decade, nursing has increasingly made use of mental health concepts. Nevertheless, there is sometimes a vague, unformed quality in our attempts to adopt preventive programs and new ways of thinking about patient care. Psychoanalytic concepts can encourage dynamic rather than static attitudes; therefore, mastery of these concepts is necessary for promoting mental health and reducing rates of mental disorders.

The direction of our efforts has also been to point up the complexity of providing modern nursing care in our mass society. Great social issues such as war, racial injustice, poverty, and environmental pollution have caused health workers to recognize our state of rapid flux and tumultuous change. Among other problems, the quality of health services is threatened by the depersonalization of nurses and patients that comes with large organizations and institutions.

Since this book is based on a psychoanalytic frame of reference, it includes discussions of child development and provides clinical case examples of normal as well as sick children. A large section is devoted to this area, since knowledge of child development is basic to understanding human behavior at all ages. Learning professional nursing care encompasses the study of conditions that influence a child's health and development, and psychoanalytic research during the past quarter of a century has provided significant evidence that the quality of psychological care a child receives in his earlier years is of vital importance to his psychic growth.

Practical as well as theoretical knowledge regarding child development has frequently been provided by psychoanalysts who specialize in studying children in institutions, at home, and in psychiatric treatment. It is through their contributions that we have learned much about normal as well as disturbed children.[5]

---

[5] Anna Freud and Dorothy Burlingham. *Infants Without Families: The Case For and Against Residential Nurseries*. New York: International Universities Press, Inc., 1944.
August Aichhorn. *Wayward Youth*. New York: The Viking Press, Inc., 1935.
Bruno Bettelheim. *Love Is Not Enough*. New York: The Free Press, 1950.
———. *Truants from Life*. New York: The Free Press, 1955.
Edith Buxbaum. *Troubled Children in a Troubled World*. New York: International Universities Press, Inc., 1970.

xviii *Preface*

Mental health concepts are presented throughout the text along with human development and clinical problems. The concepts concern the adaptive and defensive structures that form a basic part of human personality. Definitions and discussions of such subjects as unconscious mental functioning, defense mechanisms, psychic conflict, anxiety reactions, and transference elements are dealt with for the purpose of helping the nurse observe their occurrence in the nurse-patient relationship. Moreover, the nurse needs to identify, define, and understand the elements of her own behavior that are built into the professional role.

To supplement the text, we have selected articles primarily from nursing and medical literature that demonstrate facets of human experience with illness and illuminate the professional relationship of the nurse with the patient. These articles are discussed from a psychoanalytic point of view in order to offer the student a psychosocial and psychodynamic dimension to nursing care.

The format of this book is such that it can be used in conjunction with standard clinical nursing texts to help teach psychological concepts that are becoming an integral part of many basic nursing programs. It can also be used as a handbook for nurses who wish to review, organize, and extend their knowledge of psychodynamic findings in nursing care. It may be helpful for supplemental reading in psychiatric nursing. Hopefully, as nursing care becomes more community oriented, it can be used in conjunction with new courses as an instructional tool for students working with families inside and outside the hospital setting.

During the past twenty-five years, instructors in psychiatric nursing

―――. *Your Child Makes Sense.* New York: International Universities Press, Inc., 1949.

Margaret Ribble. *The Rights of Infants.* New York: Columbia University Press, 1943.

David Levy. *Maternal Overprotection.* New York: W. W. Norton & Company, Inc., 1966.

Selma H. Fraiberg. *The Magic Years.* New York: Charles Scribner's Sons, 1959.

Fritz Redl. *Children Who Hate.* New York: The Free Press, 1951.

―――. *Controls from Within.* New York: The Free Press, 1952.

Melanie Klein. *The Psychoanalysis of Children.* New York: Grove Press, Inc., 1932.

Sally Provence and Rose Lipton. *Infants in Institutions.* New York: International Universities Press, Inc., 1962.

Milton J. E. Senn and Albert J. Solnit. *Problems in Child Behavior and Development.* Philadelphia: Lea & Febiger, 1968.

René Spitz. "Hospitalism: An Inquiry into the Genesis of Psychiatric Conditions in Early Childhood." *The Psychoanalytic Study of the Child.* Vol. 1. New York: International Universities Press, Inc., 1945. Pp. 53–74.

―――. "Hospitalism: A Follow-up Report." *The Psychoanalytic Study of the Child.* Vol. 2. New York: International Universities Press, Inc., 1946. Pp. 113–17.

―――. "Anaclitic Depression: An Inquiry into the Genesis of Psychiatric Conditions in Early Childhood." *The Psychoanalytic Study of the Child.* Vol. 2. New York: International Universities Press, Inc., 1946. Pp. 313–42.

have taught psychoanalytic concepts along with other personality theories. Psychoanalytic theory has also proven to be uniquely suitable in providing psychiatric nurses with a deeper understanding of the meaning of the "one-to-one" therapeutic relationship. Psychiatric nurses first became involved in studying the reactions of nurses and patients in this relationship because the nature of their work usually provided them with the opportunity to focus primarily on the patient's emotional, rather than physical, problems.

In working with psychiatrists, psychiatric nurses were provided with additional insight regarding the meaning of a "therapeutic relationship." They were trained to gain some awareness of their feelings and responses toward patients, as well as to appreciate the feelings and responses of their patients. Furthermore, part of the training of a psychiatric nurse was guidance in understanding and control of this therapeutic relationship. For the most part, however, teaching and texts in this field have primarily focused on psychopathology and psychiatric treatment.

The most recent task of the psychiatric nurse is to assist in integrating this information for application to general nursing care. This book is intended as a response to an increasing need for information, courses, and texts focusing on the life cycle and the psychosocial aspects of personality development for nurses. While this volume is designed for nurses, it may also be of interest to others who help the patient cope with stress and physical illness.

The ultimate objective is to contribute to the understanding of certain dynamic components of nursing care. By identifying specific familiar elements within the nurse-patient relationship, the nurse may systematize her knowledge and use it in order to be of maximum help to her patient.

As nurses participate in research projects individually or as part of multidisciplinary teams, a fuller understanding of psychoanalytic psychology is a significant preparation for their investigations of the influence of psychosocial factors on patient care. For example, we have included within our bibliography reports on the research in nursing by Jacqueline Holt Vandeman and Florence Erickson. In addition, we have provided other examples of nurses working with psychiatrists and social workers in interdisciplinary teams that use psychoanalytic concepts for their frame of reference.[6] Thesi Bergmann, a psychoanalyst, acknowledges the assistance of

---

[6] Jacqueline Holt Vandeman. "Children's Recall of a Preschool Age Hospital Experience After an Interval of Five Years." In *Communicating Nursing Research—The Research Critique*. Marjorie Batey (ed.). Boulder, Colorado: Western Interstate Commission for Higher Education, University East Campus, July, 1968. Pp. 56–70.

Florence H. Erickson. *Play Interviews for Four-Year-Old Hospitalized Children*. Monograph of the Society for Research in Child Development, Inc. Vol. XXIII, Serial No. 69. No. 3. Child Development Publications. Yellow Springs, Ohio: The Antioch Press, 1958.

nurses in contributing to her research on children in hospitals.[7]

Nursing education and practice require a direct confrontation with all phases of life. In her clinical experience, the nursing student soon witnesses human birth and death. She also quickly comes into contact with people of various ages and from every socioeconomic and cultural background. Nursing educators see today that scientific theory can assist nurses in providing a unifying conceptual framework within which they can carry out clinical practice.

Nursing education has become less didactic and more informal, encouraging students to observe and discuss their own clinical observations and experiences. In this text, we recommend the case study method of approaching the understanding and learning related to the psychological aspect of patient care. Students and graduates should be encouraged to discuss their own clinical cases in order to apply directly the information offered in this text. In addition references at the end of each chapter provide more detailed sources for further study.

The first chapters of the book consider infancy, childhood, and adolescence. The next sections take up the early and middle phases of adulthood. In the last section of the book, we explore the emotional aspects of aging and the dilemmas faced by the patient, by his family, and by the nurse, when faced with dying and death.

Since this work represents an interdisciplinary effort, we are indebted to the fields of nursing, social work, medicine, psychiatry, and psychoanalysis. The opportunity for us to cross the traditional boundaries between schools and disciplines has been an educational experience for us both.

We recognize that many behavioral scientists feel that "the age of the individual has passed." Much emphasis has been placed on group behavior and on the role of the individual in the larger society. The informed nurse is exposed to a variety of psychological and social theories, such as role theory, communication theory, and behaviorism. Each approach has adherents and critics; each has made useful contributions. In this text, we have used psychoanalysis and its applications without attempting to delineate contrasting points of view.

Psychoanalytic theory, like all other theories, has its limitations, since it has not been completely explored and developed. Just as Freud conceded,

"As you know, we have never prided ourselves on the completeness and finality of our knowledge and capacity. We are just as ready now as we were

---

Julina P. Rhymes. "Working with Mothers and Babies Who Fail to Thrive," *American Journal of Nursing*. September, 1966. Pp. 1972–76.

[7] Thesi Bergmann, *Children in the Hospital*. New York: International Universities Press, Inc., 1966.

earlier to admit imperfections of our understanding, to learn new things and to alter our methods in any way that can improve them." [8]

Nevertheless, it is our hope that the nurse can use this approach to help her develop her own critical judgment regarding those methods and theories that best serve her in responding to patients' needs. Nurse-patient interaction is a "face-to-face" relationship, but it must also be experienced as a mind-to-mind and heart-to-heart relationship if it is to be a mutually gratifying experience for the nurse and her patient, and if the nurse is to continue to play an essential role in patient care.

LAWRENCE H. SCHWARTZ
JANE LINKER SCHWARTZ
Seattle, Washington

---

[8] Sigmund Freud. "Lines of Advance in Psycho-Analytic Therapy." In *The Standard Edition of the Complete Psychological Works of Sigmund Freud.* James Strachey (ed.). Vol. XVII. London: The Hogarth Press Ltd., 1957. P. 159.

chapter one

THE NURSE AND HER PATIENT

Introduction

Today, the field of nursing is in a state of rapid transition brought about by the advancing technology of twentieth-century medicine. In response to many changes in hospital and community situations, nursing education is reaching for help outside the field of medical research. The century-old affiliation of nursing with medicine is now being extended to include collaboration with the social and behavioral sciences.

Although this incorporation of the behavioral sciences into nursing is a relatively new development, nurses have long been aware of the psychological complexities associated with illness and patient care. Florence Nightingale's *Notes on Nursing* (1859), the first clinical textbook for nurses, shows a sensitive awareness of the whole patient. She sees him as a person with an illness, confronted with an entirely new set of environmental expectations. As she notes:

Volumes are now written and spoken upon the effect of the mind upon the body. Much of it is true. But I wish a little more was thought of the effect of the body on the mind. You who believe yourselves overwhelmed with anxieties, but are able every day to walk up Regent Street, or out in the country, to take your meals with others in other rooms, etc., etc., you little know how much your anxieties are thereby lightened; you little know how intensified they become to those who can have no change; how the very walls of their sick rooms seem hung with their cares; how the ghosts of their troubles haunt their beds;

how impossible it is for them to escape from a pursuing thought without some help from variety.[1]

With the assumption that nursing care should be centered on patients, rather than primarily on treatment and disease, nursing education is currently based on a recognition of the interrelationship of the social, emotional, and pathological factors that influence health and illness. In our agreement with the belief that nursing care is incomplete if it is only procedure-oriented, the emphasis in this text is on the "total" patient experience and the nurse-patient relationship.

In the article "To Nurse and to Nurture," Bruno Bettelheim states, "Rightly or wrongly, the public image of the nurse is that of an efficient and obedient helper of the physician, who shows little concern for the emotional needs of the patient." Most nurses would reject this view of themselves. Initially, at least, the outstanding motivating factor in choosing nursing as a career usually is the wish to help others. Nursing educators also try to select students who they feel are warm, concerned, and interested. Bettelheim adds:

> I believe that the true virtue, the true calling of the nurse, consists . . . in the two aspects contained in the very name of the profession: to nurse and to nurture; to feed the body and to nurture the soul.[2]

Nursing education and clinical experience afford each student the opportunity to view segments of human life from birth to death. The nurse's professional responsibilities bring her into uniquely close personal contact with people who are either physically ill or injured.

For the student or graduate nurse actively engaged in patient care, the nature of the work is stimulating and challenging, with each day unlike the one before. Tensions can arise, however, from a constant need to accommodate oneself to a variety of intense situations in a short span of time. The nurse sets her pace and plans her day in response to many patients' needs, not all of which can always be met.

As Hedi Freund notes:

> All who work with people in pain and trouble must steel themselves against sentimentalism. As with physicians, so it is with the nurse. She must keep calm in the face of pain, excitement, and panic. But there are many times when her "professional attitude" becomes an armor that permits her to go about her duties unaffected by pity, concern, or love.[3]

---

[1] Florence Nightingale. *Notes on Nursing.* Philadelphia: J. B. Lippincott Company, 1946. P. 34.

[2] Bruno Bettelheim. "To Nurse and to Nurture." *Nursing Forum.* Summer, 1962. Reproduced in this volume, pp. 20 to 29. See p. 21.

[3] Hedi Freund. "Listening with Any Ear at All." *American Journal of Nursing.* August, 1969. P. 1653. Reproduced in this volume, pp. 29 to 36. See p. 35.

The student soon recognizes the commitment of nursing service in the hospital facility and its need to provide round-the-clock observation and care for all patients. Menzies noted, "The nursing service, therefore, bears the full, immediate, and concentrated impact of stresses arising from patient care."[4]

Sickness or disability places the usually healthy person in the unaccustomed role of "patient." Once a person assumes this role, society exempts him from many of his routine social responsibilities. He is often placed in an enforced state of childlike dependency as a result of his illness and the care that he receives, with an intensification of feelings and increase in psychological stress. The nurse may observe the patient express feelings of appreciation, affection, and gratitude, or equally strong feelings of anger, depression, fear, and despair.

Again, Florence Nightingale understood the strain of illness when she commented:

> I think it is a very common error among the well to think that "with a little more self control" the sick might, if they chose, "dismiss painful thoughts" which "aggravate their disease," etc. Believe me, almost any sick person, who behaves decently well, exercises more self control every moment of his day than you will ever know until you are sick yourself. Almost every step that crosses his room is painful to him; almost every thought that crosses his brain is painful to him; and if he can speak without being savage, and look without being unpleasant, he is exercising self control . . . .[5]

Apprehension, uncertainty, waiting, expectation, fear of surprise, do a patient more harm than any exertion. Remember, he is face to face with his enemy all the time, internally wrestling with him, having long imaginary conversations with him. You are thinking of something else.[6]

In redefining the scope of the nurse's tasks in patient care, the uniqueness of this situation must be taken into consideration. Bedside nurses often deal with the intimate details of patients' bodily functions, which laymen consider either embarrassing or unattractive. Many patients who "prepare" for their doctor's visit may feel more free to "be themselves" with the nurse, especially with one directly responsible for their physical care. As a result, certain patients will wish to discuss questions and problems with the nurse that they will not mention to the doctor out of fear, ignorance, or embarrassment.

Encounters between nurses and patients usually take place in the tradi-

---

[4] Isabel E. Menzies. *The Functioning of Social Systems as a Defense Against Anxiety*, a Report on a Study on the Nursing Service of a General Hospital. Tavistock Pamphlet No. 3. London, England, 1961. P. 5.
[5] Nightingale. *Notes on Nursing*. P. 35.
[6] *Ibid*. P. 22.

4 The Nurse and Her Patient

tional setting of hospitals or clinics. Such surroundings are familiar and even reassuring for the nurse, but not for the patient. Hospital environment and procedures are often strange and frightening for the incoming patient, contributing additional emotional stress to the physical and psychological discomfort from which he is already suffering.

Sometimes, in addition to the stress of physical illness, the patient may suffer from "culture shock." We use this term to describe "the effect that immersion in a strange culture has on the unprepared visitor."[7] The patient's inability to cope with the hospital environment may be likened to the feeling of an American living abroad in an unfamiliar place, who, at times, may experience frustration and confusion without the use of his native language and his usual psychological cues. The patient may regard the medical jargon so frequently used by hospital personnel as such an unfamiliar language that it can cause a breakdown in communication, contributing to the patient's disorientation, his misunderstanding of procedures, and his inability to cope with his illness.

The hospital environment sharply differs from the patient's home and work setting. There are so many different cues to react to that the radically new circumstances may make him feel more like a victim than a patient. On the other hand, the hospital forms an important and familiar part of the nurse's social landscape. Much of what she learns during her training is centered on her organization of orderly or mechanical procedures, the purpose of which is to achieve predictable, controllable results in patients.

Is it any wonder that the nurse and the patient may find themselves at seeming cross purposes as they together confront the patient's physical disease? The matter-of-fact instructions given by doctors and nurses may seem too businesslike or even callous to the patient. Hospital timetables, machinery, routine, and hurried pace rob the patient of a good bit of his feeling of individuality.

Not only the patient, but also the student may wish to revolt against the new technology. The basic concern of the patient is that even while his life is being saved, he lacks personalized care; the student, on the other hand, complains that the program isn't sufficiently individualized for his interests. The basic nursing student sometimes also complains about not being treated as an individual. Nursing schools, particularly at the graduate level, have greatly broadened their variety of courses in order to give the student more free range of choice and individual consideration.

As a nurse broadens her own outlook, she can become increasingly aware of feelings and attitudes implicit in the nurse-patient relationship. She can appreciate why many of the so-called "little things" she does for patients often assume great significance for them.

---

[7] Alvin Toffler. *Future Shock.* New York: Random House, 1970. P. 12.

Despite the stress of physical illness, the patient is expected to conform to certain role expectations in order to "cooperate" with those who treat and care for him, including nurses. Meanwhile, there are role expectations for nurses as well. Reciprocal interaction between the nurse and patient implies a relationship in which each party has preconceived expectations of the other.

Part of the stress of the nurse's role stems from the fact that she must interact effectively not only with the patient and his family, but with his physician, with hospital administrators, with other nurses, and with paramedical personnel. Since these relationships can make major demands on the nurse's time, energy, and skills, they place her under considerable strain. What actually happens to nurses as they are asked again and again to assume an intermediary position in which they must translate the doctor's "orders" to the patient and interpret the patient's physical and emotional response to the doctor?

The nurse's behavior can skillfully bridge the gap between the patient and the hospital environment. Stress may bring the personal problems of a patient to the attention of the staff, and the nurse often is needed to share the burden. Dorothy W. Smith portrays one type of problem the nurse may encounter:

> . . . People differ in the extent to which loss of privacy distresses them, and in the type of exposure that is most threatening to them. For some, physical exposure may be especially threatening; for others, the need to discuss personal affairs may be more so. However, loss of privacy in either of these ways has the potential of causing humiliation and anxiety. In fact, some individuals are so disturbed by the exposure of personal concerns to others that, once the crisis is past, they may be angry at the person who saw them exposed, or they may even push the experience out of awareness. . . . Sharing the patient's confidences presents many challenges to one's judgment and discretion. It is a privilege for the nurse to receive a patient's confidences, but it can also be a burden and, sometimes, a heavy one.[8]

Reactions of the patient to illness and hospitalization present the nurse with a wide variety of behavior. She may observe awesome displays of courage, dignity, and fortitude in the face of extreme suffering, or, on the other hand, childlike outbursts of fear and feelings of helplessness in response to minor procedures or symptoms. Inconsistent behavior is far from uncommon.

The dignity and worth of the individual are frequently mentioned in nursing literature as important for the nurse to remember. Ideally, the nurse is expected to accept the patient as he is, despite a natural preference for

---

[8] Dorothy W. Smith. "Patienthood and Its Threat to Privacy." *American Journal of Nursing*. Vol. 69, No. 3 (March, 1961). Pp. 508–13.

some patients over others. Many times patients behave in ways repugnant to some nurses. What is acceptable behavior to one nurse may not be to another, depending on her own sense of values and the way she views her patients. Hedi Freund writes:

> When he becomes a patient, the human being asks for complete acceptance of his illness as well as his personality, no matter how bizarre. As a sick being, the patient craves permission to become infantile, dependent, and demanding without punishment or isolation.[9] Paralyzed by fear, in constant need of reassurance, the asker of innumerable questions, the patient most in need of human contact is quickly labeled a "pest" and shunned. Only if he can learn to play "patient," which often means playing a game of cheerful endurance, false compliance, and repressed anger, does he get affection, albeit in the mushy form of "How are we feeling today?" and, "Have we taken our medicine?" [10]

Other possible responses are discussed by Anna Freud in regard to child and adult patients.

> A normal adult who is nursed through a severe illness cannot help feeling at the same time that he is exposed to a series of indignities. He has to renounce ownership of his own body and permit it to be handled passively. He is dressed and undressed, fed, cleaned, washed, helped with urination and defecation, turned from one side to the other, his nakedness exposed to nurse and doctor, regardless of sex, of decencies and conventional restrictions. He is, as it were, under orders, subjected to hygienic routine which implies a major disregard for his personal attitudes and preferences. Characteristically enough, many adults sum up this experience as being "treated as a baby," or, as a "complete return to the conditions of their childhood."
>
> On the other hand it would be a mistake to conclude from such statements that the situation of being nursed, by virtue of its similarity to infantile experiences, is less upsetting to the child than to the adult. Observation, as well as theoretical considerations show that the opposite may well be the case.[11]

The nurse is expected to deal appropriately with numerous and diversified responses, although she may have no knowledge about the patient other than a description of his physical condition and the treatment recommended by the physician. Administrative and supervisory obligations often sharply limit the time a nurse can spend in direct patient care. Now that improvement in medical care has made hospitalization brief for most patients, the nurses may have even less time to become well acquainted with their patients.

From the nurse's point of view, adaptation to different patients is not always easy. There are times when anxious, depressed, helpless, and de-

---

[9] Freund. "Listening." P. 1650.
[10] *Ibid.*
[11] Anna Freud. "The Role of Bodily Illness in the Mental Life of Children." *The Psychoanalytic Study of the Child.* Vol. VII. New York: International Universities Press, Inc., 1952. P. 71.

manding patients can tax even the most competent nurse and cause her to feel reluctant and unprepared to cope with their emotional distress.

The impact of psychoanalysis showed the world the importance of unconscious motivations in determining behavior. It is frequently brought to the attention of nurses that all behavior has meaning. If the nurse does not understand certain kinds of responses that the patient makes, perhaps she does not know him well enough, in her brief contact with him, to understand or interpret his behavior. Lydia Rapoport writes:

> Human behavior is complex, but we believe it is potentially understandable. Motivating forces in behavior are both rational and irrational. We are often puzzled and upset by the irrational components but there are scientific means to appraise this irrationality and to learn to work with it. We believe that people have an infinite capacity to grow, develop, and change; the extent of this capacity may vary, of course. But there is inherent in everyone's personality makeup a force that pushes toward physical and mental health.[12]

Furthermore, from the field of psychoanalysis we learn that every new experience, even in middle life or old age, is likely to have meaning for a person in terms of his earlier history or childhood experiences. This insight forms an important frame of reference for the nurse, even though she does not usually have the opportunity or the need to explore the patient's total life history.

Bettelheim in his article suggests that the hospital experience is particularly crucial for a child. It not only has immediate importance but also may influence adulthood. Bettelheim emphasizes the psychoanalytic concept that anxiety is present in every human being regarding the intactness or integrity of his body. He writes:

> Everything that threatens our body threatens in some sense our very existence. Hence, we respond to it with massive anxiety though it often remains unconscious, however powerfully it affects our entire being: The younger the child and the more primitive his thinking, the more drastic his notions of what may happen to him and the more radical his fantasies.[13]

Bettelheim's article stresses the point that

if we wish to secure emotional health for children, we must try to look at what they see and recognize what worries them. . . . The more time we take out to talk to them about their anxieties, the better we will know how they see the world, and the better we will be able to help them with their feelings.[14]

Later, when we discuss children's hospital experiences, we will cover in detail some of their fantasies about illness.

[12] Lydia Rapoport. "Motivation in the Struggle for Health." *American Journal of Nursing*. Vol. 57, No. 11 (November, 1957). P. 1455.
[13] Bettelheim. "To Nurse and to Nurture." P. 73.
[14] *Ibid*. P. 76.

8   The Nurse and Her Patient

It is easy for the nurse to understand that a young child may feel fearful of his confinement in a hospital. Children's fears are sometimes obvious, but it is also important to remember that the adult has his fears, too, despite the fact that adults often learn ways by which they can disguise their feelings. In addition to fear, regression frequently accompanies illness. Later, from a psychodynamic point of view, we will explain why this occurs.

Dealing with patients' fears, most of which the nurse cannot know, is a difficult task. In caring for the physical needs of patients as efficiently as possible, it is easy for the nurse to believe that the most desirable patient is a compliant or "good" patient. For the nurse, it is perhaps helpful to remember the analogy of the "good child" in the classroom. It took many years for teachers to understand that sometimes the compliant child was not always the healthiest mentally.

Illness necessarily makes a human being focus on his problems, disengaging himself from his former environment. This disengagement especially occurs in a long illness, when the patient is dependent and hospitalized for many months. Betty MacDonald, in her autobiographical account of contracting tuberculosis, writes:

> At first, when my visitors told me of happenings in the outside world, I was vitally interested and relived each incident vividly with the telling. Then gradually, insidiously, like night mist rising from the swamps, my invalidism obscured the real world from me, and when the family told me tales of happenings at home, I found them interesting, but without strength, like talk about people long dead. The only real things were connected with the sanitorium. The only real people, the other patients, the doctors, and the nurses.[15]

She describes further the disruptions in one's life when illness occurs.

> Getting tuberculosis in the middle of your life is like starting downhill to do a lot of urgent errands and being hit by a bus. When you regain consciousness, you remember nothing about the urgent errands. You can't even remember where you were going. The important things now are the pain in your legs; the soreness in your back; what you will have for dinner; who's in the next bed.[16]

In attempting to understand patients and their problems, the nurse must not only draw on her knowledge and skills, but also learn to use her personality as a tool in giving professional service to others. She needs to examine her personal values and beliefs. As Lydia Rapoport, a social worker, recalls:

> At one time, I felt that too much of such searching could lead to a self consciousness which might reduce one's capacity to act. I have now learned

---

[15] Betty MacDonald. *The Plague and I*. New York: J. B. Lippincott Company, 1958. P. 47.
[16] *Ibid.* P. 11.

that self examination, whether on a professional or an individual level, can enhance one's capacity to act more productively.[17]

Today, as nurses increasingly see themselves as more than technicians, there is an increasing emphasis on gaining a professional identity. Rapoport writes:

> The struggle to gain professional status is an important one for nurses and social workers. The status question is still an open one in the academic world and in society at large. Fears have been expressed that we are becoming over-professionalized, that we will lose qualities of humanism. This is a complex problem and I am not sure I really understand the full implications of these fears. But I think somehow there is a basic distortion in the assumption that scientific knowledge about human behavior, motives, and needs, and scientific knowledge of ourselves in relation to how we meet these needs, will in and of itself devitalize the real values of the helping process.[18]

In an attempt to structure the nurse–patient relationship, it is not necessary to dehumanize it. In the next section, we will discuss in detail some of the problems regarding the patient's feelings toward the nurse and the nurse's feelings toward the patient. As Hedi Freund states:

> No mother reacts to all her children identically; no teacher can truly like all her pupils equally. We strangle our real feelings when we say we "like everybody," and we deny our humanness when we pretend that we treat all patients and clients alike.[19]

Transference Elements in the Nurse–Patient Relationship

For many years in her nursing career, Miss Ames had preferred to work with critically ill and dying patients. Later, during a period of psychotherapy, she became curious about this interest. She and her psychiatrist discussed the fact that she had been four years old when her mother had died from cancer. She remembered her feelings of helplessness and fear as she witnessed the course of the disease. Shortly following her mother's death, her father died after an automobile accident. When her psychiatrist explored her feelings about these events, she began to realize that her work with critically ill patients was related to an attempt to master the earlier feelings those events had aroused. She was doing for her patients what she had been unable to do for her mother and father.

[17] Rapoport. "Motivation in the Struggle for Health." P. 1456.
[18] *Ibid.* P. 1457.
[19] Freund. "Listening with Any Ear at All." Reproduced in this volume, pp. 29 to 36. See p. 34.

In Miss Ames' case, it appeared likely that she had unconsciously transferred or displaced some aspects of her earlier, unresolved conflicts about dying and death onto the nursing situation. The patients then represented, to some extent, those earlier, important persons in her life who had been sick and died.

Human behavior is characterized by a powerful tendency to repeat itself. This is especially true if the behavior is rewarded. Learning in general, and some forms of psychotherapy, are based on this fact. The repetition of behavior also occurs with great persistence in situations where there are unresolved unconscious conflicts. In these cases, the repetitive behavior represents an attempt to master the anxiety associated with the original circumstances or an attempt to find a new and more satisfactory solution to the conflict. Repetition in the attempt to master anxiety is seen in the recurrent nightmares that often follow a traumatic situation; in such episodes, the anxiety has been too much for the person to deal with adaptively at the time the traumatic event occurred.

Freud noted early in his psychoanalytic work that patients often seemed to treat him as though he represented one of the important persons from their early lives. The treatment process tended to lead to the reactivation of earlier forms of behavior and attitudes, which then became attached to or "transferred" to the person of the analyst through a "false connection." He referred to this phenomenon as *transference,* and felt that it represented a reliving in the analysis of the patient's memories, displaced onto the current situation.[20] The recurrence of such childhood feelings and behavior patterns reflect unresolved developmental conflicts, and the transference represents a renewed attempt to resolve these conflicts with a new figure in the present.

Although at first the term "transference" was reserved for describing an aspect of psychoanalysis and psychotherapy, it later became apparent that the elements of transference existed in a wide variety of human relationships. Transference manifestations have been described in other professional relationships, such as those of the social worker, teacher, lawyer, minister, nonpsychiatric physician, and nurse.

Mrs. Cole, a forty-five-year-old married woman, entered the hospital for a hysterectomy. Following successful surgery, she found herself wishing consciously for her mother to take care of her. She felt especially dependent on Mrs. R., the nurse on the evening shift. When Mrs. R. was not on duty, Mrs. Cole felt especially lonely and apprehensive. Gradually, she became aware that she expected Mrs. R. to treat her as though she were a sick child. She had responded to Mrs. R. as though the nurse were her

---

[20] Sigmund Freud. *Fragment of an Analysis of a Case of Hysteria.* Standard Editions of the Complete Psychological Works of Sigmund Freud. Vol. VII. London: The Hogarth Press, 1905. Pp. 116–17.

mother. The fact that Mrs. R. looked a little like the patient's mother made such a transfer of feelings and expectations especially easy.

Nurses observe how patients may misinterpret and distort communications, too, in a seemingly irrational fashion. The sick patient does not always view his doctor or the medical staff in a realistic manner. He may react to his doctor's directives as he once did to his father's orders. For some patients, this attitude may mean overcompliance, while for others it leads to stubborn resistance.

Insofar as these reactions are unrealistic, and if they result from an unconscious displacement on to the doctor or nurse of earlier feelings about important persons, they may be properly referred to as having transference elements.

The proper application of the concept of transference requires that the nurse have a clear understanding of the implications of the term. Transference in the strict sense refers to an aspect of the psychoanalytic situation. Karl Menninger defines transference as "the unrealistic roles or identities unconsciously ascribed to the therapist by the patient in the regression of the psychoanalytic treatment and the patient's reaction to this representation as derived from earlier experiences." [21]

Freud writes:

What are transferences? They are new additions or facsimiles of the impulses and fantasies which are aroused and made conscious during the progress of the analysis; but they have this peculiarity, which is characteristic of their species, that they replace some earlier person by the person of the physician. To put it another way: a whole series of psychological experiences is revived, not as belonging to the past, but as applying to the person of the physician at the present moment.[22]

Often we ignore the real characteristics of the other person and behave as if the relationship were quite different from its reality. For instance, the relationship between the nursing instructor and the student may shift to be similar to that of the mother-daughter relationship, or sister-younger sister, mother-infant, or boss-worker. Harry Stack Sullivan described these distortions quite clearly under the name "parataxic distortions"; they may be defined as those patterns of interpersonal feelings and behavior in which *me* and *you* are experienced in terms of some former relationship, so that the reality of the present situation is ignored to some degree.

The reason that it is important for the psychotherapist to recognize transference is that he must accept the fact that the patient is treating him somewhat on the basis of previous important relationships in his life. In

---

[21] Karl Menninger. *Theory of Psychoanalytic Technique.* New York: Basic Books, Inc., 1958. P. 81.
[22] Freud. *Op. cit.* P. 116.

therapy, if this distortion is overlooked and accepted as reality and then mutually reciprocated by the therapist, the therapy is not only interfered with, but may be destroyed.

Psychoanalytic treatment encourages the development of transferences. In this way, the patient tends to repeat in the treatment various derivatives of his important early experiences. Instead of simply remembering the past —which he also does—the patient strives to relive it by casting the analyst in roles from the patient's childhood environment. The analyst may become father, mother, sibling, teacher, and so forth. In this way, the patient "externalizes" certain conflicts, which then can be studied, understood, and perhaps resolved.

Transferences may be positive, that is loving, tender, sexual, protective, and so forth; or they may be negative, with the expression of anger, jealousy, irritability, or rejection. Whether "positive" or "negative" or a mixture of the two, transference feelings are characterized by being relatively independent of reality, by representing a repetition of earlier feelings, and by being stimulated largely by unconscious factors.

The intensity of transference feelings is lessened when there is a focus on reality elements, when the appointments are infrequent and relatively brief, and when the therapist is an active participant in the verbal exchanges between himself and the patient.

Of course, there are all shades of psychotherapy and counseling, from the psychoanalytic setting characterized by 50-minute appointments four to six times a week for several years, to the brief, supportive contacts nurses usually have with their patients.

Helen Harris Pearlman, in discussing transference elements in a caseworker–client relationship, states that

> in casework practice, our effort is to maintain the relationship on a basis of reality, that is, to keep both client and caseworker aware of their joint purpose, their separate and realistic identities and their focus upon working out some better adaptation between the client and his current problem situation. Transference manifestations need to be recognized, identified, and dealt with as they occur. But the effort is to so manage the relationship and the problem solving work as to give minimum excitation to transference.[23]

It is significant that there is very little, if anything, written in the nursing literature regarding transference, although the nurse and nonpsychiatric physician are often involved in transference distortions in their relationships with their patients. A woman whose husband had just died, for example, reacted with a show of intense anger directed toward the doctor. Until then, she had seen him as a kindly, fatherly person. Underlying these

---

[23] Helen Harris Pearlman. *Social Casework.* Chicago: University of Chicago Press, 1957. Chap. VI. P. 78.

positive feelings was the conviction that, in some magical fashion, he could protect her husband from dying, as she believed her father had protected her during childhood. Her intense feelings of helplessness and anger were partly the result of her disappointment in the doctor (father). Another factor in those cases where the nurses and doctors are the undeserved object of the survivors' wrath is the displacement onto them of the anger, helplessness, and frustration engendered by the death of a loved one.

Nurse–patient relationships are subject to distortion because of the tendency of physically ill people to regress to more childlike modes of behavior, thinking, and feeling as part of the usual adaptation to illness. Nurses are often expected to be all-giving mothers, and if they do not fulfill these expectations, certain patients will react as though they have been rejected or mistreated in spite of objective evidence to the contrary.

In the hospital setting, the patients' seeing doctor and nurse as father and mother is to some extent based on an unconscious reënactment of childhood illness. Nursing supervisors and instructors need to be aware of these phenomena, not only to help their staffs and students work with patients, but also because the supervisor often finds that her students enter into a counseling relationship with her.

For example, a middle-aged supervisor, Mrs. M., became upset when she discovered that one of her students had complained about her. The student felt that Mrs. M. had been "bossing her around and telling her what to do." This was especially distressing because it was the way the student's mother had always treated her. Mrs. M. explained that she didn't see the student as a daughter, but realized that the girl did remind her of a younger sister who had often made her angry by refusing to follow her advice or take directions from her. In this case, there were transference distortions on the part of both Mrs. M. and her student. Difficulties had ensued because neither person was aware at first of the feelings that were contributing to their reactions.

The existence of sexual feelings for nurses or doctors on the part of patients is not uncommon. These are by no means always irrational, and may be reciprocated as in any other relationship. However, the roles and duties of nurses and physicians combined with the needs and expectations of patients create situations where transferences are especially likely to occur.

The considerate, wise physician-father and the tender, solicitous nurse-mother are ready-made love objects for suffering and frightened or unhappy and frustrated patients. It is for this reason and because of the legal complications that can result from misunderstandings that the male physician routinely has another woman present when he performs a vaginal or other gynecological examination. During physical examinations, patients often feel and sometimes express sexual impulses. Occasionally, a patient becomes jealous and angry when she feels that the doctor is not paying sufficient attention to her. Because physical contacts with patients are often intimate ones, the nurse, as well as the doctor, needs to be aware that even essential nursing procedures may elicit sexual fantasies or anxious withdrawal on the part of the patient.

Grief and mourning are sometimes the setting for transference distortions. Despite the fact that the nurse has given a deceased patient the best possible nursing care, the grieving relatives may express anger and even become abusive as a result of their need to rid themselves of a feeling of helplessness. At such times, the nurse, too, may feel a sense of failure and frustration. One of her motivations for choosing a career in nursing may have been to heal people and to keep them from dying. Such a nurse may feel depressed and worthless following the death of a patient.

Nurse–patient relationships are frequently subject to distortions because the nurse must often work in highly charged emotional situations with the patient, who is suffering moderate to severe stress. Illness, financial deprivation, war, grief, loneliness, and death may make it easy for the patient to develop intense feelings toward the nurse.

One of the most difficult tasks in nursing—as in psychotherapy—is to learn how to manage one's own emotional reactions to patients when the bases of the reactions are largely unconscious. For example, a nurse who has conflicts and unresolved fears concerning her sexual feelings may unconsciously avoid or reject certain patients or, on the other hand, act in a seductive fashion without being aware of her behavior. By the same token, a nurse with unconscious resentment toward her mother may not consciously realize why she becomes irritable with many of her elderly women patients. Another nurse may not recognize or accept her own dependent needs, and may thus react with hostility or avoidance to the very old, the very young, or the helpless of any age, who may wish to lean upon her emotionally for prolonged periods of time.

Inappropriate responses to patients based on unconscious conflicts may be termed *countertransference*. Nurses, as well as therapists, may display such feelings and behavior toward their patients. Karl Menninger has called attention to a number of practical indicators of countertransference problems in psychoanalysis.[24] Some of these criteria can be usefully adapted to the nurse–patient relationship.

Arguing or feeling very angry with a patient often indicates that the nurse as well as the patient has a problem. If this happens, she should attempt to find out why she feels that way. The wish to assume total responsibility for a patient's care, or the feeling that the solutions to all of a patient's problems rests with the nurse, may also be a sign that counter-

---

[24] Menninger. *Theory of Psychoanalytic Technique.* Pp. 84–90.

transference is at work. The nurse should be alert to her responses and to behavior toward any one patient that is markedly different from her usual manner toward her patients. Whenever the nurse finds herself behaving in a fashion unusual for her, she should consider the possibility of countertransference.

The nurse represents to the patient certain values, standards, and behavior. The task of becoming a professional person means that the nurse should learn to deal with conflictual distortions in her own life and attempt to resolve contradictions that interfere with her nursing behavior. Good supervision and sometimes counseling or psychotherapy are necessary for the nurse better to understand the unconscious currents in herself and in her relationships with her patients or colleagues.

In the nurse–patient relationship, the nurse is not usually expected to function as psychotherapist. Often, however, patients seek emotional support and appreciate the nurse's ability to provide comfort, reassurance, and counsel. A calm, competent nurse can, by her very manner, soothe a patient who is anxious and concerned. Many times words are neither necessary nor appropriate to convey to the patient interest and solicitude for his well-being.

We feel it is important for the nurse to gain insight into some of her patient's problems; at the same time, she must use the utmost tact to avoid making penetrating comments that neither are solicited nor lie within the bounds of the relationship. This need for tact is equally felt in the relationship between supervisors and their students. Furthermore, the recognition of transference elements in the nurse-patient or teacher-student relationships should not be the occasion for blame or condemnation.

There is a universal human tendency to identify oneself with persons who offer nurture and satisfaction of needs. This process is especially significant in various types of learning throughout life. If a supervisor treats her students with understanding and respect, the students thereby will become better able to treat their patients in a like fashion. On the other hand, if transference distortions occur and interfere with the supervisor–student interaction, the student's effectiveness with her patients will very likely be adversely affected.

Transference distortions, based as they are on unconscious conflicts, are the inevitable consequence of human encounters. Recognition of these distortions should lead to constructive attitudes and changes within the nurse. One of the best methods of maintaining perspective in one's relationship with patients is a periodic review by a constructive critic. Thus, the nurse may wish to systematically share her professional experience with a reliable colleague, an understanding supervisor, or a professional psychotherapist. Sharing various experiences is vital to maintaining a realistic view of oneself. One of the most important aspects of supervision is to bring in an uninvolved third person who has the ability to detect distortion in the nurse–patient relationship. For example, Miss Jones, a middle-aged nurse, was upset because a young veteran whom she had cared for following major surgery, told her that he "loved her." Thereafter, she experienced tension and anxiety whenever it became necessary to care for him, and found herself wishing to avoid him.

Miss Jones discussed this problem with her supervisor. Her supervisor encouraged Miss Jones to consider her reactions to the patient in more depth. What emerged was that Miss Jones felt embarrassed that a young man could have such intense feelings for a woman of her age. Miss Jones became uneasily aware of her own attraction for this particular patient.

Her supervisor not only was understanding and accepting of these feelings, but was able to help Miss Jones gain perspective regarding the patient's unconscious wish for mothering, which seemed to be the source of his seductive attitude. The supervisor also helped Miss Jones to realize that her feelings (and his) need not be acted upon, and thus would not interfere with her patient's care.

Our emphasis on the unconscious determinants of behavior in this chapter as well as elsewhere in this book is not intended to convey the impression that we recognize no other factors at play in thinking and acting. The mature person is characterized by his capacity to make choices and decisions based on a realistic, conscious appraisal of his environment and his emotional reactions. Most of the nurse's procedures and interactions with patients and colleagues should be relatively uninfluenced by transference elements or other distortions resulting from conflict. By the same token, most of the nurse's developmental conflicts will have long since been resolved and integrated into her personality.

In order to understand more of the implications of transference and to gain a fuller understanding of patients and nurses, it is necessary to study the psychosocial development of the individual. In Chapter 2, we begin by introducing some of the psychodynamic concepts which are a necessary background for viewing the manner in which the personality develops.

Suggested Readings on Transference Elements in the Nurse–Patient Relationship

Nunberg, Herman. *Principles of Psychoanalysis: Their Application to the Neuroses.* New York: International Universities Press, 1955. Pp. 245–46.

Orr, Douglass W., M.D. "Transference and Counter-transference: A Historical Survey." *Journal of the American Psychoanalytic Association.* Vol. II, No. 4 (October, 1954). Pp. 621–70.

———. *Professional Counseling on Human Behavior: Its Principles and Practices.* New York: Franklin Watts, Inc., 1965. Pp. 116–19.

Pattison, Mansell, M.D. "Transference and Countertransference in Pastoral Care." *The Journal of Pastoral Care.* Vol. XIX, No. 4 (Winter, 1965). Pp. 193–202.

Sterba, Richard, Benjamin H. Lyndon, and Anna Katz. *Transference in Casework.* New York: Family Service Association of America, 1948.

Waelder, Robert. *Basic Theory of Psychoanalysis.* New York: International Universities Press, 1960. P. 253.

Wolstein, Benjamin. *Transference—Its Meaning and Function in Psychoanalytic Therapy.* New York: Grune and Stratton, 1954.

Suggested Readings on the Nurse–Patient Relationship

Abdellah, Faye G. "Frontiers in Nursing Research." *Nursing Forum.* Vol. V, No. 1 (1966). Pp. 28–38.

Baziak, Anna. "Prospects for Change in Nursing." *Nursing Forum.* Vol. VI, No. 2 (1967). Pp. 134–54.

Benne, Kenneth D. and Warren Bennis. "What Is Real Nursing?" *American Journal of Nursing.* Vol. 59, No. 3 (March, 1959). Pp. 380–83.

Brinling, Trudy. "Tearing Down a Wall." *American Journal of Nursing.* Vol. 71, No. 7 (July, 1971). Pp. 1400–3.

Brown, Esther Lucile. *Nursing for the Future.* New York: Russell Sage Foundation, 1948.

———. *Nursing Reconsidered: a Study of Change.* Part 1: *The Professional Role in Institutional Nursing.* Philadelphia: J. B. Lippincott Company, 1970.

———. *Nursing Reconsidered: a Study of Change.* Part 2: *The Professional Role in Community Nursing.* Philadelphia: J. B. Lippincott Company, 1971.

Freeman, Ruth B. "Practice as Protest." *American Journal of Nursing.* Vol. 71, No. 5 (May, 1971). Pp. 918–21.

Hall, Benita L. "Human Relations in the Hospital Setting." *Nursing Outlook.* March, 1968. Pp. 43–5.

Henderson, Virginia. "The Nature of Nursing." *American Journal of Nursing.* Vol. 64, No. 8 (August, 1964). Pp. 62–8.

Johnson, Dorothy E. "Today's Action Will Determine Tomorrow's Nursing." *Nursing Outlook.* Vol. 13 (September, 1965). Pp. 38–41.

Kalisch, Beatrice J. "An Experiment in the Development of Empathy in Nursing Students." *Nursing Research.* Vol. 20, No. 3 (May-June, 1971). Pp. 202–11.

Lenarz, Dorothea M. "Caring Is the Essence of Practice." *American Journal of Nursing.* Vol. 71, No. 4 (April, 1971). Pp. 704–7.

Leonard, Robert C. "Developing Research in a Practice-Oriented Discipline." *American Journal of Nursing.* Vol. 67, No. 7 (July, 1967). Pp. 1472–75.

Merton, Robert K. "The Search for Professional Status." *American Journal of Nursing.* Vol. 60, No. 5 (July, 1960). Pp. 662–64.

Mussallem, Helen K. "The Changing Role of the Nurse." *American Journal of Nursing.* Vol. 69, No. 3 (March, 1969). Pp. 514–17.

Pellegrino, Edmund D. "The Communication Crisis in Nursing and Medical Education." *Nursing Forum.* Vol. V, No. 1 (1966). Pp. 45–53.

Peplau, Hildegarde. "Specialization in Professional Nursing." *Nursing Science.* August, 1965. Pp. 268–87.

Perrine, George. "Needs Met and Unmet." *American Journal of Nursing.* Vol. 71, No. 11 (November, 1971). Pp. 2128–33.

Peters, Norma J. "The X Factor in Nursing." *R.N.* Vol. 34, No. 7 (July, 1971). Pp. 39–43.

Pollak, Otto and Pauline A. Vincent. "Human Relations in Nursing Consultation." *Nursing Forum.* Vol. IX, No. 1 (1970). Pp. 85–89.

Stein, Leonard I. "The Doctor-Nurse Game." *Archives of General Psychiatry.* Vol. 16 (June, 1967). Pp. 699–703.

Walker, Dorothy J. "Our Changing World—Its Challenge to Nursing." *Nursing Forum.* Vol. IX, No. 4 (April, 1970). Pp. 328–39.

Wollowick, Annette. "Will the Nursing Profession Become Exinct?" *Nursing Forum.* Vol. IX, No. 4 (April, 1970). Pp. 408–13.

DISCUSSION OF SELECTED READINGS

We have included in this section articles by writers outstanding in other fields who have formulated their views regarding patients and their care.

The first selection is by Dr. Bruno Bettelheim, founder of the Orthogenic School in Chicago, who has spent a lifetime working with children. Some of his better-known works are *Love is Not Enough* and *Truants from Life*. In the following article, he turns his attention to the nurse-patient relationship. Dr. Bettelheim is especially concerned with the intense and often irrational fears of children. Furthermore, he explains how childhood fears can later influence adult reactions to illness. Dr. Bettelheim gives clinical case illustrations of the problems a child faces when the nursing staff does not see the hospital environment through his eyes. This provocative reading allows for much general discussion by nurses regarding Dr. Bettelheim's philosophy, observations, and suggestions.

In the second article, Hedi Freund, a social worker and educator, is concerned with some of the specific problems the adult experiences in the hospital. She provides, in her article, the opportunity for nurses to discuss their ideas regarding "professional status" and the ways these attitudes affect the nurse–patient relationship. She also points out the nurse's need for self-awareness and identifies certain similar problems that nurses as well as social workers may have with their clients.

In the third article, Dr. Edward Auer, a psychiatrist,[*] discusses the anonymity of the patient, who is often lost sight of in our technologically complex hospital settings. Dr. Auer discusses the importance of the patient's interaction with the staff, and he acknowledges the place of transference feelings as they can affect this relationship. He gives clinical examples that illustrate how previous life experiences influence staff–patient reactions toward each other. Dr. Auer also discusses dependency and regression as they relate to the patient's method of coping with his illness and his anxiety.

[*] Professor of Psychiatry at St. Louis University.

The selected readings in this section and in the bibliography are included to help the nurse gain some of the wisdom necessary for studying the underlying psychological factors in human behavior.

To Nurse and to Nurture

by Bruno Bettelheim, Ph.D. *

Rightly or wrongly, the public image of the nurse is that of an efficient and obedient helper of the physician, who shows little concern for the emotional needs of the patient. This was illustrated recently when a well-known psychiatric children's institution was to be changed into a psychiatric children's hospital. The greatest source of fear and resistance to the change among child-care workers at the institution was that registered nurses would have to be added to the staff. Their main objection was that nurses would be too obedient to physicians, would in general side with physicians against the child-care staff. This, of course, is a biased and stereotyped judgment of the nursing profession. But I submit that the stereotype has enough validity that when it turns out to be invalid the experience is exciting and rewarding. Exactly such an experience comes to mind now.

An adult patient had undergone major surgery and was now recovering, slowly if uneventfully. But late one evening he took what to him seemed a serious turn for the worse; he felt there were subjective and objective signs that he was sinking fast. He asked for the resident, who came and examined him but saw no reason to change the orders left by the attending physician for the night. He then asked the resident to contact his physician, but the resident declined because of the lateness of the hour, and because, in his opinion, there was no cause to. Several hours passed, the patient's condition worsened and he became desperate. The head nurse, if she did not recognize the condition of his body, certainly recognized his state of mind and promised to speak to the resident again. This she did, but the resident's reply was the same. At this point the patient knew panic. He begged the nurse to call his physician; but she was under orders not to do so. Moreover, since she had already talked with the resident making the call would go directly against his orders. By this time it was well into the night. The patient was in a state of despair when the nurse

---

* Bruno Bettelheim. "To Nurse and to Nurture." Nursing Forum. Vol. 1, No. 3 (Summer 1962). Pp. 60–75.

remarked noncommittally that she would see what she could do. About 15 minutes later the patient's physician was at his bedside, the nurse having taken it upon herself to break the rules and call the doctor herself. It is only incidental to my story that the physician decided to change the program of treatment, with beneficial results for the patient.

I relate this, because with due respect to the physician we do not know if the patient's rapid recovery was due to the changed medical regimen or to the radically changed emotional conditions within him. At one moment he felt trapped inside a vast institution that paid no attention to his desperate personal needs. By the nurse's single act he felt he was once more in the company of human beings, willing to take grave risks for his physical and emotional well-being.

For this nurse's courage a citation once existed in my native Austria. Among soldiers, obedience and valor are the highest qualifications one looks for. But in the eighteenth century a great Austrian empress created a new and higher order of merit. Unlike our medal of honor, this honor was conferred not for courage beyond the call of duty but for the courage to disobey it. In particular, this knight's cross of valor was conferred only on soldiers who went against the orders of a superior officer during combat and, in so doing contributed to victory or at least helped in averting defeat. Unfortunately there was no one to confer the cross of the Empress Maria Theresa on the nurse of my story. But both physician and patient told her how much it meant to them that she had risked grave personal censure to help a human being in distress.

The True Virtue of Nurses

In ancient India, more than three thousand years ago, nursing was a male profession but was recognized as a very special calling. According to an early medical treatise in Sanskrit, "the physician, the drugs, the nurse and the patient constitute an aggregate of four." Each of them needs particular virtues in order to add to the cure of the disease.

Nurses were healers long before they became adjuncts of physicians. Nurses' proud tradition, at least in Western society, is much more one of uplifting the downtrodden, of rekindling the spirits of the sick, of ministering to body and mind, than that of dispensing medication, administering injections, or taking specimens for analysis. I believe that the true virtue, the true calling of the nurse, consists neither in following doctor's orders nor in administering prescribed treatments (though she ought to do both conscientiously), but in the two aspects contained in the very name of the profession: to nurse and to nurture; to feed the body and to nurture the soul. Just as the infant is nursed by his mother, nursed in body and soul, so the nurse should nurture the body and soul of her patient. And this makes it a peculiarly feminine calling, whether the nurse is male or female. Much as we have learned that the mental health of an adult depends on how well his mother nursed him in body and soul as an infant, so the recovery of a patient will, added to medical care, depend on how well you administer tender nursing care to his body and soul.

True, in these days of psychosomatic medicine, it becomes harder and harder, with certain diseases, to know where the treatment of the psyche, the mind, or of the soma, the body, should take precedence. But let us also remember that while many patients who require nursing care are beyond help by medicine proper, no patient, least of all the terminal case, is beyond help where his feelings are concerned.

Perhaps the time has come for the pendulum to swing back. During the last hundred years it was important to put nursing on a scientific basis and make it into a profession. Perhaps now, without relinquishing advances, it is time we began to pay more attention to the uplifting of spirits, which is no less essential to nursing than the healing of the body.

How curative that can be for the mental patient is shown, for example, by the Japanese institution of the *tsukisoi*. Actually these are women below our level of graduate nurses and should be compared to aides in our hospitals. They act as motherly helpers to mental patients, both male and female. It is a one-to-one relation, each patient having his personal *tsukisoi*, particularly in private psychiatric hospitals. His *tsukisoi* is with the patient twenty-four hours a day, seven days a week. She sleeps in the same room with him, and serves as housekeeper, companion and caretaker. Thus, the *tsukisoi* often sees her role as parallel to what might exist between a good mother and her child, or to how an older sister functions as a mother to a younger sibling. They really nurse the patients, and the improvement among those who can enjoy the services of such helpmate is really astonishing, at least as seen from our Western experience.

Desirable as such a regime might be, particularly in the nursing care of children, it would not seem practical to institute in our hospitals. But there is something in between nursing care for a patient that runs seven days a week, twenty-four hours a day, and one that takes account only of the physical well-being of a patient but not also his emotional needs; a care that is more concerned with efficiency in the care of the body than with an unhurried ministering to the feelings of the sick.

Nursing may not be one of the oldest professions of women but it is certainly one of the oldest professional activities women have practiced in our culture. It is, moreover, one of three professions with which every human being has direct, meaningful contact. These three professions are nursing, teaching and medicine. But nursing comes first, because it stands at the very beginning of our lives. Two of these three are largely prerogatives of the fair sex, and all three are related (or should be) to problems of mental health.

No doubt all three professions, and many more, give a great deal of lip service nowadays to their concern with mental health. But how much time and energy do they, in fact, devote to this task they acknowledge is so important? Speaking of a profession I am more intimately familiar with—education—and using it to highlight parallel conditions in nursing, I am always impressed with how often teachers claim that the mental health of their children is of paramount concern to them. But when we investigate the degree to which they are willing to go to promote emotional health at the expense of academic achievement, then a different picture emerges. What they then appear to believe is that emotional health should be an incidental by-product of the teaching of subject matter. Unfortunately this is not so.

Unless we plan for emotional health, neither in nursing nor in education, will we gain it for the children in our care. On the contrary, if we concentrate mainly on teaching subject matter in class, or on medical care in nursing, we may actually impede mental health. As long as our teachers remain committed to efficiency alone as an educational goal, they will do a poor job in the field of mental health. As long as nurses are committed to an efficient discharge of their nursing duties, there will be little they can do to help the patient with his mental health. Perhaps I should quote Justice Frankfurter here. "I don't like a man to be too efficient," he said. "He's likely to be not human enough." If we are serious about mental health, we must free ourselves from the fetish of efficiency.

WHAT CAN NURSES DO FOR THE EMOTIONAL HEALTH OF CHILDREN IN SHORT-TERM CONTACTS?

The nurse's contact with the patient in my story was very short: a bedside visit and a phone call of a moment's duration. But its consequences were most far-reaching for the patient's recovery.

To Nurture the Soul

I do not know if the tale conveyed what the emotional state of a patient can be like. He feels himself suddenly projected from the friendly environment of his family into one that seems not only alien, but basically an inimical world, however helpful. This is by no means a contradiction. A world can be dedicated to helpfulness and still seem inimical—because it is helpful to our bodies but unfriendly to our feelings. The hospital climate is not created, of course, by nurses, and I am well aware that they, too, suffer from the factory-like efficiency that pervades some of our large modern hospitals, just as do patients, as well as professionals who must work in such a setting. But it is the nurse—because of the traditions of her calling, and her public image—of whom the patient expects not only skilled care, but also help with his emotional needs. He feels doubly let down when she disappoints him in the latter respect. And what is true for adults, who should (and often do) understand the whys and wherefores, is doubly true for children, who are mainly in the dark.

We all know how anxious a child is when he first meets a nurse, particularly in a hospital setting. We also know that nothing so distracts from anxiety as getting busy doing something, while anxiety increases if we have to stand by doing nothing, waiting to see what will happen. All too often in this situation—though there are many laudable exceptions—the nurse does not ask the child what's wrong with him, where it hurts, or how long he's been sick, but will turn to the mother with her questions. True, the mother will probably give the more correct story, though not always. But what is gained by getting the full story quickly is lost by neglecting the child's anxiety; worse, by giving him the feeling that we are not even concerned with his own view of his sickness. Weakened by his temporary infirmity, we debilitate him still more by giving him the impression that we consider him incompetent to speak for himself. And this, even before we have given him a chance to try his hand at it. About the story of his illness we have the excuse that his childish impressions might be untrue to fact. But what about his name, his age and such rote information? Why should the child not be the best source of such pieces of data? In order to gain a few seconds, we give him the feeling that even where his own sickness is concerned, he counts less than all these powerful and potentially threatening adults. All patients, even small children, are entitled to sense immediately that they stand in the center of our interest; they, and not what their parents have to say.

It is well known that to combat the patients' insecurity, particularly the child patient's, good medical and nursing care requires that we reassure them about the procedure they are about to undergo. We must explain to them what they are going to experience, and also the reasons why it is necessary to inflict it on them. Most nurses do explain things to the child. But after that, how much time do they give him to really understand what it's all about? At best they repeat their explanations; but if a second explanation is not accepted or understood, most nurses become restless because they feel too much time is being wasted.

As parents and teachers we all know that for a child to learn and understand even a simple paragraph may require repeated re-readings of the same story. And this is for stories cut to the order of the child's comprehension, dealing with facets of life with which he is well familiar. Compare this with the situations laden with anxiety, such as when a child has to get an injection or submit to minor surgery—not to speak of more traumatic interferences with his body. Why, then, do we expect him to accept and be able to master the experience of medical interferences, after one or, at best, two or three short explanations? The less the child understands, the more likely the nurse is to get frustrated in her efforts to explain. And the more nervous her explanations become, the more likely she is to give up. Actually the less the child is able to follow explanations, the more he shows us how anxious he is. Therefore, the more time we should take, and the more patient we have to become.

Here I would like to add that the mental health of human beings consists very largely of the conviction that they are able to predict the future correctly. If we believe that we can predict future events, we can prepare for them. Even if we cannot avoid painful experiences, at least they do not hit us out of the blue. At least they do not prove to us that we were stupid not to know what was about to befall us. That is why mental health thinking in nursing requires careful and truthful preparation for what is about to happen to the child. In our explanations we should not go into gory details, but without scaring the child we must tell him the truth. Then, if a painful experience is inflicted on him, he at least has the reassurance that "they told me beforehand; therefore I don't have to be afraid that some terrible new thing is about to happen; they would again have told me beforehand."

Our efforts to explain what is going to happen are interfered with by our not wanting to worry the child, and sundry methods are used to keep him from worrying. True, excessive worry is detrimental and a sign of poor mental health. But so is not worrying about the future at all. In many ways I am more concerned for the mental health of a person who does not worry about bad events in the future than about the person who does worry, so long as his worries are within normal limits. Worrying is a way of working through bad experiences before they happen, so that we are better prepared for them and they don't hit us too suddenly when we are unprepared and hence vulnerable. Thus good mental health practice in nursing care would include giving the patient enough time, but not too much time, to prepare himself for the experience he is anxious about before it happens.

After careful investigation of psychological stress among surgical patients, the conclusion was reached that anxiety before an operation can be highly useful in preparing patients emotionally for a surgical experience. The type of emotional relief the patient feels after surgery is directly related to the kind and amount of anticipatory fear he experienced. The study shows that a moderate degree of such fear is desirable, but an extremely high degree is likely to result in intense operative fear, with postoperative difficulty in adjustment. Further, an extremely low degree of anticipatory fear is likely to result in postoperative resentment.[1] Even more reason to take time out and make sure that our preparations, and above all our inner attitude in preparing the child, should enable him to experience and master moderate anticipatory anxiety, but not too intense a degree of it.

A considerate nurse lets the child play with the instruments she is going to use on him, or provides trial experiences such as letting the child give an injec-

---

[1] I. L. Janis. *Psychological Stress: Psychoanalytic and Behavioral Studies of Surgical Patients.* New York: J. Wiley & Sons, 1958.

tion to an orange. This is a very good way for the child to master some of his feelings about injections, but unfortunately it fails to prepare him for the pain he is going to experience when the needle does not enter an orange but is pushed into his skin. So it is preparation only for the externals. Unless warnings go with it about the pain to be experienced, the whole effort remains beside the point as far as preparation for the emotional impact of pain is concerned. True, there is basically no preparation for pain. But much is to be gained through trust in a human being who spends a great deal of his time and serious effort in preparing us for the painful experience. While we must still endure the pain, we have gained a friend to be trusted. Compare this with pain inflicted by someone who fooled us about it. Whatever the situation, it is always damaging to the emotional well-being of children to be told what is not true, such as that the injection won't hurt, that he will only feel a little prick, or that it tickles. Far better to say that it will hurt, but that the pain will not last.

Another important principle of good mental health concerns the person's ability to have appropriate emotional reactions to events. This is so important that we can almost gauge by it the degree of mental health or mental illness. Therefore it is important not to expect or to encourage children to show emotional reactions that are not in line with their feelings. To tell a child he is a good child for not crying or screaming when we expose him to painful procedures means to encourage bad mental health practices. Contrary to this principle, children are rarely encouraged to have appropriate feelings. Instead they are expected or told to do the opposite: to keep a straight face and not to fight back when it hurts. This is so prevalent in hospital practice that I am tempted to conclude that for nurses and doctors the good patient is often the one who temporarily shows severe signs of poor mental health, and the other way around.

Here, as in so many cases, our procedures seem more conditioned by our wish to protect our self-image as a kind, helpful person who does not hurt children, than by what is best for the patient. It is unrealistic to expect a child who is hurt or in pain to be able to recognize our good intentions and therefore not express his feelings or fight back. That so many patients conceal their true feelings proves only how widespread poor mental health is in our society, or how little they trust us.

Basically, children have only the two defenses when confronted with nursing care that includes potential pain. They can verbally complain or show physical resistance. This is a natural reaction and should be recognized and accepted as such rather than criticized. True, the problem is then the adult's. There are other children who give us much less trouble but store up trouble for themselves. These are the children who become completely passive as if they were saying to us, "I am completely in your hands. Do whatever you like with me, you know best." Such giving up of decision making, of the freedom to react to one's own life experiences, is a bad omen for mental health and emotional well-being. Therefore the child should be watched carefully for such passive surrender and not encouraged in it, though the initial tendency is to consider such a child a good patient. True, it is convenient and permits you to go through your procedures easily and speedily. But this is the crux of the matter. Very often the easier it is to dispense nursing care, the poorer it is for emotional health. There are no rules here, but often the more difficult nursing care becomes, the better it is promoting good mental health. This is hard to accept, and even harder to set into everyday practice.

So far I have dealt with obvious relations between nurses and children, and about common situations. But what of the more hidden anxieties that every child brings to his contact with nurses? One of the greatest anxieties of every human being is his fear for the integrity of his body. Everything that threatens our body threatens in some sense our very existence. Hence, we respond to it with massive anxiety though it often remains unconscious, however powerfully it affects our entire being: The younger the child and the more primitive his thinking, the more drastic his notions of what may happen to him and the more radical his fantasies. We need only remember all the awesome changes that happened to Alice in Wonderland, all of which children accept as both possible and probable. Compare this with what might happen to the hero in our own novels, or what an adult accepts as possible or probable.

The adult surgical patient may fear a slight error on the part of his physician, a needle forgotten, a medication dosage slightly off, a dressing put on too tightly or removed too early. But the child patient fears that the medication will poison him, that the surgeon will take out his heart and put another one in its place, that his leg will remain permanently short, that his parents or friends won't be able to recognize him after the physician is through with him. Everything seems possible in the child's wonderland of his fantasies. Any little cut needed for removing a splinter foretells the most radical cutting off. Therefore nothing is more dangerous than the so-called "jokes," told to alleviate the child's anxiety, such as telling him we are going to cut his finger off, or his leg, when actually we are just dressing a small wound. Since what we tell him as a joke is exactly what he fears may happen, such remarks only increase his anxiety to an unbearable pitch.

Wise mental health practice suggests that we keep in mind the exaggerated fears of children whether they voice them or not. We should neither jokingly exaggerate what we are going to do, nor give them empty reassurances that it won't hurt at all. Both are untrue to fact. Instead, I would suggest that in talking to the child we begin by telling him that we know how terrified he is that we might inadvertently cut too deep or too much, or do some other permanent damage; that this is an anxiety most children feel when confronted with certain types of nursing care, but that these are irrational fears; that in reality we are simply going to take out a splinter or remove an infected hangnail.

No medical interference, not even the slightest, should be treated as a joking matter because of the great anxiety children feel about their bodies, and the danger they think might come from adults. The best we can do is to recognize the anxiety and show by our behavior that because we recognize it we make allowance for it; but that we also know, and they will soon find out, that their anxiety was unrealistic. Unless we openly recognize their often unspoken anxiety, nothing we say or do will convince the child that we understand what he is feeling and have compassion with his physical pain and with his mental suffering.

This brings me to the most basic principle we must keep in mind if we want to safeguard mental health in our dealing with children. It is the need to see things through their eyes as well as ours. To all this I have been alluding from the start. When we tell the child that we will inflict only a little cut—because to us it is only a little cut—we speak from our own frame of reference, not from his. As the child sees things, little cuts are the dangerous forerunners of radical cuts, of severe damage to his body. Most of our explanations, most of our attitudes to the child, are based on thinking from our own frame of reference, whereas the emotional well-being of the child would require that we see everything from his frame of reference before we see it from our own. Our explanations should first be geared to how the child looks at things. Because only after we have shown we understand him will he be ready to accept that what we say about things, how they look from our own frame of reference, may also make sense.

Let me use a very simple example. A child had to stay in the hospital for a physical illness. Up to a point he recovered nicely. But once out of bed he developed a severe psychological disturbance—or so it seemed, because for hours on end he stood transfixed at a window, in a state of catatonic rigor, and couldn't be budged. All efforts to entice him away came to nothing. His health declined, too, as he stood there without moving, without eating, without talking. Things went from bad to worse until one day a nurse instead of trying to induce the child to give up his position by the window came and joined him. She stood by for a long enough period of time to discover that he was looking out at the place where corpses were being loaded for removal. It was only when she looked out of the window with the eyes of the child did she realize that he was glued to this watching post in order to assess how many people had died in the hospital that day; that he was trying to figure out his chances for survival, given the number of corpses removed daily. Once this anxiety was understood and could be discussed with the child, he was eventually able to give up his place by the window, rejoin human company and return to normal living.

If we wish to secure emotional health for children, we must try to look at what they see and recognize what worries them. We must try to see the nursing experience through the eyes of the anxious child. The more we take time out to talk with them, about them, about their anxieties, the better we will know how they see the world, and the better we will be able to help them with their feelings.

Listening with Any Ear at All
*by Hedi Freund, M.S.W.**

This article was born under the duress of a flight between New York and Chicago. The weather was pea soup; the proposed landing at Detroit was out of the question; and we needed to refuel. On my lap were several magazines carrying air line advertisements describing, not the safety, speed, or efficiency of service, but the beauty, virtue, and sociability of stewardesses. No marriage broker could have written more loving copy.

As the pea soup outside thickened, the anxiety inside increased. I looked at my neighbors and saw confusion and fear. Slowly my attention focused on the air line's representatives—the beautiful, ever-smiling stewardesses, so pert in their Pucci outfits. Surely, I thought, they are "in" people; they know something; some of the pilot's godlike assurance has rubbed off on them.

The passengers began to press anxiously. "Where are we?" "What time are we expected to land?" "Have you ever flown in weather like this?" "What is a crash landing?"

The stewardesses' gazes began to shift. "You must ask the pilot that." "Everything is taken care of as well as can be expected."

Well, we made it, and the unruffled beauties took phonograph-like leave, "Have a good day! Have a good day! Have a good day!"

It was then that I remembered another time of stress when I had needed, but not found, the comfort of a human relationship, the security of feeling that there was a beating heart beneath the crisp, white uniform, a concerned head beneath the perky, starched, little hat.

It was during a brief hospitalization for a minor operation that I had felt similar fear, anxiety, and dread. Dependency had stirred in my usually adult ego, and now I remembered my clumsy efforts at reaching out to the figures walking in and out of my room.

* Hedi Freund. "Listening with Any Ear at All." *American Journal of Nursing*. Vol. 69, No. 8 (August 1969), 1650–1653.

Mind you, I had really not wished weather information on the plane, nor did I in the hospital expect a chemical analysis of Probanthine or a rundown on the course of my disease.

What I wanted was something else, something hard to put in everyday language. Was it Linus' blanket? My old teddy bear? Visitors? Chocolate? Roses?

Then the other day I saw a cartoon of a little, frail human being looking up into the sky while nuclear missiles were dropping. He was picking up the telephone to say as his last message, "Operator, I love you."

Then, I understood that what I had wanted was a brief, two-way relationship, an extended hand that did not hold a thermometer, a friendly face without a forced display of teeth, and a human voice that addressed me as a person. I had wanted to feel closeness, acceptance, and understanding on a simple level.

Sidney Jourard points out that loneliness seems to be a part of every illness, and no matter how secure the person, feelings of anonymity, fear, worry, the "shearing of identity" take place in the medical institution and tend to retard healing.[1]

When he becomes a patient, the human being asks for complete acceptance of his illness as well as his personality, no matter how bizarre. As a sick being, the patient craves permission to become infantile, dependent, and demanding without punishment or isolation.

Paralyzed by fear, in constant need of reassurance, the asker of innumerable questions, the patient most in need of human contact is quickly labeled a "pest" and shunned. Only if he can learn to play "patient," which often means playing a game of cheerful endurance, false compliance, and repressed anger, does he get affection, albeit in the mushy form of "How are we feeling today?" and, "Have we taken our medicine?"

Well, what of it? Is this really the nurse's business? Nurses have valuable information about the patients' symptoms, but many have not yet become interested in the patient *qua* patient.

In most instances, the nurse is used to promote efficiency. In Jourard's words:

> [She is one who] institutes clear manipulations to make the patient do what he is supposed to do, so that the system of the hospital will work smoothly, work will get done faster, and the patient will be less of a bother to care for.[2]

If this is, indeed, her role, then we cannot expect her to spend time with matters that impede smooth functioning, such as patients' feelings. Today's nursing educators, however, know that smooth functioning and efficient operations are not enough. There is much evidence that "the hip in room 245" is

---

[1] Sidney Jourard. *The Transparent Self.* New York: D. Van Nostrand Co., 1964.
[2] *Ibid.* P. 149.

changing to, "the middle-aged woman who is weepy all the time and who has had no visitors since her arrival."

Social Therapists

If we can acknowledge that sick people act like frightened people, and that frightened people act like disturbed people, then we no longer need to think of the uncomfortable, troublesome patient as "emotionally disturbed," "psycho," or "crazy." We then accept, even expect, that much of the behavior exhibited in the psychiatric service of the hospital will be duplicated in the other services. The nurse, then, no longer functions as what William Schofield terms a "combination clerk-watchdog," but rather as the "social therapist," described by Esterson.[3, 4]

In my work as a teacher of social workers in a graduate school and a psychiatric outpatient clinic, I have become aware of many similarities in the theories and practices of the professions of nursing and social work. Social workers, too, have been described as "social therapists," but they have also been called "social watchdogs."

Where nurses have been criticized for their distance from patients, social workers have been accused of inching too close, of meddling and snooping. Social work has been scolded for being psychiatry's handmaiden; has not nursing been attacked for being medicine's underpaid relative? These positions may shift and change, but both social work and nursing will always deal with persons in some kind of trouble, will always provide the links between the patient's needs and his and society's resources.

In social work education, we teach the student to approach the client from the biologic as well as the social and psychologic points of view. The student learns that the elements of trust, understanding, empathy, and acceptance are as important as financial assistance and medical intervention. What is of most consequence, he becomes aware of the importance of his own role in the helping process. The student learns that his role when performed with wisdom and feeling, not unlike that of a nurse or a physician, might determine the patient's recovery or functioning.

The opportunities for positive intervention are limitless. The following three abbreviated case histories are examples of simple situations where ombudsmen— no matter of what profession—might have done much to help a temporarily disabled human being in trouble.

[3] William Schofield. *Psychotherapy; the Purchase of Friendship.* Englewood Cliffs, N.J.: Prentice-Hall, Inc., 1964. P. 34.
[4] A. Esterson and others. "Results of Family-Oriented Therapy with Hospitalized Schizophrenics." *British Medical Journal.* Vol. 2 (December 18, 1965). 1462–65.

Three in Trouble

Fanny G., aged 62, is in the surgical ward of a metropolitan hospital for recurring melanoma. Mrs. G. has four children, for whom she was the sole support during their minority after the death of her husband 30 years ago. She is an intelligent, strong-willed woman, used to attacking problems through logic and action. She has always been able to fix things for herself and her family. There was never anybody to depend on. In the hospital, she is bewildered and frightened. Her daughter, mother of three, can only come to see her after regular visiting hours and not at all on weekends.

Mrs. G. feels she has to see her as much as possible, because this daughter recently lost a child. Mrs. G. has always had trouble sleeping; she needs to pace at night. Will this be permissible? Last night she waited a long time for medication. What would happen if she were in great pain? Is there a short cut? She knows it is "crazy," but all of a sudden she is beset by fears of fire. She is all bandaged up. Where is the fire exit? How would she get out? The nurses seem too far removed to answer such infantile questions and the doctor would only laugh at her.

During the day many doctors—at least they wear white jackets—walk in and out. Who are they? Some do not speak English. Is she a teaching case? Does that mean that she is very sick? Have they chosen her case because it is hopeless? Will they experiment on her? Her own doctor is a good man, efficient, and kind. He is very busy, of course. The other day she wrote a list of questions, but she was too embarrassed to read from it.

Peter M., aged 55, is a furniture repairman. He is in the hospital for the first time in his adult life. He is six feet four and weighs 240 pounds. He had been a marine for 17 years and was an amateur boxer. His friends call him a "tough guy."

He is on urology and the tentative diagnosis is kidney stones. He is in considerable pain. He does not know how much time needs to elapse between doses of medication. He asked the aide, who offered to ask someone else, but he did not think he should disturb the nurse. She seemed to be too busy and efficient.

As a sergeant in the service, he had plenty of experience giving orders. Now he finds it difficult to obey them. He has other concerns also. His son quit high school some months ago and he really should talk to the principal. He is not at all sure whether his job will be held for him, and he does not know how long he will have to stay in the hospital. The doctor could only say, "We'll see how it goes."

Sometimes the pain gets so unbearable he cries. This is the worst. He cannot stomach a crying man. A few times, a nurse entered his room while he was crying and he was terribly embarrassed. He tried to make light of it by cracking

Listening with Any Ear at All 33

a joke, but this did not seem to work. The other day while the nurse was helping him he was so overcome by pain that he grasped her hand. She withdrew hers quickly and he felt ashamed and unmanly. He thought the nurse had looked at him with disgust. He believed he should be able to control himself better, but he had never experienced this kind of pain before.

Janet R. is 24. She gave birth to a 10-pound girl two days ago. She has had a bad pregnancy and a worse delivery. She gained only 14 pounds and weighed 105 just before delivery. No one has come to see her. She received a few cards; that is all. The nurses have exchanged significant glances, and she thinks she has heard someone whisper in the hall that she is not married, despite the ring on her left hand.

Janet would like to talk a little. She asks the nurse if she is married. Does she have children? How many and what ages? She asks many times for the hour when the mail gets delivered. She even asks the nurse's advice about naming the baby. When she thinks no one is about, she buries her face in the pillow and sobs.

These are everyday cases. Probably in each case the discharge note will read "Uneventful recovery." If these patients had had a relationship with a helping person, would it have mattered? Perhaps it would not have affected recovery in these instances, but persons familiar with René Spitz' work know that the difference in many cases might mean life or death.[5]

Bedside Manner

Social workers call their relationships with their clients, "the soul of casework." They have learned that, with a good relationship, a client will experience therapeutically desirable changes, will develop courage to bear life's vicissitudes, to test his strength during adversities, and will be more able to accept the inevitable, whatever this might be.

This kind of relationship is not necessarily dependent on many months of labor. It begins the moment the social worker meets his client and should begin when the nurse and patient first encounter each other.

There is much talk about bedside manner and what it does. Real bedside manner means understanding the interrelationship between psyche and soma, as does the use of placebo. Good bedside manner can be learned and taught. It is the armamentarium of most helping professions, though tied to neither bed nor office. Bedside manner includes an understanding of common basic needs. Felix Biestek, a priest and social worker, names seven basic human needs which such professionals as nurses and social workers will come to know.[6]

[5] Rene Spitz. "Anaclitic Depression." In *Psychoanalytic Study of the Child.* Ruth S. Eissler and others (ed.). Vol. 2. New York: International Universities Press, Inc., 1946. P. 313.
[6] F. P. Biestek. *The Casework Relationship.* Chicago: Loyola University Press, 1957.

They are the need:

- To be dealt with as an individual rather than a case or type
- To express feelings, both negative and positive
- To be accepted as a person of worth
- To receive sympathetic understanding of and response to the feelings expressed
- To be neither judged nor condemned for his difficulty
- To make his own choices and decisions
- To have confidential information about himself kept as secret as possible.

Basic Needs

We know that persons in trouble have a deep need to communicate. Witness a person who has gone through an ordeal such as a fire, an accident, or an attack. He seems almost obsessed with the need for catharsis, for telling over the same story, for reliving it until he incorporates it into his life.

The frequently given advice of, "Cheer up," or, "You mustn't think about it," is park-bench advice and not worthy of a professional helper.

Nonjudgmental Attitudes

Questions of worthiness and unworthiness have no place in professional behavior. Our Anglo-Saxon heritage and the Protestant ethics on which much of our thinking is based make it difficult for us not to condemn the human being while condemning his deed or behavior. Somewhere tucked back in our minds is the secret feeling that the unwed mother needs no anesthetic during delivery, that the criminal's agony from a gunshot wound need not be helped.

No words are needed to transmit to a patient, already excruciatingly sensitive, our disdain, or criticism, our disapproval. The law, the courts, and, ultimately perhaps, a higher being will judge. The clinic, the hospital, the consulting room are there for mending and healing.

Still another concept bears consideration: "self-awareness," a term much used in social work. In simple terms, this deals with the usual tendency to react to others in an irrational and unpredictable manner and the understanding that this tendency is predicated on past life experiences.

No mother reacts to all her children identically; no teacher can truly like all her pupils equally. We strangle our real feelings when we say we "like everybody," and we deny our humanness when we pretend that we treat all patients and clients alike.

The fault lies not in differential treatment. It lies in our lack of awareness of the feelings behind the treatment. It behooves our professional selves to understand our own prejudices (yes, we all prejudge), our tendencies to cubbyhole, our habit of comparing unrelated persons. The nurse must ask herself whether she sees her patient D. or a person who reminds her of her mother, her father-in-law, a childhood teacher, or an old enemy. She must ask herself whether she rejects *a priori* certain behavior or habits and how this development took place within her.

Professional Attitude

Finally, a word about "professional attitude." Many sins are committed under the guise of this pretense. There is, of course, an attitude which sets apart the involved person from the bystander. All who work with people in pain and trouble must steel themselves against sentimentalism. As with physicians, so it is with the nurse. She must keep calm in the face of pain, excitement, and panic. But there are many times when her "professional attitude" becomes an armor that permits her to go about her duties unaffected by pity, concern, or love.

If the student nurse is anything like the student social worker, she comes to the profession with these feelings well developed. She generally is a concerned, warm, interested person wanting to reach out, but also afraid of her own softness and vulnerability. (See a recent poem by Rebecca Beam, entitled "Nursing Is . . . .") [7]

Somewhere in her schooling she begins to reject these parts of herself. She begins to imitate the efficient, the cold, and the detached, expecting that she must erase all that is human in her before she can become a real professional.

Just as a young nurse might hide her fear of witnessing pain and her disgust at seeing excreta, so a young social worker denies his despair at seeing social ills and his anger with social resources. A character armor is being developed.[8] What to the incoming student seems clear—a sobbing child must be comforted by hugs—becomes a problem during the middle part of preparation when the young social workers worry about "infantilizing," "fostering dependency," and exhibiting unprofessional behavior. They squelch their spontaneous selves and behave as they think they should.

It is probably then that the stereotyped smile, the patterned speech, and the stilted language are born. And yet the warmth is still all there. It is within the stewardess, the nurse, the social worker—the desire for closeness, for giving and obtaining comfort (yes, patients are a great source of comfort if only one dares to make use of them), for being human in the face of suffering. Perhaps we could change our modes of advertising; perhaps something could be added to the stewardesses' designer hats and the nurses' caps. Perhaps a concerned face,

---

[7] Rebecca Lee Beam. "Nursing is. . . ." (Student Page). *American Journal of Nursing.* Vol. 68 (November, 1968). P. 2412.

[8] Wilhelm Reich. *Character-Analysis.* Trans. Theodore P. Wolfe. 3d ed. New York: Orgone Press, 1949.

indicating a concerned heart, might become the trademark of TWA as well as the ANA. Then I will more willingly fly in fog or lie in traction next time.

The Invisible Patient
by Edward T. Auer, M.D. *

Who is the invisible patient? I submit that all patients in our hospitals today are somewhat invisible at all times, and that all are totally invisible some times. Not long ago, I was asked to see a patient in consultation. Reviewing his chart, I found that the clinical clerk, a junior medical student, had written an excellent history that included a graphic description of the patient as a person. The intern's work-up was relatively brief, and the resident's note consisted of only several sentences. As I read the progress notes, I found no further reference to the patient. Typical notes read: "Upper G.I. series normal, will order a cholecystogram"; "Cholecystogram normal, will order small bowel films"; and so forth. A review of the chart and a discussion with the house staff made it quite apparent that the staff was treating the chart; the patient had faded from view.

No one can seriously doubt that certain patients fade from view when the staff is focusing its attention on another patient who is acutely or critically ill. Who can argue with the nurse who fails to prepare a patient for a cholecystogram because she is too busy looking after a patient in diabetic coma or one suffering from congestive heart failure? To give more attention to the more serious health condition seems perfectly logical, until the patient who is thereby neglected happens to be you.

There is no substitute for a real-life experience. You cannot appreciate what it is like to be "invisible" unless you have experienced it yourself. Even so, anyone can imagine the kind of thoughts that go through a patient's mind when an identification bracelet is put on him and he is told that its purpose is to help the staff avoid getting him mixed up with other patients.

These are some of the obvious ways in which we lose sight of the patient. They seem to be related to increased specialization, to the complexity of the hospital organization, to emphasis on science in medicine, etc. Although technical and scientific progress is important, we in the health professions must strive to determine whether or not we have adequately defined our goals. Are we

* Edward T. Auer. "The Invisible Patient." *Hospital Progress*. Vol. 50, No. 12 (December 1969). Pp. 55–59.

working effectively and cooperatively in the pursuit of a common goal—the efficient and effective delivery of care to the individual patient?

Aside from the rather catastrophic experience of being distinguishable from other patients only as a result of an ID bracelet, there are also less obvious ways in which our perception of the patient and of ourselves in relation to him can be distorted. Let me illustrate this for you with several brief examples. Some years ago, I worked with a very competent physician. He was regarded as an excellent teacher, and was always praised by the house officers for his scientific skill, as well as his sincere interest in their patients on the wards. He came to see me one day to discuss a problem that was markedly hindering his personal development. When confronted with wealthy patients, he experienced a certain degree of animosity which resulted in a performance far below his usual standards both as a person and as a physician. In brief, his clinical abilities were inhibited by his envy and hostility toward those in life who had more than he. As a result, he could not serve these people effectively and, therefore, lost opportunities to do so. He was completely unaware of the reasons for his behavior under these circumstances.

Recently, an intern discussed a case with me that was causing him much concern. It involved a patient with a history of coronary disease who was being uncooperative in the treatment program outlined for him. He would not stay at bed rest, would not stop smoking, and so forth. The feelings of apprehension and annoyance that the patient's behavior was causing this physician were obvious. They were doing little to improve the patient's attitude. When I pointed out to this intern that the clinical and electrocardiographic findings did not really justify the stringent controls that were being prescribed and that I could not understand the reasons for his degree of concern, he told me that the day before this man was admitted, a young woman, who had a coronary and who was at bed rest for three weeks under his care, had stood up beside her bed and suddenly died. He said he did not want that to happen again. Apparently he was more concerned with this previous experience and his reactions to it than he was with the realities of his current patient's problem.

These examples illustrate the way in which previous life experiences, both recent and remote, conscious and unconscious, influence the reactions of a physician toward a patient. The following example demonstrates the fact that the patient may be similarly affected. A relatively young woman, with a history of two previous episodes of coronary occlusion, was admitted to a hospital complaining of chest pain. The treatment program prescribed for her included complete bed rest, cessation of smoking, restriction of visiting, and so forth. The house staff and nurses became both concerned and annoyed at her failure to cooperate in this program. They told her that her failure to do so was endangering her life. In spite of their warnings, she continued to get out of her bed, to adjust it, to walk down the hall, to use a phone, and to smoke several packs of cigarettes each day.

The patient's past history revealed that, prior to her initial episode of coronary disease, she had been severely depressed and had made a serious attempt to take her own life. It was quite apparent from her behavior and from a subsequent psychiatric examination that she did not share her physician's concern for her life. Once her emotional illness was recognized and treatment for it was initiated, her desire to live returned and, with it, her ability to cooperate in her treatment program. It is important to point out that the staff's annoyance with this "uncooperative patient" served to increase the patient's self-destructive drives.

These brief histories illustrate the fact that individual perceptual experiences are influenced by personalities, which are, in turn, the product of a person's previous life experience. These are not unusual stories. They are the stories of human beings who are ill and of other human beings who are trying to understand them and their illnesses in order to help them. This is the challenge—to see the patient as a human being and to encourage those who come in contact with him to appreciate their role in the total treatment process. The care of the patient begins with his first contact with a member of the hospital staff. Will this contact be a therapeutic one? Will the admission clerk really be interested in more than whether or not the patient is covered by insurance? Will the ward clerk realize that the patient is more than the "ulcer Dr. Jones is expecting?" Will the laboratory technician see the patient as more than a "stat count and urinalysis?" How many of those involved in the patient's care will be thinking of him as a human being like themselves—a person who is ill and frightened and who is delivering himself to the care of a group of strangers?

How do we in the health professions react to the frightened and defensively hostile patient, who replies to a question about why he has come to the hospital with the unfriendly retort, "That's what you're supposed to find out." Do we recognize his fear and try to relieve it or do we become defensive ourselves and intensify it? Are we prepared to understand that human beings react to illness by becoming more dependent? Do we accept the fact that it is quite normal for human beings, faced with a threat of any sort, either to mobilize and fight it or to flee from it? Are we aware of the way in which these basic human responses influence the behavior of patients? Can we recognize, for example, that a patient who has sustained an injury at work and becomes angry and irritated at the delay he experiences in the emergency room might really be fearful not only of the injury itself, but also of the impact that the time lost from work might have on his job security as well as on the economic security of his family?

Reactions of patients toward their illnesses not only influence their behavior but the response of the hospital staff toward them, as well. Hospital personnel, like school teachers, respond best to those patients who are most cooperative. Often, you will hear the comment: "Mr. Jones is a good patient . . . he doesn't give us any trouble." Many times this reflects the maturity of Mr. Jones and the efficiency of the staff. Often, however, it reflects the fact that Mr. Jones either does not have the courage to speak his mind or does not feel he has the right to do so.

Conversely, it is always interesting to observe the techniques used to cope with the patient who is quite demanding. Often, no one makes any effort to determine the cause of this patient's complaints. It is quite true that the patient's attempt to control his environment may be related to deep-seated personal insecurity. It may be equally true that it is the result of a threat to the individual that is associated with his illness. In neither case is it appropriate to overindulge the patient; on the other hand, it is inappropriate to frustrate and frighten him in the hope that he will either toe the line or sign out and "stop bothering us."

Up to this point, I have focused attention on aspects of the problem of the "invisible patient" that are commonly associated with a treatment situation. I would like to turn briefly to a discussion of several other factors that influence patients and health professionals alike.

The first of these is peoples' attitudes toward money. From my own experience, I do not recall having ever encountered an individual who could be described as truly objective when his money was involved. The extremes represented by the person who feels that everyone is out to take his money from him and the person who still believes in Santa Claus are easily recognized. The fact that people want the best care and do not care what it costs is not an unfamiliar problem. Just as many people, however, need care and do nothing about it, because they are afraid they cannot afford it. Unfortunately, this latter group does not concern us as much.

Neither the patient nor the hospital is well served by unreal attitudes toward money that might exist in the patient, the physician, the house staff, the nurse, the office manager, or the administration. However, I am the first to acknowledge the difficulty inherent in trying to modify the attitudes of such a diverse group. Unfortunately, third party financing of medical care provides a convenient scapegoat for many of the conflicting opinions and attitudes toward the cost of health care, and I expect it will continue to do so. It also accounts for some of the unrealistic attitudes that physicians, patients, administrators, and board members have in regard to hospital costs. I do believe, however, that health personnel and hospital staffs must make every effort to realize that the patient's pocketbook is as real and reactive a part of him as are his vital organs. His money should be handled, therefore, with the same maturity, dignity, and respect as they are. Not long ago a well-known comic strip dramatically suggested that the patient was "invisible" until the "fiscal fog" had lifted. I hope that this fact is not commonly true in real life.

The second factor concerns the way in which our personal blind spots interfere with our ability to see one another, to recognize common goals and objectives and to work effectively toward them. This factor must certainly contribute to our inability to really see the patient. For example, some years ago I had the uncomfortable experience of living through a serious rift between a group of physicians and their administrator and hospital board. I knew many of those involved on both sides of the issue. It was apparent throughout the struggle that concern for the primary mission of the hospital—patient care—disappeared in the heat of personal struggles for power. On the other hand, I also had the privilege of serving for many years on the staff of a hospital that enjoyed excellent relations between the medical staff, the hospital administration, and the board of trustees. This hospital experienced differences of opinion, but these differences were always concerned with determining the best way of providing better patient care.

Although it is relatively easy to point out the causes of the invisible patient problem, it is much more difficult to effect solutions. I would like to be able to say that it is to physicians that the health professions should turn for help in attempting to make the patient visible. There was a time when the physician knew and cared about the whole patient. But it is unreal to think we can turn back to those "good old days." Similarly, in the past, nurses often knew as much about a patient and his family as the doctor did and were interested in and concerned about them. But, as scientific skills in medicine and nursing have increased, the complexity of hospital functions has also increased. In developing the profession of hospital administration we have created serious problems for patients. The problem is not unlike that faced by the patient who can find a doctor to take care of his liver, another to take care of his prostate, another to take care of his hemorrhoids, but none to take care of him.

Those interested in the sociology of illness tell us that an accumulation of stressful life situations precedes the onset of illness. More importantly, they indicate that illness begets further stress which, in turn begets further illness. Does it follow then that a patient who, for example, is given an overwhelming bill and is pressed to pay it, is potentially impaired in his ability to do so as a result of such pressure?

The success or failure of treatment is often contingent upon what happens after the patient leaves the hospital. Does he have a place to stay, the necessary nursing care, ample food, someone who cares about him? Does anyone ever look into these questions? Or does the hospital's concern stop when the patient walks out the door? Are not the house, the family, the job, the neighbors that he leaves behind when he comes to the hospital and returns to when he is discharged as much a part of him as that which he physically entrusts to our care? I believe they are. They are just not in our field of vision.

In terms of the future of the invisible patient, I hope that the hospital of the future will become a community health center in the true sense of the term. In addition to treating acute and chronically ill patients, such a hospital would participate in programs of health education and preventive medicine. To accomplish such a goal, those involved in delivering health care must rethink and rework many of the current concepts of medical care. A community health center will mean not only a central place where meaningful records can be kept, but also a place where a team of individuals dedicated to total patient care can work together. The task of realizing such a goal has become too big for any one of us in the health professions to assume individually. We must join forces in our search for the invisible patient if we ever hope to be able to really see him.

chapter two

INTRODUCTION TO PSYCHOANALYTIC CONCEPTS

Psychoanalysis was developed by Sigmund Freud (1856–1939), a Viennese physician and neurologist. In the introduction, we discussed the great impact of Freud's ideas on American culture. Philip Holzman, in discussing the nature of the theory of psychoanalysis, writes:

> What has been called psychoanalytic theory is actually many theories that are loosely tied together—microtheories linked with each other. . . . One such group consists of psychoanalytic theories of thought processes such as memory, perception, attention, consciousness, action, emotion, and concept formation; another group is concerned with psychoanalytic conceptions of development; and still another group is a complex of clinical psychoanalytic theories focused on psychopathology and treatment.[1]

Psychoanalysis was formed from observations of human behavior, and constant revision of models and theories has been a part of its progress. In this chapter, the historical presentation focuses on the first psychopathological problems studied by Freud in a clinical setting. In addition, there is a brief introduction to some frequently used psychoanalytic terms and a discussion of the divisions of the mind as conceptualized by psychoanalysis.

Psychoanalysis is widely recognized as a method of depth psycho-

---

[1] Calvin S. Hall and Gardner Lindzey. *Theories of Personality.* 2d ed. New York: John Wiley & Sons, Inc., 1970. Pp. 29–61.

therapy for emotional disorders. Our focus, however, is not on the therapeutic implications of psychoanalysis but rather on the basic contributions of psychoanalysis to our knowledge of human growth and development as well as normal and abnormal behavior. In order to understand Freud's discoveries and subsequent developments in psychoanalysis, it is helpful to take note of a few historical facts.

Freud, who was born in Freiberg, Moravia, studied medicine at the University of Vienna and graduated in 1881. During the ensuing four years he did postgraduate work in neuroanatomy, neurophysiology, and neurology, and published a number of scholarly scientific papers.

As a neurologist, Freud realized that his medical training had not prepared him to understand and treat successfully those numerous patients whose diagnosis was "hysteria," and who in that era were referred to neurologists for treatment. These patients suffered from a wide variety of symptoms ranging from epileptic-like seizures, paralyses, and anesthesias to anxiety and irrational fears, none of which seemed to have an organic origin.

During the middle and late nineteenth century, such symptoms were thought to be the result of local morphological changes in the tissues. The modern era of medicine had just emerged, and the discoveries of Lister, Pasteur, Koch, and others had already led to the introduction of new scientific laboratory methods in medicine. One great discovery followed another as medicine aspired to become more of a science than an art. These momentous discoveries, however, led to a mechanistic trend in medical practice.

One of the first reactions against this attitude came from Jean Charcot, a French physician who was then considered to be the world's leading neurologist. Charcot refused to concern himself exclusively with the hysterical patient's physical symptoms, because he recognized the necessity of considering the relationship between the patient's mental and physical responses.

In 1885, Freud went to Paris to study with Charcot, who at that time was experimenting with hypnosis as a treatment method for hysteria. Charcot had observed that "unconscious" thoughts could influence conscious behavior. In other words, he recognized that behavior could be influenced by psychological motives of which the subject was not aware.

Freud, greatly impressed with Charcot's methods, returned to Vienna, where he and Joseph Breuer, an internist, attempted to apply Charcot's methods to the treatment of a hysterical patient. Under hypnotic trance, this young woman recalled long-forgotten distressing experiences. Furthermore, she expressed strong emotions related to those experiences, with which she had been unable to cope at the time the events had occurred. Freud and Breuer called this method "cathartic hypnosis." Their patient,

Anna O., named the method the "talking cure," since she felt improved after these sessions.[2]

After using hypnosis on a series of patients, Freud abandoned it, largely because of the temporary nature of the symptomatic improvement. He continued, however, to encourage his patients to express verbally all of their thoughts and feelings, a method that came to be known as "free association." Freud's study of the mind through the use of hypnosis and free association convinced him that by far the greater part of mental functioning in healthy as well as emotionally ill people takes place unconsciously. Under hypnosis, patients remembered and verbalized painful early experiences, but on awakening had no recollection of what had been so dramatically expressed only moments before.

It seemed that the conscious, aware self could not tolerate certain "forgotten" memories. These could come to the surface of the mind only when the conscious self was more or less eliminated by hypnosis. There appeared to be an obstacle to recalling certain events and feelings. This psychological resistance against remembering emotions, wishes, and attitudes was termed "repression." [3]

These unconscious contents, kept from awareness by repression, were by no means inert or passive, but instead continued to exert a pressure for discharge. Freud discovered that certain everyday occurrences such as slips of the tongue, momentary forgetting, losing objects, accidents, and so forth, could often be traced to temporary circumvention of the repressive barrier by these unconscious forces. He referred to these events as the "parapraxes of everyday life." In addition, he understood psychoneurotic symptoms as representing disguised derivatives of forbidden wishes, which had been repressed but which had circumvented the repressive barrier and had found expression in the symptoms.

Patients often told Freud their dreams and fantasies (daydreams) as well as recollections of their childhood. Through the analysis of his own and his patients' dreams, Freud penetrated many of the secrets of dreams. He discovered that dreams have psychological meaning and that they serve an essential intrapsychic function. Eventually, Freud learned how to decipher the strange language of dreams and thereby uncovered basic truths about the human psyche. He concluded that most dreams serve to discharge tensions and conflicts that have their origins in early childhood,

---

[2] Sigmund Freud. *The Standard Edition of the Complete Psychological Works of Sigmund Freud.* Vol. 22, *New Introductory Lectures* (1933). London: The Hogarth Press, 1957. P. 73.

[3] Charles Brenner. *An Elementary Textbook of Psychoanalysis.* Garden City, N.Y.: Doubleday & Company, Inc., 1957. P. 45.

even though the dreams may be triggered or colored by everyday events and current emotional states.

According to Freud, the core dream conflicts arise from unconscious sexual and aggressive attitudes, and from conflicts, especially those with parents and siblings during the early years of life. Since these conflicts could not be successfully resolved in childhood, they had been repressed.

In the adult, these feelings and thoughts, usually heavily disguised, would break through the repression barrier during sleep and appear in dreams along with more recent feelings and ideas.

In 1899, he published his monumental work, *The Interpretation of Dreams*. This book, often considered Freud's most significant publication, treats extensively all aspects of dreaming and delves particularly into the unconscious meaning of dreams.[4]

Freud's psychoanalytic treatment method included the analysis of the patients' dreams, memories, and current thoughts and feelings. A basic feature of his clinical theory was that the mature psyche of the adult could learn to deal effectively and realistically with the painful emotions and ideas that the child's immature mind was forced to repress. The aim of psychoanalysis became that of helping to bring these unconscious memories and feelings to consciousness. Then, those unruly forces associated with the memories could be "domesticated" and brought into harmony with the conscious moral and social standards of the adult personality.

Freud did not discover the existence of unconscious mental processes. Philosophers, poets, and physicians long before Freud speculated on unconscious types of thinking. He did, however, describe and clarify the powerful unconscious forces that influence so much of our thinking and behavior. The consideration of these dynamic psychological forces within the individual and in his interactions with his environment comprises the psychodynamic view of mental life.

As Freud's psychoanalytic experience progressed, he also approached human psychology from a developmental point of view. He sought to relate the neurotic behavior observed in his patients to significant childhood experiences and reactions. As psychoanalytic knowledge advanced, it became increasingly evident that such experiences (often forgotten or unconscious) were important determinants, not only of neurotic symptoms, but of normal behavior as well.

During the past twenty-five years, psychoanalysts such as Anna Freud, René Spitz, John Bowlby, David Levy, Margaret Mahler, Sylvia Brody, and Erik Erikson have studied infants and children in their developing family

---

[4] Sigmund Freud. Standard Edition, Vols. 4 and 5. *The Interpretation of Dreams* (1900).

46 Introduction to Psychoanalytic Concepts

and social interactions, thereby contributing immeasurably to our understanding of personality development.[5] Their influence, which has found its way into pediatric as well as psychiatric nursing, has had a profound effect on child-rearing practices and on the care of infants.[6]

The individual, the family unit, and society with its cultural patterns have all been studied extensively. Each area has its own students, research methods, and scientific terminology. A satisfactory integration of these overlapping and related behavioral sciences still lies in the future. However, a major effort to bridge these artificial gaps between the person, his family, his society, and his culture was begun in *Childhood and Society,* by Erik Erikson, a psychoanalyst and cultural anthropologist.[7] Erikson's theme is the continuing lifelong interaction and mutual regulation between child, family, and society. In order to illuminate these ideas, he discusses the stages of the human life cycle. To each of eight stages—infancy, early childhood, play-age, school-age, adolescence, young adulthood, maturity, and old age—he assigned biological drives and necessities, psychological experiences and conflicts, and social tasks and transactions. Erikson emphasized that the outcome of each stage is determined to some extent by those that come before and, in turn, will influence those that follow.

Erikson's major focus was on childhood and adolescence. In addition, however, he called attention to the importance of certain crucial events throughout life.

---

[5] Anna Freud. *Normality and Pathology in Childhood.* New York: International Universities Press, Inc., 1965.

———. *The First Year of Life.* New York: International Universities Press, Inc., 1965.

John Bowlby. *Attachment and Loss.* Vol. 1, *Attachment.* New York: Basic Books, Inc., 1969.

———. *Child Care and the Growth of Love.* Baltimore: Pelican Books, Inc., 1963.

David Levy. *Maternal Overprotection.* New York: W. W. Norton & Company, Inc., 1966.

Sylvia Brody. *Patterns of Mothering.* New York: International Universities Press, Inc., 1956.

Erik H. Erikson. *Childhood and Society.* New York: W. W. Norton & Company 1963.

Mahler, Margaret. *On Human Symbiosis and the Vicissitudes of Individuation.* Vol. 1, *Infantile Psychosis.* New York: International Universities Press, Inc., 1968.

[6] Florence Blake and Howell Wright. *Essentials of Pediatric Nursing.* Philadelphia: J. B. Lippincott Company, 1963.

Charles K. Hofling, Madeleine M. Leininger, and Elizabeth A. Bregg. *Basic Psychiatric Concepts in Nursing.* Philadelphia: J. B. Lippincott Co., 1967.

Hildegard Peplau. *Interpersonal Relations in Nursing.* New York: C. P. Putnam's Sons, 1952.

[7] Erikson. *Childhood and Society.*

Most recently, psychoanalysts have turned their attention to problems of identity, the meaning of "self," and the understanding of how the person adapts to his environment.

Psychiatric nursing has long included psychoanalytic concepts in clinical care of individuals and groups. Psychiatric nurses have, in addition, attempted to transmit some of these concepts to general nursing, especially in the areas of pediatrics and maternal-child care.

Preconscious and Unconscious States of Mind

At this juncture, it seems appropriate to attempt a clarification of a few terms commonly found in the psychoanalytic literature. These are *preconscious* and *unconscious; id, ego* and *superego*. Since these terms do recur, both in the text and the reprints, the student should have some understanding of them before turning to the study of the life cycle which begins in Chapter 3.

A fundamental assumption of psychoanalysis assigns meaning to such diverse and apparently meaningless phenomena as dreams, psychoneurotic symptoms, slips of the tongue, and momentary forgetting. Regardless of how irrational the thought or behavior pattern may appear, its form and content is assumed to have been determined by antecedent experiences and mental associations. Since these factors are usually multiple and complicated, and usually involve unconscious processes, complete explanations are not always possible. This does not, however, alter the fact that mental phenomena do make sense if one knows enough of the determining chain of ideas or events which preceded them.

From the psychoanalytic point of view, mental functioning is a complex, dynamic, ongoing process of which only a small portion is within one's awareness. Consciousness, which represents only the outer layer of mental activity, is usually closely related to the immediate perceptual and adaptive needs of the individual. Most psychic processes are not conscious, that is, they lie outside of immediate awareness.

A large group of thoughts, memories, and feelings closely allied to consciousness may be brought to awareness without great effort through concentration. These include most of the usual data of thinking, recalling, and feeling, since relatively few thoughts or perceptions can be held in the immediate focus of conscious attention. Such mental processes are referred to as *preconscious.*

Both preconscious memories and thoughts as well as deeply buried indifferent memories may correctly be described as *unconscious,* simply because they are not within one's consciousness. Freud's monumental discoveries about *unconscious* mental forces, however, refer especially to those vital and dynamically powerful urges, memories, and reminders of emotional conflicts that date back as far as earliest infancy.

It is not possible to observe directly these unconscious mental processes. We can, however, by observing the derivatives of these repressed forces, realize that unconscious processes may continue to exert a major impact on thoughts and behavior long after the original events have been "forgotten." A few examples are the powerful feelings of sibling rivalry, the desire to remain forever a dependent infant, and the child's wish to take the place of one or the other parent. Disguised derivatives of these or other unconscious contents may appear in adult consciousness in dreams, fantasies, slips of the tongue, psychoneurotic symptoms, personality traits, and patterns of relationships.[8]

The Divisions of the Mind
(Id, Ego, and Superego)

A "model" of mental functioning may help us to visualize the interaction between the parts of the personality and between the personality and the environment. The final model of the mind which Freud settled upon was first described in 1923. At that time, he described the adult personality as consisting of three major systems: the id, the ego, and the superego. Each of these structures has its own functions, principles, dynamisms, properties, and mechanisms. The relationship between these three systems is intricate and intimate and has been the object of detailed study by psychoanalysts and psychologists.

It is often difficult to disentangle the relative importance of one mental agency as opposed to another, and behavior nearly always includes to some degree the influence of all three agencies interacting with each other.

Since much of the psychoanalytic and dynamic psychiatric literature refers to this model of the mind, it is worthwhile for the nurse to be familiar with it. It is also important to bear in mind that this model is a hypothetical, abstract view of the way the mind may work. There is no reason to think that it has any organic equivalents in the brain, even though there may be some crude approximations between certain parts of the brain and some of the functions of the psychic apparatus.

The *id* is that primitive portion of the mind that is the repository of the basic sexual and aggressive drives. It is completely unconscious. It stands, so to speak, on the border between the bodily sources of energy from the chemical and physiological processes which go on throughout life, and the psychological functioning we have begun to describe in these pages.

[8] Brenner. *An Elementary Textbook of Psychoanalysis.* P. 45.

In other words, the id is that division or agency of the mind in which the physical needs and demands of the body are (in theory) "translated" or "transformed" into psychological and emotional terms.

Sigmund Freud wrote:

[The id] is the dark, inaccessible part of our personality; what little we know of it we have learned from our study of the dream work and of the construction of neurotic symptoms, and most of that is of a negative character and can only be described as a contrast to the ego. [The id] is filled with energy reaching it from the instincts, but it has no organization, produces no collective will, but only a striving to bring about the satisfaction of the instinctual needs subject to the observance of the pleasure principle. The logical laws of thought do not apply in the id and this is true above all of the law of contradiction. Contrary impulses exist side by side without cancelling each other out or diminishing each other. . . . There is nothing in the id that corresponds to the idea of time. . . . The id, of course, knows no judgements of value: no good and evil, no morality.[9]

The id, then, by its very nature is blind, impulsive, and irrational; moral and ethical values are unknown to it. It consists of sexual and aggressive energies and pressures seeking outlets. The id stands for a portion of our mental functioning of which we are totally unaware in a direct sense, except insofar as id impulses manifest themselves in dreams, slips of the tongue, neurotic symptoms, and so forth. When repression occurs, the forbidden ideas, wishes, or impulses become part of the id.

The ego [10] is that portion of the mind that develops in response to the need of the infant to adjust to the environment. It mediates between the id and the outer world. The ego, then, performs highly important functions that serve adaptation by permitting the person to obtain drive satisfaction with a minimum of frustration, anxiety, and guilt; and with a maximum sense of competence and reasonable achievement.

The ego must distinguish between what exists only in the mind and things in the external world.

Sigmund Freud writes:

The relation to the external world has become the decisive factor for the ego; it has taken on the task of representing the external world to the id—fortunately for the id, which could not escape destruction if, in its blind efforts for the satisfaction of its instincts, it disregarded that supreme external power. In accomplishing this function, the ego must observe the external world, must lay down an accurate picture of it in the memory-traces of its perceptions, and by its exercise of the function of "reality testing" must put aside whatever in this

---

[9] Freud. *New Introductory Lectures.* Pp. 73–74.

[10] The term "ego" is *not* used here as synonymous with "self," although that usage was current in psychoanalysis before 1923.

picture of the external world is an addition derived from internal sources of excitation. (i.e., Those stimuli which come from within the mind itself.) [11]

It is in the ego that Freud places the functions of rational thinking and the sense of time. The ego is capable of perceiving, planning, and carrying out the necessary actions to achieve satisfaction within the limits set by the external environment.

A major function of the ego is to perform a synthetic and executive function, integrating and acting upon the often conflicting demands of the impulses, the moral judgments of the conscience or superego and the requirements of the external world. This is not an easy task, and often the ego is placed under great stress.

The ego is said to be best characterized by its functions. The ego controls many of our actions and selects what instincts will be satisfied and in what manner. It performs an integrative function in responding to the demands of the id, the superego, and the external world. Its principal role is to mediate between instinctual needs of the human and the demands of the external environment. A partial list of functions assigned to the ego would include perception, learning, memory, reality, testing, control of motility, and the acquisition and use of language. The manner in which the id impulses are controlled and the derivative form in which they are expressed is within the province of the ego. Self-preservation is a function of the ego.

The defense mechanisms (or mental mechanisms) that serve to maintain the equilibrium of the personality are under the control of the ego. We will have much more to say about the ego and its functions as we proceed with our description of the personality and the manner in which the individual functions psychologically in health as well as under the stress of illness.

Psychoanalysts at first were particularly concerned with manifestations of deeply unconscious, or id, impulses and the derivatives of them that appeared in the forms of symptoms, irrational behavior, inhibitions of functioning, and so forth. More recently, however, the ego has been studied extensively by psychoanalysts and other students of the mind because it is more directly accessible to study than the id, and because it reveals much about normal as well as abnormal behavior and thinking.

Under the stress of illness or injury, ego functions are ordinarily weakened, and the nurse may see signs of distorted perception, memory problems, poor reality testing, and the emergence of considerable anxiety, severe irritability, or changes in self-concept.

The third agency of the mind that Freud delineated is the *superego*,

---

[11] Freud. *New Introductory Lectures.* P. 75.

which does not appear in well-developed form until about the age of six or seven. Although precursors begin to make their appearance during the first few years of life. The superego is the internal representative of the traditional values and ideals of society as interpreted to the child by his parents and enforced by them through a system of rewards and punishments.

Small children, at first, do not manifest any internal inhibitions or compunctions against pleasure seeking. Their parents or surrogates gradually instill in them such inhibitions. By giving affection and by threats of loss of love or by means of punishment, the parents exert enormous power and control over the psychological development of the child. There remain, deep in the superego, unconscious memories, and distortions of memories, of early and fearsome parental prohibitions with real or imagined threats of bodily punishment, illness, and rejection as the price for expressing forbidden aggressive or sexual impulses. In the superego, derivatives of these long-forgotten impressions or experiences still remain in many adults and contribute to irrational guilt reactions, depression, and suicidal attempts.

In other words, the superego in the older child and adult serves a somewhat similar guiding and moral function within the individual that the parents did for the child during the first years of life. When a forbidden impulse is expressed or is about to be expressed, the superego can assume the function of creating a sense of guilt and the possibility of some vague punishment.

The very word "superego" expresses Freud's view of this agency as a higher or overseeing portion of the ego itself. Insofar as the attitudes contained in the superego coincide with those of the ego, there will be little or no conflict or friction between these two agencies of the mind. On the other hand, where tension exists between them, anxiety, guilt, and symptom formation may result.

In summary, the tripartite model of the mind in which the ego, id, and superego are the three systems provides a framework in which can be placed the various psychological processes and functions that characterize the personality.

Hall and Lindzey note:

> Under ordinary circumstances these different principles do not collide with one another nor do they work at cross purposes. On the contrary, they work together as a team under the administrative leadership of the ego. The personality normally functions as a whole rather than as three separate segments. In a very general way, the id may be thought of as the biological component of personality, the ego as the psychological component, and the superego as the social component.[12]

[12] Hall and Lindzey. *Theories of Personality*. Pp. 29–61.

Suggested Readings on the Life of Sigmund Freud

Costigan, Giovanni. *Sigmund Freud—A Short Biography*. New York: The Macmillan Company, 1965.

Freud, Ernst L. *Letters of Sigmund Freud*. New York: Basic Books, Inc., 1960.

Freud, Martin. *Sigmund Freud: Man and Father*. New York: Vanguard Press, Inc., 1958.

Jones, Ernest. *The Life and Work of Sigmund Freud*. Vols. 1–3. New York: Basic Books, Inc., 1953.

———. *The Life and Work of Sigmund Freud*. Edited and abridged by Lionel Trilling and Steven Marcus. New York: Basic Books, Inc., 1961.

———. *Sigmund Freud—Four Centenary Addresses*. New York: Basic Books, Inc., 1956.

Rieff, Philip. *Freud: The Mind of the Moralist*. New York: The Viking Press, Inc., 1959.

Suggested Readings on Psychoanalysis

Alexander, Franz. *The Scope of Psychoanalysis*. New York: Basic Books, Inc., 1961.

Brenner, Charles. *An Elementary Textbook of Psychoanalysis*. Garden City, New York: Doubleday & Company, Inc., 1957.

Freud, Sigmund. *Abstracts of the Standard Edition of the Complete Works of Sigmund Freud*. Edited by Carrie Lee Rothgeb. U.S. Department of Health, Education, and Welfare. Washington, D.C.: U.S. Government Printing Office, 1970.

Hendrick, Ives. *Facts and Theories of Psychoanalysis*. New York: Alfred A. Knopf, Inc., 1958.

Herma, Hans and Gertrud Kurth, editors. *A Handbook of Psychoanalysis*. Cleveland: The World Publishing Company, 1963.

Holzman, Philip S. *Psychoanalysis and Psychopathology*. New York: McGraw-Hill Book Company, 1970.

Jones, Ernest. *Papers on Psychoanalysis*. Boston: Beacon Press, 1961.

Klein, Melaine. *Contributions to Psycho-Analysis* 1921–1945. New York: McGraw-Hill Book Company, 1964.

Menninger, Karl. *Man Against Himself.* New York: Harcourt, Brace, and Company, 1938.

———. *A Psychiatrist's World: Selected Papers of Karl Menninger.* Vols. I and II. New York: The Viking Press, 1959.

———, with Martin Meyman and Paul Pruysor. *The Vital Balance: The Life Process in Mental Health and Illness.* New York: The Viking Press, 1963.

Menninger, William. *A Psychiatrist for a Troubled World: Selected Papers of William C. Menninger.* Vols. I and II. New York: The Viking Press, 1967.

———. *Psychiatry: Its Evolution and Present Status.* Ithaca, New York: Cornell University Press, 1948.

Munroe, Ruth L. *Schools of Psychoanalytic Thought.* New York: The Dryden Press, Inc., 1955.

Redlich, Fritz and June Bingham. *The Inside Story: Psychiatry and Everyday Life.* New York: Vintage Books, 1953.

Trilling, Lionel. *Freud and the Crisis of Our Culture.* Boston: The Beacon Press, 1955.

Waelder, Robert. *Basic Theory of Psychoanalysis.* New York: Schocken Books, 1964.

chapter three

INFANCY

Early Infancy

The human personality evolves out of the interaction between the individual and his social and physical environment. Genetically transmitted traits and potentials provide the biological basis for physical maturation and mental development.

Our discussions focus on the psychosocial aspects of personality and the events of infancy and early childhood that provide the foundation for the adult personality. It is not possible to understand adequately adult mental life without some knowledge of early human development. For the nurse, this knowledge is doubly essential, since her work includes intimate contact with both children and adults.

The birth of the infant, with the shock of transition from life within the uterus to life in the outside world, calls forth maximal adaptational responses. Although at that moment the infant becomes separate from its mother in a physical sense, he is totally dependent on a mothering person for his very survival.

Human beings are endowed with relatively few of the innate determinants of behavior known as instincts, which provide animals with stereotyped behavioral reaction patterns. Such behavior is demonstrated in the migrations of birds, spawning habits of fish, and mating rituals of mammals. Many instincts guarantee the survival of animals by asserting themselves very early in life. They also allow animals to become independent and self-sufficient while still very young. Animal behavior, which is largely determined by instincts, has an intraspecies sameness and predictability that is much less apparent in humans.

In human society the enormous variety of individual, family, and cultural differences reflects the relative paucity of specific instinctual endowment. One result is that the environment, especially that of the family, exerts a major influence in shaping the personality of the individual.

The long period of helplessness and dependency that characterizes the human infant is unknown among other animals. <u>The severance of the umbilical cord marks the infant's first progress toward independence.</u> But the human infant or small child, if left to his own devices, would soon die. The complete dependency of the immature child underlines the importance of his need for nurture and protection by persons closely involved with his well-being. In the nuclear family of western society, with which we are most familiar, the mother first, and the family later, are the forces most often in the key position to influence the child's personality development. Both parents are important in providing for the child's changing needs, and the family provides the dynamic structure and framework for channeling much of the child's behavior. It is the first social system in which the child, through the directive influence shown by parental attitudes, learns the basic mores of his society. Family patterns and child-rearing practices are undergoing changes which may ultimately be far reaching. Within our social system, however, the mother–child relationship remains the first and most significant one of all.

THE MOTHER AND INFANT AS A BIOLOGICAL AND PSYCHOSOCIAL UNIT

During pregnancy, the mother and her child are a biological unit, unseparated and in many ways mutually dependent. Prenatal care was established in order to protect both mother and child, while the mother carries the pregnancy to term.

Although conception is the beginning of life for the fetus, the pregnancy, represents also a stage of development for the mother. Long before they are physiologically able to bear children, little girls are interested in infants. For many women such an interest continues throughout their lives, whether or not they become mothers. Since the capacity to provide good maternal care is independent of the experience of motherhood, men as well as women may possess maternal attributes.

A "maternal instinct" is relatively weak in human beings compared to that in lower animals. It is probably limited to such manifestations as milk flow at the sound of a crying infant, heightened awareness of and response to the infant's cries, and some diffuse urges to hold, cuddle, and nourish the baby.

It seems likely that most of what we consider "maternal behavior" is learned; that is, it evolves out of innumerable experiences throughout life—but especially in childhood—which lead to identifications, self-images, and personality traits that later are activated when maternal responses are called for. Almost all women are made aware of being "female" from a very early age, probably well before the end of the first year. The responses of those around infants are consciously and unconsciously reactive to the gender of the infants. These responses reflect individual idiosyncrasies, family customs, and cultural attitudes toward men and women. Thus it is that girls "feel" feminine and boys "feel" masculine long before sexual-genital differences are clear to them.[1]

As a result of these factors, it is customary (though not necessary) that little girls of two or three begin playing maternally with dolls or with little siblings, whereas boys generally are encouraged directly and subtly into more "masculine" activities. Tender, maternal behavior in both boys and girls may represent identification with mother, love for a baby sibling, a defensive reaction against hostile urges toward a sibling, or a combination of these and other factors.

Since families in our society often encourage maternal behavior on the part of fathers as well as mothers, it is not surprising that many normal men are capable of giving excellent maternal care. Nor is it surprising that some women have had their maternal tendencies thwarted by sexual conflicts, jealousy, and competition with mother, rivalries with little brothers and sisters, and other conflicts. The result may be women who have difficulty accepting and expressing maternal impulses. Thus it is that many men are as capable of providing maternal care as are women, while some women seem to lack the skills and sensitivities of what we consider the "good mother." The male nurse, for example, may possess a firm sense of his masculinity and yet find satisfaction and professional success in nursing because of his capacity to express helpful derivatives of maternal behavior toward his patients.

Maternal Attitudes and Skills

Early experiences. Just as a woman's early development may or may not prepare her psychologically for marriage, childbearing, and child care, nursing students show a wide range of differences in aptitude when they begin clinical training in obstetrical and pediatric units. They may have, as

---

[1] Robert Stoller. *Sex And Gender: On The Development Of Masculinity And Femininity.* New York: Science House, 1968.

children, often "played the role" of mother or nurse, caring for dolls, animals, or younger children. Whatever her past experience, the nurse is frequently referred to as a "mother surrogate." [2] Nursing in many ways is similar to the mother-child relationship. The empathy that the nurse feels toward her patient is not unlike feelings a mother may experience toward her child, and a nurse may become a "mother figure" for her patients. Those nurses who have cared for younger brothers and sisters or who have had children of their own usually find it easier to work with infants and children in the hospital. One of the responsibilities of nursing education is to provide all nursing students the opportunity to acquire these skills.

Pregnancy. From the time she becomes aware of having conceived, the mother has an emotional response to her pregnancy, to her unborn child, and to the dramatic changes in her body during pregnancy. Parenthood brings with it new duties and demands. While the physiological process of "normal pregnancy" is the same for all women, the psychological impact is different for each woman. A young, highly paid actress or model at the height of her career is likely to have very different responses to her changing body from those of a woman whose life centers on her home and her family. And, obviously, an unwed mother who plans to relinquish her baby views her pregnancy very differently from a young married woman who eagerly awaits the birth of her first child.

Despite the popular assumption that babies are "blessed events," some adults do not wish to have children. Reasons may be conscious or unconscious and may range widely. They include fears about childbirth, sexual identity problems, concerns about world or national social instability, financial problems, health factors, and dislike of babies and children. One woman wrote to the *London Observer,* on September 25, 1966:

> My first conscious reason for not wanting children is that I've never yet met a child that I would like to have permanently around my life. Certain children for brief, well defined periods, maybe—but not all day. I find babies irritating at best, rather disgusting at worst. Young children bore me and I think their demands on one's time and tolerance outrageous. I prefer the company and conversation of adults.

Birth. While most mothers are delighted with their babies, some express negative attitudes. An unhappily married woman may look at her newborn son and comment with disgust, "He looks just like his father. I suppose I'm in for more trouble." The number of children a woman has borne can also influence her reactions. Mrs. Jones may complain of the burden placed on her family by the birth of her fifth child. She may say,

---

[2] Sam Schulman. "Basic Functional Roles In Nursing: Mother Surrogate and Healer." *Patients, Physicians and Illness.* E. Gartly Jaco (ed.). New York: The Free Press, 1958. Pp. 528–37.

"I like kids, but my husband's a longshoreman, and the work has been unsteady. There's not enough money to buy all the things the rest of us need."

The interactions between the mother and infant are influenced by many other factors. The sex of a baby is often of considerable importance to its mother. Her reaction to its sex may be a clue to her ability to accept the child's sexual identity and role in later life. Birth order is significant. In our own culture, babies—the firstborn especially—may cause the mother to feel anxious, uncertain, and incompetent. The first child is handled differently from his later brothers and sisters, who are born to a more experienced mother.

For many women, their babies represent their most important creative production. Their sense of worth as women is tied to the normality of their infants. The baby represents an extension of the mother's self, a part of her own body expelled to the outside world for all to see and evaluate. As a result, new mothers show an understandable curiosity and concern about the physical intactness of their newborn infants and wish to undress and examine the baby at the earliest opportunity. Twins, premature infants, retarded children, and children with birth defects greatly complicate the maternal–child relationship. If there are defects in her child, the mother may have feelings of guilt, anger, and depression, which can lead to a crisis.

A woman's spontaneous reactions to pregnancy and motherhood often reveal important facts about her personality and conflicts. These reactions, however, tend to become modified with time. Multiple factors are at play in all human behavior. Initial responses of a new mother eventually become only a small part of an increasingly complex relationship as the mother takes her baby home from the hospital and begins to assume total responsibility for his care.

Mothering skills can be learned, and childless women may become highly skilled at infant care. Furthermore, many young fathers who calmly quiet crying babies and handle their children with tenderness and understanding, clearly demonstrate that men too can "mother" an infant. Much about an infant's care can be learned by observation of the way the mother holds her child while carrying out tasks such as feeding and bathing. The nurse can be extremely helpful to the mother by demonstrating methods of properly holding an infant, since new mothers often lack this knowledge.

Reva Rubin suggests that a distinction be drawn between maternal and obstetrical care. She writes:

> Maternal nursing care must include obstetrical nursing care but it goes beyond obstetrical nursing in scope and in ultimate objectives. It presumes a basic education and training in nursing in which obstetrics is only a necessary

part of the whole of nursing skill and knowledge available to the practice of maternity nursing.[3]

Nurses, like mothers, have personality variations that may affect their ability to care for infants. For example, Margaret Freis noted:

> It has been found that nurses in hospitals caring for newborns affect the amount of activity displayed by the infant. The author has observed that when active-compulsive nurses bathed and weighed infants, these infants reacted with more startled responses than when cared for by a "quiet" nurse.[4]

The nature of the mothering received by the nurse will affect her manner of providing substitute maternal care to her young patients.

The Newborn Child

The oral stage. The first year of life, the period of infancy, comprises the *oral stage* of childhood development.[5] This term, as used in personality theory, reflects the primary importance of the mouth as a source of pleasure during this period of life. The baby needs to take in nourishment in order to survive. He expresses pain or physical discomfort by crying, and derives pleasure and comfort from sucking. The mouth area is richy supplied with sensory nerve endings and becomes the main focus for the relief of tension and the achievement of gratification through early infancy. Any available object eventually ends in his mouth, and as a normal part of his development, he sucks his fingers and thumb. The need for pleasure sucking is separate from the need for nourishment. Babies who are comfortably fed will continue to suck on the nipple, pacifier, or their own fingers or hands. It is as though nature has provided for the area of the mouth and lips to be a source of sensual pleasure in order to assure that the intake of essential nutrition will be accomplished at this critical early stage of life.

Until the sucking reflex is well established, the new mother may have some difficulties in her first attempts to feed her infant. Bernfeld notes, regarding the infant and sucking:

> It is by no means an ordinary reflex; on the contrary, sucking is a very complicated act, which is not altogether understood in all detail. . . . The act of sucking proper is performed within the mouth, in which the tongue, gums, cheeks, and lower jaw act as a suction pump. Swallowing is closely associated

---

[3] Reva Rubin. "Basic Maternal Behavior." *Nursing Outlook.* Vol. 9, No. 11 (November, 1961). P. 683.

[4] Margaret Fries. "The Child's Ego Development and the Training of Adults in His Environment." *The Psychoanalytic Study of the Child.* Vol. II. New York: International Universities Press, Inc., 1946. P. 89.

[5] Clara Thompson with Patrick Mullahy. *Psychoanalysis: Evolution and Development.* New York: Thomas Nelson and Sons, 1950. P. 35.

60 *Infancy*

with sucking, but only after the fluid has reached the mouth. . . . Crying and sucking are complementary processes in the newborn when awake, and to a certain extent in older infants too. . . . The hunger cry is nothing more than a preliminary step to sucking. The newborn is incapable of making an intentional movement to put something into its mouth.[6]

Establishment of patterns. During the first months of life the infant's activities consist mainly of eating, eliminating, and sleeping. He normally sleeps about twenty hours a day, but unbroken sleep seldom lasts more than two hours, at which times it is interrupted by hunger or some other discomfort. Infants usually fall asleep quickly, sleep lightly, and are awakened easily. The newborn usually awakes crying, and the crying attracts the attention of the mother. Crying is the infant's means of signaling for help and expressing discomfort and dissatisfaction.

During the first six months or so, the infant experiences the world in a passive fashion. He takes in whatever his environment has to offer, physically and emotionally. If the mother can provide adequate psychological and physical care of the infant during these early months, the normal infant usually responds by being what the mother describes as a "good baby" or a "happy baby." As the immature infant copes with the mechanics of life, a mutual adaptation usually results between the mother and child. Dissatisfaction on the part of either the mother or infant can disturb the balance of this relationship.

Individual differences. Babies, like all other people, are individuals, and their appetites may vary during the first few days of life. Sooner or later the baby will indicate what kind of child he is by his rhythm of eating and sleeping and by the problems he presents. The personality of the child may emerge quite early, and the compatibility of the mother and child, or lack of it, can often be seen in their early relationship. A very active, alert mother, for example, may not respond favorably to a quiet, rather phlegmatic, though otherwise normal, child.

Fries writes, in regard to individual differences:

Infants vary in response to stimuli. There is a quiet infant, the moderately active infant and the active infant. For example, a restriction to movement that is frustrating to the active child may not be so to the quiet child, whereas situations which are real obstacles to the quiet type are easily overcome by the active.[7]

Methods by which the infant learns. The baby's physical responses are almost totally unorganized as compared to the behavior of mature adults. His needs are urgent and his patience limited. Since he is completely

---

[6] Siegfried Bernfeld. *The Psychology of the Infant.* Trans. Rosette Hurwitz. New York: Brentano's, 1929. P. 24.

[7] Fries. "The Child's Ego Development." P. 88.

unable to put any of his feelings into words, his mother, as she gets to "know him," must learn from his nonverbal cues what he wants and needs.

Fenichel comments:

Infants and small children live mainly according to the "pleasure principle." They obey every impulse, have no interest except to get rid of their tensions. Their continual attempt to do whatever they like doing right at the moment, is restricted only by the inhibiting force of their physical limitations.[8]

As the mother cares for her infant, it is important for the nurse to remind her that much of his earliest learning comes through the sense of touch. A restless baby is often soothed by being picked up, bathed, walked with, and held. The face and head of an infant are especially sensitive. The gentle stroking of the head is calming to a restless infant, as are changes in position. Gentle but firm holding of an infant gives him a sense of contentment and security.

Infants in turn soon learn to cling to their mother and to seem to enjoy and derive gratification from touching her body. John Bowlby writes:

There is in infants an in-built propensity to be in touch with and to cling to a human being. In this sense there is a "need" for an object independent of food, which is as primary as the "need" for food and warmth.[9]

The need to attach himself to his mother and to cling to her, as well as to be held and touched by her, has been studied by psychologists, especially by Harlow. In his work with monkey infants, he discovered that there is no substitute for the warm responsive maternal body, but that the infant monkeys develop far more normally when they can attach themselves to a terry-cloth covered wire dummy "mother" than when all they have is a wire frame with no cloth around it to which to cling. While it is always necessary to caution against drawing conclusions regarding human behavior from animal experiments, Harlow's work seems to extend and to verify tentative conclusions made by observers of human infants.[10]

In addition to touch, the infant experiences his environment through his mother's eyes, ears, and sense of smell. Holding, cuddling, singing, rocking, and talking to an infant help to make even the briefest encounters pleasurable for both baby and mother. The young infant needs regular physical contact with a mothering person, and should be held and carried periodically, even if no physical care is needed.

Infants who are born with certain congenital sensory defects such as

[8] Otto Fenichel. "The Means of Education." *The Psychoanalytic Study of the Child.* Vol. 1. New York: International Universities Press, Inc., 1945. P. 281.

[9] John Bowlby. *Attachment and Loss.* Vol. I. New York: Basic Books, Inc., 1969. P. 178.

[10] Harry F. Harlow and Robert R. Zimmermann. "Affectional Responses in Infant Monkeys." *Science.* Vol. 130 (1959). P. 421.

blindness, deafness, or kinesthetic impairment require special sensory gratification to make up for these deficits. In fact, Solnit and Senn stress the particular value, for such infants, of being cuddled.[11] Infants who are born blind should be offered special opportunities to develop their hearing and their sense of touch. With adequate educational and training opportunities, these children can develop into emotionally healthy adults.

Much of the nurse's work involves touch contact with patients. Lianne Mercer, a nurse, writes:

> Touch has many meanings. It can be interpreted as the acknowledgement of a person's presence, a display of love, an act of aggression, an arousal of sexual desire, and a desire for comfort and a feeling of physical closeness. How one person interprets the touch of another depends upon each person's cultural background and his feelings at the time and upon the nature of the relationship. It is a primitive way of communicating and frequently reaches a person when nothing else will. The mother comforts the infant by holding him close. For many centuries healing has occurred through the "laying on of hands." The therapist sometimes touches the schizophrenic patient to maintain contact with him.[12]

The extra dimension. Much of what goes on between infant and mother is a "silent language." The mother learns what the infant's feelings are by observing, holding, and handling it. The baby in turn gradually becomes equally "tuned in" to its mother's moods and reactions. This "empathic" quality permits both individuals to experience with a part of themselves what the other person seems to be feeling. Empathy—as used here—refers to the capacity to become aware of feelings or emotions of another. It is in these earliest months of life that the precursors of adult empathy appear. The six-month-old infant, for example, who does not understand words can be acutely aware of, and respond to, tension, resentment, and anxiety in those persons who care for him. Infants cannot for many months experience themselves as beings separate from their mothers. The empathic adult, however, retains a sense of his own individuality while remaining able to consider and to act on his empathic responses. Throughout life much important communication in close relationships occurs in an empathic, non-verbal fashion.

For the sensitive nurse, the capacity to empathize with her patients is essential. When the nurse helps the new mother with her baby, she may wish to consider with the mother all aspects of the baby's physical and emotional nurturance and maintenance. Activities that seem routine, such as feeding, changing, and bathing an infant, should not be treated merely

---

[11] Milton J. E. Senn and Albert J. Solnit. *Problems in Child Behavior and Development.* Philadelphia: Lea and Febiger, 1968.

[12] Lianne S. Mercer. "Touch: Comfort or Threat?" *Perspectives in Psychiatric Care.* Vol. IV, No. 3 (1966). Pp. 20–25.

as physical care. Instead, the mother (or nurse) should view these activities as opportunities to demonstrate her affection for her baby.

Reva Rubin writes:

> The beginning mother tends to use her fingers, then her hand, then her arms as appendages not too well connected with her body. There is an orderly sequence and progression from one phase of handling and touch to another. So universal is this progression, that we have begun to use it as an index of how the mother feels about herself and about her relationship with her infant and to assess her readiness and capacity for increasing maternal behavior.

She writes further:

> The first, and sometimes most dramatic, maternal behavior observed is the mother's concern for her ability to function in a mothering capacity. We are all familiar with the physical manifestations which reveal the intensity of meaning the first mothering acts have for the primipara: the sweating palms, the flushed or perspiring face, the body held tense and rigid throughout the act, the predominantly silent concentration with which she carries out her task. Upon the completion of the task, she is ready, to the point of eagerness, for the baby to be taken from her and the fatigue and exhaustion she then manifests serve as further indicators of how intensely meaningful this mothering act has been for her. We see this behavior repeated through various tasks: the first time she feeds her child, the first time she changes her child, the first time she dresses or bathes her child.[13]

Margaret Ribble states:

> It is obviously true that unwise attention prolongs dependency and thus spoils a baby. But mother love is a good deal like food, we do not stop giving it because the child may get too much or the wrong kind. It has to be expressed regularly, so that the child expects it. A little at a time and frequently, is the emotional formula.[14]

Behavior and food. One of the most important maternal tasks is that of feeding the infant. Nurses working on obstetrical and pediatric floors quickly become aware of the enormous demand for information as mothers present a variety of questions in regard to infant feeding. For both mother and baby, feeding can represent mutual satisfaction or conflict and struggle. If the mother is able to nourish her baby successfully, one major hurdle is surmounted on the way to a mutually gratifying relationship. Food becomes symbolically equated with life, health, and growth, but most especially with mother love.

---

[13] Reva Rubin. "Basic Maternal Behavior." *Nursing Outlook.* Vol. 9, No. 11 (November, 1961). Pp. 683–85.

[14] Margaret Ribble. *The Rights of Infants.* New York: Columbia University Press, 1943. P. 13.

Feeding for all human beings is closely connected with feelings. Nurses are aware that patients are affected by the emotional climate surrounding eating. Eating disorders are frequently connected with psychological disturbances throughout life.

The issue of breast versus bottle feeding is frequently raised by new mothers. On this issue, Selling and Ferrano state:

> No formula has yet been devised which will enable the bottle to give the love, security, affection and pride that even an infant seems to be able to gather from the mother's affectionate embrace when he nurses from her.[15]

They therefore advise that at least a part of the child's food should be, if possible, supplied by the breast during part of the first year. New mothers often ask nurses about breast feeding and express concerns about inadequate milk supply, various nipple problems or about the effect of breast feeding on their figures. Some young mothers feel embarrassed by the sexual pleasure that often accompanies breast feeding. Benjamin Spock discusses some of the questions young mothers ask nurses. His well-known and widely used book provides a good reference for some of the questions patients ask. Spock notes:

> The most convincing evidence of the value of breast feeding comes from mothers who have done it. They tell of the tremendous satisfaction they experience from knowing that they are providing the baby with something no one else can give him, from seeing his devotion to the breast, from feeling his closeness. It is too seldom mentioned that after a couple of weeks the act of nursing becomes definitely pleasurable for the mother—it's intended to be. A woman doesn't get to feel like a mother, or come to enjoy being a mother, or feel the full motherly love for her child just from the fact that a baby has been born to her. With her first infant particularly, she becomes a real mother only as she takes care of her child. The more success she has in the beginning in doing her part and the more visibly her baby is satisfied by her care, the sooner and the more enjoyably she slips into the role. In this sense breast feeding does wonders for a young mother and for her relationship with her baby. She and her baby are happy in themselves and feel more and more loving to each other.[16]

Nurses have an opportunity, and an obligation, to offer practical counsel and emotional support for problems that arise concerning feeding, and the more experienced, trained, and knowledgeable she is about the practical aspects of infant feeding, the more qualified she will be to offer this kind of help.

[15] L. S. Selling and M. A. Ferraro. *The Psychology of Diet and Nutrition.* Norton: 1945, cited by Edward Lehman. "Feeding Problems of Psychogenic Origin—A Survey of the Literature." *The Psychoanalytic Study of the Child.* Vols. III, IV. New York: International Universities Press, 1949. P. 462.

[16] Benjamin Spock. *Baby and Child Care.* New York: Pocket Books, 1946. Pp. 72–73.

Nursing an infant is not always an easy task for the young mother. The importance of a quiet unhurried atmosphere seems essential, especially for the inexperienced mother. Stresses that create tension and anxiety can interfere with the mother's breast feeding. Cultural differences greatly influence the freedom the mother feels to nurse her child. Some women can nurse their children "anywhere," others prefer to be left alone or with few people around them. The "let down" reflex that influences the release of breast milk is frequently inhibited if the mother feels tense, hurried, embarrassed, or angry while she is trying to nurse her baby.

Many mothers choose not to breast feed their babies because of personal preference or their need to meet responsibilities that interefere with a breast feeding schedule. Other women bottle feed their babies because of illness, breast infections, or other unforeseen circumstances. Finally, some women, in spite of their best efforts, are simply unable to breast feed their babies to the mutual satisfaction of mother and infant. Breast feeding is not an essential requirement for a happy baby. Bottle fed babies with loving mothers can thrive as successfully as breast fed babies.

If the bottle is the main source of milk, it should be given to the infant in a manner that simulates breast feeding as closely as possible. The mother or nurse should at least help support the bottle, and ideally the baby should be held in the same position as if it were at the breast. It is important for the infant to experience a sense of closeness.

The hospital nursery and pediatric units can assist the nurse by providing a rocking chair for her use while she is bottle feeding children. "Propping bottles" in nurseries and pediatric wards is an example of a mechanized approach to infant and child care. Obviously, time is the reason most frequently given. Dehumanizing methods sometimes intrude greatly in hospitals where crucial work must be done and the number of staff is correspondingly limited.

Resolution of this problem requires information and education, so that detrimental activities can be avoided and better methods found for feeding infants and children. Sometimes, auxiliary workers, parents, and volunteers help greatly to humanize infant and child care by assuming these responsibilities.

There is a vital connection between the infant's hunger for adequate physical nourishment and his need for a continuing supply of love and maternal care. This state of affairs is expressed by the term "dependency," a state most clearly evident in the infant's total reliance on his environment for all aspects of his survival and growth. Fenichel describes this situation in psychoanalytic terms:

It is characteristic of children that they very deeply need love and affection from persons in their environment. This is a psychic component of the biological helplessness of the human infant. The infant is wholly dependent on external care and would perish without it. He slowly develops the feelings that grown-ups who can either give or withhold satisfaction are omnipotent. The self-esteem of the child is dependent on the flow of these supplies. When a child is loved, he feels powerful, when neglected, he feels helpless and in danger. . . .[17]

Frustration tolerance. The needs of the infant assert themselves through the gradual mounting of tension. When this tension becomes uncomfortable or painful, the child becomes restless and may cry. These responses are signals to the mothering person. A crying baby can evoke such powerful maternal responses in women that mothers of infants will awaken from sound sleep at the first whimpering of their child. If the infant's tension is not relieved, the frustration increases and may lead to frantic, uncoordinated agitation with screaming, and finally exhaustion, followed by brief sleep. Then the pattern repeats itself until the infant is satisfied or gives up its attempts to find relief and becomes apathetic.

Infants vary in their tolerance to frustration and in manner of expressing it. Even in the nursery it has been noted that some babies are more active than others. Some infants seem able to tolerate cold or pain for longer periods than others. The same variation may be seen in their feeding habits. The development of mutual regulation between mother and baby requires that the mother (or nurse) recognize the pattern of her baby.

The infant becomes increasingly able to tolerate hunger and mild discomforts as physical maturation and psychological development progress. Meanwhile the responsive, loving mother (or her substitute) repeatedly reinforces the infant's experience of need satisfaction within a reasonable time. Gradually he becomes able to defer satisfaction of his needs for longer periods of time, secure in the expectation that satisfaction will come.

Frustration is the other side of the coin of satisfaction. Without it, there is little motivation to seek solutions in one's environment and thus develop new modes of behavior. René Spitz writes:

> For the child's welfare does require frustration. . . .
> . . . Without unpleasure, without that measure of frustration which I would call age-adequate, no satisfactory ego development is possible.[18]

A child undergoes frustrations naturally and inevitably in the process of growing up; he can escape them only if his parents are unduly permissive. Thus frustration within the limits of the infant's tolerance provides the psychological exercise, so to speak, that stimulates the infant's mental structures to grow, and leads to the early forms of socialization.

During this early period we assume that the infant at first experiences

---

[17] Fenichel. "The Means of Education." P. 285.
[18] René A. Spitz. *The First Year of Life.* New York: International Universities Press, Inc., 1965. P. 148.

himself and his environment as one global whole. Only gradually over a period of many months does he begin to differentiate himself psychologically as an individual, separate from the breast, his mother, and his surroundings. This rudimentary awareness that there is an outer world separate from his body can scarcely as yet be called knowledge. Gradually, however, through innumerable transactions between himself and the people and objects in his environment, the infant gradually learns to take into account the opportunities, demands, and limitations of his surroundings. His urgent needs for physical, sensual, and social gratification slowly become tempered and modified by his need and his wish to adapt to the realities and frustrations of the world around him.

The smiling response. One of the early forerunners of social development is the "smiling response."[19] As early as four weeks or as late as three months, the baby's mother notices—invariably with great pleasure—that her infant looks at her face and smiles at her. This naturally evokes a delighted smile from her that in turn reinforces the baby's smile. The remarkable fact of the matter is that all babies of his age will smile in response to seeing even a crude facsimile of the upper part of a full-face view of the human face!

This vital interaction sets in motion an exchange that in time does become highly personal, as the baby begins to recognize its own mother. Eventually the baby prefers its mother's face and presence to all others' faces and presence. The smiling response thus has highly important adaptational implications, since it serves to strengthen the vital bond between the mother and child, the bond that has been growing since birth and is so essential for the child's physical and psychological growth.

Deprivation of maternal care. From about the third to the fifteenth month, the presence of a mothering person is so essential to the baby that prolonged separation from the mother or from an adequate substitute can lead to very serious consequences. One result may be that the infant, in order to survive in a world without a consistent, adequate mothering person, must bypass the phase of growth in which an intimate mother–infant relationship is established. Instead he must seek precociously to adapt and relate to other individuals in order to receive as much gratification as is possible under those circumstances. While such children may be highly adaptable, they may have serious problems in forming and maintaining intimate significant relationships.

Interestingly enough, one of the early descriptions of the serious pathological conditions that can result from prolonged absence of maternal care during these months was made by a nurse, Jane Lester, whose article is reproduced in full on pages 99 to 101.

[19] *Ibid.* P. 20.

68   Infancy

Such workers as John Bowlby, Anna Freud, Sally Provence, Rose Lipton, and René Spitz have carried their observations to the point where it now can be stated with certainty that during the first few years of life, the child must receive more than simply adequate physical care to develop normally.[20] In cases of emotional deprivation, severe physical and psychological symptoms can occur. Provence and Lipton, in speaking of institutionalized infants, note:

In the first three to four weeks of life motor behavior of the institutionalized infant was not different in any way that could be measured from that of infants cared for by their mothers. The first easily observable difference occurred in the second month and concerned a specific characteristic in the way the infant reacted to being held. There was a decrease in the extent to which they made appropriate postural adjustments to being held or carried. They did not adapt their bodies well to the arms of the adult, they were not cuddly, and one noted a lack in pliability. We do not refer to hypertonicity or muscle spasticity. All reflex behavior was normal. The best description is that they felt like sawdust dolls; they moved, they bent easily at the proper joints, but they felt stiff or wooden as they were perceived through the holder's own sensory apparatus. It was difficult to put into words the impression the infants conveyed. However, what the infant's body conveyed to the body of the holding person was real and distinct.[21]

René Spitz summarizes his early work in the area of emotional deprivation and discusses quantitative and qualitative factors in emotional deprivation. Spitz accidentally came upon an institution where a group of infants who had experienced normal mother-child relationships during the first six

[20] John Bowlby. *Maternal Care and Mental Health.* Geneva: World Health Organization, Monograph No. 2, 1951.
———. "The Nature of the Child's Tie to His Mother." *International Journal of Psycho-Analysis.* Vol. 39 (1958). Pp. 350–73.
Anna Freud and Dorothy Burlingham. *War and Children.* New York: International Universities Press, Inc., 1943.
———. *Infants without Families.* New York: International Universities Press, Inc., 1943.
Sally Provence and S. Ritvo. "Effects of Deprivation on Institutionalized Infants: Disturbances in Development of Relationship to Inanimate Objects." *The Psychoanalytic Study of the Child.* Vol. 16. New York: International Universities Press, Inc., 1961. Pp. 189–205.
René Spitz. "Hospitalism." *The Psychoanalytic Study of the Child.* Vol. I. New York: International Universities Press, 1945.
———. "Hospitalism: A Follow-up Report." *The Psychoanalytic Study of the Child.* Vol. II. New York: International Universities Press, 1946.
René Spitz and K. M. Wolf. "Anaclitic Depression: An Inquiry into the Genesis of Psychiatric Conditions in Early Childhood." *The Psychoanalytic Study of the Child.* Vol. II. New York: International Universities Press, Inc., 1946. Pp. 313–42.
[21] Sally Provence and Rose Lipton. *Infants in Institutions.* New York: International Universities Press, Inc., 1962.

months of life were then separated from their mothers, placed in an institution, and deprived of substitute mothering for several months. These infants were given what was presumed to be good physical care. Spitz used the term "hospitalism" to describe this state of almost total emotional deprivation.

These infants developed a syndrome characterized by increasing signs of what in adults would be called depression. After three months, Spitz observes:

> . . . the children refuse contact, they lie prone in their cot most of the time, a pathognomonic sign. Insomnia sets in, loss of weight continues. There is a tendency to contract intercurrent diseases; motor retardation becomes generalized. [There is] inception of facial rigidity.[22]

Spitz referred to this disorder as "anaclitic[23] depression" to suggest that the main cause lies in the absence of the mother on whom the infant had depended for physical and emotional satisfaction. Interestingly enough, a precondition for anaclitic depression is that prior to separation the infant should have been in a good relation with his mother. Other forms of deviant behavior resulted when the relationship had been a poor one before separation.

Spitz found that if the child with anaclitic depression was once again restored to his mother within three to five months, the condition was largely reversible, although the long-range effects are still unknown. Where separation and emotional deprivation are complete for more than five months, the children may develop severe disturbances in the development of object relationships. Ultimately, such children may develop marasmus (progressive emaciation) and have a high mortality rate. Fortunately, such prolonged and severe emotional deprivation is very unusual. Most children's institutions are now aware of these problems and attempt to provide psychological stimulation and affection as well as physical care for infants.

"Failure to thrive" is a term used to describe infants who do not gain weight and grow as expected, when, in many instances, no organic defect can be found. Maternal deprivation either inside or outside an institution can be a cause of a "failure to thrive."[24] A clinical example of a maternally deprived child is described by Ingles. She writes of Maria an 11-month-old child who weighed slightly more than a new born infant:

> As I looked down at her that first morning, I saw all of this—but most of all I saw her wide-open, terrified eyes; they seemed to reflect a summary of all

---

[22] René Spitz.
[23] From the Greek word *anaklinein*, meaning "to lean upon."
[24] Camille Legeay. "A Failure to Thrive; A Nursing Problem." *Nursing Forum*. Vol. 4, No. 1 (1965). Pp. 56–71.
   Julina P. Rhymes. "Working Mothers and Babies That Fail to Thrive." *American Journal of Nursing*. Vol. 66, No. 9 (September, 1966). Pp. 1972–76. Also reproduced in this volume, pp. 102 to 110.

tragedy. . . . She stopped crying, but looked at me with distrust and anger. It was the anger in her eyes which gave me hope: she was still fighting . . . I massaged Maria with oil, gave her some passive exercises, and dressed her in a gay yellow jacket, diapers, and blue rubber pants. She looked like an unhappy underfed rag doll.[25]

Provence and Lipton also note that nonthriving infants, deprived of adequate mothering, may both "look" as well as "feel" like rag dolls.[26] Nonthriving children can be seen in private homes where the mother is present as well as in institutions. A mother with physical or emotional problems may be unable to satisfy her child's needs for love and affection.

Long before the syndrome of "hospitalism" was described by Spitz and later by other writers, Lester wrote in 1915:

It has been observed that babies in an asylum never laugh, or even cry, except when in severe pain. . . . and it is quite reasonable . . . that the child also suffers when separated from its mother. Let each nurse remember this fact and do all she can to fill the mother's place.[27]

In reviewing literature on maternal deprivation, Casler notes:

It is more likely that deprivation of maternal love can have ill effects only after specific affective responsiveness has been achieved by the child (usually at about the age of six months). Ill effects found in children maternally deprived before this age probably have some other cause.

Evidence is accumulating, both on the human and the animal level, that this "other cause" is perceptual deprivation—the absolute or relative absence of tactile, vestibular, and other forms of stimulation.[28]

The important factor of pre-existing good maternal care was emphasized also by Sylvia Brody in her 1960 study of 150 orphans between the ages of 2 and 3.

[The infants] took on a faraway, dazed expression, and showed increased disturbance when an adult tried to make contact and screamed. This distinctive clinical picture was found in 19 out of 123 infants, in all of whom it occurred during a separation from the mother of three to four months' duration and disappeared after the mother came back. No infant whose mother was not sepa-

---

[25] Thelma Ingles. "Maria, the Hungry Baby." *Nursing Forum*. Vol. 5, No. 2 (1966). Pp. 36–47. Also reproduced in this volume, pp. 97 to 99. See pp. 93 to 95.

[26] Provence and Lipton. *Infants in Institutions*. New York: International Universities Press, Inc., 1962.

[27] Jane Elinor Lester. "The Psychic Principle in Nursing Infants." *American Journal of Nursing*. Vol. 16, No. 2 (November, 1915). Pp. 109–11. Also reproduced in this volume, pp. 99 to 101. See p. 101.

[28] Lawrence Casler. *Maternal Deprivation: A Critical Review of the Literature*. Monographs of the Society for Research in Child Development. Vol. 26, Serial No. 80, No. 2 (1961). Evanston, Ill.: Child Development Publications.

rated from him developed this syndrome. The severe depression is interpreted as a reaction to the loss of the love object, the mother, a reaction that brings about gross arrest of the infant's ego development. It occurred with greater frequency and severity in cases where the mother-infant relationship had been good prior to the separation and no severe depression occurred where the relationship had been notably bad. This implies that it is more difficult to substitute a satisfactory love object than an unsatisfactory one and that the greater the loss the greater the readiness for depressive reaction.[29]

In the hospital, those infants who have had good mothering may react more strongly and have a more obvious depression when they are hospitalized or separated from their mothers than those infants who have not had adequate mothering prior to the hospitalization.

Brody emphasizes the reversibility of this condition in the infants she studied. The same would be true of those infants who are hospitalized for physical illness. If separation is not too prolonged, and if some attempt is made to provide substitute care, the depression and other accompanying symptoms are reversible and may have no long-lasting ill effects.[30]

The ill effects of separation from the mother may be seen in children of all ages, but especially in those under six or seven. The pediatric nurse may observe this phenomenon in infants and young children who must be separated from their mothers for varying lengths of time because of physical illness or injury. They may show signs of apprehension, anxiety, and depression if their mothers are not made available to them or an adequate substitute is not provided. Freer visiting hours which allow the mother, when possible, to help care for her infant have helped to ease this problem.

On the maternity floor, most mothers and babies are healthy. In our discussion of early child development, we have suggested the need to strengthen, as necessary, the mother's patterns of adaptation to her infant in order to promote positive mental health.

We have also described situations in which gross maternal deprivation in the infant can lead to emotional and physical problems. As we have seen, psychoanalytic research has shown that trauma or stress to the infant can have an impact on his life as an adult.

Caring for the Damaged or Premature Child

Complications related to childbirth cause the mother increased stress in coping with her infant's problems. Situations such as prematurity, congenital defects, and illness may cause the mother to have mixed feelings about her infant.

[29] Sylvia Brody. *Patterns of Mothering.* New York: International Universities Press, Inc., 1956. P. 115.
[30] *Ibid.*

The article by Jane Kallaus, a nurse instructor in maternal-child nursing, states:

> One of the hardest jobs I have as a nurse is to care for a woman who gives birth to a deformed baby. Pain and suffering are frequently encountered in my work, but this is a special kind of sorrow. This new mother feels sadness, a feeling completely different from the joy she expected. And the sadness comes at a time of physical exhaustion following the effort of childbirth. The woman's reaction may be dramatic and will depend on the type and severity of the deformity, as well as on her past experiences.[31]

Mothers who give birth to a deformed child are often in a state of acute grief, because they have lost the perfect baby they imagined they would have, and instead have received a damaged child. These painful emotions evoke, frequently, a sense of inadequacy in the mother. We have previously mentioned that the child symbolizes to the mother an extension of herself.

Kallaus notes that

> cleft lip and cleft palate are particularly disfiguring for the baby and alarming for the mother to see for the first time.[32]

Not only is there an aesthetic problem of the baby with a cleft palate, but the mother is also faced with the mechanics of feeding.

It is frequently emphasized that the doctor should give the mother information as soon as possible regarding birth defects. Veronica B. Tiza and Elizabeth Gumpertz, a physician and a social worker, found in their study that the mothers who suffer most are those not given information promptly and whose babies are not shown to them promptly.[33] Kallaus confirms this observation in her article (see Footnote 31).

Physicians, like other people, may postpone difficult, painful tasks, and the hours that elapse between the birth of a deformed child and telling the mother can cause a mother only increased anxiety as she wonders what has happened to her infant. Kallaus emphasizes that the nurse, by withdrawing from a patient at this time, can also cause additional harm; and she stresses the importance of the nurse's accessibility to the patient during this crisis.

Nurses are increasingly trained to understand that reactions to a damaged child can represent an actual loss of gratification to the mother. The mother can suffer grief not unlike that which she might experience if the child had died. The mother may also blame a variety of circumstances, for which she may feel either guilty or angry, for the deformity.

[31] Jane Kallaus. "The Child with Cleft Lip and Palate." *American Journal of Nursing*. Vol. 65, No. 4 (April, 1965). P. 120.
[32] *Ibid.*
[33] Veronica Tiza and Elizabeth Gumpertz. "The Parent's Reaction to the Birth and Early Care of Children with a Cleft Palate." *Journal of Pediatrics*. Vol. 30 (1962).

The phases of grief are discussed in the excellent article by Kallaus, "The Child with Cleft Lip and Palate" (Footnote 31). Just as in the case of hearing of a death, the mother who hears about her deformed child first experiences a feeling of numbness and disbelief. Kallaus notes:

> A helping relationship between the patient and nurse will comfort the patient a great deal at this time. The nurse must fashion her approach according to the patient's reaction. The patient may want to cry, or she may be unable to cry or to talk about her baby. She may be angry and try to find the answer by blaming herself, or God, or the hospital, and persons in it. If the nurse realizes the need for this type of behavior, she will not be offended personally when the patient seems unreasonable in her demands or uninterested in her child.[34]

This article further emphasizes the fact that the way a mother responds to her baby's deformity depends on her own personality and the way she is able to handle grief. The length, depth, and nature of the resolution of mourning will significantly influence the mother's relationship with her child. Lindemann suggests that the normal grief reaction takes six months to one year to resolve.[35] In addition to grief, the mother must face many medical, surgical, and orthodontic problems. Later, as the child grows older, there may be speech problems. And all of these problems add up to a significant emotional strain for both the parents and the child. The long-term plan for rehabilitation of children with congenital defects strongly points up the need for immediate attention to give the mother emotional support as she goes through mourning.

Gerald Caplan emphasizes that:

> "a person in crisis both feels a greater need for help than when he is in his usual psychological state, and *is usually more easily influenced* during this period than at other times." [36]

Helpful intervention by the doctor and the nurse, as well as by other people like social workers, may greatly increase the parents' ability to deal with a defective child.

Any defect may give rise to grief and stress in the mother. For an example, Albert Solnit discusses retardation. He notes that just as pregnancy is a "crisis" in which there is no turning back, so too with the physical or mental defects found in some newborns. Solnit adds:

> The irretrievable nature of the retardation adds to the mother's trapped feel-

---

[34] Kallaus. "The Child with Cleft Lip and Palate." P. 122.

[35] Erich Lindemann. "Symptomatology and Management of Acute Grief." *American Journal of Psychology*. Vol. 101 (September, 1944). P. 141.

[36] Gerald Caplan and Henry Grunebaum. "Perspectives on Primary Prevention." *Archives of General Psychiatry*. Vol. 17 (September, 1967). P. 238.

ing—she has failed to achieve what she so laboriously prepared herself to create or produce. Fathers too will have similar or related reactions. . . .[37]

Whenever a premature, retarded, or damaged infant enters the family it presents special needs, sometimes difficult for other family members to accept. If there are other children they may resent the time and attention the mother must give to this one child. The husband may also be under stress when his wife pays more attention to the young baby than to him or to other members of the family. The visiting nurse or social worker can be especially helpful when the mother's full attention is on the child. <u>The nurse can help both parents by focusing her attention on them as well as on their infant</u>.

The highest rates of prematurity and complications in pregnancy are in the low socioeconomic groups and among young nonwhite women. It is often hypothesized that these are the people who have the least access to good medical and nursing care.

Because prematurity is a complication of pregnancy and is closely associated with fetal and neonatal death, it is important for the public health nurse to be aware of the need for increased prenatal observation. She can serve a real function in encouraging and helping these young mothers to go to clinics for prenatal care.

As a result of poor nutrition, inadequate or total lack of prenatal care, and psychosocial stress, a significant number of defective children are born to low-income families. While we do not know many of the causes of mental retardation, we do know that severe malnutrition, as well as specific nutritional deficiencies, have been shown to be associated with mental defects. The public health nurse can be particularly helpful in discussing with young mothers in these socioeconomic groups proper diet and the need to avoid injuries and infections at this critical time.

Not only is prenatal care important in avoiding complications of pregnancy, but after the delivery of a child the mother may continue to need support from her physician and from nurses and social workers as necessary. The young, poor mother who has a premature child often has the fewest resources to cope with its needs if it survives, and will need special help.

It is well known that the premature infant poses many difficult problems for the mother. Occasionally, the premature child may also have neurological defects or a low intelligence quotient. One of the first fears that confronts a mother who has a premature infant is the thought that his life is in jeopardy. It is not unusual for a mother to experience "anticipatory grief" as she faces her concern about survival of the infant. David Kaplan has noted additional problems with which the mother must cope at this time. She has to accept the feelings of failure that may result from not delivering

---

[37] Albert J. Solnit and Mary H. Stark. "Mourning and the Birth of a Defective Child." *The Psychoanalytic Study of the Child.* Vol. 16.

a normal, full-term baby. According to its weight and physical condition the infant may be separated from the mother and remain in the hospital from one week to as long as three months. During this time the disruption of the normal family process of relating to an infant is another difficulty.[38]

From the outset, with a premature infant or a child who is seriously ill, the mother has to prepare herself for the possibility of the infant's death. If it does survive she should respond with new hope and anticipation. The nurse should take every opportunity to encourage the mother of a premature infant, when possible, to follow weight gains and new feeding patterns and to accept the fact that if the child gets through the early critical months, it can catch up and become a normal child, provided that the mother is able to meet special needs and accept its slower early growth patterns.

If the infant needs prolonged hospitalization, the mother often goes home and leaves him in the hospital. This separation may be an added disappointment to her. Changes in pediatric practice and hospital policy now allow much more frequent visiting of parents on the pediatric ward, and mothers are often encouraged to stay with and, when possible, help care for their infants.

Besides suffering from the separation, the young mother may feel afraid of the hospital. Frequently she is coping with realistic fears as to the severity of the child's illness or deformity as well as feeling anxious and guilty about the child's condition.

Prolonged illness or congenital defects that require repeated surgery deprive the parents of their usual time and energy for leisure activities. After the baby leaves the hospital the mother may find much of her time taken up with his care, and may feel less able to relate to capacity to engage in her husband, friends, and family. Husbands and wives are often unable to spend enough time alone, and their sexual relationship may be disrupted. The husband may feel that his wife is spending too much time with the baby and that "the baby's needs always come first."

After a young infant has been ill, a significant number of parents continue to share a room with the baby. The mother frequently loses sleep as she gets up to look after the child. Further pregnancies may cause a young mother great concern, since she may be hesitant to run the risk of having another "sick child."

Traditionally it is a mother who cares for the child and takes him to the doctor's office or for hospital visits. She is often responsible for carrying out medical procedures and giving medicine. With a sick child, a mother is often tired and preoccupied, and she may misinterpret or misunderstand information given to her by the physician. The community health nurse can often be helpful in encouraging the father to visit the hospital and the physi-

---

[38] Caplan, Gerald. *Prevention of Mental Disorders in Children.* New York: Basic Books, Inc., 1961.

cian's office to share the burdens of the child's illness. Mothers often complain that fathers don't understand what they are going through.

Morris Green and Albert Solnit emphasize that placing a child (or infant) on the "critically ill" list in hospitals again confronts the parent with the grim information that the child may die.[39] If the child survives, parents often recall how they "almost lost him." Later, these same children may pose additional problems if parents have not been able to adequately cope with their feelings concerning the child's illness.

A group of clinical features has been described which constitute "the vulnerable child syndrome." It was noted by Green and Senn that young children who are expected by their parents to die may be treated differently from other children if they survive. Parents may become overly protective, indulgent, and solicitous of the child long after he has recovered from handicaps, prematurity, and illness. The child may find it difficult to go on to new experiences, especially when a separation from the mother occurs to go to school or to leave her for brief intervals.

Some parents find it difficult to "set limits" with children that have almost died. These children may be disobedient, irritable, and uncooperative. Since not all children who recover from a critical illness develop this "vulnerable child syndrome," it was hypothesized by Solnit and Green that only certain families are affected, depending to a large extent upon the past experiences of the parents.

Treating a child "specially" when he is sick can later become disadvantageous to both the parent and child after the child recovers. Therefore, once a child completely recovers, it is helpful for the doctor and nurse to point out that no special precautions are necessary for his care.

William Carey, a pediatrician, wrote in discussing seriously ill children:

> Probably a goodly number of children emerging from health crises in early infancy evolve into children and adults who are generally considered normal by themselves and others. What the percentage and circumstances of this favorable outcome may be nobody can say at this time. It may be that most mothers and infants do all right if the crisis is not too overwhelming and if the other circumstances are not too disruptive of the mother's ability to adapt.[40]

Infant Death

It is extremely difficult for the nurse working on obstetrical service, where birth is usually a happy event, to witness the death of a newborn. We discuss death, grief, and mourning later in the book, but some explana-

---

[39] Morris Green and Albert Solnit. "Reactions to the Threatened Loss of a Child: a Vulnerable Child Syndrome." *Pediatrics*. Vol. 34 (1964). P. 53.

[40] William Carey. "Psychological Sequelae of Early Infancy Health Crises." *Clinical Pediatrics*. August, 1969.

tion of grief as a process must necessarily be given at this point. Shakespeare, in *Macbeth*, wrote, "Give sorrow words. The grief that does not speak knits up the overwrought heart and bids it break." [41] In more modern language, the implication is that grief cannot be permanently postponed and the longer it is inhibited the more severe may be the feelings when they finally emerge.

The death of an infant is especially painful for the mother, who has anticipated over the long months a normal and healthy child. Not only is she most vulnerable after the delivery because of her fatigue and hormonal shifts, but this may be her first experience with death itself. One young mother, when told about the death of her infant said, "It's all like a dream, I can't believe it." This sense of numbness, which represents a form of denial, is often experienced when a person is confronted with news of death. Many mothers, of course, will cry, but some people cannot cry, especially in front of others. The mother may also feel angry. This anger is a phase of grief called "protest."

The young mother may feel anger over trivial episodes and there may be feelings of general irritability and bitterness. She may express feelings of self-reproach built around something she might have done or omitted that caused the death of her infant. She also may feel "jumpy" and experience a sense of turmoil. One mother stated that the most painful part of the loss of her infant was being kept on an obstetrical service. While she was kept in a private room with the door closed, and the nurses made frequent attempts to visit and speak with her, she was constantly confronted with hearing the crying of other people's babies. This raises the question of the advisability of keeping a patient who has suffered the loss of her newborn baby on an obstetrical ward after her delivery.

In this chapter the concept frequently emphasized is that the early months of infant care are of great significance to the child as well as the mother. Discussions that help nursing personnel to implement the most advanced psychological knowledge can help them provide better care. It is the responsibility of the obstetrical and pediatric specialties in nursing and medicine to expand preventive services and to help provide an entire range of human resources by using all members within the health disciplines.

Later Infancy

THE OLDER INFANT

Testing Reality

The first year of life, or oral stage, may be divided into 2 phases. The earliest months are characterized by passive intake and dependent receptive-

---

[41] Shakespeare. *Macbeth* in *The Complete Works*. New York: Harcourt, Brace, and Company. P. 1212.

78   Infancy

ness. During the latter half of the first year, oral behavior becomes more active and aggressive. For most babies the eruption of teeth becomes the first persistent painful or frustrating experience that is not relieved by crying responded to more or less rapidly by the mother or her substitute. If the baby is being breast fed, the new teeth may also lead to sudden and disconcerting withdrawals of the breast and even to the termination of breast feeding.

Along with his new-found ability to bite, chew and spit out food, the older infant begins to show the first signs of hostility and negativism toward people and objects. This tendency to express both hostile and loving (or libidinal) impulses becomes especially prominent as the infant enters the toddler stage during the middle of his second year.

By the time the infant becomes a toddler, he has made a great deal of progress in personality development and has taken major steps in adapting to the world. Functions such as control of the voluntary muscles, ability to defer satisfaction of inner needs, and effective use of eyes, ears, and other senses have begun to be firmly established.

There is by then a close bond between mother and child, although he is also able to recognize and respond to other people within his family and his immediate environment. The child has learned something about his own body and has a rudimentary sense of self. He has begun to be able to "test reality" after a fashion. However, he still does not know the difference between what is considered right and wrong in his society except insofar as he discovers that some of his behavior consistently brings love and approval while other activities evoke disapproval from important adults.

He has become intensely curious and wishes to explore his world. He takes a much more active role in feeding himself. His communication is immeasurably aided by a new capacity to use words to convey his needs and feelings.

These early infantile needs reflect the most fundamental physical and psychological processes. They include the need for adequate nourishment, warmth, and freedom from pain, as well as the need for physical contact and closeness to the mothering person. In addition, the infant requires perceptual and sensory stimulation in order to provide nutriment for psychological growth.

The infant and his mother comprise his total world. As a result, repeated experiences of need satisfaction (adequate mothering) encourage the development of what Erikson refers to as a sense of *basic trust*, whereas repeated or excessive frustrations or pain may contribute to an underlying tone of *basic mistrust*.[42]

---

[42] Erik Erikson. *Childhood and Society.* New York: W. W. Norton & Company, Inc., 1950. P. 247.

Resolution of Conflicts

Erikson has attributed a core or "nuclear" conflict to each of 8 stages of development through childhood and throughout life. His theory, a blend of psychoanalytic and social theory, suggests that a relatively successful resolution of the basic conflicts associated with each level of development provides an essential foundation for the successful resolution of the next level of development. The manner in which each of these conflicts is resolved has an important influence on shaping the adult personality. In addition he assigns certain social and psychological tasks to each stage of life which the ego of the individual needs to complete in order to progress to more mature achievements.

To the earliest stage of life, that of infancy, Erikson assigns the nuclear conflict of *basic trust* versus *basic mistrust*.[43] If a satisfactory mutuality has been established between the infant and his mother (or mother substitute), the infant learns to anticipate that its needs will be satisfied. Since these needs involve the most fundamental life processes, satisfaction of them contributes to a feeling that experiences generally will be satisfying. People will —within reason—respond to one's important needs. Basic trust (or its opposite, mistrust) can underlie the individual's attitude toward life and toward other persons throughout life.

Such basic attitudes are by no means always clearly manifested in behavior, nor is the person necessarily aware of them. On the contrary, an outward show of great trust and hopefulness in an adult may mask unconscious fears of being deeply disappointed, while a "pessimistic" person may harbor an underlying naïve trust in the world.

During illness, these early attitudes or combinations of them often emerge as the patient is placed in a helpless and relatively infantile position where he must rely on his physicians and nurses for his very survival.

The experiences of infants and children, then, are not simply mentally recorded and then forgotten. They underlie and color the behavior, feelings, thoughts, and dreams of adults as well as children. For example, oral pleasure related to the infant's pleasure in nursing is derived by children and adults from eating, chewing gum, smoking, talking, drinking, and so forth. Our language is replete with references to orality in such expressions as "I'm fed up," "You look good enough to eat," "I can't swallow that."

Affection, satisfaction and self-esteem are connected with food and eating. Unrealistic feelings of deprivation and emptiness may be manifestations of unsatisfying early oral experiences. At a physiological level, unconscious oral conflicts may affect digestive functioning.

As a result, many psychopathological symptoms seem to have at least

[43] *Ibid.*

part of their origin in the oral period. A few of these are alcoholism, compulsive eating, obesity, functional stomach distress, and peptic ulcer.

It should be noted, however, that these and all other such disorders are determined by multiple factors that can occur throughout life and serve to reinforce the early, oral elements.

There are also serious problems with relationships that result partly from a lack of mutuality during this early time of life. Individuals who have failed to develop mutuality may have a very low frustration tolerance and make insatiable demands for attention and love. Some tendency to develop these traits may be inborn, but they also probably reflect inadequate gratification in the earliest months of life. To sum up, everyone continues to derive some pleasure throughout life from oral activities or perhaps suffer symptoms or unhappiness as a result of unresolved conflicts related to oral functions.

Eating Behavior and the Child's Adjustment

It has long been noted that eating behavior may serve as an indicator of the child's general adjustment. In the case of sick children the picture is much more complicated. The nurse is especially aware of the child's "intake and output" in the hospital environment. Each child at a given age has an average expectable performance level, and part of the nurse's responsibility is to understand normal ranges of physical and emotional behavior. Nurses need to be aware of the complex interaction between physical and mental factors in the child's eating habits. Loss of appetite is also an important consideration in identifying physical illness, since it helps to determine the degree of health or illness.

For the nurse, the oral stage is of special significance because of the vital importance of feeding in nursing procedures and in the life of the patient. Feeding and digestive difficulties can give some indication of beginning pathology in the infant, as well as some clues regarding the mother-infant relationship.

As the child gets older, he may show emotional disturbance by refusing food, overeating, or staying overweight. Nurses are very familiar with patients of all ages who cannot or will not follow a diet, even at times when their lives depend on it.

An example was Mrs. R., a 68-year-old woman who weighed 235 pounds. Mrs. R. had a severe coronary condition that required her to lose weight in order to reduce the strain on her heart. Mrs. R. carefully listened to the doctor and public health nurse when they told her why she must lose weight.

In spite of her conscious wish to cooperate, Mrs. R. found herself unable to diet successfully. She felt depressed and miserable when she deprived herself of food. The gratification she derived from eating was too important for her even though she was aware of the risk to which her obesity exposed her.

The nurse on her weekly visits was upset and annoyed because Mrs. R. not only did not lose weight, but gained even more during her illness. The nurse failed to realize that Mrs. R. could not tolerate the painful emotional hunger that accompanied her attempts at dieting.

The problem of alcoholism is similar to the problem of excessive and compulsive overeating. Both represent emotional problems that are often difficult to treat, and tend to arouse negative reactions in nurses and doctors. In order to work effectively with patients with such problems, the nurse should be aware that the oral symptoms represent a maladaptive attempt to satisfy infantile needs that take precedence over reason and logic.

Rejection of food also may be an emotional response to a given situation. In the pediatric unit a young patient may refuse to eat when the nurse tries to feed him but accept food readily from his mother should she arrive at feeding time. The adult patient, too, if isolated or anxious, may reject food as a symbol of his unhappy state.

This stage of infancy or orality represents the foundation of psychosocial development. All that comes after will inevitably be affected to some extent by the events of that period of life. There can be no denying the vital significance of the first and most important human relationship, that between the infant and his mother.

THE NURSE AND CRISIS INTERVENTION

In earlier times mothers shared their infant care responsibilities with relatives, older children, and hired help. Today, they often face this vital task alone. During a crisis, it is frequently to the professional person that they must turn for help.

The nurse needs information, not only to understand developmental tasks, but to help when a crisis arises that interrupts or delays the developmental tasks necessary for the infant's physical and emotional progress. In preventive psychiatry and community mental health there is much emphasis on early detection of problems so that the mother can cope with the essential tasks of infant care. Coping behavior can be interfered with when the mothers' usual pattern of functioning is disorganized by a crisis situation. Acceptable coping behavior implies that the mother accomplishes her tasks in a manner satisfactory to herself, her infant, and the group in which they live.

If the mother cannot cope and she must face a crisis, she needs professional help. Julina Rhymes, in her article, "Working with Mothers and

Babies Who Fail to Thrive" demonstrates how both the mother and infant can greatly benefit from professional intervention (p. 102).

Child Abuse

Elizabeth Elmer, a social worker, attempts to explain through the use of clinical case material, the severe problems that mothers can have with children, particularly in cases of child abuse.[44] It is easy for the nurse who observes an infant battered and in the hospital to be angry toward the responsible parent. Miss Elmer's research demonstrates the sad fact that parents who beat, neglect, and abuse their children are themselves suffering from serious emotional problems. Blaming the parent helps neither the child nor the parent. Miss Elmer has carefully studied the kinds of problems present when child abuse occurs.

The community health nurse may be the first person who identifies child abuse; perhaps it is through her agency that child abuse cases are called to the attention of the authorities. In these cases, she has a responsibility to both the parents and the child. Elmer notes, "Abusive families can sometimes be helped by what might be termed 'cool mothering' in which members of the community persistently make themselves readily available, but do not push beyond what parents can tolerate in the way of a relationship." [45]

Child abuse is an example of a situation in which a nurse may find herself unable to cope with problems alone. Medical and social work help is usually essential in combining forces to properly treat families in crisis. The seriousness of a crisis situation furthermore requires that the nurse not turn her back and forget that it exists.

Crises may well cause strong feelings in the nurse, especially when she sees a helpless infant deprived, neglected, or beaten. This is one circumstance in which it is understandable for the nurse to have value judgments. There are some parents and some children with whom the nurse may find it difficult or impossible to work. Coping with parents who neglect and batter children requires a good deal of insight into their personality dynamics.

The cooperation of medical, legal, and social agencies may also be necessary in working with the severe problems connected with child neglect and child abuse. We suggest that all nurses familiarize themselves with Elizabeth Elmer's monograph, *Children in Jeopardy*, which is a detailed report of neglected and abused children and their families.[46]

---

[44] Elizabeth Elmer. *Children in Jeopardy: The Study of Abused Minors and Their Families*. Pittsburgh: University of Pittsburgh Press, 1967.

[45] Elizabeth Elmer. "Child Abuse: The Family's Cry for Help." *Journal of Psychiatric Nursing*. July–August, 1967. P. 338.

[46] Elmer. *Children in Jeopardy*.

Awareness of Crises

Nurses, as human caretakers, should be conversant with various kinds of crises, which often disorganize an individual's usual pattern of functioning. Many of the young patients that the nurse sees experience feelings of frustration and helplessness during a period of crisis. All aspects of crises, however, are not negative, and Caplan observes,

> The individual may emerge from the crisis with increased adaptive capacities and confidence in his ability to tolerate stress and to cope. On the other hand, he may emerge with lower adaptive capacities and a greater vulnerability to mental disorder. Therefore, we can say that crises represent mental health turning points. The individual will be helped or hindered in finding a healthy outcome by his family and friends.[47]

Dr. Caplan has consulted extensively with public health nurses and has suggested that they, along with doctors, lawyers, teachers, clergymen, and social workers, can be extremely helpful in times of crisis. Dr. Caplan discusses mental health consultation with visiting nurse associations and suggests that nurses who are unable to understand particularly difficult cases should have access to consultation services to enable them and their supervisors to work out methods of helping their patients.

Sometimes nurses are particularly concerned about patients' becoming too dependent upon them. Caplan notes in this article,

> Individuals in crisis are more dependent; however, long-term dependency does not appear to be fostered by active intervention during a crisis. In fact, the more help given during the crisis, the more independent are the clients when the crisis has been resolved. Undue dependency is also avoided by dealing with current realities, rather than exploring the antecedents of the problem.[48]

Allowing the parents to verbalize their fears concerning their infant's health may help them to diminish some of the apprehension and anxiety they may have endured silently. Mothers may also have distorted perceptions of their sick children, and allowing them to discuss their views may help them toward healthier attitudes.

The nurse is sometimes surprised that when a mother talks about a child that was ill as an infant, she may recall some of the feelings she had at the time of the crisis in vivid detail, and may break down and cry as she experiences again her earlier anxieties and fears. Solnit suggests that these delayed reactions and pathological aftereffects represent a "persistent, disguised,

---

[47] Gerald Caplan and Henry Grunebaum. "Perspectives on Primary Prevention." *Archives of General Psychiatry.* Vol. 17 (September, 1967). P. 238.

[48] *Ibid.* P. 240.

mourning reaction that was evoked by earlier life threatening illness of the child." [49]

Infantile colic and abdominal pain may be related to early infancy health crises. When medical reasons have been ruled out, the child complaining of abdominal pain may be demonstrating his anxiety by displacing it onto a limited part of the body.

After the child leaves the hospital, the visiting nurse can provide the parents with the opportunity to air their concerns and fears. Frequently, when an infant is acutely ill in the hospital, everyone is so preoccupied with life-saving measures that not until the mother is home alone with her child is she able to discuss many of her feelings about the crisis. Sometimes, the crisis does not exert its full emotional impact until after it is over.

A mother with a sick baby often needs emotional support. The pediatrician may not pay sufficient attention to nontechnical descriptions of the child's illness in talking with her. Medical terminology may be unclear, and the mother may not want to bother the doctor because he is "too busy." Again, the nurse who is in the office of a pediatrician, or is working on a pediatric ward, must be alert to the way in which the parents are able to receive information and the way they interpret the actions of the pediatrician.

William B. Carey, a pediatrician, notes:

Evidence is accumulating that health threats or actual illness during early infancy may produce psychologic problems in some children, the result of a complex interaction of the mother, the child, and the situation. Similar experiences arising later in childhood seem to have a less disruptive effect.[50]

Dr. Carey suggests that the term "neonatal crisis syndrome" might be better than "the vulnerable child syndrome." He emphasizes that the mother's reactions to the baby's illness can affect the way she handles her child afterwards. He also notes that the mother's concerns about the child may be very different from the doctor's. He suggests:

It seems that the more dramatic or early the illness, the greater the problem of adaptation for the mother.[51]

Dr. Carey has found that the mother's vulnerability to emotional trauma may come from having inadequate knowledge of her child's illness, or limited intelligence, or negative feelings about "child rearing in general or this

---

[49] Green and Solnet. "Reactions to the Threatened Loss of a Child: A Vulnerable Child Syndrome." P. 53.

[50] William B. Carey. "Psychological Sequelae of Early Infancy Health Crises." *Clinical Pediatrics.* Vol. 8, No. 8 (August, 1969). P. 459.

[51] *Ibid.* P. 460.

child in particular." [52] The temperament of the child is extremely important in determining the way that the mother views him. A sick child is often irritable and difficult to comfort, and poses many more problems to the mother than one who is easygoing.

Prevention of Emotional Problems

At each level of child development, tasks vary for both child and mother. Once conflicts arise that are unresolved, they can lead to more serious problems. This is the reason that concepts from preventive psychiatry are especially important in the mental health of both children and adults.

Dr. Gerald Caplan, as a leader in community psychiatry, has carried out extensive studies relating to the psychosocial and sociocultural contributions to mental disorder.[53] This model of viewing emotional illness comes originally from public health concepts of prevention. Dr. Caplan suggests that only within the last decade have many psychiatrists become interested in extending their skills beyond their office practice into community mental health.

For the student unfamiliar with preventive psychiatry, there are three main types of prevention: primary, secondary, and tertiary.

Primary prevention refers to the efforts made to reduce emotional disorders through "modifying the environment and strengthening individual capacities to cope with situations." *Secondary prevention* "aims at reducing the duration of cases of mental disorder which will inevitably occur in spite of the programs of primary prevention." The emphasis here is on "casefinding, diagnostic, and remedial services so that mental disorders are detected early and are dealt with efficiently and effectively." *Tertiary prevention* "aims at reducing the community rate of residual defect which is often a sequel to acute mental illness." The purpose of these three types of prevention is to reduce the occurrence of emotional problems and to deal with them through physical and psychosocial resources within the community. Dr. Caplan's work is essential reading for those nurses who wish a thorough discussion of this aspect of mental health.[54]

Dr. Caplan raises thoughtful questions regarding preventing emotional problems. For example, he states:

> It is clear from this review of the literature on primary prevention, that much has been learned from clinical experience and research; yet, unfortunately, it must be admitted that what is known is often not used. To cite one example,

---

[52] *Ibid.* P. 460.

[53] Gerald Caplan. *The Theory and Practice of Mental Health Consultation.* New York: Basic Books, Inc., 1970.

[54] Gerald Caplan and Henry Grunebaum. "Perspectives on Primary Prevention." *Archives of General Psychiatry.* Vol. 17 (September, 1967). P. 331.

the short-term effects of hospitalization on infants and small children are well known and thoroughly documented, and yet it remains true that all too few hospitals take into account the emotional needs of the child patients. . . .[55]

The nurse, as a citizen, is part of what has been called the "throwaway society." We clutter our environment with discarded paper, plastics, and bottles. The health disciplines must face, however, the greatest waste within our culture—our neglect and disregard for the mental and physical health of thousands of our infants and children.

Suggested Readings on Infancy

BOOKS

Ackerman, N. W. *The Psychodynamics of Family.* New York: Basic Books, Inc., 1958.

Ames, Louise Bates. *Child Care and Development.* New York: J. B. Lippincott Company, 1970.

Berlin, I. N. *Bibliography of Child Psychiatry with a Selected List of Films.* Washington, D.C.: American Psychiatric Association, Inc., 1963.

Bettelheim, B. *Love Is Not Enough.* New York: The Free Press, 1950.

Buxbaum, Edith. *Troubled Children in a Troubled World.* New York: International Universities Press, Inc., 1970.

———. *Your Child Makes Sense.* New York: International Universities Press, Inc., 1949.

Deutsch, Helene. *Psychology of Women. Vol. 2. Motherhood.* New York: Grune & Stratton, Inc., 1945.

Fraiberg, Selma H. *The Magic Years.* New York: Charles Scribner's Sons, 1959.

Freud, Anna and Dorothy Burlingham. *Infants Without Families: The Case For and Against Residential Nurseries.* New York: International Universities Press, Inc., 1944.

Gardner, George F. *The Emerging Personality: Infancy to Adolescence.* London: Hutchinson & Co., Ltd., 1970.

Gesell, Arnold. *The First Five Years.* New York: Harper & Row, Publishers, 1940.

Gesell, Arnold, and Frances L. Ilg. *Infant and Child in the Culture of Today.* New York: Harper & Row, Publishers, 1943.

[55] Caplan and Grunebaum. "Perspectives on Primary Prevention." P. 344.

Levy, David. *Maternal Overprotection.* New York: W. W. Norton and Company, Inc., 1966.

Lidz, Theodore. *The Person.* New York: Basic Books, Inc., 1968.

Maier, Henry. *Three Theories of Child Development.* New York: Harper & Row, Publishers, 1969.

Mussen, Paul Henry, John Janeway Conger, and Jerome Kogan. *Child Development and Personality.* 3d ed. New York: Harper & Row, Publishers, 1969.

Murphy, Lois Barclay. *The Widening World of Childhood: Paths Toward Mastery.* New York: Basic Books, Inc., 1962.

Piaget, J. *The Origins of Intelligence in Children.* New York: International Universities Press, Inc., 1952.

Ribble, Margaret. *The Rights of Infants.* New York: Columbia University Press, 1943.

Schilder, P. *The Image and Appearance of the Human Body.* New York: International Universities Press, Inc., 1950.

Stendler, Celia Burns. *Readings in Child Behavior and Development.* 2d ed. New York: Harcourt, Brace, and Jovanovich, 1964.

Winnicott, D. W. *The Child and the Outside World.* New York: Basic Books, Inc., 1957.

ARTICLES

Ainsworth, M. "The Effects of Maternal Deprivation: A Review of Findings and Controversy in the Context of Research Strategy." *Deprivation of Maternal Care: A Reassessment of its Effects.* Geneva: World Health Organization, Public Health Papers 14, 1962. Pp. 97–159.

Bakwin, H. "Emotional Deprivation in Infants." *Journal of Pediatrics.* Vol. 35 (1949). Pp. 512–21.

———. "The Hospital Care of Infants and Children." *Journal of Pediatrics.* Vol. 39 (1951). P. 383.

Benedek, T. "Adaptation to Reality in Early Infancy." *Psychoanalytic Quarterly.* Vol. 7 (1938). Pp. 200–14.

Bergman, P. and S. K. Escalona. "Unusual Sensitivities in Very Young Children." *The Psychoanalytic Study of the Child.* Vol. 314 (1949). Pp. 333–52.

Bibring, G. L. and others. "A Study of the Psychological Processes in Pregnancy and of the Earliest Mother–Child Relationship." *The Psychoanalytic Study of the Child.* Vol. 16 (1961). Pp. 9–72.

Bowlby, J. "Childhood Mourning and Its Implications for Psychiatry." *American Journal of Psychiatry.* Vol. 118 (1961). Pp. 481–98.

———. "Grief and Mourning in Infancy and Early Childhood." *The Psychoanalytic Study of the Child*. Vol. 15 (1960). Pp. 9–52.

———. "The Nature of the Child's Tie to His Mother." *International Journal of Psycho-Analysis*. Vol. 39 (1958). Pp. 350–73.

Bowlby, J., M. Ainsworth, B. Boston, and D. Rosenbluth. "The Effects of Mother–Child Separation: A Follow-Up Study." *British Journal of Medical Psychology*. Vol. 29 (1956). P. 211.

Casler, Lawrence. "Monographs of the Society for Research in Child Development." *Maternal Deprivation: A Critical Review of the Literature*. Vol. 26, Serial No. 80, No. 2. Evanston, Ill.: Child Development Publications, 1961.

Erikson, E. H. "Growth and Crises of the Healthy Personality," in Conference on Problems of Infancy and Childhood, Transactions of the 4th Conference, 1950. Ed. by M. J. E. Senn. New York: Josiah Macy, Jr., Foundation, 1951.

———. *Identity and the Life Cycle—Psychological Issues*. Vol. 1, No. 1. New York: International Universities Press, Inc., 1959.

Escalona, S. K. "Emotional Development in the First Year of Life," in Conference on Problems of Infancy and Childhood, Transactions of the 6th Conference, 1952. Ed. by M. J. E. Senn. New York: Josiah Macy, Jr., Foundation, 1953.

Escalona, S. K. and G. Heider. *Prediction and Outcome*. New York: Basic Books, Inc., 1959.

Escalona, S. K., M. Laitch, and others. *Earliest Phases of Personality Development; A Non-Normative Study of Infant Behavior*. Monographs of the Society for Research in Child Development. Vol. 17, Serial No. 54, No. 1. Evanston, Ill.: Child Development Publications, 1952.

Freud, A. "The Mutual Influences in the Development of Ego and Id." *The Psychoanalytic Study of the Child*. Vol. 7 (1952). Pp. 42–50.

———. "Psychoanalysis and Education." *The Psychoanalytic Study of the Child*. Vol. 9 (1954). Pp. 9–15.

———. "Some Remarks on Infant Observation." *The Psychoanalytic Study of the Child*. Vol. 8 (1953). Pp. 9–10.

Fries, Margaret E. "Research in Problems of Infancy and Childhood: A Survey by Lillian Malcove." *Psychoanalytic Study of the Child*, Vol. I (1945). Pp. 405–14.

Provence, S. and S. Ritro. "Effects of Deprivation on Institutionalized Infants: Disturbances in Development of Relationship to Inanimate Objects." *The Psychoanalytic Study of the Child*. Vol. 16 (1961). Pp. 189–205.

Winnicott, D. W. "Transitional Objects and Transitional Phenomena." *International Journal of Psycho-Analysis*. Vol. 34 (1953). Pp. 89–97.

DISCUSSION OF SELECTED READINGS

The following articles are included to assist the nurse in discussing mother-infant interaction. These selections provide clinical examples that demonstrate the application of psychodynamic concepts.

On the following pages we have included two developmental schema charts by Drs. Milton Senn and Albert J. Solnit. Dr. Senn, formerly director of the Child Study Center, Yale University, is Sterling Professor Emeritus of Pediatrics and Psychiatry. Dr. Solnit is Director of the Child Study Center, Yale University. These charts were used in their book, *Problems in Child Behavior and Development*.

The nurse's first responsibility is to understand normal behavior and the usual tasks for the infant and mother. Acceptable behavior, as it tallies with the task in process, is shown in the left-hand column of the charts. Such behavior indicates a favorable relationship between the infant and the mother. Pathological problems at various stages of child development are described in the right-hand column.

The first charts give a brief overview of the usual tasks for the infant from birth to six months, and the second set of charts describes the infant's tasks from six to eighteen months, as well as outlining some of the mother's major tasks. In addition to helping the nurse in caring for patients, the charts should also prove helpful to her as a mother or mother substitute.

In extreme pathological problems of infancy, we often find "an unwilling mother," as Anna Freud terms her. The "unwilling mother" may be completely unable to function in the maternal role and may show signs of severe depression and excessive guilt. Thelma Ingles, a consultant to the Rockefeller Foundation, describes her nursing care of a baby with such a mother in "Maria, The Hungry Baby." This article is a careful clinical account of a child who was sick, as well as maternally deprived. It illustrates the response of an infant who had previously failed to thrive, and her progress when given understanding and skillful nursing care.

The next selection, by Jane Lester, is an attempt to demonstrate to the nurse that observant nurses have for a long time been aware of the influence of the care the child receives on his growth and emotional development. It was published in November, 1915, over a quarter of a century before René Spitz made his valuable contributions regarding "hospitalism." Lester observed what Dr. Spitz later proved: that when a child is separated from the mother or receives inadequate care, he suffers intensely and may eventually die. Articles such as Jane Lester's and Thelma Ingles' help us understand the kinds of contributions nurses can make to better patient care.

The last selection is by Julina P. Rhymes, a nurse and Assistant Professor at the Yale University Child Study Center. As a member of an interdisciplinary team, she studied 13 babies who failed to thrive, and found, that the mothers, too, needed nursing care. The mothers had certain common characteristics and tended to resist help. Mrs. Rhymes, in her article, offers some practical suggestions which should help these babies and mothers to grow.

DEVELOPMENTAL SCHEMA CHART *

The Newborn and Young Infant (Birth to 6 Months)

Tasks in Process

INFANT	MOTHER
To adjust physiologically to extrauterine life.	To sustain baby and self physically and pleasurably.
To develop appropriate psychologic response.	To give and get emotional gratification from nurturing baby.
To assimilate experientially, with increasing capacity to postpone and accept substitutes.	To foster and integrate baby's development.

Acceptable Behavioral Characteristics

INFANT	MOTHER
Copes with mechanics of life (eating, sleeping, etc.)	Provides favorable feeding and handling. Gets to "know" baby.
Body needs urgent.	Develops good working relationship with baby.
Reflexes dominate.	
Has biologic unity with mother.	Has tolerance for baby.
Establishes symbiotic relationship to mother.	Promotes sense of trust.
	Learns baby's cues.
Sucking behavior prominent.	Applies learning to management of baby.
Cries when distressed.	
Responds to mouth, skin, sense modalities.	Interacts emotionally with baby.
	Encourages baby's development.

---

* Milton J. E. Senn, M.D., and Albert J. Solnit, M.D., *Problems in Child Behavior and Development*. Philadelphia: Lea & Febiger, 1968.

Is unstable physiologically.
Functions egocentrically.
Is completely dependent.
Has low patience tolerance.
Is non-cognitive; expresses needs instinctually.
Develops trust in ministering adult.
Begins to "expect."

Has reasonable expectations of baby.

Minimal Psychopathology

INFANT

Feeding and digestive problems.
Sleep disturbances.
Excessive sucking activity.
Excessive motor discharge.
Excessive crying.
Excessive irritability.
Hypertonicity
Difficult to comfort.

MOTHER

Indifference to baby.
Ambivalence towards baby and its needs.
Self-doubt and anxiety.
Intolerance of baby's characteristics.
Over- or under-responds to baby.
Premature or inappropriate expectations.
Dissatisfaction with role of motherhood.

Extreme Psychopathology

INFANT

Lethargy (depression).
Marasmus.
Cannot be comforted.
Unresponsive.
Infantile autism.
Developmental arrest.

MOTHER

Alienation from baby.
Severe depression.
Excessive guilt.
Complete inability to function in maternal role.
Overwhelming and incapacitating anxiety.
Denies or tries to control baby's needs.
Severe clashes with baby.
Vents life's dissatisfactions on baby.

DEVELOPMENTAL SCHEMA CHART

The Older Infant (6 to 18 Months)

Tasks in Process

INFANT	MOTHER
To develop more reliance and self control.	To provide a healthy emotional and physical climate.
To differentiate self from mother.	To foster weaning, training, habits.
To make developmental progress.	To understand, appreciate and accept baby.

Acceptable Behavioral Characteristics

INFANT	MOTHER
More stable physiologically.	Derives satisfaction from serving baby well.
Heightened voluntary motor activity and exploration.	Responds appropriately to baby's signs of distress.
Higher level of patience tolerance.	Aware of baby's inborn reaction pattern.
Instinctual needs in better control.	Has more confidence in own ability.
Strong selective tie to mother.	Gives positive psychologic reassurance (fondling, talking, comforting).
Stranger differentiation.	Shows pleasure in baby.
Increased verbality, play and sensori-motor behavior.	Keeps pace with baby's advances.
Discernible social responses; joyful in play.	Is accepting of baby's idiosyncrasies.
Outbursts of negativism and anger.	
Sensory modalities important.	
Emergence of idiosyncratic patterns.	
Demonstrates memory and anticipation.	
Begins to imitate.	

Minimal Psychopathology

INFANT	MOTHER
Excessive crying, anger and irritability.	Disappointed in and unaccepting of baby.
Low frustration tolerance.	Misses baby's cues.
Excessive negativism.	Infancy unappealing.
Finicky eater, sleep disturbances.	Impersonal management.
Digestive and elimination problems.	Attempts to coerce to desired behavior.
Noticeable motility patterns (fingering, rocking, etc.).	Over-anxious or over-protective.
Delayed development.	Mildly depressed and apathetic.

Extreme Psychopathology

INFANT

Tantrums and convulsive disorders.
Apathy, immobility and withdrawal.
Extreme and obsessive finger-sucking, rocking, head-banging.
No interest in objects, environment or play.
Anorexia.
Megacolon.
Inexpressive of feeling.
No social discrimination.
No tie to mother; wary of all adults.
Infantile autism.
Failure to thrive.
Arrested development.

MOTHER

Neglect or abuse of baby.
Rejection of the maternal role.
Severe hostility reactions.
No attempt to understand or gratify baby.
Deliberately thwarts infant.
Complete withdrawal and separation from baby.

Maria, The Hungry Baby

by Thelma Ingles, M.A., R.N.*

When Maria came to our hospital in Cali, Colombia she was eleven months old and weighed seven and a half pounds. Her domelike head seemed enormous above her starved, skeletal body. All of her subcutaneous fat had been sacrificed to feed her vital organs. The lobes of her protruding ears looked like curves of parchment paper. What hair she had was dry, patchy, and the color of hay. Her swollen abdomen exaggerated the emaciation of her ribbed chest and shrunken pelvis. Her spindled arms and legs were folded close to her body as if she were trying to protect herself from the harm of an unpleasant world.

As I looked down at her that first morning, I saw all of this—<u>but most of all I saw her wide-open, terrified eyes; they seemed to reflect a summary of all tragedy</u>. Her face was torn with wrinkled movement and huge tears ran down her cheeks, but only a dry, tired sound came from her mouth. I picked her up, held her closely, and talked with her. She stopped crying, but looked at me

---

* Thelma Ingles. "Maria, The Hungry Baby." *Nursing Forum.* Vol. 5, No. 2 (Spring 1966). Pp. 36–47.

with distrust and anger. It was the anger in her eyes which gave me hope: she was still fighting.

Maria became my patient. For two weeks I went to the ward each morning to hold her and to feed her. After three or four days, she seemed to expect me. She would stare at each person who passed her bed, and dismiss them. When I arrived she began to cry out her message, "Don't forget me." Occasionally, I would try to talk with her before her food arrived. This she objected to loudly—"Let me eat first, and then we can chat."

At first, when I put her back to bed after her breakfast, she would hunch up in a fetal position and cry. I discovered that when I covered her with a sheet, she stopped crying. She would grab her "security blanket," pull it up around her face, and tuck a corner into her mouth. Only her alert eyes were exposed, always watching, watching.

After several days, Maria began to gain a little weight and to seem less tense. However, alone in her bed, she never fully relaxed her tense position. There were so many different people on the ward, so much movement, that she seemed afraid to relax.

At the end of two weeks, I had to stop my daily visits to Maria. I talked with the ward aides who would be giving her care, explained the things she liked and didn't like, and asked them to hold her often and talk with her.

It was ten days before I had a chance to return to see Maria. I was shocked when I saw her because she looked worse than she had the day she arrived on the ward. Her eyes were turned upwards; only the whites showed. When I spoke to her, she slowly pulled her pupils down, looked at me with recognition, and then, with an air of despair, once again secluded herself. Her chart showed that she had lost most of her weight gain, and that she was running a fever.

I went to the staff physician and said angrily, "What has happened to *my* baby?" He commented quietly, "I think she has missed her mama." Overwhelmed with guilt, I asked permission to take Maria home with me for the weekend. He explained that this was unorthodox procedure, but after consulting with the ward resident physician, he decided that it might nonetheless be wise procedure. I asked, "What shall I feed her?" and was told, "Use your own judgment."

Maria and I started for home. We stopped only long enough to buy her a minimal wardrobe—all bright colors—and some baby food—Incaparina, a cheap but very nutritious prepared food, an expensive formula, and pablum.

When we arrived at my apartment, I wondered what kind of a reception my maid would give Maria. Lucila had emphatically turned down my request for a dog or a cat. How would she react to a baby? Lucila first looked at Maria with surprise; then her face filled with tenderness, and she repeated over and over, "Pobrecita, pobrecita" (poor little one). Maria was welcome.

While Lucila held her, I prepared Maria's quarters—a couch in my bedroom. A dresser drawer, padded with a foam rubber pillow and placed on the middle of the couch, made an excellent crib. A large beach towel was arranged for the diaper changing routine. The opposite end of the couch became the closet for Maria's new clothes.

While Lucila prepared lunch, I massaged Maria with oil, gave her some passive exercises, and dressed her in a gay yellow jacket, diapers, and blue rubber pants. She looked like an unhappy, underfed rag doll.

High on our list of needs for Maria was food. I sat down to feed her with an air of grim determination. She ate well at first, her eyes taking in all the newness of her surroundings with interest. Then she slowed down, but I was persistent: each time she opened her mouth I popped in a spoonful of soup or formula. She tried to tell me she had had enough, but I was so anxious for her to eat that I failed to get the message. Finally, with no alternative, she vomited. Lucila explained to me that the real problem was that I had given her soup and milk at the same meal. "You must never feed a baby salty things and sweet things together."

I rocked Maria for a while and then put her to bed. Although she was obviously very sleepy, she began to cry; she did not yet feel secure enough to be alone. So I rocked her until I felt it was safe to feed her again. This time I was more circumspect; when she slowed down, I slowed down, and when she anchored her upper lip over her lower lip, I stopped. She accepted her bed gracefully, and with her security sheet held tightly to her face, went promptly to sleep.

While she slept, I cooked. This was my first experience in preparing Incaparina. It has to be sifted to remove all foreign matter and then is added to water and boiled for fifteen minutes. Like a pudding, it needs to be stirred constantly. I kept running to the bedroom to look at Maria, to be sure that she was breathing properly. During one trip, the Incaparina collected in the bottom of the pan, and when I returned I found a burned mass. So I started over again, but first I quietly moved Maria's bed to a chair near the kitchen where I could see her while I cooked. How frightening are the anxieties of a new mother!

For supper, Maria had her first carrots. With the initial spoonful, her eyes opened wide, and she looked at me while she moved them about a bit in her mouth. Then she swallowed and opened her mouth for more. Carrots were in! She ate two ounces of carrots, four ounces of Incaparina, and four ounces of formula. I propped her up in her chair, and she watched me eat my dinner. She took note of each movement between dish and mouth.

At nine that evening I washed Maria's hands and face and dressed her in her new blue nightgown. I decided to try a bottle of formula. She absolutely refused the bottle; in fact, she screamed when I held it in front of her. I wondered whether she had had a bad experience with a bottle, perhaps too hot a formula, or whether she had figured out that spoon-feeding takes longer.

By the time the formula was downed, I was almost asleep, but not Maria. In her bed she was quiet as long as I rocked the bed. I put a loud ticking clock beside her head, hoping she would recall the peaceful haven of her mother's womb. It didn't work. I tried my music box; this was fine as long as I continued to rock her bed. At midnight I gave her some more formula and put her back to bed, but again she cried. I thought she might have a stomachache, so I walked with her. She snuggled her head close to my neck and enjoyed the hike. Finally, at three in the morning I moved her, bed and all, into my bed, and we both went to sleep.

Giving Maria her morning bath was a real hurdle. I had no bathtub and was sure the shower would have little appeal. She ended up in my carefully scrubbed bidet and protested the ignominy. After the bath, I rubbed her with oil and moved her bed to the balcony, where she had a sunbath. In the warm sun, she went to sleep and slept until noon. She awoke with a big appetite and cried loudly to be sure I heard her.

For lunch she ate four ounces of thick soup. Lucila insisted that sick babies should have fresh soup, and she had prepared it from various vegetables cooked with chicken. I took an opposing view to the inclusion of lettuce, but gave in, as I wanted to maintain Lucila's interest. The blender turned all of the vegetables, including the lettuce, into a puree. Maria seemed to really like the soup; in fact, I could hardly keep the spoon going fast enough between dish and mouth. For dessert she had a banana blended with her formula.

After lunch, I propped her up beside the record player. She loved the music, and was content as long as I was in sight. If I left the room, she would cry. If the record player stopped, she would cry. At two o'clock, I gave her some Incaparina, and she went to bed without protest. I woke her at four-thirty because I wanted her to sleep that night.

After a small lunch of pablum, formula, and banana, I propped her in her chair (Lucila called her the "Queen"), tied a string around a gizzard, and gave it to her to suck on. I pinned the other end of the string to the sheet, so that the slippery gizzard was always within reaching range. While she sucked with vigor on the gizzard, I read aloud to her.

At eight that evening I decided to crowd the calories; she ate four ounces of thick soup, four ounces of Incaparina, and three ounces of formula. It took her a full hour to finish her bedtime snack. After a short rock she went to bed and almost immediately was asleep. My alarm clock woke us both at six o'clock. We had to get up early so that I could get both of us ready for our return to the hospital by eight.

In the hospital, we weighed Maria and found that she had gained 200 grams in a day and a half. It was apparent that home cooking agreed with her. I asked permission to take her back home, and this time her visit was made official. She was assigned to my "nursing home" for an indefinite period of time. I learned that her parents lived in the high Andes, some seventy miles from the hospital. In view of the fact that they had not been to see her, it seemed likely that Maria might stay weeks with me.

During the following week many changes took place in Maria, not only physically, but also psychologically. We worked out a routine that would permit me to spend as much time with her as possible during the hours when she was awake. I fed her at six in the morning and bathed her, and then she watched me eat and get ready for work. Before I left, I put her to bed, with her music box beside her. Lying on her abdomen, she would go to sleep immediately. After two days she gained enough strength to turn her head from one side to the other. (When she first came to the hospital, she had a bedsore on the back of her flat head and on her coccyx, so I assumed that lying on her abdomen was a new experience for her.)

When she woke at ten or ten-thirty, Lucila fed her and sat her in her special chair in the living room. Sometimes when I came home at noon, I would find the broom in the middle of the room and Lucila either rocking Maria or walking the floor with her. Maria learned to put out her arms as a gesture that she wanted to come to me. I talked with her while Lucila got my lunch ready, and then she joined me at the table and watched me eat. Afterwards I fed her and held her until two, when I returned to work. She went to bed quietly and around four woke for her afternoon feeding. Again, Lucila fed her and took her to the living room, where she was waiting for me when I arrived at six.

She was such fun to come home to: she always seemed glad to see me. During the cocktail hour she sat on my lap and opened her mouth each time I lifted my glass. I got her a jigger of orange juice, and we took turns sipping. After our cocktails, she had her dinner and then joined me at the table. After dinner, I washed her and put on her night clothes. We rocked and listened to records. She enjoyed music, everything from "Hello Dolly" to Brahms. She liked me to keep time to the music by patting her.

One evening we had as guests a young couple who paid a great amount of attention to Maria. She responded to the socialization by refusing to go to bed; at ten-thirty she was still among us. This was the only time she awoke during the night. At three o'clock she took some formula with no interest: most of all she wanted to be with people.

During the week, we experimented with various kinds of new foods. Pureed calves liver was a great success. Maria seemed to know she needed proteins. Pureed apricots were less successful; she puckered up her mouth and looked at me with a sour face. Mixed with Incaparina, the apricots were more acceptable. She liked baked potatoes with butter and loved to suck on a piece of tough steak. I always watched her carefully as she drooled over her steak, but as she had no teeth I didn't have to worry about her biting off a piece.

As the week progressed Maria's urinary output increased, and her abdomen became less swollen. She was cooperative in having just one bowel movement a day, called "po-po" by Lucila. This occurred right after breakfast. I would place a paper towel under her and await results. Because of her poor muscle tone, this event was difficult for her. I helped her by pressing on her lower abdomen. The great quantity of feces which she delivered was astonishing—but then, she was consuming a lot of food.

By the end of the week, two teeth were beginning to emerge from her gums. She gained enough strength to hold her head erect with support, and to move it from side to side, not with agility, but at least to move it. Her fever ended after four days. She had had a persistent chronic pneumonia since her admission to the hospital and coughed often, especially at night. By elevating the foot of her crib and standing her on her head a few seconds each morning, I helped her to bring up the pooled mucus in her lungs. Too, as she grew stronger, she was able to use her intercostal muscles more effectively.

Even more exciting than her physical changes were her psychological gains. From a tense, terrified little animal, she became a relaxed, sweet little girl. The edges of fear were always near the surface, but she learned to trust Lucila and me. In the beginning, if we went out of the room and left her alone, she would immediately cry. After two or three days, she would sit quietly watching the door for our return; then she moved to carrying on with her own activities, regardless of our presence or absence.

Finding suitable toys for her was a problem, because she had so little strength in her hands and arms. Our first successful toy was the cellophane wrapper from a package of cigarettes, crunched into a ball. She could hold this, and it made a gentle noise when she played with it. From playing with this, she learned about her hands. She would hold them in front of her face, move her fingers, and watch the whole process with interest. Her second toy was a plastic letter-opener with a leather crocodile head on one end. She would hold this up in front of her and try repeatedly to get the head into her mouth. As her strength increased this became a dangerous weapon, and we exchanged it for a Brazilian goodluck piece made of balsam.

As Maria became more proficient in the use of her hands, I tried giving her two toys at the same time. When she had one toy I would hand her a second. At first she would drop her toy and reach for the other. Then, she learned that she could use both hands and would hold tightly to one toy while she took the other. And then, I really tested her intelligence. When she had one toy in her left hand, I would stand on her left side and hand her a second. She would drop her toy and take the second in her left hand. Finally, she learned that she could transfer the one toy to her right hand and accept the second, thus losing neither.

At the end of the six o'clock feeding, I would hold her dish in front of her so she could smear her hands in the remaining soup or Incaparina. This was great fun. During mealtime, I began to play a game with her. I would say "hum," pause, and then say it again. Very soon, like a little parrot, she began to respond with a "hum." Occasionally, I would surprise her with a "hum hum." At first she would make no response to the double sound—but would look up at me. After a while she learned that she, too, could say "hum hum."

At the end of the week, I took Maria to the hospital to see her physician. She had gained more than a pound during one week. There was no question about returning home with me. While she was in the hospital she seemed somewhat tense. I couldn't believe that she recognized where she was, but I do know that we were both very happy on our trip home.

That night, for the first time, Maria smiled. I had the feeling that it was the first time she had smiled in a very long time; I even wondered if she had ever smiled before. She didn't seem to know quite how to do it. I thought that possibly my need for her to smile was so great that I was misinterpreting a grimace for a smile. But the next morning she was full of smiles, even to the point of making minimal laughing noises. She responded with pleasure to a kiss on the top of her head. Before, when I kissed her, she screamed with anger or fear.

That afternoon they called me from the hospital to say that Maria's father had come to take her home. I was shattered, but I bundled her up and packed her clothes and all the food available. In the hospital, both the physician and I tried to persuade her father to leave her with me for two more weeks. He said that his home was a long way from the hospital and that transportation was expensive. I offered to pay his expenses, but he said he was afraid that if he took the money he would spend it for other things and then not have any left for the trip. I offered to bring her to him, but he said that he lived two miles from a road. In the end, there was no choice: he was going to take her home.

I insisted upon feeding Maria before she left. While I fed her, the doctor explained carefully to her father the important aspects of her care—her need for love and for food. He described the procedure for preparing the Incaparina and extolled its virtues as a cheap, nutritious, and valuable food.

After I had finished feeding Maria, I carried her to the bus and, with sadness, gave her father his baby. And then she was gone.

The Psychic Principle in Nursing Infants

by Jane Elinor Lester, R.N. *

In a recent paper by Dr. Zahorsky on Problems of the Foundling Home, he asks, Why do babies in asylums develop so slowly and imperfectly in spite of a very plentiful supply of food? We all know that there are some mothers or nurses who

---

* Jane Elinor Lester. "The Psychic Principle in Nursing Infants." *American Journal of Nursing.* Vol. 16, No. 2 (November, 1915), 109–11.

have a wonderful influence on the growth of a child. There are others who lack this innate faculty. In the past few years great progress has been made in caring for infants in asylums and hospitals but to quote Schlössman: "This is the astonishing and obscure thing, why in the hospital we cannot succeed with such a minimum of care, as in the private homes." The psychic theory is very much favored by some, and Birk in a recent article says <u>"It is not a question only of individual care and of some one paying especial attention to the child but the nursing must be of such character as to produce an inner satisfaction."</u> He emphasizes the spiritual contact between child and nurse. Freund admits that the home environment stimulates nutrition and growth in some way. Most of us are ready to admit that some psychic influence is present which causes disturbances in nutrition in particular. If this is true how very essential it is that a nurse caring for children should have sympathy and be able to tell when a baby is hungry, or in pain, or merely uncomfortable. I am convinced that this branch of nursing is very important and that in order to obtain the best results the mother or nurse must love children. We are glad to note that the idea that a woman who has reared one or more infants at home can properly care for an asylum is preposterous and is no longer tolerated.

There are two motives which, knowingly or not, rule the life of every one. The first is egoistic. Over against this is the altruistic motive. A nurse is bound to adjust her life between the ideals of egoism and altruism. Reasonable service for others is indispensable that we may truly serve ourselves. Each nurse when she enters private or institutional practice in a certain sense is going into business. She has something to sell. She looks for a market. If you would succeed financially you take your pay. But the pay in mere dollars is not altogether gratifying. You must give of your soul. Whether in literature, art, or nursing, if you do not get into "the soul of things," you miss the object of real vital importance. With her knowledge of the nature and cause of disease acquired while in training, a nurse is able to see plainly the far reaching results of her profession and thus ought to be able to do some social welfare work by instruction and example in the prevention of disease. We know that disease is never wholly an individual matter. Some diseases are predominantly social. Consequently her relation as nurse must involve a relation to the whole social body. She ceases to be a mere seller of merchandise and becomes a servant of the people. Society already places explicit duties on her and by implication requires many more. Her highest aim should be to lead society in the great movement of eliminating disease and in this nurses become real captains of health. This means a broad responsibility and a more dignified station. Nurses like doctors ought to be active leaders of public sentiment. Most of them endorse the many health movements although they feel that in so doing it means a diminution in their business. Every conscientious nurse practices those methods of routine in her professional work which are calculated in a measure to limit the spread of disease. Through our associations we carry on an active and valuable campaign of education and assist in every form of social uplift. It is true that the medical profession may justly claim the credit of many important accomplishments in sanitation and public hygiene. While we admit that the foregoing statements are true, it is equally true that a sick child may receive very careful skillful nursing through a severe illness and yet when it recovers be left in an environment which is not conducive to growth and development. It is not enough that nurses should be well trained in asepsis, or that the nurse who feeds the babies should not handle anything but the bottles. It is of course essential that the baby's milk, including the bottles, should be clean, but after all, the actual formula of milk modification and cleanliness is only of secondary importance if the environment is such that the child has not that "inner satisfaction." For those children who must necessarily remain in an institution or asylum much can be accomplished by the nurse. Even foundlings may make good citizens. Much has been accomplished in recent years by public lectures on pre-natal care and by organizations for the prevention of infant mortality, and also for the prevention of blindness, but why not have an organization whose purpose it is to investigate the environment existing in public institutions for our sick children? Many nurses have undoubtedly observed in hospitals and also in private practice, that procedure by which a patient at large expense of money and effort is brought to a condition of health and is then turned back to the environment which was the real cause of disease. While this is to be regretted in the case of an adult who may be able, in some cases, to modify his environment, change his employment, or his habits of living, it becomes an actual social crime when the patient is a little child who can in no way change its environment.

It has been observed that babies in an asylum never laugh, or even cry, except when in severe pain. Every child should be stimulated to exercise and made to laugh. We realize that when a mother is separated from her child she undergoes great mental anguish and it is quite reasonable to suppose that the child also suffers when separated from its mother. Let each nurse remember this fact and do all she can to fill the mother's place. Let every nurse consider the social background of her patients and be a real force in all that tends to brighten the life of every little child. Pull your oar joyfully in that "teamwork of nurse, educator and social worker" whose object is "the care of the people in trouble." Surely the homeless child left in an institution without the mother's care is in trouble. Make that home in the meanwhile the "House of Love" for that child.

Working with Mothers and Babies Who Fail to Thrive

by Julina P. Rhymes *

Though all children do not grow at the same rate, there is an expected growth pattern to which babies normally conform. Why some infants do not gain and grow at the expected rate is not clearly understood, as in many instances no organic cause can be determined.

The normal growth rate during the first year of life is relatively greater than in any comparable period postnatally. During this year, the baby's average increase is 50 percent in length and 200 percent in weight (1).

Interest in environmental and psychologic factors as possible contributing causes of failure to thrive in infancy is increasing (2–10).

In a recent study designed to explore some of these factors, I participated in intensive investigation of 13 babies who failed to thrive although no organic cause was discernible. The babies ranged in age from 12 weeks to 27 months. The investigation focused on the babies' environments, especially that part created by mother-infant relationships. An attempt was made to look at total family situations, including factors in the mothers' pasts which may have had a bearing on their mothering ability.

Participating in the study were a pediatrician, a child psychiatrist and, occasionally, staff social workers. Both the pediatrician and I, the pediatric nurse, acted as participant observers while caring for the babies and their mothers during the time the babies were hospitalized for diagnostic evaluation. The period of hospitalization averaged about 10 days.[1]

Although generalizations about the total population of babies who fail to thrive cannot be made from a study of this size, our findings suggest that the babies' mothers in this study were also failing to thrive, that their emotional resources had been depleted and needed replenishing before they could give freely of themselves to their infants. Thus, we provided care and treatment for mothers as well as the babies.

---

* Julina P. Rhymes. "Working with Mothers and Babies Who Fail to Thrive." *American Journal of Nursing.* Vol. 66, No. 9 (September, 1966), 1972–76.

[1] For a more detailed report of methodology and findings, see Martha F. Leonard, Julina P. Rhymes, and A. J. Solnit, "Failure to Thrive in Infant: A Family Problem," *American Journal of Diseases of Children,* Vol. III (June, 1966), 600–12.

The theoretical framework of our study is the concept of motherhood as a developmental phase in a woman's life (11–14). According to this theory, the quality of motherliness, that biologic and emotional phenomenon that enables a woman to respond in a meaningful way to an infant's helplessness and need for care, does not always immediately accompany biologic motherhood. On the other hand, it may be present to a high degree in a woman who has never conceived or given birth to a child (15).

Typically, motherliness is enhanced and enriched under the impact of the reproductive process, but does not begin at that point. Its development begins in a woman's own infancy and continues throughout her lifetime, even through the experience of mothering successive children.

A host of cultural, environmental, and psychologic factors influence the quality of motherliness. Important among these are the way the mother was mothered while in her infancy and childhood and her subsequent continuing and maturing relationships with emotionally supportive persons (16).

Therese Benedek describes the deep-rooted passivity of the pregnant woman, a withdrawing into herself, a wish to be taken care of, to be given to (17). These needs carry over well into the postpartal period. Gerald Caplan likens an expectant mother to a battery that needs charging and states that, unless she gets adequate love during this period, she may have difficulty subsequently in giving love and affection to her child (18).

Ideally, the baby's father and close family members provide this emotional support. The baby, too, helps to satisfy the mother's receptive needs through her strong identification with him, particularly when she nurses him. In the normal, intimate, reciprocal relationship between mother and infant, both grow and develop together. Occasionally, they may be mismatched in temperament and tempo. If a baby is not as vigorous, or perhaps as passive, as the mother expects or desires, her responses to him may be adversely affected, with a circular influence on the baby's response.

Families Studied

In the light of this theory, our study findings have increased our understanding of how to help a baby who fails to thrive in the absence of discernible organic cause by helping his mother. In all of the families in our study, the relationship of the mother to the nonthriving child was disturbed. With some, neither mother nor infant seemed able to satisfy the other. Most of the mothers had difficulty perceiving and assessing their babies' needs correctly, and were frustrated and angered by their infants' unsatisfying responses. Some babies had certain characteristics or behavior that aroused conflicted responses from their mothers.

Our investigation revealed that these babies and their families had many common characteristics. All families but one were experiencing severe stress, sometimes even crisis. Most had disturbed marital relations. They had a host of other emotional, social, and financial problems. The mothers were carrying the stress without adequate help from their husbands, mothers, or other significant persons. They tended to lead lonely lives, without satisfying adult companionship, organizational membership, or recreational outlets.

Nonthriving Mothers

The mothers had been inadequately or insufficiently mothered in their own infancy and childhood. One mother, because of her own mother's mental illness, was reared in a foster home where she was harshly treated and was forced to submit to the sexual advances of her foster father. Another was reared from the age of 5 years by an 18-year-old sister because of the death of her own mother. Others grew up in chaotic, unstable home environments.

Most of the mothers had physical or emotional health problems. In all but one instance, disturbing events were associated with the pregnancy or delivery of the nonthriving child, which could have adversely influenced the mother's expectations of the baby before birth or her acceptance of him afterward.

A mother who had a serious, recurrent kidney infection regarded the baby as a threat to her life during pregnancy. She reported that he kicked so hard in utero that he fractured one of her ribs, and she believed her pelvic bone was being "split apart."

Another mother believed her baby was defective from birth, because labor was induced 10 days early and the baby was slightly jaundiced. She reported that a physician stayed with the baby for seven hours after birth, and, although she was assured that the baby was healthy, she secretly felt that "things were never quite right" with this baby.

The fathers were either absent from the home altogether, or else worked long hours and were unsupportive and uninvolved in family life. For the most part, they were passive and ineffectual, or irresponsible and childlike as husbands and fathers.

All of the pregnancies were unplanned and the babies, during pregnancy, were unwanted. In speaking of women who have unwanted pregnancies, Anna Freud uses the term "unwilling mothers" and says that expecting them to fulfill a task forced on them is too much (19).

In the study, only one baby was a first child. The mothers of the others had been successful in their nurturing of one or more children in the past.

All of the babies were bottle fed from birth. Most of the babies had histories of feeding difficulties, vomiting, sleep disturbance, or excessive irritability dating from the neonatal period.

The nonthriving children gave rise to feelings of guilt and inadequacy in their mothers. The mothers were often incapacitated by depression and anxiety.

It is heartening and significant that, despite manifold problems, these mothers and infants were helped during the brief period of hospitalization. Mothers and babies both seemed to begin to thrive during that time and, as far as is known from limited follow-up of six months to one year, have continued to make satisfactory progress at home. While they were in the hospital, the babies gained weight, vomiting stopped, and irritability lessened. Acceleration in development often accompanied the improvement in nutrition. Most mothers gradually relaxed and began to enjoy their babies.

Nursing Care of the Babies

The baby who fails to thrive needs the same kind of care all babies need: sure, gentle, loving handling while being fed, bathed, and changed. He needs to be cuddled close to the human body, rocked, smiled at, talked and sung to, and played with. These ministrations not only bring the infant comfort and pleasure, but they promote his mental, emotional, and social development. A baby derives maximum benefit from care that includes warmth, spontaneity, and enjoyment of him in response to his constantly changing needs.

Many of these babies showed signs of maternal understimulation as evidenced by varying degrees of retardation in their social, motor, adaptive, and language development. Babies who have not been exposed to enough of the various kinds of stimulation that are normally provided by adequate mothering may lack pliability. They may be stiff and unyielding when cuddled, or slow in smiling, cooing, and, later, in using language. They are often slow in their ability to turn over, sit, stand, and walk without support. They may be inept at handling toys and unable to enjoy them. They may be unresponsive to invitations to such playful activity as pat-a-cake or peekaboo. They may exhibit no obvious expected distress at being left by their mothers nor show fear of strangers at the age when such fear would be appropriate. They often respond in the same way, without discrimination, to all.

The nurse's task, in addition to providing for the baby's physical needs, is to promote development by exposing the baby to a variety of experiences normally provided by a loving mother (20).[2]

These infants should not be subjected to the scheduled, routine, impersonal care that is often the lot of hospitalized infants. The nurse should respond to such a baby's signals of distress rather than make him wait for care and comfort.

Even within the limitations of hospital routine, a nurse may provide important

---

[2] An excellent discussion of the kinds of stimulation mothering activities supply is available in Provence and Lipton, *Infants in Institutions*, chapters 4 through 16.

stimulation by singing and talking to the baby as she bathes and feeds him. She can offer him toys and engage him in play. During the periods when he must be left alone while awake, the nurse can hang a colorful Cradle Gym within his reach or position him so that he can see the activity around him. If there is no activity in his room, he may benefit from being taken to the nurses' station in a carriage.

Continuity of care by a minimum number of mother-substitutes is desirable, not only for the baby, but for the nurses, who must become sensitized to the infant's characteristic rhythm and pattern of response. It takes time for a nurse and a baby to become accustomed to one another, especially as these babies often present difficult problems in care. Feeding difficulties and vomiting are common. The baby may be hypertonic and irritable, or extremely unresponsive. Each baby has a unique combination of needs to which a nurse must adapt and respond.

Even during brief hospitalization, a baby's development may accelerate with the right kind of care. Because hospitalization is usually brief, an important function of the nurse is to help the baby's mother respond to him appropriately. For this reason, mothers should be encouraged to come to the hospital to observe and share in their babies' care.

Optimal Therapy

In looking for reasons for improvement in the babies, it seemed that our most valuable therapeutic agent was our personal contacts with the mothers. Some mothers were partly relieved to find that their infants had no organic disease. Others, who were close to physical and emotional exhaustion, seemed to benefit from the brief respite from the total responsibility of infant care. In some cases, the temporary, partial separation of mothers from their infants seemed to break the circuit of tension; but, more important, we believe, was the benefit derived from the supportive relationships that were established. The fact that these mothers were helped to cope in positive ways with distressing situations may have given them strength to cope more adequately with subsequent problems at home.

The nurse might add a new dimension to a mother's awareness and appreciation of her baby simply by pointing out and attaching importance to his unfolding skills as she observes them. For example, she might say, "See how he is learning to play with the rattle? He has more interest in it now, because we have been enjoying it with him." Very often, a mother is not aware of the effect of the stimulation provided by even such simple mothering activities as offering the baby toys and playing with him or moving him from room to room with her as she does her housework so that he may enjoy and learn from her company.

The object in giving care to the mother is to support her in uncovering her inner capacities to mother and to help her establish a satisfying relationship with her baby. One hopes that if she is helped to recognize the baby's needs and meet them adequately, the resulting satisfaction and well-being and responsiveness in the infant will increase her self-confidence and promote pleasure in her mothering.

Because these mothers are usually emotionally deprived and, at the same time, burdened by stress, one of the most important functions of the nurse is to help supply emotional nurture in a way that can be accepted by the mother without encouraging her overdependence. The nurse does this by using herself creatively in providing warm, accepting, nonjudgmental help. This is not always easy to accomplish.

Characteristically, these mothers are difficult to reach. They often fail to visit their babies in the hospital, or, if there, are polite but guarded, aloof, and passively resistant to help. Sometimes, they are defensive and competitive with the staff.

It may be that they fear too close relationships with supportive persons because they have previously been hurt by those on whom they relied for sympathy and help. They appear to displace their own feelings of anger at the baby onto the staff, or look for someone to blame for their real or imagined shortcomings. The nurse may be viewed as a threat if she is perceived as giving more competent care than the mother. A mother may resent the nurse's intrusion on her relationship with her child.

It is not unusual for a mother to openly find fault with the nursing care, especially if the baby has improved markedly. One mother accused the nurses of not charting her baby's vomiting. Another claimed the nurses lied about her baby's gain in weight. It seemed as though some of the mothers deliberately tried to provoke counter-hostility in the staff, possibly to relieve their own guilt or to justify their resentment.

Helpful Nursing Attitudes

The nurse may have trouble avoiding feeling annoyed, but these mothers are quick to sense critical attitudes, no matter how correct the nurse's surface behavior. The nurse who harbors poorly handled negative feelings may unwittingly reinforce a mother's expectation of rejection and blame. The mothers need a great deal of acceptance and understanding guidance if they are to benefit from their association with the hospital staff rather than be made to feel even more inadequate.

A nurse, to function effectively, must have a genuine interest in the mother as a worthwhile person who is worthy of her respect and attention regardless of her shortcomings. This cannot be feigned. The key to this kind of acceptance is *understanding*. If a nurse imagines what being in the mother's place is like and wonders how she herself would handle the same problems, she is apt to be less judgmental.

Every nurse, of course, has her own characteristic way of relating. Some seem to know intuitively how to get along well with all patients. Others sometimes have to work at forming helpful nurse-patient relationships. The following techniques, which are offered as suggestions, have been found to be useful in working with mothers who are politely on guard or who are openly defensive and antagonistic.

Helping Non-Thriving Mothers

The nurse is usually more effective if she avoids the role of expert or authority figure and, instead, engages in a friendly, informal relationship with the mother as an ally or collaborator in the care of the baby; if, in effect, she says to the mother, "Look, your baby is, indeed, difficult to feed and comfort. Let's put our heads together and see what we can do to make him happier." The nurse, more than any other member of the medical team, is in a favorable position to do this. She has the opportunity for a close, more continual association with the mother and appears to be a less-threatening status figure than either the physician or social worker.

It seems to work well if the nurse avoids giving direct advice or suggestions and teaches instead by example and casual conversation with the mother as they work together. If the nurse comments informally about her observations of the baby, his behavior may become more meaningful to the mother, perhaps increasing her appreciation of him as well as helping her to evaluate his needs more accurately. When a mother obviously needs explicit direction in her mothering activities, the nurse will be more effective if she supports the mother in following the doctor's advice rather than being directive herself.

Letting the mother move at her own pace in taking over her baby's care is helpful. Giving the care should not be expected of her, nor should her prerogative be usurped. One tense, 19-year-old mother of two children visited her baby in the hospital every day. Under the circumstances, she had a legitimate reason for leaving her two-year-old child in the care of a neighbor, and she seemed to benefit from the resulting, temporary relief from responsibility. While in the hospital, she was allowed to spend many hours curled up in a comfortable chair by her baby's crib. She occasionally held and fed the baby, but expressed no desire to do more. As hospitalization continued, she gradually relaxed and seemed to gain strength from her association with the supportive, accepting nursing staff. By watching the nurses handle her difficult baby calmly, she gained self-confidence and, when finally able to assume the baby's care, demonstrated that her own mothering skills had improved.

Another mother was dictatorial and aggressive in assuming the total care of her baby, even though her method of mothering left much to be desired. She was openly critical of the nurses and left instructions for them to follow whenever she went out of the room. The nurses, instead of reacting defensively, were permissive and gentle in allowing her to prove herself. After a few days, she relaxed and became eager to relinquish her infant's care to the nurses, from whom she also seemed to gain strength and a more realistic understanding of her baby's problem.

A nurse may be of help simply by listening attentively to the mother as she expresses her feelings. The resulting catharsis may relieve the mother's tension, and, sometimes, just being able to put her problems into words may lead her to a more realistic assessment of them and enable her to grapple with them more successfully. This also serves to increase the nurse's knowledge of the mother. If the mother feels understood, accepted, and respected, even though her expressed feelings are negative, her self-esteem may be bolstered. The nurse may also promote the mother's self-respect and confidence by praising any signs of strength. When possible, acting on the mother's suggestions is helpful. A nurse might even solicit these by asking, "What seemed to work best with the baby at home?" or, "Why don't we try this and see whether it helps?"

The nurse might allay the mother's feeling of blame by speaking of her own difficulties in handling the baby and stating that he does present a challenging problem in nurturing. This can be done optimistically with the attitude that the problems in infant care are not insurmountable and that mother and nurse can work them out together.

If the opportunity arises, the nurse might encourage the baby's father and other family members to support the mother. Referrals to appropriate community agencies might help so that a public health nurse can continue the supportive care that began in the hospital. In such cases, the nurse who cared for the baby in the hospital can insure more meaningful continuity of care after a referral if she shares her knowledge and experience with the public health nurse in a direct and continuing manner.

References

1. Jeans, P. C. and others, eds. *Essentials of Pediatrics.* 6th ed. Philadelphia: J. B. Lippincott Co., 1958. P. 13.
2. Bowlby, John. *Maternal Care and Mental Health.* 2d ed. World Health Organization, Monograph Series No. 2. Geneva, Switzerland: World Health Organization, 1965.
3. Widdowson, E. M. "Mental Contentment and Physical Growth." *Lancet,* Vol. 1 (May 28, 1951), 1316–1318.
4. Coleman, Rose W. and Provence, Sally. "Environmental Retardation (Hospitalism) in Infants Living in Families." *Pediatrics,* Vol. 19 (February, 1957), 285–92.

5. Patton, R. G. and Gardner, L. I. "Influence of Family Environment on Growth; the Syndrome of Maternal Deprivation." *Pediatrics,* Vol. 30 (December, 1962), 957–62.
6. Barbero, G. J. and others. "Malidentification of Mother-Baby-Father Relationships Expressed in Infant Failure-to-Thrive." In *The Neglected—Battered Child Syndrome.* Ed. Helen C. Boardman and others. New York: Child Welfare League of America, 1963. Pp. 13–28.
7. Elmer, Elizabeth. "Failure-to-Thrive; Role of the Mother." *Pediatrics,* Vol. 25 (April, 1960), 717–25.
8. Blodgett, F. M. "Growth Retardation Related to Maternal Deprivation." In *Modern Perspectives in Child Development.* Ed. A. J. Solnit and Sally Provence. New York: International Universities Press, Inc., 1963. Pp. 83–93.
9. Patton, R. G. and Gardner, L. I. *Growth Failure in Maternal Deprivation.* Springfield, Ill.: Charles C Thomas, Publisher, 1963.
10. Stott, D. H. "Abnormal Mothering as a Cause of Mental Subnormality. Part I. A Critique of Some Classic Studies of Maternal Deprivation in the Light of Possible Congenital Factors." *Journal of Child Psychology and Psychiatry,* Vol. 3 (April–June, 1962), 79–91.
11. Benedek, Therese. *Psychosexual Functions in Women.* New York: Ronald Press, 1952.
12. ———. "Parenthood as a Developmental Phase." *Journal of the American Psychoanalytic Association,* Vol. 7 (July, 1959), 389–417.
13. Deutsch, Helene. *Psychology of Women.* Vol. 2. Motherhood. New York: Grüne and Stratton, 1945.
14. McFarland, Margaret B. and Reinhart, J. B. "The Development of Mother-Illness." *Children,* Vol. 6 (March–April, 1959), 48–52.
15. Deutsch. *Psychology of Women.* P. 166.
16. *Ibid.* P. 20.
17. Benedek, Therese. "The Psychosomatic Implications of the Primary Unit: Mother-Child." *American Journal of Orthopsychiatry,* Vol. 19 (October, 1949), 6–13.
18. Caplan, Gerald. *Concepts of Mental Health and Consultation.* U.S. Children's Bureau Publication No. 373. Washington, D.C.: Government Printing Office, 1959. P. 49.
19. Freud, Anna. "Safeguarding the Emotional Health of Our Children; An Inquiry Into the Concept of the Rejecting Mother." In *Casework Papers.* Proceedings of the 81st annual forum of the National Conference of Social Work. Atlantic City, N.J., May 1954. New York: Family Service Association of America, 1955. P. 9.
20. Provence, Sally and Lipton, Rose. *Infants in Institutions.* New York: International Universities Press, Inc., 1963.

chapter four

PRE-SCHOOL CHILDREN

The Toddler Stage

INTRODUCTION

The toddler stage refers to those months and years during which the child begins to take his first steps and gradually develops the ability to walk confidently. Some normal children begin to walk before twelve months and others acquire this skill only toward the latter half of the second year, and this stage continues until about the end of the third year. The child acquires verbal skills, increases his intellectual achievement, improves his physical coordination, and achieves voluntary control over his bladder and bowel sphincters.

His new physical skills are enhanced by what seems to be boundless energy. The manageable baby slides into this much more active and vigorous stage, often to the surprise and dismay of parents. He slowly moves away from his mother, first by creeping and crawling and then by walking. With all of these new skills, a child begins to develop autonomy, a sense of independent self.[1] This process of self-definition continues during the ensuing years and is not truly completed until after adolescence.

[1] Erik H. Erikson. *Childhood and Society*. New York: W. W. Norton & Company, Inc., 1963. P. 82.

At the beginning of this stage, the toddler's mother continues to be his primary love object. However, as his consciousness widens, he shows increasing interest in other members of his family and in his peer group. By the end of this stage, he walks and runs with confidence and vigor. His aggressive impulses become channelled into large-muscle activities, and he is liable to damage or destroy objects as he playfully investigates them.

The voluntary muscles provide the toddler with the mobility to explore his new world. The extent of restraint imposed upon the toddler will vary according to the circumstances and customs of his family and his culture. One of the reasons that toddlers require so much supervision is that their natural wish to explore is coupled with an inability to identify danger. For this reason, this stage is sometimes known as "the age of accidents." American mothers have the added responsibility of guarding their toddler against dangers such as poisons, fires, automobiles, and water hazards. In America half a million children are accidentally poisoned every year, and three-quarters of these victims are under four years of age.[2]

Meals, dressing, and toilet training are all affected by the toddler's need for independence. These areas can early become battlegrounds for the mother and child. It is not without reason that some unprepared parents refer to their toddlers as "the terrible twos." Children at this age show a wide range of emotional responses. They can be playful and happy one moment and angry and tearful the next. The nurse may note a toddler happily playing one moment with a toy, and crying the next when another child tries to take it away.

Child rearing practices vary widely in American society. The toddler who lives in a house with many expensive, breakable objects may be trained differently from the child who grows up in a family without such objects. Generally speaking, the nurse should advise mothers to keep breakable and dangerous items out of reach of the toddler.

Nurses in children's hospitals are aware of the number of children who come into the emergency room after ingestion of medicine or injury arising from their inability to discriminate between dangerous and benign objects. The nurses are aware that some mothers underprotect and others overprotect their children. Both extremes can give the nurse important clues regarding the mother-child relationship.

THE DEVELOPMENT OF MOTOR SKILLS

Nurses, through their understanding of child development, can help the mother learn the kind of person her child is and accept his developmental

---

[2] Gene Accas and John H. Eckstein. *How to Protect Your Child.* New York: Sandranita Associates, 1968. P. 1.

limits, as well as his emerging abilities. <u>Limits and skills vary a great deal from child to child.</u>

The obvious pleasure that the child gets from body activity and independent movement leads him to especially enjoy being undressed and walking around without clothes. It is important to help mothers understand that children, especially when they get up in the morning and after a bath, like to be free of clothing for a time if the day or room is warm enough.

The aggressive energy that the toddler shows is natural, and forcible restriction of bodily activity tends to increase the child's destructive tendency as well as interfere with his sense of personal freedom. Prolonged restriction of activity through either illness or injury is especially difficult for a toddler to accept, and may contribute to later problems, especially relating to the expression of hostility.

The well-equipped nursery school with a trained staff is an excellent place for the nurse to observe healthy children learning their roles, developing physical and motor skills as well as making emotional progress. The well child and the sick child may be at opposite ends of the spectrum. For this reason, the nurse needs to be familiar enough with normal development to assess where each child she cares for is on the scale. For example, the nurse will be aware that the two-year-old is much more active and sure of himself than he was at 15 to 18 months. He is less likely to fall, he climbs and runs much more frequently, and is less likely to lose his balance.

DEVELOPMENT OF INDIVIDUALITY

In many ways, because of his mobility, the toddler increasingly becomes a companion to other family members. He can be loving, affectionate, and warmly responsive, despite the normal negativism seen during this stage. The child frequently may say "no" even when he means "yes," or will do just the opposite of what he is told to do. He may one moment find his mother lovable and at the next moment intolerable. Intense loving, dependent feelings and behavior alternate unpredictably with anger and rejection directed at parents, siblings, and other children.

This is often a difficult time for the mother too. For some women, the experience of closeness to an infant is hard to relinquish. Furthermore, the toddler is by no means always lovable or responsive to her wishes. The existence of the contrary feelings of love and hate, seeming to be present at the same time or in rapid alternation, is termed *ambivalence*.[3] <u>The concept of ambivalence suggests that in all important relationships there is usually a mixture of both loving and hostile feelings.</u> Ambivalent attitudes and be-

[3] Theodore Lidz. *The Person.* New York: Basic Books, Inc., 1968. P. 177.

havior are universal in human beings, but they are especially prevalent during the early toddler stage.

Physically ill patients often experience and express considerable ambivalence towards medical and nursing personnel. In sick persons there is often a reawakening of the conflict between a desire to yield to the dependence enforced or encouraged by illness and treatment on the one hand, and the wish to be independent and grown up, on the other. The result is that nurses may become the objects first of clinging, demanding behavior from their patients, and then of resentment and hostility when patients feel ignored or unrelieved of symptoms. These regressive behavioral manifestations in sick adults are reminiscent of normal behavior during the toddler stage.

TEMPER TANTRUMS

Temper tantrums represent motor discharges of affective states.

During the toddler age temper tantrums are fairly common since speech has not been fully established. Temper tantrums represent an outlet for conflict, frustration, and distress. A positive relationship with an adult can have a stabilizing effect on a child who is subject to temper tantrums by helping him to diminish his fear, anger, and anxiety. The child then learns a better way to test his limits without having to resort to a tantrum. In the young child, there is less emotional stability and occasional temper tantrums are part of his learning to cope with his frustrations.

Just as a child who has been restrained physically may have temper tantrums, so too the child who is raised in an overly permissive atmosphere can frequently be very restless and irritable.

Whenever a child is tired, sick, or anxious, he will revert to earlier forms of behavior. Anna Freud notes,

> At the end of a long nursery school day, for example, temper tantrums will occur, good manners will disappear, impatience and urgency of wishes will be more obvious, even in the most adaptive child. This is "normal." No development goes forward in a straight, progressive line. It is usual for every human individual during his period of growth constantly to take temporary steps backward, without on the whole giving up or harming his forward development.[4]

Temper tantrums are not isolated incidents, and it is important for the nurse as well as the mother to understand the total situation in order to deal with it.

---

[4] Anna Freud. *Research at the Hampstead Child Therapy Clinic and Other Papers.* London: The Hogarth Press, 1970. P. 328.

MENTAL AND VERBAL DEVELOPMENT

The toddler's vocalizing and babbling with energetic gestures mature into speech, which begins to take the place of close bodily contact, especially between the mother and the infant. The child begins to express his feelings and needs through words, instead of crying when unhappy or in pain. Being able to make his wants known helps him to be understood by others and can relieve some of his frustration.

The toddler shows a surprising increase in the ability to understand language. Words gradually gain discrete meanings and become symbols to identify objects, feelings, qualities, and relationships between objects. As a child increases his vocabulary, he also increases the precision with which he is able to use words. When a child is about two years old, he begins to use two- to four-word expressions, such as "mama go bye-bye," and "nice doggie." By the time the child is three years old, he begins to ask questions ("Why?" "What's this?"), and his comprehension expands rapidly.

A child's language development greatly depends upon his parents' verbal as well as nonverbal communication with him. The importance of the mother or a consistent caretaking person to the child's speech development is emphasized by Edith Buxbaum. She notes:

> The mother's voice, comforting and promising from the very beginning of a baby's life, is the voice of feeling and of love. In many cases, young children who had just started to talk either stopped talking or made no further progress when their mothers left them to take a job during the day. Whatever function has been acquired is to some degree dependent on a continuation of the relationship to the mother.[5]

Nurses frequently see the toddler in the hospital become verbally uncommunicative once he is separated from his mother.

THE IMPORTANCE OF PLAY

Children enjoy many types of physical and emotional play. They often invent games and construct their own materials, thus developing their creativity.

Aggression is an important part of the child's development, and play helps to express this aggression in a more acceptable form. Children play, not only for pleasure, but to master anxiety. Playing, itself, is therapeutic

---

[5] Edith Buxbaum. *Troubled Children in a Troubled World.* New York: International Universities Press, Inc., 1970. P. 15.

and is an important part of the child's life. It is largely through play that the child begins to socialize with other children and to develop emotional relationships.

Children do not play like adults, but they frequently imitate adults and "the work of adults." The young child practices being an adult by keeping house, cooking, driving the car, and dressing up like an adult. Play is the method by which the child expresses himself and learns about life.

Expensive toys are not essential for children. Pots and pans, cardboard boxes, old magazines, and catalogues can provide the child with a source of pleasure. The toddler often likes to tear pages out of books, and for this reason, he should be provided with cloth and cardboard books at home and in the hospital.

Creative materials such as playdough and clay are helpful to the child at home and in the hospital because they allow him the opportunity for pounding, shaping, and molding. A blackboard with white or colored chalk can also be useful. Crayons, with large sheets of paper provide another opportunity for expression.

Large plastic and wooden blocks are also fun for the toddler. While in the hospital, he can especially enjoy take-apart toys, pull toys, and simple large puzzles. Toddlers also enjoy music and rhythm. Instruments such as drums, cymbals, triangles, toy xylophones and accordions, along with records, provide a means for emotional expression.

In recent years, the study of children's drawings in relation to normal and abnormal child development has been increasingly emphasized. Books by Burns, Kaufman, and DiLeo illustrate this mode of enhancing our understanding of children through the study of their drawings.[6]

The young child requires adequate time to play out of doors. He needs to play with materials that help to develop his large muscles through running, jumping, climbing, and pounding. The jungle gym is an example of climbing equipment that also provides a social experience.

Another basic play item for the young child is a sandbox. The nurse who has observed children in a nursery school or at the beach will recognize how sand and water play provide the child with the opportunity to make mudpies and to play with his cars and trucks. This is especially helpful for the child who is being, or who has recently been, toilet trained. Mud and dirt offer an opportunity for the child to "make a mess" in a socially acceptable manner. Water itself, is also very important to the toddler. For this reason, he can also have an especially good time in the bathtub and enjoy making bubbles with soap flakes.

---

[6] Robert C. Burns and S. Harvard Kaufman. *Kinetic Family Drawings*. New York: Brunner/Mazel, Inc., 1970.

Joseph H. DiLeo. *Young Children and Their Drawings*. New York: Brunner/Mazel, Inc., 1970.

TRANSITIONAL OBJECTS

Teddy bears, dolls, and soft or hard toys are often used by the young child for dramatic play and provide a temporary substitute for mother, father, siblings, or friends. Children like to take these objects to bed at night, or at times when they feel lonely, depressed, or anxious. This is one of the important reasons why the child should be able to take such objects from his home to the hosptial. The term transitional objects is described in detail by D. W. Winnicott.[7]

It may be difficult for the nurse to understand that a small dirty piece of blanket can be a precious object for the young child. She has only to recall Linus with his blanket in the comic strip Peanuts to see the value of this symbol to the young child.

The child in the hospital can be given another source of security and reassurance if his mother leaves objects like her gloves or an old purse. These help the child to feel that she has left something of value for which she will surely return.

PLAY THERAPY

Play therapy has been used by child analysts for nearly half a century in the treatment of emotional disorders of childhood. The use of play as a treatment was introduced early by therapists such as Anna Freud, Sigmund Freud's daughter, and Melanie Klein.

Play therapy in hospitals is called by some "Mental First Aid." [8] The use of dolls and other toys in conjunction with experienced therapists can help provide the sick child with better methods of coping with his illness. There is an increasing need for further exploration regarding the use of play therapy in pediatric units.

ROUTINE AND THE TODDLER

Although the two-year-old explores readily, he likes things to continue the way they have been. New routines with new clothes, new places, and new things to eat may be especially upsetting to him. The nurse may find, for example, that when a child of this age comes into the hospital, merely changing his own clothing to a hospital gown may be extremely distressing.

[7] D. W. Winnicott. *Playing and Reality*. London: Tavistock Publications Limited, 1971. Pp. 1–25.

[8] Anna Freud. *Research at the Hampstead Child-Therapy Clinic and Other Papers*. London: The Hogarth Press, 1970. P. 430.

SLEEP

Ritual becomes very important at this age. His bedtime hour is most effective if it is accompanied by routine. Encouraging parents to slow down the tempo at bedtime or naptime is important. Roughhousing with the father may be fun, but it is not conducive to quietness and rest. In most instances, reading is a much better preliminary activity to bedtime than active play. The child will enjoy hearing the same stories read over to him night after night. He will often fill in words in a story that has been read to him repeatedly, before he can read himself. In discussing bedtime, Louise Bates Ames writes:

> Bedtime isn't always an easy experience for anyone—child or adult. It isn't always easy to get children to bed, to keep them in bed, to get them to sleep, or to keep them asleep. And, clearly, it isn't easy for children to leave the day's activities, the family group, and—at the final moment—their mother, and to accept being left alone in the dark.[9]

The young child should have a quiet place in which to sleep. This is a time when he can usually benefit by having his own room. It is very important for the nurse to have some idea of where a child sleeps at home. It is not unusual in the homes of poor and underprivileged children to find that the child, even at this age, occupies the parents' bedroom. This is not satisfactory for the child or the parents, since both need a sense of privacy.

Sleep requirements change for the toddler, and he may begin to omit one of his daytime naps. These, like food requirements, vary from child to child. Part of a toddler's routine is related to his family's. Small children need a balance of rest and activity and, for this reason, a nap can be a good way to give them a quiet time during the day. The two-year-old may make excuses for not going to sleep—for needing to go to the bathroom, to have a drink of water, a glass of milk—and may offer a variety of reasons for staying awake. Many children at this age are afraid of the dark and a soft light will help them to sleep more comfortably. Sickness may disturb sleep patterns, and children in the hospital may suffer from insomnia, nightmares, and restlessness.

Children may continue to take a bottle at this stage, especially at bedtime. Weaning occurs best when done gradually, with the daytime bottle usually discontinued between the first and second year. Some mothers who nurse their babies wean them from breast to bottle within the first six months. Some children are weaned from the breast or bottle to a cup as early as the middle of the first year. An important function of the nurse is

[9] Louise Bates Ames. *Child Care and Development.* Philadelphia: J. B. Lippincott Company, 1970. P. 159.

to help the mother feel relaxed about this process, in order to make it as pleasant as possible for her and her child. The nurse may find that the toddler who comes into the hospital and has been ill may go back to using a bottle for brief periods of time.

THE FAMILY AND THE TODDLER

We have previously discussed the function of the family in its role in providing food, shelter, and the material necessities of life. As the infant proceeds to the toddler stage, it is important to consider his development within the family. The family is the primary group that will contribute to the health and strength of the emerging personality of the child. The public health nurse, particularly, works with family groups and is perhaps most aware of the equilibrium within this unit. Failure of the family to function adequately can bring about mental and social disorder. We are aware that certain families are "multiple-problem families," whereas others stay predominantly trouble-free. In the early sections, we have emphasized the mother's role; as the child develops, however, we see the whole family as responsible for the cultivation of learning and the support of individual creativity. As the toddler develops, it is the family that molds the kind of person, to a large extent, that he will be. For one thing, it helps him form his identity as a man or a woman.

The toddler frequently emerges from the family setting to the nursery school or day care center. At this time the effect of separation from the mother becomes paramount, and a few children may find it too painfull. The community health nurse may be helpful in pointing out to mothers that there are individual differences in this area of development, as well as the others we have discussed. Disturbances seen in the nursery school child may reflect disturbances within the family structure. Emotional problems in the child may make it necessary to have him referred, with his parents, for professional help.

With our emphasis on the role of the mother in child care, it is important that we remember the father's role from the birth of the child. He may participate in the actual care of the baby from the outset. As the infant becomes a toddler, the father's relationship to him becomes increasingly important. The process of socialization includes companionship with the father and other family members, as well as with the mother.

The high divorce rate in the United States suggests that large numbers of children are brought up with one parent during the early years of their lives. About one-third of the couples divorced in the United States had a marriage with an average duration of less than six years. Many young children lose one or both parents at the vulnerable age of two or three.

At the age of three, a child cannot be sure a parent who has left will ever return. The toddler lives from moment to moment, day to day, and will not understand comments such as "Mommy will be back tomorrow" or "next week," because these phrases express ideas that are beyond his immediate experience. The anxiety experienced by the toddler as a result of brief separations from his parents is often intensified by feelings of guilt relating to struggles with his parents over such issues as cleanliness, aggression, and independence. When the child's parents separate or when he becomes ill, he may feel that he has caused these events by being a bad boy or bad girl. It is not unusual for young children in cases of divorce, for example, to blame themselves. An older child of four may be able to say: "Why doesn't Daddy like me any more?" or "Why doesn't Daddy come to see me?"

In families where there are emotional difficulties, the child may be a problem at home and at school in his attempts to deal with the separation experience. Unhappiness and incompatibility between parents makes the home a disturbing place, and a child can suffer from a parent's "emotional divorce" in many ways just as much as from a legal divorce.

When parents are separated, the child's mother may become depressed and withdrawn. The child therefore not only misses the absent parent but also feels the emotional loss experienced by the remaining one. He may identify with the depressed mother and become sad and withdrawn; he may also suffer from neglect or from clinging overprotection.

The young child whose father goes to war or spends long periods away from the family may also suffer from the effects of temporary separation. Ideally, a child should have two compatible parents throughout his life.

Where a father is not present, mothers may feel that they have to "make up to their children for not having a father." Not having a father can be a serious handicap, but more important is that the mother and the child learn to adjust as well as possible under adverse circumstances.

One of the most traumatic events that can happen to a young child is the death of a parent. Although the first awareness of death usually appears between the ages of two and four, children's ideas about death are poorly formed even by the age of four. Deaths of relatives or pets can also be most upsetting to a young child. In our section entitled "Death, Grief and Mourning," we discuss in detail some of the problems that arise when a child loses a parent through death.

TOILET TRAINING

By about 18 months, the child's nervous system is mature enough to permit the beginning of voluntary control over the sphincters of the bladder and rectum. Ribble observes that "readiness to begin control of elimination usually coincides with the ability to stand alone and to take the first steps." [10] In earlier times, toilet training was often begun long before 18 months. This type of training depended on reflex rather than voluntary activity, and had to be undertaken by a mother who was alert to the elimination patterns of her baby. She had to "catch" him at the proper time and place him on the potty. It was not unusual, in the interest of establishing early toilet regularity, for these mothers to use routine enemas or suppositories.

Although such efforts may succeed outwardly, children cannot achieve their own mastery over these functions at such an early age. Early toilet training does not necessarily lead to psychopathology, but it may be one factor in the development of psychological symptoms or maladaptive personality traits; for example, those related to fears concerning loss of control of impulses or of making messes of one sort or another.

It seems advisable to help each child to establish bowel and bladder control in his own reasonable time so that he can thereafter regard the accomplishment of sphincter control as the result of his growing maturity. It is largely because of the love of his parents and the fear of their disapproval and punishment that the child gradually begins to give up the pleasure of leaving his stool where and when he pleases. He discovers that when he deposits it at the proper time and in the proper place, his mother is pleased. To the child, the delivery of the bowel movement can be a kind of "gift" to his mother.

If the mother treats elimination as a "necessary evil," her feeling will interfere with the toilet training. The more the mother can make this training pleasant and easy, the less danger there is of getting into a battle with the child. One of the common problems of children who have difficulty in toilet training is stool retention. The child with this problem feels angry, insecure, and unwilling to give up his stool, and he may retain it for some time. While stool retention during the toddler stage is usually a consequence of toilet training conflicts, retention beginning at an earlier age may also involve physical factors such as megacolon.

Mothers who have previously established close, positive relationships with their children generally have fewer toilet training difficulties than others. Women who are severe and punitive are likely to use harsher toilet training methods. Too, these women are likely to be severe and controlling about obedience, masturbation, and sex play. Sears states:

We get the impression of a rather pervasive quality of strictness in the mothers who are most severe in toilet training. They seem to have been seeking

---

[10] Margaret Ribble. *Personality of the Young Child.* New York: Columbia University Press, 1955. P. 26.

to achieve more mature standards of conduct at a faster pace than other mothers. They had more of a tendency to drive rather than to lead their children, and they used a more punitive kind of discipline.[11]

When we hear of a child under 18 months who is "completely toilet trained overnight" or "in a few days," we can usually assume considerable readiness or preliminary preparation. It is true that some children seem suddenly to decide to "train themselves," but ordinarily the process takes weeks or months. As Selma Fraiberg points out:

Many parents do not know that normally the process of toilet training, including bladder control, can take many months, and we can expect occasional relapses until well into the fourth year.[12]

Bladder control is usually begun about the same time as bowel training. Just as a child may retain his stool, he may also hold onto urine. Concerning bladder control, Josselyn notes:

Urinary training, as bowel training, is not possible without severe strain on the child until the second year of life. Control is generally more difficult to establish and accidents are more frequent. Relapses occur when the child is mildly emotionally disturbed by minor illnesses or is absorbed in his own activities. A child should not be considered enuretic until he is three or four years of age.[13]

Children vary in their wish to sit or stand when urinating, and some toddlers prefer their own "potty" where they can sit comfortably. Children usually prefer a potty that sits directly on the floor, so that their feet can touch the ground. This squatting position increases the ability to exert lower abdominal pressure. (It is for the same reason that this position is preferred for childbirth by women in certain societies.) Toddlers may be afraid of falling into the toilet, and a smaller seat can give him a sense of security.

The early toddler stage is sometimes called the *anal phase*, the term Freud used when he discussed psychosexual development.[14] In Erikson's scheme of development, the child who is fortunate in his physical and psychological growth and resolves the conflicts of the anal stage will develop a sense of autonomy based on his capacity to control his own body and give pleasure and satisfaction as the result of this control to important adults in

---

[11] R. R. Sears. E. E. Maccoby, and H. Levin. *Patterns of Child Rearing*. New York: Harper & Row, Publishers, 1957. Pp. 121–22.

[12] Selma H. Fraiberg. *The Magic Years*. New York: Charles Scribner's Sons, 1959. P. 99.

[13] Irene M. Josselyn. *Psychosocial Development of Children*. New York: Family Service, 1948. P. 62.

[14] Philip S. Holzman. *Psychoanalysis and Psychopathology*. New York: McGraw-Hill Book Company, 1970. P. 116.

his life. If the outcome is not so favorable, the child may tend to develop a sense of shame or doubt concerning his capacity to control himself and his impulses.[15]

Erikson further comments:

> What enduring qualities are rooted in this muscular and anal stage? From the sense of inner goodness emanates autonomy and pride; from the sense of badness, doubt and shame. To develop autonomy, a firmly developed and convincingly continued state of early trust is necessary. The infant must come to feel that his basic trust in himself and in the world (which is the last treasure saved from the conflicts of the oral stage) will not be jeopardized by this sudden violent wish to have a choice, to appropriate demandingly, and to eliminate stubbornly. Firmness must protect him against the potential anarchy of his as yet untrained judgment, his ability to hold on and to let go with discrimination. His environment must back him up in his wish to "stand on his own feet" lest he be overcome by that sense of having exposed himself prematurely and foolishly, which we shall call shame, or that secondary mistrust, that looking back which we shall call doubt. . . . *Autonomy vs. shame and doubt*, therefore, is the second and a clear conflict, the resolving of which is one of the ego's basic tasks.[16]

Continence and control are demanded of the child just when conflicts over self-control are at a new height. The toddler alternates between surprising pliability and unreasoning stubbornness.

It is during the toddler stage that the child first begins to be conscious of having a front and behind to his anatomy. The "behind" of the body comes to represent for the child his vulnerability to those who would attack his sense of autonomy. Adults, too, show similar anxieties about being approached or attacked from the rear. Erikson highlights the significance of this part of the body, especially to children:

> For this reverse area of the body, with its aggressive and libidinal focus in the sphincters and in the buttocks, cannot be seen by the child and yet it can be dominated by the will of others. The "behind" is a small being's dark continent, an area of the body which can be magically dominated and effectively invaded by those who would attack one's power of autonomy and who would designate as evil those products of the bowels which were felt to be all right when they were being passed.[17]

Nursing procedures often require that the anal area and buttocks are approached, treated, stimulated, or hurt. Anna Freud notes:

---

[15] Erik Erikson. *Childhood and Society*. New York: W. W. Norton and Company, Inc., 1963. Pp. 84–85.
[16] *Ibid.* P. 84.
[17] *Ibid.* Pp. 253–54.

124 Pre-School Children

Intrusive procedures

Suppositories and enemas have been given and temperatures taken in the child's anus for countless years without any such question being asked; then came the discoveries of the people that work with the child's mind and who found that this particular body opening has a number of functions. One is a pure bodily function, namely that of elimination; but there is also a secondary function which is to provide excitation for the child and, especially at certain ages and stages of development (approximately between two and four years) excitation of a very strong and pleasurable kind. Thus, whenever doctor, nurse, or mother, for purely medical reasons interferes with that part of the child's body, a secondary effect is set in train. The child feels excited. This is pleasurable until he learns that this is not a very nice kind of pleasure. After that, he feels violently upset by such interference with his body. This reaction has, in time, become rather widely known, and has made people wary of interfering with that body opening.

Then an additional piece of information was added. These actions not only provide bodily excitation at the moment, but the accumulated bodily excitement in the anal region may set up certain trends of development which will be unwelcome later on. They strengthen the importance of these anal sensations and keep them going at a time that the child should have outgrown them and substituted other, for example, genital excitations for them. . . . If temperatures can be taken under the arm, there is no need to excite the child anally. If suppositories have to be given for some important reason, then it has to be, and one has to risk the side effects.[18]

It is the research of the psychoanalysts that has led physicians and nurses to take a second look at medical and nursing care procedures used for young children at this stage of development and to understand some of the emotional risks involved.

The bowel has long been known to be subject to mild and severe disorders as a result of psychosomatic imbalance. Sudden diarrheas are often recognized to have a basis of anxiety as well as organic causes. Constipation often occurs when patients are depressed and regressed. Functional colitis and itching of the anal area may represent somatic concomitants to emotional conflicts or stressful life situations.

All nurses who have contact with patients need to understand psychological, social, and physical aspects of development of anal control, and the conscious or unconscious feelings and fantasies related to this stage of development. Derivatives of these conflicts can be expected in patients who have diseases that affect this area. The ulcerative colitis patient, for example, can become extremely upset over his lack of control of defecation. He may need to defecate at inopportune times when he does not have easy access to a bathroom. This problem can interfere with his work and his

---

[18] Anna Freud. "Answering Pediatricians' Questions" in *Research at the Hampstead Child Therapy Clinic and Other Papers*. London: The Hogarth Press, 1970. Pp. 379–406.

ability to deal with other people. After surgery, the colostomy patient, particularly in the early months of trying to adjust to his surgery, may have social problems related to his inability to control his defecation. The patient who has urinary problems or soils himself may experience a deep sense of shame. He is often afraid that the nurse will become like the disapproving parent if he fails to maintain bowel or bladder control.

Nurses and doctors need to develop ways of overcoming their own dislike of observing and handling human excrement. One of the major problems in training medical personnel at all levels is to encourage skills necessary to treat and care for sick people without forming emotional barriers between the patient and staff. Observation by the nurse of the patient's bowel and bladder functioning may be important, since illness and bed rest may change these habits.

In early childhood, feeding disturbances can be related to toilet training. Anna Freud writes:

> There is a feeding disturbance which comes roughly between two and four years, at the time when the child first becomes overinterested in anal products, and then turns against the whole subject; much of the child's disgust of the feces is apt to go over to food and to exclude certain forms, consistencies, and colors in food. These are the children who suddenly refuse to eat spinach or chocolate sauce, or sauces of any kind, who are very suspicious of brown things, and certain shapes. I remember a three or four year old boy coming to the table in the nursery and finding on his plate some small sausage, and with an expression of disgust put it on the ground where he thought it belonged. He felt this was not edible and should hardly be touched. Disturbances in this group are not serious as children outgrow this phase of disgust, usually when their toilet training is fully established.[19]

PEER RELATIONSHIPS

The toddler's first relationship with other children outside the home may be in nursery school, where he may be taken as early as two and one half years. Activities with other children in his own age range give essential new experiences to the young child, even if he engages only in parallel play. In nursery school, he begins to relate to other children as an equal, rather than as a child in an adult world.

Maladaptive behavior on the part of the child can cause him problems in nursery school where many types of aggressive behavior are demonstrated. Aggression in boys of this age is often tolerated more than aggression in girls, and seems to detract less from the boy's popularity.

[19] Anna Freud. *Research at the Hampstead Child Therapy Clinic and Other Papers.* London: Hogarth Press, 1970. P. 398.

One of the reasons that nursery schools have gained popularity is that the neighborhood may not provide satisfactory play opportunities. In addition, the increasing numbers of women who are working or attending school have created a nationwide movement to provide day care centers for their children. Since high-quality child care outside the home is difficult to achieve, these centers could become little more than "dumping grounds" for small children who have no other place to go. The interests of the children, their mothers, and society are best served if the highest standards are required of such institutions. Nurses can play an important part in helping to set standards for these programs.

AUTOEROTISM AND MASTURBATION

During the early years of life, most infants discover that they can obtain pleasure from stimulating the genital area. This discovery is almost universal among boys, and very common with little girls, although their anatomy may preclude such discovery until later in childhood.

Autoerotism, in its broadest sense, usually refers to self-stimulation of the skin, mouth, anal area, or any other part of the body, which causes the infant or child to feel sensually aroused. Generally, the term "masturbation" refers to such stimulation applied to the genitals. "Autoerotism" has, in the minds of many, been so identified with the subject of masturbation that the terms have, in effect, become synonymous. Some authors prefer the term "autoerotic" because they feel it less objectionable than the term "masturbation," so they substitute one word for the other. Here, masturbation is defined as any form of deliberate self-manipulation of or application of pressure to the sexual organs for pleasure and for the release of tension.

In the infant's first half year, he discovers his fingers and toes, and later in much the same way he finds his genitals. Because he derives pleasure in manipulating his genital organ from the beginning, he may return to this area for satisfaction. Under stress, or when suffering from anxiety or fear, many children will turn to this form of behavior to reduce painful tensions. Loneliness, boredom, and physical pain may cause hospitalized children to masturbate for a sense of comfort and satisfaction. Children may learn to substitute the exciting and soothing sensations of masturbation for inadequate or absent parental attention and affection.

Social or religious attitudes toward masturbation all too often lead adults to take a negative, punitive, or at best, an ambivalent view toward it. Some nurses respond to such behavior in their young patients with anxiety, discomfort, or disapproval. Intellectually, most nurses recognize that masturbation is a part of normal sexuality, but emotionally, it may be difficult for some nurses to accept it. They may fear that masturbation is abnormal or even harmful. By now, sex education has convinced most knowledgeable people that masturbation is universal, and is practiced by infants, children, and by many adults. Any harm that comes from masturbation results from the guilt that may accompany it, induced either by disapproving adults or by the child's fear of the sexual and aggressive fantasies that may accompany his masturbatory activities. Normally, children keep their sexual activities to themselves, so that the nurse usually does not have to concern herself with the situation. Selma Fraiberg writes:

> Two and three year olds are sometimes very casual in the ways in which they handle themselves. In games or in quiet periods the hand may stray to the genital region and the child seems quite unconcerned about the presence of adults or other children. It is usually unnecessary to comment on this to very little children. As the child grows older he tends to restrict his occasional masturbation to moments when he is alone. We consider this a normal development which goes along with the child's growing social sense. We support this realization by the child that masturbation is a private affair not because it is shameful or bad, but because it is one of a number of things which are regarded as private acts.[20]

The Toddler in the Hospital

The emotional needs of a sick or injured child vary individually as much as his needs for food or medication. In recent years, there have been in-depth studies of the emotional significance of childhood illnesses that require hospitalization. Among them is James Robertson's film "A Two-Year-Old Goes to the Hospital," which is an excellent presentation of the trauma experienced by the child who is hospitalized.[21]

For over twenty years Robertson has written and filmed material relating to children in the hospital, and has documented information regarding brief separations in early childhood.[22]

The hospitalized child may be subjected to unusual stress from physical discomfort, separation from parents, and other kinds of emotional strain.

---

[20] Fraiberg. *Op. cit.* P. 215.

[21] James Robertson. *A Two-Year-Old Goes to the Hospital.* Suffolk, England: Concord Films Council, 1952. (New York University Film Library, New York.)

[22] James Robertson. *Young Children in Hospital.* 2nd ed. London: Tavistock Publications Ltd., 1970.

James and Joyce Robertson. *Young Children in Brief Separation*: No. 1: Kate, aged two years five months; in fostercare for 27 days. London: Tavistock Child Development Research Unit, 1970. (New York University Film Library New York.)

———. No. 2: Jane aged 17 months; in fostercare for 10 days. London: Tavistock Child Development Research Unit, 1968. (New York University Film Library, New York.)

Factors such as the medical or surgical procedures being used are important in evaluating the stress that a child must undergo. Additional considerations are the discomfort involved in diagnostic tests, and the severity and length of the child's illness. In assessing a child's capacity to cope with illness it is helpful to learn something of the mother-child relationship before hospitalization. Problems with the mother may be accentuated during hospitalization when both the mother and child are under stress.

Changes in pediatric practices and in hospital policies allow much more frequent visiting and participation in ward care by parents. These have been regarded as hallmarks in programs aimed at preventing emotional trauma during hospitalization for physical illness in children. Occupational and educational play opportunities in pediatric units have also been found useful ways of applying therapeutic and psychological concepts. Through play, the young child often can be assisted to express his thoughts and feelings and to achieve some mastery over his anxiety. Skillfully used by trained hospital staff, play therapy can help the child express fears and resolve some of the conflicts regarding his illness and hospitalization. Familiar toys and games brought from home to the hospital can be a tie to the child's former environment.

Undirected play allows the child free time so that he does not feel that he is being "managed" by nurses, doctors, or parents. Unfortunately, children who are sick or who suffer disabilities are often deprived of fun and play.

REACTIONS OF PARENTS TO A CHILD'S ILLNESS

Realistic fear over the severity of the child's illness, and overt anxiety and guilt about having contributed to it are only some of the feelings that parents must often face when a child is hospitalized. These feelings affect his adjustment to the hospital.

Well-adjusted parents are frequently able to participate effectively in caring for their sick child—feeding him, playing with him, and putting him to bed. The capacity of the parents to control their own feelings, to give emotional support to the child, and to accept the realities of his illness are important in determining not only his response to hospitalization but can also affect the course of his illness. Anxiety in the parent can also be aroused from repressed hostility toward the sick child, and may prevent parents from participating in their child's care. In these cases parents may need supportive psychotherapy to adjust to their child's illness.

In poorly adjusted parents, extreme anxiety, depression, and acting out of sadistic impulses toward the sick child are sometimes observed. Ambivalence, even on the part of well-adjusted parents, is not unusual considering the aggression many sick children show during or following hospitalization.

Studies repeatedly show that well-adjusted parents whose children are hospitalized seem happier when they are able to visit freely. Parents usually find it easier to tell their children truthfully when they are going to leave and when they will return when there are flexible visiting regulations. Prugh notes:

> The common conception that crying occurs more frequently among children whose parents visit frequently was found to be erroneous. . . . Also there is no indication that cross infection is any greater.[23]

SEPARATION ANXIETY IN CHILDREN FROM TWO TO FOUR YEARS

For a two- to four-year-old child, separation from parents often causes intense anxiety. Anxiety associated with fear or anger is usually most acute when the parents leave the hospitalized child to go home. Crying, apprehensive behavior, outbursts of screaming, and acute panic when the child is approached by another adult are frequently seen. Occasionally, the nurse may also observe somatic complaints such as urinary frequency, inability to eat, diarrhea, and vomiting. Homesickness, withdrawal, and depression—at times resembling the anaclitic type described by Spitz—can be seen in young children, particularly when they first go into the hospital. Toddlers may reveal overwhelming anxiety through feeding behavior, including anorexia, overeating, and refusal to chew food, often in combination with smearing of food or the demand for a return to bottle feeding. Regressive changes in toilet behavior involving loss of bladder or bowel control are often seen early in hospitalization.

Fear of the bedpan or toilet and concerns regarding changes in toilet behavior may burden the sick child, as may guilt and fear of punishment concerning wetting or soiling. Separation fears can be partly alleviated if the child is allowed to have familiar toys or other articles that remind him of home.

REGRESSION AND ILLNESS

Anna Freud describes regression as follows:

> In their mental growth, children do not take a straightforward path, but, as it is popularly expressed, take "two steps forward and one back." This refers

[23] D. G. Prugh, E. M. Staub, H. H. Sands, R. M. Kirshbaum, and E. H. Leninan. "A Study of the Emotional Reactions of Children and Families to Hospitalization and Illness." *American Journal of Orthopsychiatry.* Vol. 23 (1953). P. 74.

to all their functioning, from control of motility, speech, bladder and bowel control, ability to wait, social adaptation, honesty, fairness, etc. The capacity to function on a high level of achievement is in itself no guarantee that the performance will be stable; on the contrary, it is more normal for the child, and a better guarantee for later mental health if, during the state of growth, he reverts occasionally to more infantile modes of behavior before these are abandoned: from being toilet trained to messing, from sensible speech to nonsense talk, from play with toys to body play, from constructiveness to destructiveness, and from social adaptation to pure egoism.[24]

When children are ill, they may show such regressive behavior as loss of vocabulary with a return to noncommunicative crying. Recently acquired skills like walking and running may become clumsier and less coordinated.

Illness in children, as well as in adults, is often referred to as causing "stress." If a child is unable to cope with the stress, he is apt to become anxious or show signs of regression to a less mature level of integration.

In her observations at the Hampstead Nurseries, Miss Freud noted that when children were under the impact of traumatic experiences such as loss of parents by death or separation, regression was frequent. Illness may be traumatic, too. Psychoanalytically speaking, a child in the anal phase during illness will often regress to the oral stage. A child in the phallic phase may regress to the anal stage during illness. These regressions may also be accompanied by ego impairment and with speech disturbances, perceptual distortions and poor reality testing.

REGRESSION AND CHANGES IN EATING HABITS

Regression in the pre-school child can be seen in certain oral-dependent longings. A child who has fed himself at home may wish to be fed; another may revert to thumbsucking; another may refuse to eat when a nurse offers feed, but eat when his mother is at hand. Children show a strong need at this age to command the situation at mealtimes and whenever possible, a child should be allowed to make his own choices of food. This will permit him to maintain at least one important area of control in a situation where independence has been replaced by dependence and activity by passivity.

If the child feels comfortable with the nurse, he may often accept food to please her. On the other hand, if he is anxious or upset, he may fight to control and frustrate the nurse as well as trying to control and frustrate his mother.

[24] Anna Freud. *Research at the Hampstead Child-Therapy Clinic*. London: The Hogarth Press, 1970. Pp. 413–14.

AGGRESSIVE DRIVES AND HOSPITALIZATION

Aggressive and infantile behavior can be observed in the hospitalized pre-school child, who may show outbursts of intense anger, coupled with guilt and anxiety. Inhibition of aggressive drives is manifested in some children, together with restlessness, hyperactivity, and irritability. Thumb sucking and rocking are common, and are associated with withdrawal and masturbation.

DENIAL AND ILLNESS

The pre-school child may deny his illness or the loss of a loved object—as when his mother leaves him. A little boy alone in the hospital insisted that his mother was waiting in another room. Another child with an acute illness kept saying, "I'm all well now. . . . I want to go home."

COMMUNICATION AND SUPPORT

Florence Blake, a pediatric nurse specialist, writes on the crisis of childhood illness:

> How the child copes with this crisis is dependent upon the physical and emotional energy he has at his disposal, the ego strength he has to draw upon from past experiences, and the quality of the support he gets from his environment. . . . The child who has acquired trust and self-realization in his home and has maintained these personality strengths throughout the pre-operative and post-operative period in the hospital, seeks to regain and retain them post-operatively.[25]

During hospitalization, children express directly and indirectly a need for physical closeness to maintain their integrity and equilibrium. This is the reason that in hospitals rocking chairs and nurses with time to hold and pick up children are essential. This is also the reason that in current pediatric practice mothers are usually allowed and in many cases encouraged to help take care of their sick children. It has been recognized that resignation and the feeling of helplessness and despair, which often plague the hospitalized child, consume energy that is necessary for his continued progress. Resignation increases a child's mistrust of his environment and adversely influences his feelings about himself.

[25] Florence Blake. "In Quest of Hope and Autonomy." *Nursing Forum*. Winter, 1961–1962. P. 14.

When possible, the child should be allowed some form of activity since this discourages regression and dependency. Mobility allows the preschool child the necessary activity for healthier coping. As Mason puts it:

> If he acknowledges his feelings and expresses them in play or talk, the child can learn to deal with his environment promptly and appropriately, and his growing maturity helps him cope better with future pain and frustration.[26]

In the pediatric ward, nursing assignments should be based on a higher nurse–patient ratio than in most other sections of the hospital. Mason reports that some hospitals have used "mother banks" in an attempt to find substitute mothers for hospitalized children. It seems unfortunate that with our large, aging population more of these people cannot be employed in hospitals to provide this service. Many older women could work part time to be with a sick child when neither a nurse or a mother is available for more than brief periods. One person to stay with the child through a variety of treatments and tests can be most supportive.

The child's psychological response to illness is sometimes characterized by a feeling that his condition is self-induced and that hospitalization is punishment for misbehavior. This response is also seen in primitive tribes and in some adults in our culture, who assume that a sick person has done some misdeed and is being punished by illness. In biblical times, people assumed that badness was punishable by plague or sickness. When young children are ill, they frequently have a sense of guilt and fear that they are being rejected or abandoned.

Ability of parents to cope adequately with their own fear, guilt, and anxiety helps to reinforce the child's constructive reactions to his illness. Parents help to determine how secure a child is within himself and in his environment. An important function of the mother or her substitute being in the hospital is to help keep the child's anxiety and fears within his limits of tolerance. With the toddler, a consistent caretaking person is essential since a variety of nurses and doctors may confuse him. In pediatric units, where volunteers work for brief periods, it is better to assign them to work with school-age children rather than with toddlers. Fragmented care of these young children gives little gratification to either the nurse or the child. Child psychiatrists or staff members with appropriate knowledge in child development can be most helpful in group discussions regarding specific problems in understanding the hospitalized child's behavior.

---

[26] Edward A. Mason. "The Hospitalized Child—His Emotional Needs." *New England Journal of Medicine*. No. 8 (February 25, 1965). Pp. 406–14. Reproduced in this volume, pp. 157 to 174.

Research by Dr. Florence Erickson, Chairman of the Department of Pediatric Nursing at the University of Pittsburgh points up the range of fears, real or imaginary, that children have in the hospital.[27] She tells of one six-year-old who became pathetically frightened when a nurse explained to her that she was about to inject dye for an X-ray examination. Near panic, the child cried out, "They're going to put *die* in me!" Another somewhat older girl watched horrified, Erickson reports, as a lab technician took blood from her arm with a pipette. Turning to her mother, the girl shrieked, "Tell him to stop drinking my blood." Erickson notes that medical gadgetry is scary to children. They are mistrustful of anything unfamiliar, especially when it seems to be of that class of things they have always been told to avoid. Erickson writes,

> The attachment of wires to the head for encephalograms, for instance, is considered unsafe by children who have been warned about electric wires and electric equipment. One little girl pleaded with the technician who was setting up the electroencephalogram, "Don't write on my hair. My mommy won't like it."[28]

Illness generally involves going to bed and being cared for. While many adults can permit themselves this dependent experience, Anna Freud has observed that, unlike adults, young children do not regress with such pleasure. Sula Wolff notes:

> Some children, for whom the mastery of independent eating, washing and toiletry was accomplished in the face of great longing for dependency and passivity do not give up these achievements easily. They become difficult and intractable patients. Other young children lapse readily into a state of helpless infancy from which they had only just emerged and may have to relearn many of their social skills during convalescence.[29]

RESPONSE TO PHYSICAL RESTRICTIONS

Orthopedic conditions or chronic illnesses such as tuberculosis and rheumatic fever may necessitate weeks or even months in bed, perhaps being immobilized, adding much stress to illness.

Medical and surgical problems requiring restraint place an added bur-

---

[27] Florence Erickson. *Nursing Outlook*. Vol. 6, No. 9 (September, 1958), 501–4. 501–4. Reproduced in this volume, pp. 148 to 157.

[28] Phylis Feinstein, "There Are Cures for Fear, Too." *The New York Times Magazine* (October 26, 1969). P. 122.

[29] Sula Wolff. *Children Under Stress*. London: The Penguin Press, 1969. P. 53.

den on the staff who have daily contact with a child who is undergoing often intense emotional and physical frustration. In general, motor restrictions increases expressions of aggressive feelings, both in toddlers and in older children. In fact, it is not unusual for patients who are paraplegics or who are in body casts to become verbally abusive, since they cannot act out their feelings in motor ways. Edith Buxbaum notes:

Aggression must have an outlet, and it finds this outlet in the motor apparatus. Hyperactivity in children can often be traced back to severe early restrictions. The reactions, in these cases have continued long after the original cause was removed. I remember a four-year-old girl who constantly ran through the schoolhouse up and down the stairs; when we tried to stop her, she had a temper tantrum. We learned that the child had spent more than a year before starting the school term in a "body cast." [30]

Prolonged nursing care of a child by the mother can result in maternal overprotection and the stimulation of apprehension. Anna Freud has pointed out that parents undergo a change of attitude when their children become ill. In their efforts to get the child to eat, they may adopt methods of force feedings, to keep him at rest they may restrain him physically, and even the most truthful parent may resort to deceptions.

BASIS FOR REACTIONS TO HOSPITALIZATION

Sula Wolff, in her book notes the various reactions of children to hospitalization. The child will be affected by his hospitalization according to his age, his personality, and past experiences, and what actually happens to him in the hospital.[31]

In order fully to understand the impact of hospitalization on the child, the nurse needs some information from the parents, if possible, before and after the event. Florence Erickson and Jacqueline Holt give examples of how nurses are studying these problems.[32]

Freud has taught us that traumatic experiences may not be fully inte-

---

[30] Edith Buxbaum. *Troubled Children in a Troubled World*. New York: International Universities Press, Inc., 1970. P. 46.

[31] Sula Wolff. *Children Under Stress*. London: The Penguin Press, 1969. P. 53.

[32] Florence Erickson and Jacqueline Holt. "Play Interviews for Hospitalized Pre-School Children." Unpublished research report, School of Nursing, University of Pittsburgh, 1964.

Jacqueline Holt Vandeman. "Discussion of the Method and the Clinical Implications from the Study 'Children's Recall of a Preschool Age Hospital Experience After an Interval of 5 Years." *The Research Critique of the Western Interstate Commission for Higher Education*. Vol. 17, July 1968. Pp. 56–72.

grated at the time of the trauma, and that only months and years later can the person appreciate the total impact of the trauma.[33]

Children under the age of four tend to show more manifest disturbance while in the hospital and to have more frequent emotional sequelae after discharge than do older children.

MODERN MEDICINE AND SURVIVAL OF CHILDREN

Advances in pediatric knowledge, and in medical and surgical treatment of children, especially those with congenital abnormalities, have led to a greater rate of survival. Infanticide, once not uncommon, is still practiced in primitive societies. In earlier times, any child who was born defective often did not survive; today, even children born with abnormalities of the heart, spine, or kidneys may survive with treatment. All these children have been exposed since birth to prolonged hospitalization and major surgery, and their parents have faced the possibility that their child may die.

THE CHRONICALLY ILL CHILD

From the outset, the severely unhealthy child does not develop normally. Illness limits the child's motor activities and restricts his interaction with other children his own age, thereby placing an added burden on his psychological development as well as his physical progress. For the chronically ill child, emotions such as despair, anxiety and guilt can be significant not only in the onset of disease, but in the delay of recovery.

Mothers of physically defective children often suffer from chronic feelings of guilt, despite rational explanations and reassurances. They may feel convinced that they must have done something wrong, and have helped to bring about the illness or defect.

The Child from 3–6

Between three and six years of age, the child develops better control over his impulses. The three-year-old moves from parallel to cooperative play and is easier to get along with. If he lacks companions, he may develop an imaginary playmate with whom he talks. This playmate, either a child or an animal, represents the strong need for companionship at this age.

---

[33] Robert Waelder. *Basic Theory of Psychoanalysis.* New York: Schocken Books, 1964. P. 41.

136 Pre-School Children

The four-year-old displays a wide range of behavior from quiet to noisy to cooperative and indifferent. His vocabulary allows him to express himself more freely and he enjoys dramatic play. These pre-school children are learning to separate from their mother and are becoming more independent. A good nursery school provides the child with a period of brief separation from mother and with the opportunity to be with his own peer group.

This long step into the outside world is not always easily accomplished and sometimes needs to be effected over a period of time before the child is comfortable about having the mother leave him. The nursery school provides the child with opportunities to learn basic social and emotional skills in human relationships. The pre-schooler learns to put his feelings into words, to share, to wait his turn, and to stand up for himself. As the child learns, he changes, and he learns best when he enjoys his education. He needs guidance to learn rather than punishment.

The five-year-old often has kindergarten experience that provides him with a physical, intellectual, and emotional challenge that he enjoys at this age. Many teachers and parents find this a delightful stage because the child obeys much more easily and is more self-contained and mature.

The child at six becomes increasingly independent and able to focus on school and learning. He is usually able to leave his mother for a time at school and to turn to his teachers for new ideas and learning. It is not unusual, however, for a child initially to feel excessive fatigue and a half-day of school is frequently enough for many first-graders. The school nurse and teacher need to remember that the young child going to school has a compressed schedule of eating, dressing, and leaving home, often for the first extended time in his life.

Oedipal Stage

As the growing child separates emotionally and physically from his mother and is able to accomplish more for himself, he gradually develops a sure sense of the boundaries of his psychological self and of his body. He shows great interest and curiosity in his body and the way it functions, and becomes concerned about its intactness and well-being. This interest in and love for himself and his body is called *narcissism*. In a general sense, this term refers to the self-love that all persons feel in varying degrees. Although narcissism is at a height from about age three to age six, a healthy concern and affection for one's physical and mental self is a regular component of the normal personality.

During the early years of life, when narcissistic trends are at their height, the child is especially vulnerable to real or imagined damage to his body or to the feelings of self-love that have grown out of the experiences of being cared for and nurtured by loving parents.

During normal development, the major source of conflict in children from three to six springs from what Freud has termed the *Oedipus complex*. On this subject, Erickson writes,

... The increased locomotor mastery and the pride of being big now, and almost as good as father and mother, receives its severest setback in the clear fact that in the genital sphere, one is vastly inferior; and furthermore that not even in the distant future is one ever going to be the father in sexual relationship to the mother or the mother in sexual relationship to the father. The very deep consequences of this insight make up what Freud has called the "Oedipus Complex." [34]

Oedipus, the hero of the Greek myth, was the son of King Laius and Queen Jocasta. At the time of his birth, the oracle prophesied that he would kill his father and marry his mother. The sense of horror aroused by such a prophecy caused his parents to order Oedipus to be put to death. Through a series of events, determined by fate and therefore outside the control of the persons involved, the infant Oedipus survived and the oracle's dire predictions eventually came to pass. When Oedipus and his mother-wife Jocasta discovered what had befallen them, she committed suicide and Oedipus blinded himself. These events are dramatically described by Sophocles in *Oedipus Rex*.

Freud discovered those impulses and anxieties that he later grouped under the term Oedipus complex both in the psychoanalysis of his patients and in himself. Whether the Oedipus complex must occur in all human beings or whether it is only an artifact of Western society remains an unanswered question. It seems clear, however, that most children in American and European families pass through a stage of life in which the sexual impulses of the small child are directed mainly at the parent of the opposite sex, while competitive, hostile, and aggressive impulses are aimed at the parent of the same sex.

In addition, reverse patterns, with sexual feelings directed toward the parent of the same sex and competitive impulses toward the parent of the opposite sex, also occur. Ordinarily, however, these feelings (the "negative" Oedipal feelings) are less powerful and less significant than the "positive" Oedipal constellation.

The small child, therefore, has sexual impulses and hostile, competitive ones toward both parents at various times. As a small boy gradually becomes more clearly identified in his own mind as male, he tends to identify

---

[34] Erik Erikson. *Childhood and Society*. New York: W. W. Norton & Company, Inc. 1963. P. 87.

himself with his father and older brothers and reveals much more graphically his affectionate and sexual impulses toward his mother. The little girl develops similar identifications with her mother, and ultimately directs most of her sexual feelings toward her father. The child's own observation of physical differences, of variations in clothing, and of some differences in feminine and masculine interests prepare him for the next important step of establishing his psychological acceptance of his own sex.

The Oedipal period brings the problem of sexuality to the foreground. The little boy senses a new element in relationship to his mother, the girl to her father. Romantic fantasies develop, and this is the time when the little girl announces that she will marry her daddy. Masturbation increases as a means of discharging sexual tensions. The way a child is treated by parents at this time is of paramount importance. If the rival parent continues to love him and does not get unduly angry, the child is reassured. He comes to realize that he cannot take his father's place, but can grow up to be a man like him and find a wife for himself.

The Oedipal child is interested not only in the functioning of his own body, but also in the bodies of persons around him. The main focus of his sensual, pleasurable feelings shifts to the genitals and there is curiosity about the functions of all the sexual organs. Freud referred to this stage of psychosexual development as the *phallic urethral* stage.

It is during this time that children enjoy seeing, with a sense of excitement, the nude bodies of other children, as well as their own. In addition, they may derive a thrill from exposing themselves to adults and to other children. Tendencies towards exhibitionism or excessive modesty in the adult or older child usually originate during this stage.

During this stage, girls learn that they are equal to, or surpass, boys in size, physical capacities, and intelligence, but that there are physical differences in their genital organs. The little girl becomes aware that the boy has a penis, while she has none. It is helpful, at this time, to remind the little girl that she can have babies later on even though it is only partially reassuring that at some far distant time she will have breasts and be able to bear children.

The differences between the sexes become particularly highlighted at this time of life by the perceptions of childrn concerning their sexual organs. Their sexual gender, however, has been determined by innumerable interactions between them and the persons in their environment ever since their birth.

At the time they are born, babies are identified as male or female on the basis of the appearance of the external genitalia. This determination of gender sets into motion various reactions on the part of the parents, doctors, nurses, and others, which tend to reinforce and establish firmly the sexual identity of the child. These reactions include such simple matters as choice of room, clothing, and blanket colors, as well as more complex ones such as behavior of siblings, relatives, and teachers. Added to these phenomena are the more widely social reactions of churches, schools, and the larger community. As a result of these factors it is likely that the sense of maleness or femaleness is well established by the time the child is a year old, and firmly fixed by age three or four.

On those rare occasions where there is some physically apparent ambiguity in the infant's sex, early diagnosis and appropriate corrective measures are vital to prevent severe psychological conflict and trauma.

During the Oedipal stage, the child has heightened feelings of sexuality, narcissism, and rivalry with his parents—particularly the parent of the opposite sex. All these factors combine to make the child particularly vulnerable to fears about bodily damage or mutilation. According to the psychoanalytic point of view, these fears are intimately related to the anxiety engendered by the child's hostile, competitive impulses toward the parent of the same sex and the resulting fears that these impulses will cause retaliation by that parent.

In the boy, these fears are focused on his penis, and he dreads losing that organ, or being "castrated." (As used in psychoanalytic literature, this term refers to loss of the penis; not to the removal of the primary sexual organs, the testicles). In addition to specific "castration" terrors, boys and girls of this age fear bodily mutilation generally, and thus it is that surgical or medical procedures performed on children at this time of life are usually potentially more traumatic psychologically than those that occur at other ages.

These feelings and attitudes seem to the adult to be highly unreasonable, and thus should be susceptible to correction by rational explanation. It is often difficult for adults to appreciate the difference between the thinking of children and that of normal adults. Anna Freud wrote of this important matter as follows:

> What blocks understanding here is the normal adult's unfamiliarity with a child's subjective, irrational, emotional approach. . . . Any intercurrent infection, caught inadvertently, is understood by many children as the consequence of naughtiness and revives the memory of things eaten, warm clothing and rubbers discarded, or fought against, puddles walked into, etc., in the face of parental prohibition. What weighs on the child . . . is a confirmation of the belief that wrongdoing, however secretly performed, is open to punishment and that other, still undetected misdeeds whether actually carried out or merely contemplated in fantasy, will likewise be followed by retribution of some kind. This idea . . . arouses intolerable pangs of conscience irrespective of whether fate metes out the supposed "punishment" in the form of rheumatic illnesses, or in the milder form of common colds, sore throat, upsets of the stomach and digestive tract.[35]

[35] Anna Freud. *Research at the Hampstead Child-Therapy Clinic and Other Papers,* 1955–1965. London: Hogarth Press, 1970. Pp. 422–23.

140 Pre-School Children

Each stage of development has its own sources of anxiety. During the first year of life, separation from mother is the main cause of anxiety and can be devastating if prolonged and if the child is left without adequate maternal care. While separation from mother remains a serious basis for suffering during the toddler stage, the major cause for anxiety in the two- to four-year-old arises from fears surrounding his love relationship with his parents. He fears that this love may be lost and that the parent might disapprove, reject, or even abandon him. Therefore, fear of loss of parental love may be considered as the core cause of anxiety during the anal stage. Then, as we have just noted, during the Oedipal period, the fear of retaliatory castration or mutilation as a result of sexual and aggressive impulses toward his parents leads to anxiety.

The resolution or passing of the Oedipus complex occurs at about the age of six or seven. At this time, the child gradually renounces many of his sexual and rivalrous wishes toward his parents. Sexual fulfillment is delayed until physical maturation occurs after puberty. With the resolution of the Oedipus complex, the stages of infantile psychosexual growth are completed and the child enters into the school-age years, sometimes called *latency,* which usually lasts from the ages of six through ten years.

During the latency period, the child is ready to direct his energies to school work and other socializing activities. The term latency refects the fact that there is often a diminution in the direct expression of sexual attitudes and behavior until after puberty begins. The route through which the resolution occurs is generally that of repression of many of the conflicts, anxieties, and impulses associated with the Oedipal and earlier stages of development, and a concomitant identification with the parent or parent surrogate of the same sex. This identification paves the way for a later relationship with a person of the opposite sex and tends to establish even more firmly the sense of gender, which has been growing since the earliest time of life.

The four- to six-year-old child identifies with his parents in many ways. Such children not only imitate their parents physically and become excellent mimics—often to the consternation of the parents and the amusement of outsiders—but in addition, take on certain core attitudes pertaining to vocational, sexual, social, and moral aspects of life. The resolution of the Oedipus complex and the various identifications that occur contribute a large part to the firm establishment both of the ego and of the superego. Before the Oedipus stage passes, the child tends to behave obediently or to misbehave mainly on the basis of whether he will be punished or will receive love and approval from his parents. As the Oedipus complex passes, the child's psychic development permits him to "internalize" approval and disapproval. From that time on, he begins to be able to "know" within himself the difference between right and wrong and to lay down standards of behavior and rules of conscience that will thereafter guide much of his behavior.

After the resolution of the Oedipus complex, a fourth source of anxiety can be described, one that results from a sense of self-criticism and "guilt." Thus, the child, rather than fearing separation from parents, or loss of love from parents, or castration, begins to suffer pangs of conscience. Although the conscience, or "superego," ideally should be a guide and provide a model as well as a necessary degree of self-criticism, it becomes in some people a threatening, punitive, hypercritical part of themselves. One result may be feelings of guilt and depression even in the absence of any objective basis for these feelings.

In Erikson's eight stages of man,[36] the phallic-urethral and Oedipal phase is the third. During these years, the child normally achieves the capacity for, and a sense of, what Erikson terms "initiative." At the same time, there are numerous opportunities for feelings of guilt to result from his activities, fantasies, and interactions with other people. The nuclear conflict lies between the forces that encourage the development of initiative and those that would lead to deep and lasting feelings of guilt. Normally, the balance is in favor of a sense of initiative, with a much less strong tendency toward guilt.

The sensitivities and conflicts that occur during the Oedipal stage of life persist in some fashion throughout life. Overly strong reaction to the need for surgical intervention, fears pertaining to nursing procedures, and parental transferences toward physicians or nurses may be derivatives of Oedipal conflicts that are either unresolved or are reawakened by illness or hospitalization.

The discovery and elucidation of the Oedipus complex is often considered to be one of Freud's greatest discoveries, even though its details and its universality may continue to be the subject of further study and validation. In order to understand the development of adult personalities in our culture and clarify some of the reactions of patients undergoing medical care, some knowledge of the Oedipal conflicts and the manner in which they are resolved is essential.

Suggested Readings on the Pre-School Child

Accas, Gene and John H. Eckstein. *How to Protect Your Child.* New York: Sandranita Associates, 1968.

Altschal, A. *Psychology for Nurses.* London: Balliere, Tindall and Cassell, 1971.

Anthony, James E. and Cyrille Koupernik, eds. *The Child in His Family.* New York: John Wiley & Sons, Inc., 1970.

Balint, Alice. *The Early Years of Life.* New York: Basic Books, Inc., 1954.

---

[36] Erik H. Erikson. *Childhood and Society.* New York: W. W. Norton & Company, Inc., 1950. Pp. 86–87.

Berlin, Irving. "Working with Children Who Won't Go to School." *Children*. Vol. 12, No. 3 (May–June, 1968). Pp. 109–12.

Berlin, I. N. "Some Reasons for Failures in Referral for Psychiatric Care for Patients with Psychosomatic Illnesses." *Annals of Internal Medicine*. Vol. 40. (1954). Pp. 1165–68.

Berlin, I. N., Gwen McCullough, E. S. Liska, and S. A. Szrek. "Intractable Episodic Vomiting in a Three-Year-Old Child." *The Psychiatric Quarterly* (April, 1957). Pp. 228–49.

Blake, Florence and Wright F. Howell. *Essentials of Pediatric Nursing*. New York: J. B. Lippincott Co., 1963.

Bowlby, John. *Attachment,* Vol. I, *Attachment and Loss.* New York: Basic Books, Inc., 1969.

———. *Child Care and the Growth of Love.* Baltimore: Penguin Books, 1963.

Bronfenbrenner, Urie. *Two Worlds of Childhood.* New York: Russell Sage Foundation, 1970.

Buxbaum, Edith. *Troubled Children in a Troubled World.* New York: International Universities Press, Inc., 1970.

———. *Your Child Makes Sense.* New York: International Universities Press, Inc., 1961.

"Casework Services for Parents of Handicapped Children." Reprints from *Social Casework*. New York: Family Service Association of America, 1957.

Coles, Robert. *Children of Crisis*. Boston: Little, Brown & Company, 1964.

DeSchweinitz, K. *Growing Up*. 3d ed. New York: The Macmillan Company, 1953.

Despert, J. L. *Children of Divorce*. New York: Doubleday & Company, Inc., 1953.

Elmer, Elizabeth. *Children in Jeopardy*. The Study of Abused Minors and Their Families. Pittsburgh: University of Pittsburgh Press, 1967.

Erikson, Erik. *Identity Youth and Crisis*. New York: W. W. Norton and Co., Inc., 1968.

Emerson, Laura. "There's Always Time." *American Journal of Nursing*. Vol. 67, No. 9 (September, 1967). Pp. 1857–58.

Fisher, Seymour and Sidney Cleveland. *Body, Image and Personality*. New York: Dover Publications, Inc., 1968.

Fiske, A. "Psychology." *American Journal of Nursing*. Vol. 23 (1923). Pp. 1011–14.

Fraiberg, Selma H. *The Magic Years*. New York: Charles Scribner's Sons, 1959.

Freud, Anna. *Research at the Hampstead Child-Therapy Clinic and Other Papers.* London: The Hogarth Press, 1970. See Chapters III, V, VI, VII, X, XIV, XVI, XIX, XX.

———. *The Ego and the Mechanisms of Defence.* London: The Hogarth Press, 1946.

———. *The Psychoanalytical Treatment of Children.* London: Imago Publishing Co., Ltd., 1946.

Freud, Anna and Dorothy Burlingham. *War and Children.* New York: International Universities Press, Inc., 1943.

Furst, Sidney, ed. *Psychic Trauma.* New York: Basic Books, Inc., 1967.

Ginott, Haim G. *Between Parent and Child.* New York: Avon Books, 1965.

Greenacre, Phylis. *The Quest for the Father.* New York: International Universities Press, Inc., 1963.

Ginsburg, Herbert and Sylvia Opper. *Piaget's Theory of Intellectual Development.* Englewood Cliffs, New Jersey: Prentice-Hall, Inc., 1969.

Hadfield, J. A. *Childhood and Adolescence.* Middlesex, England: Penguin Books Ltd., 1962.

Hartup, W. W. and Nancy L. Smothergill. *The Young Child.* National Association for the Education of Young Children, 1967.

Holt, John. *How Children Learn.* New York: Dell Publ. Co., Inc., 1967.

Hyde, Naida D. "Play Therapy—The Troubled Child's Self Encounter." *American Journal of Nursing.* Vol. 71, No. 7 (July, 1971). Pp. 1366–70.

Ilg, Frances and Louise Bates Ames. *Child Behavior.* New York: Harper & Row, Publishers, 1955.

James, Vernon L., Jr. and Warren E. Wheeler. "The Care-By-Patient Unit." *Pediatrics.* Vol. 43, No. 4 (April, 1969). Pp. 488–94.

Klein, Melanie. *Contributions to Psycho-Analysis 1921–1945.* New York: McGraw-Hill Book Company, 1964.

Lavy, David. *Maternal Overprotection.* New York: W. W. Norton and Company, 1966.

Leonard, George B. *Education and Ecstasy.* New York: Dell Publ. Co., Inc., 1968.

Lichtenberg, Philip and Dolores G. Norton. *Cognitive and Mental Development in the First Five Years of Life.* Chevy Chase, Maryland: National Institute of Mental Health, 1970.

Lowenfeld, Margaret. *Play in Childhood.* New York: John Wiley & Sons, Inc., 1967.

Lynd, Helen. *On Shame and the Search for Identity*. New York: Science Editions, Inc., 1961.

Mahler, Margaret Schoneberger. "On Sadness and Grief in Infancy and Childhood; Loss, and Restoration of the Symbiotic Love Object." *The Psychoanalytic Study of the Child*. Vol. 16. Ruth S. Eissler, Anna Freud, and others, eds. New York: International Universities Press, Inc., 1961.

Mead, Margaret. *Male and Female*. New York: Dell Publ. Co., Inc., 1949.

Nelson, C. Alice. "Why Won't Stevie Drink?" *The American Journal of Nursing*. Vol. 61, No. 7 (July, 1961). Pp. 44–48.

Oswin, Maureen. *The Empty Hours*. London: The Penguin Press. 1971.

Plank, Emma. *Working with Children in Hospitals*. Cleveland: Western Reserve University, 1962.

Rothenberg, Michael B. "Child Psychiatry—Pediatrics Liaison. A History and Commentary." *Journal of the American Academy of Child Psychiatry*. Vol. 7, No. 3 (July, 1968). Pp. 492–509.

Salk, Lee. *Your Child from 1 to 12*. New York: New American Library of World Literature, Inc., 1970.

Schultz, Nancy V. "How Children Perceive Pain." *Nursing Outlook*. Vol. 19, No. 10 (October, 1971). Pp. 670–73.

Schwartz, Lawrence H., Jessie Snider, and Jane E. Schwartz. "Psychiatric Case Report of Nutritional Battering with Implications for Community Agencies." *Community Mental Health Journal*. Vol. 3, No. 2 (Summer 1967).

Silberman, Charles E. *Crisis in the Classroom*. New York: Vintage Books, 1970.

Spock, Benjamin. *Baby and Child Care*. Des Moines, Ia.: Meredith Press, 1946.

Spock, Benjamin and Marion O. Lerrigo. *Caring for Your Disabled Child*. New York: The Macmillan Company, 1965.

Winnicott, D. W. *The Child, The Family, and the Outside World*. Middlesex, England: Penguin Books, Ltd., 1964.

Wolff, Sula. *Children Under Stress*. London: Penguin Press, 1969.

DISCUSSION OF SELECTED READINGS

First, we present Solnit and Senn's developmental charts on the toddler and pre-school child. These charts give the nurse a brief overview of the tasks in process for the toddler and the pre-school child, as well as some of the major duties of the mother. Some of these relate to separation from the mother and attendant problems, as well as sexual identity, development of initiative and development of a sense of right and wrong. As before, the charts show the range from normal development through severe psychopathology.

Following these charts is an article, "Reactions of Children to Hospital Experience," by Florence Erickson, who is the chairman of the Department of Pediatric Nursing at the University of Pittsburgh. By creating play routines that simulated hospital life, Erickson was able to record the reactions of preschool children to their hospital experiences. She particularly stresses their anxiety over being separated from their parents and their fear of possible physical harm.

The article "The Hospitalized Child—His Emotional Needs" by Dr. Edward Mason, Assistant Clinical Professor of Psychiatry, Harvard University, emphasizes hospitalization as an important emotional event in the life of a child. He stresses, as do the other authors, the importance of the mother to the child's welfare during illness and hospitalization. Mason notes that as early as 1923, A. Fiske in *American Journal of Nursing* urged liberalized visiting rules in hospitals.

Mason gives an excellent summary of the work done by psychoanalysts during World War II who studied children in institutions and the effects of separation from mothers. Again, he emphasized, "Separation from the mother is considered the chief traumatic factor for the younger child."

Dr. Mason's article is especially helpful from a historical and practical point of view in discussing such questions as parental visitation, the colors of nurses' uniforms, and the types of ward activity that are conducive to a more relaxed atmosphere. Discussion of this article and the other previous articles can give nurses many ideas about how to implement newer and better methods in pediatric nursing care.

In the text we have discussed in detail the role of the parents with the child in the hospital. It would be helpful for nurses to discuss their experiences with specific parents and children and how they have coped with each situation. In order for specific details to be worked out, it would probably be beneficial if nurses could discuss their feelings about the problems of having parents on pediatric wards.

DEVELOPMENTAL SCHEMA CHART *

The Toddler and Pre-School Age (Under 5 years)

Tasks in Process

CHILD	MOTHER
To reach physiologic plateaus (motor action, toilet training).	To promote training, habits and physiologic progression.
To differentiate self and secure sense of autonomy.	To aid in family and group socialization of child.
To tolerate separations from mother.	To encourage speech and other learning.
To develop conceptual understandings and "ethical" values.	To reinforce child's sense of autonomy and identity.
To master instinctual psychologic impulses (Oedipal, sexual, guilt, shame).	To set a model for "ethical" conduct.
To assimilate and handle socialization and acculturation (aggression, relationships, activities, feelings).	To delineate male and female roles.
To learn sex distinctions.	

Acceptable Behavioral Characteristics

CHILD	MOTHER
Gratification from exercise of neuromotor skills.	Is moderate and flexible in training.
Investigative, imitative, imaginative play.	Shows pleasure and praise for child's advances.
Actions somewhat modulated by thought; memory good; animistic and original thinking.	Encourages and participates with child in learning and in play.
	Sets reasonable standards and controls.
Exercises autonomy with body (sphincter control, eating).	Paces herself to child's capacities at a given time.

* Milton J. E. Senn, M.D., and Albert J. Solnit, M.D., *Problems in Child Behavior and Development*. Philadelphia: Lea & Febiger, 1968.

Pre-School Children

Feelings of dependence on mother and separation fears.
Behavior identification with parents, siblings, peers.
Learns speech for communication.
Awareness of own motives, beginnings of conscience.
Intense feelings of shame, guilt, joy, love, desire to please.
Internalized standards of "bad," "good"; beginning of reality testing.
Broader sex curiosity and differentiation.
Ambivalence towards dependence and independence.
Questions birth and death.

Consistent in own behavior, conduct and ethics.
Provides emotional reassurance to child.
Promotes peer play and guided group activity.
Reinforces child's cognition of male and female roles.

Minimal Psychopathology

CHILD

Poor motor coordination.
Persistent speech problems (stammering, loss of words).
Timidity towards people and experiences.
Fears and night terrors.
Problems with eating, sleeping, elimination, toileting, weaning.
Irritability, crying, temper tantrums.
Partial return to infantile manners.
Inability to leave mother without panic.
Fear of strangers.
Breathholding spells.
Lack of interest in other children.

MOTHER

Premature, coercive or censuring training.
Exacting standards above child's ability to conform.
Transmits anxiety and apprehension.
Unaccepting of child's efforts; intolerant towards failures.
Over-reacts, over-protective, over-anxious.
Despondent, apathetic.

Extreme Psychopathology

CHILD

Extreme lethargy, passivity or hypermotility.

MOTHER

Severely coercive and punitive.
Totally critical and rejecting.

Little or no speech; non-communicative.
No response or relationship to people, symbiotic clinging to mother.
Somatic ills: vomiting, constipation, diarrhea, megacolon, rash, tics.
Autism, childhood psychosis.
Excessive enuresis, soiling, fears.
Completely infantile behavior.
Play inhibited and non-conceptualized; absence or excess of auto-erotic activity.
Obsessive-compulsive behavior; "ritual" bound mannerisms.
Impulsive destructive behavior.

Over-identification with or overly submissive to child.
Inability to accept child's sex; fosters opposite.
Substitutes child for spouse; sexual expression via child.
Severe repression of child's need for gratification.
Deprivation of all stimulations, freedoms and pleasures.
Extreme anger and displeasure with child.
Child assault and brutality.
Severe depression and withdrawal.

Reactions of Children to Hospital Experience

by Florence Erickson, R.N., Ph.D.*

In recent years, we have become increasingly aware of the traumatic effects of hospitalization on children, especially during their pre-school years. Studies by Freud and Burlingham, Bowlby, and others have indicated that much of the trauma can be attributed to separation anxiety, which is more marked in children under four years of age (1, 2). In addition to separation anxiety, preschool children have intense fears of body mutilation, as Jessner and Kaplan have portrayed in their report on fears aroused by the operative procedure (3).

Children also show severe reactions to other procedures of bodily intrusion (temperatures, enemas, hypodermic or other injections, and so on) many times out of all proportion to the pain of the procedure. Anna Freud has said that the small child reacts more to the fantasy aroused by the procedure than to the procedure itself (4). Very little is known about children's interpretations of intrusive procedures, and that has been gleaned in retrospect by analysts or through

---

* *Nursing Outlook.* Vol. 6, No. 9 (September, 1958). Pp. 501–4.

the empathy of doctors and nurses who have observed hospitalized children's play and emotional reactions.

In the hospital, the nurse is the one who most often prepares the child for the intrusive procedure, carries it out, or assists the doctor or technician in carrying it out, and comforts the child following it. The question was raised "Could she give more effective preparation and more specific help to the child in the assimilation of intrusive procedures if she had more knowledge of how children tend to interpret these procedures?"

The play interview was chosen as the method of studying children's feelings about procedures of bodily intrusion, so we might answer our question. Play has been recognized as an integral part of child life for a long time. Freud emphasized that children repeat in their play everything that has made a great impression on them in order to become master of the situation.

The unpleasant nature of an experience does not always unsuit it for play. If a doctor looks down a child's throat or carries out some small operation on him, we may be quite sure that these frightening experiences will be the subject of the next game, but we must not in that connection overlook the fact that there is a yield of pleasure from another source. As a child passes over from the passivity of the experience to the activity of the game he hands on the disagreeable experience to one of his playmates and in this way revenges himself on a playmate (5).

Piaget further explained this same theme when he said, "Although play sometimes takes the form of repetition of painful states of mind, it does so not in order that the pain shall be preserved, but so that it may become bearable, even pleasurable, through assimilation to the whole activity of the ego" (6).

Erik Erikson recognized the child's need for solitary play in the presence of a sympathetic adult when he said, "Solitary play remains an indispensible harbor for the overhauling of shattered emotions after periods of rough going in the social seas. . . . For to play it out is the most natural self-healing measure childhood affords" (7).

Because children react strongly to experiences which are intrusive in nature, and which violate body integrity, we selected for the study pre-school children who were in the stage of development in which intrusion seems to be more threatening. Erikson describes them as being "dominated by the intrusive mode. They intrude into other bodies by physical attack; into other people's ears and minds by aggressive talking; into space by vigorous locomotion; into the unknown by consuming curiosity" (8). Children at this age level tend to interpret others' attitudes and feelings as a reflection of their own, assuming that others have impulses toward them which are similar to their own.

Children of preschool age, also, are at the stage of development in which they have a strong love attachment for the parent of the opposite sex. At the same time, they are aware of their dependence on the parents and their inability to compete with someone who is so much larger. This conflict gives rise to feelings and thoughts for which the child expects to be punished. A hospital experience at this age level is likely to be interpreted by the child as punishment, or even as an attempt to eliminate him.

Setting up the Study

We chose twenty hospitalized children four years of age for the study, and divided them into two groups of ten each. The children in one group were interviewed three times following discharge from the hospital: at one-week, one-month, and two-month intervals. The children in the other group were interviewed every other day during hospitalization plus one week, one month, and two months after hospitalization. Ten nursery school children who had not been hospitalized served as a control group, and each child in the group was interviewed once in the nursery school playroom.

Five boys and five girls were in each of the three groups. The children in the study groups were hospitalized for not less than two nor more than twenty days, for medical or surgical conditions. Their parents were interviewed and were willing to have the children participate in the study.

Three categories of intrusive procedures were chosen for the study:

1. Oral procedures, such as the administration of pills and medicines, and oral examinations using tongue blades.
2. Anal procedures, such as rectal temperatures and enemas.
3. Cutaneous procedures, such as injections, blood tests, intravenous fluids, and transfusions.

Such clinical equipment as a hypodermic syringe, a thermometer, medicine cups, and other things used in carrying out intrusive procedures, were made available to the children in play interviews. An additional variety of small toys such as a car, a gun, and doll furniture was added to the equipment to increase the range of selection, as were doll figures which represented a nurse, a doctor, a mother, a father, a boy, and a girl. The dolls were contour type, stuffed cloth, ranging in height from five to eleven inches, and had detailed sex characteristics. Each doll was completely dressed in clothing made of materials similar to the materials used for real clothing, and, except for the shoes, which were sewed on, all the clothing was removable. The doctor doll wore a white laboratory coat over dark shirt and trousers, the nurse wore a white uniform and cap; the children each had a hospital type gown in addition to their regular clothing. Sheets, blankets, and pillow were available for the doll bed.

Interviewing Technique

Each play interview was set for one hour, but if a child terminated his play in less than that time, no attempt was made to encourage him to play longer. The observer wore nurse's uniform during hospital interviews and was known as a nurse to the children. She recorded all of the child's conversation and action in running narrative form, and tried to be accepting of the child and his play—neither approving or disapproving of what he chose to do. She made no attempt to alter the play unless it became dangerous. For example, if a child threatened another child with the hypodermic syringe he was told, "We only use that on doll people." No specific object was brought to the child's attention, and his questions were reflected back to him unless he seemed to need a definite answer or explanation. If the child requested or seemed to want help in dressing the doll figures, or tying or buttoning clothes, the observer helped him.

In the first interview the observer introduced herself, showed the child the toy bag, and asked if he would like to play while she did some writing. The observer removed the toys from the bag, naming each one, and assembled the hypodermic syringe and removed the thermometer from its holder. She then sat beside the child and recorded while he played. In successive interviews, the child usually removed the toys from the bag, and the observer made no attempt to name them or to assemble the syringe unless the child requested this.

A code was devised to facilitate the analysis of the data: the letter "R" meant to reject; "T"—to touch; "P"—to play with; and "I"—to inject. Each interview was coded and the results recorded on a data sheet, revealing trends in play.

Differences Noted

There were some differences between the play of the children in the hospitalized groups and the children in the control group. Children who had not been hospitalized were more active in their play than children who had been hospitalized, and they tended to engage in a wider variety of play activities, moving more quickly from one thing to another. Hospitalized children were in general more listless, easily distracted by sights and sounds, and more constrained in their play, seeming to move more slowly and deliberately. Not until the third home interview was the play of the children who had been hospitalized comparable to the play of the children in the control group, and the hospitalized boys did not reach the level of activity of the boys in the control group in any interview. This did not seem to be related to the children's physical condition during home interviews.

Both the children in the hospitalized and in the control groups gave medicines and pills as though the oral route were the accepted and natural way to give them. They showed more understanding of the reason for giving medicine this way than in giving it by anal or cutaneous routes. For example, Kit gave her doll a pill and explained, "She has a little headache. She needs one of the white ones. She has a runny nose, too. I'll have to give her nosedrops." Some children ate the pills and explained, "For my cough." To many of the children the pills seemed to represent a gift from the observer, especially after they discovered that they were candy. They would find the box early in the interview, eat the pills, and remind the observer to bring more the next time. Carl routinely transferred the pills into a battered aspirin box which he carried in his pocket. In general, the children gave oral medications with much the same feeling tones as they gave feedings. A few of the hospitalized children used dropper, spoon, and bottle for self-mothering, particularly in the first hospital interview.

The tongue blades were used mostly for probing by the children in all three groups. They poked them into the car, the toilet, the tub, and the cups. They used them to flick cotton out of the test tube and to push it back in again. A few hospitalized children held a tongue blade to the mouth of a doll figure. One child commented as she held a tongue blade to the nurse figure, "I dorry we have to do dis to you. Open you mouth. Not gonna hurt you. Just gonna do dis." Sonny explained that a tongue blade is to hold your mouth open. Anne commented, "This the doctor thing. Stick it in my tongue." The children did not seem to know why adults use tongue blades. Could they have represented adult curiosity? Or adult hostility?

The children tended to interpret anal procedures as though they were not very "nice." Much of their reaction seemed to be related to their feeling that taking off the panties is bad or indecent. Many children never removed the panties of doll figures; instead, they carefully pulled them up when they undressed the dolls. Several asked, "All right to take off panties?" Others removed them and looked guiltily at the observer.

Most of the hospitalized children tried to avoid the thermometer the first time they saw it. None of the boys, and only two of the girls, took rectal temperatures on doll figures during the first hospital interview. Sonny handed the thermometer to the observer and said, "You can take that home." Nora drew back when she saw the thermometer and said, "No." Ann said soberly, "I cry when I get my temperature." Some said, "Give a pinch," or "It jag," as they used it. Some said it hurt, others said it didn't. Ruthie told her mother that the nurse awakened her at night to give a "shot in the boom-boom." She had had no injections during her hospitalization. In her first interview she picked out the thermometer and said, "Gonna give a shot in the boom-boom," and proceeded to take the rectal temperature of the girl figure. All but one child used the thermometer during some interview. Sonny explained, "My mommy take it in my mouth. Nurse don't."

She afraid you bite it." Several children practiced taking oral temperatures on themselves.

Some children followed the procedure of taking rectal temperatures very accurately. Barbara put the thermometer under the nurse doll's arm and shook both the nurse and the thermometer. She helped the nurse doll rub the tip of the thermometer with cotton; then, held the thermometer as though taking the rectal temperature of the girl doll figure. When she removed the thermometer, she said, "All done," shook the nurse and the thermometer, then just the thermometer. She held the arm of the doll figure as though taking a pulse, stared off into space and commented, "Have to see what time is."

Most of the children who had had enemas showed some distaste for this procedure. Some rejected the equipment and commented, "Not for me," or "I don't like it." Ruthie gave the doctor figure an enema because "He's bad." Betty took the mother figure and said, "I'm gonna give her an operation because she didn't have operation." She undressed her, selected the rectal tube and asked, "Does it go in the rear end?" She placed the tip of it inside the mother's panties and remarked, "She's getting an enema." Then she used the intravenous tubing the same way and said, "She needs some more." She held it to the umbilicus, saying, "In her belly," and to the genital area and said, "And in here." She danced the doll up and down, chanting, "Dancing in the rear end." In a later interview she examined the enema equipment and then defended herself verbally: "You put this in little girl. Not in me, huh? Cause I'm big. I'm all better. I have a gun."

Most of the children in all three groups reacted to the hypodermic syringe as though it were a dangerous weapon. They tried to avoid it when first exposed to it in an interview. A few of them took it apart very gingerly, put it back in the case and closed the lid. Some commented, "I'm gonna put this away." Bucky pointed at it and said, "You better put that away." Sonny touched it with the tip of the intravenous tubing and asked, "Is this a real one?" A little later he insisted, "Me don't want that. Take that back home. Me don't want it." Levy, in a study of hostility patterns in sibling rivalry, found that escape movements were by far most frequent in three- and four-year-old children (9).

Although the children attempted to avoid the syringe, most of them could not resist handling it repeatedly. They practiced taking it apart and putting it together. They felt the needle, jabbed it into some object such as the car, the toilet, or the bed, and talked incessantly about it in their attempts to muster enough courage to use it on doll figures. Sonny expressed what many of the children seemed to feel. "This what I like but I don't like to get it. I just like to give it to somebody else."

None of the hospitalized boys used the syringe for injection on doll figures during the first interview. Three out of five girls used it either on their own doll or a doll figure. All but one child used the syringe in this fashion during some interview. Some used it repeatedly, others only once. Some clenched their teeth and rammed the needle into a doll figure, even screwed it around, while others gently pricked doll figures with it.

Mike carefully avoided the syringe in his first interview by playing in another part of the room. Finally he picked it up, looked at it with a grimace and put it down fast. He turned his back to it and did not look at it again. During his next interview he picked it up and looked at it, but again put it down and backed away. He knelt, leaned forward and looked at it intently, then backed up and busied himself with other toys. Suddenly he picked up the syringe. He breathed more heavily as he pulled out the plunger and pushed it back into position. He put it on the floor but immediately picked it up, took it apart, and put it in the case. He took the rectal temperature of the mother figure, then took out the hypodermic syringe. He grunted as he screwed on the needle. He looked at the mother figure and at the observer, then gently jabbed the buttocks of the mother figure and said, "Her cryin'." He withdrew the needle, showed the observer the spot and said, "Put in there." He put the syringe away, took her temperature again, laughed aloud and said, "Pinch." He assembled the syringe, stuck the needle into the abdomen of the nurse figure and said, "Her cryin' again." When his sister appeared in the doorway, Mike said, "Here goes," and went on a wild spree of jabbing one doll after the other.

Sandy suspended the mother figure on the needle and commented, "Hanging." The syringe was dropped like a bomb, used like a knife, and aimed like a dagger. Even the terminology used by the children in relation to the syringe indicated violence. It was most commonly referred to as a "shot," and at times was equated with the gun. Some children used the gun immediately before or after using the syringe.

Margie, who seemed to interpret her whole hospital experience as punishment, helped the doctor doll to hold the gun to each child while the nurse pulled the trigger. When she first saw the nurse figure she commented, "This will be a gun-shooter." Margie had received daily injections of penicillin during hospitalization. In a home interview she sat examining the syringe and commented, "Shot dem once a day."

The syringe was called a pin, a pincher, a needle, a penicillin, a polio shot, a sticker, and a "dag." Barbara looked at it one day and commented, "That thing pinch every time. Every morning." As they used it on doll figures the children made such comments as, "The pin goes in, huh?" "Makes a hole, huh?"

Some children carried out the injection procedure very carefully. Although Connie was angry after blood had been drawn from her arm, she sponged the buttocks of the doctor figure with gauze before she rammed the needle into him. Betty commented as she sponged a doll figure before injection, "Have to wet her bum." Jerry forgot on one occasion to sponge the doll figure before injection. He looked sheepishly at the observer and said, "Look what I forgot." There was no indication that the children understood that the purpose of the sponging was to cleanse; it seemed rather like ritualistic behavior.

Children who had experienced receiving intravenous fluids or blood transfusions tended to interpret these procedures as painful and gave no indication that they understood why they were done. They recognized the equipment, used it at times on doll figures, or verbalized as Betty did, "One day the doctor put a needle in my ankle. I cried." Anne said, "I had a needle. Shot in my hand. I didn't like it." A few children who demonstrated these procedures had not been subjected to them but apparently had seen other children receive them.

A few children during the play interviews reproduced illness experiences which had occurred previous to their hospitalization. Barbara picked up the rectal tube in one interview and commented, "Once I was at Arlene's and I drinked turpentine. And I went to the dokker and he put one these in my nose. I didn't want it." She tried to insert the tube into the nose of the doctor doll. Barbara's mother verified that about six months previously Barbara had been taken to the emergency room and her stomach lavaged with a tube introduced through her nose.

A few hospitalized children seemed to be unable to play during an interview because of their concern about what was happening to children around them. During one of Sonny's interviews in the hospital, a child was returned from surgery to a cubicle nearby. She was encased in a Risser jacket and was receiving a blood transfusion. Sonny watched with wide eyes and then commented, "Look at what she gets. That what Denny got. One blood and one water." He fingered through the toys but couldn't seem to concentrate on them. He kept glancing furtively across the hall although he could not see what was happening there. He looked worried and said to the observer, "They tried take that big thing off last night. They had . . . Oh my they had something that make lotta noise!" (Electric cast cutter.) A little later he repeated, "They tried take that big thing off last night."

Anne is an example of how the children used the play interview to work through crises in their life situations. She had been admitted for an emergency appendectomy two months after her cousin Nancy had died in the same hospital. Anne was placed in an oxygen tent and received intravenous fluids for two days following surgery. The nurses were not aware of the cousin's death but charted daily that Anne was inconsolable, almost hysterical, and fought all procedures. In her first play interview Anne looked politely at the toys, then chose crayons and tablet and began to draw. She commented, "My Mommy needs to see me. She'll get me and take me home. When I go home I'll see my Mommy and Daddy. And I'll see Linda, too." She paused, then added without looking up, "Nancy is up in Heaven." The observer asked, "What happened to Nancy?" Anne replied, "Nancy sick and last night the doctor gave her a shot. Just like me. But Nancy still sick. She not here anymore." The observer commented, "But you got well and soon you will go home." Anne smiled slightly and agreed. Then she began to play a game in which she hid objects and brought them back. She placed a pill in a medicine cup, placed a second cup inside the first and said, "It's all gone." Then she removed the top cup, showed the observer and said, "I got it." She used a tongue blade to flick a cotton ball in and out of the test tube. She talked continually: "He's back up. He's lost. He's back out and he's lost." She repeated this over and over and laughed aloud. She opened and closed the lid of the hypodermic case and said, "He's gone." Then she tried to fit the car, the thermometer, the boy doll, and the mother doll into the hypodermic case. She commented, "Now it's lost. Now it's in." She continued this game throughout the hour. We could ask the question, "What is death to a little child?"

During Anne's next interview, a child was returned from surgery under anesthesia. Anne stopped her play, sat staring at the child and picking her nose. She seemed unable to resume play despite the observer's explanation that the child would soon awaken.

Confirming an Hypothesis

Although this was a pilot study concerned with a relatively small number of experimental subjects, it confirmed the hypothesis that when 4-year-old hospitalized children are given opportunity for play with clinical equipment and other accessories for projective play, they are able to express their feelings about their experiences. The data presented clear evidence that the majority of the children studied perceived no protective intent of the adults behind the procedure, but rather, considered them as hostile in intent with the exception of procedures in the oral area. The consistency with which the children studied interpreted invasion of the anus and skin as hostile is of considerable theoretical significance.

References

1. Anna Freud and Dorothy T. Burlingame. *War and Children*. Ed. P. R. Lehrman. 2d ed. New York: International Universities Press, Inc., 1944.
2. John Bowlby. *Maternal Care and Mental Health*. Geneva, Switzerland: World Health Organization, 1951.
3. Lucie Jessner and Samuel Kaplan. "Observation of the Emotional Reactions of Children to Tonsillectomy and Adenoidectomy." In *Problems of Infancy and Childhood; Transactions of the Third Conference, . . . 1949*. Ed. Milton J. E. Senn. New York: Josiah Macy, Jr., Foundation, 1950. Pp. 97–156.
4. Anna Freud. "The Role of Bodily Illness in the Mental Life of Children." *Psychoanalytic Study of the Child*. Vol. 7 (1952). 69–81.
5. Sigmund Freud. *Beyond the Pleasure Principle*. New York: Liveright Publishing Corp., 1950. Pp. 12–16.
6. Jean Piaget. *Play Dreams and Imitation in Childhood*. Trans. C. Gattegno and F. M. Hodgson. New York: W. W. Norton & Company, 1952. Pp. 148–49.

7. E. H. Erikson. *Childhood and Society.* New York: W. W. Norton & Company, 1950. Pp. 194-95.
8. *Ibid.* P. 83.
9. David Levy. "Hostility Patterns in Sibling Rivalry Experiments." *American Journal of Orthopsychiatry.* Vol. 6 (April, 1936). 183-257.

The Hospitalized Child— His Emotional Needs

by Edward A. Mason, M.D.*

Hospitalization as a significant psychologic event in childhood has been a focus of concern, investigation and action for two decades. The postwar interest in psychiatry, combined with the therapeutic controls made possible by antibiotics, encouraged a surge in the trend toward humanizing the care of children. During the decade 1944-53 several basic studies were undertaken that gave rise to dramatic and frequently controversial revisions; in the following decade the changes seem to have been less publicized but more widespread. Because these changes have often been on the basis of personal conviction more than on empirical evidence, objections have risen among physicians of opposite persuasions. This review of progress in the understanding of the emotional responses of children to short-term hospital care will summarize the developments so as to point up successes and gaps, as well as current developments.

The National Health Survey states that 851,000 children were discharged from hospitals in 1960, and that 9 out of 10 of these children were cared for in general hospitals (1). Thus, the welfare of these children is a concern not limited to pediatricians, pediatric nurses and child psychiatrists, although it is these specialists who have been most involved in the "battle waged and won" (2) for liberalized visiting hours on pediatric wards. Even beyond the practical issues pertinent to every hospital that admits children, there is value in studying the experience of hospitalization for the knowledge it can provide about personality adjustment and development. Any stressful life event is worthy of study, but here is one that is readily accessible for observation. Unfortunately, research efforts have been scarce. There are studies to be corroborated, and more age-specific, depth and longitudinal studies are needed. Common sense and a sensitivity to the child's reactions are important assets for the professional in setting out hos-

* *New England Journal of Medicine,* Vol. 272, No. 8 (February 25, 1965). Pp. 406-414.

pital policies, but the limitations of breadth and objectivity make studies based on qualitative assessments alone of less value than controlled studies with adequate follow-up observation. On the other hand, research is not the only basis for change: it is often handicapped by a lack of objective criteria for measuring emotional distress and by control groups unsatisfactory for the study of a single variable. In the field of hospitalization reactions, it appears that action has typically resulted from the efforts of a person whose orientation is based on accumulated clinical experience, with research findings serving as incidental justification or as the end product of the change.

Order of Concerns

The primacy of the physical condition of the hospitalized child is unquestioned. Surgical and medical considerations have always been the chief determinants of procedures and arrangements, although personnel, facilities, finance and local custom are closely linked. Optimal diagnostic and therapeutic skills are directed toward recovery and rehabilitation without medical complication. It was the danger of infection and crossinfection introduced by visitors that for so long was the reason for excluding parents from the wards. The study by Watkins and Lewis-Faning (3) illustrates the basis for revision of these notions that others have found by experience (4): no longer can the dread of crossinfection justify keeping mother and child apart.

There is common acceptance of the value in strictly medical response of taking into account the emotions of the child. For example, the presence of the mother can dramatically revive a child's interest in getting well, and improve his eating, sleeping or general behavior (5, 6). A second level of professional concern is for the psychologic welfare of the child; this has been taught by such pediatric leaders as Powers (7), and support has been added by the frequent history among child-guidance patients of the onset of a behavior disorder after operation or hospitalization (8, 9).

A third area of concern is administrative, although it involves medical and administrative staff equally. Never intended to affect patient care adversely, the concern about efficiency of service meant that some tasks received priority, and those with the least bearing on achievement of the primary goal were discouraged. For example, in some hospitals it was considered necessary to protect the busy intern from questions by parents about a child's diagnosis or progress (10). Space limitations have to some extent dictated policy about permitting mothers to sleep next to their children. There is no doubt that a new building makes a new policy easier to introduce, but changes have frequently been made in old facilities where the staff favored them.

The fourth area of concern has been a more recent one. The family, especially the mother, is of such importance to the child's welfare that the total response of the group to the illness and hospitalization of one of its members is now taken into account. <u>The younger the patient, the more vital the protection of his source of nourishment and the fostering of the optimal relationship to mother, father and siblings</u>. Inevitably, a mother feels some guilt about her child's becoming ill or about leaving him in the hospital. Such guilt or any severe anxiety can alter her response toward the child so as to impair their relationship (11). In addition, the mother is typically left feeling helpless when her mothering tasks are taken over by the hospital staff. The impact on the rest of the family, although less intense, may also be significant. Consideration of the long-term adjustment of the child in the broader network of family and neighborhood may appear to stretch the limit of responsibility of hospital staff; yet the prevention of iatrogenic disturbance and the promotion of health are basic medical goals.

Early Writings

As early as 1923, a plea for liberalized visiting appeared in the professional literature. Fiske (12) urged the recognition of the "deeper feelings of life" and stressed the need to set an example for trainees so as to recognize "the natural affection and solicitude of parents for their children." She warned that otherwise nurses would "ignore family affection and consider the solicitude of relatives as something that interferes with the comfortable performance of their duties and not to be put up with." Brenneman (6) and Bakwin (5) pointed out the "almost 100% mortality rates for infants under one year in institutions" and, believing that this was at least partially due to the lack of mothering, instructed the staff to hold and stimulate hospitalized infants and invited parents to visit when possible. <u>The mortality rates declined, and individual cases dramatized the therapeutic potential of enlisting a mother's help in getting a child to eat.</u> The dramatic evidence of the psychologic and physiologic influence of an institutional setting has been documented by such persons as Spitz (13), Goldfarb (14) and Lowrey (15). A. Freud and Burlingham (16), from their work in residential war nurseries, contributed age-specific observations that were unique and have served as a basis for action since. Bowlby (17) was asked by the World Health Organization to assimilate the various studies on maternal deprivation and in 1951 presented the monograph that sparked a minor revolution in child care. Workers in all specialties have quoted his axiom: "Essential for the infant is a warm, intimate, and continuous relationship with mother in which both find satisfaction and enjoyment." He concluded that "there is no room for doubt that prolonged deprivation of young children of maternal care may have grave and far-reaching effects on his character and so on the whole of his future life," and he called for a revision in many policies with his statement that "a bad home is better than a good institution."

This single publication influenced or revolutionized policies in welfare, adoption, foster-home placement, convalescent care, day nurseries and homemaker services, as well as institutions. Praised and criticized, quoted and misrepresented, Bowlby nevertheless crystallized the concerns about the dangers of institutional care. Although he took pains to choose words carefully and to discuss the problems of short-term hospitalization separately, many persons lumped together all types of institutions and all effects. Robertson (18) focused professional attention on the behavior of 1 normal two-year-old girl during her eight days in the hospital by his film study, thereby making the impact of his and Bowlby's work more specific on short-term hospital policy. Spence (19), in 1927, Pickerill and Pickerill (20), in 1942, and Moncrieff (4), in 1950, had already adopted certain practices aimed at minimizing emotional trauma during hospitalization.

In this country Pearson (21) reported retrospective case histories to illustrate the psychic shock of operations. Jessner and her collaborators (22) had intensively and directly studied the emotional reactions of 143 children to tonsillectomy and adenectomy. Prugh and his colleagues (23) compared the reactions of 100 children to traditional medical admission with a comparable group after ward management had been reorganized. The findings of these studies and the literature before 1954 can be summarized into the following formulations:

Emotional Meaning of Hospitalization

Separation from the mother is considered the chief traumatic factor for the younger child (23). Without his customary source of comfort and support and in spite of the kindest nursing care, he is deprived of the basic trust and security that he particularly needs during illness. Illness, even without hospitalization, involves a threat, varying in children according to their culture and experience (24). The restriction of the ego because of the focus of attention on the body leaves it less able to handle other psychic demands, and fears are magnified. Beyond separation and the illness itself are the threats of the procedures, and other aspects of the atmosphere that are strange, lonely, painful and frightening (22). The common regression to more immature behavior is both a protective maneuver and a symptom of stress in response to the enforced dependency, and recent developmental achievements are often lost.

Young children are predisposed to misinterpretation of their surroundings, their fantasies and fears often lead them far from reality, and their intellectual grasp is not sufficient to help them cope by means available to older children. Most of all, they need a trusted protector nearby. Not only simple frights and annoyances, but major concerns about abandonment or annihilation confront the child (22). He frequently interprets the events as punishment, and he may react with hostility, withdrawal or apathy (23). Signs of depression are commonly observed: sadness, anorexia and listlessness. Some distress is expectable in response to separation and illness—in fact, a lack of anxiety is considered a bad prognostic sign (22). "It is better for a child to be upset than to be apathetic, burying its fears and sorrow in a colorless 'goodness' " (25).

Protest, Despair and Detachment

Bowlby (17) and Robertson (26) have described three stages in the child's process of "settling in" to the hospital routine. The first they label "protest," which is a period of crying, confusion, fright and searching for mother. This is gradually replaced by "despair," characterized by apathy, withdrawal and monotonous wailing. If the separation lasts long enough, a "detachment" occurs in the child—a turning away from his disturbing feelings toward the mother as he recovers an interest in his environment.

Responses vary in kind and in intensity according to the age and stage of development of the child. Up to six months of age, the infant has a brief upset from the change in environment, separation not being as significant as after this age, when the mother comes to be known as an individual figure. Under five years the child lacks the verbal ability, sense of time and understanding of the reasons for procedures that a school-age child possesses, so that he is apt to have the more severe and prolonged reactions. He is less able to assess reality or express himself as actively as the school-age child. In boys four to six, the fear of bodily mutilation is pronounced. Adolescents have a special problem during illness: sensitive about their normal strivings toward independence, they particularly resent enforced dependency. A child of any age has increased difficulty if there are concurrent stresses such as the birth of a sibling, recent death of a friend or relative or disruptions in family relationships (27).

After returning home, a child usually shows a temporary increase in anxiety, clinging and fearfulness, a disruption in eating, sleeping or toilet routines, and sometimes evidence of hostility. This behavior gradually drops away so that after three months it may be seen in 16 to 58 per cent of children (23, 28, 29); at six months 15 to 55 per cent (23, 30) have behavioral evidences of emotional disturbance. The effects beyond that time are difficult to substantiate. Individual retrospective case histories have traced lasting neurotic patterns to the time of hospitalization (9), and children with neurotic tendencies before operation have been found more likely to react with increased disturbances (22). Robertson (18) reports follow-up observations on the two-year-old girl whom he photographed in the hospital that demonstrate the child's susceptibility to anxiety as much as one year later when an event triggered a conscious or unconscious recall of the apparently resolved trauma.

In chronic hospitalization additional factors alter or complicate the child's emotional response: the child's focus is on lengthy treatment procedures rather than the normal developmental challenges, and families are strained to maintain positive and healthy relations with a child away from home for a long, uninterrupted period. These problems blur into those associated with institutionalization and maternal deprivation that, at first, were believed to have common sequelae. There can be no doubt that concern about children receiving institutional care was legitimate, and that those receiving short-term institutionalization in a hospital may have benefited by the attention to the whole area of maternal deprivation. The reports by Spitz (13), for example, stressed the harmful effect of extreme deprivation: three months in a foundling home would lead to "serious" disabilities, and after five months these would probably be "irreversible." Others described the effects of deprivation as leading to lower intellectual ability, poor ability to make human relations or lower frustration tolerance. None of these, however, could be directly applied to the effects of shorter deprivations. The important distinction began to be made between separation and maternal deprivation, and the implications for practice became more specific.

A Decade of Implementation

By 1954 the impact of the separation experiences during World War II and the new interest in the plight of the hospitalized child was evident in the gradually broadening scope of attempts to prevent or alleviate the traumatic effects. The findings and recommendations of the studies (17, 18, 22, 23) began to be accepted and put into practice in revised policies or programs that were characteristic of the individual institutions. As is typical in response to the realization of any complex area of need, the experience, personalities or circumstances existing in each hospital colored the solutions. Liberalized visiting has captured primary attention, particularly in England, and has mobilized considerable professional and lay support, but it is by no means the only development. At least six different areas can be identified that deserve periodic and serious consideration by all hospitals admitting children.

AVOIDING HOSPITALIZATION

The obvious (yet sometimes unacknowledged) means of reducing potential trauma is to eliminate it. Not only are patients with infectious illnesses less apt to be hospitalized now, but home-treatment services encourage the maintenance of a normal environment without depriving the child of medical supervision (31). More thought is given to the recommendation for elective operations, and fewer children are admitted for routine evaluations. The recognition of critical ages, stages or concurrent events has made it feasible to time elective procedures optimally. For example, there may be a "sensitive phase" between six and twelve months (32) during which maternal deprivation is most likely to lead to intellectual retardation. If admission to the hospital is necessary, what efforts have been made to ensure its being a *positive* experience emotionally as well as physiologically (22)?

PREPARATION

The disillusionment of children left at the hospital by parents who tell them nothing, or even mislead them, evokes grossly negative reactions (22). (Perhaps the shaken trust of a small child explains some of the hostility he later demonstrates in his negative behavior on the ward or after returning home.) Depending upon his age, an honest account of the anticipated events can help the child maintain his trust in parents and remove some of the strangeness from those events. Particularly useful with children four to eight years old is the possibility of asking the questions that may be troubling each of them, at a time neither too near nor too far from the event (33). Many books have been published to be read to the child (34), as well as films (35) and coloring books for the child (36) and pamphlets for the mother. Vaughan (30) studied the responses of two groups of children admitted for eye surgery: those "prepared" were *more* anxious on the ward, but six months later only 15 per cent had emotional sequelae as compared to 55 per cent of the control group. It is of special interest that the 15 per cent included *all* the children in the group under four. For the very young child preparation is of no value (26) because of limited intellectual grasp, span of memory or verbalization. In some cases preparation has backfired when it was made too specific; no booklet can cover all the events during hospitalization, and the proper balance between general and specific preparation is therefore necessary for each child.

One unusual example of preparation is the practice at the Children's Hospital of the East Bay in Oakland, California, to encourage visits by nearby nursery-school groups (37). The children are given a tour and a treat, and if any must subsequently be hospitalized, they appear to adjust more easily to the ward. Another related possibility is that the improvements, expanding interests and community relatedness of outpatient departments will bring about a more positive orientation toward the hospital wards.

PHYSICAL ARRANGEMENTS

Many hospitals believe in the benefits of making wards more homelike. When nurses wear pastel-colored uniforms (38) preschool children are reported to adjust more quickly, parents to be more relaxed, and the nurses to feel less fatigue. Certainly, light and color can affect mood, and perhaps that of the staff as well as the children. Gay decorations, the provision of toys and a play area for their use, the ever present television set and the central dining table for all ambulatory children are notable transformations. Changes in the character and levels of noise and activity often accompany these. Whereas fewer children now need to be restricted to bed, the atmosphere during much of the day resembles a more normal sample of child behavior. They may retain favorite possessions, wear ordinary clothing and sleep in beds more like their own. Not only less rigid, oppressive, frightening, austere and solemn (as some wards had been considered), the new arrangements give children the opportunity to be more active psychologically as well as physically. The benefits of activity are several: children can be of significant help to one another if they are allowed mobility (39); and the change from passivity to activity allows a healthier coping (40). If he acknowledges his feelings and expresses them in play or talk, the child can learn to deal with his environment promptly and appropriately, and his growing maturity helps him cope better with future pain and frustration. Activity discourages repression and dependency, which, although expectable in limited amounts, may increase and complicate immediate adjustment and subsequent personality development.

VISITING (4)

The older patterns of not allowing parents to visit their children at all, or only during a limited period such as two hours once a week, have given way to a variety of patterns that allow flexibility. It has been found that relaxation of rigid rules has allowed the children to be more relaxed about an anticipated visit, parents can share visiting responsibilities and integrate them into their own work and home schedules, and the staff members learn more and help patients better by having more natural contacts with parents. No longer widely held are the past objections to liberalized visiting that were based on fears of crossinfection, crowding, interrupting routines, abuse of rules by parents and harm to children (41, 42). The reasoning for the latter was that the child's upset after his parents left was due to the visiting itself. The wail as the bell signaled the end of visiting hour for a week was difficult to avoid, and also difficult to take. It soon began to be realized that a cry when parents leave is natural, and that the child might suffer less than if he were not visited at all. The cry is a release of feelings of grief about separation and anger about being left; it is more appropriate than the excessive control or absence of these emotions. A respect for the child's right to have and to express these emotions promotes the optimal manner for each child to handle them (26, 39).

The child "lives from day to day: he depends on the evidence of his senses and his understanding of the situation is fragmentary at best. A loving mother who remains absent is a figure whom he is incapable of conceiving" (43). Younger children cannot understand the enforced separation, and neither can the mothers. By regular visiting, by assisting in the ordinary care of their children and by being considered the best judges of their children's needs, mothers can be more relaxed. They naturally feel anxiety for their children and guilt if they cannot protect them from pain and unhappiness. The opportunity to help on the ward benefits them and their children, as well as other children whose parents are not visiting. Also, rather than being considered competitors and demanders of nursing attention, they are seen as collaborators (41). One study of two years' experience with daily visiting (44) in England showed that parents made 90 per cent of possible visits and that 77 per cent of all children were visited every possible day in spite of the high cost and time in travel. Ratings of the children's behavior after the visits showed upset more frequent in the younger (86 per cent among children one and two years old, as against 32 per cent among those ten and twelve years old). Among the older children this dropped after four days, but the younger children continued to show the *same amount of* upset after visitors left regardless of the length of their hospital stay.

By 1954 the practice of liberalizing visiting hours on children's wards in America was gaining momentum. One survey (42) in New York City in February of that year showed that 32 per cent (24) of the hospitals with pediatric beds permitted daily visiting as compared with 35 per cent (26) that allowed visiting only once or twice a week. Many reported recent or pending changes, and a follow-up report four years later (45) showed more changes: the number permitting daily visiting doubled (65 per cent). No hospital by 1958 limited visiting to once a week, and of the 18 hospitals new to the survey, 15 (83 per cent) permitted daily visiting. In addition, the hours were increased or more flexible in half the original group, and decreased in only 2 hospitals.

A more recent survey by Geppert (46) of instructions to parents from 190 hospitals with approved pediatric residency training showed only 6 per cent to have less than daily visiting. Twelve had recently liberalized visiting rules, and 1 had just reduced the time from unlimited to four hours daily.

A survey by me of the visiting arrangements in Boston hospitals during October, 1964, revealed that daily visiting was allowed in all but 2 hospitals, and these limited their pediatric admissions to tonsillectomies. Out of 15 hospitals in the city that admit children 8 currently encourage or make it possible for a parent to live in. Two have had such facilities for many years, and at the other extreme, 1 liberalized its arrangements to a major way as recently as December, 1962. On private floors there is greater flexibility, and often availability of a room determines whether a mother can live in. It is my impression that a staff doctor would need only to make a strong request for living-in arrangements to make it possible. Public pressure and a certain level of competition between hospitals will be a significant factor in their moves to satisfy the needs and reasonable wishes of the community's children, parents and practitioners.

MOTHER'S STAYING

"It is paradoxical that when a young child needs his mother most, when he is ill and perhaps in pain, she is generally not allowed to be with him for more than brief visits" (26). A more adequate provision for the needs of the child would be the arrangement for 1 person to remain with the child through all treatments, procedures, tests, examinations and moves. The child can establish a supportive and trusting relation more easily when there is consistency. For this reason, nursing assignments have tried to give responsibilities for fewer children to each nurse (47), thereby providing an atmosphere mutually conducive to a closer tie between nurse and child. Some hospitals have organized "mother banks" (48) and find that these substitute mothers who give intensive care to a deprived infant can stimulate a more normal responsiveness, reduce the infant's gastrointestinal symptoms and shorten his hospital stay. The supply of such women will never meet the need, and the logical solution, of course, is to allow a child's own mother to be present.

In many countries and in some areas of the United States it has long been expected that a mother will accompany her child on admission. In 1953 there were 3 hospitals pioneering this policy in areas where it had not been the established practice: Amersham Hospital in Buckinghamshire, England; the Royal Hospital for Sick Children in Aberdeen, Scotland; and the Hunterdon Medical Center in Flemington, New Jersey. MacCarthy et al. (49), at Amersham, had tried gingerly, for three years, admitting mothers one at a time. The success of the program led to its establishment on a regular basis for all children under five, sometimes older children "if they are specially dependent or cannot understand English," and all children with "cerebral palsy, mental defect, mongolism, blindness, or any handicap causing emotional dependence." A film by Robertson (50) documents the benefits during 1 child's hospitalization at Amersham. It also demonstrates that a staff dedicated to meeting the emotional needs of mother and child can find its work aided, rather than hindered, by such imaginative use of a traditional ward. Refusing to exclude "difficult mothers," the staff stresses understanding that the origin of some aggressiveness may lie in the mother's anxiety or guilt and that such negative feelings may be fostered by her "being kept in the dark about the facts of the case" (49).

The Royal Aberdeen Hospital for Sick Children opened a new unit in 1953 with one wing providing rooms for 12 mothers to be admitted with their infants. Craig and McKay (51) allow a mother to choose, offer her instruction while she is caring for her infant and encourage her to have visitors or to leave the ward as she wishes. They report that in 1955, 36 per cent of medical admissions were accompanied by the mother for at least part of the time. The average length of stay was shorter on this wing, which may represent the advantage such a facility offers in the establishment of breast feeding and the treatment of feeding difficulties (50 per cent of medical admissions for that year). This facility is limited to children under one year, however, and 80 per cent of those admitted are less than six months of age.

In the United States, when the Hunterdon Medical Center opened in 1953, it instituted a program for children of all ages that allows mothers to remain or visit freely (52). The success of such programs has often been discussed in professional meetings, but the spread to other hospitals has been slow. In 1962 only 15 per cent of hospitals with approved pediatric residencies allowed parents to stay overnight (46). In 1963 replies from half the 300 hospitals questioned by a national women's magazine revealed only 14 that permitted living in (53). A far greater number, probably the majority, permit parents to stay as long as they wish when a child is on the danger list. Wessel and Simon (53) ask why hospitals should deny any mothers living in on the basis of "difficulty" when that is not the criterion used for providing any other essential such as oxygen or intravenous fluid therapy.

Solnit (54) has described the therapeutic uses of admitting mother and child together, especially for helping the child master separation anxieties, bodily self-control or ambivalent feelings toward parents. Feeding problems resulting from disorders of parent-child relationships can be observed and treated more readily in a therapeutic setting.

A study by Hamovitch (55) undertook an evaluation of the Parent Participation Program at the City of Hope Medical Center. Two thirds of the 82 children were considered to have benefited. It had been hypothesized that the children under five would be helped most, and although this group gave more evidence of "separation anxiety" in spite of parent participation, they were just as able to adjust as the school-age children. The program reduced the reciprocal anxiety that was evident among the parents of this youngest group. Most significantly, when parents did *not* participate, the children demonstrated the classic patterns of response to the emotional trauma of hospitalization.

There are several indications of professional interest in the family as a significant therapeutic ally. For example, an integral part of the plans for the new Kennedy Institute at Johns Hopkins Hospital is the provision of a residential service to house parents so that they will be actively involved, instructed, supported and given practice in the habilitation efforts for their handicapped children. This represents the trend toward a broader and wiser use of hospital space and professional skills. Architects and physicians are working together to assist this development (56). The even broader challenge of integrating hospital building plans with urban redevelopment so as to benefit both the community and the hospital has been accepted by the Tufts-New England Medical Center. One activity there is its "Study for a New Design Concept for a Children's Hospital," financed by the United States Public Health Service. Using behavioral scientists, architects and medical staff, it is grappling with issues of space, financing, work patterns, referral channels, family participation, therapeutic trends, personnel shortages, psychologic responses and many more (57). Its results are awaited both in the form of a specific plan for a new Boston Floating Hospital and in the recommendations that will be of use wherever new pediatric construction is being considered.

STAFF RELATIONS

Quite apart from the changing physical arrangements or procedures, the significance of staff attitudes in dealing with children is recognized. The emphasis on truthfulness is benefiting the child patient whereas in the past it was considered acceptable, and even advisable, to keep him uninformed. A specific example of the place of truthfulness in the event of death on a children's ward has been described by Plank (58).

By showing respect for the child as an individual, hospitals support children so that they can cope with their concerns and uncertainties. From studies that explore the meaning of various procedures it is known that some are more disturbing than others. Erickson (59), for example, shows that children are less upset by procedures involving the mouth, whereas intrusion of the skin or the anus is often interpreted as "hostile." For this reason information and preparation before such procedures can minimize misinterpretation, although it is acknowledged that the information is not as important as the attitude of the professional at the time. An honest and comforting approach, rather than cajoling or threatening, is conducive to better coping response. It may not be possible to allow the child the authority to determine when the needle will be inserted (60), but he might be allowed a more active role in his own care (39).

Readily observed, but not always acknowledged, is the difference in care received by different children on the same ward. Sometimes a showering of "tender loving care" on the ward darling has been accepted as normal and inevitable, but a concern for the impact on that child as well as the emotions of the others and of the staff has led to studies which explore the variables determining the quality of care. Pavenstedt (61) points out that lower socioeconomic status and cultural communication handicap deprives many children of the optimal hospital care. Spitzer and Sobel (62) have suggested that certain personal characteristics of children affect the quality and quantity of their hospital treatment according to whether they are liked or disliked. They have shown a correlation between staff liking of a school-age child and his showing the type of behavior that fulfills staff expectations (cooperation, respect, appreciation and increasing acceptance of hospital socialization). Also, the more frequently these children exhibited immature behavior (failure of emotional control, acting "childish," crying, whining and so forth), the less well liked they were. The authors contend that patients who make the staff feel effective in carrying out their duties tend to be preferred to those who evoke feelings of ineffectiveness and helplessness. The circular nature of this process becomes apparent and necessitates increased recognition of the emotions of the hospital personnel and the preventive opportunities that can be seized in an understanding of "immature" behavior without responding negatively.

In a study of the emotional problems associated with hospitalized burned patients, Long and Cope (63) outline the aspects of psychologic stress for the children and emphasize the need to understand and deal with reactions that may antagonize the therapists. If a child interprets the painful treatment as punishment he may react with anger, which can be expressed in aggressive outbursts or in a barrier of apathy that provides a lack of staff interest. These authors advise that "whenever a patient's resistance to a procedure provokes a subjective feeling of frustration, irritation, or anger, it may indicate that the child misconstrues the procedure," and the staff persons should explain and reassure the child.

The importance of communication is recognized for effective care, but it is seen to be handicapped by such factors as the tendency toward increasing specialization and separation of the professions. If a physician spends less time with patients because of conflicting demands and shorter hospital stays (the average for children is now six and four-tenths days vs. thirteen and one-tenth days thirty years ago) (10) he may more quickly refer the child to a specialist in the quest for efficiency. To counteract the more impersonal and mechanical care of patients, physicians and nurses have turned for assistance to other professional groups. The work of occupational therapists, physiotherapists, nursery-school teachers and recreational therapists has long been considered important on children's wards (58, 64). The social worker has traditionally been given the role of listener, counselor, enabler and communication clarifier. The increasing capability of this profession to offer case work to hospitalized children or their parents parallels the awareness of its potential value. A recent account by Richman (65) details aspects of the technic, content and results of this type of support. In this example the social worker's help to a child undergoing heart surgery was perhaps lifesaving and certainly made this critical and frightening period one of emotional growth. These professions, as well as the elementary-school teachers, volunteers, public-health and welfare workers, trustees and many others, take part in a variety of significant activities that benefit the hospitalized child. One of the newest specialties is that of social group work; it has begun to serve patients in a few hospitals by constructive use of groups to encourage better coping mechanisms. By providing the type of play situation or activity that allows freedom of verbal and physical expression, the social group worker may support the recognition and communication of feelings about separation, isolation, procedures or hospital life (39, 63, 66). He must evaluate the requirements for individual patients and of the entire ward, he must maintain limits, as well as be permissive, he must be intuitive about recognizing a child's hostility, guilt, depression or anxiety, and yet he must not take it personally if any of these negative feelings are expressed toward him. Training and experience are essential in such tasks, as is the ability to work collaboratively with other professions and thereby to contribute toward the overall hospital goal of concern for the whole child and his family.

Discussion

Out of the "controversy and emotionally-colored convictions" that were stimulated in the forties by a concern about "hospitalism" and maternal deprivation has evolved a body of knowledge that substantiates the potential trauma of hospitalization to the child's psychologic development. Tempered by evidence that the young child's response today is not apt to resemble the "hospitalism" of two decades earlier (67), the subject is included regularly in professional instruction, and there is a steady advance in recognition of its importance.

A committee appointed by the British Ministry of Health in 1956 on arrangements in hospitals for the welfare of children took note of the advances in medicine, the increased awareness of children's needs and the movement toward a new concept of child care in hospitals. Its report in 1959 (41) spells out practical information and makes recommendations on many aspects of hospital arrangement, procedures and professional training. The Minister of Health agreed with these and asked that they be implemented, including unrestricted visiting on children's wards and the possibility of admitting mothers with their children. In spite of this official support, however, it was said in 1962 that the report "has largely been disregarded and there are comparatively few children's wards where either of these recommendations is practised" (68). Robertson (69) has published letters written during 1961 by British parents with praise and criticism for various hospital attitudes and practices, and he has also encouraged mothers to form a committee and stimulate action. Some parents point a damaging finger at the apparent ignorance or refusal of some hospitals to follow a humane approach, much less to accept and implement the recommendations of the Platt report. At the same time it is recognized that some British hospitals acted quickly and enthusiastically.

Variations in hospital facilities in any country are to be expected, but the gaps in the United States are surprisingly wide and resistance to change surprisingly strong. Pediatric residents, a group that might represent current attitudes, in a recent study were frank in expressing their resentment about parents' living in because they see it as a deterrent to the child's adjustment (55). The same group considers discussions of social and emotional matters as "gossip sessions." Residents at first feel self-conscious about lacking experience and yet later come to see the psychologic benefit to child and parent of living in. Resistance to change is not restricted to residents, of course, and need not be blamed altogether on fear of the new or of upsetting tradition (70). In the concern about the emotional impact of hospitalization some exaggeration may have resulted from the wish to call attention to the problem. Steam certainly has spread from the controversies over maternal deprivation, and there may have been some scapegoating of the hospital as responsible for any subsequent disturbance in the child. Yet the clinical case descriptions and the reports of experiments in hospital care mobilized a genuine and valuable widening circle of changes. Revisions are always necessary when a balance is maintained among changing personnel, technologies, insights and philosophies. The value of the experimental approach is that it keeps the field open rather than forces the acceptance of an outmoded solution or a premature new plan. This also means that the best parts of the old and the new plans can be merged. For example, while the evidence mounts that indicates the potential trauma of the separation of mother and child, there is evidence that occasional separation is therapeutic (71). A further example is the use of the traditional parent interview along with a new type of group meeting to achieve a better understanding of the parents' emotional reaction and its implication for the child's recovery (11).

Following the effort to develop the preventive approach wherever possible, medicine has identified hospitalization as a noxious factor that may influence the future mental health of a number of children and their families. Community-wide efforts are indicated to reduce hospitalization or by educational support and policy adjustment to minimize its potential trauma. The characteristics of those most endangered have been outlined: the child from seven months to four years of age; one with a violent, severe or unusual health threat; or a child with earlier emotional problems or poor family relations. Technics to identify these children and studies of their responses to alternative programs of care must be developed.

Considering hospitalization as a crisis means that it is seen as a significant time of stress as well as an opportunity for learning (22, 72, 73). This aspect may enable the medical professions to move away from the emotions and defensiveness that have been associated with the subject. The support of reality-based, adaptive and adjustive technics among children while maintaining the optimal therapeutic environment and now broadening the considerations to include the mother and the family appear as the current goal. On reflection it is obvious that the goal was not different two decades ago or more; it is basically the same goal and even the same challenge, and the difference lies only in the means.

References

1. United States Department of Health, Education and Welfare, Children's Bureau. Schiffer, C. G., and Hunt, E. P. *Illness among Children, Data from U. S. National Health Survey.* 107 pp. Washington, D.C.: Government Printing Office, 1963. (Publication No. 405.)

2. Mercer, M. E. Emotional aspects of feeding children in hospitals. *Pub. Health News* **44**:9–11, 1963.
3. Watkins, A. G., and Lewis-Faning, E. Incidence of cross-infection in children's wards. *Brit. M. J.* **2**:616–619, 1949.
4. Moncrieff, A., and Walton, A. M. Visting children in hospital. *Brit. M. J.* **1**:43, 1952.
5. Bakwin, H. Loneliness in infants. *Am. J. Dis. Child.* **63**:30–40, 1942.
6. Brenneman, J. Infant ward. *Am. J. Dis. Child.* **43**:577–584, 1932.
7. Powers, G. F. Humanizing hospital experiences: presidential address *Am. J. Dis. Child.* **75**:365–379, 1948.
8. Levy, D. M. Psychic trauma of operations in children and note on combat neurosis. *Am. J. Dis. Child.* **69**:7–25, 1945.
9. Edelston, H. Separation anxiety in young children: study of hospital cases. *Genet. Psychol. Monogr.* **28**:1–95, 1943.
10. Rothman, P. E. Note on hospitalism. *Pediatrics,* **30**:995–999, 1962.
11. Lewis, M. Management of parents of acutely ill children in hospital. *Am. J. Orthopsychiat.* **32**:60–66, 1962.
12. Fiske, A. Psychology. *Am. J. Nursing* **23**:1011–1014, 1923.
13. Spitz, R. Hospitalism: inquiry into genesis of psychiatric conditions in early childhood. In *Psychoanalytic Study of the Child.* Vol. 1. 423 pp. New York: Int. Univ. Press, 1945. Pp. 53–74.
14. Goldfarb, W. Effects of early institutional care on adolescent personality. *J. Exper. Educ.* **12**:106, 1943.
15. Lowrey, L. G. Personality distortion and early institutional care. *Am. J. Orthopsychiat.* **10**:576–585, 1940.
16. Freud, A., and Burlingham, D. *War and Children.* Second edition. Edited by P. R. Lehrman. 191 pp. New York: Int. Univ. Press, 1944.
17. Bowlby, J. *Maternal Care and Mental Health.* Second edition. 179 pp. Geneva, Switzerland: World Health Organization, 1952. (Monograph No. 2.)
18. Robertson, J. *Two Year Old Goes to Hospital.* New York: New York University Film Library, 1953. (Fifty-minute, 16-mm. sound film and discussion guide.)
19. Spence, J. C. *The Purpose of the Family: A guide to the care of children.* 68 pp. London: Epworth Press, 1946.
20. Pickerill, H. P., and Pickerill, G. M. Elimination of cross-infection: experiment. *Brit. M. J.* **1**:158, 1945.
21. Pearson, G. H. J. Effect of operative procedures on emotional life of child. *Am. J. Disc. Child.* **62**:716–729, 1941.
22. Jessner, L., Blom, G. E., and Waldfogel, S. Emotional implications of tonsillectomy and adenectomy on children. In *Psychoanalytic Study of the Child,* Vol. 7, 448 pp. New York: Int. Univ. Press, 1952. Pp. 126–169.
23. Prugh, D. G., Staub, E. M., Sands, H. H., Kirschbaum, R. M., and Lenihan, E. A. Study of emotional reactions of children and families to hospitalization and illness. *Am. J. Orthopsychiat.* **23**:70–106, 1953.
24. Freud, A. Role of bodily illness in mental life of children. In *Psychoanalytic Study of the Child.* Vol. 7. 448 pp. New York: Int. Univ. Press, 1952. Pp. 69–81.
25. Moncrieff, A. Human relations in child health. I. Children in hospitals. *J. Roy. Inst. Pub. Health* **26**:57–64, 1963.
26. Robertson, J. *Young Children in Hospitals.* 136 pp. New York: Basic Books, Inc., 1958.

27. Jackson, K., Winkley, R., Faust, O. A., Cermak, E. G., and Burtt, M. M. Behavior changes indicating emotional trauma in tonsillectomized children. *Pediatrics* **12**: 23–27, 1953 .
28. Jackson, K., Winkley, R., Faust, O. A., and Cermak, E. G. Problem of emotional trauma in hospital treatment of children. *J.A.M.A.* **149**:1536–1538, 1952.
29. Eckenhoff, J. E. Relationship of anesthesia to postoperative personality changes in children. *Am. J. Dis. Child.* **86**:587–591, 1953.
30. Vaughan, G. F. Children in hospital. *Lancet* **1**:1117–1120, 1957.
31. Lightwood, R., Brimblecombe, F. S. W., Reinhold, J. D. L., Burnard, E. D., and Davis, J. A. London trial of home care for sick children. *Lancet* **1**:313–317, 1957.
32. Ainsworth, M. D. Effects of maternal deprivation: review of findings and controversy in context of research strategy. *World Health Organ. Pub. Health Papers* **14**:97–165, 1962.
33. Robertson, J. Mother's observations on tonsillectomy of her four-year-old daughter. In *Psychoanalytic Study of the Child*. Vol. 11. New York: Int. Univ. Press, 1956. Pp. 410–427.
34. Sever, J. A. *Johnny Goes to the Hospital*. 32 pp. Boston: Houghton, Mifflin Co., 1953.
35. Premier Films. *A Place to Get Well*. Chicago: American Hospital Association, 1961. (Twenty-minute, 16-mm., sound, color film.)
36. King Features. *Henry*. Buffalo: The Children's Hospital, 1958.
37. "Through looking glass." *Hospitals*. **43**:47–49, January 16, 1960.
38. Bradshaw, C. E., and Cheng, N. C. Pastels in pediatrics. *Nurs. Outlook* **11**:361–363, 1963.
39. Mason, E. A. *Children in the Hospital*. Chicago: International Film Bureau, 1962. (Forty-four minute, 16-mm., sound film and discussion guide.)
40. Jessner, L. Some observations on children hospitalized during latency. In Jessner, L., and Pavenstedt, E. *Dynamic Psychopathology in Childhood: With 15 contributors*. 315 pp. New York: Grune, 1959.
41. Great Britain, Platt Committee. *The Welfare of Children in Hospital*. 42 pp. London: Her Majesty's Stationery Office, 1959.
42. Liberal visiting policies for children in hospitals: report by Citizens' Committee on Children of New York City, Inc. *J. Pediat.* **46**:710–716, 1955.
43. Editorial. Visiting children in hospital. *Lancet* **2**:1138, 1953.
44. Illingworth, R. S. and Holt, K. S. Children in hospital, some observations on their reactions with special reference to daily visiting. *Lancet* **2**:1257–1262, 1955.
45. *Progress Report on Visiting Policies*. Prepared by Citizens' Committee on Children of New York City, June, 1958.
46. Geppert, L. J. Pediatric visiting hours and policies. *Pediatrics* **31**(1):158–160. Part 1, 1963.
47. Bielicka, I., and Olechnowicz, H. Treating children traumatized by hospitalization. *Children* **10**:194, 1963.
48. Fineberg, H. H., and Jones, E. C. Mother back in children's hospital. *J.A.M.A.* **174**: 2153, 1960.
49. MacCarthy, D., Lindsay, M., and Morris, I. Children in hospital with mothers. *Lancet* **1**:603–608, 1962.
50. Robertson, J. *Going to Hospital with Mother*. New York: New York University Film Library, 1958. (Forty-five minute, 16-mm., sound film.)

51. Craig, J., and McKay, E. Working of mother and baby unit. *Brit. M. J.* **1**:275–277, 1958.
52. Hunt, A. D. Experiment in teamwork. *Child Study* **74**:10–14, 1956.
53. Wessel, M., and Simon, N. Why can't mothers stay in hospitals with their children? *Redbook Magazine*, pp. 41–84 (August), 1966.
54. Solnit, A. J. Hospitalization: aid to physical and psychological health in childhood. *J. Dis. Child.* **99**:155–163, 1960.
55. Hamovitch, M. B. *The Parent and the Fatally Ill Child*. 152 pp. Duarte, California: City of Hope Medical Center, 1964.
56. Nuffield Foundation, Division for Architectural Studies. *Children in Hospital: Studies in planning; A report of studies made by Division*. 115 pp. Fair Lawn, New Jersey. Oxford, 1963.
57. Kennedy, D. A. Personal communication.
58. Plank, E. N. *Working with Children in Hospitals*. 36 pp. Cleveland: Western Reserve Press, 1962.
59. Erickson, F. Reactions of children to hospital experiences. *Nurs. Outlook* **5**:501, 1958.
60. Bochner, A. K. *One Child's Experience in Our Hospital*. Cleveland: University Hospitals, 1960. (Forty-seven minute, 16-mm., sound film.)
61. Pavenstedt, E. Child guidance service in municipal hospital. *Children* **10**:207–212, 1963.
62. Spitzer, S. P., and Sobel, R. Preferences for patients and patient behavior. *Nursing Research* **11**:233–235, 1962.
63. Long, R. T., and Cope, O. Emotional problems of burned children. *New Eng. J. Med.* **264**:1121–1127, 1961.
64. Tisza, V., and Angoff, K. Play program and its function in pediatric hospital. *Pediatrics* **19**:293–302, 1957.
65. Richman, H. A. Casework with child following heart surgery. *Children* **11**:183–188, 1964.
66. Frey, L. A. Social group work in hospitals. In *New Perspectives on Service to Groups: Theory, organization, and practice—social work with groups, 1961*. 160 pp. New York: National Association of Social Welfare, 1961. Pp. 92–103.
67. Schaffer, H. R., and Callender, W. M. Psychologic effects of hospitalization in infancy. *Pediatrics* **24**:528–539, 1959.
68. Cooper, C. Children in hospital with mothers. *Develop. Med. & Child Neurol.* **4**:644–646, 1962.
69. Robertson, J. *Hospitals and Children, a Parent's-Eye View: A review of letters from parents to the Observer and the B.B.C.: With a foreword by Sir Harry Platt*. 159 pp. New York: Int. Univ. Press, 1962.
70. Stein, A. Resistance to psychological prophylaxis in hospital pediatrics. *J. Pediat.* **55**:497–503, 1959.
71. Howells, J. G. Child-parent separation as therapeutic procedure. *Am. J. Psychiat.* **119**:922–926, 1963.
72. Caplan, G. *Prevention of Mental Disorders in Children*. 425 pp. New York: Basic Books, Inc., 1961.
73. Langford, W. S. Child in pediatric hospital: adaptation to illness and hospitalization. *Am. J. Orthopsychiat.* **31**:667–684, 1961.

chapter five

MIDDLE CHILDHOOD

Between the ages of 5 and 12, the child enters school and encounters the wider world of his peers and social group. Sigmund Freud termed this time of life *latency,* believing that during this period children experience marked diminution in the pressures of sexual and aggressive drives and an increased capacity to channel these drives into social and intellectual activities.

The diversion of sexual energies into nonsexual activities and aims is termed *sublimation.* Sublimation is active throughout life as the ego rechannels drive energies into socially acceptable aims. During latency, the resolution of oral, anal, and Oedipal conflicts results in increased ego control over the instinctual drives. This ego control contributes to greater social conformity, educability, and personality stability.

In latency, personality traits and patterns emerge that reflect reactions against infantile sexual and aggressive behavior. Messiness gradually gives way to cleanliness; aggression and cruelty are replaced by sympathy and concern for others; exhibitionistic tendencies yield to modesty; and greediness and selfishness are supplanted by cooperation and willingness to share.

This vital process of socialization involves the alteration of infantile drives through the medium of the ego as the child learns to adapt to and fit in with his family, his peer group, and the wider society.

These achievements are not easily won or maintained. Emotional conflicts, family problems, or physical illness may lead to temporary breakdowns of these recation formations and sublimations. In time, however, the new psychological and social patterns and traits become firmly established.

During middle childhood, the child's intense ties to his family and home expand to include his peer group, his school, and his neighborhood. The parents, however, continue to be of first importance in providing the child with the background security, support, and guidance that are essential for his continuing emotional development.

Although the earlier conflicts and tensions associated with family intimacy now become somewhat lessened, the child faces new areas in which he must prove himself and which present to him emotional hazards and challenges. His new problems include rivalry with other children, concern about the approval or disapproval of teachers, and frustrations as well as satisfactions in his efforts to master the tools of his society, both intellectual and technological.

During this period, he consolidates the identifications and ego functions that lead to an increased certainty about his self identity and his sexual role. His perception of the world widens immeasurably as he becomes more and more aware of people and things outside his family and himself.

For many children, entering school represents the first regular separation from their mothers, and it lasts over a period of many hours each day. Thus, the teacher may become the first consistent substitute for the mother. Teachers exert considerable influence especially insofar as the child transfers some of his emotional attachments to them from his parents.

School Adjustment Problems

The school nurse may note that emotional and physical problems that had not appeared in relationship to the parents may, for the first time, show up in school and manifest themselves in the classroom in relation to the teacher. When the child enters school, the separation may be more difficult for certain mothers, who have been dependent on the companionship of their children for emotional support and security, than for the child. Sometimes children of these mothers experience anxiety or fears about school and show hypochondriacal concerns and physical symptoms that represent a means to keep them at home with their mothers. In such cases, it is essential that the mother be involved in any attempt to work with the child's problems, since more often than not the mother's conflicts are being expressed through the child's behavior.

Those children who come from culturally or economically disadvantaged homes or communities may first show problems in adjusting when they enter school. The schools reflect the interest and attitudes of the middle and upper classes in our country and have only recently begun to take cognizance of the means of communication, the educational requirements, and the physical needs of the poor. As a result, poor children may find themselves at a loss to deal with the material presented to them at school and may react with withdrawal, behavior problems, or physical symptoms and thus come to the nurse's attention.

Public health nurses and school nurses especially are faced with the dilemmas presented by families that have no roots in a community or are poor and are therefore the least able to prepare their children for school. Children from such families may be ill as a result of poor nutrition, inadequate housing, and poor sanitation. All of these environmental factors will affect the schoolwork of the child, and the nurse may be able to play an important role in helping to evaluate the basis for school failure in the children from such settings.

Preparing For Adult Roles

During latency, the child begins to learn about occupations and careers that may interest him later in life. He also learns to use the intellectual and other skills that the school and home teach him, developing a sense of industry that enables him to compete successfully in his environment.

Erikson sees the danger at this stage of development as "an estrangement from himself and his tasks—the well-known *sense of inferiority.*" [1] This may be caused by an insufficient solution of the preceding conflict. The child may still want his mommy more than knowledge; he may still prefer to be the baby at home rather than the big child in school; he still compares himself with his father, and the comparison may arouse a sense of guilt as well as of inferiority. Family life may not have prepared him for school life, or school life may fail to sustain the promises of earlier stages in that nothing he has learned to do well so far seems to count with his fellows or his teacher. And then again, he may be potentially able to excel in ways that are dormant and need to be encouraged now if they are not to be lost.

It is at this point that wider society becomes significant to the child by admitting him to roles preparatory to the actuality of technology and economy. Where he finds out immediately, however, that the color of his skin or the background of his parents rather than his wish and will to learn are the factors that decide his worth as a pupil or apprentice, the human propensity for feeling unworthy may be fatefully aggravated as a determinant of character development.[2]

As with all the stages of development that Erikson describes, this one presents a conflict, the resolution of which may be in one of two directions.

---

[1] Erik Erikson. *Identity, Youth and Crisis.* New York: W. W. Norton & Company, Inc., 1968. P. 124.
[2] *Ibid.*

The sense of inadequacy, in this stage, may be balanced or outweighed by the growing sense of industry—the child's desire to, and ability to, perform various tasks skillfully. Ideally, the child will emerge from this period with a secure sense of his capacity to work at age-appropriate tasks and to show competence in his work as he enters puberty and adolescence.[3]

During middle childhood, the child has a well-established body image and is able to understand, to some extent, the manner in which his body functions. He is able to talk and behave in a reasonably realistic fashion concerning illness when he himself is not ill and when his body is functioning comfortably. On the other hand, children during the latency period continue to be subject to many irrational fears and fantasies about illness and hospitalization. For one thing, they still are in the process of integrating and resolving the dilemmas and conflicts from earlier stages of growth and show residuals of oral, anal, and Oedipal conflicts. These fantasies and feelings will color their experiences as they continue to grow and to meet new situations.

The child of this age is accustomed to being away from home for at least brief periods of time and has become accustomed to being cared for partly by other persons, especially teachers. As a result, the hospitalization experience may not be as traumatic for him as for the toddler, for example. As Robertson points out, it is at the ages of 1 to 3 years that the child is endangered most from psychological trauma by hospitalization and separation from mother.[4]

Older children generally suffer fewer serious illnesses than very young children, with the result that they usually spend only brief periods in the hospital except when they have chronic diseases. However, when any child in this age group does face hospitalization, a complete and honest explanation should be given whenever possible in order to help him cope with the experience.

The verbal skills the child has acquired enable him to understand and express his feelings about illness and incapacitation. The ability to verbalize helps to protect him from the frustration and helplessness experienced by the toddler, who lacks the words to describe his experiences and thoughts.

In spite of good preparation, however, when children are ill, they often regress, showing behavior and attitudes that reflect earlier stages of their lives. They may manifest anxiety, unreasonable fears, preoccupation with their bodies, physical or emotional developmental arrests, and alterations and disturbances in relations with their peers and others.

Throughout childhood, children are inclined to think and react in char-

---

[3] *Op. cit.* P. 125.

[4] James Robertson. *Young Children in Hospital.* London: Tavistock Publications, 1970. P. 87.

acteristic ways, very different at times from the ways in which adults think and react. Because adults do repress many of the experiences, feelings, and thoughts that occurred during their early years, they often have difficulty understanding the way children think. Although nurses frequently work with small children, they too, may be subject to the same kinds of misunderstanding unless they are especially sensitive to the differences between children and adults in think and experiencing.

As far as surgery is concerned, Bergman notes that "any interference with the child's body, whether major or minor, is likely to arouse fantasies and fears with regard to being attacked, mutilated, or deprived of a valuable part of himself." She points out that there is surprisingly little difference whether the intervention is serious or insignificant.[5]

David, an intelligent and healthy nine-year-old patient, sustained a superficial scalp wound while at a summer camp near his home city. He was at a party playing with the other children when he fell against a table edge. Later, he was able to report many of his reactions to his parents, who picked him up at the emergency room of a hospital near the camp, where the wound was easily and quickly sutured by a physician aided by a nurse.

David described how frightened he was when he saw and felt the blood pouring from the wound. He was convinced that he would literally bleed to death. Finally, the bleeding was stopped and he was taken to the hospital. Fortunately, his twelve-year-old brother was with him and joined the counselor on the trip to the hospital.

At the emergency room, he asked if the counselor or his brother could sit with him during the treatment. This request was summarily refused. Then he was taken into the examination room and was placed on a table. At this point, towels were placed over his head and he was covered with a sheet. He described the heat, the loneliness, and his fear that "the doctor was going to cut the top of [his] head off." He said, "I wish that nurse would have held my hand." He recalls no attempts to explain the procedure, only admonitions to be a "big boy."

On the way home, he seemed like a much younger child. He clung to his parents and upon arriving home decided to sleep with his toy leopard, which he had discarded some months before. He talked on and on about the experience and then for days expressed his concern about the removal of the sutures. It was almost a month before the experience began to fade from his consciousness.

A minor accident, a superficial scalp wound, and a rapid surgical repair are routine matters to doctors and nurses, but to a little boy, they are events of great and often lasting significance.

[5] Thesi Bergman with Anna Freud. *Children in Hospital.* New York: International Universities Press, Inc., 1965. P. 136.

Repression in Middle Childhood

One of the truly major achievements of the child is the ability to verbalize, which usually begins during the second year of life. The capacity to attach words to feelings, things, and ideas permits an increasing mastery over the instinctual drives and over the environmental stimuli and objects to which the child must adapt. At first, as we have seen in the previous chapters, the verbalizations of the child tend to reflect his more infantile and primitive thought processes, which seem mostly bound to immediate satisfaction of needs and to the reduction of unpleasant sensations. The child's verbalizations are characterized by illogic, magical thinking, distortions of perception, and attempts to deal with anxiety-producing situations.

With the completion of the Oedipal stage, around the age of 5 or 6, there also appears a major advance in the child's capacity to repress or forget many of the anxiety-producing events of the first years of life. An extraordinary fact is that the first five years of life are largely relegated to the unconscious part of the mind and remain inaccessible to conscious awareness except for isolated events that may be recalled spontaneously.

Under hypnosis, in psychoanalysis, or under other unusual circumstances, these early memories may be recaptured; although even then, most of the events of the first five years of life remain subject to amnesia as a result of repression.

Repression, a basic mental mechanism, was the first to be described by Sigmund Freud, as indicated in Chapter Two where his early discoveries are discussed. Although repression may occur in an inconsistent fashion during the second to the fifth year of life, it is after the age of 5 or 6 that massive repression, or childhood amnesia, occurs. For this reason, reactions to a hospital stay or illness during the first five years of life are largely forgotten, incompletely recalled, or distorted by older children and adults.

These experiences, and the distortions that accompany them, persist unconsciously and continue to exert influence long after they are forgotten. Derivatives of them reappear in personality traits, psychoneurotic symptoms, and relationship patterns and during periods of regression such as dreaming and later illness. Even children during middle childhood show signs of repressing many earlier experiences.

Dr. Holt's study was aimed at determining the recall "of the details of a former hospitalization by 30 children after a five-year interval."[6] All

---

[6] Jacqueline Holt Vandeman. "Discussion of the Method and the Clinical Implications from the Study 'Children's Recall of a Preschool Age Hospital Experience After an Interval of 5 Years.'" *The Research Critique of the Western Interstate Commission for Higher Education.* Vol. 17 (July, 1968). P. 56.

the children had been hospitalized when they were three, four, and five years old. This report not only describes a carefully conceived and carried out nursing research project, but is one of the few such projects that attempt to deal with the psychodynamic aspects of physical illness in children. In keeping with the facts of infantile amnesia, Dr. Holt states:

> The elements missing from the childrens' recall of a former hospital experience were one of the most striking findings of this study. The missing elements seem to cluster around the themes of loneliness, isolation, and separation. . . . The childrens' perception of the hospital appeared as a colorless, stark, blank place containing few people and things.[7]

She notes that the separation theme seemed to be a major recurrent one and felt that the caretaking procedures in the hospital were not only rarely mentioned, but usually experienced as painful and intrusive. She indicates that restriction of activity "was perceived by the children as restraint." Many of the children's memories were neutral or somewhat positive, "being confined to a crib was one of the few negative elements directly verbalized by the children."[8]

She discovered that those children with the most verbal recall of the hospital and illness seemed to understand their disease most completely and seemed most objective about the experience. Interestingly enough, the study found that even though more than half the children said that they knew the name of their illness and why they had been hospitalized, "deeper probing proved only seven children out of the total of thirty had a good understanding of those illnesses." She adds, "This finding indicates the fallacy of parents and hospital personnel assuming, because the child can parrot the name of his illness, he understands the illness or what has happened to him."[9]

Part of the study pointed to the negative influence of illness and hospitalization on the development of a normal body image. Holt found that even children who had chronic diseases requiring repeated treatment, including operations, recalled very little of their hospital experience. "It was as though the whole complex of disease, illness, and hospitalization had been distorted, blocked out, or clouded over."[10]

It was of interest, too, that the families of children who had chronic illnesses considered those children significantly different from the other children in the family. Holt found that "the majority of the mothers of the children in this study saw their children as different from others, and one wonders if this had not contributed to the large number with distorted or age-inappropriate body images." She adds, "Professional health personnel

[7] *Ibid.* P. 67.
[8] *Ibid.* P. 65.
[9] *Ibid.* P. 69.
[10] *Ibid.* P. 70.

need to become more aware of the necessity of relating occurrences that are separated by years in order to understand better the child's current development." [11]

Thus, important experiences of illnesses and hospitalization with the attendant diagnostic and therapeutic procedures can be repressed by children if these events occurred in the first few years of life. However, the forgetting does not mean that the experiences have lost their influence. On the contrary, the lack of ability to remember, verbalize, and thereby master some of the anxiety associated with the event may be a source of considerable conflict throughout childhood and into later life.

One of the bases for severe anxiety and apprehension in adults regarding certain medical procedures is the experience in early childhood of having been ill or having undergone surgery and being unable to remember clearly the events or master the anxiety associated with them.

DISCUSSION OF SELECTED READINGS

The following material is provided to give some guidelines on clinical applications of the previous text material. In the developmental scheme chart by Solnit and Senn the typical behavior for a child in his middle childhood years (5 to 12) is described. Normal parent–child interaction is compared with minimal and extreme psychopathology.

The second article by Carolyn P. Stoll, Assistant Professor of Nursing, University of Michigan School of Nursing, Ann Arbor, describes the hospital experiences of three girls admitted for burn injuries. The article describes the psychologic and behavioral changes involved in their stay. Through the use of patient profiles, Carolyn Stoll describes such responses as regression, anxiety, aggression, and withdrawal. Even though regression is often a necessary part of illness, this response may be disturbing for the staff or the patient to accept.

The author points out that group discussions allowed the nurses the opportunity to assess their methods of coping with patients' problems and she felt that these discussions were as important as other plans for patient care. Group discussions allow problems to be seen from a new vantage point and often solutions can be found once specific problems have been discussed.

DEVELOPMENTAL SCHEMA CHART *
School Age and Pre-Adolescence (5 to 12 years)
Tasks in Process

CHILD	PARENT(S)
To master greater physical prowess.	To help child's emancipation from parents.
To further establish self identity and sex role.	To reinforce self-identification and independence.

* Milton J. E. Senn, M.D., and Albert J. Solnit, M.D., *Problems in Child Behavior and Development*. Philadelphia: Lea and Febiger, 1968.

184   *Middle Childhood*

To work towards greater independence from parents.

To become aware of world-at-large.

To develop peer and other relationships.

To acquire learning, new skills and a sense of industry.

To provide positive pattern of social and sex role behavior.

To acclimatize child to world-at-large.

To facilitate learning, reasoning, communication and experiencing.

To promote wholesome moral and ethical values.

Acceptable Behavioral Characteristics

CHILD

General good health, greater body competence, acute sensory perception.

Pride and self confidence; less dependence on parents.

Better impulse control.

Ambivalence re dependency, separation and new experiences.

Accepts own sex role; psychosexual expression in play and fantasy.

Equates parents with peers and other adults.

Aware of natural world (life, death, birth, science); subjective but realistic about world.

Competitive but well organized in play; enjoys peer interaction.

Regard for collective obedience to social laws, rules and fair play.

Explores environment; school and neighborhood basic to social-learning experience.

Cognition advancing; intuitive thinking; advancing to concrete operational level; responds to learning.

Speech becomes reasoning and expressive tool; thinking still egocentric.

PARENT(S)

Ambivalent towards child's separation but encourage independence.

Mixed feelings about parent-surrogates but help child to accept them.

Encourage child to participate outside the home.

Set appropriate model of social and ethical behavior and standards.

Take pleasure in child's developing skills and abilities.

Understand and cope with child's behavior.

Find other gratifications in life (activity, employment).

Are supportive towards child as required.

Minimal Psychopathology

CHILD

Anxiety and oversensitivity to new experiences (school, relationships, separation).

PARENT(S)

Disinclination to separate from child; or prematurely hastening separation.

Signs of despondency, apathy, hostility.

Lack of attentiveness; learning difficulties, disinterest in learning.

Acting out: lying, stealing, temper outbursts; inappropriate social behavior.

Regressive behavior (wetting, soiling, crying, fears).

Appearance of compulsive mannerisms (tics, rituals).

Somatic illness: eating and sleeping problems, aches, pains, digestive upsets.

Fear of illness and body injury.

Difficulties and rivalry with peers, siblings, adults; constant fighting.

Destructive tendencies strong; temper tantrums.

Inability or unwillingness to do things for self.

Moodiness and withdrawal; few friends or personal relationships.

Foster fears, dependence, apprehension.

Disinterested in or rejecting of child.

Overly critical and censuring; undermine child's confidence.

Inconsistent in discipline or control; erratic in behavior.

Offer a restrictive, overly moralistic model.

Extreme Psychopathology

CHILD

Extreme withdrawal, apathy, depression, self-destructive tendencies.

Complete failure to learn. Speech difficulty, especially stuttering.

Extreme and uncontrollable anti-social behavior, (aggression, destruction, chronic lying, stealing, intentional cruelty to animals).

Severe obsessive-compulsive behavior (probias, fantasies, rituals).

Inability to distinguish reality from fantasy.

Excessive sexual exhibitionism, eroticism, sexual assaults on others.

Extreme somatic illness: failure to thrive, anorexia, obesity, hypochondriasis, abnormal menses.

Complete absence or deterioration of personal and peer relationships.

PARENT(S)

Extreme depression and withdrawal; rejection of child.

Intense hostility; aggression towards child.

Uncontrollable fears, anxieties, guilts.

Complete inability to function in family role.

Severe moralistic prohibition of child's independent strivings.

Responses of Three Girls to Burn Injuries and Hospitalization
by Carolyn P. Stoll, R.N., M.N.Ed.*

Not all children evidence psychologic sequelae as a result of hospitalization. The burn-injured child, however, seems particularly vulnerable to the stresses of treatment, and personality disturbances have frequently been attributed to hospitalization or to the injury itself.[1, 2, 3, 4]

Burn injuries are sudden and frequently critical. There is no time for preparation of the child for frightening treatments and a strange hospital environment. During the first few days following admission to the ward, the child is usually cooperative and appreciative of all aspects of care. Subsequently, however, the pattern changes, and the child becomes irritable and demanding, causing considerable concern and frustration for the nursing staff. Management appears to be more difficult because of psychologic problems arising from the child's feelings about his injury and the treatment procedures involved. He often sees doctors and nurses as punitive persons because of their part in painful dressing changes, baths, and operative procedures.

Reactions of aggression, regression, and depression have been noted to occur throughout hospitalization, and feelings of sadness and abandonment may result from lengthy separation from parents and families.[5] Fears of death persist for long periods and there may be exaggerated fear of disfigurement and crippling.[6]

* Nursing Clinics of North America. W. B. Saunders and Company, Vol. 4, No. 1 (March, 1969). Pp. 77–87.

[1] R. T. Long and Oliver Cope. "Emotional Problems of Burned Children." New England Journal of Medicine. Vol. 264 (June, 1961). 1121–23.

[2] Joan M. Woodward. "Parental Visiting of Children with Burns." British Medical Journal. Vol. 2 (December, 1962). 1656–57.

[3] ———. "Emotional Disturbances of Burned Children." British Medical Journal. Vol. 1 (April, 1950). 1009–13.

[4] D. A. Hamburg, Beatrix Hamburg, and Sidney deGoza. "Adaptive Problems and Mechanisms in Severely Burned Patients. Psychiatry. Vol. 16 (February, 1953). 1–20.

[5] Long and Cope. "Emotional Problems of Burned Children."

[6] Aldo Vigliano, L. W. Hart, and Frances Singer. "Psychiatric Sequelae of Old Burns in Children and Their Parents." Orthopsychiatry. Vol. 34 (July, 1964). 753–61.

Treatment and Nursing Care
of Three Patients

This study of the reactions of three young girls to burn injuries and treatment was done while the writer functioned as a clinical specialist on a surgery ward at Babies and Childrens Hospital, Cleveland. The girls sustained second- and third-degree burns and were hospitalized for approximately the same period of time. The body areas of their burns were markedly similar. Except for a brief time when Furacin and silver nitrate dressings were used, all of the girls were treated with Sulfamylon acetate cream,[7] daily baths, and physical therapy. All of the girls were maintained on Foster frames although one was able to be transferred to a regular bed several weeks prior to discharge.

Care for the girls during the early weeks of hospitalization included intravenous fluid therapy, urinary catheter drainage, antibiotics, Sulfamylon cream, frequent vital signs, and rotation of frames every two to four hours. All of the girls were noted to have brief periods of confusion and disorientation during this early phase of illness. It was necessary for two nurses to be in constant attendance in order to provide observation and care required by the four girls in a partitioned area.

Tub baths were instituted in the first week of care and were initially carried out on the unit by a team of nursing and physical therapy personnel. A whirlpool agitator was placed in the tub to assist in the removal of the hardened Sulfamylon cream from the body. After six to eight weeks the girls were well enough to be transported to the physical therapy department for baths in a Hubbard tank.

Sulfamylon cream was applied liberally to all burned areas following baths, and to denuded areas whenever needed. The cream had the consistency of soft butter, was often very difficult to apply, and appeared to be very irritating to the children for a period of 10 to 20 minutes following application. No clothing or linen was permitted to come in contact with areas to which the cream had been applied. Cradles were used to keep sheets from touching the girls' bodies and only one sheet previously impregnated with the Sulfa cream was permitted to cover the frame. (As treatment progressed, a large dressing pad with the cream was placed between the body and the frame.) The girls frequently complained of being cold even though blankets were placed on top of the cradles, and cast dryers were used to provide additional warmth in the air. As areas of grafting increased, the girls did not experience the intense chilling noted in the

---

[7] Sulfamylon acetate cream is produced by Winthrop Laboratories. It was instituted for investigation and evaluation in the treatment of burn patients by Dr. Robert Miller at Babies and Childrens Hospital. The compound will be manufactured commercially following approval of the Food and Drug Administration.

first months of care. Initially the girls were not permitted to wear clothing at any time. Later, as precautions were relaxed, special tent-like gowns were allowed for ambulation.

All of the girls received both homografts and autografts during their hospitalization. From the time of admission, sedatives and analgesics appeared to be of little value for relief of pain and apprehension during debridement and treatment periods.

The writer gave direct care to the girls for one to three hours a day, five days a week, for a period of four months. Frequent conferences were held with the nursing staff and a multidisciplinary team to plan and evaluate care for the girls.

Patient Profiles

SUSIE

Susie, a thin, energetic, 5-year-old white girl was burned when plastic drapes being worn for "dress-ups" were accidentally ignited by her teasing brother. Susie's mother applied lard to all of the burned areas before taking her to a nearby hospital. She was immediately transferred to Babies and Childrens Hospital where her injuries were estimated as second- and third-degree burns covering 50 per cent of her body. Following six days of treatment with silver nitrate wet dressings, her therapy was changed to applications of Sulfamylon cream. Susie underwent three procedures for autografts and two for homografts. She remained in the hospital for 146 days.

Susie was one of five children of a lower income family residing 150 miles from the hospital. Her parents did not visit frequently although her father would stay for two consecutive days every three or four weeks. Both parents were very quiet and seemingly uncomfortable in the hospital setting. The mother demonstrated a flat affect and was known to have had a mental illness three years previously. The father showed considerable warmth and sensitivity toward Susie and his apprehension about her condition was clearly evident.

JENNY

Jenny was an amiable, talkative white girl of 9 years of age who was injured while attempting to burn the trash. She was treated with Furacin dressings at her home hospital and transferred to Babies and Childrens Hospital five days following her injury. She had sustained second- and third-degree burns of approximately 40 per cent of her body, and portions of the burned areas were infected. Sulfamylon therapy was instituted on the second day of her hospitalization, which totaled 139 days. Jenny underwent four procedures with anesthesia: one for debridement and three for autografting. Homografts were applied twice without anesthesia.

Jenny came from a family of fifteen children. Four siblings died in early childhood and a sister was born during Jenny's hospitalizations. Both of Jenny's parents had multiple health problems. Her father was unable to work and minimal income was provided by welfare agencies. In spite of their poverty and a driving distance of 100 miles, Jenny's family visited frequently and remained for long periods. They demonstrated genuine concern for their daughter as well as the other burned children on the unit.

DORIS

Doris was a shy, attractive Negro girl of 6 years of age. She was injured when her dress caught fire on a hot plate being used to heat the room. Doris was admitted to Babies and Childrens Hospital two hours following her injury, having first been taken to an emergency room of another hospital in the city. Her injuries were diagnosed as second- and third-degree burns of 30 per cent of her body. She was treated with Furacin dressings for two days after which Sulfamylon therapy was instituted and continued for the remainder of her hospitalization of 105 days. Doris underwent two grafting procedures, one for homografts and one for autografts. Both procedures necessitated anesthesia.

Doris had nine siblings who were all healthy. Her mother was a very quiet, gentle woman who had a severe hearing defect. She was able to read lips on some occasions and frequently responded with an inappropriate smile when she did not understand conversations. She commented that initially her husband blamed her for the accident and she feared that other people did too. She appeared to be a warm and loving mother and usually visited four or five times each week. Doris's father visited about once a week and was described as reserved but concerned about his daughter.

Responses to Burn Injury and Treatment

ANXIETY

As one might expect, anxiety was by far the most common and pronounced response of the girls to their injuries and treatment. Fears of death, mutilation, pain, and abandonment were major sources of anxiety and were evident in varying degrees during at least three months of the recovery period.

Fear of death was probably the most outstanding fear presented by the girls. They repeatedly asked if they would get better and occasionally voiced fear that they would never get to go home. During the first critical week of Susie's hospitalization, her mother constantly sat beside her and frequently asked loudly if Susie would die. Although cautioned to refrain from this type of question in front of Susie, she was unable to do so. All of the parents verbalized fear that their children would die and their anxiety was readily conveyed to the children.

Susie, in particular, had difficulty in sleeping and often begged for someone to remain with her at night. Late in her convalescence she revealed some meaningful thoughts about sleep. She dramatically described the way in which she had been burned and the manner in which she had been taken to the hospital, as follows:

> . . . and then my daddy wrapped me up and took me to the hospital and he wouldn't let me go to sleep, but he told me not to go to sleep or I wouldn't wake up . . . and he kept waking me up.

The hospital did not have a special area designated as a burn unit and therefore the girls were placed in an enclosure that was only partially partitioned from the rest of the ward. A fourth girl, Tina, who was more seriously burned, was also situated in this same enclosure. The nature of treatment for all four girls was identical and understandably they constantly compared their progress with one another. During the fourth week of care Tina died suddenly. Although she collapsed while sitting in full view of the other three girls, death actually occurred behind closed curtains after Doris and Jenny had been removed from the room. The staff did not discuss Tina's absence with the three girls and they were reported to have had a restless night. In the morning, following an explanation of Tina's death, Jenny commented: "I told my dad she was dead, but nobody said anything so I didn't ask the nurse. I saw her drop in the chair." Doris later stated softly, "I know she died, my sister told me." Susie stared with wide eyes and said nothing although she voiced fear of sleeping alone. Tina's death was discussed with Susie on several occasions thereafter as her withdrawn behavior seemed to indicate fears and concerns about death, but she was still unable to verbalize her feelings. Interestingly, three months later when Tina's name came up in a conversation, Susie talked freely of Tina's death with the following comments:

> I saw her all the time—they put things on her neck—all the people came and they had machines and tubes and they put them on her neck—and they put the oxygen tent on her—and she was bleeding—and they ran back and forth—and she didn't ever come back.

Susie appeared to perceive the danger of death but she did not appear to have advanced beyond the level of prelogical thinking. She seemed to have little understanding of relations of causality or the concept of finality of death. Late in her recovery, Susie asked if Tina were staying at another hospital and when she was coming back.

A severely burned 6-month-old infant died ten days following the death of Tina. Death occurred four days after her admission to the unit. The girls were given truthful explanations regarding the infant's critical condition, treatment, and subsequently her death. Doris expressed concern that the nurses did not feed the infant by bottle; however, in general, the girls asked very few questions about the infant, which seemed to indicate the fear and threat felt by them in the situation.

A superstition about death presented stress to Jenny some months later. By chance her bed was moved to the position where Tina and the small infant had died. Following a very restless night, Jenny admitted:

It's spooky—this is where two people died—right on this spot! In West Virginia, they believe that if you stand on the spot where somebody died, they'll come back to get you! I was scared that those kids would get me. I couldn't sleep all night.

The girls had an unusual experience with death. Midway through their hospitalization period the head nurse, who had worked closely with the girls, was killed in an auto accident. The girls discussed the accident freely and Jenny perceptively told of her observations regarding the sadness apparent in the nurses at this time.

Fear of mutilation was constantly apparent and was a major cause of anxiety for the girls. During and following baths, blood oozed from their burned areas. As the covering of Sulfamylon cream dissolved in the water, superficial blood vessels, damaged by the burns, bled freely. The bleeding would continue for three to five minutes following the bath, usually necessitating the application of light pressure. On several occasions it was necessary to suture small blood vessels on Susie's chest, buttocks, and back. All of the girls screamed hysterically while staring wildly at the bleeding, always refusing to look away. Unfortunately, when bleeding occurred in the tub, the appearance of blood-stained water suggested a far greater blood loss than was actual, which further magnified the girls' fears. Explanations and reassurance were seldom heard because of the uncontrolled screaming during the procedure. After repeated discussions, Susie and Jenny verbalized that they feared that the bleeding would never be stopped.

Debridement periods evoked marked anxiety and screaming in all of the girls. Efforts to maintain reverse isolation precautions necessitated that all treatments be carried out in the small enclosure on the unit, so the girls were exposed to each other at this difficult time. The children were terrified of the debridement periods even though they could later state that the experience had not really been painful. It appeared that they feared that the doctor was removing healthy skin rather than dead tissue. It also seemed that they were afraid their bodies would fall away when the skin was gone. Susie cried, "He's [the doctor] taking my skin off . . . don't let him pull it off, he's hurting my skin . . . it won't hold together!" All of the girls received blood transfusions and seemed to understand the need for blood replacement, which contributed further to their fear of bleeding. Late in the recovery period, the girls continued to show considerable anxiety whenever minimal bleeding occurred.

Fear of crippling and disfigurement contributed to the girls' level of anxiety. Susie declared that she knew that she would never be able to stand and walk with her legs straight. She felt certain that girls who could not straighten their legs could never go to school or play outside. The staff inadvertently reinforced fears of crippling when they stressed the need for exercises to prevent contractures. Jenny talked about the ugliness of the burned areas and expressed gratefulness that she wouldn't have scars on her face.

Susie showed pronounced *fear of abandonment*. Her parents' visits were infrequent and they made no attempt to phone or write. Reassurances that her parents loved her and could not visit because of the long distance from her home brought about reactions of anger and doubt. When her father did stay for weekends, he usually left while Susie slept without telling her so that he would be spared the anguish of her sobs protesting his departure.

Feelings of *guilt* related to the actual burn incident caused a considerable increase in Jenny's anxiety. Upon admission to the unit, when Jenny was asked how her accident occurred, she hung her head and softly murmured, "I was playing with matches!" She often referred to her behavior as having been "bad" and "wrong" and acknowledged that her burns were punishment for not minding her parents. Doris became very silent when the others talked about their accidents and her replies were not audible when other children asked her how she had been burned. Susie was quick to blame her brother for causing her injuries and at one time saw him from the window of the hospital and shouted, "You just wait—I'll get you when I get out!"

Grafting procedures were generally viewed positively as they were equated with improvement in the appearance and the condition of the injured areas. There seemed to be visible relief when increased areas were covered, and Jenny demonstrated a marked change in affect following her first autografting procedure. She became much more talkative and social and seemed much more aware of her surroundings. Although the operative days were frightening, reactions of the girls did not seem extreme. Days following grafting procedures were thought to be desirable because baths, exercises, and ambulation activities were omitted for a temporary period. In all instances Negro skin was used for homografts. While waiting to be called for surgery one day, Jenny expressed concern over the use of "dark skin." She repeatedly requested reassurance that the dark skin would never stay on permanently.

Fear of pain produced by tub baths and application of Sulfamylon cream evoked considerable crying and screaming prior to the activity. Immersion in water appears to cause sensations of intense pain and stinging for burn patients and Sulfamylon is reported to cause brief periods of discomfort immediately following contact. Initially the girls cried and complained of "burning" during both procedures; however as time progressed, their reactions before, during, and following these activities were extreme, with periods of hysterical screaming for as long as 20 minutes following cream applications. Soon, even preparation for baths and cream application brought about marked apprehension and crying. Because cream application had to be completed in the enclosure during the early stages of treatment, cries from one child would cause considerable apprehension in the others. It appeared that fear and apprehension were responsible for the hysterical reaction rather than the actual pain experienced.

Susie's feelings regarding the tubbing procedures were demonstrated in play interviews on two occasions. She would take the little girl doll and repeatedly push it under the water in the doll tub. She then angrily said to the doll, "There, now I've got you under the water and you can't come out 'til I let you." She then looked up and said, "She doesn't like it." On the next occasion she talked about how much the doll screamed when she was in the bathtub.

Independent behavior with active participation in treatment procedures was encouraged. As might have been expected, Doris was the first to assist with her own cream applications and eventually was able to take over this activity completely. Susie progressed to assisting with partial application of cream. Jenny never wished to apply her own cream but eventually took full responsibility for removal of the cream as well as portions of dead tissue during her whirlpool baths.

REGRESSION

Regression was a major defense mechanism for all of the girls at some period in their treatment. Susie was noted to have a more intensified reaction in this area than the other two girls. Probable factors contributing to her increased regression were: (1) her youth, (2) the severity of her burns, and (3) the long periods of separation from her parents and family.

Shortly after admission Susie returned to more immature behavior such as thumbsucking (even though her thumb and hands were edematous, cracking, and bleeding), and voiding and defecating on her frame. Tooth grinding became pronounced during sleep. Susie frequently exhibited her anger with her family and the staff by soiling. She had stools during her bath on several occasions and usually on her frame when immobilized for long periods. She began to speak in a whisper and avoided normal voice tones for one month, except when experiencing pain. Later in her hospital stay, Susie could verbalize her anger with her parents for leaving her in the hospital. Occasionally she refused to eat although she rarely refused fluids.

Regression exhibited by Jenny included long periods of whimpering, crying, and generally demanding behavior. Refusal to eat was common in the early weeks of her treatment; however, her appetite became insatiable during the later recovery period.

Doris demonstrated regression in bowel and bladder control, although such occasions were infrequent. Refusal to eat and comply with simple requests was frequently noted in the first two weeks of her hospitalization.

It should be emphasized that the nature of burn injuries and their treatment imposes enforced dependency upon these patients. Although ambulation was begun in the early weeks of care, tolerance to activity was minimal at first and the girls were confined to frames for the major portion of the day. They were not even permitted to turn themselves from an anterior to posterior position for several weeks. Thus, continued dependency and regression was unavoidably fostered in the acute phase of care.

AGGRESSION

Display of aggression was usually confined to treatment procedures and appeared to be a response to overwhelming apprehension and frustration. Aggression was generally verbal; however, Doris actively kicked and hit at personnel during her first week in the hospital. Susie often directed her anger at the personnel during treatments by shouting loudly, "I hate you!" "I hate you!" throughout an entire procedure which might be 30 minutes in duration.

Motility offered by ambulation and occupational therapy activities appeared to provide a necessary outlet for tensions and anxiety, and seemed instrumental in reducing aggression. An advantage of the Sulfamylon cream was that such therapy allowed the girls to ambulate as soon as parental fluid therapy was discontinued and cumbersome dressings were not used.

WITHDRAWAL

Withdrawal was demonstrated by all of the girls for varying lengths of time. Jenny tended to become easily depressed if her parents failed to visit for two or three days. She would become very quiet, eat very little, and object to ambulation. On one occasion her depression appeared to be related to the fear that her parents no longer loved her, as was revealed in the following statement: "My father doesn't want me home because I'll soil the sheets" (soiling referred to oozing serum mixed with the treatment cream). "Maybe they won't ever want me to come home!"

Doris and Susie also appeared to withdraw in response to long separations from their parents. For Susie, however, there appeared to be the added component of her anger with the staff and with herself for losing control during tub baths in physical therapy.

NURSING STAFF REACTIONS

Although intensity of the response of the nursing staff varied with the individual, all of the nurses voiced anger and frustration with the girls' behavior at some time. On several occasions the writer found it necessary to leave the girls temporarily to control anger aroused by their behavior. Certainly the most difficult task for the nurses was the application of the Sulfamylon cream. Feelings of helplessness experienced during this painful procedure produced extreme frustration and, often, exhaustion among the staff. Group discussions of the nurses' manner of coping with the patient's screams, aggression, and regression were as valuable as were discussions of plans for patient care.

In conclusion, it appeared that the reactions of these three girls were similar to reactions of burn children reported in the literature. Sulfamylon cream, however, appeared to afford opportunities for earlier ambulation and motility, thus lessening the severity of these reactions. Assessment of individual patient responses and coping strength offered a valuable and necessary approach to nursing care.

chapter six

ADOLESCENCE

A major task in becoming an adult is the development of a sense of identity. The child slowly evolves a frame of reference from which he views the rapidly changing, often chaotic world. The adolescent faces many new demands: independence from his family, the need to integrate his new-found sexual maturity, the establishment of meaningful and working relationships with peers of both sexes, and decisions regarding his life work and goals.

With the onset of adolescence, major psychological, social, and biological changes begin. Normal adolescent development does not occur on a smooth continuum. New situations are often challenging to the adolescent and may be viewed with anxiety. There are sometimes sudden and intense romantic attachments, unexpected aggressive outbursts, heightened involvement in school activities, and increased group involvement. Even in healthy adolescents, this may be a time of considerable turmoil. This turmoil at times aggravates or initiates psychological symptoms and leads to behavioral problems.

Adolescence refers to those psychosocial and physical maturation processes that are initiated by puberty and that end with the attainment of young adulthood. Although the terms adolescence and *puberty* have often been used interchangeably, more recent usage defines puberty primarily as the onset of physical changes that begin to occur in girls between the ages of 10 and 12, and in boys between the ages of 12 and 16. The hormonal changes and growth that occur during the period of puberty are gradual, and there is considerable individual variation. The age of the onset of puberty may be affected to some extent by culture, geography, and the socioeconomic level of the individual as well as by inborn factors.

Many physiological and anatomical changes accompany puberty; for example, development of primary and secondary sex characteristics and changes in weight, height, muscular development, and body proportions. Changes also will occur in the adolescent's coordination and strength. For some adolescents, these changes will be rapid, occurring in a period of one or two years; in others, the rate of growth may extend to five or six years. Rapid growth may produce psychological problems for the adolescent, who must learn to cope with much change quickly.

The onset of puberty and adolescence is never sudden, although it sometimes may appear this way to parents as well as to the child himself. A period of one to three years prior to the onset of puberty is referred to as the *prepubertal* or *early adolescent* period.

This phase includes the changes in physical development characterized by the beginning of puberty. Social and psychological attitudes, however, remain similar to those of the latency child until a year or more after puberty sets in. The second stage of *mid-adolescence* is characterized by the more marked alterations in behavior considered typical of the teen years. There is increased interest in sexual exploration, rebellion against parental authority, and involvement and conformity with peer groups.

Late adolescence marks a turn toward more adult concerns such as career, marriage, and parenthood. There is a consolidation of the personality and a beginning sense of identity as a mature person.

Some adolescents greet oncoming sexual maturity with a positive attitude, and seem prepared to accept the physical as well as the psychological concomitants of their growth. These are the youngsters who are most likely to experience relatively trouble-free early adolescence.

Other children are emotionally unprepared for pubertal changes and try to deny them and to go on living as if nothing had occurred.

While many youngsters fall into the "neurotic" group, the majority of young people fall somewhere between the extremes of acceptance and rejection of adolescence. They neither have a smooth, asymptomatic adolescence, nor are chronically disturbed and emotionally upset. In an article entitled "Adolescence," Anna Freud writes on the subject of normal adolescence. She says:

> Adolescence is by its nature an interruption of peaceful growth and . . . the upholding of a steady equilibrium in the adolescence process is in itself abnormal. Once we accept for adolescence disharmony within the psychic structure as our basic fact, understanding becomes easier.[1]

[1] Anna Freud. "Adolescence." *Psychoanalytic Study of the Child.* Vol. 13 (1958). Pp. 255–78.

Adolescence is one of the critical periods in life in which severe disturbances may occur and pass over or persist as permanent emotional disorders.

Adolescence in general is characterized by some emotional instability, with occasional outbursts of tears, anger, and impulsive behavior alternating with compliant, docile, and loving behavior. During later adolescence, the young person begins to assume more adult responsibilities and manifests increased control of his impulses. Prepubertal anxieties, with their sexual and aggressive conflicts, begin to yield to a growing biological (and especially hormonal) stability and to new-found ego capacities, which in turn increasingly control the sexual and aggressive impulses.

The conflicts that most adolescents suffer from are derived from several sources. Physical changes are often rapid and unsettling, especially for girls during the establishment of menstrual regularity. The upsurge of sexual feelings that accompanies the onset of menses in girls and the genital changes in boys arouses in them echoes of conflicts about sexuality which existed during the Oedipal stage. Parents and siblings remain primary objects of sexual and aggressive impulses, as was the case in early childhood. However, now the boy or girl is faced with the fact of oncoming sexual maturity and physical strength, which permits equality with or superiority to parents who once seemed unassailable because of their size and strength.

The maturation of the sexual organs leads to increased sexual drive, which stimulates sexual daydreams and wishes. Nocturnal emissions, often accompanied by erotic dreams, begin to occur in boys, and both boys and girls may seek sexual outlet through masturbation.

Nocturnal emissions (the involuntary discharge of semen during sleep), which is a normal occurrence for adolescent boys, can nevertheless be fraught with embarrassment and guilt. In addition, boys often have unexpected erections. These events at first may cause the adolescent boy to feel helpless and not in control of his body. Old feelings of shame and anxiety about bedwetting may be temporarily revived by the nocturnal emissions.

In spite of widespread education about masturbation, many youngsters experience painful feelings of guilt and anxiety because of the conscious and unconscious fantasies associated with it. Moreover, the adolescent, in resolving his infantile ties with his family, often has overt or thinly disguised sexual feelings and fantasies about parents or siblings. Such feelings can produce considerable uneasiness and remorse.

False ideas and unreasonable fears pertaining to masturbation persist. For example, some boys fear that the act will render them less potent as adults. Another common fear is that masturbation, especially "excessive" masturbation, will cause acne, nervousness, or even mental illness. While it is true that compulsive masturbation may be a distressing symptom of emotional conflict, the act of masturbation itself does not produce any physical or mental disorder.

Adolescence   199

The adolescent's need for strenuous physical activity, intense peer group social interaction, and constant distraction may at least partially represent maneuvers in the battle against the temptation to masturbate when he is alone. Blos notes:

> Masturbatory activity may appear in displaced form without genital manipulation or sexual phantasy: these cases remind us of a host of masturbation equivalents involving other body parts or compulsive hand-object manipulation. Scratching, nose-picking, cuticle tearing, nail biting, hair twisting, pencil chewing, endless play with rubber bands or other objects; all these activities can be considered masturbatory equivalents.[2]

Freud's "Three Essays on the Theory of Sexuality," published in 1905, provided the first scientific explanation of autoerotic activities and their origin.[3] In the essay on infantile sexuality, Freud pointed out that the child has feelings of pleasure in various parts of the body starting at birth, and that autoerotic behavior begins in infancy as the baby strives to duplicate pleasurable feelings it has experienced. Freud noted that the infant becomes aware of its sex organs through sensations produced by urination, and also through the washing and rubbing to which it is subjected in the course of being bathed and cleaned by the mother. This essay marks the beginning of an enlightened attitude toward masturbation and other manifestations of sexuality in childhood, but it took nearly forty years before Freudian-oriented psychiatrists were able to influence their medical colleagues to rewrite medical textbooks.

The onset of menstruation is usually the definitive sign of the beginning of puberty in girls. When her regular menstrual cycle is established, the girl tends to become more stable and to achieve better integration and organization of her personality. She is confirmed as a woman. Girls who have unresolved psychological problems related to accepting the role of a woman may express them in connection with this function. The age of the onset of menstruation is important: If it occurs too early, the child may be upset, yet if it does not occur until 15 or 16 years of age, the failure to menstruate may be equally distressing.

Unfortunately menstruation may be experienced as a "curse" to be suffered or a burden to be borne. The influence of social, family, and peer attitudes about menstruation on the girl's attitudes is great. Primitive taboos about the shamefulness, dirtiness, or dangerousness of this normal function may lead to apprehension and anxiety in young girls and women. Such atti-

[2] Peter Blos. *On Adolescence: A Psychoanalytic Interpretation.* New York: The Free Press, 1962. P. 163.
[3] Sigmund Freud. "Three Essays on the Theory of Sexuality" from *The Standard Edition of The Complete Works of Sigmund Freud.* Translated by James Strachey in collaboration with Anna Freud. Vol. 7. London: Hogarth Press, Ltd., 1953.

tudes and reactions can exert an unfavorable influence on the girl's later acceptance of her feminine roles as well as on her overall self-esteem.

Physical discomfort is quite frequent during the establishment of regular menses, and sometimes the dysmenorrhea continues sporadically throughout adolescence. In addition to irregular menses girls may experience tension, cramps, backaches, headaches, anorexia, and weakness with their menstrual periods.

If the girl is prepared poorly or if she has conflicts about her femininity dating from her earlier years, she may react negatively to menstruation and to physical symptoms accompanying it. Menstrual bleeding for some of these girls may represent unconscious "proof" that they have been genitally mutilated or wounded. While few girls would think this at a conscious level, such fantasies may be revived by the menstrual flow and may play a part in the girl's reaction to her menstrual cycle. Kestenberg notes that adolescents who suffer with menstruation and attach fearful fantasies to it are unable to accept or retain clear explanation:

The onset of menstruation makes it possible for the girl to differentiate reality from fantasy. What she knew and what she anticipated can now be compared with how it happened to her. The sharpness of the experience, the regularity of it, the well-defined way of taking care of it, the sameness of the experience as compared with her anticipation of it all provide release. It helps the girl structuralize her inner and outer experiences.[4]

Regularity of menstrual flow helps to foreshadow steady progress in ego organization. A mother who treats menstruation as a shameful experience (a curse), and does not foster pride in growing up and being a woman, disrupts a girl's emotional development. Societal or masculine attitudes that disparage women's sexuality can also contribute to feminine self-depreciation.

Parental attitudes toward physical and sexual matters are of great significance in determining the smoothness with which the adolescent adapts to his physical changes. If the parents' reactions are defensive, confused, or guilt-ridden, the child must turn to peers or to other sources for information and support. For these reasons the nurse should be educationally and emotionally equipped to respond to the needs of adolescents who may consult her for advice and counsel about the physical and psychological occurrences of the adolescent years.

Many adolescents secretly worry about being homosexual because, from time to time, they are aware of homosexual thoughts and impulses. "Crushes" on members of the same sex are not unusual during this de-

---

[4] Judith Kestenberg. *Adolescents, A Psychoanalytic Approach to Problems and Therapy.* Sandor Lorand, M.D., and Henry Schneer, M.D., eds. New York: Harper & Row, Publishers, 1961. P. 34.

velopmental stage. Overt homosexual practices are not uncommon in early adolescence, especially among boys. Kinsey reports that many adolescent boys engage in homosexual activities and that such experiences rarely interfere with normal heterosexual development.[5]

Girls appear to be more fearful of homosexual activity. A pair of girls may be involved in breast play, and less frequently in mutual masturbation. Where sex play occurs among girls it usually involves a pair, seldom a group.

Independence from the Nuclear Family

When family life is not harmonious and demands are unrealistic or excessive, the adolescent may need help from others to work out the physical and emotional problems that interfere with normal adjustment. Fortunately, most problems arising during adolescence are handled more or less effectively within the family. Rebellious behavior exhibited by the teenager may or may not upset the family balance, depending on the inherent strength of the family. Family strengths include a stable marriage, consistent forms of child rearing, open communication, clearly defined roles, a flexible and understanding attitude about sexuality, and the capacity to set reasonable limits on aggressive behavior.

The direction of adolescent growth is clearly toward emancipation from the family. At adolescence, the interaction of parents and child is conditioned by their mutual knowledge of the child's eventual departure. One of the essential tasks of parents is to help their child leave them without causing him to feel that he is either abandoned or an abandoner. The period begins with the child almost entirely dependent on his family, needing its say-so for what he can and cannot do; still tied to parents emotionally; still clinging to their ideas and ideals. It ends with the child reaching into adulthood—freer to make up his own mind about what he will and will not do, about his own beliefs and values—and, if need be, looking elsewhere than the family for love and support.

Adolescence is a preparatory stage of life in our culture, a stage before being an adult, with many responsibilities and much competition. It is primarily a time of learning social, intellectual, physical, and mechanical skills and of acquiring psychological and emotional awareness and maturity.

This learning takes time, so the adolescent's departure from home is gradual. Usually, in early adolescence the child continues to live at home, but situates his interests and emotions in the world of peers.

[5] Alfred Kinsey, Wardel Pomeroy, and Coyde Martin. *Sexual Behavior in the Human Male.* Philadelphia: W. B. Saunders Company, 1948. Pp. 320–21.

In primitive societies, duties and responsibilities are fixed and traditional. Therefore, preparation for adult life is usually easier. In those cultures where pubertal boys and girls take on adult roles, adolescent problems either do not exist or are minor. Instead, puberty signals the beginning of adult life. In industrialized, modern societies like ours, however, the young person often requires many more years of dependency to learn the skills to equip him for his role in society.

Peter Blos, in his work *On Adolescence, A Psychoanalytic Interpretation*, writes:

> There is no societal agreement in western culture as to the age at which an individual ceases to be a child, or ceases to be an adolescent, and becomes an adult. The age definition of maturity has varied at different times, and it varies today in different localities.[6]

During the late 1920s and early 1930s, a number of systematic anthropological field studies of primitive societies opened a new area of thinking about personality development—the socialization process in human instincts. Two books by Margaret Mead, *Coming of Age in Samoa* and *Growing Up in New Guinea,* discuss this period.[7]

In Samoa, the child follows a relatively continuous growth pattern. Young persons see birth and death near their home, and many have seen a partly developed fetus, the opening of dead bodies, and occasional glimpses of sex activities. The child is not considered basically different from the adult. Sex is not repressed or inhibited by society but is considered natural and pleasurable. Homosexuality, promiscuity, and other sexual activities which, because of their social and moral stigma, divert emotional development toward neuroses in American society, or may result in an unsatisfactory marriage, are seen as relatively harmless in Samoa. They are considered simply "play," and are without moral weight. In Samoan society, most sexual experiences follow a gradual, continuous line of development without severe interruptions, interferences, or restrictions. By contrast, in Western society many experiences approved for adults are restricted or forbidden for children.

In Samoa, girls only six or seven years old are sometimes responsible for caring for and disciplining younger siblings. Thus, each girl is socialized and develops responsibility by early involvement in family duties. The boys at an early age learn the simple tasks of reef fishing and canoeing; the girls, after they are released from their duties as nursemaids for their younger brothers and sisters, work on plantations and help carry food for the village. No basic change takes places during the adolescent period; the degree of

---

[6] Blos. *Op. cit.* P. 10.
[7] Margaret Mead. *Coming of Age in Samoa.* New York: Morran, 1928. P. 62. *Growing Up in New Guinea.* New York: Apollo, 1962.

responsibility increases and the quality of the work increases as the child grows stronger and matures. In our society, especially in urban and suburban communities, the shift from nonresponsible play to responsible work usually occurs rather suddenly during adolescence. Frequently, this shift is a part of adolescent conflict.

After pointing to some of the variations between cultures and indicating the problems with which adolescents are faced in American society, the Group for the Advancement of Psychiatry writes:

> It should now be clear that some of the manifestations of adolescents are not only specific to, but are partially caused by, the culture. Comparative and anthropological considerations are useful to give perspective, to alert us to the arbitrariness and contingency of much of our cultural handling of adolescence, and even to offer possible alternatives and modifications. The biology of puberty is universal, but human reactions to puberty always occur within a particular culture, and adolescence becomes fully intelligible only through an awareness and understanding of the culture which surrounds it.[8]

The problems of adolescence then, as we define them, are essentially those of middle-class Western culture, and would be very different, or insignificant, in more primitive societies, or in those with other types of family organization than our own.

In other times and other places, children of this age would begin to seek mates and roles outside the family, establishing their own households and carrying on independent lives. In our culture, however, young people remain with their families, often completely dependent on them for physical sustenance, while at the same time becoming adults with attitudes and needs at variance from those of their parents. One result is strong reliance on peer groups, with which young people share experiences and heroes. Often during adolescence, group influences become stronger than those of the family and to a considerable extent replace family ideals and controls.

The economic problems attendant upon early marriage cause many young people to wait. This delay leads to sexual problems, since sexual maturity is reached early in adolescence and interest in the opposite sex is at a high peak during these years. While there is no doubt that sexual customs and social attitudes are changing markedly away from traditional American puritanism, many young people still have sexual conflicts and sexual tensions that cause them considerable anguish.

During adolescence, the boy's libidinal attachment to his mother has finally to be relinquished, and he must also free himself from the dominance of his father. Unsuccessful attempts to resolve these Oedipal conflicts may

---

[8] Group for the Advancement of Psychiatry. "Normal Adolescence." Vol. 6, Report No. 68 (February 19, 1968). P. 785.

result in neurosis and raise obstacles to the successful selection of a heterosexual love object. The resolution of the Oedipus complex in adolescence is a slow process, reaching into late adolescence. It probably is fully accomplished only when, in the normal course of events, the individual establishes himself in his own family.

The marked bodily changes that occur during adolescence require changes in the self-concept, since the adolescent's idea of what he looks like and how he appears to others must shift quite drastically. Reorganizing the self-concept is not an easy task and requires constant reassessment of one's bodily changes, and how the persons in one's environment are reacting to these changes.

Erikson views adolescence as a time when a successful synthesis of social, psychological, and physical changes and challenges leads to a sense of "identity." [9] The failure to achieve a sense of identity at this stage leads to "role diffusion," with deep and distressing feelings of doubt and confusion about one's social, psychological, or occupational role.

The normal physical and psychosocial changes during adolescence at times produce inevitable feelings akin to role diffusion. In order for the adolescent to emerge as a potentially mature adult, however, the crisis of ego identity versus role diffusion needs to be resolved in favor of a secure sense of identity.

The period of adolescence is ordinarily one of good physical health, so nurses have relatively little contact with adolescent patients. Although serious physical illness is not common during adolescence, the rate of accidents is quite high, and accidents are the leading cause of physical incapacitation among adolescents.

Venereal disease rates are also high during adolescence. Many adolescents begin having sexual intercourse, but may lack both the information and the caution necessary to prevent venereal disease. Unwanted pregnancy also may be a hazard for the adolescent girl who is poorly prepared to cope socially and emotionally with sexual feelings and with the realities of sexual relationships.

During recent years, there has been an increase in the number of adolescents who attempt or commit suicide. There are many causes for suicide and suicide attempts, but their high rates among young people may well include the same dissatisfactions that have led to the widespread use of a variety of mind-altering drugs.

A major concern during the past ten years has been the increase of drug use among high school and college students. The greatest attention, public discussion, and alarm has been expressed over the use of marijuana because

---

[9] Erik Erikson. *Childhood and Society.* New York: W. W. Norton and Company, 1963. P. 235.

of the frequency of its use and the medical, legal, and social questions such use raises.

Other drugs, however, are at least as important, if only because of their greater potential harm. These include the hallucinogens such as D-lysergic acid (LSD), mescaline, and psylocibin. A particularly harmful group of drugs are those stimulants related to methedrine ("speed"), too often prescribed in diet pills. Then there are the well-known and widely used sedatives and tranquilizers, misuse of which probably far exceeds legitimate use.

The tragic effects of addiction to the "hard drugs," i.e. heroin, morphine, demerol, etc., are well known and have been widely publicized. A more complete discussion of drug use and abuse is beyond the province of this text. However, the widespread experimentation and habitual use of drugs by adolesecnts makes it essential that nurses acquire accurate and sophisticated information about this subject.

For the nurse, the drug problem poses a heavy personal responsibility. The nurse, like the physician, has easy access to many medications. The young nurse may herself be tempted to experiment with drugs. The potential dangers of taking mind-altering drugs must not be overlooked by those responsible for the care of other people.

As adolescence draws to a close, if the young person has had some success in deciding upon a career and coming to terms with his sexual role and needs, he will be consolidating his personality and gaining a sense of wholeness that provides a foundation for success with the tasks of adult life.

The Group for the Advancement of Psychiatry concludes its monograph on adolescence with the following statement:

> Ideally, the resolution of adolescence is characterized by (1) the attainment of separation and independence from the parents, (2) the establishment of sexual identity, (3) the commitment to work, (4) the development of a personal moral value system, (5) the capacity for lasting relationships and for both tender and genital sexual love in heterosexual relationships, and (6) a return to the parents in a new relationship based upon a relative equality.[10]

Suggested Readings

BOOKS

Ackerman, Nathan W. *The Psychodynamics of Family Life*. New York: Basic Books, Inc., 1958.

───. *Treating the Troubled Family*. New York: Basic Books, Inc., 1966.

[10] *Ibid.* P. 829.

Aichhorn, August. *Wayward Youth.* New York: The Viking Press, Inc., 1935.

American Medical Association. Committee on Alcoholism and Drug Dependence. "Dependence on LSD." *Journal of American Medical Association,* Vol. 202 (1967). Pp. 47–50.

American Medical Association. Committee on Alcoholism and Drug Dependence. "Dependence on Cannabis" *Journal of the American Medical Association.* Vol. 201, No. 6 (1967).

Beck, Aaron T. *Depression. Clinical, Experimental, and Theoretical Aspects.* New York: Harper and Row, Publishers, 1967.

Blos, Peter. *On Adolescence: A Psychoanalytic Interpretation.* New York: The Free Press, 1962.

Cohen, Sidney. *The Beyond Within: The LSD Story.* New York: Atheneum, 1964. Rev. ed., 1967.

Freud, Sigmund. "Three Essays on the Theory of Sexuality" from *The Standard Edition of the Complete Works of Sigmund Freud.* Translated by James Strachey in collaboration with Anna Freud. Vol. 7. London: Hogarth Press, Ltd., 1953.

Green, Hannah. *I Never Promised You a Rose Garden.* New York: Holt, Rinehart, & Winston, Inc., 1964.

Grinspoon, Lester. *Marihuana Reconsidered.* Cambridge, Mass.: Harvard University Press, 1971.

Hall, G. Stanley. *Adolescence: Its Psychology and Its Relations to Physiology, Anthropology, Sociology, Sex, Crime, Religion, and Education.* Vols. 1 and 2. New York: Appleton-Century-Crofts, 1904.

Havighurst, R. J. and H. Taba. *Adolescent Character and Personality.* New York: John Wiley & Sons, Inc., 1949.

Horman, Richard E. and Allen M. Fox, eds. *Drug Awareness: Key Documents on LSD, Marijuana and the Drug Culture.* New York: Avon Books, 1970.

Jersild, A. T. *The Psychology of Adolescence.* 2d ed. New York: The Macmillan Company, 1963.

Josselyn, Irene M. *The Adolescent and His World.* New York: Family Service Association of America, 1952.

Keniston, Kenneth. *The Uncommitted: Alienated Youth in American Society.* New York: Harcourt, Brace, & Jovanovich, 1965.

———. *Young Radicals.* New York: Harcourt, Brace & Jovanovich, 1968.

Kesey, Ken. *One Flew Over the Cuckoo's Nest.* New York: Viking Press, 1962.

Kinsey, Alfred C., W. B. Pomeroy, and C. F. Martin. *Sexual Behavior in the Human Male.* Philadelphia: W. B. Saunders Company, 1948.

Kobler, Arthur L. and Ezra Stotland. *The End of Hope. A Social-Clinical Theory of Suicide.* London: Collier-Macmillan Limited, The Free Press of Glencoe, 1964.

Lindesmith, Alfred R. *The Addict and the Law.* Bloomington: Indiana University Press, 1965.

Mead, Margaret. *Coming of Age in Samoa.* New York: William Morrow & Company, Inc., 1928.

Menninger, Karl, M. Mayman, and P. Pruyser. *The Vital Balance.* New York: The Viking Press, Inc., 1963.

Milbauer, Barbara and Gerald Leinwand. *Drugs.* New York: Washington Square Press, 1970.

Mussen, P. H., J. J. Conger, and J. Kagan. *Child Development and Personality.* 2d ed. New York: Harper & Row, Publishers, 1963.

Piaget, Jean. *The Growth of Logical Thinking from Childhood to Adolescence.* New York: Basic Books, 1958.

Reich, Charles A. *The Greening of America.* New York: Random House, 1970.

Schofield, M. *The Sexual Behavior of Young People.* Boston: Little, Brown & Company, 1965.

Stone, L. J. and J. Church. *Childhood and Adolescence.* 2d ed. New York: Random House, Inc., 1968.

Sullivan, H. S. *The Interpersonal Theory of Psychiatry.* New York: W. W. Norton & Company, Inc., 1953.

Symonds, Percival M. and A. R. Jensen. *From Adolescent to Adult.* New York: Columbia University Press, 1961.

Weiner, Irving B. *Psychological Disturbance in Adolescence.* New York: John Wiley & Sons, Inc., 1970.

Wittels, Frit. "The Ego of the Adolescent." In K. R. Eissler, ed. *Searchlights on Delinquency.* New York: International Universities Press, Inc., 1949. Pp. 256–62.

World Health Organization. Statements on Drug Use. *Bulletin of the World Health Organization.* Vol. 32 (1965). Pp. 727–33.

ARTICLES

Ackerman, N. W. "Adolescent Problems: A Symptom of Family Disorder." *Family Process.* Vol. 1 (1962). Pp. 202–13.

Bakwin, H. "Suicide in Children and Adolescents." *Journal of Pediatrics.* Vol. 50 (1957). Pp. 749–69.

Bernfield, S. "Types of Adolescence." *Psychoanalytic Quarterly.* Vol. 7 (1938). Pp. 243–53.

Blanchard, P. "Psychoanalytic Contributions to the Problems of Reading Disabilities." *Psychoanalytic Study of the Child.* Vol. 2 (1946). Pp. 163–87.

Bruch, Hilde. "Psychological Aspects of Overeating and Obesity." *Psychosomatics.* Vol. 5 (1964). Pp. 269–74.

Condon, Alice and Arlene Roland. "Drug Abuse Jargon." *The American Journal of Nursing.* Vol. 71, No. 9 (September, 1971). P. 1738.

Dorpat, Theodore L. "Evaluation and Management of Suicide Reactions." *Medical Times* (December, 1963).

———. "The Relationship of Physical Illness to Suicide." In *Suicidal Behavior*, ed. H. L. P. Resnik. Boston: Little Brown and Company, 1968. Pp. 209–19.

———. "Evaluation and Management of Suicide Reaction." *Medical Times.* Vol. 91 (December, 1963). Pp. 1212–18.

Elkind, D. "Egocentrism in Adolescence." *Child Development.* Vol. 38 (1967). Pp. 1025–34.

Fleck, S. "Pregnancy as a Symptom of Adolescent Maladjustment." *International Journal of Social Psychiatry.* Vol. 2 (1956). Pp. 118–31.

Freud, Anna. "Adolescence." *Psychoanalytic Study of the Child.* Vol. 13 (1958). Pp. 255–78.

Foreman, Nancy Jo and Joyce V. Zerwekh. "Drug Crisis Intervention." *The American Journal of Nursing.* Vol. 71, No. 9 (September, 1971). Pp. 1736–39.

Friedenberg, E. Z. "Discussion of Erik Erikson's 'Eight Stages of Man'." *International Journal of Psychiatry.* Vol. 2 (1966). Pp. 306–7.

Helfat, L. "Parents of Adolescents Need Help Too." *New York State Journal of Medicine.* Vol. 67 (1967). Pp. 2764–68.

Hine, C. H. "The Role of the Industrial Nurse in the Detection and Prevention of Drug Abuse." *Occupational Health Nursing.* (April, 1969). Pp. 15–17.

Josselyn, I. M. "The Ego in Adolescence." *American Journal of Orthopsychiatry.* Vol. 24 (1954). Pp. 223–27.

———. "Psychological Changes in Adolescence." *Children.* Vol. 6 (1959). Pp. 43–47.

Kohlberg, Irving J. and Michael B. Rothenberg. "Comprehensive Care Following Multiple, Life-Threatening Injuries." *American Journal of Diseases of Children.* Vol. 119 (1970). Pp. 449–51.

Lindemann, E. "Adolescent Behavior as a Community Concern." *American Journal of Psychotherapy.* Vol. 18 (1964). Pp. 405–17.

Masterson, J. F. "The Psychiatric Significance of Adolescent Turmoil." *American Journal of Psychiatry.* Vol. 124 (1968). Pp. 1549–54.

Nealon, J. "The Adolescent's Hospitalization as a Family Crisis." *Archives of General Psychiatry.* Vol. 11 (1964). Pp. 302–11.

Nixon, R. E. "An Approach to the Dynamics of Growth in Adolescence." *Psychiatry.* Vol. 24 (1961). Pp. 18–31.

———. "Psychological Normality in Adolescence." *Adolescence.* Vol. 1 (1966). Pp. 211–23.

Spiegel, L. A. "Comments on the Psychoanalytic Psychology of the Adolescent." *Psychoanalytic Study of the Child.* Vol. 13 (1958). Pp. 296–308.

———. "Disorder and Consolidation in Adolescence." *Journal of the American Psychoanalytic Association.* Vol. 9 (1961). Pp. 406–17.

———. "A Review of Contributions to a Psychoanalytic Theory of Adolescence." *Psychoanalytic Study of the Child.* Vol. 6 (1951). Pp. 375–93.

Zwick, Sister Dorothy and Sister Maureen Brown. "Workshop on Drug Abuse." *Nursing Outlook.* Vol. 19, No. 7 (July, 1971). Pp. 476–77.

DISCUSSION OF SELECTED READINGS

In this chapter on adolescence, we have continued to use the developmental charts by Doctors Milton Senn and Albert J. Solnit, as we did in earlier chapters of child development. The chart on puberty and early adolescence provides guidelines for the general tasks in process for the child and parents. The schema provided by Solnit and Senn gives a guideline of behavioral characteristics from normal behavior to extreme pathology.

The first article following the chart is by Mary Lou Byers, a supervisor and instructor in pediatric nursing, who introduces problems encountered in the nursing care of a female teen-age patient. She describes this adolescent's response to authority figures, restricted activities, separation from family and friends, and changes in her body due to illness. She emphasizes the importance of the nurse's awareness of each patient's stress areas.

The second article, "Predictable Problems of Hospitalized Adolescents," by Herbert L. Meyer, a psychiatric nurse and supervisor, suggests that an uncooperative response to enforced immobilization may alert the staff to other problems. Mr. Meyer suggests that the adolescent may resent and appear hostile toward hospital rules and regulations since these may symbolize parental authority.

We have already discussed the adolescent's need to assert his independence and this is especially necessary for the hospitalized patient. In an example of a specific case history, Mr. Meyer found the patient had considerable conflict with parental authority and therefore a possible predictable conflict with hospital authorities.

These articles emphasize that adolescents are similar in many ways, and yet different, even though they may be in the same chronological age group.

DEVELOPMENTAL SCHEMA CHART *

Puberty and Early Adolescence (12 to 15 years)

Tasks in Process

CHILD	PARENT(S)
To come to terms with body changes.	To help child complete emancipation.
To cope with sexual development and psychosexual drives.	To provide support and understanding.
To establish and confirm sense of identity.	To limit child's behavior and set standards.
To learn further re sex role.	To offer favorable and appropriate environment for healthy development.
To synthesize personality.	To recall own adolescent difficulties; to accept and respect the adolescent's differences or similarities to parents or others.
To struggle for independence and emancipation from family.	
To incorporate learning to the gestalt of living.	To relate to adolescents and adolescence wtih a constructive sense of humor.

Acceptable Behavioral Characteristics

CHILD	PARENT(S)
Heightened physical power, strength and coordination.	Allow and encourage reasonable independence.
Occasional psychosomatic and somatopsychic disturbances.	Set fair rules; are consistent.
Maturing sex characteristics and proclivities.	Compassionate and understanding; firm but not punitive or derogatory.
Review and resolution of oedipal conflicts.	Feel pleasure and pride; occasional guilt and disappointment.
Inconsistent, unpredictable and paradoxical behavior.	Have other interests besides child.
	Marital life fulfilled apart from child.
Exploration and experimentation with self and world.	Occasional expression of intolerance, resentment, envy or anxiety about adolescent's development.
Eagerness for peer approval and relationships.	
Strong moral and ethical perceptions.	
Cognitive development accelerated; deductive and inductive reasoning; operational thought.	

* Milton J. E. Senn, M.D., and Albert J. Solnit, M.D., *Problems in Child Behavior and Development*. Philadelphia: Lea and Febinger, 1968.

Competitive in play; erratic work-play patterns.

Better use of language and other symbolic material.

Critical of self and others; self-evaluative.

Highly ambivalent towards parents.

Anxiety over loss of parental nurturing.

Hostility to parents.

Verbal aggression.

Minimal Psychopathology

CHILD

Apprehensions, fears, guilt and anxiety re sex, health, education.

Defiant, negative, impulsive or depressed behavior.

Frequent somatic or hypochondriacal complaints; or denial of ordinary illnesses.

Learning irregular or deficient.

Sexual preoccupation.

Poor or absent personal relationships with adults or peers.

Immaturity or precocious behavior; unchanging personality and temperament.

Unwillingness to assume the responsibility of greater autonomy.

Inability to substitute or postpone gratifications.

PARENT(S)

Sense of failure.

Disappointment greater than joy.

Indifference to child and family.

Apathy and depression.

Persistent intolerance of child.

Limited interests and self expression.

Loss of perspective about child's capacities.

Occasional direct or vicarious reversion to adolescent impulses.

Uncertainty about standards regarding sexual behavior and deviant social or personal activity.

Extreme Psychopathology

CHILD

Complete withdrawal into self, extreme depression.

Acts of delinquency, asceticism, ritualism, over-conformity.

Neuroses, especially phobias; persistent anxiety, compulsions, inhibitions or constrictive behavior.

PARENT(S)

Severe depression and withdrawal.

Complete rejection of child and/or family.

Inability to function in family role.

Rivalrous, competitive, destructive and abusive to child.

Persistent hypochondriases.

Sex aberrations.

Semantic illness: anorexia, colitis, menstrual disorders.

Complete inability to socialize or work (learning, etc.).

Psychoses.

Abetting child's acting out of unacceptable sexual or aggressive impulses for vicarious reasons.

Perpetuation of incapacitating infantilism in the pre-adolescent.

Panic reactions to acceptable standards of sexual behavior, social activity and assertiveness.

Compulsive, obsessive or psychotic behavior.

The Hospitalized Adolescent

by Mary Lou Byers, R.N., M.N.Ed.*

Jean, a 14-year-old adolescent was the sole occupant of hospital room 605 and had been alone there for four weeks. Her diagnosis was rheumatic fever, and she had no known previous history of the disease. Jean's heart murmur was minimal, but she required close observation. As I walked toward her room anticipating our first meeting, several of the comments that had been made about her during the morning report ran through my mind:

That girl is ordered on bed rest and she never stays in bed.

Her room is the messiest place on the ward, with bobby pins, powder, body lotion, and hair all over the bedside table, her bed, and the floor. She's always combing her hair.

She insists on pasting pictures of movie stars on the wall. It's against hospital policy to paste or stick anything on the wall, but she had a temper tantrum when we tried to take them down and we thought that would hurt her heart, so we left them there and the housekeeping department complains about it all the time.

If she does not have clean pajamas to put on, she refuses to bathe. She won't wear the hospital gowns. She says she feels undressed in them.

That radio blares rock and roll so loud! If she's not already hard of hearing, she soon will be and so will the rest of us!

The description of Jean's room was accurate even to the volume of the radio. As I entered, Jean was concentrating on applying her lipstick, a little awkward

* Mary Lou Byers, "The Hospitalized Adolescent." *Nursing Outlook*, Vol. 15, No. 8 (August, 1967). Pp. 32–34.

in manipulating the brush. Her dark brown hair was still in clips; her gray eyes looked intently through her plain plastic-rimmed glasses into the bedside table mirror. A few freckles over her nose were still showing, even though it was evident she had applied makeup and powder. Over her somewhat stocky frame she wore clean, neatly pressed light blue cotton pajamas. It was not until Jean looked up, smiled, and said "Hello," that the braces on her teeth became noticeable.

"Good morning, Jean. My name is Miss Byers and I am going to be your nurse today." Because the volume of the radio was turned quite high, I found myself almost shouting.

Jean responded with a shrug of her shoulders and a disinterested "Oh." A moment later she commented that she had already taken her bath. Then she said that if I wanted to come back later to make her bed when she was finished putting on her lipstick that that would be fine with her. I wanted to communicate to Jean that she was more important to me than just that I had to make her bed later. The radio continued to blare and I wasn't sure I had heard her correctly. Also, I felt she was rejecting me by dismissing me. Then I wondered why she wasn't more interested in talking with a nurse, even though I was a stranger to her. I raised my voice again to carry above the radio and said, "I'm sorry. I'm not sure I heard what you said."

Jean retorted, "Do you really want to?"

I nodded my head and said, "Yes, I do."

Jean then turned the radio off and said, "If you do, you are the first one who does. Most people 'shush' me all the time."

I sat down in the chair beside her bed and asked, "I wonder why?"

"Oh," she said, "I'm a big problem around here. Just wait; people will tell you about me."

I said to her, "I'd rather hear about you from you."

"People always holler at me. I never do anything the way I'm supposed to. If you're so interested in me how about getting me permission to use the phone more often?"

Jean's manner of speech irritated me and I could understand why the staff was so unhappy with her and had had difficulty in helping her deal with her problems more effectively. Jean went on to say that she wouldn't mind getting up and going down the corridor to the phone booth. When I reminded her that she was on bed rest she flipped over in her bed, faced the wall, and refused to talk with me any longer. I sat there in silence for 15 minutes. Then I told her I had to leave, but that I would try to talk to the doctor about what arrangements could be made for her to use the telephone. She shrieked loudly, "Oh, they'll say 'No.' Never mind. Don't bother." She refused to say anything else to me at that time.

During the adolescent years, when mobility and activity are so crucial, the restrictions of bed rest present many problems. Jean's reactions to her hospital experience was no exception. Our staff needed to have the order for bed rest spelled out and defined in order that our individual interpretations could be clarified and the goals of the therapy more realistically attained. One person permitted Jean bathroom privileges once a day, another person twice a day, and still another would not allow her to get up at all. Jean was confused and frightened and our inconsistency in interpreting the physician's orders only added to the problems with which she was already struggling.

Cooperative Planning

Two staff nurses, one assigned to day and the other to evening duty, were interested in trying to help Jean and asked that she be assigned to them. I was one of these nurses and, together with Jean, we designed plans for such special activities as sewing, painting, and other handicrafts as well as allowing for time to "talk." Every two weeks the physician, nurse, social worker, recreation therapist, and nutritionist held a conference to discuss plans for Jean's care. This meant that each person's intervention with Jean could be more meaningful because they had knowledge of the total care plan and could follow it. It also helped to limit the number of people Jean was required to relate to, and thus conserved her energy and provided more carefully planned, beneficial help.

As the nurses had the opportunity to observe and care for Jean they became more able to pick up cues of needs not readily recognized. For example, it occasionally happened that a patient on the ward became dangerously ill. At these times, Jean's sensitivity was heightened. She kept the volume of her radio down and her persistent requests to make phone calls decreased greatly. The quietness which pervaded her room was in direct contrast to the usual lively atmosphere. One day Jean questioned me about a child in a nearby room.

"What's wrong with that kid? Does he have rheumatic fever?"

When I asked Jean why she wondered if he had rheumatic fever, she said, "Oh, he looks pretty sick. One of the kids told me sometimes people die from rheumatic fever, and I don't even feel sick. Will I get lots sicker if I don't stay in bed?"

As the shock of separation from home wore off and she became more able to express her fears about her illness, Jean sought out information concerning her condition from both the physicians and nurses. The medical and nursing staff held weekly conferences with Jean to clarify some of her questions. Her parents came to these sessions whenever they could.

"What's the mitral valve, and what if it doesn't work right?" "But my heart doesn't hurt." "Will I be able to go to the beach and swim when I get out of the hospital?" "What does it mean that my heart may be diseased?" "What does a diseased heart look and feel like?" "I don't feel anything wrong." The answers to such questions taught Jean a great deal about her disease and about caring for herself.

These serious inquiries were followed by others which were just as important to Jean, "When will they get these braces off my teeth? They're so 'icky.' Boys don't like girls with braces on their teeth."

Some Special Problems

Jean's refusal to permit more than one physician to examine her at any one time persisted throughout her hospitalization. She clutched her pajama top, making it impossible for anyone to listen to her heart from the front of her chest. Although the medical staff was very impatient with this behavior, Jean held her ground and, I might add, won the battle. In a firm indignant tone she exclaimed, "I'd just die having all those doctors see me. There are at least five of them and some are so young!" The nurse who was responsible for Jean discussed this problem with the physician and it was arranged that a nurse would always accompany the physician when he visited Jean and wished to examine her. Jean changed into a hospital gown temporarily while the examination was done and the physician took special care to avoid exposing her any more than necessary.

Other crises arose during Jean's 16-week hospitalization. One day the nutritionist reported that Jean was fasting and refusing most of her food. When the nurse investigated this report, Jean said, "With all this bed rest jazz, I've gained eight pounds since I've been here and I don't want to get fat." So she was placed on a low-calorie selective diet; but, occasionally, when she couldn't resist temptation, Jean supplemented her diet with popcorn, to the intense chagrin of the nutritionist.

On Wednesday of each week, Jean was scheduled for a venipuncture as a sample of her blood was needed to determine her eosinophile sedimentation rate. This procedure was often quite painful because Jean's veins were difficult to locate and stabilize. At first, she wept profusely and screamed throughout the whole procedure, but she always held her arm perfectly still even when the physician had to try more than once to find a blood-yielding vein. Later on, she was able to control her screaming, but she still wept every time a specimen of blood was taken. Because her activity restrictions were reduced whenever her sedimentation rate remained within certain limits for a period of time, Jean awaited the results of this test eagerly. This was the best criterion she had for judging the progress she was making toward recovery.

Jean's activity was gradually increased and staff members, viewing this as progress, shared their enthusiasm with her. Confusion about "up privileges" was kept to a minimum. Jean and her nurses still worked together in planning her schedule and wrote it out in duplicate. One copy of her activity sheet was attached to her nursing care plan, and the other was given to Jean for her personal reference. After Jean was permitted greater activity, she was able to talk about how "icky" she had felt when she was on complete bed rest. She said with disgust and revulsion, "I'm nothing, lying there in bed." Occasionally, she would want to extend her activity, and her copy of the activity sheet would disappear mysteriously. Most of the time, however, she tolerated her restrictions quite well and the staff felt that this was because she was one of the active planners of her schedule and thus was kept aware of her progress.

Features of Care Plan

The general areas of concern in preparing a plan for this adolescent's care included her reactions to: (1) authority figures; (2) restricted activity; (3) separation from family and friends; (4) changes in her body which are normal for the developmental period she was experiencing; and (5) the physical and psychological changes she sensed in her body because of her illness.

There are many patients like Jean, not only on pediatric units, but also in general hospitals. Under the best of circumstances, the teenager is subject to many uncertainties which influence his self-concept. When illness intervenes, these uncertainties multiply, thus increasing the tensions and frustrations characteristic of this age group. One cause of Jean's early difficulty in adjusting to hospitalization was that, although adolescence is the time when the process of emancipation from parents accelerates, Jean had not been prepared for this abrupt departure from home. Her premature, forced separation from family and friends was very upsetting to her. Possibly the disease process also played a part in lowering her capacity to tolerate the restrictions imposed by day-to-day life within the hospital.

The rapid physical growth spurt and hormonal changes that take place during adolescence produce tension and stress in and of themselves. When illness creates additional stress, the nurse has a responsibility to help make this undesirable situation as tolerable as possible. By keeping at a minimum the number of people with whom Jean had to relate, and by respecting her need for privacy, we hoped to reduce her tension and frustration. Allowing her to participate actively in planning for her care helped both her and the staff to broaden their understanding of the total problem she was experiencing. Keeping her informed of the overall plan for her care helped reduce her fears and fantasies about her illness.

If the nurse-patient interaction is to be a therapeutic one for the teenage patient, the nurse needs to be able to perceive the cues which indicate the areas where the patient is experiencing stress. These provide the guidelines for effective nursing intervention.

At the time Jean tolerated "up" activity for four hours without signs of physical fatigue, plans were initiated for her discharge from the hospital. At first, she had doubts about going home. The public health nurse from her community visited with Jean and her parents several times while she was still in the hospital. Jean learned she would receive careful health supervision at home and she began to look forward more eagerly to returning home. The public health nurse made suggestions about possible rearrangements of rooms and furniture in Jean's home to minimize her activity, especially going up and down stairs. In addition, the physician requested a "homebound teacher" for Jean so that she could continue her education at home until she was able to return to school.

My last meeting with Jean before she left the hospital was very different from the first one. She had sent a message asking me to come to her room to see her. When I arrived, her eyes were overflowing with tears. In one hand she held a small, neatly wrapped package and with the other hand she fumbled with a tissue, attempting to dry her eyes. She sobbed, "It's so silly to cry about going home when I've waited all this time to go, but I'm sad about not being able to see the people here anymore." I told her that I hoped she would plan to visit when she returned to the clinic, because I would miss her, too, and wanted to see her again as a visitor in the hospital and not as a patient. Jean hadn't realized it was possible to come to the unit to visit and this news seemed to help her feel better. She handed me the small gift (something she had made herself), and asked me not to open it until after she had gone. She also took my address and asked me to write to her.

Initially, Jean wrote weekly. She told me of her activities, accomplishments, and interests. Three months after her return home, she was able to attend school. Her clinic visits became more and more infrequent. The exchange of letters gradually lessened, but she continues to write a short note each year at Christmas time.

Bibliography

Blake, Florence G., and Wright, F. Howell. *Essentials of Pediatric Nursing*. 7th ed. Philadelphia: J. B. Lippincott Co., 1963.

De Groot, Jeanne-Lampl. "Adolescence." *The Psychoanalytic Study of the Child*. Vol. 15. 95–103.

Erikson, E. H. "Youth and the Life Cycle." *Children*. Vol. 7 (March–April, 1960). 43–49.

Gallagher, J. R. "Rest and Restriction; Their Conflict with an Adolescent's Development." *American Journal of Public Health*. Vol. 46 (November, 1956). 1424–28.

Jacobson, Edith. "Adolescent Moods and the Remodeling of Psychic Structures in Adolescence. *The Psychoanalytic Study of the Child*. Vol. 16. 164–83.

Josselyn, Irene M., and others. "Anxiety in Children Convalescing From Rheumatic Fever." *American Journal of Orthopsychiatry*. Vol. 25 (January, 1955). 109–19.

Predictable Problems of Hospitalized Adolescents

by Herbert L. Meyer, R.N., M.S.*

This is the story of Jim, age 19, who awakened in the hospital after an automobile accident. His male companion had been killed. Jim's cervical spine was fractured. After two days he was placed on a Stryker frame and in cervical traction.

His reaction to enforced hospitalization and the events which accompanied it posed a number of problems that might have been expected.

A great deal has been written about the traumatic effects which any threat to body strength and image may have on an adolescent. A young victim will be faced with many adjustments which can be especially difficult if they come at a time when he is still striving for personal identity and is already struggling with the normal problems of development.

He may be impatient with restrictions and react with hostility because his plans are disrupted. Resentment of hospital rules and regulations may represent an extension of rebellion against parental authority from which he is trying to emancipate himself. On the other hand, placid acceptance of restrictive rules and hospital routines may fit neatly into our stereotype of the "good" patient but, in fact, may be evidence of denial and regression.

Because his parents are legally responsible for him and only their consent is required for his treatment, the hospitalized adolescent usually is given few opportunities to participate in making the decisions which affect him. Any rebuff or temporary rejection can be especially traumatic if not accompanied by a degree of loving concern such as we hope would be experienced in his home situation. Above all, in this striving for independence, the adolescent expects, and has a right, to be included in the decisions which affect his treatment and prognosis. He should be advised of the therapeutic measures which are planned for him and he should be consulted in matters concerning his care. He needs to be accepted as an individual personality with unique worth and special attributes.

Because of his insecurity and his feelings of anxiety, the adolescent needs constant reassurance about his progress. He should be encouraged to participate

* American Journal of Nursing, Vol. 69, No. 3 (March, 1969). Pp. 525–28.

in his own care and to socialize with his peers insofar as this can be done within the framework of the medical regimen.

If, in addition, an adolescent patient is subjected to enforced limitation of motion from restricting therapeutic devices, such as Jim's cervical traction and frame bed, problems of a physical and an emotional nature can be anticipated.

Almost two decades ago both the physiologic and metabolic changes which occur in normal subjects as a result of immobilization were demonstrated by Deitrick.[1] More recently, Spencer and his associates studied the effects of immobilization on 18 quadraplegic men. They concluded that the physiological effects of immobilization are profound and demonstrable, although there may be some differences in degree of effect on ill or disabled patients as opposed to healthy subjects.[2] Studies of the psychologic effects of sensory deprivation associated with immobilization have also been reported.[3] Kottke describes psychologic effects with accompanying sensory deprivation:

Emotional response to diminution of activity will vary depending on the degree of sensory deprivation and the dominant personality factors of the individual. The immediate emotional response to limitation of activity is similar to that in other situations of stress and persons may show evidences of insecurity with anxiety and dependence or aggressiveness and hostility. Anxiety, hostility, tension, complaints of discomfort and changes in patterns of sleep all may occur in varying degrees depending on the personality of the individual. The greater the degree and the more prolonged the limitation of activity and isolation, the greater will be the regression toward dependency and primitive emotional response.[4]

Urging a comprehensive approach to the problem of immobilization, Levy points out that the profound physical and psychologic changes observed in healthy experimental subjects can only be increased in the ill person who is beset by stressful factors in addition to his illness:

This anxiety may become greater when the patient senses that he is not being told the nature of his condition or the reasons for various mystifying and frightening procedures. In such a state of mind he is less able to withstand pain, isolation and immobilization. This is especially true when the patient has no idea how long he might be in this state.[5]

---

[1] J. E. Dietrick and others. "Effects of Immobilization upon Various Metabolic and Physiologic Functions of Normal Men." *American Journal of Medicine.* Vol. 4 (January, 1948). 3–36.

[2] W. A. Spencer and others. "Physiologic Concepts of Immobilization." *Archives of Physical Medicine.* Vol. 46 (January, 1965). 89–100.

[3] Philip Solomon and others. "Sensory Deprivations." *American Journal of Psychiatry.* Vol. 114 (October, 1957). 357–63.

[4] F. J. Kottke. "Effects of Limitation of Activity upon the Human Body." *Journal of the American Medical Association.* Vol. 196 (June 6, 1966). 830.

[5] Roland Levy. "Immobilized Patient and His Psychological Well-being." *Postgraduate Medicine.* Vol. 40 (July, 1966). 74.

He suggests that the regression to be expected in all hospitalized patients will probably be more manifest in those who are dependent on others for almost total care. Although most patients make a good adjustment to these additional stresses, others may

. . . make excessive demands, display irrational fears, and reject many aspects of the treatment program. Others show marked dependency, are clinging and helpless and seek constant attention and reassurance. . . . Other patients who cannot accept illness and its associated dependency may refuse to take medication or [may] attempt premature ambulation when strict bed rest is indicated.[6]

Levy also stresses the anxiety which bedside teaching and consultations can create, and the additional burden which is placed on the man who, in the past, has depended on display of physical prowess and activity for relief of tension and anxiety. He suggests encouraging as much self-care as possible, occupational and recreational therapy, constant reassurance, good communication as to the nature of his condition, and frequent visits by friends and family. He urges that placement in a private room be avoided.

Jim's Early Course

It was 5:30 in the morning when Jim was admitted to the hospital. He had been thrown from his car during the accident and was unconscious on arrival at the emergency room. He regained consciousness shortly after admission and was aware of the tragedy which had claimed the life of his companion.

He complained of pain in his neck and anterior chest. Physical examination revealed tenderness in the posterior aspect of his neck. X-ray examination confirmed the fracture of the second cervical vertebra with separation of the body from the posterior arch. Neurologic examination was negative. The patient's neck was immobilized with a Thomas collar. Two days later, because of continued angulation at the site of the fracture, Jim was placed on a Stryker frame, Crutchfield tongs were inserted in his skull, and 10 pounds of traction were applied.

Very early in his hospitalization Jim firmly established himself as persona non grata. According to the staff, he rebelled against authority, was belligerent and demanding, and refused to cooperate in his treatment. He would ease the traction on his neck and place towels under his head although he knew his neck should be in continuous hyperextension. He withdrew behind the security of his cubicle curtains and, while thus secluded, engaged in what was described as petting sessions with his girl friend who stayed at his side virtually night and day. As a result of these activities the curtains were removed and regular visiting

[6] *Ibid.*

hours enforced. Other retaliatory methods were also employed to demonstrate disapproval of his conduct, and the patient became even more belligerent and uncooperative. On one occasion he struck out at an aide, hitting her in the abdomen. Also, he was reported as being overly bold and suggestive in some of his remarks to the nurses and aides, calling them "chicks," and inviting them to view some of his reading material which was described as frank pornography. This behavior and the disciplinary measures used in retaliation resulted, in time, in rejection by the staff and further isolation of the patient.

The patient complained that there was no one in the ward to talk to but old men, whom he especially resented. He stated that he drew the bedside curtains so that he could be alone to think about his problems and, at times, enjoy the companionship of his girl friend who was the only one whom he wished to see and from whom he derived strength and comfort. He insisted that they did nothing which they considered wrong and, besides, he asked, if their relationship was carried on in private, "Whose business is it?"

Above all, Jim consistently and bitterly resented the failure of members of the staff to consult with him in the matters which concerned their plan for his care, what they proposed to do with him, the details of his condition, and a host of related grievances. When he was asked one day how he was getting along, he replied with bitterness and intensity: "They don't tell you nuthin'—they get my old man off in a corner and then it's p-s-s-t, p-s-s-t, p-s-s-t—then he comes back and tries to tell me what's going on. He's all right, but probably forgets half of what they tell him. Why don't they talk to me? After all, it's my body that's being operated on, not theirs!"

Problems with Authority

Granted that much of this resentment may have been a highly exaggerated response to the situation or symptomatic of the emotional effect of enforced immobilization, it nevertheless was a true reflection of the patient's interpretation of the events as he saw them and the feeling tone which accompanied them. As a result, it produced chronic resentment, hostility, and mutual withdrawal of the patient and personnel.

In the course of a number of interviews with this patient and with his family, I was able to elicit evidence of other areas of problem behavior and potential conflict. On one occasion the patient recounted with considerable relish how he and his friends had succeeded in evading their responsibilities under Selective Service by deliberately getting into difficulties with the law so they would be placed on probation.

He was expelled from school at an early age and his mother told how he "went his own way" while still quite young, drifting slowly out from under parental influence and authority. She described his frequent conflicts with his father, usually over the late hours which he persisted in observing. She described periods when Jim seldom talked to his parents for days at a time and was absent from home except to eat and sleep. One of her laments was that they had probably tried to give their son "too much." She indicated that both she and her husband had had a difficult economic struggle and hoped to spare their children some hardships.

The father was described as a heavy drinker, short in stature, belligerent, outspoken, and intensely concerned with every phase of his son's illness. Jim, himself, admitted to considerable drinking with the gang and the usual amount and manner of adolescent sexual experimentation. A certain social ambivalence was indicated as the patient described gang activities on one hand, but on the other a solitary, lonely search for values and identity.

It appeared that the patient's youth and early development had not been especially unusual but certainly was characterized by early and nearly complete withdrawal from parental influence, by gang activities symptomatic of delinquency, and by considerable conflict with parental authority. Evidence was given of parental pampering and attempts to buy the boy's love and cooperation. One could foresee the difficulties that such conditioning would cause when the boy was subjected to the stresses of illness, immobilization, and conflict with the hospital autocracy.

Jim evinced no apparent guilt over the death of the young man who was riding with him the night of the accident. He dismissed it with the curt rejoinder, "It was his fault . . . he was messing around." We had no way of knowing if the details as he recounted them were true, and even if they were, whether anyone could be as immune as he seemed to be to the violent death of another human being. We knew that the accident had brought with it a host of additional problems for this young patient. He had been served with a subpoena in a civil action because of his companion's death. He feared trouble with the law because he was violating probation, inasmuch as he was drinking and was out after prescribed hours on the night of the accident. One of his laments was the loss of his new Corvette sports car which had been demolished in the accident. He spoke of this car with great affection and the pitch of his voice and the look in his eyes was mute testimony to the intensity of his attachment to it.

Four weeks after Jim's admission, a cervical fusion was done because of the continued displacement and angulation of the body of the second cervical vertebra on the third. Approximately three weeks later, the Crutchfield tongs became displaced and had to be reinserted. The patient refused to consent to this last procedure but it was done in spite of his protests. His father signed the necessary consent.

During the night, approximately two weeks later, the traction rope broke. The patient got out of bed without calling the nurse and was discovered in the morning sitting beside his bed with a pair of Crutchfield tongs hanging down his back—a ludicrous picture of one seemingly insistent on having the last word.

After this episode, a plaster Minerva jacket was applied. The patient had a final trip to the operating room for curettage of infected burr holes before he was ready for discharge.

Staff Rejection

Many of these problems had developed before I became involved in the care of this patient, but it was nonetheless possible to modify some of them and assist the staff to a better understanding of what had occurred.

All agreed that the patient could have been involved in planning his care and could have been kept better informed as to his progress. Better communication, successfully substituted for the punitive measures might have elicited the patient's cooperation. A number of interviews revealed Jim's deep resentment about the lack of information he was given regarding plans for his care and his exclusion from any participation in these plans. These observations were discussed with members of the staff and some remedial measures were belatedly taken.

The mechanism of rejection by the hospital staff which had only succeeded in driving the patient into deeper withdrawal and hostility was explored and accepted. The reasons for these reactions were discussed with the patient and he seemed to have a better than expected understanding of his own resentment of authority as well as some appreciation for the decisions which had been made, perhaps without his express consent, but because of certain legal responsibilities for his care. It was felt that the patient's unwillingness or inability to cooperate with the treatment program and his disruptive ward behavior may have been based on some unconscious mechanism of denial or self-destruction but this was not demonstrated.

However, we could conclude that he had not as yet completed the adolescent task of establishing either his personal identity or a workable set of values. His peer group had led him into antisocial, group-type activities considerably at conflict with parental, spiritual, and societal values. He manifested extreme insecurity when not supported by the gang and turned with anxiety and possessiveness to the one person capable of supplying emotional support—his girl friend. He exhibited the classical, spiritless, bored, "anything for a kick" attitude of many youths who are searching for a purpose in life and a meaningful definition of living. His preoccupation with sex would lead one to the conclusion that in this area, also, he was still immature, still insecure in his manliness.

The weeks which followed our planned efforts to understand Jim saw a gradual improvement in his attitude and behavior, and staff members became friendlier and more accepting of him.

Adolescents will always be a part of our society and their search for a maturity will inevitably be characterized by ambiguity, stress, and anxiety. Some will make but a tenuous adjustment. A considerable number will need assistance from the helping professions as they strive to achieve healthy maturity or as they meet the stressful problem of illness. With this group, things mechanical (including war, demonstrations, and motor vehicles) become a hazard to life, limb, and emotional stability. Therefore, we can expect that many more adolescents will require health care as a result of sudden, unexpected, and ill-timed accidental injuries. The challenge of their physical care will be no less important than that of their emotional needs, especially those which have origin in the well-known, but not too well understood, phenomena of immobilization and sensory deprivation.

Whether the stresses of their illness and hospital experience will represent growth toward maturity will depend to a considerable extent on professional intervention during this period. And the degree to which professional people are aware of their own needs will relate directly to their effectiveness in perceiving and supplying the comprehensive care young patients require.

Bibliography

Bueker, Kathleen. "Adolescents Need Attention." *Amer. J. Nurs.* **60**:372–376, March, 1960.

Cholcher, Mary, and Burtis, Mary. "Teens Together." *Amer. J. Nurs.* **64**:104–105, July, 1964.

Daubenmire, M. Jean, and others. "Adolescence in the Hospital." *Nurs. Outlook* **8**:502–504, September, 1960.

Eisenberg, Leon. "Developmental Approach to Adolescence." *Children* **12**:133–135, July–August, 1965.

Erikson, E. H. *Childhood and Society*, rev. ed. New York: W. W. Norton and Co., 1964.

King, Joan M. "Denial." *Amer. J. Nurs.* **66**:1010–1013, May, 1966.

Pressey, Sidney, and Kuhlen, R. G. *Psychological Development Through the Life Span.* New York: Harper and Brothers, 1957.

chapter seven

ADULT STAGE

The adult patient is the recipient of most nursing care. In the preceding pages we have attempted to show that it is essential to study the development of the person from his earliest years in order to understand the adult's personality and the manner in which the adult patient responds to illness, injury, and hospitalization.

The earliest studies and theories of personality development considered the infant and child in detail, but usually stopped at adulthood. Of course, it was recognized that marriage, pregnancy, parenthood, menopause, aging, and so on, represent challenges and stresses during adulthood. Erik Erikson, in *Childhood and Society,* however, systematically applied the concept of developmental stages to adult life as well as to childhood.[1]

We have already enumerated and described briefly the first five stages of Erikson's schema and the nuclear conflicts that characterize them. He then delineates three stages in the adult.

The first is the post-adolescent or young-adult period. The second is maturity, and the third is old age. During each of these stages, the individual is faced with characteristic life experiences and internal conflicts. The manner in which he resolves these conflicts and adapts to the circumstances of his life will be determined to a considerable extent by the manner in which he has resolved the nuclear conflicts associated with earlier stages.

---

[1] Erik H. Erikson. *Childhood and Society.* New York: W. W. Norton & Company, Inc., 1963.

In young adulthood, the person strives to achieve at least the first phase of sexual (genital) maturity. He seeks a sense of *intimacy* with a person of the opposite sex and should be able to express and integrate the earlier, more childish modes of sexuality under the influence and impact of a more mature sexual life. Insofar as he is unable to achieve intimacy, he may experience a sense of *isolation* and distance from others. Thus, the nuclear conflict of early adulthood would be between the achievement of intimacy and the experience of isolation. Where circumstances preclude the achievement of this type of intimacy, significant professional relationships and friendships may provide at least a partial solution to this conflict.

During the middle years, Erikson refers to a sense of *generativity* leading to productive and creative work. In women, this may include child rearing as well as career achievements. The opposite pole from generativity during these years may be a pervasive feeling of *stagnation*. In the section on Middle Age, we consider this conflict in more detail.

During old age, the individual sums up his life consciously and unconsciously. In addition, he responds to the evaluations of his family, friends, and colleagues. If he has been fortunate, he experiences a feeling of *ego integrity*, of having lived a worthwhile life. He has a sense of wholeness and a satisfying continuity with his past. If he has not been so fortunate, he may feel a sense of *despair*. The numerous problems associated with aging in our culture make this time of life even more difficult than it might otherwise need to be. We discuss these and other elements involved in aging in Chapter 9.

Reactions to Illness

The adult personality is the product of a long developmental sequence, much of which we have already described. While changes in body and mind may continue throughout life, by the time an individual has passed through adolescence his physical structure has been completed and his mental apparatus is fully formed. Changes that occur during adult life are of a different magnitude from those that occur during childhood. They are slower, and the increment of change is smaller.

When a person is physically well and emotionally healthy, his total functioning is smooth. Adaptation to his environment, satisfaction of his needs, and social interactions proceed relatively effortlessly and with a minimum of subjective discomfort. The individual feels and behaves as though he is in control of his impulses and feels in harmony with his superego ideals and demands. Under most circumstances, he is able either to satisfy his needs without excessive delay or frustration or to defer satisfaction without undue anxiety or conflict. His ego is capable of making choices that seem best for the total equilibrium of his personality.

Each person develops psychological and behavioral adaptational patterns which serve to cope with the threat of emotional disequilibrium under normal circumstances. These patterns become incorporated into ego functioning and are called *mental mechanisms* or *defense mechanisms*. This ego activity is largely unconscious, although the resulting thoughts, feelings, or behavior may reach awareness. Just as one is not aware of the digestive processes or of the actions of the nerves and muscles during physical acts, so one is not conscious of most of the operations of the mind.

For instance, as the nurse goes about her work efficiently and without serious conflict, she is usually relatively unaware of strong reactions to individual patients, anxiety about nursing procedures, or irritation with physicians or colleagues. It is only when she feels particularly annoyed at a patient, or unduly protective of one, or when she realizes that she has forgotten to carry out an important medication order, for example, that one can observe transient and usually minor interruptions in her mental functioning and behavior.

By the same token, the patient with whom the nurse has contact is not only physically different from the way he was before his illness or injury. Usually he has also reacted emotionally to the stress of the physical disorder. His psyche has been required to make shifts in order once again to regain some sense of mental balance. It is when such disequilibrium threatens the person that he is apt to experience the feelings associated with anxiety.

No one is able to achieve maturity without having undergone some psychological trauma. The capacity to tolerate stress varies with each individual. A minor procedure may greatly upset one patient, whereas another patient will scarcely notice it. Nurses, too, vary in their capacity to tolerate stress. Some nurses find the operating room experience or intensive care units too demanding or upsetting. Other nurses find such places exciting, challenging, and stimulating. There are limits, however, to the amount and the types of stress any person can withstand.

Fear and anger in small doses stimulate the ego, thereby increasing its efficiency. With repeated prolonged or severe psychological traumata, however, the intensity of these emotions may heighten until the ego is overwhelmed and loses much of its effectiveness.

During illness the person often feels helpless and dejected because of the changes in himself and in his environment precipitated by the illness. The patient must surrender a good deal of his usual freedom and become a passive partner to the activities of the doctors and nurses on whom he relies for treatment and protection. As long as the medical staff can demonstrate their ability to care effectively for him, the patient feels relatively safe. Illness, helplessness, and dependence on others tend to produce responses reminiscent of early childhood. His difficulties are additionally accentuated by the direct effects of his illness, fatigue, and loss of sleep. Intense anxiety can result from such circumstances. Helplessness and anxiety cause the patient to feel insecure and may impair his capacity to relate to others. He may fear and avoid the hospital staff or become uncooperative with nursing procedures.

Object loss refers to the loss of a person or thing which has special value or meaning to an individual. The concept of object loss is often applied in relation to death and dying and other significant separation experiences.

Object loss also may be experienced following loss or damage to parts of the body through amputation, mastectomy, paralysis, brain damage, severe scarring, etc. These patients often experience grief reactions accompanied by feelings of depression, withdrawal and lowered self-esteem. Such reactions are especially marked when the loss either symbolically or realistically seems likely to interfere with occupational, social or sexual functioning or attractiveness.

Nurses who help patients face the loss of organs through surgery must bear in mind some of the various problems which confront him. The meaning to a patient of loss of certain internal organs may be seen by the importance of a specific body organ. In the case of cardiac surgery, the patient may experience a stronger response than one having an appendectomy, as the heart possesses an important psychic life-giving representation.

ANXIETY

Anxiety is a universal emotion. Anxiety and fear are identical feeling states. The term "fear," however, is sometimes used when there appears to be a realistic or objective basis for such a reaction. An example of fear would be the feelings a patient experiences when confronted with a diagnosis of cancer. Anxiety, on the other hand, usually applies where there seems to be less "objective" basis for the feelings of apprehension. At times, anxiety occurs for no apparent reason. This is sometimes referred to as "free-floating anxiety." On other occasions, the reasons seem inadequate to account for the strong reactions experienced by the patient. An example is some patients' near-panic when it becomes necessary to draw blood for laboratory tests. Since both terms describe the identical feeling state, we will use them interchangeably with the meaning clarified by the context.

Anxiety is one of the normal, biological reactions to danger, becoming pathological only when experienced in excessive quantity or when persisting without apparent provocation. It is a subjective feeling tone that accompanies physiological reactions that occur predominantly in the sympathetic nervous system and its innervated smooth muscles and glands, in preparation for or during external emergencies.

An especially graphic description of anxiety is the following one by Margaret Neylan:

> Anxiety may be defined as a feeling tone of anticipation, generally unpleasant. Physiologically, it is manifested in the "fight or flight" mechanism which is triggered by a release of a comparatively large amount of adrenalin into the blood stream. Respirations become rapid and more shallow, pulse accelerates, color changes, generally toward pallor, but sometimes there is flushing. Common gastrointestinal symptoms that may occur are "butterflies in the stomach," nausea, cramps, vomiting, and diarrhea. Appetite may be decreased or occasionally increased. Usually perspiration increases, particularly of the palms of the hands, the soles of the feet, and the axillae.
>
> Muscles are generally tensed, often giving rise to tremor, taut facial expression, and rigid body stance. One of the results of this may be a certain lack of coordination leading to clumsiness and manual errors. If this muscular tension is maintained, tension headaches or backaches may occur. Frequency of micturition is common. Eyeballs may be slightly more protuberant and pupils tend to dilate, giving the appearance of a "glassy-eyed stare." Changes in blood pressure can be expected. Often the skin shows goose-pimples. In fact, the frightened person may say, describing this, "My hair stood on end." Often a dryness of the mouth is reported.

Every nurse has observed that it is often difficult or impossible to ascertain whether an anxious reaction is based on realistic considerations or springs from a fear of the unknown or a reawakening of a deep-seated conflict within the patient. A clinical example of a mixture of fear and anxiety might help to clarify these differences.

A 60-year-old man who previously had been in excellent health developed acute abdominal pain. He was referred by his physician to a hospital, where a diagnosis of acute gall bladder disease was made and an exploratory operation performed. The gall bladder was found to be normal and the patient recovered rapidly from the effects of the surgery. He was sent home within a week. Shortly thereafter, an EKG, which had been done almost as an afterthought just prior to his discharge, revealed that his symptoms had been caused by an undiagnosed myocardial infarction. At this point, the patient was called at his home and urged to return immediately to the hospital. Although he no longer had any physical discomfort, he was placed in an oxygen tent and treated as though he was acutely ill. Not surprisingly, he experienced marked apprehension and became tense, agitated, and depressed. The nursing staff noted that he was wakeful and needed constant reassurance. The physicians prescribed sedatives and were concerned about the patient's emotional condition.

The patient's family informed the treating physician that their father had always been a man who relied strongly on intellectual understanding for a sense of security. Furthermore, he needed to be able to assist in his treatment program if at all possible. The family suggested that the treating physician offer a complete explanation to the patient of his condition, its treatment, and its prognosis.

The physician followed this suggestion and the patient almost immediately became more comfortable. He recovered from the infarction with remarkably little residual effect. In his case, ignorance was not bliss, but instead caused him to feel helpless and acutely apprehensive. He commented later, "Once I understood it, I could adapt to it."

In this clinical example, it seems reasonable that a man who had been misdiagnosed, told he is well, and then informed that he has had a coronary occlusion and placed in emergency treatment would have every realistic basis for feeling fearful and apprehensive. On the other hand, as his recovery proceeded, he continued to be anxious and apprehensive beyond what one would expect under the circumstances. This continuing anxiety reflected less the realistic concerns he had first experienced than a reaction to his feelings of helplessness, impotence, and lack of understanding of what had happened to him. His usual adaptational methods, which included intellectual mastery and active participation in conducting his life, were temporarily out of his grasp. The result was that he felt increasingly frustrated and anxious. When the situation was corrected by his doctor, the patient almost immediately began to improve.

When anxiety is not overwhelming, it can serve a useful function by alerting the person to the existence of some threat within himself or in his environment. If it becomes overwhelming and approaches panic, however, then all functioning is paralyzed. Severe anxiety is one of the most uncomfortable feeling states human beings can experience. To be overwhelmed by anxiety is the epitome of feeling helpless, infantile, and vulnerable to the very worst that the world and one's inner impulses can offer.

The sense of mastery or autonomy, which we examined earlier in terms of child development, is a very important aspect of human psychology. The feeling that one has the capacity to determine one's activities and destiny is interrupted when a patient falls ill. This can be a most distressing aspect of illness. Illness and surgery often bring the person face to face with concerns about death. Such an eventuality, even though it may be remote, leads both to fear and to severe anxiety. This is particularly true in surgery. Even a relatively simple procedure, such as a tonsillectomy or a herniorrhaphy, can induce anxieties and fantasies associated with mutilation and death. The fact is that no matter how minor a surgical procedure is, it carries with it some physical and psychological risk.

Bernard Kutner notes some of the problems associated with surgery.[3]

---

[3] Bernard Kutner. "Surgeons and Their Patients: A Study in Social Perception." In *Patients, Physicians, and Illness.* E. Gardley Jaco, ed. New York: The Free Press, 1958.

He mentions that some specific types, such as colostomy, limb amputation, radical mastectomy, craniotomy, hysterectomy, and orchidectomy carry with them the actual or probable loss of a bodily part and the function that that part serves. Operations involving the genital organs, eyes, and skull are thought to present the greatest danger of psychological disruption. Such operations are realistically feared, because they are serious. Furthermore, they are accompanied by apprehension regarding the future.

An example is a case of a 21-year-old American soldier who was sent home from Vietnam with a badly injured arm. His doctors told him amputation might be necessary. This young man became moody and depressed, did not want to see his family, and was especially upset when he was unable to pick up his infant son because of the damage to his arm. This physical limitation was accompanied by feelings of inadequacy as a wage earner, as a father, and as a husband. This was especially traumatic for him since he had been an outdoorsman, an athlete, and had worked with his hands. The injury required major changes in his way of life and in his self-concept.

Goffman notes that illness and disability may have the effect of cutting the individual off from society and from himself, thereby "spoiling his identity." [4] The person handicapped by illness or through surgery feels different and is often treated differently by society. He may no longer feel worthwhile or accepted, especially when he has been "stigmatized" by his illness. Obvious bodily changes through radical surgery change his self-concept and threaten his body intactness. Changes in one's image may occur even when one has no easily identifiable external bodily change, as in the case of a person who has experienced a mental illness.

Nurses are frequently in a unique position to observe changes in the patient's self-concept and to intervene in helping him rebuild a damaged self-concept. The nurse often helps the patient with new appliances, equipment, and clothing that help to make these changes less obvious. Her acceptance of the patient can give him a sense of comfort that he may find difficult to achieve in many other relationships.

Reactions to hospitalization are shaped by the patient's illness, his prognosis, the accommodation in which he is housed, and significantly, by his preconceived image of the institution. Although the hospital is especially equipped to deal with diseases, many persons assign negative connotations to it; the hospital is a place where suffering is concentrated, bodies are mutilated, and people are taken to die. Sometimes treatment is feared as much as or more than the diseease. The persistence of such fears and anxieties often interferes with the healthy convalescence of the patient.

It has been shown in repeated studies that the patient who is prepared

---

[4] Irving Goffman. *Stigma: Notes on the Management of Spoiled Identity.* Englewood Cliffs, N. J.: Prentice-Hall, Inc., 1963. P. 87.

for surgery makes a speedier recovery than the patient who is emotionally unprepared.

The stress of an operation may even cause some patients to become psychotic prior to surgery.[5]

Research has been conducted in intensive care units where the patient is subjected to monitoring, frequent examinations by the physician and nurse. In the case of open-heart surgery, which is major surgery, the patient in addition may have a tracheotomy, making it difficult, if not impossible for him to speak, and relay his feelings to the nurse or doctor. These patients all too frequently become psychotic; certainly there are indications of sensory deprivation. The intense threat to life, the isolation from relatives, and the preoccupation of the staff for serious medical and surgical implications cause the patient as a person to be lost in the shuffle. The sights and sounds in the intensive care unit are enough alone to make an inexperienced person extremely upset and frightened. Staff working in these units are under extreme stress because the death rate is high with patients, the tension level is high, and the risks are high. In the reprinted article, "The Irony of the ICU," pp. 275–78 in this text, Rome writes of the potential psychological dangers to nurses and patients in the use of intensive care units.[6]

The nurse therefore should be aware that an anxious response in hospitalized patients may represent their reaction to the totality of the hospital experience. For the nurse, the physical aspects of the hospital and the procedures that take place within its walls tend to become routine. Nursing and laboratory procedures seem logical and understandable. To the patient, however, these same procedures and this same setting may evoke deep-seated fears and anxious fantasies of illness, pain, suffering, and death. Though these reactions are especially prevalent in children, they occur as well in many adult patients.

NARCISSISM

Apprehension or anxiety is related to the threat of loss of what is needed or loved. Love, affection, interest, care, or devotion are psychological and behavioral aspects of the libidinal or sexual drive. In infancy and early childhood, intaking trends are prominent in relation not only to food and drink, but also to love and attention. The child is "narcissistically" preoccupied with his own somatic and psychological needs. This infantile narcissism gradually diminishes as the child grows older and more secure. He

---

[5] E. Gartley Saco. *Patients, Physicians and Illness.* New York: Free Press, 1958.
[6] Howard Rome. "The Irony of the ICU." *Psychiatry Digest.* May, 1969. Pp. 10–14.

then becomes able to love other persons while still retaining a normal quantity of narcissism or self-interest.

When a person feels emotionally strong and physically healthy, his narcissism is relatively intact. He feels confident and self-assured. Illness and death are unpleasant but remote possibilities. When accidents and illnesses occur, they are experienced as blows to one's narcissism insofar as it applies to his body, just as rejection and criticism are affronts to one's narcissism as it applies to his personality and his conception of himself as a psychosocial being.

Physical illnesses or disabilities are almost invariably experienced and reacted to as narcissistic wounds. The individual feels "hurt" and suffers from a sense of loss (loss of physical intactness) and depression. There is a weakening or a shattering of feelings of omnipotence and invulnerability, which all healthy persons have to some extent.

Of course, every adult "knows" that illness, accidents, old age, and death are the inevitable accompaniments and outcome of life itself. Nonetheless, hidden within each of us is the secret certainly that we will be spared. *Others* fall ill and die, accidents happens to *them,* but these events do not occur to *us.*

So it is that when the nurse cares for her patients, she is interacting with persons whose narcissism has been damaged. Many patients are incredulous that fate could have attacked them so wrongfully. They desperately need to rebuild their narcissistic "supplies." They want and need love and tenderness, care, and attention. At the same time, they are often depressed and irritable, intolerant of delay, and demanding toward nurses, doctors, family and friends. Their behavior may be seen as the result of their wish to be restored to physical and emotional health so that their sense of narcissism will once again seem intact. They want this to occur instantly, and feel frustrated and impatient when it does not occur as they wish. Such reactions may be considered normal in many people. Persons who ordinarily are patient, considerate, and independent may become irritable, depressed, and overly dependent patients.

DEFENSE MECHANISM

We have already alluded to anxiety and fear as it is experienced *consciously*. Sigmund Freud suggested, however, that small doses of anxiety that are stimulated on an *unconscious* level by threats to the equilibrium of the personality may serve an important triggering function to the ego by setting into motion certain mental operations.[7] Their purpose is to reduce

---

[7] Sigmund Freud. *Inhibitions, Symptoms and Anxiety.* Stand. Ed. Vol. XX. London: The Hogarth Press. Pp. 77–175.

the possibility of the development of conscious, overwhelming anxiety that can interfere with functioning. He referred to this unconscious anxiety as "signal" anxiety.

This signal anxiety, in modern terms of automation, serves a "feedback function" in alerting the psychic apparatus to the threat of some inner disequilibrium. Then the ego unconsciously proceeds to choose from its resources an appropriate means of dealing with the imbalance. Often what is called forth is one or another of the various mental defense mechanisms. These mental operations or clusters of feeling, thinking, and behaving are grouped into categories. They were described systematically by Anna Freud in *The Ego and the Mechanisms of Defense*.[8] Since then, psychoanalysts and psychologists have studied the development and operation of defense mechanisms in detail and have added substantially to our knowledge about the manner in which the ego carries out its work, mediating between internal impulses while adapting to the external world.

Repression. We have already alluded to a number of significant defense mechanisms as we discussed Freud's early work and as we described the development of the individual through infancy and childhood. In Chapter Four, we discussed repression and its contribution to infantile amnesia and to keeping from consciousness those impulses and conflicts that might interfere with ego functioning throughout life.

Repression occupies a unique place in psychoanalytic theory and practice. Freud considered it one of the three "cornerstones" on which the analytic theory of the neuroses is based.[9]

Brenner writes:

> Repression consists in an activity of the ego which bars from consciousness the unwanted id impulse or any of its derivatives, whether memories, emotions, desires, or wish-fulfilling fantasies. All are as though they did not exist as far as the individual's conscious life is concerned. A repressed memory is a forgotten one from the subjective point of view of the individual in whom repression has taken place.[10]

The repressed impulse continues to exert pressure for discharge from the id. It requires a constant counterforce from the side of the ego to maintain the repression. Repression is initiated in the first place to bar access to consciousness those impulses or their derivatives that would lead to anxiety or guilt. It may occur throughout life when unconscious, unacceptable impulses threaten to become conscious and disrupt the equilibrium of the personality. The ego's counterforce is weakened in some cases of psychosis,

---

[8] Anna Freud. *The Ego and the Mechanisms of Defense.* 1939.
[9] Sigmund Freud. *Psychoanalysis.* Standard Edition, 1926. Vol. 20. P. 2677.
[10] Charles Brenner. *An Elementary Textbook of Psychoanalysis.* Garden City, N.Y.: Doubleday Anchor Books, 1955. P. 89.

severe anxiety, or psychoneurosis, as well as in febrile or toxic states. Repression then begins to fail and derivatives or direct expressions of the repressed impulses may appear.

Patients who are acutely ill or are emerging from surgical anesthesia may verbalize or behave aggressively or seductively, thereby expressing impulses usually repressed. The same is true in alcoholic or drug intoxication. The repression is usually reinstated following recovery from the acute situation, although psychosis following surgery or drug intoxication sometimes persists.

Another more normal manner in which such unconscious mental processes may reveal themselves in nurses is discussed in Beate Brann's article, "Unconscious Motivation and Medication Errors." [11] Nuring procedures are especially strict in the area of medication administration. The potential for serious harm from medication errors is great, and the measuring and administration of medication is usually entirely the nurse's responsibility. While errors undoubtedly can result from fatigue, distraction, ignorance, or inexperience, it is well to keep in mind that unconscious motivation can cause nurses to make medication and other errors in their nursing procedures. In Brann's reported cases, there is no evidence given of conscious rancor or intention to injure any patient. Instead, it seemed likely that in most of these cases, there were unconscious repressed impulses related to (1) emotional involvement with patients, (2) frustrations in the nurse's therapeutic efforts with chronic patients, or (3) the nurse's conviction that the medication was of little or no value.

Other unconscious attitudes that might be at play include resentful feelings toward the physicians, sexual feelings toward patients, and defensive hostility directed at patients who do not improve. Finally, the nurse may unconsciously resent nursing colleagues or supervisors.

These are but a few speculations about some of the repressed motivations that might contribute to causing a nurse to make medication errors. More lengthy, in depth interviews in each case would be required to understand some of these factors more fully. Since unconscious impulses may be powerful and can overcome ego controls, nursing practice quite rightly calls for careful, methodical routines that help the nurse avoid medication errors even when disruptive unconscious impulses may be present.

The following case illustrates the power of unconscious impulses. A young nurse, working in an army hospital, was assigned to the ward for prisoners in the stockade. One young patient was especially flirtatious. The nurse recognized that she found him somewhat attractive, but at the same time felt it necessary to maintain her professional and personal distance.

[11] Beate Brann. "Unconscious Motivation in Medication Errors." *Journal of Psychiatric Nursing*. July–August, 1966. Pp. 362–70.

One evening, she was to administer twenty drops of belladonna to him. A half hour following her giving the medication, the patient reported that he felt strange, that his eyes were blurry and he thought something was the matter with him. Upon checking her records, the nurse realized that she had inadvertently administered ten times the does that had been prescribed. In a state of near panic, she called the physician, who reassured her that while the dose was large, the medication was not very toxic and the patient would recover.

She realized later that her error had been related to consciously unwanted sexual feelings aroused by this young man, which had been largely repressed. She was deeply resentful and angry that he stimulated such conflicts in her and retaliated against him without any conscious wish to do so. Fortunately, serious medication and treatment errors happen infrequently. Nurses, however, should be aware that unconscious forces are active, both in their personal contacts with patients and in their nursing procedures.

Suppression. Suppression, in contrast, is a *conscious* putting aside of a thought or feeling, which can then easily be retrieved from memory. This is, of course, different from repression, in which case the mechanism is unconscious and direct retrieval from memory of the thought or feeling is rarely possible. For example, an experienced nurse, faced with a serious acute burn case or accidental mutilation, consciously suppresses feelings of revulsion or horror or any other intrusive feelings or mental images which might otherwise interfere with carrying out her professional responsibilities. Then, when the emergency has passed, she recalls the details and feels the full emotional impact of the experience.

Denial. Among other defense mechanisms is denial. Here, the ego bars to consciousness the awareness of a reality that is too painful for the ego to tolerate. Nurses are familiar with the operation of this mechanism in patients who are suffering from terminal cancer or brain damage or who cannot bear to face the disability occasioned by severe accident or amputation.

Denial is by no means always pathological. It often serves an essential adaptational function. For some patients, it is vital for their sense of well-being that they be permitted or even encouraged to retain their denial of impending death or disability. On the other hand, there are times when denial operates to interfere with adequate cooperation with adjustment to an illness or to hospital procedures. In these cases, the patient may have to be confronted tactfully with his tendency to deny the facts and be helped to face reality as best he can.

An all-too-frequent case is that of a woman who discovers a suspicious lump in her breast but delays seeking diagnosis. At first she *denies* that it is possible for her to have a serious lesion. In extreme cases, patients will finally consult the doctor with far advanced tumors whose presence they had refused to perceive in spite of the most obvious signs and symptoms.

The presence of denial is seen, too, in men who refuse to alter their diets or life styles following serious cardiovascular illness. They simply deny the existence of life-threatening disease and continue to live as though they had never been ill. Some of these patients rationalize their behavior by stating that they simply can't or won't change. But denial appears to be a prominent mechanism in these cases and often is responsible for premature death.

At a recent clinical seminar, a nurse, Miss R., expressed annoyance toward a patient with terminal carcinoma who continued to deny the imminence of her death in spite of severe symptoms and obvious debilitation. While describing the patient, Miss R. chain-smoked cigarettes! A nurse colleague then confronted Miss R. with her own behavior which reflected denial of the overwhelming evidence for a causal relationship between smoking and lung cancer. The ensuing discussion pointed up the widespread use of denial and how powerful a mechanism it is. Furthermore, it became clear that for Mrs. R's patient, the use of denial was vital to whatever sense of stability and equanimity she could muster in the face of death.

What should be emphasized is that denial, like all other mental mechanisms, takes effect unconsciously. The person does not voluntarily or willfully choose to repress or to deny. The ego seeks to achieve the most stable equilibrium possible, taking into account the internal and environmental factors and making use of those mental operations that seem most suitable to the situation. Denial is to external reality what repression is to the inner reality of instinctual drives.

Displacement. In the section on transference in Chapter One, transference was described as a special example of the mental mechanism of displacement. Displacement refers to the unconscious substitution of a new object for one toward whom the feelings were originally directed. Nurses, for example, often receive the criticism and hostility of patients who are angry or disappointed with their physicians or family members. Another example is of the nurse who is resentful of the manner in which a colleague or physician has treated her, but is unable to express her feelings toward that person. She may then go home and be irritable and angry with her husband or children for no sufficient or apparent reason. She has *displaced* her feelings of resentment and hostility away from the person toward whom they were originally aimed onto someone else.

Isolation. Excrement, infected wounds, colostomies, burns, the ravages of cancer—all must be treated with professional dignity by the nurse. Poorly controlled feelings of aversion, disgust or revulsion might otherwise be expressed to the detriment of the nurse–patient relationship. Sometimes repression is set into motion in such cases, causing both the negative feelings *and* ideas to be barred from consciousness.

Another mental defense which occurs frequently in such circumstances is called *isolation*. When isolation is operative, only the potentially disruptive feelings are banished from consciousness (repressed) while the thoughts about the experience remain within consciousness. The feeling is thus deemphasized and isolated from the ideas that originally accompanied it. As a result of the process of isolation, most nurses eventually *feel* little or no aversion to emptying a bedpan, for example, even though they may still *think* about the distasteful aspects of the task.

Reaction formation. In the section on the toddler stage, there was discussion of how, in the normal course of development, pleasure in bowel activity and enjoyment of sadistic activities toward animals and other children become converted through the process of psychological growth and socialization into something like their opposites. Instead of experiencing fascination with and pleasure from bowel functions, the child learns to behave as though defecating is a dirty, unpleasant act in which he is not supposed to express interest or curiosity except as a matter of health. By the same token, the early meanness and aggression shown by many small children turn to pity and concern about others as the child matures. Children go through stages in which they can scarcely bear to see an insect swatted or hear about an animal dying, even though only a few months or years before they were fascinated by pain and death. The mental mechanism leading to these changes is called reaction formation. Bibring et al. write that this implies "the management of unacceptable impulses by permitting the expression of the impulse in an exactly antithetical form; in effect the expression of the unacceptable impulse in the negative." [12] As a result of reaction formation, impulses towards sadism or cruelty may later be channelled into kindness and pity. Exhibitionistic tendencies may be manifest through reaction formation by excessive modesty. Early infantile fascination with filth and dirt may be converted into overconcern about germs and excessive cleanliness.

Magical thinking. The giving up of reality testing in the interest of making wishful thinking come true was referred to as a normal component of childish thinking. Adults may also use it illogically in order to avoid awareness of external danger or as a way of attempting to fulfill certain needs. Superstitions are manifestations of magical thinking.

Regression. A phenomenon with which nurses are familiar is regression, since patients often show a return to some earlier or less mature mode

---

[12] Grete Bibring et al. "A Study of the Psychological Processes in Pregnancy and of the Earliest Mother-Child Relationship." *Psychoanalytic Study of the Child.* Vol. 16 (1961). P. 69.

of functioning during illness and hospitalization. In a nursing seminar, the question arose as to the meaning and significance of regression during illness. Most of the nurses present felt that regression was to be avoided and that it was the nurse's job to prevent it insofar as possible in those patients under their care. This suggestion showed misunderstanding of the meaning of regression, since regression may represent an adaptive manner of dealing with a situation that arouses conflict and anxiety. Bibring et al. describe regression as a "return to a previous state of functioning to avoid the anxieties and hostilities involved in later stages; a re-establishment of an earlier stage where conflict is less. . . . It is a 'way out,' and, as it were, a flight into earlier modes of adjustment." [13]

There can be regression in thinking, feeling and behavior. During illness, the usual modes of achieving satisfaction are often barred to the individual, and therefore he sometimes returns to behaving in more infantile fashions in order to achieve certain essential gratification. Patients who are ordinarily independent and self-assured may become dependent and clinging to the nursing staff and doctors. The implication here is that regression need not be a permanent or necessarily a pathological mode, but may represent the most practicable adaptation to a situation that otherwise cannot be dealt with effectively.

It is true, of course, that regression when continued too long may interfere with the healing process. For this reason, it is the nurse's responsibility to be sensitive to the changes in the patient's condition that may warrant encouragement of his independence or a return to more adult modes of functioning. The point we wish to make here, however, is that evidence of regression is not in and of itself evidence of a negative, antitherapeutic situation. Instead, it may be the patient's way of dealing with the physical and emotional trauma of illness and hospitalization.

An example of regression that was required to assist in the healing process is given by Eleanor Cockerill in her article, "Reflections on My Nursing Care." [14] This article describes how it was necessary for the author to "fully accept the necessity for spoonfeeding during the first 5 or 6 postoperative days." Furthermore, she refers to the "abrupt shift from adult to infant role and from independent to dependent status" which "called for a quick shifting of gears on [her] part." Thus, nurses had to help the patient to accept a more infantile regressed situation during the postoperative period in order to assist in her recovery.

On other occasions, patients may regress to more infantile modes of bowel and bladder functioning or may become irritable, clinging, whining, or depressed. In these cases, the nurses may be helpful by accepting the

[13] *Ibid.* P. 69.
[14] Eleanor Cockerill. "Reflections on My Nursing Care." *American Journal of Nursing.* Vol. 65, No. 5 (May, 1965). Pp. 83–85.

patient's temporary regression, showing empathy and sympathy, and then encouraging the patient to try to behave more in his usual fashion so that he can be more cooperative and participate more fully in nursing procedures.

Withdrawal. A commonly observed mechanism in ill patients is withdrawal. In this situation, the individual may be depressed and may turn his attention, feelings, and thinking to himself and to his illness with little interest left for his environment or other persons. This withdrawal may be either self-involvement (narcissicism) as a result of illness or other crisis, or a way of avoiding a situation that might lead to increased anxiety. In the case of physically ill persons, some degree of withdrawal is to be expected and should not be considered abnormal, since physical disorder compels the ego to invest interest and energy in one's physical self. Withdrawal may be associated with depression and detachment of feelings from persons and things in the environment. It is only when it persists beyond a reasonable time and interferes with the patient's physical recovery or with his emotional functioning that it can be considered pathological.

Projection. Projection is a common defense mechanism, both in normal mental states and in psychopathology. Projection refers to the attribution of undesirable impulses to agencies or persons outside the self. In this way, aggressive, sexual, or punitive impulses are not experienced as belonging to one's self. Instead, they seem to be coming from some other person or thing. Then the individual reacts to the supposed source of these impulses as though they were from outside himself rather than from within his own mind.

Mild forms of projection include those cases in which a patient becomes convinced that a member of the nursing staff doesn't like him—"has it in for him." When this seems clearly not true, it is likely that the patient, unbearably angry and frustrated about some aspect of his illness or treatment, attributes the anger and rejection to the nurse in question.

Another example would be that of a patient who accuses the nursing staff of intentionally giving her smaller doses of pain medication than had been ordered. Such patients are unable to express their disappointment in the failure of their bodies as indicated by the continuing pain. They are unconsciously furious with their doctors and nurses ("parents") for not relieving their discomfort. The outcome may be accusations of carelessness, inadequate attention, and so on.

In its more extreme pathological forms, projection is manifested by marked suspiciousness and delusions of persecution. In such cases, patients may accuse nurses of poisoning them or attempting to harm them in some other way.

On the other hand, patients who accuse nursing staff of minor or major treatment errors or of acts of hostility may be at least partly correct. Nurses do on occasion behave tactlessly or untherapeutically toward a patient. His response then will not be a "projection," but an appropriate reaction to the nurse's treatment of him. Hostile behavior towards nurses or other care-givers should not automatically be disregarded on the basis that it is "projection."

Identification. Identification is a mental mechanism that describes the innumerable and varied changes brought about through modeling the self or some part of the self after another person or one of his characteristics. Identification begins during the first week after birth and goes on throughout life. The infant first imitates his mother's expressions, postures, and movements.

As he develops, many of his attitudes and personality traits represent identifications. The moral standards the child perceives in his parents are, through a form of identification, internalized to form part of the conscience or superego.

The adolescent identifies with his peers and with the current teen-age idols. Children (and adults) identify with teachers, politicians, and each other. Some identifications are unconscious, while others are at least partially conscious. Student nurses consciously and unconsciously attempt to emulate teachers or supervisors. After a while, certain attitudes that were acquired consciously may become unconscious. Examples may be found in behavior and attitudes toward patients and the manner of treating nursing colleagues and other medical personnel. Identification may be called unconsciously into play as a result of conflict. A nurse may identify with an unduly strict or controlling supervisor whom she dislikes. The nurse then tends to behave towards her patients the way the supervisor behaves towards her. Also, some nurses identify with the doctors or hospital administration, while others identify more with their patients.

Patients often identify with one another. Usually, the identification is based on similarity of illness or symptoms. A patient in a room with a dying person may begin to feel certain he too is dying and become depressed and more symptomatic. The behavior of ill persons is sometimes determined —at least in part—by early identifications with sick parents or siblings. Many of these adult identifications are shifting and transient, while those that contributed to building the personality are much more deeply imbedded and lasting.

Sublimation. The diversion of sexual energies into nonsexual activities and aims is termed sublimation. This mechanism is especially prominent during the middle childhood or latency years as for example, the child transforms sexual curiosity into an interest in science and other knowledge; voyeuristic trends are altered to appear as enjoyment of drama; messiness can be expressed through art work, and so on. Since mental mechanisms rarely appear in simple, uncomplicated forms, it is likely that these examples of sublimation also include repression, reaction formation, and other mechanisms.

Sublimation is active throughout life and contributes to adult career choices and hobbies. Sublimation is not a sign of psychopathology, but instead an aspect of normal psychological and social development.

Rationalization. Rationalization refers to the attempt to justify behavior, attitudes, or beliefs that might be unacceptable to one's ego or superego. The justification takes the form of fallacious reasoning or the misapplication of the truth. This is a very frequently used mechanism, and it is often very difficult or impossible to decide how much of an explanation is factual and how much represents an attempt to explain away the incident in a seemingly rational fashion.

While the list of mental mechanisms could be extended even further, those we have described are among the most widely used. Whether specific mental mechanisms are used in the service of normal functioning or whether they represent the basis for symptoms or personality disorders depends on the totality of the circumstances surrounding their use.

Psychosomatic Aspects of Illness

DEVELOPMENT OF PSYCHOSOMATIC MEDICINE

We have described some of the psychological and emotional reactions which patients manifest in conjunction with physical illness or injury. The course of an illness may be materially affected for better or worse by the nature of doctor–patient or nurse–patient relationships as well as by occurrences in the hospital.

Of even greater significance, however, are factors such as early childhood experiences, personality constellation, the course of vital family relationships, and the presence or absence of significant life stress prior to and during the patient's illness.

The mutual influences of physical illness, psychological states, and social interactions have been of interest to physicians throughout recorded history. Since the end of the nineteenth century, however, the relationship between physical illness and emotions has become the subject of serious and methodical scientific study.[15, 16] Prior to that time, Western man had tended to

---

[15] Chase Patterson Kimball. "Conceptual Developments in Psychosomatic Medicine: 1939–1969." *Annals of Internal Medicine.* Vol. 73 (1970). P. 307.

[16] Joseph Breuer and Sigmund Freud. *Studies on Hysteria* (1893–1895). Vol. II, in *The Standard Edition of the Complete Psychological Works of Sigmund Freud.* Ed. and trans. by James Strachey. London: The Hogarth Press, 1955. Pp. 1–240.

consider psyche (soul) and soma (body) as separate systems, even though their effects on each other had long been recognized. A basic difficulty in studying this relationship, however, lay in the fact that bodily reactions can be studied objectively, whereas emotional or psychological reactions are, to a considerable extent, subjective experiences. Thus, there have been two approaches to the study of man—a physical one and a mental one.

The psychosomatic approach attempts to study the mind-body problem from a unitary point of view and to reconcile observations from both the somatic and psychological spheres.

Freud's early work with the psychoneuroses compelled him to consider the mind-body problems since he frequently treated physical reactions to emotional conflicts. He described paralyses, anesthesias, pains, vomiting, visual disturbances, etc., as manifestations of "hysteria." In these cases, he ascribed to the physical symptomatology a "symbolic" function. That is, the patients would unconsciously attempt to resolve sexual conflicts by developing physical symptoms as "substitutes" or "conversions." These symptoms would then symbolically express important elements of the unconscious conflict. For example, partial blindness might symbolize both the wish to see a forbidden sexual scene as well as the self-imposed punishment for the wish. The paralysis of a soldier in combat could represent the wish to escape—and the fear of escaping—a terrifying situation in which he felt conscience-bound to remain.

The organs involved were generally the voluntary musculature and the sensory organs. The implication of these discoveries was that these particular organ systems seemed uniquely suited to express specific unconscious fantasies, feelings, and impulses. Furthermore, these conversion symptoms seemed to bind the emotional tensions associated with the conflicts so that the patient suffering from these disorders rarely evidenced or experienced severe anxiety.

In 1920, Cannon published his classical work describing laboratory experiments in which he found that the organism responds to fear and rage as though preparing physiologically for fight or flight.[17] In other words, emotional states can activate major physiological responses, which are appropriate to the situation signified by these emotions.

Studies of the relationship between emotions and physiological states have been productive of many of the most important advances in psychosomatic medicine. These studies have included investigations of hormonal systems and their responses to stress and emotion.

In an extensive review of the concept of psychosomatic medicine from 1939 to 1969, Kimball notes:

The hope of these workers is to arrive at a basic physiology and biochemistry

---

[17] W. B. Cannon. *Bodily Changes in Pain, Hunger, Fear and Rage.* New York: Appleton-Century-Crofts, 1920.

of the emotions and defenses whereby illness characterized by organ responses mediated by these hormones may be understood. These workers observe specific responses secondary to specific environmental stresses. They feel, after Selye, . . . that the response, although it may be simultaneously adaptive for the organism in handling the stress, may also lead to disease (diseases of adaptation) by upsetting the internal balance of the body. In one way or another an organ system reaction once sensitized to respond to a stressful event may continue to do so with stereotyped and overused responses to similar or even to different stress processes.[18]

Meanwhile, other groups were investigating the relationships between specific diseases and personality characteristics and traits. On the basis of this approach, Dunbar developed the Personality Specificity Theory of Disease.[19] She identified eight illness states in which she felt psychosomatic relationships could be established: fracture, coronary occlusion, hypertensive cardiovascular disease, anginal syndrome, rheumatic heart disease, cardiac arrhythmias, rheumatic fever, and rheumatoid arthritis. On the subject of such states, Kimball writes:

For example, patients with hypertension were observed as having a need to keep peace and having conflicts over seeking satisfaction within themselves or devoting themselves to achievement of external, long-range goals. Obsessive and compulsive traits with perfectionistic inclinations were also noted. Conflicts between aggressivity and passivity were seen as erupting in occasional outbursts of rage. Patients with rheumatoid arthritis were identified as quiet, sensitive individuals who combined posing as a good sport with ingratiating appeal for sympathy beneath which much hostility was present. These patients had many neurotic traits that were viewed as defenses against guilt and depression related to sexual conflicts. Trends toward perfectionism, cleanliness, orderliness, and punctuality were also noted.[20]

During the 1940s, Franz Alexander undertook to apply specific psychoanalytic insights to the study of certain physical diseases.[21] The Chicago studies carried out by Alexander and other psychoanalysts focused on a group of diseases in which specific emotional conflicts seemed to play an unusually significant role. These diseases included peptic ulcer, ulcerative colitis, rheumatoid arthritis, essential hypertension, bronchial asthma, hyperthyroidism, and neurodermatitis. Alexander and French later wrote:

It is well known from everyday experience that emotions such as fear, anger, resentment, guilt or embarrassment have definite physiological effects. The best known examples are weeping, laughing, blushing, and losing bowel or bladder

[18] Kimball. "Conceptual Developments in Psychosomatic Medicine." P. 308.

[19] H. F. Dunbar. *Emotions and Bodily Changes: A Survey of Literature on Psychosomatic Interrelationships.* New York: Columbia University Press, 1954.

[20] Kimball. "Conceptual Developments in Psychosomatic Medicine." P. 309.

[21] Franz Alexander. *Psychosomatic Medicine, Its Principles and Applications.* New York: W. W. Norton and Company, Inc., 1950.

control under the influence of fear. All these examples are, however, transitory processes occurring in everyday life in all healthy persons. What the systematic psychosomatic studies have shown is that not only transitory physiological changes can be caused by emotions, but that sustained emotional strain may lead to chronic disturbances of physiological functions and in this way cause bodily diseases.[22]

Contrary to many overly simplified views of psychosomatic research, there has never been any attempt to claim that the presence of psychological features alone explain these diseases. Alexander also emphasized that two other elements must be present. There must be an "X" factor, that is, some vulnerability of the involved organs or organ systems that is either constitutional or acquired very early. Finally, a situation or conflictual life circumstance often precedes the onset of the disorder.

The psychological phenomena involved are generally unconscious. For example, powerful infantile dependency needs may exist outside of awareness. These may be, and often are, masked by an apparently independent life style and by considerable success in the business or professional world. When persons with these needs lose an important source of dependent gratification, their reaction may be manifested somatically. For example, a man who is successful and enjoys a secure position may be consciously pleased and flattered to be offered a position of greater responsibility and higher salary. However, his unconscious concerns about the loss of the security and dependent gratification offered by his previous job may activate powerful infantile longings to be fed and cared for. These unconscious wishes are repressed, and the conflict becomes channelled and expressed somatically through motility and hypersecretion of his stomach. These factors, combined with organic predisposition (such as a tendency of his stomach to hypersecrete), not uncommonly leads to the development of peptic ulcer.

Individuals who have unconscious hostility and resentment toward persons whom they fear to alienate and whose love they fear to lose tend to develop essential hypertension.

In other words, there are specific chronic unconscious emotional conflicts and feeling states that are partially expressed through certain organs or organ systems. Persistent psychophysiological outflow involving invulnerable organ systems often leads to psychosomatic disease. Once the disease process (arthritis, ulcer, hypertension, and so on) is well established, then further pathological alterations may occur. Eventually, these organic pathological changes become independent of the emotional factors that may have contributed to the onset in the first place. For example, essential hypertension may show a definite relationship to emotional states in its earliest stages. If the elevation in blood pressure persists, however, irrever-

---

[22] Franz Alexander and Thomas Martin French. *Studies in Psychosomatic Medicine.* New York: The Ronald Press, Inc., 1948. P. 26.

sible vascular damage in the kidneys, enlargement of the heart, and thickening of the walls of the arteries and arterioles may occur. The hypertension is then sustained as much or more by pathophysiological factors as by emotional ones.

A psychophysiological theory of specificity is briefly summarized by Alexander and Selesnick as follows:

> Chronically preparing to fight, the hypertensive individual has a dysfunction of the circulatory apparatus. The arthritic is one who gets ready for flight but inhibits his urge: his symptoms occur in joints that are closely related to the musculo-skeletal system. The patient with neodermatitis longing for physical closeness, has disturbances in the organ of contact. The asthmatic is inhibited in verbal communication, and an organ necessary for this function (the lung) is disturbed. The peptic ulcer patient longs to be fed and a lesion in the upper gastro-intestinal tract develops. Only in ulcerative colitis, are there as yet no direct psychophysiological correlations.[23]

The pathways through which the emotions influence physiology and lead to pathology have been studied intensively in recent years. For example, the hypothalamus has been a focus of study because of its influence on the regulation of emotions and neuro-endocrine activity.

The stress reactions, with special emphasis on the adrenals, have been of interest to psychosomatic researchers. H. Selye[24] originally described the general adaptation syndrome, in which the adrenal hormones play an essential role in defending the body tissues against trauma. Selye felt that exhaustion or dysfunction of these mechanisms could lead to what he termed the "diseases of adaptation," such as hypertension or peptic ulcer.

Selye's and other studies relate man's health to his social environment. Frustrating life situations that place conflicting demands upon humans have been shown to increase susceptibility to all forms of illness. Holmes and Rahe[25] found a remarkable 8 per cent correlation between the incidence of significant life stress and the onset of illness within a two-year period after the stress. They have not as yet offered an explanation for this phenomenon.

Other researchers, such as Benedek and Rubenstein,[26] have studied the relationship of the menstrual cycle to emotional reactions.

Nasal responses to threat and conflict have been intensively investigated

---

[23] Franz Alexander and Sheldon T. Selesnick. *History of Psychiatry.* New York: Harper & Row, Publishers, 1966. P. 395.

[24] Hans Selye. *The Stress of Life.* New York: McGraw-Hill Book Company, 1956.

[25] T. H. Holmes and R. H. Rahe. "The Social Readjustment Scale." *Journal of Psychosomatic Research.* Vol. 11 (1967). Pp. 213–18.

[26] T. Benedek and B. R. Rubenstein. *The Sexual Cycle in Women: The Relation Between Ovarian Function and Psychodynamic Processes. Psychosomatic Medicine Monographs.* Vol. 3, Nos. 1 & 2. Washington, D. C.: National Research Council, 1942.

by T. H. Holmes, T. Treuting, and H. G. Wolff.[27] They found that nasal reactions to humiliation, frustration, and resentment include redness of the nasal mucous membranes, marked swelling of the nasal turbinals, profuse secretion, and obstruction. They inferred that these local nasal reactions are attempts of the organism to shut out an unfavorable environment.

Hinkle and Wolff[28] studied the psychosomatic aspects of diabetes mellitus. Kimball summarizes their work as follows:

> Noting that diabetes mellitus is a notoriously labile and unpredictable syndrome, they (Hinkle & Wolff) explored the relationship of life stress to fluctuations in the patient's symptoms and physiology so far as the diabetic condition was concerned. Using the interview method previously described and following blood glucose, ketones, and fluid balance, they followed patients in long-term studies. They concluded:
>
> 1. Life experiences may play an important role in determining the onset and possibly constitute a factor in the cause of diabetes mellitus.
> 2. There was a specificity and uniformity to the stressful situation precipitating ketosis—namely, conflicts that threatened the real or symbolic dependency of the individual, usually on a parent or parent-surrogate and in which there was an inability to express anger or hostility for fear of further disrupting this relationship.
> 3. Conflictful situations in which the individual was able to express his hostility did not result in ketosis.
> 4. When the individual avoided situations in which his dependent relationships might be threatened, during which situations anxiety prevailed, hypoglycemia developed.
>
> Thus, it was not only the situation but also the way in which the individual coped with the situation that determined his physiological response.[29]

Engel and his co-workers at Rochester have conceptualized what they refer to as a "giving-up–given-up" syndrome, which they believe is often a nonspecific determinant in the onset of both physical and psychiatric disease.[30] These concepts are described and clinically illustrated in the article in this volume "A Life Setting Conducive to Illness, p. 266.

[27] T. H. Holmes, T. Treuting, and H. G. Wolff. "Life Situations, Emotions and Nasal Disease: Evidence on Summative Effects Exhibited in Patients with Hay Fever." *Psychosomatic Medicine.* Vol. 13 (1951). P. 71.

[28] L. E. Hinkle and S. Wolff. "A Summary of Experimental Evidence Relating Life Stress to Diabetes Mellitus." *Journal of Mount Sinai Hospital.* Vol. 19 (1952). Pp. 537–70.

[29] Kimball. "Conceptual Developments in Psychosomatic Medicine." P. 310.

[30] G. L. Engel. "A Life Setting Conducive to Illness: The Giving-Up–Given-Up Complex." *Bulletin of the Menninger Clinic.* Vol. 32 No. 6. (November 1968). Pp. 239–300. The article is found in this text on pp. 266 to 274.

PRESENT STATE OF KNOWLEDGE

At the conclusion of his review of the literature, Kimball writes:

In summary, a survey of the literature of the last 30 years demonstrates a decreasing preoccupation with single factors, either psychological or physical, in the cause of disease and increasing attention to the multiple factors associated with illness, which has caused many investigators to study the environmental field of the individual who becomes ill. Thus, at this time the term psychosomatic medicine applies not to a discrete set of diseases but rather to an approach to illness which studies the interrelationships of the organic, the psychologic, and the social. On the basis of these researches, the following formulations may presently be made:

All illnesses have psychosocial aspects that influence their cause, precipitation, manifestation, course, and outcome.

Cause-and-effect relationships between psychic and somatic processes are of lesser significance than establishing the interrelatedness of psychological, social, and organic processes and their effect on one another in the ill patient.

The study of how an individual adapts to stresses biologically and psychologically and on what underlying factors these responses depend has become a major area of psychosomatic research.

There is no fundamental difference between mental and physical illness, but all illnesses have psychological and somatic components.

There is no special treatment of psychosomatic diseases as opposed to any other diseases, but in the treatment of all illnesses there are therapeutic procedures that are required for the psyche as well as for the body.

The approach to the individual suffering from a specific illness is specific depending on the idiosyncracy of the patient's life situation, which includes, in addition to attending to the disease process, attending to the psychological and social correlates.

These interrelationships and correlations can be made by the physician only if he pursues an interview method that will allow the patient to make these associations.

Patients confronted with particular procedures and illness situations may experience these in similar ways. The physician identifying what this common experience is will be able to help his patient anticipate and adjust to this experience.

Anxiety, grieving, and depression are a part of the illness experience of all patients. Attention to these factors on the part of the physician by permitting and encouraging his patient to express his feelings will facilitate adjustment.

A recognition of the patient's personality characteristics will assist the physician in structuring his relationship with the patient in a manner that will be most therapeutic.[31]

[31] Kimball. "Conceptual Developments in Psychosomatic Medicine." P. 310.

250 Adult Stage

In spite of the numerous advances made in psychosomatic areas, the field remains in its infancy, for the relationships between body and mind are exceedingly complex and elusive. From the point of view of nursing care, there are psychosomatic elements in all patients' illnesses, if the term is used in its broadest sense.

Suggested Readings on the Adult and Illness

Alexander, F. *Our Age of Unreason*. Philadelphia: J. B. Lippincott Company, 1942.

Bettelheim, B. *The Informed Heart*. New York: The Free Press of Glencoe, 1960.

Bibring, Grete, and Ralph Kahane. *Lectures in Medical Psychology*. New York: International Universities Press, Inc., 1968.

Cannon, W. B. *The Wisdom of the Body*. New York: W. W. Norton & Co., Inc., 1932.

Caplan, Gerald. *Principles of Preventive Psychiatry*. New York: Basic Books, Inc., 1964.

Cummings, Jonathan W. "Hemodialysis-Feelings, Facts, Fantasies." *American Journal of Nursing*. Vol. 70, No. 1 (January, 1970). Pp. 70–76.

Dollard, J., et al. *Frustration and Aggression*. New Haven: Yale University Press, 1939.

Dorpat, Theodore L. "Phantom Sensations of Internal Organs." *Comprehensive Psychiatry*, Vol. 12 (1971). Pp. 27–35.

———. "Emotional Reaction to Surgery." *Yale Scientific Magazine*, Vol. 32 (1957). Pp. 53–60.

Dudley, D. L. in collaboration with C. J. Martin, M. Masuda, H. S. Ripley, and T. H. Holmes. *The Psychophysiology of Respiration in Health and Disease*. New York: Appleton-Century-Crofts, 1969.

Duff, R. S. and A. B. Hollingshead. *Sickness and Society*. New York: Harper & Row, 1968.

Dunbar, H. F. *Emotions and Bodily Changes*. 2nd ed. New York: Columbia University Press, 1939.

———. *Psychosomatic Diagnosis*. New York: P. B. Hoeber, Inc., 1943.

Engel, George. *Psychological Development in Healthy and Diseased Children*. Philadelphia: Saunders, 1962.

———. "A Unified Concept of Health and Disease." *Perspect. Biol. and Med.* Vol. 3 (1960). Pp. 459–85.

Freud A. *The Ego and the Mechanisms of Defense.* London: Hogarth Press, 1937.

Freud, S. *Group Psychology and the Analysis of the Ego.* London: Hogarth Press, 1922.

———. *The Ego and the Id.* London: Hogarth Press, 1927.

———. *The Problem of Anxiety.* New York: W. W. Norton & Co., Inc., 1936 (a).

———. *Inhibitions, Symptoms and Anxiety.* London: The Hogarth Press, Ltd., 1936(b).

———, S. Ferenczi, K. Abraham, E. Simmel, and E. Jones. *Psychoanalysis and the War Neuroses.* London and New York: International Psychoanalytical Press, 1921.

Grinker, Roy R. and John P. Spiegel. *Men Under Stress.* Philadelphia: The Blakiston Co., 1945.

Haber, W. D. "Reactions to Loss of Limb: Physiological and Psychological Aspects." *Ann. N.Y. Acad. Sci.,* Vol. 74 (1958). Pp. 14–24.

Hamburg, D. A., Beatrix Hamburg, and S. Degoza. "Adaptive Problems and Mechanisms in Severely Burned Patients." *Psychiatry,* Vol. 16 (1953). Pp. 1–20.

Hawkins, N. G., R. Davies, and T. H. Holmes. "Evidence of Psychosocial Factors in the Development of Pulmonary Tuberculosis." *Psychosomatic Medicine.* Vol. 19 (1957).

Heilbrunn, Gert. "Psychodynamic Aspects of Epilepsy." *Psychoanalytic Quarterly,* Vol. 19 (1950). Pp. 145–57.

Henderson, J. L., and M. Moore. "The Psychoneuroses of War." *New England Journal of Medicine,* Vol. 230 (1944). P. 273.

Holmes, T. H. "Infectious Disease and Stress with Special Reference to Tuberculosis." In *The Psychological Basis of Medical Practice.* H. V. and W. Lief, editors. New York: Hoeher Medical Division of Harper and Row, 1963.

———. "Multidiscipline Studies of Tuberculosis." In *Personality, Stress and Tuberculosis.* P. J. Sparer, editor. New York: International Universities Press, Inc. 1956.

———. "Panel on Anxiety: Make More of Your Time with the Anxious Patient." *Patient Care.* Vol. 4 (1970).

———. "The Individual as a Biological Organism" in *Family-centered Social Work in Illness and Disability: A Preventive Approach.* Monograph V in series "Social Work Practice in Medical Care and Rehabilitation Settings." New York: National Association of Social Workers, 1961.

Jackson, Joan K. "The Role of the Patient's Family in Illness." *Nursing Forum.* (Summer, 1962). Pp. 119–28.

Jackson, J. K. and T. H. Holmes. "Alcoholism and Tuberculosis." In *Sociological Studies of Health and Sickness.* D. Apple, editor. New York: McGraw-Hill Book Co., 1959.

Jaco, E. Gartley, ed. *Patients, Physicians, and Illness: A Sourcebook in Behavioral Science and Medicine.* New York: The Free Press, 1958.

Jahoda, Marie. *Current Concepts of Positive Mental Health.* New York: Basic Books, Inc., Publishers, 1958.

Janis, I. L. *Psychological Stress.* New York: John Wiley and Sons, Inc., 1958.

Lidz, Theodore. *The Family and Human Adaptation.* New York: International Universities Press, Inc., 1963.

Lifton, Robert. *Death in Life: Survivors of Hiroshima.* New York: Random House, 1967.

Lindemann, E. "Symptomatology and Management of Acute Grief." *Amer. J. Psychiat.* Vol. 101 (1944). Pp. 131–38.

Mechanic, D. *Students Under Stress.* New York: The Free Press of Glencoe, 1962.

Menninger, Karl. *Man Against Himself.* New York: Harcourt, Brace and Company, 1938.

———. *The Vital Balance.* New York: The Viking Press, 1963.

———. *Love Against Hate.* New York: Harcourt, 1942.

———. *The Human Mind.* New York: Knopf, 1945.

——— and Bernard Hall, eds. *A Psychiatrist's World.* New York: The Viking Press, 1959. Vols. I and II.

——— and Bernard Hall, eds. *A Psychiatrist for a Troubled World.* New York: The Viking Press, 1967. Vols. I and II.

Menninger, W. C. "Psychological Reactions to an Emergency (Flood)." *Amer. J. Psychiat.* Vol. 109 (1952). Pp. 128–30.

Mordkoff, A. M. "The Relationship Between Psychological and Physiological Response to Stress." *Psychosom. Med.* Vol. 26 (1964). Pp. 135–50.

Ripley, Herbert S. "Changes in Cardiovascular Function Associated with Personality Reactions." *The Nebraska State Medical Journal.* Vol. 49, No. 4 (April, 1964).

——— and Joan K. Jackson. "Therapeutic Factors in Alcoholics Anonymous." *The American Journal of Psychiatry.* Vol. 116, No. 1 (July 1959).

———, and H. G. Wolff. "Life Situations, Emotions, and Glaucoma." *Psychosomatic Medicine*. Vol. XII, No. 4 (July–August,1950).

Selye, Hans. *The Stress of Life*. New York: McGraw-Hill, 1956.

Simmel, E. "Psychoanalysis and the War Neuroses," London: *International Psychoanalytic Press,* 1921. Self-Preservation and the Death Instinct. *Psychoanalyt. Quarterly*. Vol. 13 (1944). P. 161.

Steiner, M. and D. R. Aleksandrowicz. "Psychiatric Sequelae to Gynecological Operations." *The Israel Annals of Psychiatry and Related Disciplines*. Vol. 8, No. 2 (July, 1970). Pp. 186–92.

Szasz, Thomas. *Pain and Pleasure: A Study of Bodily Feelings*. New York: Basic Books, 1957.

Titchener, James. *Surgery as a Human Experience: The Psychodynamics of Surgical Practice*. New York: Oxford University Press, 1960.

Tjossem, T. D., A. R. Leider, R. W. Deisher, T. H. Holmes, and H. S. Ripley. "Emotional Reactions and Skin Temperature Responses in Children Aged Two to Four Years." *Journal of Psychosomatic Research*. Vol. 4, No. 1 (1959).

Treating, Theodore and Herbert S. Ripley. "Life Situations, Emotions and Bronchial Asthma." *The Journal of Nervous and Mental Disease*. Vol. 108, No. 5 (November, 1948).

Weisman, A. D., and T. P. Hackett. "Predilection to Death." *Psychosom. Med*. Vol. 23 (1961). Pp. 232–56.

Weiss, E., and O. S. English. *Psychosomatic Medicine*. Philadelphia: W. B. Saunders Company, 1943.

Wolff, H. G., and Helen Goodell. *Stress and Disease*. 2nd ed. Springfield, Ill.: C. C. Thomas, 1968.

Wyler, A. R., M. Masuda, and T. H. Holmes. "Magnitude of Life Events and Seriousness of Illness." *Psychosomatic Medicine*. Vol. 33 (1971).

Zetzel, Elizabeth. *The Capacity for Emotional Growth*. London: The Hogarth Press, 1970.

DISCUSSION OF SELECTED READINGS

The first selection, "The Impact of Mastectomy," is by Jeanne C. Quint, a nurse and sociological researcher, now teaching at the University of Washington School of Nursing, who describes an investigation of women who have undergone a breast removal due to cancer. She follows the patients' reactions from the preoperative period through the postoperative impact. The participating patients in the study appeared to outline three basic effects from the operation (regardless of age): a period of shock and unexpected reprisals, an adjustment to bodily appearance, and lastly, the prospect of a shortened life and possibly painful death. She notes that the period of upset was lengthened due to delays in healing, having radiation treatment, and other complications and that appearance was a major preoccupation of these women. Dr. Quint emphasized the psychologically alienating feeling of such an experience and the lack of channels of expressing these feelings during the usual tabooed everyday social interactions. The interview, in a sense, provided an opportunity for these women to vent their emotional and psychological states in an accepting situation. Dr. Quint expresses that she and the interviewers also had to face the fact that they, as women, could be in the patients' position. She emphasizes the need for better personal and professional understanding on the part of nurses to cope with the patient undergoing this type of operation.

The next selection, "A Life Setting Conducive to Illness: The Giving-Up–Given-Up Complex," is by George L. Engel, a professor of psychiatry and medicine at the University of Rochester. In this article, the author suggests that it is not by accident that a psychological state plays a "significant role in modifying the capacity of the organism to cope with concurrent pathogenic factors."

He explains the phenomenon of "dying of grief," a situation in which a sudden loss of a loved one precipitates the death of the bereaved. He also points out the occurrence of those "scared to death" during situations of danger. All were involved in circumstances about which the victims felt powerless to do anything.

Dr. Engel points out that this phenomenon occurs throughout the animal kingdom. He calls this psychologically besetting state the "giving-up–given-up complex." It consists of a state of helplessness, a lowered image of oneself, a loss of gratification from a relationship or life-role, a break of continuity between the past, present, and future, and a stirring of memories of earlier periods of giving up.

Dr. Engel describes this psychological state of limbo, in which we all have found ourselves at some time in a lesser degree. Such circumstances can provide the opportunity to help create new adaptive solutions for future crises. Those times when a resolution is not imminent for the person can become those periods when disease may intercede. The homeostasis of the organism is upset, perhaps lowering the body's usual ability to deal with pathogenic processes. The exact biological state associated with the giving-up–given-up complex is not known, but are only noted for further research. There is a significant need for scientific research to study the psychological states or life settings of patients and the extent to which they influence disease.

Howard P. Rome, a senior consultant at Mayo Clinic and professor of psychiatry at Mayo Graduate School of Medicine, reports the radical expansion of health-care service or medical delivery system. The hospital has become the focal point of these specialized medical delivery interhierarchies. The hospital, architecturally, has also expanded into specialized wings or departments, thus creating emergency rooms, surgical pavilions, administrative offices, psychiatric wards, dialysis centers, and intensive care units. Dr. Rome points out that patients assigned to these technologically frightening units can experience adverse psychological responses. The presence of such an abundance of electronic devices as oscilloscopes, automatic breathing devices, etc., and a constant flurry of white-coated staff members creates an ambiance which can be both disorientating and tension-ridden for the patient.

Unfortunately, even the nurses in these Intensive Care Units can take on a clinical, detached air as a human defense in the face of constant death confrontations.

In the fourth article, "Defenses Against Anxiety in the Nurse–Patient Relationship," Margaret Asterud, an instructor in medical-surgical nursing at Indiana University School of Nursing, deals with a real problem that occurs in many hospital stays—the seemingly assaultive and threatening actions by the hospital personnel on a patient. Many nursing practices can be very disturbing and anxiety provoking.

In dealing with children, intrusive procedures, victimization, authority figures, death, and surgical patients, Mrs. Asterud emphasizes the need for "understanding of the situation based on knowledge, observation, and tempered with individual application."

In our final selection, Samuel C. Klagsbrun, a psychiatrist and Clinical Instructor in Psychiatry at Yale University, explores the attitudes of the nurses and the nurse–doctor relationships in a small cancer unit in a general hospital. He uses small group techniques to recognize and deal with the repressed tensions and emotions involved when managing a ward with a high mortality rate. Dr. Klagsbrun worked to change the ward culture as a whole. An experiment in self-care was initiated with unusual results with a nonregressive approach emphasized.

The Impact of Mastectomy *
by Jeanne C. Quint, D.N.S., R.N.

Disfigurement and cancer are words that individually carry a negative connotation in our society. Some women personally come face to face with both simultaneously through having a breast removed for malignancy.

Traditionally in nursing mastectomy has been discussed as a treatment procedure for a disease and emphasis has been given to activities that should be done to facilitate recovery (1, 2). In like manner, studies on psychological reactions and adjustment have emphasized what is considered good professional practice (3, 4). Focus in this article is on the viewpoint of the woman who experiences mastectomy, and attention is directed toward it as a turning point in her life. The idea has been presented elsewhere that certain critical experiences can function as turning points which precipitate reevaluation and revision of one's personal identity (5).

That this operation can come as a shocking and unexpected episode is well described in the experience of one who went through it. This woman was 56 years of age, married, and had a teen-aged son. She found a small lump above her breast and went to the doctor, who removed it in the office on the assumption that it was a lipoma. To his great surprise it was malignant, and he called her and her husband to the office to tell them and to refer them to a surgeon.

The woman recalled that though only a few days transpired before she entered the hospital, she felt as though she were in a daze during the whole time. She was sure she would never "come out of it" and went to the bank and withdrew her insurance policy.

There is no doubt that the period before the operation is a very frightening one for many of these women, but this discussion will emphasize those things which they face afterward.

* The American Journal of Nursing. Vol. 63, No. 11 (November, 1963). Pp. 88–92.

Information in this article comes from an investigation of adjustment to mastectomy. Data collection began during the patients' hospitalization and continued with periodic home contacts at selected intervals during one year. In both settings, data were collected by another nurse and myself using the method of participant observation. A tape recorder was used for home conversations, but observations in the hospital were dictated onto tape shortly after they were noted. We participated in the patients' hospital care but did not assume complete responsibility for nursing care.

Participants in the study were women who entered a university medical center hospital for mastectomy during the initial six months of our hospital field work. We excluded, with one exception, women who showed evidence of metastasis to areas other than axillary nodes at the time of operation. Of the 21 women studied, 6 were private care patients, and 14 were classified as nonprivate and received medical supervision from the medical center resident staff. One changed from private to nonprivate care during the period of observation.

The women, all of whom were Caucasian, ranged in age from 38 to 79 years with the median found at 57, but those with private physicians were generally younger. All of the private group were married, in sharp contrast to the others, of whom nine were widows.

The group studied has not yet been tested against available standards for establishing socioeconomic classification, but included were representation from middle, working, and less privileged economic classes. Participation in the study was voluntary and cooperation was excellent. Only one woman chose not to continue after the first interview at home.

The participants gave us their views of the three basic changes which this operation initiates. First, it precipitates a period of shock and unexpected events. Second, it leaves a change in bodily appearance. Third, it mars the future by the prospect of shortened life and the possibility of slow, painful death.

The first look at the incision frequently comes as a tremendous shock. It strikes most forcibly when the woman stands before a mirror and looks at herself. In describing her feelings one woman said, "I'll never forget the first time I saw it. Not the lack of what you used to be but the horrible scar was what got me down. Oh, this horrible purple piece of flesh up here! I'm very self-conscious about it, and I don't want anyone to see me. I had to dress it the first day at home and that was pretty rough, too."

Shock of the Unexpected

Another woman said that while she was in the hospital she watched the doctor change the dressing and it did not bother her to look. She said that she was really prepared not to have her breast and that she felt more or less numbed or drugged and she did not give it much thought. On the night before she left the hospital, however, she sat on the side of the bed and tried to change the dressing herself. Her hospital roommate said that she didn't realize the surgery was as extensive as it was. The rommate said that she "walked over to my bed and her face was so shocked by it all."

The woman herself made this comment after she went home: "I looked at it several times but the night before I guess it seemed to disturb me the most. The part up on my shoulder I hadn't seen because I guess my gown was over it. I kind of expected to have my breast gone, but I didn't expect the incision to go as high as it did. That disturbed me a lot."

The real impact of this experience does not hit until the woman has returned home. As another woman said, "Anybody who's in the hospital is sick with something. You have plenty of company and it makes a difference. You don't think about it until you get home. You kind of begin to thaw out."

In a way the postoperative period in the hospital is like a period of shock with little overt response showing. The early period out of the hospital, in contrast, is characterized as one of agitation and upset. It was described as a "period of exhaustion," and most of the women had blue spells.

This period was one of getting accustomed to feeling as though in a cast, of learning that it is difficult to sleep because it is hard to find a comfortable position. Some women found that they could hardly tolerate lying flat on their backs because of the terrible pull. One said, "The thought goes through your mind, are you going to stay together? The pull is that terrific that you wonder whether you're doing the right thing or not."

The period was one of unexpected events. "I didn't know about the material, the stuff that drains off. I thought I was developing some kind of an infection. My whole arm was quite swollen. It didn't do that at the hospital, so I wasn't prepared for that."

The period of upset and agitation was often prolonged by such things as delayed wound healing, some other complication, or by having radiation therapy. One woman whose incision was still not healed at eight weeks found herself confined to the house by the need to apply hot compresses. "It has been confining, although this past week the doctor told me I don't have to spend an hour doing it. But then he left it up to me because he says if there is any pus still coming out he expects me to continue it, and I've had pus coming out in one particular area. So I've had to be in the house most of the time. I thought by now I'd have a chance to do more getting out."

Most women expressed surprise at the amount of pain and discomfort, the marked fatigue, the slow healing of the incision, the swelling of the arm, and jittery feelings. They expected to be feeling better by four months and frequently were amazed to find themselves going through a phase of letdown and continued exhaustion.

It was common to find that family and friends were interested and concerned at first but soon expected the patient to return to normal. One woman stated the problem clearly when she said that some persons just do not understand that you aren't the same any more. She made this statement about herself and other persons, "Now I'm learning not to pay too much attention to what they have to say. I know which people to talk to, and which people not to."

For some women, personal appearance was a major concern. For others it was a minor one. Yet all described a certain amount of self-consciousness about appearance. There was more open expression of concern by large-breasted women, some of whom had the additional problem of altered body alignment precipitated by the uneven weight distribution.

All these women were faced with two major decisions. First, each had to determine the extent of camouflage required for her own peace of mind. Second, each had the problem of choosing whether to hide the incision from others.

A Personal or Social Loss

Appearance was a major concern of a 38-year-old woman who at one time had been a model. These statements were made two months after the operation, "It looks so funny. This arm is so much bigger than this arm. See the difference. To me it just seems like it's as big as a balloon. Joe (her husband) said it's not that noticeable, but I got all shook up one day and gave away all my sun dresses."

When asked if she felt self-conscious at this time, she replied, "Yes—very, very, very! I just know everybody knows that I'm half, I'm half here you know. That's why I wear old baggy clothes to go out. I didn't even want to go to a dance that I would have before. I don't seem to be a good mixer any more."

Two months later this woman described going to dinner at a friend's home. She stated that she would not remove her coat even though everyone assured her that, "It doesn't show."

She found that she could not wear a regular brassiere because it felt too tight. The elastic was too stiff. Quite by accident she heard about a "sleeping" brassiere which was much softer and more comfortable to wear. She elected to use a make-shift falsie, as did many of these women.

The problem of camouflage was generally approached by trial and error. Some found that advice given by others did not work for them, and some were unable to use effective devices because of wound drainage or delayed healing. The latter situation was quite disturbing to those women who refused to return to social activities without a satisfactory breast replacement.

Most married women in the study did not hide the incision from their husbands. One woman, however, was so shocked by its appearance that she had not permitted her husband to view it though she had been home for three weeks. "My husband says he's never seen me wear so many clothes to bed as I wear these days. I wear a nightgown with long sleeves and a high neck and over that I wear a bedjacket."

When asked if she thought she would one day let him see it, she responded, "Oh, I think so when it's all healed and not blue any more. It looks too awful. And then when I can wear something with a bra, it won't be so bad. But right now, no!"

The Incision

Another woman in discussing the question of whether this affected her feelings about herself as a woman said, "Well, it's like I told my husband, with all the advertisements that go on, I don't think we'd be normal if we didn't give it a thought. But then it's a thing that's done with. As I said before, I can't go out and kill myself. There's nothing I can do about it, so I don't see any sense in stewing about my femininity. There's just not a thing I can say or do."

This woman was quite open in talking about her feelings to her husband, that is, feelings about herself. Her concern for what this meant to him came out in these words, "I was always quite full bosomed, and I do have a feeling that maybe it has affected his feelings, but I don't really know. This is something a woman never knows in spite of the fact that I've been able to get him to kid about it, too. I'll go out and get something kind of cute and silly and put it on and sort of perform or something and kid about it."

A woman in her thirties was asked whether her school-aged children had seen the incision. "No. They may have but—no, I haven't made any effort to show it to them if that's what you mean. I don't think I should."

She said that she had not shown the incision to her women friends, that she did not undress in front of them. She still felt very self-conscious after her appearance even though a year had elapsed since the operation. In discussing the changes this had brought for her she said, "Number one, you have to throw away all the pretty low-necked dresses. Where are the designers that will make good-looking clothes with high necks and sleeves, especially cocktail dresses? If you're invited to a dressy party, you want to look nice but it becomes such a hassle.

"You do find some salesgirls that are so belligerent. They don't understand why you're—what you're seeking. They just aren't aware of the problem that exists. Of course, there are those that I think are extremely wonderful—alteration women and dressmakers—and I seek them out."

One might get the impression that only the young married women were self-conscious and concerned about appearance. That this was not the case shows in the following quotation from a 56-year-old widow's interview four months after her operation, "I feel ashamed to go outside. I haven't been out in quite a while and I think that they're all going to look at me. So I put on a sweater and they can't see anything."

The Uncertain Future

An all encompassing problem, harder than dealing with the deformity, is the question, often not said aloud: What is my future? It is as though almost anything that happens can trigger the thoughts: Am I going to die? When? How?

The uncertainty is illustrated by a situation in which the family was told one thing and the woman herself was told another. The woman had a scirrhous carcinoma with metastasis to the axillary nodes. The surgeon told her family that there was a four-to-one chance that she probably would not live for five years. The woman herself was "given the usual encouragement," to quote one of the doctors.

Two months postoperatively, the woman talked about being depressed once in a while, "I never did that before but once in a while you just think of everything and start crying and it's over. You wonder why these things have to happen. I don't know. Things come to your mind. Maybe the kids have something they don't want to tell me. Maybe they know something. So, well, I say if it's for the worst, it's for the worst."

This woman was a widow, and her children insisted that she come to stay with them. There was such a protective atmosphere that she was not permitted to be alone with the interviewer at the first home session. It was during the second interview that she said she sensed her children knew something she did not.

Fear of Death

Four months after the operation she was asked if she ever had thoughts that she might die. She commented, "You think, maybe I did all this work, and what good is it? I still, you know, especially when you feel sick, I say, gee, maybe this is (pause). Then I say, well, there's other people that have done it. I say three, four years maybe I'll be healthy as a horse. So maybe the good Lord will help me through. So when the time comes, if we gotta go, we gotta go. The only thing is every time I sleep, I pray. I don't want to have pain."

She went on to describe a dream which had occurred three weeks before, "I get cockeyed dreams like that. I had one dream, I dreamt that my mother—she's dead you know—and she come over and she says, 'You have to go to Italy.' So I say, 'Italy, why've I got to go to Italy for?' She says, 'Well, to get well. Get well.' So she says, 'No, it's incurable!' That scared the daylights out of me. I woke up out of my sleep, I got so scared. I was really depressed."

She said that she did not talk to anybody about her operation, that she put her faith in the doctors who would do something if there was anything wrong.

262   *Adult Stage*

For many, changes in physical signs and symptoms took on new meaning and were used as cues for testing the future. A woman in her third-month interview described pains in her back that felt like hot needles. When she asked the doctor about it, he told her that this was part of healing, that the pains were associated with growing new muscle. She described what these pains meant. "I don't have any idea. I guess that's why I bugged poor Dr. B so much. At first I swore cancer was coming back. I did because—and even now—my chest is always sore. But he said no, that there was no sign of cancer. He says, 'It's just a healing; you're worrying about nothing.' But still I don't know, you just can't help it somehow or another. You're bound to worry, I guess."

Six weeks later she described what happened when she saw the doctor again, "I don't have any relief from it now. The doctor's doing nothing for it and I don't know what I'm going to do. I should go back this week for a checkup. But he takes a look at me and, see, all the time I have these pains, aches all the time. All he does is just take one look at me and say, 'Oh my, it looks fine, goodbye, toodle-oo,' and he takes off and you don't see him again.

"Well, I want him to give me some suggestion or tell me what to do for my arm swelling and this continuous discomfort I have. But he doesn't do anything and I feel like I'm going right down a rat hole."

Later in the same interview, she said that her nerves were shot, that she couldn't control herself, that she yelled at her husband all the time, and that she was miserable. She said that she knew of two women who were in mental hospitals after having this operation. She said that sometimes she saw herself doing such dumb things she wondered if she were going crazy herself.

The Doctor

The significance of the doctor is pinpointed again in the statements of another woman at her sixth-month interview, "The appearance didn't bother me particularly, I don't think, after the operation. The only thing that bothered me was recurrence. That was the thing that bothered me most. I have a little more confidence about the recurrence not happening now than I did before. I was seeing the doctor today and he reassured me. Then I do a lot of praying and, that to me, is the most reassuring thing."

The impact of this problem can perhaps best be described in the words of a woman who had just passed the five-year mark from one mastectomy and then was faced with a second one. She said that when the surgeon told her a second operation would be necessary, "I completely fell apart because, in my mind, I had heard of people that had two, never knowing anyone. But I just sort of marked them off as people that couldn't survive. And when I heard that I was going to have to go back to the hospital, it was a very trying experience.

"My immediate reaction was that I didn't want him to do any further surgery. I wanted him to let me die. I said, 'I just want you to leave me alone, and when it gets bad, that's it. I just cannot go through this again.'

"I stormed out of his office and he, in the meantime, called my husband, apparently told him to meet me. As I was walking out of the building, he was walking in."

She said that she had asked the surgeon to promise her that he would just remove the lesion no matter whether it was malignant or not and that he wouldn't do a radical operation. This is how she described what happened, "He came into my room at the hospital and said, 'I can't promise you that.' He said, 'If you want me to do the surgery, then I have to do what I think is necessary.' By that time he must have suspected something but he said, 'I cannot promise you that I will just leave you alone.'

"Well, I really prayed very hard and then I remember waking up, and there was this nurse sitting in my room. And I think this is where a nurse can play such a big part. She was the coldest cucumber that I have ever run across in my life. All I said to her was, 'Did they do a radical?' And all she said to me—and I know she couldn't say any more—was, 'The reports haven't come down yet.'

"I knew that if she said that then they must have done something. But it was her whole attitude. In fact, they asked me if she was to come back as night nurse, and I said I didn't want her. 'Please don't have that same nurse with me again.' It was extremely trying. I guess I just sort of fell apart. I just thought of having to go through all this fear all over again—even now it brings forth a great deal of emotion—of having to worry again and count off every day.

"The thing that was so, I guess, so sad was that here I had just counted off five years. You know I just counted off five years; and it was just about five years to the day practically when this happened again."

These women have described what it was like to undergo a treatment, mastectomy, which not only did not guarantee a long and happy life by removing the cancer but also inflicted them with the stigma of being half a woman, a not too happy prospect in a breast-conscious society such as ours. For these women there was a central core of loneliness, the key element being that they had few if any outlets for talking about those things which most concerned them. They were stuck with two relatively taboo subjects: a defeminizing disfigurement and the prospect of dying.

Is Any Woman Immune?

That breast cancer and mastectomy are potent subjects for women in our society is illustrated by what happened to the study staff, all of whom were women. There were two major consequences for the interviewers.

Because the interviews contained a great deal of personal and emotionally laden material, we had to come to terms in some way with our own feelings about cancer, loss of a breast, and death, not to mention a tremendous sense of inadequacy in the situation. We had to face the fact that we, too, were frightened and wanted to run away. We found it extremely difficult to permit others to talk about disturbing events when our own fears were rising.

The second consequence was that some of the women who were interviewed became worse. Some, in fact, did not survive the first year. It was hard enough to talk to those who at least superficially were recovering, but it was sometimes agonizing to watch someone go downhill, eventually to die. It was this experience which was the hardest to bear.

Even the secretaries who typed the interviews found themselves caught in the intensity of highly emotional experiences.

To continue the study, we interviewers found that we had to talk to each other to get our own reactions and feelings out in the open. Even so, it was difficult to go on. We found, just as did the women in the study, that most persons won't permit talk about upsetting things. It became apparent that professionals, like laymen, found such talk intolerable. We interviewers, too, found ourselves in a lonely position.

As one listened to these women postoperatively describe their lives in transition, one was struck by the lack of professional guidance offered to them. The major problems they faced alone, not because family and friends lacked concern or did not try to help, but usually because the latter were also caught in the tragedy and were made impotent by it.

It became evident that, as a by-product of the study, the interviewers were providing the opportunity for these women to ventilate about matters which were generally forbidden in their everyday social contacts, both familial and otherwise. They were permitted to let their hair down about what it is really like to live with a mastectomy. The interviewers, in turn, paid a price for this experience; eventually we had to face the thought: This could happen to me.

Articles in lay magazines have made it well known that breast cancer is the most common form of cancer in women (6). It is estimated that one woman in 20 can expect to have it (7). In spite of publicity to the effect that early diagnosis and mastectomy will cure, there is no guarantee of this. Breast cancer is a capricious disease as professionals and patients know (8). What woman is immune from the question: Will this happen to me?

It is not surprising to note that most women function to minimize their personal identification with the problem and make use of such protective devices as avoiding the topic altogether or keeping discussion of the operation at a sociable level.

One would expect to find that nurses, most of whom are women, act much the same as women in general; and this is indeed so. In fact, one would be surprised to find otherwise since this group not only have access to privileged information about postmastectomy recurrence and survival statistics but also have given care to women with breast cancer in varying stages. Those who have seen death and suffering from breast cancer cannot so easily minimize personal identification with it.

Nurses' Reactions

It is true that there are individual women who are able to cope with this fearful problem admirably and to offer sustenance and support to postmastectomy patients. One can find this in an office nurse who has a well-organized follow-up program in the doctor's office. One observes it in a private duty nurse giving care during the early postoperative days. One knows of a woman who had a mastectomy taking time to visit newly operated women while they are still hospitalized.

These women are unusual, however, and are rarely available to the majority of those who undergo this operation. After mastectomy, most women are not yet ready to talk while still in the hospital. Even if they were, they have little access to nursing personnel except for brief contacts centered on procedures and physical tasks. That nursing personnel do not openly initiate discussion about mastectomy and its personal meanings is the rule, not the exception.

It is not difficult to understand, however, that nurses use such a device to protect themselves from a woman's situation which they would find hard to handle. It makes even more sense when one recognizes how little preparation most nurses have had for coping with such a problem.

A student nurse recently made this response when she was asked if she had seen many women with breast cancer, "Yes, and I don't like it. It's one thing I can't stand. This sounds silly but I think I could stand to have a leg off rather than a breast, because of the idea of being disfigured."

She was asked if she had taken care of many of these women, "I think my nursing care is poorer here because I relate it to myself. I find it hard to talk, and these people are ones who need it so much. They do need a lot of care. I'm sure if I had to have a mastectomy, I'd never get used to it."

It was appropriate to say to her, "Don't feel bad. You're not alone," but one was reminded immediately that many women are going it alone with their mastectomies.

It is no small thing to have a breast removed for cancer, and adjustment to living with the change comes slowly. Most surgeons cannot offer the kind of sustained support which these women want. Perhaps this is not the surgeon's job, for what can he know of what it is like to be a woman?

For nurses to accept responsibility in this problem, however, they must be willing to forego the practice of saying, "That's the doctor's responsibility," and be willing to face a problem which offers no easy solutions. Perhaps the first step for many is to agree with the student nurse who said, "I think my nursing care is poorer here because I relate it to myself."

References

1. Alexander, Sarah E. Nursing care of a patient after breast surgery. *Amer. J. Nurs.* **57**:1571–1572, Dec. 1957.
2. Smith, Genevieve Waples. When a breast must be removed. *Amer. J. Nurs.* **50**:332–339, June 1950.
3. Bard, Morton, and Sutherland, A. M. Psychological impact of cancer and its treatment. IV. Adaptation to medical mastectomy. *Cancer* **8**:656–672, July–Aug. 1955.
4. Renneker, Richard, and Cutler, Max. Psychological problems of adjustment to cancer of the breast. *J.A.M.A.* **148**:833–838, Mar. 8, 1953.
5. Strauss, Anselm. *Mirrors and Masks: the Search for Identity.* Glencoe, Ill., The Free Press, 1959, pp. 93–100.
6. Spicer, Betty Coe. New weapons against breast cancer. *Ladies Home Journal* **79**:48, June 1962.
7. Lewison, E. F. Treatment of advanced breast cancer. *Amer. J. Nurs.* **62**:107–110, Oct. 1962.
8. Lewiston, E. F., and others. Results of surgical treatment of breast cancer at Johns Hopkins Hospital. *J.A.M.A.* **153**:905–909, Nov. 7, 1953.

A Life Setting Conducive to Illness: The Giving-Up—Given-Up Complex*

by George L. Engel, M.D.

In my view, William Menninger's most notable contribution was to help bring the science of mental health into the mainstream of American medicine, a task which he initiated largely through his role in the Surgeon General's Office during World War II. With imagination, skill, and his unusual personal qualities he succeeded in harnessing the ordinarily cumbersome administrative machinery of the military and converting it into an educational instrument. Utilizing the inescapable social disruption of the period as a demonstration laboratory, he made it possible for military physicians to verify how man's capacity to deal with the

* *Bulletin of the Menninger Clinic.* Vol. 32, No. 6 (November, 1968). Pp. 355–65. *Annals of Internal Medicine,* Vol. 69 (August, 1968). Pp. 293–300.

changes in his personal and social environment influences the balance between health and illness (1). This approach had a profound influence on young physicians, many of whom became interested in studying more systematically the association between the conditions of life and the development of illness.

I have selected this aspect of William Menninger's many contributions because it has direct bearing on my own scientific interests. I hope that the work that I will report on today will in some small way do honor to his name.

Before coming to the substance of my presentation, I wish first to acknowledge that this work represents more than 20 years of the collaborative efforts of the Medical-Psychiatric Liaison Group of the University of Rochester, past and present, notably William Greene, Arthur Schmale, Franz Reichsman, Sanford Meyerowitz, and David Tinling, and the 60 fellows and trainees who have participated in these studies over the years. For those of you who are unfamiliar with the background of our group, I must also explain that most of us have had our primary training in internal medicine and all of us work on the medical service essentially full time as physicians, not as consulting psychiatrists. Our clinical orientation is thus more that of the internist than of the traditional psychiatrist, and our patients span the full range of illnesses ordinarily encountered on a general medical service (2).

One question has been central to all of our research: Why do people fall ill or die at the time they do? What determines that a man shifts or drifts or plunges from a state of good health into illness or even dies at a particular juncture of his life? These are broad questions and obviously go beyond psychology. In essence they call for a study of man's reaction to his environment in the broadest sense and bring into the foreground the role of the mind and of the central nervous system in the regulation of the body economy.

Today I intend to concentrate on one issue only, namely the clinical characterization of a psychological state that we commonly find precedes the onset of illness. We have designated this state the giving-up—given-up complex (3, 4). I will not here attempt to document the prevalence of this sequential relationship, which in our experience is somewhere around 70 to 80 percent; nor will I evaluate the contribution of this psychological state to the subsequent development of illness. Many studies, both retrospective and prospective, strongly suggest that it is neither a coincidence nor a consequence of the illness, that it plays some significant role in modifying the capacity of the organism to cope with concurrent pathogenic factors (5–8). This position is far from proven, but in our view the evidence is sufficient to justify careful study and characterization of the state itself, whatever its role in disease pathogenesis may ultimately prove to be. For as a psychological state it must also, after all, reflect the biological condition of the organism, and its elucidation may well provide access to disease mechanisms heretofore unappreciated, particularly the role of the nervous system.

It is interesting that most lay people take it for granted that a person's frame of mind has something to do with his propensity to fall ill and even to die. Discouragement, despair, humiliation, and grief are generally thought to be conducive to illness and death, while contentment, happiness, faith, confidence, and success are associated with health. But physicians, who in their nonprofessional roles may share such notions, rarely regard this as a legitimate area for their scientific interest. Indeed, most avoid discussing such phenomena with their colleagues, relegating them to the category of curious anecdotes. Yet this is a theme which has been so commonplace in popular thinking and in folklore and literature throughout the ages, from ancient sagas to modern soap operas, that one cannot help wondering whether it is based on actual observations or whether it represents some kind of mass delusion. It always attracts popular interest and when sufficiently dramatic may appear in the form of a news item. During the past 5 to 6 years I have collected 100 items from newspapers around the world that report the occurrence of sudden death under unusual circumstances. They provide us with a good starting point for our consideration of the psychological setting of disease.

The largest group, 50, or half, are popularly referred to as "dying of grief." These people died suddenly or soon after receiving news of the death of a loved one. An additional ten died anticipating such a loss. A common item is of a husband or wife dying immediately after discovering the spouse to have collapsed or died. Some victims died when they realized the spouse was dead, others merely anticipating that he might die. The commander of the ceremonial troops at President Kennedy's funeral, a 27-year-old Army captain, collapsed and died a week after the funeral; the 52-year-old wife of the owner of the motel in which Martin Luther King was assassinated had a stroke and died the next day.

The second largest group, usually described as "scared to death," numbers 32 and concerns people who dropped dead during situations of danger. Some represented real dangers—such as riots, storms, shipwrecks, earthquakes or personal assault; others constituted a more personal type of threat—such as the hold-up suspect who dropped dead in court as he was telling his lawyer how "scared" he was, or the woman who died while phoning the police to report four teen-agers beating and robbing a bus driver in the front of her house.

Two items referred to respected citizens who died in court after being accused or convicted of a serious offense.

Perhaps the most interesting items concerned six persons who died on what should have been an occasion for joy. Three died during reunions after long separations. One report tells of a 55-year-old man and his 88-year-old father, both of whom are alleged to have collapsed and died at the moment of their meeting after a separation of more than 20 years. Another reports that a winner of $1,683 on a $2 bet at the race track died as he was collecting his money. A man died as he was receiving an ovation from his friends.

In most cases nothing reliable is available concerning either the state of health of these people prior to the fatal incident or the causes of death, but these are not our concern now. Rather we are interested in the circumstances under which they are reported to have died. By and large these settings correspond very well with what we have observed to be associated with the onset of illness in general. All involved a change in the environment about which the victim felt powerless to do anything—the sudden death or the threat of death of some important person, a real or fantasied great personal danger, a sudden humiliation or a loss of status. And all were also circumstances which we ordinarily associate with painful emotion; that is, all but the 6 people who succumbed with an excess of good fortune! But are these really exceptions? I think not, for Feldman's study of the familiar phenomenon of "tears with the happy ending" has demonstrated that the crying reflects not happiness, but an acute awareness of the loss or deprivation that marked the period of hardship or tension which culminated in the happy ending (9). Reunions after painful separations are the most obvious examples. Many of you will recall the dramatic scene on television of the mother who cried and then collapsed upon greeting her son whose funeral service as a Viet Nam casualty she had attended the day before.

How basic is this phenomenon? Let us look at another press report, this time one which I was able personally to verify. This concerns a couple, Charlie and Josephine, who had been inseparable companions for 13 years. In a senseless act of violence, Charlie, in full view of Josephine, was shot and killed in a melee with the police. Josephine first stood motionless, then slowly approached his prostrate form, sank to her knees, and silently rested her head on the dead and bloody body. Concerned persons attempted to help her away, but she refused to move. Hoping she would soon surmount her overwhelming grief, they let her be. But she never rose again; in 15 minutes she was dead!

The remarkable part of the story is that Charlie and Josephine were llamas in the zoo! They had escaped from their pen during a snowstorm and Charlie, a mean animal to begin with, was shot when he proved unmanageable. I was able to establish from the zoo keeper that to all intents and purposes Josephine had been normally frisky and healthy right up to the moment of the tragic event. No autopsy was performed, so we can go no farther in explaining the death.

I cite this example to indicate that we are dealing with a general biological phenomenon, not simply a process peculiar to an occasional oversensitive human being. Actually such occurrences among animals are well known to naturalists and zoo keepers, and the circumstances seem very similar to what we have been describing for humans. Its occurrence among animals obviously offers possibilities for experimental research.

Let us now turn to everyday clinical practice and see what we can learn about the circumstances under which our patients fall ill. Some are quite as dramatic as those reported in the newspapers. Others represent situations of prolonged or recurring difficulty, frustration, failure, or defeat, culminating in illness. But most fall in the category of the personal dramas and tragedies of everyday life, often involving circumstances that would hardly impress the casual observer as important. For example, the last patient I interviewed before writing this paragraph was a 70-year-old woman who developed congestive heart failure when her son injured his hand in an accident. Hardly a catastrophic event, yet the accident in fact reawakened painful memories of her own situation as a young widow struggling to care for her children after her husband had been killed in an accident. Already she was visualizing her son as permanently disabled, her daughter-in-law as having to raise her children by herself, and all too keenly she felt her own inability and unwillingness to live again through a situation so reminiscent of her own painful past.

Such a story is rather typical of the more subtle life settings, and serves to emphasize that the important variable is not the external situation but how the individual responds. Indeed, one cannot tell from the external event what a person's response will be. Some rise magnificently to the occasion only to fall ill under a lesser blow later on, while others succumb to the first disruption of their life pattern. Some seem to live a charmed life, seldom subjected to a serious frustration or loss, while others seem to be cursed by an evil fate that pursues them at every turn. Yet out of this complexity of responses we discover again and again one particular psychological pattern that appears especially to be associated with disease onset. In many respects it seems to constitute a final common pathway in that it may evolve in the course of many different life circumstances and in the face of many different personality characteristics. This is the pattern we have designated the giving-up–given-up complex (3, 4).

What are its essential elements? Perhaps its most characteristic feature is a sense of psychological impotence, a feeling that for briefer or longer periods of time one is unable to cope with the changes in the environment; the psychological or social devices utilized in the past seem no longer effective or available. In place of the smooth, almost effortless integration of behavior and the sense of confidence and mastery of the environment that mark effective functioning there is a disruption, a pause, an interruption, while the mind seems to search in vain for a solution. And for that period of impasse there is a profound alteration in how one sees oneself and one's environment.

How is this manifested clinically? The data from which this construction has evolved have come from the interviews of literally thousands of patients from all walks of life and with every conceivable medical illness. From descriptions by patients of their life setting and their feelings during the period antedating illness onset we identify five characteristics of the giving-up–given-up complex: (1) the giving-up effects of helplessness or hopelessness; (2) a depreciated image of oneself; (3) a loss of gratification from relationships or roles in life; (4) a disruption of the sense of continuity between past, present, and future; and (5) a reactivation of memories of earlier periods of giving-up. Let us look at each of these briefly:

(1) The patient exhibiting the giving-up–given-up complex commonly reports feelings of being at the end of his rope, at a loss, bewildered, uncertain, at an impasse. Or he may instead stress his efforts to avert or overcome such feelings,

which is only another way of acknowledging that these feelings existed. Thus, he may speak of giving up or struggling not to give up, of despair, of it being just too much or too difficult; or of being concerned that he will be unable to take it any more. Such descriptions reflect the two affects of giving up, *helplessness* and *hopelessness*. The person experiencing helplessness ascribes his feeling of impotence to failures of or frustrations from the environment, to which he looks to provide a solution. To him it seems that he is in the state that he is because the people in his life have failed or are frustrating him. Feeling himself incapable of doing anything about his own situation, he nonetheless still anticipates that some response or help from the environment will resolve his dilemma. The person experiencing *hopelessness* holds himself to account for his failure or inability to cope, and he has no expectation that any change in the environment is possible or will help. Responsible for his own fate, he feels help, even if offered, will be to no avail (5, 6).

(2) The patient's image of himself is as one who is no longer competent, in control, or capable of functioning in his accustomed manner, though he may continue to attempt to do so. Particularly after the loss of a loved one, of status, of home, or of a valued possession, he may feel himself incomplete or damaged, literally as if part of himself has been torn away, leaving a gaping wound (10).

(3) Commonly he feels less gratified or supported in important human relationships or in roles in life. Sometimes this occurs because of actual disappointments, losses or separations and sometimes because of threats to such roles or relationships. These were common themes in the newspaper items I cited earlier. Failures, rebuffs, humiliations, loss of standing in the family or the community, decline in strength or ability, thwarting of life's ambition or goal all may contribute to a feeling that even the simple gratifications of life are denied him.

(4) The sense of a continuity between past, present, and future is disrupted. This feeling of continuity, ordinarily taken for granted, only becomes conscious when it is in danger of being interrupted. Then it seems that the devices used in the past no longer are applicable and it becomes difficult to project oneself into the future, which seems uncertain, unpromising or even bleak.

(5) Patients may also be reminded of other occasions in the past when they felt helplessness or hopelessness. And when such memories involve situations never adequately resolved, there may be a cumulative effect as well. It is as if the earlier failures or losses, not really successfully mastered, constitute all too real reminders of past vulnerability and inability to cope. Such reactivated feelings may be as intense as when they originally occurred. This accounts for the "last straw" phenomenon, a relatively minor event serving to reopen old wounds with accompanying feelings of helplessness or hopelessness. A familiar example is unresolved grief, exemplified by the person who still cries years after the death of a loved one. Such a person may experience each successive loss, no matter how trivial, as symbolic of the original loss, each time with reactivation of the giving-up feelings. The occasional catastrophic response to the happy

ending, as may occur upon reunion after years of painful separation, no doubt involves this mechanism. Here the victim is overwhelmed by all the painful memories of the period of separation, none of which could be resolved as long as he could not know whether he would ever again see his loved one alive.

The psychological state we are describing is a fluid one, often quite transient or intermittent. Indeed, it is impossible to imagine how one could exist for long in such a state of limbo. Ordinarily the mind constantly and actively seeks for some solution. It scans past experience as well as the present scene in an attempt to find old solutions or devise new ones. Actually, what we are designating as the giving-up–given-up complex is in fact only an exaggeration of a normal psychological phenomenon. Everyone in this room has many times in his life been at such a psychological crossroad where, for the moment at least, the smooth flow forward was disrupted, and one seemed to whirl about directionless until finally some suitable solution presented itself. When successful, as it is most of the time, this constitutes a developmental step forward and adds to the armamentarium of adaptive solutions available for future crises. But sometimes circumstances are such that prompt resolution is impossible and, for varying periods of time, one finds oneself alternating between giving up and struggling again to find a solution. It is during such periods of psychic disequilibrium that we believe disease may supervene.

In essence, we are proposing that during such a state the total biologic economy of the organism is altered, at times in such a way that its capability to deal with certain potentially pathogenic processes is reduced, permitting disease to develop. The giving-up–given-up complex thus constitutes the psychological or behavioral reflection of a psychobiologic state. Implicit in this perspective is that the predisposition to the organic disease must already exist; otherwise the person may be psychologically distressed, but he will not become ill. Thus, we conceive this psychobiologic condition as *contributing* to the emergence of the disease; it does not cause it; nor is it a necessary or a sufficient condition for disease development.

Finally, to call your attention again to the biological side of this psychobiological reaction, let me point out that there is ample evidence in modern neurophysiology and neuroendocrinology to show that it is precisely when the central nervous system is failing in its task of processing input that emergency biologic defense systems are invoked. Such failure results when an input relevant to the organism's adjustment is too great (overload) or when no program or response to the input is available (incongruence); or, in psychological terms, when information cannot be handled promptly and effectively by mental mechanisms alone. Under such circumstances the organism has available no relevant behavior. At this point the limbic structures of the forebrain and midbrain, forming an elaborate neural circuit with the hypothalamus in the center, respond by mobilizing emergency systems to prepare the body to deal with or avoid damage. Exactly what biological activity is associated with the giving-up–given-up complex is not yet known. But having identified and characterized the complex in psychological terms, we are now in position to develop the experimental approaches necessary to define its biological dimensions and to investigate how these influence susceptibility to disease.

In closing I would like to return to a historical perspective. It was not always true that physicians disregarded the influence of the mental state of their patients. Indeed, in the 19th century in particular, few writers failed to invoke the baleful influence of grief, despair, or discouragement in predisposing to illness. None ignored the healing effects of faith, confidence, and peace of mind, and all regarded contentment and happiness as prerequisite for health and for resistance to disease. Nor did they fail to recognize that such emotions were only contributing factors, not primary causes. In 1816, Samuel Black (11) cited "ossification of the coronaries" as the "primary and original cause" of angina pectoris, but he considered "the powerfully pernicious influence of strong mental emotion or of depression passion" as a "contributing influence." He cited case examples to support his view (11). Even Freud, in a very early paper, opined that the "depressive affects are often sufficient in themselves to bring about . . . disease . . . accompanied by manifest anatomical changes." But he added, "In such cases it must be assumed that the patient already had a predisposition, though hitherto an inoperative one, to the disease in question" (12). It is interesting to speculate how it is that such insights could have vanished so completely from medical writings for so long. I recently had occasion to review the papers of my uncle, Emanuel Libman, and I was interested to discover that in a clinical report on nephritis (13), published in 1899 at the very beginning of his career, he begins the case history of his 14-year-old patient by saying, "One week ago she became very much frightened at a fire in the neighborhood at 2 p.m." I daresay in that era this was the expected thing to do. But then his imagination was captured by the exciting discoveries of bacteriology, and he began his work on bacterial infections, blood culture, and subacute bacterial endocarditis. Never again, in his numerous clinical papers, do any such allusions to life settings ever appear. I suspect that this epitomizes the issue. The psychological observations of these early writers were no doubt correct, but they were based largely on intuition and sentiment. No useful body of scientific theory and no reliable methods were available to study the problem further. With the tremendous breakthroughs in the biological sciences that began in the latter half of the 19th century, medicine acquired powerful tools with which to investigate disease. It is hardly surprising that only those aspects of disease that were accessible to study by these methods were considered scientific. Everything else was deemed unworthy of attention by serious minded physicians. Hence the efforts to develop a scientific theory of mind and behavior for the most part had to take place outside the boundaries of medicine. Those physicians who did occupy themselves with such issues either had to confine themselves to the study of so-called "mental diseases," or were excluded from membership in the medical profession, as was Freud. Curiously enough, even the brain was studied without reference to its psychological functions. But now at long last the gap is closing. The development of an organismic point of view is finally making it possible to grasp how the individual functions within an environment and how mind and brain acts as the mediators and regulators of the body economy. Such insights began with clinical observations of the impact of social and environmental changes on the person. And no one has contributed more significantly to bringing this perspective into the mainstream of medicine than William Menninger.

References

1. Menninger, W. C. Psychiatry in a Troubled World: Yesterday's War and Today's Challenge. New York, Macmillan, 1948.
2. Engel, G. L. Medical Education and the Psychosomatic Approach. A Report on the Rochester Experience, 1946–66. J. Psychosom. Res. 11:77–85, 1967.
3. ———. A Psychological Setting of Somatic Disease: The "Giving Up—Given Up" Complex. Proc. Roy. Soc. Med. 60:553, 1967.
4. Schmale, A. H. and Engel, G. L. The Giving Up—Given Up Complex Illustrated on Film. Arch. Gen. Psychiat. 17:135–45, 1967.
5. ———. Relationship of Separation and Depression to Disease. Psychosom. Med. 20:259–77, 1958.
6. ———. Object Loss, "Giving Up," and Disease Onset; An Overview of Research in Progress. Symposium on Medical Aspects of Stress in the Military Climate. Washington, D.C., U.S. Government Printing Office, 1965, pp. 433–43.
7. Engel, G. L. and Schmale, A. H. Psychoanalytic Theory of Somatic Disorder: Conversion, Specificity, and the Disease Onset Situation. J. Amer. Psychoanal. Assn. 15:344–65, 1967.
8. Thurlow, H. J. General Susceptibility to Illness: A Selective Review. Canad. Med. Assn. J. 97:1397–1404, 1967.
9. Feldman, S. S. Crying at the Happy Ending. J. Amer. Psychoanal. Assn. 4:447–85, 1956.
10. Engel, G. L. Is Grief a Disease? A Challenge for Medical Research. Psychosom. Med. 23:18–22, 1961.
11. Black, S. History of Two Cases of Angina Pectoris. Med. Chir. Trans. 7:70–83, 1816.
12. Freud, Sigmund. Psychical (or Mental) Treatment (1905). Standard Edition 7:283–302, 1953.
13. Brill, N. E. and Libman, Emanuel. A Contribution to the Subjects of Chronic Interstitial Nephritis and Arteritis in the Young: With a Note on Calcification of the Liver. J. Exp. Med. 4:541, 1899.

The Irony of the ICU *
by Howard P. Rome, M.D.

It is a truism to observe that health-care service is expanding in all directions at an exponential rate; it is now a 55 billion dollar per year industry. In 1950 it was estimated to be 12.1 billion dollars per year; by the end of 1968 it had risen 380 per cent. The demands for the delivery of this service increased at a rate in excess of comparable increases in other areas of the economy. As gauged by the Consumer Price Index, prices of health service rose almost 67 per cent from 1950 to 1965; an annual rate of increase higher than the all-goods and all-services categories. Moreover this increase affects all sectors of the health-care establishment. "Radicalized" is a current in-word; it not only connotes change but also the revolutionary direction and pace the change takes. The entire health-care system has been radicalized since the end of World War II. A reflection of this is to be seen in the revolutionary changes in the hospital component of the medical delivery system.

For example, the demand for nursing services has followed the lead of the demand for medical services. In partial but inadequate response to this demand, the traditional duties of the nurse have been parcelled out among a number of more or less restricted occupational tasks. There are the broad general divisions of nursing education, research, and patient service in a similar fashion to the divisions in the field of medicine. In the patient-service area, there are the added occupations of the orderlies, nurses' aides, licensed practical nurses (LPNs), and volunteers. The clerical-administrative functions of the hospital (ward) operations have been delegated in large part to a secretary-clerk. Then, too, there is the educational hierarchy: student nurses in training to be RNs, "diploma" nurses, as well as their instructors, teaching supervisors, and nursing school administrators. In short, as medical education and hospital practice have fissioned and produced specialties and their satellite subspecialties, the nursing profession has also recognized the utility and the need of this division of labor.

The hospital as the physical nodal point of the medical health-care delivery system matrix has become the center of these specialized medical delivery subsystems. It has also become a focal point for community health care, and increasingly it will incorporate all preventive, curative, and rehabilitative services within its purview.

* Psychiatry Digest. Vol. 30, No. 5 (May, 1969). Pp. 10–14.

Apropos of this challenge to traditional function there has been a growing, albeit laggard, development in the architectural structure of hospitals and especially of the units that serve these special functions. Thus, "wings," "pavilions," and "units" have proliferated as appendages to the main body of the hospital, each with its own staff of trained personnel and its own equipment necessary to perform its assigned task. But essentially they have been more or less walled-off compartments—not very original in their concept of design.

Thus emergency rooms, medical wings, surgical pavilions, recovery suites, administrative offices, and psychiatric wards were among the first of the specially designated facilities of the General Hospital. When the utility of physical separation into these gross divisions was demonstrated, there followed progressively smaller subdivisions [e.g., dialysis centers, poison-control units, intensive care units (ICUs)] especially designed to provide more efficiency for the convenience of administration, for the medical staff, and last of all for the critically ill patient.

In parallel the biotechnology used in these units has become more sophisticated. Those architectural and operational changes which have been made to accommodate the physical equipment and only incidentally the people they accommodate. These costly products have become obligatory equipment for large general hospitals. One observer has editorialized to the effect that the resulting scene is an "encounter not easily forgotten in the science-fiction setting of a coronary ICU. Surrounded by weird electronic equipment, facing anxious fellow patients, nurses, and attending staff, the patient is made constantly aware of the proximity of death."[1]

The designers and indeed the caretakers who work in these ICUs point to the obvious benefits to be derived from the constant vigilance that is available, the provision of skilled nursing care as a consequence of specialization. They are rightfully proud of the lessened morbidity and lowered mortality which follows from the capacity to monitor with the most advanced technologic equipment minute changes in the vital signs and functions of their patients. They consequently avoid otherwise disastrous complications. Then, too, there are other more peripheral benefits such as the economy to the hospital in allocating this expensive equipment to the place where it can get maximum use. In turn, it is said that these economies are passed on to the patient-customer; at least the rate of increase in the cost of hospital care is attenuated. Better and therefore more complete records add to the general store of medical information about the longitudinal course of not only the patient's continuing progress but also critical disease states or injuries in general as well as their complications.

But as Emily Dickinson wryly observed: ". . . We must an anguish pay/in keen and quivering ratio. . . ." for every boon. Patients as well as their caretakers who are the subjects as well as the participant-observers of these life-saving procedures have to endure a certain amount of emotional stress incidental

---

[1] Editorial. *Journal of the American Medical Association.* Vol. 205 (1968). 697–98.

to being exposed to the very environment that will help spare these lives.[2] For instance, Feindel in writing of the selection of nurses for this duty says "(They) should be able to control their emotions . . . tolerate stress . . . act effectively . . . use good judgment in emergencies. . . ." There have been many studies of untoward psychiatric consequences experienced on the nether side of the bed. Thus, this is a quality of mercy that affects him that gives and him that takes.

The etiology of these untoward psychiatric reactions of patients has been much debated: whether these reactions are in response to some coincidental physiologic insult, or are the consequence of the emotional stress of being exposed to "the science fiction setting." Perhaps it is in response to being subjected to a combination of both ordeals.

The standard procedure that obtains in most ICUs is that regardless of their status as private or ward patients, the patients are assigned to the care of the house and attending staff managing that service which means that whatever their competence technically, this is an entire group of strangers. The ICU cubicle where the patient is bedded is a segment of a larger unit. There is usually a large defibrillator with the array of syringes, needles, and stands holding parenteral solutions. The unit is equipped with a bank of electronic devices for monitoring: tape recorders, an oscilloscope that constantly displays electrocardiographic signals. There may be an additional attachment to permit analogic conversion of heart signals to an audio mode and thus warn the nearby attendants of the sudden development of a cardiac arrythmia. Inadvertently this also alerts the patient.

The typical ICU patient has an intravenous needle in place and consequently that arm (at least) is tied down. The side rails of the bed are up in place. An oxygen mask with one kind or another of the automatic breathing devices stands nearby. Depending on the size and crowded state of the unit, men and women are in the same room although separated by a curtain said to be "the dirtiest piece of linen in the hospital."[3] Although there are windows surrounding the

---

[3] "Building for Tomorrow's Medicine." *Medical World News*. Vol. 10 (1969). 30–35.

patient making privacy an impossibility, often the cubicle is kept dark or, in the case of neurosurgical ICUs, lighted 24 hours daily. The net result of either of these procedures is that the ambience they create conduces to disorientation. This potential confusion is enhanced by the fact that no radios or televisions are permitted and visitors, one per patient, are permitted for a maximum of five minutes per hour. The anxiety fulminated by these short-lived exposures ricochets from the patient to his family.

There is a flurry of nurses hovering in the immediate area as well as house-staff members within calling distance at all times, since emergencies of a serious nature occur frequently. These obviously require the presence of a team with a

[2] R. G. Druss and D. S. Kornfeld. *Journal of the American Medical Association*. Vol. 201 (1967). 291–96.

resulting increase in the "white" noise level environment and inevitably a subliminal communicated indistinct and unfocused atmosphere of excitement. To the conscious patient living in this environment, the general atmosphere vibrates with an aura of intense alertness. Periodically persons speak (literally) about the patient in muted tones at the foot of his bed but the message that comes through to him with high-fidelity is concern—also present is the specter of sudden death.

As soon as one patient is deemed well enough, he is moved, and another seriously ill patient takes his place. There is an omnipresent background of sound: muffled voices, grunts, stertorous breathing, moaning, retching, and crying. This serves as a backdrop for the periodic interruptions of a troubled sleep by routine nursing chores: temperature taking, the recording of blood pressure, giving of medications, plus the hygienic needs of very sick persons.

While the character of the ICU depends upon the kind of patient it specializes in caring for, the effect upon the nurses is, in the overall, generally the same regardless of their special duties. In order to dilute the emotional impact of this total immersion in critical sickness, depending on their personality, the attendants—particularly the nurses who are assigned to this station on a regular shift basis and who have the most to do with the personal care of these patients—shield themselves from anxiety by delivering their ministrations with a certain degree of emotional detachment. One can speculate as to the probable reasons for this anxiety. Manifestly, constant exposure to impact of death requires a defense. This is a companion reaction to the defense mechanisms used by patients exposed to the same likelihood and circumstances. La Rochefoucauld remarked, "One can no more look steadily at death than at the sun." Hence, the most conservative tactic is avoidance—a resort by which everyone who is exposed similarly escapes from a direct confrontation and thus helps deny the plaguing existential question: To be or not to be?

Although duty in an ICU is similar to, it is also a different psychologic experience than that which surgical teams are exposed to routinely. All patients in an operating room are unconscious. Except for the exposed operative site the body of the patient is draped. The surgical procedure is never more than hours in duration at most—never days. Although death here too is an ever-present contingency, its actual occurrence is infrequent as compared with the mortality of patients in ICUs. Then, too, upon death in the operating room the surgical team is relieved of the preburial preparations and the family discussion and explanations that are incumbent upon the ICU nurses.

Defenses Against Anxiety
in the Nurse–Patient Relationship

by Margaret Aasterud, R.N., M.S.

Nathan Jones shifted restively in his bed and looked at the travel-clock on the bedside table.

"Ten o'clock," he thought, "it seems like hours since breakfast."

Wincing, he splinted his right side with his hand as he turned back.

"Damn," he muttered, "I wish they'd take these adhesive things off."

Idly he wondered how long it took Miss Sears, his private nurse, to get a cup of coffee—she must have been gone at least half an hour.

Across the hall he could hear old Mrs. Lewis, who had been there before he came, imploring one of the nurses to please get her something for the pain. He knew the answer before it came; he'd heard it so often.

"I'm sorry, Mrs. Lewis: you had a hypo just an hour ago, and I can't give you anything yet."

He looked across the court. His room faced at right angles the pediatric ward, and he often waved at the children standing in their cribs or at the window. He smiled this time. The little dark-haired girl with her leg up in traction had a doll with her and was doing an effective imitative job of giving the doll a fierce injection with a plastic syringe.

Past his door a new patient was being pushed in a wheelchair. He supposed he was the one going into the isolation room since he had seen the nurses going by earlier with all the accoutrements.

Miss Sears came into the room.

"I saw your doctor downstairs; he's tied up for awhile but said to see if you couldn't walk farther today—at least twice the length of the corridor."

Nathan grimaced; neither she nor the doctor apparently knew what it was like to get out of that bed—how much it hurt and how much he worried about the sutures holding. *They* said activity was the thing, but he wished *they'd* have to try it.

All of these incidents happened in a brief space of time; none of them unusual, just routine occurrences in a typical hospital. The administrator and the nursing director were making rounds together and they agreed, "It's a quiet day."

Both they and the staff personnel would undoubtedly raise their eyebrows in surprise if someone suggested that a myriad of attacks were being made upon the patients within those walls.

But upon reflection they might agree.

"Well, yes, we do heap indignities on some of them—drawing blood, sending them to surgery, inserting gastric tubes, and so on—but it's for their own good and it has to be done."

Actually, with this statement we could have little argument; most procedures in medical practice are not pleasant, and few people voluntarily, for pleasure, would submit themselves to being poked, prodded, turned and denied food, companionship and privacy.

But we might pursue the questioning a little further and ask, "Then isn't much of what nurses do *hostile* acts?"

This will undoubtedly cause a spontaneous and emotional denial.

"Hostile, what do you mean? Our nurses aren't angry at patients; they don't go around inflicting pain for the fun of it! They're helping people regain health —sometimes you might even say they're being motherly, but doing hostile things, never. We'd fire anyone who did!"

After this outburst, we wish our phrasing had been better and that we had discussed matters more subtly and had not forced such a spontaneous denial. After all, administrative heads within a hospital can hardly be expected to admit to being responsible for hiring a staff that is hostile and aggressive to people to whom they are committed to give service.

So let's go back to our "typical" scenes.

Nathan Jones had been assaulted some days before by the surgeon's knife and the anesthesiologist's mask of unconsciousness; now he has hired someone to protect him from being alone, from the fear of inattention on the part of staff personnel. Weeks later, he will speak of this nurse-protector in words such as, "I had a good nurse; she kept me moving all right." And he will not mention the fact that he felt irritated when she left him to go for coffee or a cigarette. Nor will he say how it really felt to have someone, a stranger, wash him, clean him, keep track of his toilet habits, dress him, undress him, tell him when to move, when to get out of bed and how far to walk. Sure, he knew the jargon about everyone regressing when they were sick and how it was all right to do so. The doctors and nurses expected this, and, he suspected, encouraged it, but that didn't alter the fact that there were things he didn't like but didn't have the strength to resist. What's more, he couldn't see that it would do any good to resist since they seemed to have all the power.

The little girl on the pediatric ward was more overt about how medical and nursing procedures affected her. She transferred her anger openly onto the doll.

Mrs. Lewis had no chance at all. She couldn't get up and get medicine for her pain, which was *real* to her; it didn't occur on schedule every four hours. Her frustration built up until *nothing* was right and she soon was labeled "fussy" and "cranky." But who would call obeying the doctor's order a hostile act? After all, one can't give medication indiscriminately, and Mrs. Lewis should understand that.

The man going into the isolation room; well, that *is* different. Anyone knows it is hard to be shut off from people—most of all, *he* knows it. He is fifty-four, but it stirs almost-conscious memories of being sent to his room and the door being closed firmly behind him by his mother after bad sessions at the dinner table some fifty years ago. The sensation is almost the same: the hospital noises outside his door swell and recede just as did the family noises outside his old bedroom. He couldn't help it if he had to get that bug, could he? But it seemed as though people were treating him as though it were his fault, that he *could* help it.

We hope by now that our administrator and director will agree that what may appear to us as only good medical and nursing practice can be perceived quite differently by those towards whom these practices are directed. And, we should hasten to add, the feelings aroused by these acts are often not recognized by the patient. Consciously, the person knows that certain procedures are necessary and that medical and paramedical personnel must do what they are doing with his body and to his feelings. However, at the same time and on a different level these same people and their actions can be tremendously threatening to him. His self-image is being attacked in all manner of ways. Still he cannot realize why so many feelings are aroused in him and why he reacts the way he does—often so defensively and almost angrily. At the same time he feels compelled to push these feelings down because it is necessary to "co-operate" in order to recover.

Nurses also have trouble with their feelings about these same practices and have difficulty identifying the sources of uneasiness. In defense they resort to behavior that may be saving to a certain extent but not entirely satisfactory either to themselves or to the patients involved in the situations. Isabel Menzies identifies these defenses in a report on the nursing service in an English general hospital. These defenses, she states, have by collusive agreement become part of the structure of nursing service itself.

It is relevant to state here those which directly affect patient care by detracting positive personal factors of warmth and empathy from the situations to be described:

a. Splitting up the nurse-patient relationship—performing only a few tasks for, and having restricted contact with, any one patient.
b. Depersonalization, categorization and denial of the significance of the individual.
c. Detachment and denial of feelings.

d. Attempt to eliminate decisions by ritual task-performance.
e. Reducing the weight of responsibility in decision-making by checks and counter-checks.
f. Avoidance of change (1).

This social defense system fosters evasion; it is oriented toward helping the nurse avoid anxiety, guilt, doubt and uncertainty. It is, in fact, quite successful in leaving little room for the nurse to confront or work through situations which might provoke anxiety in herself, in the patient, or in both.

It is with some of these situations that this paper is concerned—the every-day occurrences, the every-day practices and procedures that by their very nature are threatening and should be recognized as such. They could be any one of those to which our four patients have been or will be subjected.

We cannot dispense with the situations or procedures simply because they are threatening, anymore than the surgeon can dispense with the scalpel because it is painful. But we can look at them more closely with a view toward being able to encourage some understanding of the emotions they arouse in patients and in ourselves.

The nurse's function has been delineated by Schulman as dual in nature—mother-surrogate and healer. Those functions which come under the mother-surrogate role are the ones most pleasant to the patient—the tenderness, the watching-over and the comforting (2). However, the healing functions are not usually pleasant. The injection given to the little girl was not pleasant; the forced isolation for the man was not pleasant, neither was the spacing of medication for Mrs. Lewis, nor the ambulation for Nathan Jones.

The Situations

CHILDREN

The effects of healing procedures on children are easier to identify than those administered to adults since the child has not built up the patterns of behavior that often effectively mask real feelings.

Anna Freud writes of how loss of mastery of various bodily functions such as independent eating, bowel and bladder evacuations, ability to wash, dress and undress, occasioned by nursing procedures (or by the weakened bodily condition itself) means an equivalent loss in ego control, a pull back to the earlier and more passive levels of infantile development.

Though most children renounce these ego skills and abilities fairly easily under the impact of being "nursed," they defend to the utmost their freedom of movement in the same situation. Young toddlers, who have only recently learned to walk, are known to stand up stubbornly in their beds for the whole course even of severe illnesses (3).

The heightening of aggression during and after motor restraint (as in plaster casts) is especially well known, and may appear as restlessness, increased irritability, or in the use of bad language.

In regard to feeding, Anna Freud believes that less harm is done by withholding desired foods than by urging or forcing unwelcome food on an ill child. The latter often revives feeding battles which have raged between mother and child in the nursing period (4).

The bad taste or smell of some medicines often presents a major difficulty with children. Through analytic investigation Melanie Klein has revealed the existence of repressed ideas of being attacked or poisoned by the mother. These unconscious fantasies may be linked to reality by the administration of laxatives which force the bowels to move although the child intends otherwise (5).

The punitive character of restrictive measures has always been known to parents and has been exploited by them. Sending a child to bed, confining him to his room, depriving him of favorite dishes have been used as punishments over the ages. In certain societies even the forcible administration of laxatives is used for the same purpose (6).

The conclusion has been reached by several authors that nursing and medical procedures of every variety may be more traumatic to the sick child than the physical illness itself. This is more pronounced in the child with emotional disturbances, and persons working with these children attest to how measures that seem reasonable to a cautious and thorough pediatrician merely add further elements of isolation, punishment and retaliation to the child and may signify impending mutilation or death. Specifically mentioned have been medical isolation as a symbol of separation and abandonment, and procedures with an implied threat of mutilation and castration such as buttock injections and the use of rectal swabs on boys.

One group noted the exaggerated playing-out of fantasies that the disturbed children indulged in after exposure to certain procedures: "... in an attempt to allay their anxiety, the children often eventually arrived at compulsive rituals that seemed strongly identified with the actual defenses of the nurses. This solution seemed to apply to the little girls in particular, and several of them have never relinquished a fetish-like attachment to their little charts, records, and play instruments, which keep them protected in a magical way while helping them identify with the aggressors" (7).

The defense that is built up with increasing years against feelings related to a particular procedure was investigated by Kassowitz. He found that relative to the use of hypodermic needles children up to six months of age showed no evidence of apprehension; those from one to four showed the highest incidence of more-or-less violent fear and resentment; and after five there was a steady decline of fighting defense (8).

We should not assume that the fear and resentment of pain-producing instruments disappear; rather, the desire for approval of others in being "a good girl" or "a good boy" or a "tough guy" is stronger than the desire to openly express this feeling. Aside from those few who perversely desire infliction of pain, adults have the same fear and the same resentment of these instruments.

The use of injectable medications is one of the healing functions that is easiest to recognize for what it is—a painful act. Just as the child may continue to act out his resentment over them for some time, the adult's verbal recall of a hospital experience is often punctuated with statements of the seemingly endless round of needle injections. Nursing practice seems, to many, to involve primarily this function. In the hospital the more outspoken express their feelings in an undisguised fashion, with remarks such as, "You must get a lot of pleasure out of all those needles," or, "You have a sadistic look this morning—do you have a needle with you?"

INTRUSIVE PROCEDURES

Nursing practice involves intrusive procedures which are capable of eliciting many primitive fantasies of mutilation and punishment, notably the use of gastric tubes, enemas, douches, catheterizations and rectal temperatures.

Catheterizations and douches carry with them the threat of genital mutilation. Indwelling catheters, in addition, leave exposed to the world a function that is usually reserved for the individual's privacy, but in hospitals we find drainage tubes and glass or plastic receptacles fastened onto the bed or placed on the floor where anyone may look, measure and note the contents.

An enema pertains to a sphere of action that constitutes one of the earliest modes of infantile resistance against parental interference—that of retention of feces. Janis, in a post-surgical analytic interview, elicited the information that this concept had been at work when the patient had been unable to expel an enema—the primitive language of the body saying, "I won't give in to their demands; I won't let them take anything out of my body" (9).

It is his contention that most patients find intrusive procedures (and other distressing ones) easier to bear if they are *not* told about them beforehand as this gives them time to visualize the event as a horrible ordeal and to develop vivid fantasies. The best time to give an explanation and help assuage the patient's fear of being injured is at the time of institution of the procedure. He states:

Detailed descriptions of certain physical threats, such as those involving the forcible intrusion of a bodily orifice, readily lend themselves to symbolic fantasy elaboration and are especially likely to touch off irrational, infantile fears (10).

VICTIMIZATION

Medical and nursing procedures do not always go as planned: a lumbar puncture goes on for what seems an interminable time if there are arthritic changes and the needle cannot be inserted easily; an intravenous can require the exploring of three veins instead of the expected one; a catheterization is sometimes not successful until the fourth catheter is used; a bedpan is not always removed promptly, or a liquid diet might be continued when the patient could be on a regular diet.

The patient's irritation and frustration over these events seem to us to be magnified out of all proportions to the objective situation. He may express statements to the effect that the person initiating the procedure is incompetent, ill-trained and should get someone who can do it better. Why this intensified reaction? Janis hypothesizes in the following manner:

If an episode of stress impact produces actual physical suffering and if the degree of perceived victimization is greater than had been expected beforehand, the episode will tend to be unconsciously assimilated to early victimization experiences which had evoked in the child feelings of intense disappointment concerning the behavior of one or both parents. The disappointments that are rearoused stem from painful episodes which had been interpreted by the child as excessive punishment caused by an angry or rejecting parent and which did not terminate in the usual degree of reconciliation.

The reactivated disappointment will be manifested as an "aggrievement" reaction (a combination of rage and grief) and will be externally directed toward danger-control authorities (resentment and retaliation against parent-surrogates) and/or inwardly directed toward the self (lowered self-esteem, self-punitive asceticism, feelings of hopelessness).

Sometimes rage rather than grief is the reaction to deprivation. . . . Given a stress episode of unexpectedly high victimization, the probability that disappointment reactions will take the form of externalized rage toward danger-control authorities (or toward other parent-surrogates) will be increased by the presence of any external cues which tend to reactivate childhood experiences of resentment against the parents for unwarranted punishment. . . . These cues include any action on the part of a danger-control authority which is perceived as deficient behavior and which resembles the apparent deficiencies of one's parents at times when seemingly unfair, excessive, or undeserved punishment was inflicted. . . . The child may have said (silently or aloud), "I don't deserve this, you didn't warn me that I was doing anything wrong; you don't love me anymore so I don't love you; you are the bad one, not I!" (11)

AUTHORITY FIGURES

Since doctors and nurses are looked upon as authority figures it is interesting to note that Freud states there is, in primitive peoples, a strong unconscious share of hostility toward all such figures. There is a distrust as well as a veneration even of a good ruler because there is no confidence that the ruler will use his tremendous power to the advantage of his subjects; surveillance is thus considered justified. (The public surveillances operating over the professions in our own cultures are many—the oaths, licensures and actual taboos. Those capable of being most hurtful are those that are watched most closely.)

Freud states another mechanism at work in the attitude toward authorities:

The importance of a particular person is extraordinarily heightened and his omnipotence is raised to the improbable in order to make it easier to attribute to him the responsibility for everything painful which happens to the patient. Savages really do not act differently toward their rulers when they ascribe to them power over rain and shine, wind and weather, and then dethrone or kill them because nature has disappointed their expectations of a good hunt or a ripe harvest (12).

The nurse or doctor may be unconsciously identified with a former authority figure who has withheld love and attention. Now this figure is here giving attention, and there may be an over-compliance to "please mother" or "please father" and so keep this attention coming.

Should the patient ascertain, by overt or covert signs, that these parental figures of doctor and nurse disagree, a great deal of anxiety may be created— as in the child when mother and father argued or there was continued stress between them. On the other hand, a patient whose early pattern has been to perpetuate disagreement—playing the parents against each other for his own end—may find his present situation ripe for such manipulative techniques; a behavior which may reap short-term gains for him but seldom an ultimate benefit.

The close physical care of the nurse may arouse early childhood feelings and fantasies in both the giver and receiver of this care. The most primitive elements of these feelings stem from the infant's feeling of omnipotence, of being able to control others and to deal out destruction. At the same time he fears these impulses and is anxious about his ability to control them. Greed, frustration and envy easily replace a loving relationship—the child may lash out at a parent or a sibling with a violence that surprises the adult (13).

In his belief of omnipotence the infant feels that any hurt which comes to mother is his fault; the anxiety created in patients by disagreements among personnel would seem to be heightened by this unconscious fantasy.

DEATH

A source of strong primitive feelings of denial and fear among nurses and patients alike is a death on the hospital unit. The taboo of the dead would appear to be exceedingly strong in our twentieth-century culture, though it is not always given the name of taboo. We prefer to teach that our reactions to the dead should be *respect*, or even *reverence*. However, it would appear that *taboo* is still the correct term to apply.

Witness what happens immediately after a death: The body is taken to an isolated area, and there begins an almost magical ritual; each discrete task in the procedure of "Care of the Body after Death" is performed as though it were all-important. Even the identification tags are placed in exact spots—the left wrist, or the great toe of the right foot.

Should only one person be free to care for the body, that person will invariably wait for another to "help" her, although the task, in fact, could be done by one person. And, although the deceased may have been bathed but a few hours before death, the nurses are seen to don gowns over their uniforms. (Primitive cultures render "unclean" the person who has touched a corpse, and that person is segregated from society for a period of time.)

The voices are lowered as the body is prepared, and if we listen carefully we note that the deceased's name is seldom mentioned; it has become "he" or "she," "the body," or "the old man with cancer," even though shortly before death he was talked of and addressed by his given name.

In primitive races there is a widespread prohibition of pronouncing the *name* of the deceased. Freud again explains this as an outcome of considering the dead person's name as a part of his personality, and therefore subject to the same taboo. Calling a dead person by name can also be traced back to contact with him, which is visited with severe taboo (14).

During the preparation of the body other personnel somehow find time to come into the room on some pretense or another (or carefully avoid coming in—the same thing). The desire to violate a taboo continues in the unconscious; in this case it could be to watch others violate the taboo of touching the dead.

The evidence of taboo continues as the deceased is taken to the morgue, past closed doors and into an elevator locked behind the group. Two persons guide the cart, one of whom is a nurse and a woman. One or two male orderlies taking a body to the morgue alone is almost universally unacceptable.

Nursing is past the stage when personnel were instructed not to tell other patients that a death had occurred, but the reluctance to do so continues, and we usually impart the information only when directly questioned. This may very well not be totally accounted for by the expressed reason, "The effect is depressing," but also by the unconscious taboo on names, and the consequences which result from contact with the dead. Patients may associate their nurse or nurses as those having had contact with the deceased so that they are unconsciously reluctant to have the nurse care for them or touch them. This would seem to be substantiated by historical "uncleanness" associated with those who care for the dead. In society we can find evidence of the same taboos. Consider, for example, the undertaker to whom there are often twinges of aversion. Financially he may be successful, but rarely does he attain positions denoting community leadership or elevated social prestige.

Their own feelings and patients' reflected ones are often verbalized by nurses who, after caring for the dead say, "I'd like to go home and change my uniform before I take care of anyone else."

Immediately preceding an imminent death and after a death an atmosphere of unnatural calm pervades the unit. Patients make few requests; they are often to be seen doing things by themselves with which they required assistance before. They tell nursing personnel to "go on and help someone else; I can take care of this." Nurses are seen to take pains to do small, thoughtful things that they have previously been "too busy" to do. In general, everyone seems anxious to please everyone else and to do the right thing.

This type of behavior is often seen in children. When one child hurts himself or is punished by an adult another child present will often announce how good he is or seek reassurance in various way from the adult to attest to the fact that he is a good boy.

Janis makes the same observation of pre-surgical patients. He states that people facing danger will attempt to ward it off by making sure they do not deserve to be punished, often by imposing stringent self-controls and attempting to live up to purified moral standards (15). Since the threat of death is the greatest of dangers it is not surprising to see this "good" behavior in any ward where one of the members suddenly turns critically ill.

SURGICAL PATIENTS

Abandonment of social restraint, Janis states, occurs only after the danger is past; a statement we are quite aware of in everyday life, but frequently fail to recognize in hospitals as contributing to the actions of patients which may antagonize the nurse's sense of propriety. Reinforcing the cause for self-indulgence is the patient's temporary separation from his primary group and from other persons who reinforce adherence to the norms of conventional morality. "In this respect, the surgical ward of a hospital may resemble a displaced persons' camp. Surgical patients are temporarily uprooted and put in a new social milieu where norms and conventions, especially with regard to body exposure and manipulation, are no longer valid" (16).

Although there is some degree of abandonment of social restraint, Janis also observes that post-surgical patients are relatively optimistic with a dominant mood of benignity. This is fortunate since these are the patients who receive the brunt of most of the painful and intrusive procedures—drains, probes, swabs, stomach tubes, adhesive tapes, intravenous and intramuscular medications and the gamut of manipulations. At the same time, the relative ease with which the patient accepts these procedures lessens nurses' anxiety on administering them and at causing discomfort and pain. Nurses unused to the daily use of such procedures often suffer quite intensely when forced to use them. This was true in the previously mentioned study done on a child-psychiatry ward, in which the observation was made that the nursing personnel seemed unconsciously to experience the injections, medical isolation and operative procedures as punitive instead of healing in nature. The authors' additional comment was that they believed an unconscious conflict over sadomasochistic problems may determine the choice of nursing specialization, as is so often the case with the physician [17]. Their observation is further confirmed by studies done on the personality comparisons of medical and surgical nurses [18] and psychiatric and nonpsychiatric nurses [19].

Although the dominant mood of post-surgical patients has been found to be relatively benign, there are many for whom this does not apply. The actions of these patients foster withdrawal and hostility on the part of personnel, who often remark, "I can't understand it; he was so cheerful and friendly before surgery."

This paradoxical situation was investigated by Janis also, who, on the basis of his studies, formulated the following hypotheses:

1. Persons who display a moderate degree of anticipatory fear before being exposed to physical stress stimuli (pain, bodily discomforts, and severe deprivations) will be less likely to develop emotional disturbances during or after the stress exposure than those persons who display either a very high degree or a very low degree of anticipatory fear.
2. Persons who display an extremely high level of anticipatory fear or anxiety during the "threat" period will be more likely than others to display intense fear of body damage during the subsequent crisis period, when exposed to actual stress stimuli.
3. Persons who display an extremely low degree of anticipatory fear or anxiety during the "threat" period will be more likely than others to display reactions of anger and resentment toward danger-control authorities during the subsequent crisis period when exposed to actual stress stimuli [20].

Patients who react with high pre-operative and high post-operative fear are hypothesized to be those in whom repressed childhood fears are reactivated by the slightest threat of actual danger, and they tend to react as though they were facing an enormous danger. These same persons cannot gain the usual degree of emotional relief from the reassurances given by authoritative figures—the underlying source of anxiety remaining unconscious and the fear reaction tending to persist ("neurotic anxiety").

A patient with low pre-operative fear may be intellectually denying the danger—a defense which works only when no salient danger stimuli are present. In the postoperative period, pain and stress stimuli are present, and he is experiencing more suffering than had been expected beforehand. A low level of pre-operative fear may be, in addition, due to inadequate advance warnings from doctors and nurses.

A moderate amount of anxiety then prepares the person for danger, but the person who runs into danger without preparatory anxiety is subject to fright (21).

Although these hypotheses were worked out in regard to surgical patients, their implications are evident for all types of danger situations on all clinical units: the woman in labor; the patient facing unpleasant diagnostic studies such as a lumbar puncture; the psychiatric patient facing electro-shock, and so on.

OTHER PRACTICES

The scope of nursing practice includes many areas where there is a minimum of actual physical dangers for the patient, but we cannot exclude these from our consideration. The withholding of attention or the art of ignoring can be the most hostile practice of all. It is an affront to the patient's concept of himself as an individual, as being important, deserving of notice and worthy of respect. He may respond to acts of inattention by becoming aggressive and demanding —a response usually met by further withdrawal or defensive counter-aggression on the part of personnel, or he may himself withdraw, feeling that the struggle to command attention is not worth it, perhaps, that he is not worthy of notice.

Although we have discussed some of the intrusive procedures, it should be emphasized that these include not only the mechanical ones, but the subtle (and often not-so-subtle) invasions of privacy of feelings—the highly personal questions often asked for no other reason than that of curiosity, and the witnessing of emotions and family situations not normally open to the view of strangers. There is, in many instances, an unnecessary lack of tact and a frequent thoughtlessness on the part of the very person who is in the stronger position and can better afford to be the more considerate. The patient is in a peculiarly helpless state; he cannot resist becoming the "interesting case" or "the one with the bad burn." Neither is it easy to resist the insidiously familiar terms he does not ask for —the use of the first name and the superficially endearing word.

Conclusion and Implications

Lest it should seem that nurse practices are primarily assaultive actions, we should hasten to emphasize what we have known all along—that most patients come through hospitalizations with their defenses still intact and their personalities unscathed. The human being is capable of withstanding a vast amount of stress, a fact attested to by the remarkable survival of people under the impact of wars, calamities, poverty and misfortunes of all types.

The average patient does not emerge from a hospital experience with a permanent wariness, distrust and resentment of therapeutic practices and the persons who administer them. Our four initial patients will return home. Nathan Jones will return to his job and friends who inquire how he feels and tell him that it is good to have him back—statements that reward him for the three weeks of absence. He thanks them for their cards, and goes about getting caught up in his job.

Mrs. Lewis's pain gradually subsides, and with it much of her "fussiness." By the time she leaves the hospital she is showing two of the student nurses how to knit, and they, in turn, are spending extra time helping her walk out to the sun-porch in the afternoon.

The little girl on the pediatric ward gave up mistreating her doll soon after the penicillin injections were stopped, and she is happily contemplating playing with the puppy her parents bought for her at home.

The man who was being wheeled into the isolation room still has unpleasant memories of it—when he thinks about it, which is seldom, since he has been so busy with the accumulated office work that his wife has brought home for him.

However, the fact that people have the saving mechanisms of suppression and repression should not invite us to ignore the implications of certain of these nursing practices. To some patients, they will be very disturbing, and the anxieties created difficult for them to manage or to forget. The effect upon nursing personnel of using the practices and procedures is often insidious, but the defense systems erected are evident on any hospital unit.

To the writer, the following implications are apparent:

1. Certain nursing practices and procedures should be recognized as being threatening to the patient, either consciously as a source of pain and discomfort, or unconsciously reactivating childhood fears of mutilation, abandonment, deprivation and other parental punishments.
    a. Intrusive procedures involving body orifices are best explained at the time of institution, not at some time preceding, and only the necessary details should be given.
    b. Fear of a procedure may be minimized by thoughtful use of terminology; for example, a patient may retain "some warm oil" but not "an oil enema."

2. Intrusive procedures may be psychological as well as physical; and may be more threatening.
    a. Keeping patients from being "thrust into roles" is the responsibility of and an attitude perpetuated by the person in charge of a ward. By

his or her manner of address to and reference of patients, a feeling of maintaining individual dignity is adopted by other personnel.

3. Many of the healing practices are unconsciously viewed as punitive by nurses, creating anxiety in them and the erection of defenses against these feelings.

   a. If the nurse is uncomfortable in a certain working area or in specific situations it is well to talk it over with an able and understanding person. The nurse may, of course, not be able to change the situation, but may be saved from developing the cold, unfeeling, impassiveness often assumed in carrying out an unpleasant task.

4. Patients who evince either a very high degree, or very low degree of pre-danger anxiety may be expected to show excessive emotional manifestations after the danger period is over.

   a. This should become an automatic cue for personnel to spend additional time with them in the pre-danger period, creating opportunities and openings for these patients to talk about their feelings toward the stress situation.

   b. Advance warnings and explanations of the stress situation should be made to all, but especially to those with very low pre-danger anxiety.

   c. Those with very high pre-danger anxiety may accept reassurance from the highest authority figures in the situation, but not from lower-authority figures. Sometimes they will accept it from neither, and this should be another automatic cue that difficulty may be expected in the post-danger period.

5. A death on a hospital unit causes strong emotional feelings in patients and personnel. Primitive taboos concerning the dead are manifested in many ways; the effect on those personnel who must violate these taboos is often unrecognized and the necessary support is not given.

   a. At the risk of over-simplification of this point, it would seem extremely important that head nurses always assign more than one person to the care of the deceased.

   b. If possible, these persons should be given some time off the unit after the task, even if only for a few minutes.

   c. A supervisor, upon knowledge of a death, should make it a point to get to that unit immediately; her presence alone implying, "I know this is difficult, but we're all with you."

   d. Similarly, patients who have known the deceased or have been in the room with him need additional support.

It is increasingly less difficult to deal with feelings when the events causing them are known and recognized; this is one of the prime bases of mental health. This paper has attempted to point out certain nursing areas that are charged with feeling for both patients and nurses. It must be stressed, however, that being able to recognize these areas is only the first step. We may, for instance, be aware that a certain procedure is anxiety producing, but have little understanding of *why* it is so for this individual. We are prone to make broad general statements about this "why" aspect and tend to accept obvious, superficial answers. Perhaps we often excuse behavior rather than trying to understand it, and the reasons we give as to why a patient acts or responds as he does are our own rationalizations, given not from lack of interest but from a lack of knowledge.

Intelligent action can be taken only with some understanding of the situation based on knowledge, observation and tempered with individual application. Intervention then becomes meaningful and limited to the necessary scope of adjustment as opposed to probing followed by a ready-made solution. If there can be no meaningful solution, we may then know why and be comfortable with this knowledge. No action is often preferable to a baseless "remedy," even though the latter be applied with the best of intention.

References

1. Menzies, Isabel E. P. "A Case-Study in the Functioning of Social Systems as a Defense against Anxiety," *Human Relations* **31**:95–121, 1960.
2. Schulman, Sam. "Basic Functional Roles in Nursing: Mother-Surrogate and Healer," in Jaco, E. Gartly (Ed.), *Patients, Physicians, and Illness*. Glencoe, Illinois, The Free Press, 1958, pp. 528–537.
3. Freud, Anna. "The Role of Bodily Illness in the Mental Life of Children," in *The Psychoanalytic Study of the Child*, 1952. New York, International Universities Press, Vol. VII, p. 72.
4. *Ibid.*, pp. 73–74.
5. *Ibid.*, p. 74.
6. *Ibid.*, p. 74.
7. Sutton, Helen A., Eugene I. Falstein, and Ilse Judas. "Emotional Reactions to Medical Procedures and Illness in a Hospital Child Psychiatry Unit," *American Journal of Orthopsychiatry* **28**:180–187, 1958.
8. Kassowitz, Karl E. "Psychodynamic Reactions of Children to the Use of Hypodermic Needles," *AMA Journal of Diseases of Children* **95**:253–257, 1958
9. Janis, Irving L. *Psychological Stress*, New York, John Wiley and Sons, 1958, p. 83.
10. *Ibid.*, p. 387.
11. *Ibid.*, pp. 163, 169, 171.
12. Freud, Sigmund. *Totem and Taboo*, New York, Random House Modern Library, 1946, pp. 67–69.
13. Menzies, I., *op. cit.*, pp. 98–99.
14. *Ibid.*, pp. 73–76.
15. Janis, I., *op. cit.*, p. 148.
16. *Ibid.*, p. 214.
17. Sutton, H., E. Falstein, and J. Judas, *op. cit.*

18. Lentz, Edith M., and Robert G. Michaels. "Comparisons Between Medical and Surgical Nurses," *Nursing Research* **8**:192–197, 1959.
19. Navran, Leslie, and James C. Stauffacher. "A Comparative Analysis of the Personality Structures of Psychiatric and Nonpsychiatric Nurses," *Nursing Research* **7**:64–67, 1958.
20. Janis, I., op. cit., p. 217.
21. Ibid., pp. 218–221.

Cancer, Emotions, and Nurses

by Samuel C. Klagsbrun, M.D.*

The small cancer research unit in a major East Coast university hospital was unique in many ways. It was tucked away in a corner off a main corridor and was screened in by a glass partition that architecturally demonstrated its separateness. It was the only service to which no house staff was assigned. It was funded in a different way from all the other services. And it was the only service in the hospital that had little hope for success in its struggle to ward off death.

The patient population was selected for research purposes. If a patient experienced a remission, he was discharged to the outpatient clinic and followed by the same medical and nursing staff that worked on the inpatient unit. The entire staff got to know the patients, their families, and their friends on an intimate basis.

The psychiatric consultation service of the hospital had been called in from time to time by the cancer research unit to help in the management of difficult patients. We became aware of the tremendous strain the patients placed on the medical and nursing staff. To a great extent the staff saw these patients as walking dead; and since "One should not speak ill of the dead," the staff felt constrained to keep their feelings about the patients to themselves.

But the angry feelings—and guilt at having those feelings—did exist and were very evident in the approach of the staff toward the patients. There was covert rejection of the patients' emotional needs, especially in the face of terminal illness. Numerous struggles between patients and staff took place over such medical issues as the side effects of some of the experimental drugs being used. The patients complained of being used as guinea pigs. "Uncaring doctors"

* *American Journal of Psychiatry.* Vol. 126, No. 9 (March, 1970). Pp. 71–78. © 1970 American Psychiatric Association.

and "unavailable nurses" were phrases that were often repeated to anyone who would listen.

This was the setting, then, in which the following pilot project was attempted.

The psychiatric consultation service assigned me to work as the cancer unit's own psychiatrist in an attempt to analyze and develop a workable approach to the problem of patient management on a cancer unit. I decided that the best approach was to try to alter the ward culture as a whole rather than to deal separately with each patient management problem. The assumption was that the patients' morale and behavior could be improved greatly if they could continue to see themselves as functioning and productive human beings. Meeting these goals would require the creation of an anti-regressive atmosphere. And the creation of such an atmosphere would depend largely on the nursing staff. The nurses spent much more time with the patients than anyone else; therefore, their impact was likely to be more pervasive than anyone else's influence on the patients.

Meetings with the Nurses

My first job was to make the nurses aware of the importance of their role. After receiving clearance from the medical staff, I began to hold weekly meetings with the nursing staff. The initial object of the one-hour-a-week meeting was to discuss patient management problems. No hint or suggestion was made to indicate that the ultimate object was to deal with the ward culture or with the nursing staff's feelings toward the patients. The reaction of the staff to the appearance of a psychiatrist in their midst was a mixed one. They were gratified to have this effort made on their behalf by a medical service of the hospital, but they also felt self-conscious and somewhat threatened. An initiation phase began. Problems of an emotional nature were not brought up at all. Instead, matters pertaining to drug dosage, organic illness, or the care of weeping sores on the buttocks of patients sent in from other units rose to the surface. My medical competence was thoroughly tested during this period, and only when it became obvious that I was comfortable as well as interested in these aspects of a patient's care were the nurses willing to accept me as a member of the staff.

The head nurse, an extremely competent and perceptive person, broke the ice one day by saying, "Now look, ladies, this is a psychiatrist. Why don't we tell him things he's supposed to know about?"

With that, a flood of feelings began to come out. Many of these were directed not toward the patients, as might have been expected, but toward the medical staff in charge of the unit. What the nurses complained about most bitterly was the lack of emotional backing by the medical staff, rather than the demands of the patients or the depressing nature of their work.

The following incident exemplified their feelings: A middle-aged woman, well known to the staff, had died a few days prior to our weekly meeting, and the mood of the unit was still low. The nurses spoke of their sense of despair and frustration. At one point, a member of the staff turned toward a large bulky brown bag sitting on the floor in the corner of our room. "Those are her clothes," she said. "I haven't called the family to pick them up."

"This patient was different," another nurse said. "She tried so hard. She was always cheerful, and when she was sent home last time to continue her treatment in the clinic she was so happy."

"And yet other patients have gone through the same thing," I commented. "There must be something different about her."

"It's the way we feel about what the doctors did on the night she died. We saw she was going, and we called the family in to be with her. We also notified the doctor on call, who knew there was nothing he could do. We had earlier decided not to use any heroic measures since there was no way for her to continue her life. The doctor said that we should help the family accept the inevitable and to let him know when she had died. That was it. I was so angry at his coldness I could have cried. But what can you do? I had to control myself because the family was there and there were other patients to take care of."

"What happened when she died?" I asked.

"The family kept asking, 'Is the doctor coming?' It was terrible. I told them that he had left all the necessary orders, but they kept on asking when he would be coming. Finally, they left after she died. We all cried and they thanked us for what we had done. We felt terrible."

"And the clothes?"

"I guess we just don't want to face them. . . . The doctors never come in when there's a situation like this. It's as though the research drug is the most important thing. If it can't be used anymore, they just lose interest. Oh, I guess that's not true, but it's not fair for them to leave this stuff to us to handle."

The meeting continued and cooled down as the nurses spoke up, with less and less anger being directed at the doctors. Finally, at the end, one of the nurses volunteered to call the family to pick up the brown bag of clothes.

The following week the nurses seemed more guarded and distant, as though they had revealed too much in the previous session. In order to let them deal with their feelings about their doctors with some degree of safety and distance, I decided to use another hospital setting as an example of the problem they had raised. I described a meeting the psychiatric consultation service had held with the surgical, medical, social service, and psychiatric staff of a major hospital devoted exclusively to cancer research. We were interested in exploring the emotional effects of some of their radical work on cancer patients. The medical staff had been placing patients in "life islands" for the purpose of keeping them in a sterile atmosphere during periods of low white counts while they were under anti-metabolite treatment. They hoped thereby to prevent infections. These patients lived for weeks in a plastic bubble with ultraviolet light shining constantly. The hospital had also been doing hemicorporectomies on patients in the hope of eliminating extension of the disease. In response to some of our questions, one surgeon had summed up his feelings very clearly when he said, "If I thought about what I was doing to a person, I couldn't do it. But I don't think that that is my job."

I asked the nurses for their reaction. After talking about how gruesome they thought these research procedures were, they moved on to discuss the purpose of the procedures. Finally they came around to appreciating the truth and honesty of the surgeon's remarks. As one nurse put it, "If our doctors had to worry about all the nausea and vomiting a drug caused, they probably would feel terrible about prescribing it. I guess that puts us right in the middle. We'll have to handle the patients."

"They give the drug and we stand there with the emesis basin," another added.

Recognition of Doctors' Feelings

What emerged from that meeting was a much clearer recognition and understanding of the doctors' need for distance as well as the nurses' own central role in the care of the patient. The exciting part of the meeting was that for the first time the nurses seemed able to accept the emotional burden of the patients without expecting to be supported by the doctors. What was left unsaid was that given the backing of a psychiatrist, they were able to free their doctors from answering their needs and thereby allow the doctors to spend more time in the labs.

Once the nurses' role was clarified, they began to look at their patients in a more critical way. They became less frightened of being put upon and therefore more open to learning. The methods patients used to express their needs were recognized more quickly. Management problems were analyzed from the point of view of "What is the patient really asking for?" The nurses became sophisticated in recognizing subterfuges for the expression of anxiety. The number of complaints—calling for nurses, turning of nighttime into daytime, repeated questions about what is really in the I.V. bottle—all these were now understood as expressions of fear, and the nurses became quite free in calling the shots as they saw them.

"Let's talk, Mrs. Jones. You really don't need the bedpan again, do you?"
"I know you didn't call, Mr. Brown, but you look sad. Anything I can do?"

The nurses were encouraged to seek out contact before the patients created a crisis situation that required their presence. They now understood that symptoms were often communications on a nonverbal level. In addition, my willingness to use more tranquilizers and antidepressants gave them a sense of confidence. They knew that methods of control were readily available in case of severe agitation and depression that they felt unable to handle. They experienced a marvelous new sense of freedom and openness. "When I told Mr. Smith that if I were in his shoes, I'd be asking many more questions than he was asking," reported one nurse, "I could actually see the tension coming out of his face."

This free and easy approach, however, soon led to complications. Patients were now communicating their worries to the nurses, and many of them asked fairly direct questions about their prognoses. The nurses felt comfortable in talking openly to the patients about anxiety or depression, but they felt they were overstepping their boundaries when patients started asking them about diagnoses, prognoses, and medications. The most frequent question raised was what to tell the patient in response to the question, "Am I going to die?"

The experienced nurses, who really understood their patients and the patients' families, could judge what answer was expected of them.

One example was that of a husband who had refused to bring his sick wife to the hospital because he was sure that the staff would tell her her diagnosis, and he was convinced that she would not be able to tolerate the truth. His wife, on the other hand, asked the nurses not to tell the husband that she had cancer because she was sure he needed to protect her from the truth, since that helped his manly image. But she also knew he would probably be unable to keep it to himself and would feel terrible if he blurted it out to her. She was trying to protect him. The nurses had no difficulty in refraining from talking to him about her illness while listening and talking to the patient about how she was doing.

A second example of courage coupled with wisdom was one reported by a nurse the day after a sad experience. An old woman who was failing rapidly called in one of the nurses and said simply, "I am dying. I feel it is the end, isn't it?" The nurse looked at her and said quietly, "Yes." The nurse sat down next to the old woman, took her hand and held it. "I don't want to die alone," the woman said. "I'll stay with you. You won't be alone," the nurse answered. The woman said, "That's good." And she died in ten minutes, with the nurse holding her hand.

As the nurses got to know their patients better, they realized that the patients were not dead yet and that even those who seemed to see themselves as dead could emerge from the grave in response to crises in their families or to important external events.

Experiment in Self-Care

Now everybody was ready for the next step: a radical experiment in self-care. Many of the patients who were in bed did not really need to be there for medical reasons; they simply retired to their beds as part of their withdrawal. The nurses had come to understand that. They began reorganizing the unit. They urged patients to take passes and to leave the ward. They made demands on the patients by asking them to get involved in such projects as sewing and art work. As much as they could, they pushed the patients into activity.

The patients' reaction to the new hustle-bustle varied. Those patients who saw themselves as terminally ill at first resented the expectation that they could take care of themselves. They saw it as further evidence that they were being abandoned by the world. On the other hand, those who found themselves grasping for any bit of evidence that proved they were not sick—or at least not dying—quickly latched on to the new idea that they were still responsible, functioning, and productive people. This group, in fact, began edging the nurses out of jobs and taking over some of the nursing tasks.

For example, one of the first changes made in the ward was to have the patients fix their own beds. Next they were to get their own water and ice. The nurses were a bit fearful of this revolutionary step, and they were upset when the sick patients saw it as a rejection of their needs. But the patient-activists on the ward surprised everybody. They began taking the water and ice to the patients who were too sick to care for their own needs. Then they took over the linen closet and made up beds for the very sick patients. They began eyeing the desk jobs. They wanted to answer the phone and type the admission forms. Finally, they took over the responsibility of running errands to other parts of the hospital. The "revolution" reached the point where the nurses were able to have each new admission oriented to the ward by a welcoming group of older patients.

The ward acquired a new culture. As the weeks went on, the activists took over the ward, and it was quite common to see a patient get up in the morning with an I.V. drip going into one arm, make his bed with the other, then carry trays of food to the bedridden and explain the new system to the practical nurses who were occasionally assigned to the ward.

The most important step taken, however, was the communal dining room. We decided that providing a nucleus for socialization would add to the atmosphere of liveliness and stimulate the patients further. The dieticians, who took part in all our meetings, arranged for food trays to be brought to a separate room where the patients would gather to eat. This was a major breakthrough that allowed lonely and isolated patients to talk to fellow patients. Now the patients discovered new communal strength that came from shared experience. Patients began organizing evening activities, with the inevitable showing of slides of the latest European trip. Afternoon snacks were delivered to the dining area, and an accumulation of puzzles, cards, and books found its way there. Life was suddenly being lived.

As the experience continued, some of the patients who had had remissions and had gone home began coming back when their illnesses progressed. A com-

Adult Stage

mon reaction was a sense of relief at returning to a culture that treated them as though something was still expected of them. Some patients had visibly regressed at home, but under the competitive spirit of the ward they too returned to greater activity. Their demands for nursing attention diminished, and they appeared happier.

The self-care atmosphere periodically broke down in the face of actual death and the overwhelming illness of patients, and the nurses learned that in order to maintain this culture they had to nourish and support it. A change in the patient population had to be countered with a renewed nursing effort to teach the new admissions about the ward culture. If the old-time patients of the ward outnumbered the new ones, the culture was protected. Otherwise the authority of the nurses had to be brought into play to back self-care until the new patients could be acculturated.

Effect on Medical Staff

The impact on the medical staff of the changing culture was interesting. In the beginning they continued to maintain their distance from the patients. But as the ward atmosphere changed more and more, they began asking about the new regulations being instituted. The influence of the ward upon the medical staff was felt to be complete when one of the nurses reported the newest order she had received. The doctor had written "Patient must eat lunch in communal dining room." The doctor explained that he had noticed that the patient was slipping into a depression and was beginning to regress. He felt that a medical order pushing her into the ward atmosphere would be helpful. This gave us a clue to something we had not been aware of before—namely, that the medical staff had not necessarily ignored the emotional aspects of patient care: they had simply felt they had little to offer. Once it became obvious that there was something that could be done, they turned to it as much as everyone else did.

The increased level of activity of the patients as well as the high level of psychological sophistication of the nursing staff were proven beyond a shadow of a doubt in one incident. A 39-year-old man with cancer had been admitted, and his sexy young wife was a constant visitor. He caught on to the spirit of self-care to such an extent that he decided that he was going to live as normally as possible while he had to be on the unit. The nurse who barged in and found him in bed one day with his wife walked out without another word. At our next meeting, after the giggling died down, the nurses discussed the man's need for denial. They had some serious doubts about whether to forbid this unusual activity on the unit. The final consensus was that it was too much of a radical departure for the ward to handle, and they should not allow it to continue. The fact that they saw it first in terms of patient need and second in terms of ward management showed that the conversion had been accomplished.

In a summary session that was taped, the staff reviewed the history of the experiment after 18 months. The unanimous conclusion was that the changes in the ward were of major importance to the patients. The nurses spoke of the increased will to live that they had noted. They pointed out that patient care was more efficient. And most of all, from an administrative point of view they realized that the turnover rate of nurses, which had been very high, had decreased markedly. Now nurses wanted to work on the unit.

What are the psychological implications of this experience? Certainly the work of some of the investigators reported in the *Annals of the New York Academy of Sciences* in January 1966 (1, 3–6) shows some correlation between the onset of cancer and the experience of an emotional loss. The implication that such a connection exists in the onset of illness suggests that its remission, or at least its management, may be equally influenced by emotional factors of a positive nature. The effect of a positive ward culture must therefore be considered worthy of research.

Aside from considering the course of the illness, we can think about the equality of life that the patient lives. Palliation need not only be thought of in terms of physical pain; it can also be seen as a legitimate goal to achieve on an emotional level. The response of the patients to the idea that they were expected to function on an adult level decreased their anxiety, dependency, and feelings of being a burden and thereby added to their well-being. The quality of their remaining life was improved.

One of the reactions we frequently see in sick patients is that of shrinking horizons over a period of time. The patient loses interest in the world outside the hospital, then in the life affairs of friends and family, and finally in the ward. At the end, he becomes focused on his own life functions. Maintaining his interest in the surrounding world as long as possible and making him feel responsible for it retards this process and keeps him feeling fulfilled for a longer time.

Conclusion

This clinical report suggests an approach quite different from that implied by Kurt Eissler in his famous book, *The Psychiatrist and The Dying Patient* (2). Eissler encouraged the patient's defense mechanism of denial by allowing the patient to imbue his therapist with magical qualities. The therapist enhanced this image by showing concern, bringing gifts, and behaving in a protective way toward the patient. The method implied was "I will take care of you." In contrast, the experience of our cancer unit led us to feel that we could successfully support a patient's denial by using an antiregressive approach.

It might be valuable to test these different approaches in a research project. We certainly do not have the complete answer yet. Our experience indicated that many of our patients did well clinically in the atmosphere we had created.

However, I am not convinced that this approach works well during the period just before death. This period is still an unknown entity from a psychological point of view.

There were two main "make-or-break" points in our pilot project when things could have gone very differently from the way they did. The first took place at the initial meeting with the nurses. By focusing the goals of this meeting on patient management rather than anything more radical, I made the road easier for myself. The nurses were able to get to know me without feeling threatened. I could then suggest more significant changes, knowing that I had a comfortable relationship with the staff.

The second point occurred when the nurses decided that they were ready to take a chance and run the ward differently. Without making a major issue of it, I spoke to the medical staff individually and encouraged them to show interest in and appreciation for the project. I pointed out that the more responsible the nurses were made to feel in their involvement with the ward, the less they would burden the medical staff with minor problems. As it turned out, the medical staff became fascinated with the project and invited us to report on it at one of their scientific research conferences.

In any attempt to change a ward culture, as we did, a good deal of ground work with key people on an informal level becomes necessary. We prepared the medical staff and made sure to discuss all changes with the head nurse, the nursing supervisor, the dietician, and the hospital administration.

Finally, I would like to offer one more observation—the importance of sharing. We all realized that our ability to talk about death and cancer with the patients and to bear their needs without closing ourselves off from them grew in direct proportion to our ability to share our own anxieties at our group meetings. The more we talked together, the more easily we could listen to our patients. As a side note, I was able to serve as a sounding board for the patients and the nurses because I was able to unburden myself at psychiatric consultation service rounds. It seems that if the system works, it does so on all levels.

The implications of this project apply to the hospital as a whole. From a financial point of view the program offers the possibility of reducing costs in that patients may need fewer aides. From a personnel point of view it suggests greater ability of staff by decreasing turnover rate. And from a humane point of view, it offers dignity.

References

1. Green, W. A. The Psycho-Social Setting of the Development of Leukemia and Lymphoria. Ann. NY Acad. Sci. **125**:794–801, 1966.
2. Eissler, K. The Psychiatrist and the Dying Patient. New York: International Universities Press, 1955.
3. LeShan, L. An Emotional Life-History Pattern Associated with Neoplastic Disease. Ann. NY Acad. Sci. **125**:780–793, 1966.

4. Muslimm, H. L., Gyarfas, K., and Pieper, W. J. Separation Experience and Cancer of the Breast. Ann. NY Acad. Sci. **125**:802–806, 1966.
5. Paloucek, F. P., and Graham, J. B. The Influence of Psycho-Social Factors on the Prognosis of Cancer of the Cervix. Ann. NY Acad. Sci. **125**:814–816, 1966.
6. Schmale, A., and Iker, H. The Psychological Setting of Uterine Cervical Cancer. Ann. NY Acad. Sci. **125**:807–813, 1966.

Discussion

John Reckless, M.B., Ch.B. (Durham, N. C.).—This interesting paper focuses upon a small cancer unit tucked away in a general hospital where patients with cancer were sent for treatment under conditions that for many of them inevitably meant death—either upon their first admission to the unit or a subsequent return to the ward. The author is to be commended for his description of a technique that involves an hour of work on the ward each week by the visiting psychiatrist, with techniques aimed at improving the staff morale so that there is more efficient management of patients and with the patients assuming more responsibility for their physical and emotional care while in this unit.

There are several major areas of discussion that arise from this paper. The first concerns the attitudes of the nurses and focuses also upon the nurse-doctor relationship. It was noted that there was originally high turnover of nurses in this unit and that patients did not seem to receive the best type of care because of the turnover and because of the lowered morale of the nursing staff. The type of specialty ward described in this paper seems to be developing in a number of hospitals in this country: there is a movement away from general wards in which patients with different kinds of diseases are cared for together toward a small unit oriented to a specific disease, such as the unit described in this paper. It is evident that concentrating one kind of patient with serious illness and a high mortality rate on one ward can provoke a major emotional stress in the nurse, for she has no patients with recoverable illness and a more positive prognosis with which to counterbalance the emotional strain occasioned by the gravely ill patient. Often, because of the frustration engendered in this situation, the nurse expects more of the physician than he is able to provide, with resultant discord and frustration occurring in the nurse-doctor relationship.

Problems in the nurse-doctor relationship in this kind of unit have two major elements. In a treatment situation where there is a rotation of house staff to the unit, the long-stay nurse often has more direct experience with the type of care needed on the unit than does the rotating intern. A second frustration can occur because of the increasing preoccupation in some teaching hospitals with care aimed at the molecular or cellular level and not at the level of human experience. The nurse is caught up in a two-fold bind by the physician's preoccupation with the discrete rather than the general and by her own inability to motivate the physician to recognize the importance of the patient's more human needs.

This is not necessarily the fault of the physician but rather is a reflection on the way in which we reward the house staff with prestige for work at this level. However, this does not help the nurse, who has to spend more time than the physician involved in the daily lives of the patients. Also, the physician's avoidance and withdrawal from the patient care situation can only intensify the nurse's feeling of frustration and isolation.

Another question concerns the way in which we treat our patients. One wonders whether or not patient treatment practices are structured for the convenience of the physician and the nursing staff or rather reflect the most appropriate way in which to care for the patients. We know that patients can respond to what they see as inelegant care by the physician or a noncaring attitude on the part of the hospital staff by assuming a demanding and complaining role in regard to the ward structure. In fact, patients "needle" us to get attention and we often needle them in reprisal. It is always easier to prescribe medication than to give of our time and empathy. With these diverse frustrations and experiences on the unit, Dr. Klagsbrun is to be commended for his techniques of recognizing and then restructuring the ward milieu of these gravely ill patients.

His use of small group techniques in which professionals are invited to discuss how to better manage their patients and the tensions involved both in the intrafamily structure and also their own intrapsychic structure reflects the techniques described in the early 50s by Balint of London (1) and Watters of New Orleans (2, 3). These techniques can be considered helpful not only in terms of the diminished nurse turnover within the unit but also in the improvement in direct patient care. An additional use of the group technique is as a teaching device to help the staff become more knowledgeable in recognizing and managing emotional illness.

The use of the self-care system by the patients reflects a trend started in geriatric practice and in the self-care system wards of some general hospitals but is different in that these patients were in a unit where many of them were gravely ill.

The techniques described here lend themselves as models to many of the specialized units springing up around the country and offer a way in which the limited psychiatric manpower problem can be eased.

References

1. Balint, M. The Doctor, His Patient and the Illness. New York: International Universities Press, 1957.
2. Watters, T. A. The General Practitioner and the Third Dimension. J. Med. Ass. Georgia 51:567–572, 1962.
3. Watters, T. A. Continuing Education Programs in Psychiatry and Their Evaluation. Boulder, Colo.: Western Interstate Commission for Higher Education, 1964.

chapter eight

MIDDLE AGE

Nurses may find it difficult to realize that middle age can present a life crisis just as earlier developmental phases do. Judd Marmor, a psychiatrist, states:

There are many familiar developmental crises common to all human beings: the crucial first year of life, the adaptive stresses of the second and third years, the Oedipal period, the separation crises of the first school attendance and then of going away from home for the first time, adolescence, the first employment, first heterosexual experiences, marriage, and parenthood.

Each of these has been the subject of extensive study. But there is a particularly important developmental crisis in life—the middle years—which has not received sufficient attention as an inevitable aspect of the aging process.[1]

Middle age is generally assumed to be a leveling-out period, when one begins to accept a slower pace. Unfortunately, this is not always the case, as a close view of this stage of life will show. Perhaps the reader will gain a new appreciation for the concept of *change of life*.

Middle age is a relatively new mass phenomenon. Today, four out of five Americans live to at least age 60, and the average age of adult workers is 45. While our total population increased 98 per cent in the last half century, those of middle age have increased 200 per cent.

We have discussed child development in great detail, but most patients seen by a nurse are adult, and of these, many are middle-aged. The signs of wear and tear on the human body most frequently show for the first time at

[1] Judd Marmor. "The Crisis of Middle Age," *R.N.* November, 1967. P. 63.

this stage of life. In addition to somatic illnesses, middle-aged persons normally show physical evidence of aging. Marmor writes:

> As people reach their middle years, they can no longer ignore the *physical* evidences of the aging process. There comes a moment in life when the decreased elasticity of the skin, the accumulating wrinkles, and the coarsening of features force themselves into a person's awareness in a way that the psychologically healthy can no longer deny. There is the inevitable moment when a man, catching sight of the back of his head in a three-way mirror, realizes that the balding stranger is, in fact, himself. For the woman there is the sagging of her once-firm breasts, the beginning of menstrual irregularity, then the cessation of menstruation. For both men and women there is the slackening of muscular activity and the tendency toward weight increase, with the subsequent never-ending struggle between oral craving and oral frustrations.[2]

Certain illnesses and disabilities occur more frequently during this stage of the aging process. There is a gradual slowing down of the basal metabolic rate, so that decrease in caloric intake is often necessary to maintain the same body weight. A man who was an athlete in his youth may find himself considerably overweight as his physical activities decline and his eating habits remain the same. Many diseases that were once considered part of the process of aging can now be averted or arrested through educating the public regarding proper diet, exercise, and better methods of coping with stress.

This time is often called the *climacteric,* a term that implies certain psychological as well as physiological changes. Of the relationship between the climacterium and the menopause, Benedek writes:

> Although the terms menopause and climacterium often are used as if they were interchangeable, the former should be reserved for one aspect of the period, the cessation of the menstrual flow, while climacteric or climacterium incompasses the more general bodily and emotional processes which coincide with menopause or follow it, and which are not necessarily causally related to it. However, characteristic of the climacterium these manifestations may be, they are dependent upon the previous history of the individual; they are motivated by trends which, woven into the personality of the mature woman, may be reactivated by the internal changes associated with that period.[3]

The woman who has proceeded well throughout her twenties and thirties may experience psychological stress with the onset of the menopause. She may express concern about mental illness, obesity, cancer, diminution of sexual life, and hirsutism, and she may very well feel more comfortable discussing such problems with the nurse rather than the doctor, feeling more

---
[2] *Ibid.*
[3] T. Benedek and B. B. Rubenstein. *The Sexual Cycle in Women.* Washington, D.C.: National Res. Council (Psychosom. Med. Mono. Vol. 3, Nos. 1 & 2). Vol. 8 (1942). P. 307.

confident of another woman's understanding and sympathy. The nurse needs a clear idea of the biological stresses involved in middle life.

Some women react to the diminution of estrogen during the menopause with such symptoms as hot, tingling flashes, sweats, headaches, vertigo, fatigue, arthralgias, and irritability. Often, these symptoms are functional rather than organic, but they are too frequently dismissed as "just the change of life." The importance of periodic checkups for women of this age group should not be underemphasized, since sometimes much more serious illnesses begin with symptoms often ignored as merely products of the menopause.

From the psychodynamic point of view, a consideration of the menopause must include an awareness of the connections between menopausal reactions and the woman's attitudes about her menarche and menstrual cycle, her feelings and conflicts about sexuality and femininity, and her relationship and identification with her own mother.

The changes in hormonal levels throughout the normal menstrual cycle are manifested not only in signs and symptoms directly related to ovulation and the menstrual flow, but in subtle psychological and sexual responses that are often masked by everyday activities. These show up, however, in dreams, fantasies, sexual responsiveness, and mood shifts, as discussed in detail by Benedek and Rubenstein.[4] The mature woman's adaptation to the menstrual cycle serves as an integrating factor throughout her reproductive years. The loss of this function requires major psychological adjustments at a time when many other stresses are apt to be present as well.

Married women, for example, face a variety of stresses, particularly in the late forties. Despite today's high divorce rate and childless marriages, most women are wives, mothers, and housekeepers. At middle age, they often give up part of these responsibilities. Children begin to leave to go to college, to marry, or to seek jobs out of town. The middle-aged woman's husband, if successful, may be at the height of his career and deeply immersed in business or professional activities.

Obesity, too, is often so serious during this time of life that it becomes a psychiatric problem. Much middle-age overweight is due not to poor metabolism but to overeating, a symptom of stress or frustration.

At the same time that the middle-aged person is urged to keep physically fit, he may be able to eat better than at any time in his life. Not only women, but men tend to gain added weight between the ages of 30 and 40, and find themselves unable to refuse second portions of food.

Middle life may also bring the unmarried business or professional woman additional concerns about her professional status and financial security.

[4] *Ibid.*

Women are increasingly outliving men in our society. It is often suggested that many men's lives could be prolonged if their wives could help share their husband's economic burdens, as well as their mental burdens.

Although her work may be much less during this time with children who are grown or nearly grown, many women complain that being married to busy executives and professional men bothers them. Helping a husband to switch from a very strenuous life to the slower pace is often difficult for both people.

Middle age, in many respects, accompanies changes in family life. Statistics emphasize the fact that the crisis period for marital happiness has been found to be in the late forties and early fifties for women, and in the fifties for men. This period, when identification with children must be broken, is difficult for husbands as well as wives. A couple may find themselves alone for the first time in many years, and those who have been especially child-oriented may suddenly find that they have few other interests in common—not even hobbies or meaningful common goals.

The main threats to adjustment in middle life appear to be "middle-age fatigue," and middle-age discontentment. Although the executive or professional man is at the peak of his earning power, he may find himself threatened by younger men with new knowledge and training who challenge his position of authority. He has many professional and business obligations, but is likely to find that he can no longer play the vigorous game of tennis or handball he used to.

Many women are concerned at this point with the diminution of libido, and may be surprised that sexual interest is rekindled when the fear of pregnancy is gone. Sometimes a source of stress and anxiety between the middle-aged woman and her husband lies in the fact that the husband has lost some of his sexual interest and potency.

Nurses are sometimes asked what forms of activity are best for middle-aged people. Usually, if people are in good health, walking each day is highly recommended, and ten to fifteen minutes of virorous exercise are very helpful in maintaining fitness.

Many texts delineate middle age as those years between 30 and 60, but demographers prefer the years 45 through 64. Retirement at 65 is considered a good index for the end of middle age and entrance into old age. Obviously, chronological age is a very poor guideline in the evaluation of each individual. Some people are old at 30, whereas others are youthful in attitudes and appearance well into their sixties.

Gerontologists are studying the middle years to help provide measures that will help people cope with their old age. The field of pediatrics emerged as a result of physicians focusing their care on children. It is suggested that a new discipline, "mediatrics," may develop to care for the middle-aged.

Today, there are over 35 million Americans between the ages of 40 and 60. Middle age is not entirely without advantages. Gray hair and changes in figure may be concurrent with increased status in the community, when successful men and women reach recognition and satisfaction. The man of middle years is often called upon to advise church committees and professional boards. Middle-aged members are often used in organizations to avoid reckless decisions, being considered more deliberate and judicious than younger persons.

Life is not the same at 50 as it is at 25, nor are we the same people at different ages. If a middle-aged person becomes ill, he will find that his recuperative powers are not what they were. Suddenly late hours, very taxing schedules, and a rapid pace make the middle-aged person aware that he is not able to keep up with the same speed as before.

Shakespeare saw human life in a series of stages, from birth to death. The developmental cycle is not new to man. The psychological and biological systems continue to interact with the social environment. Physical symptoms do not exist in a vacuum, and the biological changes of middle age affect an individual's psychological makeup as well.

The middle-aged crisis is sometimes called "the foolish forties." Simone de Beauvoir [5] and Anne Morrow Lindbergh [6] mention similar observations regarding the behavior of middle-aged women. Both authors see this as a possible period of second adolescence.

Marriages of twenty years or more may suddenly come to an end. Middle-aged men and women, bored with the emptiness of their lives and with their partners, may seek new work or new companions. Edmund Bergler also notes middle age as a possible time of emotional second adolescence for men.[7] He suggests that men in their mid- to late forties may undergo a kind of rebellion that can affect all aspects of their lives, including marriages, jobs, friendships, and social commitments.

As at all stages, the way the person has handled his life crises will affect the manner in which he reacts to middle age. Unmistakable signs of aging may be experienced as a profound blow to one's narcissism. Both men and women may become unhappy, withdrawn, and irritable as painful revision of their self-concepts becomes necessary. In our youth-oriented culture, the aging person sometimes feels out of place and somehow undesirable. These feelings often lead to the pursuit of simulated youth by means of cosmetics, hair dye, plastic surgery, "young" styles in clothes, and behavior more suitable for the young. When these and similar mechanisms fail, the tensions and

---

[5] Simone de Beauvoir. *The Second Sex.* New York: Alfred A. Knopf, Inc., 1953.
[6] Anne Morrow Lindbergh. *A Gift from the Sea.* New York: Pantheon Books, Inc., 1955.
[7] Edmund Bergler. *The Revolt of The Middle Aged Man.* New York: A. A. Wyn, 1964.

conflicts sometimes emerge as somatic preoccupations or become attached to organic disorders. This is the stage when many women and not a few men go to their doctors with psychosomatic symptoms or retreat into hypochondria.

The adolescent may say that he is "turned off," reflecting his boredom with life, school, and parents. The middle-aged person may also express boredom with his job, spouse, and work, and depression regarding the world in general. The middle-aged person's children remind him of his past and his aging parents represent his future. Middle-age is a time for reassessment.

Erikson views this time of life as one wherein the mature person must provide direction for the next generation. He refers to the constructive and satisfying achievement of this aim as "generativity." These accomplishments may result from parenthood or from serving as model or teacher for the children of others. Productivity and creativity also would be included in generativity. Insofar as the person fails to achieve the fulfillment implied by generativity, he may be subject to a sense of personal defeat and self-impoverishment, which Erikson calls "stagnation." [8]

Suggested Readings

Bibring, Greta and Ralph Kahana. *Lectures on Medical Psychology.* New York: International Universities Press, Inc., 1968.

Fried, Barbara. *The Middle Age Crisis.* New York: Harper & Row, Publishers, 1967.

Jaques, Elliott. "Death and the Mid-life Crisis." In *Death Interpretations.* ed. Hendrik M. Ruitenbeek. New York: Dell Publishing Co., Inc., 1969.

Kinsey, A. C., W. B. Pomeroy, C. E. Martin, and P. H. Gebhard. *Sexual Behavior in the Human Female.* Philadelphia: W. B. Saunders Company, 1953.

Pitkin, Walker. *Life Begins at Forty.* New York: McGraw-Hill Book Company, 1932.

Vedder, Clyde B. *Problems of the Middle Aged.* Springfield, Ill.: Charles C Thomas, Publisher, 1965.

[8] Erik Erikson. *Childhood and Society.* New York: W. W. Norton & Company, Inc., 1963. Pp. 266–68.

DISCUSSION OF SELECTED READINGS

The following articles deal with the middle years, which, especially in women, represent usually much more than the end of their reproductive years. Dr. Francis J. Braceland, a psychiatrist, and senior consultant at The Institute of Living, in his article, notes that this time may signal for many women the feeling that their worthwhile years have ended.

He discusses the depression that can occur during middle age. Frequently, in addition to depression, some women complain of boredom, especially at a time when their husbands are finding their most productive years professionally. Now, there is currently much discussion about the middle years and for some people, these years can become most rewarding and productive. While childbearing may be over for many of these women, many more married women with children are starting to go back to work. Only a generation ago, a woman at 40 might have nothing to look forward to but grandmotherhood—a wonderful and yet not completely satisfying occupation for many. A nursing education is one of the types of careers very much suited for women who have worked when they were younger and who wish to go back to work. We have already discussed the fact that our lives are open-ended and that the past connects with the future.

In his article on middle age, Dr. Judd Marmor, Clinical Professor of Psychiatry, University of California, describes how the loss of the youthful self-image, increased frequency of illness and greater likelihood of death, loss of love from a "tired" marriage, and other psychological and biological changes affect the woman in this crisis stage. Middle age, in short, is whatever one chooses to make it.

On the positive side, for the middle-aged woman in contemporary American society, the feelings that were once focused on daily family routine are now freer so that she is better able to devote time to her husband and other interests outside of the home. American society, with increased liberation of the woman can introduce her to a new world beyond her home.

Emotional Problems (During Middle Age)*
by Francis J. Braceland, M.D.

Though contemporary literature, medical and lay, presently is deeply concerned with the problems and gyrations of today's young folks, it does occasionally take a side excursion to consider the plight of the aged. Rarely, however, is it occupied with the problems of middle age which, though it lacks the drama of the other two extremes, is presently bearing the burdens of both, and sometimes unfairly being blamed for their problems.

It is true that there has never been a time when it was not open season for deploring unrest in the young; the antics of the present crop seem to demand rather constant attention. With all that is happening, some parents could be forgiven if they endorsed the wish expressed in Shakespeare's Winter's Tale (III-2) that there would be no ages between 10 and 23!

For there is nothing in between but getting wenches with child, wronging the ancientry, stealing and fighting.

Though there was nothing in the Bard's lament about smoking pot or taking "trips", there was a faint hint of today's problem—namely of youth's resistance to growing up "as if they were being snared into a trap." However, that anonymous writer was most prescient who wrote, "The denunciation of the young is a necessary part of the hygiene of older people and greatly assists in the circulation of their blood." It is these older people we would like to discuss here, particularly the female in middle life—in the fifth and sixth decades of their journeys, for they frequently come under medical scrutiny.

Middle age is a neutral period, except for those who are in it. Medically speaking it is the most interesting stage of life and for the individual it should be the time of the greatest fulfillment. Medical advances and the increased life span have postponed middle age for a decade or more, and more people now attain to that period than ever before. While the bogeys about middle life and the menopause are not as ubiquitous or powerful now as they were in earlier times, some of them still do persist. Hair styles, changes in dress, and the "liberation of the female" have made a marked difference in feminine outlook, yet

* *Medical Insight.* Vol. 2, No. 5 (May, 1970). Pp. 16–21.

physicians regularly see women who, having raised families successfully and attained reasonably comfortable economic circumstances in middle life, begin to show neurotic symptoms. The children have married and departed, and husbands are successful and pleasantly neglectful—there is no longer anyone to fuss over or minister to. The "empty nest syndrome" becomes evident and the "need to be needed" asserts itself.

In the normal woman, one of the most potent causes of anxiety and mild neurotic symptoms in middle life undoubtedly is her concept of herself as a human being and the belief in her usefulness and importance. All of her life she has cherished ideas of her own self-worth and guarded her prerogatives, and now in middle life there is a threat to that ideal which is both conscious and unconscious. In addition to her fears concerning the loss of her reproductive function, there is also the vague spectre of dimly approaching old age. Lessening of responsibility, fatiguability, loss of friends through death, etc. and perhaps fear of future economic stress and beginning dependence, all add up and increase her basic insecurity.

Understandably, some of the symptoms of the basic anxiety in the female might become fixed upon the pelvic organs, for there is in the women of this age group an awareness of marked physical changes taking place in their reproductive system at this time. Not infrequently, therefore, these women visit the physician with gynecologic complaints which upon careful examination reveal only normal changes. Thus the physician may be witness to the manifestations of neurotic symptoms in the "normal" female and he has the first opportunity to practice a form of preventive psychiatry, should he be minded to do so.

That the pelvic area is a potent source of concern has been known for a long time. Instances of it abound throughout medical history. Older clinicians more often than not, wisely took what we would call today a psychosomatic approach to the problem. Braxton Hicks in the Croonian Lectures in 1877 stated: "After the change is completed the system improves. The many irritations connected with menstruation and pregnancy are gone and changes in the individual show that many of the earlier troubles were functional without prominent lesion." On the other hand, A. F. Currier was ahead of his time when he wrote in his treatise *The Menopause* published in 1897: "I can never see the sense nor the logic of the traditional teaching repeated generation after generation that the menopause was a time and experience which matron and maid alike should approach with fear and awe."

We will forego reviewing the anatomical and physiological changes which take place in various tissues and organs during and following upon the menopause, for they are well known, and we are more interested here in the emotional stresses upon women at that time. All can agree that it involves a period of waning ovarian function, but the argument as to treatment and the wisdom of prescribing estrogen therapy during the menopause and in the post-climacteric years still goes on. The proponents for and against seem to be equally adamant about their beliefs.

If waning ovarian function were the only thing which happened at this period then the substitution of estrogens would be understandable and indeed necessary, but a lot of other things are happening to women in this age group. There are subjective symptoms as well as those due to retrogressive anatomical changes taking place in the accessory genital organs. Though there is a difference of opinion regarding the cause of these symptoms, the consensus at present is that these are due not to glandular or hormonal changes but rather that they are functional, i.e. they are of emotional origin. A majority of women negotiate this period of life with no emotional upheavals and no psychiatric symptoms at all, though it is of course recognized that pre-existing neuroses may be reawakened at this time, as they may be at any period of stress.

The climacteric acts as a period of physiological and psychological stress. There is no clinical difference in the manifestations of emotional symptoms which arise at this time; they are the same as those which appear at other stressful periods. The word "climacteric" has been mentioned several times. It is associated with the involutional period of a woman. The word stems from "climacter," which is the round of a ladder. The implication is that thus far the individual has been ascending and now has turned downward. This is an unfortunate and untrue association of words.

If a woman is to develop symptoms at this time of life, they usually are those of depression or anxiety reactions. Their development is closely related to the capacity or the incapacity of the individual to adapt to changes taking place in her internal or external world. The depression can be slight, moderate, or severe and consist of a loss of interest, loss of appetite, insomnia, irritability, pessimism and fatigue. Whatever its intensity and however it comes on, there is a period of intense psychic suffering which is part of it, also accompanied by various disturbances of a physical nature.

If the person is keeping pace with all of the changes which are taking place in either her internal or external world, she can be said to be adapting and is at peace with the environment. If the adaptive methods (which incidentally are learned mechanisms) fail, however, the individual is at odds with her world and her security is threatened and anxiety arises. The forces which break down these mechanisms may all be subsumed under the heading of stress. In diagram, then, the story would be: Stress, acting upon the individual's adaptive mechanisms, threatens the individual's basic security, producing anxiety which in turn forces the individual to mobilize all of her resources or defenses against the stressful situation. If these defenses are inadequate, the individual continues in a state of anxiety.

If a woman has successfully handled the anxieties of her emotional development in the past, the chances are very good that she will do so again at this period of life. The menopause is a natural phenomenon and nature places no hazard upon it. It is only the particularly rigid and unadaptable person who has difficulty when faced with the need for a change in outlook. Variability typifies the situation of women in middle age and it is unjustifiable to attempt to blanket them all into one great group. There are various types of personalities, with various kinds of environments and adaptive mechanisms, who meet various kinds of stress, and it is obvious that diverse reactions will be called forth.

People who are basically secure will have no difficulty in effecting the transition required of them. Should the person be vainglorious or proud of some particular physical characteristic, she will feel threatened and equate the loss of beauty with aging. She sees herself as less attractive and is unable to accept this fact. These are the women who say to the doctor that they "feel like an old witch," and while this is said to evoke protestation of flattery, actually they are expressing deep mortification over growing older. Some of these women even feel that their marital-physical relationships are at an end. Often a simple statement of the fact that sexual desire outlasts reproductive capacity by a long time, made by the physician to a woman having this anxiety, would be sufficient to completely dispel it. In compensation for these feelings there is sometimes a strong urge on the part of these women to experience motherhood once more.

This period of life may be very difficult for the childless woman who may be overwhelmed by the thought that her possibilities in this sphere are over. In like manner, the unmarried woman may become depressed, as she realizes that the possibility of her having offspring of her own has passed.

These fears, associated with the waning or loss of sexuality, are often displaced, and secondary fears and anxieties arise in their stead. Such phobic reactions are commonly expressed as fear of death, cancer or other organic disease, or the fear of insanity. As stated before, unfortunately this period of life has been looked upon traditionally by many women as a time of certain trouble and as a real organic and psychological hazard, just as many people expect to be seasick when embarking upon a sea voyage.

While we are at it we might mention one other physical happening at this point; namely, the increase in weight, thought to be inevitable at this period of life, and to be mysteriously connected with glandular changes. Actually the "middle age spread," for the most part, is due to the same reason that spread at other times of life is due—the ingestion of too many calories—overeating. The proof of this, of course, lies in the fact that not all menopausal women are affected in this fashion. If it is pointed out that it occurs frequently in mothers whose childbearing period is over, it can also be noted that they more frequently are prone to cook for the family and hence are more exposed to tasting, sampling, and frequent snacks than are their sisters who are employed away from the home. Admittedly this may prove to be a simplistic explanation of a complicated problem. There is talk of a thermogenic difficulty in obesity, but one thing sure is that a reduction of carbohydrates can lead to a considerable reduction in calories.

Thus we see that the outlook in modern middle life indeed can be a very hopeful one—it is not at all necessary to have several difficulties once thought to be the accompaniment of middle age. One need not become ill emotionally; one need not feel that she is "going upon the shelf" or preparing for a quiet corner by the hearth; and one need not add to one's girth. All of these have been bogeys for women at various times, and they have been and still are the cause of many unnecessary anxious moments. For some women, the advent of middle life really portends the beginning of a delightful and pleasant autumn with many of the worrisome pressures of earlier times abated.

How can the physician help the woman who is passing through this phase of her life? First of all, she is entitled to a thorough physical examination so that the doctor who is going to guide her through this period will be aware of any organic threats to her basic security. Secondly, her physical symptoms should be treated symptomatically. Replacement therapy with estrogenic substances should be used judiciously and chiefly to alleviate the vasomotor symptoms. They are of little or no assistance with accompanying emotional symptoms. Detailed discussion of the indications, contraindications, and techniques of estrogen administration, however, is not within the scope of this presentation.

As to the management of the mild anxiety and depressive symptoms, many women can be assisted with them by the establishment of a warm, friendly relationship with a physician who listens to her story with sympathetic, benevolent attention, who is objective, who does not judge her severely, and who speaks to her in common-sense terms about the present and the future, and who takes time to do this ungrudgingly. These women are under real stress and they need support. If the emotional problems are of greater magnitude and symptoms of anxiety and depression are severe, then the doctor may need the aid of his psychiatric colleagues who are trained to cope with the more intense emotional reactions.

Fortunately, the contemporary physicians' armamentarium affords medications which can aid in the handling of the milder anxieties and depressive feelings, but they should be dispensed with care and the patient must be kept under the physician's surveillance. The doctor also has to keep in mind the fact that depressed people are at times potentially suicidal and this possibility is often accentuated in the middle age group. This is the time when failures seem to be most poignant and the possibility of recouping losses or re-arranging one's life seems almost to be impossible. Most of the problems arising in this period are not beyond help, but if the person believes them to be, the situation is just as serious as if they truly were irremediable. While the physician cannot change many of the situations which face the patient, he can change her attitude toward them. Depression today is regarded as a treatable illness—the main requisite is its early recognition and the proper handling of it.

No other group of patients makes as many demands upon the doctor's time as do the menopausal women, nor do others require so much reassurance and personal encouragement. Often the appreciation of these patients becomes a source of professional gratification to the physician who has patiently and skillfully led them, supported them, and educated them through this trying period.

To summarize: (1) The menopause physiologically means the end of a woman's reproductive life; psychologically it means that she has to reorganize her feelings about her own sexuality. (2) The climacterium refers to that period of a woman's life following cessation of menses during which many changes occur, physical, physiological, metabolic, psychological, sociological, etc. (3) A majority of women are able to adapt or make adjustments to the changes of the climacteric without severe emotional upheavals. (4) Of those emotional reactions seen in women during the menopause, anxiety and depression are the most common. These reactions are not specifically characteristic of the climacteric but they can be if the climacteric represents a specific form of stress to the woman and, particularly, if she does not have sufficient adaptive mechanisms to handle such stress. (5) Her ability to handle stress during this period of her life is dependent upon her basic personality make-up, which is predetermined before she enters the period of her menopause. Her capacity to adapt to stress is immediately concerned with her capacity to give and to receive without mixed or ambivalent feelings. The physical and emotional aspects of the menopause are so intimately intertwined as to render them practically inseparable.

Lastly, the physician who is called upon to assist the woman undergoing these changes should have a comprehensive knowledge of the woman as a total personality, a biosocial individual, a psychosomatic unity; and the physician to treat her should be the one who knows her best and whom she trusts the most. His working principle should be that middle age and indeed old age are periods of life as normal as any of the others and they should be as full, as rich, and as healthy. Perhaps then he can communicate this belief to some distressed people.

The Crisis of Middle Age *
by Judd Marmor, M.D.

There are many familiar developmental crises common to all human beings: the crucial first year of life, the adaptive stresses of the second and third years, the Oedipal period, the separation crises of the first school attendance and then of going away from home for the first time, adolescence, the first employment, first heterosexual experiences, marriage, and parenthood.

Each of these has been the subject of extensive study. But there is a particularly important developmental crisis in life—the middle years—which has not received sufficient attention as an inevitable aspect of the aging process.

Why is middle age a crisis period? There are four major reasons: physical, cultural, economic, and psychological.

As people reach their middle years, they can no longer ignore the *physical* evidences of the aging process. There comes a moment in life when the decreased elasticity of the skin, the accumulating wrinkles, and the coarsening of features force themselves into a person's awareness in a way that the psychologically healthy can no longer deny. There is the inevitable moment when a man, catching sight of the back of his head in a three-way mirror, realizes that the balding stranger is, in fact, himself. For the woman there is the sagging of her once-firm breasts, the beginning of menstrual irregularity, then the cessation of menstruation. For both men and women there is the slackening of muscular activity and the tendency toward weight increase, with the subsequent never-ending struggle between oral craving and oral frustrations.

Now, none of these manifestations is an actual somatic pathology. Thus the point is that quite apart from any specific pathological syndromes that may occur, the normal physical changes in the middle years constitute a series of critical emotional stresses for all people.

The second type of stress is *cultural*. This stress is especially severe in the United States, where youth and physical vigor are so highly valued. Perhaps this high valuation is a carry-over from our frontier days, when youth and vigor were essential to survival. Regardless of the reason, it is worth noting that this aspect of American culture does not exist to the same degree in Europe and Asia.

* Judd Marmor, "The Crisis of Middle Age," R.N., Vol. 30, No. 11 (November, 1967), 63–68.

Another relevant cultural factor is the great emphasis Americans place upon individual success, as measured in terms of prestige, wealth, or power. To fail to have achieved such success by middle age creates a significant stress for the average American.

The middle years also bring with them many increased *economic* stresses. There is still a prejudice against hiring older people, particularly outside the professions. Moreover, today's children require support for a longer time because of prolonged education and training. In addition, the middle-aged person often is faced with the heavy economic burden of supporting aging and ailing relatives. This latter burden may be somewhat eased today by Medicare; but the steady increase in their *own* medical expenses may well continue to be a serious economic threat to the middle-aged. Too, the insidious diminution in purchasing power caused by inflation is an additional source of financial strain.

Most important, however, are the *psychological* stresses. Separation loss is a key psychological stress that occurs in many forms during this period: the loss of the youthful self-image; the increased frequency of illness and death among relatives and friends; the loss of children who leave home; and the loss of love in the "tired" marriage where intimacy has been replaced by mutual toleration, and sex takes place without passion or tenderness.

In addition to these four overt stresses, there are two other significant stress factors that are usually unconscious. The first is the *loss of the fantasy hopes of youth*—hopes of fame, accomplishment, wealth, and romance. One of the fundamental adjustments most people who have not achieved their fantasies have to make in middle age is to face the hard fact that fulfillment has become improbable. This involves a profound problem in self-acceptance and in a person's willingness and ability to compromise with inexorable reality.

The second factor—and perhaps the most challenging one—is that the physical changes of middle age force an inescapable *confrontation with the fact of mortality*. The defenses which worked so well in youth—the illusion of immortality and the denial of one's own ultimate death—can no longer be maintained. The result is a marked increase in the anxiety that comes when one is forced to acknowledge the limits of existence and one's own ultimate nonexistence.

It is interesting that all these stresses affect women differently from men. In their middle years, women manifest psychiatric disorders three to four times as frequently as men. This is certainly not due to their greater physiological vulnerability to the aging process, for American women maintain their youthful appearance at least as well as men do, and, indeed, the cosmetic industry helps them to maintain the illusion of youth far better than men are able to. The evidence strongly suggests, rather, that the reasons for the difference are cultural and psychological.

First, there is much greater emphasis in our culture on the importance of beauty and youth in women than in men. Second, the cessation of menses is an *obvious* narcissistic injury as compared to the more insidious, less visible diminution of virility in aging men. Third, the woman's loss of reproductive capacity at menopause is in direct contrast to the preservation of this capacity in men. Finally, the majority of women still form their identities as mothers and wives, within the family, rather than as persons in the outside world. But in middle age, the woman's functional role as mother and wife becomes less important as her children become less dependent and her husband less attentive. Consequently many middle-aged women feel as though they are being discarded or retired to a cultural ash heap, while their husbands still feel relatively needed and involved in the outside world. (Ironically, this functional difference is reversed in the 60s and 70s when the woman becomes more useful and needed in the grandmother role than is the man of comparable age!)

Naturally, the manner in which any individual man or woman deals with these normal stresses of middle life depends upon highly personal and idiosyncratic factors. These, for both sexes, are:

1. The individual's basic ego-integrative capacity; i.e., his capacity for flexible adaptation in contrast to emotional rigidity.
2. The nature of his interpersonal relationships—the character of his marriage and of his relationship to his children, other relatives, and friends.
3. His sense of continuing usefulness, which depends on the extent of his functional relationships and the degree of self-fulfillment they afford.
4. The breadth of his interests in the outside world.

Generally speaking, the degree of impact made on the individual by the middle-age stresses is determined by the strength of the foregoing factors. In short, the weaker the individual's ego-adaptive capacity, the more limited his interpersonal relationships, the less his sense of usefulness, and the narrower his interest in the outside world—then the more critical is the impact.

There are four major patterns of response to these stresses, all but one of them defensive. (Each, of course, is subject to considerable idiosyncratic variation.) The first is *denial by escape*. The people who use this defense try to avoid facing their inner anxieties by engaging in compulsive activity. This is why so many of the middle-aged fear being alone or with wife or husband only, and are constantly escaping into the wasteland of TV, movies, card games, and parties.

Another common defense is *denial by over-compensation,* with efforts to recapture the lost feelings of youth. The woman who uses this defense is apt to embark on a desperate search for the romance and love that have gone out of her own marriage, while the man may seek to brighten his tarnishing self-image by embarking on a series of sexual conquests.

If these two common defenses fail to work, then various forms of *decompensation* may appear: anxiety states, depressive reactions, apathetic surrender, rage. These are the psychological "disorders of the menopause."

On the other hand, many a middle-aged man or woman is able to meet the stresses of the middle years head on and deal with them successfully. Such a person achieves a state of higher *integration* than he has previously achieved—an integration that brings an added dimension of emotional maturity, a heightened awareness of self and of others, a lessening of narcissistic self-involvement, an increase in the capacity to serve others, and a greater ability to find pleasure in the achievement of his children and of youth in general. He also experiences a renewed capacity for productivity and creativity; and, finally, a deeper appreciation of the complexity and the rich bitter-sweetness that characterize our temporary sojourn on this planet of laughter and tears. As Longfellow has written:

> *For age is opportunity no less*
> *Than youth itself, though in another dress.*

chapter nine

OLD AGE

Aging in Other Cultures

One of the earliest efforts to organize studies and theories regarding aging was a volume, *Senescence, the Last Half of Life,* by G. Stanley Hall.[1] It was published in 1922, following a comparable study he had made on adolescence. By the 1940's, publications on the aging process accelerated, and a pioneering study on aging in more than seventy preliterate societies, *The Role of the Aged and Primitive Society,* was published by Leo Simmons in 1945. He noted:

As far back as we can go, the hands of the aged had reached out for little food when they could do nothing more—and they have not been entirely ignored, nor always filled.[2]

Simmons discusses the frequency of food-sharing among Indian tribes throughout the United States. It was a rule of the Omaha that the one elected chief should be a generous man, one who would remember the poor and the aged. The Iroquois also felt a great responsibility for food sharing: their aged spent their last days moving from house to house among members of the clan. The Navajos have been "hospitable," assuring food when it was

---

[1] G. Stanley Hall. *Senescence, the Last Half of Life.* New York: Appleton-Century-Crofts, 1922.
[2] Leo W. Simmons. *The Role of the Aged in Primitive Society.* New Haven: Yale University Press, 1945. P. 20.

available not only to their own people but to guests and strangers.

In many primitive societies, individuals who survived to old age were ascribed the distinction and prestige of high power, superhuman ability, and immense knowledge. Hence, they often were revered as magicians, priests, and healers.

Simmons comments that the salient fact about respect for the aging, historically, is its widespread occurrence.

Some degree of prestige for the aged seems to have been generally universal in all societies. This is so general that it cuts across many cultural factors which have appeared to determine trends and other topics related to age.[3]

Respect for the aged has been influenced by codified laws, where old men sat in council and served as judges. Their opportunities under such situations were great, and aged women also tended to gain, especially when they too had some authority in government. When aged men have control in primitive societies, initiation of the young is part of their responsibility, and their prestige appears thereby to be increased.

Knowledge, wisdom, and experience are the social assets that make the aged the custodians of folk wisdom, as Simmons confirms in numerous examples of folk customs.[4] They have been the historians, in that they treasured up the memories of travel incidents and passed them to younger generations. They have traditionally given comfort and counsel to the discouraged and the bereaved. When writing and records were unknown, a lucid mind, a good memory, and seasoned judgment were recognized assets to the group.

General Needs of the Aging Person

Social relationships provide the greatest security for individuals, especially in old age. With declining physical vigor, the old person has to rely more and more on family and other personal relationships involving reciprocal rights and obligations. In its last stages, the body is feeble, the mind is sometimes hazy, and the lightest chores may become difficult and burdensome; in societies where they have not possessed deeply entrenched rights, the aged face indifference, neglect, and actual abuse. This treatment is known in primitive societies and is certainly not unknown in contemporary American culture.

Throughout human history, the family has been the safest haven for the aged, the most important and long-lasting. Although other supports crumble and disappear, the aged can cling to kin as their protectors, and hopefully,

[3] *Ibid.* P. 79.
[4] *Ibid.*

can find in family relationships opportunities for effective social participation well into senility.

The process of aging is frequently viewed in narrow chronological terms, especially in setting age requirements for employment. In contemporary America, 65 seems to be the most commonly used boundary between "youth" and "aged." The Social Security Act uses age 65 to determine precisely when individuals become eligible for specific benefits (62, for women). Industry has been influenced by the federal system and often use 65 as the age for mandatory retirement. In other countries, such as Japan, mandatory retirement may come as early as 55. Obviously, the person's career influences his retirement age. Professional football and basketball players may find themselves too old for their work by 30; but a lawyer, a physician, or a teacher may be able to continue his professional pursuits well into his sixties and seventies and even later.

There has been growing dissatisfaction with using the mid-sixties as a demarcation point between youth and old age. With better health and improved medical care, many professional people, as well as executives, have worked into their seventies and eighties effectively. Widows are, after periodic changes in Social Security laws, eligible for benefits at an earlier age. Obviously, federal legislation has been most helpful in providing funds for our aging population, but retirement plans, federally and individually, have often phased out lives long before productive ability has ceased.

At present, there are important differences in level of formal education between our young and old. This gap will be less pronounced as our better-educated younger people become the aged of tomorrow. There is no doubt that future generations of aged persons will have more years of formal schooling than their present-day counterparts.

Many persons who are now old began to work in very early childhood, and lack the education to perform any job except the one from which they are forced to retire. Thus, many healthy, vigorous people spend years in idle boredom. Today's better-educated young people may have alternatives unavailable to most of the current aged. A second career may be possible for many of them after retirement, and is even becoming increasingly possible for the present middle-aged generation.

The Family and the Aged

Full care of aged family members that extends over months or years may exceed the financial capacity of a normal family. This problem arises particularly when chronic diseases require extended nursing and hospital care. Such care, if attempted by the family alone, can destroy it, damaging all generations. With the institution of Medicare and extension of Social

Security benefits, long-term care receives some help from society, but it is obvious that this help must increase, with extended national insurance benefits and professional health agencies. Nurses need to understand why these services have been provided and may need to be extended. They should also understand that inability to provide extended care for the elderly need not represent a failure of family responsibility.

Despite claims to the contrary, many children do continue to face their responsibilities to their elderly parents. Although many older persons move into retirement colonies or into moderate climates, the preponderance of evidence shows that most elderly people remain in the states in which they have always lived. They may prefer to live in their home state for a variety of reasons: first, it is not as easy to move in old age as it is when one is younger. It requires money, the ability to give up old ties and familiar places, and often a complete separation of generations. Eighty per cent of older people with living children still live either in the same household with one of their children, or less than one hour away from one of them.

The fields of nursing, medicine, and social work are split over the question of the responsibility the family has for its aged members, in view of the fact that many older people need not only private family care, but also social care.

Modern society has created many new conditions for family life. The modern family as a primary social unit has to cope with a great increase in the proportion of aged members surviving into their seventh, eighth, and ninth decades. Life expectancy has extended from 54.1 years in 1920 to well over 70 years in 1962. Since the nineteenth century, the proportion of the total American population over 65 has increased from 4 per cent to 9 per cent, of which nearly a third are more than 75 years of age.

With our mobile society, maintenance of traditional family ties has proven increasingly difficult. Even a dedicated, affectionate child may find it difficult to make frequent visits to a parent who lives far away. Transportation, lack of time off, and family responsibilities make it difficult to meet responsibilities toward aging parents. For this reason, society has increasingly assumed some of the children's burdens.

The social and psychological needs of the aging person can become enormous. Elderly people rarely like to be completely isolated and enjoy frequent visits from younger adults, especially true if there have been strong affectionate bonds between family members. Grandchildren symbolize a very important goal in their total life experience—an extension of themselves—and many grandparents are extremely patient and kind with young children. For the young child, grandparents often seem much more relaxed, happier, and more flexible than their parents. As we mentioned in the section on primitive cultures, this compatibility between the oldest and the youngest generation was an important aspect of the extended family.

Chronic Illness and Aging

Illness, disability, and pain usually become chronic with increasing age but the aged sick, like our mentally ill, are often hidden from the general public in hospitals or nursing homes where they are isolated, psychologically and socially and must then turn with increasing necessity to the medical and nursing professions for care. Unfortunately, health workers who see these people as hopeless can, by their sense of futility, cause serious psychological damage to patients.

Chronic illness taxes to the utmost the physical and psychological resources of the individual and his family. In acute illness, the patient is temporarily removed from his environment, but a long-term illness forces him to change his entire way of life. However, one advantage of aging is that chronic illnesses progress more slowly than in the younger person. Malignant tumors, which grow rapidly and metastasize quickly in younger patients, are slowed in development; diabetes mellitus, critical in youth, is less so in the aged.

Cancer is often associated with aging because it strikes older people with greater frequency than the young, but there is also increasing protection against it. Early detection through the use of periodic checkups, surgery, and prevention through the avoidance of unnecessary risks, such as exposure to overdoses of radiation or sunlight and cigarette smoking, help avert cancer's onset.

Illness then becomes more prevalent among the old. Such diseases as diabetes mellitus, arteriosclerosis, acute coronary thrombosis, and cerebral vascular accidents are also a common affliction of the old. With the onset of all these diseases, there is needed not only immediate medical management but a continued, vigilant therapy for the rehabilitation of the patient.

Chronic illness inevitably changes the relationships between people. Blindness, deafness, and other disabilities impede communication and often restrict physical activities. Physical handicaps frequently cause the patient to feel inferior, isolated, and "different." The old person who becomes deaf may learn to communicate through sign language. The blind require new adjustments to auditory and tactile perception. Hypertension and diabetes restrict the diet and add to the other deprivations of aging.

SENSORY DETERIORATION

Vision undergoes changes from middle age onward. It is helpful for the nurse to teach patients to adapt their behavior to growing limitations in vision. For example, patients should be taught that it may take a long time for eyes to adapt to a change in light, as in walking from a light to a dark room. The older person needs to wait for his eyes to adjust rather than proceeding blindly, risking falls, disorientation, and crashing into objects. He should be encouraged to use good general illumination in his own living quarters, and good illumination should be provided when he is adapting to the hospital.

Cataracts are one of the more common sensory impairments, but clear vision can ordinarily be restored through surgery. Fear of cataracts is often present in older patients who have neglected to have their eyes examined, and it is helpful for the nurse to explain that removal of cataracts today is a relatively routine procedure.

Progressive loss of hearing is more likely than loss of vision to have negative personality consequences. Since the inability to hear sometimes brings on such associated symptoms as irritability, suspiciousness, and even paranoid symptoms, the use of hearing aids can hardly be too strongly recommended. A period of training following the acquisition of a hearing aid is essential; otherwise, it may not be used. The simpler types of hearing aids may be necessary for older patients. The community health nurse may be especially familiar with the elderly patient who cannot make his hearing aid "work." Sometimes, this problem reflects the patient's confusion, but in other instances it may be related to an unconscious wish not to hear, as a kind of withdrawal from the environment.

The blunting of tactile sensation, another common handicap, will result in difficulty in object discrimination through touch. Of greater seriousness is that there are fewer cues from the soles of the feet, which ordinarily assist the person with reduced visual acuity in unfamiliar surroundings.

THE TOLERANCE OF STRESS

Older patients frequently show little symptomatic response to acute disease. A knowledge of this is extremely important to the nurse and physician who have his care. In making a diagnosis, a doctor no longer depends on pain, fever, and the physical findings that he might evaluate in the younger patient. Paul Starr notes:

> The elderly man may have perforation of a viscus with little reaction; he may have lobar pneumonia without cough or pain, and with low grade fever; he may have a ruptured appendix with generalized peritonitis without local or systemic signs. The older woman may break her femur and still hobble around. Such tolerance of acute stress is dangerous because the body becomes defenseless and fatal progression may occur without medical intervention.[5]

[5] P. Starr. *The Care of the Geriatric Patient.* E. V. Cowdry, ed. St. Louis: The C. V. Mosby Company, 1968. P. 45.

The hospital nurse who has an elderly patient fall out of bed, or the community health nurse who cares for one with a low-grade fever, needs to keep in mind that in many ways the older patient will not show illness in the same fashion as the younger.

Successful prevention, control, and cure of chronic illness mean that the patient must be treated along with his disease. While the problems of long-term illness and geriatric medicine are not identical, they often overlap. Mastery of chronic disease becomes a task of psychological as well as physiological adaptation. The rapidly increasing number of chronic diseases also presents a serious economic problem, and in old age the ability of the ill to pay high medical and hospital costs may decline markedly. The uninsured person who relies solely on his earned income feels intensely insecure and anxious when he becomes ill, and his rehabilitation cannot be undertaken without concern for his financial support.

In acute illness, the family of the aging person may be willing to make extreme financial sacrifices because it feels that the illness is temporary and well-defined. Insurance companies, relatives, and charity organizations tolerate acute illnesses far better than long-term ones; thus, the expense of a chronic illness often cannot be afforded or underwritten for extended periods of time. The rapidly rising costs of medical, nursing, and hospital care have placed these services out of the range of anyone without some form of financial assistance. It is for this reason that increases in Social Security have been legislated by means of such programs as Medicare.

PROTECTIVE SERVICES

In chronic illness, many aged persons may need either hospital or nursing home care and management of the transition between the hospital and home is especially difficult. Unfortunately, many patients end up in nursing homes and hospitals merely because no adequate home care is available. There is a growing conviction that many such patients do not require institutional care and attention and that, in fact, they suffer many undesirable effects from prolonged depersonalizing institutional care.

In view of the shortage of general community facilities, the people involved in hospital and extended care facilities must take leadership in providing special services for patients, or in stimulating over-all community support so that these patients can be, whenever possible, sent back into the community.

Mental disturbance in the elderly creates a need for what has become known as protective services. Preliminary studies by the National Council on Aging suggest that although many persons are capable of staying in their own communities, this capacity is sometimes affected by temporary mental problems. Periods of gross absentmindedness, neglect in the management of funds, or inability to provide themselves with minimal personal safety will quite occasionally cause these people, especially those without families, to end up in mental institutions.

Aberrations in behavior of this nature are not necessarily dangerous, but they do require protective care. Most vulnerable are those older persons living alone who may have no one to pay their bills, or look after their homes or rooms during an absence. It is generally agreed that protective services can undoubtedly prolong community residence for such persons. There is a great need for people to assist the elderly during these brief periods of emotional or physical decompensation. Obviously, the family, when willing and able, is the first line of defense in protecting them, but unfortunately, too many older people lack friends or family to assist them in this role.

There is a great need to improve the social organization to meet these common human needs through coordinating a network of services that would permit the individual to select those that meet his requirements. Major gains in our knowledge have served to counteract the stereotyped view of the aged and allow a positive approach to the challenges that cluster around aging as a major transitional point in the human life cycle.

It is clear that older people are, at any given time, usually less fortunate than younger people. Preparation for changing housing needs and many of the other negative factors of old age may be avoided by "anticipatory socialization," and when necessary, by professional intervention at earlier stages in the life course of the individual.

Nurses may see the problem of aging in a dynamic perspective by focusing on the distinction between their own present condition and their future, visualizing some of the possibilities of professional intervention, both individual and societal.

Abnormal Psychological Reactions to Aging

EFFECTS OF SENILITY

As physical weakening lessens control over the emotions, easier lapses into laughing or crying may occur. Senility also may accentuate personality traits with much more than the normal deepening of character that accompanies usual kinds of aging.

The senile patient may be concerned and upset about his memory defects, may show intellectual slowness and difficulty in making judgments, and with this become querulous and confabulating. Not remembering a trend of events, he may fill in with inaccurate stories or facts, and show irritability and oversensitivity when questioned regarding this. Sometime, excessive sexual activity or ritual exhibitionism occurs, which may represent an attempt to deny the loss of attractiveness or potency.

Aging men may experience and act on sexual impulses that take on socially and biologically forbidden directions, often leading to accusations of exhibitionism, aggressive sexual offenses against young girls, or homosexual assaults against boys.

A withdrawal and return to earlier types of behavior may begin, with a lessening of ambition and dislike of change. Defensive measures often include taking extensive time with routine, repetitious chores. The older person has fewer bonds with people and becomes preoccupied with his food and his bowels; he may also at this stage hoard worthless objects or pieces of paper. He often becomes less considerate and affectionate, and may even regress to complete isolation and alienation.

It is not unusual to see confused states in older patients in the presence of even mild physical illness, for normally there is a slowing down of evaluation and responses to perception. Moderately senile patients, when not depressed or excessively confused, need no special attention during illness, but severely senile patients may require attention and protective supervision. Where there is increasing helplessness, temporary confusion, and delirium, it is important that the nurse provide a protective figure, either herself or another, on whom the patient can rely. Sometimes a dependable family member or another patient can assume this role. It would be extremely helpful in hospitals if there were more volunteers who just spent their time being with patients, talking with them, and helping them to stay in contact with reality. Some older patients become disoriented as much from sensory deprivation as from any other cause.

Paranoid trends are frequent in the senile patient, especially if earlier personality traits were tinged with a suspicious attitude. Feeling rejected and unwanted is conducive to delusional ideas, and frequent among older patients' complaints is that they have been robbed, are poverty-stricken (when they are not), or are being poisoned.

In some cases, the aging person may feel a loss of self-respect that can lead to depressive symptoms. He complains of feeling sad, tired, or worn out, and becomes preoccupied with his various lifetime disappointments. He may complain or present a state of helplessness in which he feels unable to read, concentrate, or accomplish anything. In addition to the normal slowing of pace, severely depressed patients become even more slow. They may not want to eat, and they may lose weight. Suspiciousness, guardedness, and oversensitivity are common in older sick patients.

Personality characteristics from a patient's adult life, such as depression, often emerge in a stronger form in later life. Aging brings strong dependent needs, difficulty in controlling impulses, and a discrepancy between ideals and standards on the one hand, and the ability to achieve them on the other. Senescent changes of the body, especially loss of attractiveness and strength, cause one of the major serious disturbances among the old.

ANXIETY STATES AND PSYCHOSES

Anxiety states are essentially the same at whatever time of life they occur. A "free-floating" type of anxiety may permeate the thoughts and behavior of the individual. This is characterized by physiological derivatives of strong emotional reactions: overbreathing, increased skeletal tensions, visceral disturbances, tremors, headaches, perspiring, nausea, diarrhea, and a sense of impending danger. The attacks may occur without any apparent precipitating event, and the elderly individual may be convinced that he is seriously ill or that there is impending death.

In general, the circumstances of later life and maturity that lay the basis for anxiety neuroses are a lack of security—circumstances where the individual is less welcome, less useful, less valued, and more dependent than in earlier years.

Senile psychoses and psychoses with cerebral arteriosclerosis together constitute the great bulk of serious mental illnesses in the elderly. Early manifestations of senile psychosis are a deterioration of personal habits and loss of moral inhibitions, with severe untidiness occurring later. Insomnia, restlessness, and wandering from the home are common. In many cases delusions, hallucinations, and paranoid tendencies occur.

Paranoid tendencies can have unfortunate results since the patient becomes suspicious of the family, and often reverses commitments he has made. As the psychosis develops, symptoms of intellectual deficit are quite apparent, immediate memory is seriously impaired, and the patient lives in the past, indulging in reminiscences about friends and events in the distant past. Abstract thinking is no longer possible, although the patient may retain the ability to perform concrete activities.

Arteriosclerotic psychosis is associated with damage due to hardening of the cerebral blood vessels. The average age of onset is 66, although the disease may appear in people as young as 45. The symptoms usually have an abrupt onset. The patient becomes incoherent, restless, and often hallucinates; intellectual processes decline; memory and judgment are defective. The defective judgment may also affect moral standards. The patients complain often of depressive feelings and a fear of impending failure of physical and mental powers.

OTHER CAUSES OF MENTAL CHANGE

Some disorders are associated with specific toxic agents—barbiturates, bromides, and alcohol can cause delirious toxic reactions in elderly people. Infections that affect the meninges and the brain can cause symptoms of delirious intoxication.

The term "paranoid reactions" is widely used to cover a group of conditions, mostly of short duration, but occasionally chronic, that arise in adverse circumstances and are characterized by suspiciousness and referential ideas. The person is often oversensitive or otherwise abnormal.

The stereotype of the aged mentally ill patient is one who suffers from intellectual deterioration and behavioral disturbances associated with chronic, irreversible structural changes in the brain. This structural damage is usually ascribed to a cerebral circulatory disorder or to a so-called senile brain disease but cerebral hemorrhage and cardiac failure can also cause acute brain disorders.

Some patients have histories of frequent falls, from which head traumas can occur; these, as well as major surgical procedures, may have the clinical manifestations of an acute brain syndrome. Pulmonary diseases such as pneumonia or advanced emphysema or tuberculosis can also interfere with brain functioning.

Because both physical and mental balance is very delicate in the older person, there may be multiple reasons for changes in behavior. It is important for the nurse to realize that a patient may have acute brain disease and suffer from an affective disorder without necessarily progressing to a chronic disease. In older age groups, patients frequently show a perplexing mixture of symptoms: disorientation, disturbed awareness, memory difficulties, depression, elation, anxiety, ideas of persecution, phobias, obsessions, and even hysterical conversions. However, it is just as important not to be primarily concerned with affixing descriptive labels as it is when working with other age groups.

Care for the Aged Mentally Ill Patient

Institutional care is traditional for the older person who becomes mentally ill but institutionalization, at best, may be of itself a traumatic experience.

Only 8 per cent of the United States' population is over 65; yet 26 per cent of the new patients admitted to mental hospitals are over 65, and the proportion of older people in the population is steadily expanding. The problems of geriatric mental illness, therefore, demand increasing medical and social attention. Mental hospital staffs state that older patients are admitted not because of mental illness alone, but because communities are reluctant to provide other facilities. A survey of geriatric patients admitted in June, 1950, to California mental hospitals indicates that 55 per cent of them could have been cared for outside a mental hospital had suitable facilities existed.

The emphasis in the treatment of the mentally ill has been shifting in recent years from hospital to community care. There is no doubt that there is a tremendous need in the community to work for better ways of keeping the aged out of mental institutions. The greatest threats to old age are the long-term chronic illnesses, disability, and mental illness, with subsequent institutionalization and complete loss of independence.

Depression in elderly persons is often a response to the loss of highly valued physical or mental attributes. One nurse noted recently that a college professor who had depended upon his intellectual skills and activities reacted with depression and mourning to his diminished intellectual capacity after suffering from a stroke at the age of 70. An equivalent loss of mental capacity may be of less consequence to a man who spent most of his life doing manual labor. One such person was a day laborer in his early fifties who suffered a stroke. He, too, became depressed, and although he appeared unconcerned about some diminution in mental capacity, he mourned grievously the loss of his sure and steady hand.

The severe depressions that accompany organic brain syndromes in aged people may result less from tissue damage than from this emotional reaction, especially when a person is faced with new or stressful tasks and discovers that he is unable to carry them out successfully. Old habits and old memories persist best as the brain fails: recent memories and newly learned skills slip away quickly.

Emotional Health and Physical Functioning

Until recent years it was considered axiomatic that sexual feelings became diminished or vanished with age. The work of Masters and Johnson [6] has emphasized that active sexual life frequently persists into the sixties and seventies, and occasionally into the eighties. It appears that boredom, unhappiness, and depression are much more commonly the cause of marked diminution in sexual vigor than the actual processes of aging.

The nurse should accept that patients of all ages, from childhood to senescence, have a capacity for sexual feelings and response, except when physical illness or emotional factors are sufficiently inhibiting.

[6] William H. Masters and Virginia E. Johnson. *Human Sexual Response.* Boston: Little, Brown and Company, 1966.

The ability to continue functioning in an active and integrated fashion often depends on social and emotional factors. In old age there is often a surprising discrepancy between the state of the psyche as judged by outward functioning and the condition of the brain as gauged by the electroencephalogram.

It is common for a nurse to see rapid deterioration in patients who are ill and who lose a husband or wife with whom they have a dependent and satisfying relationship. Such an example was a man of 75 (Mr. R.) with severe cardiovascular disease and widespread arteriosclerosis, including a large arteriosclerotic plaque in the septum between his right and left ventricles. Any deviation from a strict low-salt diet would lead immediately to oedema and to cardiac decompensation. Despite two or three years in this condition, he managed to retain his fluid balance through the careful attention and psychological support of his wife. They had been married for nearly half a century, in a mutually gratifying relationship that had afforded each considerable comfort and support as they grew older. Unfortunately, his wife developed a carcinoma of the bowel. For about a year following her first surgery, she showed no recurrence, and both continued to lead an active and relatively contented life. Her carcinoma then recurred, and she began a slow, downhill course, during which Mr. R. rapidly showed progressive signs of cardiac and renal failure and arteriosclerotic brain disease. As his wife became weaker, Mr. R. suffered personality changes, becoming depressed, irritable, and at times confused and disoriented. His deterioration almost exactly paralleled the physical deterioration of his wife. The nursing staff and his physicians noted that Mr. R. asked to attend his wife's funeral and at that time showed little interest in living longer. He requested that no further treatment be given to him at the time of his final cardiac failure; he survived his wife by just two weeks. His physician speculated that had his wife lived and remained in good health, Mr. R. could have lived and functioned at a reasonably good level for a few more years. This dramatic example is no different from many other cases in which physical and mental failure follows the loss of a long-standing, vital relationship.

Need for Hospitalization

The major crisis facing the older person is a need for hospitalization. This need often comes up without adequate warning, requiring financial outlays too large to anticipate. It has been estimated that nine out of every ten persons age 65 or older will be hospitalized at least once in their remaining lifetimes, and two out of every three will be hospitalized more than once.

With the steady increase in the number of persons over 65, their health will be a growing problem, for more old people means more sick people. It is in response to public sentiment regarding the need to assume care of the aged that the Medicare Program became law in 1965.

There is a definite relationship between the state of a person's health and his feelings of dignity and self-respect. Older persons who feel neglected and rejected are more likely to think their health is poor. Unfortunately, there is a distrust of and distaste for old people in our society, and it is no wonder that large numbers of them feel desolate, depressed, and sick. The solution of this problem lies in some basic changes in the American value system. Recognition of the fact that an ever increasing number of our citizens will be among the elderly could do much to encourage programs to help solve their health problems, particularly their mental health problems.

Hospitalization can contribute to the disorientation of older people. They may react like young children when separated from their homes and families. We have previously discussed how frightened and bewildered younger people—even middle-aged or adult patients—are in their new surroundings. Because the aged have a decreased capacity to adjust to a new environment, the hospital is even more upsetting to them. Furthermore, the aged often see the hospital only as "a place to die." They may find it very difficult to go to the hospital, feeling that they will be permanently isolated and separated from their families. Traditionally, many older people have preferred to be sick and to die at home, but American culture has changed in the last generation or two, so that our very sick and our dying seldom are given the choice of being in a familiar environment at the close of life.

Psychodynamics of Old Age

In one of Freud's earlier papers, he discusses the appreciation of psychoanalytic techniques as therapeutic measures:

Near and above the 50's, the elasticity of the mental process on which the treatment depends, is lacking. Old people are no longer educable, and on the other hand, the mass of material to be dealt with would prolong the duration of the treatment indefinitely.[7]

In 1898, Freud stated, "Psychoanalysis loses its effectiveness after the patient is too advanced in years." [8]

[7] S. Freud. *Sigmund Freud on Psychotherapy—Collected Papers.* Vol. I. London: Hogarth Press, Ltd., 1904. P. 288.
[8] *Ibid.* P. 288.

Freud comments on the lack of "elasticity of the ego" in older people, which results in fixed opinions and reactions. In addition to becoming more rigid as they get older, Freud pointed out, people are more objective in their assessment of reality, but may also become more aware of childhood conflicts.

Abraham, modifying Freud's position, demonstrated that psychoanalytic therapy *was* applicable to older people.[9] Later workers have also tried psychoanalytic therapy with older people and concluded that psychoanalysis, slightly modified, was at least partly applicable as a therapeutic method and was definitely applicable as a research instrument.

In discussing analytic treatment of the depressions of old age, some psychoanalysts refer to the "inverted Oedipus complex," wherein aged and dependent individuals regard adult offspring as they formerly regarded their own parents. Older persons may feel considerable ambivalence when they who once guided now have to be responsible to their children.

Old age is a period in which many attitudes, desires, and dissatisfactions previously suppressed or kept under control may emerge in verbal or emotional expression or in action.

The Nurse, the Doctor, and the Aged Patient

Already an increasingly large number of patients in a physician's office are 65 years or older. Nurses need to be aware that elderly people, like people in other age groups, are apt to see their doctor in times of crisis, but that they should also be encouraged to visit a physician for preventive care and may need added assistance because of memory problems and their physical difficulties in getting to and from the doctor's office.

The nurse may see the aged as infirm, dependent and as an institutional problem. In fact, however, only 4 per cent of the population 65 years of age and over live in institutions, only 13 per cent live with their children or other relatives; and even within this group, children or other relatives may be dependent on the aged person rather than the reverse. In fact, with the growing number of four-generation families, it is not uncommon to find aged persons living with other persons over 65.

One important social fact in the United States is that 20 per cent of men 65 years old and over are widowed, whereas 55 per cent of the women 65 years old and over are widowed.

Preventive mental health services should be available in the community for the elderly, just as for the rest of the population. Psychiatric consultation and treatment too often are not available to aging persons because of the distance that they have to travel to receive care, the cost, and the

[9] Karl Abraham. *Selected Papers on Psychoanalysis*. New York: Basic Books, Inc., Publishers, 1953. P. 316.

lack of facilities. Often, although older people seem to be suffering from acute mental illness, their disorientation results from strains created by their loss of role, their changes in physical health, and their family's negative attitudes toward them, and as such need not threaten their independence. It is helpful for the older person if he knows his doctor over a long period of time. Periodic comprehensive health examinations allow the patient to become familiar with the doctor's office and establish a relationship with his physician.

Nurses are needed in homes for the aged where patients are allowed to move from residential wings to nursing care, and back to residential wings. Another area where nurses are increasingly employed is in nursing homes, where the trend is toward large, rather than small, homelike units. These facilities require round-the-clock skilled nursing care and rehabilitation services. Standards vary from state to state and from institution to institution, and, unfortunately, while national accreditation and standards are being worked out, some homes are grossly understaffed and inadequate. Nurses are also providing foster homes, or boarding homes, where older persons participate in family living. In these cases, nurses take in isolated older patients who need care, but who are usually ambulatory and do not require hospitalization.

Planning for the Aged Patient

Doctors and nurses often find the aging patient difficult to manage. Since the aged remind us disconcertingly of our own future, their physical signs of debilitation are upsetting to even an experienced physician or nurse. The elderly are often troubled by serious problems in communication; if they have had strokes or are hard of hearing, it is difficult for them either to understand directions or to relate their ideas. Intractable or terminal ailments may make them become surly or taciturn. Doctors and nurses often feel mounting frustration in working with the chronically ill aged patient; yet these patients continue to turn to us with hope and desperate pleas for cures.

Careful distinctions need to be made with the aged, just as with any other group of patients, for older individuals display as wide a range of personality types as do younger or middle-aged persons. An example of such categorizing exists in two homes for the aged run by religious agencies. In one, the older married couples are separated in private rooms. No married couples are allowed to share a single room, despite their generous size. The policy of the home is simple. The director and the board have concluded: "All elderly people are, or tend to be, irritable and naturally cannot get along with their spouses. Therefore, all elderly people should be separated in private rooms."

Mr. Jones and his wife were married over sixty years, with fourteen children and a large number of grandchildren. They had been compatible throughout their years of marriage, and when it was necessary to separate them in this retirement home, Mr. Jones became very upset. Both of them were mentally clear; they were sturdy, and had to give up their farm mainly because of the physical problems of managing their large old farmhouse. The thoughtless policy of the administration in separating these people is an example of the way the elderly are sometimes unfairly categorized.

In another private retirement home in a different city, the policy is that all married couples who come into the home *must* occupy the same room. Mr. and Mrs. Smith, in their mid-seventies, had not had a compatible marriage but have never seen fit to get a divorce. They had lived together out of mutual necessity. To require that they live together is another example of the inability of a staff and board of directors to consider individual personalities and problems.

Such set policies related to the aged give some idea of the extent of stereotyping. Aging involves every life, every relationship, and every home. In order to better understand the aging process, the field of social and physical gerontology has developed to study the impact of aging upon individuals in society.

Suggested Reading

BOOKS

Benedek, Therese. "Personality Development." In *Dynamic Psychiatry*. Eds. F. Alexander and H. Ross. Chicago: University of Chicago Press, 1952.

Burgess, Ernest W., ed. *Aging in Western Societies*. Chicago: University of Chicago Press, 1960.

Cavan, Ruth Shonle, Ernest W. Burgess, Robert J. Havighurst, and Herbert Goldhammer. *Personal Adjustment in Old Age*. Chicago: Science Research Associates, 1949.

Cumming, Elaine and William E. Henry. *Growing Old. The Process of Disengagement*. New York: Basic Books, Inc., 1961.

Erikson, Erik H. *Childhood and Society*. New York: W. W. Norton and Company, Inc., 1950.

Jaeger, Dorothea and Leo W. Simmons. *The Aged Ill*. New York: Appleton-Century-Crofts, 1970.

Kastenbaum, Robert, ed. *New Thoughts on Old Age*. New York: Springer Publishing Co., Inc., 1964.

Koller, Marvin R. *Social Gerontology.* New York: Random House, Inc., 1968.

Laether, Herman J. *Problems of Aging—Sociological and Social Psychological Perspectives.* Belmont, Calif.: Dickenson Publishing Co., Inc., 1967.

Riley, Matilda White, John W. Riley, and Marilyn E. Johnson, eds. *Aging and Society.* New York: Russell Sage Foundation, 1964.

Simmons, Leo W. *The Role of the Aged in Primitive Society.* New Haven, Conn.: Yale University Press, 1945.

Simpson, Ida Harper, and John C. McKinney, eds. *Social Aspects of Aging.* Durham, N.C.: Duke University Press, 1966.

Wasser, Edna. *Creative Approaches in Casework with the Aging.* New York: Family Service Association of America, 1966.

Williams, Richard H. and Claudene G. Wirth. *Lives Through the Years—Styles of Life and Successful Aging.* New York: Atherton Press, 1965.

Wolff, Kurt. *The Biological, Sociological and Psychological Aspects of Aging.* Springfield, Ill.: Charles C Thomas, Publisher, 1959.

Zinberg, Norman E. and Irving Kaufman, eds. *Normal Psychology of the Aging Process.* New York: International Universities Press, Inc., 1963.

ARTICLES

Buck, Pearl S. "Creativity and the Aging American." *Psychosomatics.* Vol. 8, No. 4 (July–August, 1967). Pp. 28–32.

Burnside, Irene M. "Grief Work in the Aged Patient." *Nursing Forum.* Vol. 8, No. 4 (1969). Pp. 416–27.

Cumming, Elaine. "Further Thoughts on the Theory of Disengagement." *UNESCO International Social Science Journal.* Vol. 15 (1963). Pp. 377–93.

———. "New Thoughts on the Theory of Disengagement." *International Journal of Psychiatry.* Vol. 6, No. 1 (1968). Pp. 53–67.

Frenay, Sister Agnes Clare and Gloria L. Pierce. "The Climate of Care for a Geriatric Patient." *The American Journal of Nursing,* Vol. 71, No. 9 (September, 1971). Pp. 1747–50.

Gage, Frances Bolard. "Suicide in the Aged." *The American Journal of Nursing,* Vol. 71, No. 11 (November, 1971). Pp. 2153–55.

Gress, Lucille D. "Sensitizing Students to the Aged." *The American Journal of Nursing,* Vol. 71, No. 10 (October, 1971). Pp. 1969–70.

Gunter, Laurie M. "Students' Attitudes Toward Geriatric Nursing." *Nursing Outlook,* Vol. 19, No. 7 (July, 1971). Pp. 466–69.

Hahn, Aloyse. "It's Tough to Be Old." *American Journal of Nursing.* Vol. 70, No. 8 (August, 1970). Pp. 1698–99.

Havighurst, R. J. "Personality and Patterns of Aging." *The Gerontologist.* Spring, Pt. 2, 1968. Pp. 20–23.

Kastenbaum, R. "The Foreshortened Life Perspective." *Geriatrics.* Vol. 24, No. 8 (1969). Pp. 126–33.

Mead, Margaret. "Ethnological Aspects of Aging." *Psychosomatics.* Vol. 8, No. 4 (July–August, 1967). Pp. 33–37.

LeRoux, Rose and Donna Arlton. "The Foster Grandparent Program." *Nursing Forum.* Vol. 8, No. 4 (1969). Pp. 405–15.

Wolff, K. "Depression and Suicide in the Geriatric Patient." *Journal of the American Geriatrics Society.* Vol. 17, No. 7 (1969). Pp. 668–72.

DISCUSSION OF SELECTED READINGS

The first article in this section is written by Marya Mannes, an outstanding American writer and critic. She discusses her feelings about aging with some interesting personal observations.

Miss Mannes mentions the problems women sometimes have after their children grow up as well as the possible loss of their husbands, either through death or divorce. She suggests that while aging often diminishes female beauty it does not give us a reason to "stop us keeping our bodies as flexible and our tissues as resilient as exercise and air can make them." She points out that swimming has been of great interest to her, as well as walking and short exercise to help her feel better and look better.

In this country we may view older people as being mostly in a taking, dependent position. Miss Mannes comments, " . . . The most enobling distinction of age is to give rather than to take. The capacity to love is timeless, and as in anything, time should increase rather than diminish it." Nurses may wish to discuss this point of view regarding individual older people. While physical strength may decrease as part of the aging process the importance of the older person in sharing wisdom, guidance, and knowledge with younger generations should not be underestimated.

The aging represent a high risk group in terms of disease and mortality. Unfortunately, younger nurses may find it difficult to relate to these patients because they have had little previous experience with grandparents or older friends. Nurses may turn away from this clinical specialty because they see this time of life as the loss of hope and the stage during which death occurs.

Working with older patients, however, can be gratifying for the nurse. Many senior members of our society could participate effectively if their social value and needs were properly recognized. Our rapidly changing society has lagged in services available for our older population. We have no blueprint for easily solving these problems but there is every indication that comprehensive planning is necessary for this large segment of our society.

In the second article, Mary Louise Conti, an instructor in Community Health Nursing, discusses the loneliness of old age. In line with the statistics about aging, we recognize that the older person may outlive his friends and relatives, finally finding himself dependent and alone. The elderly patient often views the hospital as his last stopping point before death occurs.

Mrs. Conti discusses several case examples of the way loneliness affects the life and health of the old person. She concludes, "The integration of generations has much to offer both in information exchange and as a challenge for both the young and the old."

Of Time and the Woman

by Marya Mannes *

I feel very much like one of those figures on top of an operating table in television, surrounded by thirty-six doctors and the chief surgeon telling the interns, "You see before you the body of an aging woman." Well, here it is.

But I still think that what time does to the woman depends less on time than on the woman. What woman? Who is she? For whom do you speak?

That is why this must be largely a subjective account. Not because I consider myself especially significant or especially typical, but because it is the only subject on which I am, of necessity, an authority.

Oh, there are, of course, conditions of mind and heart and body which all of us share when we grow older. We lose our children because they no longer need us. We lose our husbands either through death or choice. We lose physical beauty. We lose most of our options.

Most of us suffer the same kinds of pains and frustration, emotional and physical. And we are now more than ever humiliated by a society so oriented to the young that we are given no place in it. We know that we were born too early and possibly will die too late.

But beyond these common states, each woman responds to time in a different way because she has led a different life. And perhaps I have led a life more different than most.

At the outset, in any case, I must confess that I do not feel old. As my father did, I resent the arbitrary measurements of time (who invented it, anyway?) which is, in effect, one more label by which to put the hapless and helpless

* *Psychosomatics.* Vol. 9, No. 4, Sect. 2 (July–August, 1968). Pp. 8–11.

human into categories regardless of individual difference. Some days I feel sixty and some days I feel thirty-nine, and when, for instance, I open a magazine like Time and see a quote attributed to me followed by the sum of my years, I cry "What has that got to do with it? Whose business is it, anyway?"

To be honest, however, I must attribute this feeling of relative agelessness to luck. I inherited from both my parents a strong and resilient constitution, a passion for ideas and expression, and above all the living example of people dedicated to something outside themselves. They were both professional musicians with a strenuous and fascinating life of their own. Nevertheless they never allowed it to diminish the love and attention bestowed on their two children. My mother was no less a wife and mother because she was also a concert pianist; and I have never since then had any patience for the long-prevalent theory that a woman must choose between home and vocation.

A third piece of luck, beyond inheriting this living example and a healthy body, was that as a little girl I would tell my father all of the things I wanted to do when I grew up. I wanted to be a great actress, a great sculptor, a great writer. He said "You can be anything you want to be. Don't set any limitations on yourself."

How many parents say this to a girl, even now? Instead, how many mothers start to groom their daughters from the age of eight onwards for the marriage market and for a life clearly bounded by what is called "woman's role?" And how many women grow old too soon precisely because of this pre-conditioning, this limitation of ceiling?

For I have been thinking a long time that the single greatest factor in aging is rigidity—the resistance to change and growth in mind as well as in body. Another word for this is habit; the repetition of patterns which throttle the life of human beings; habit in thinking, habit in feeling (which ends in *not* feeling), habit in eating, habit in the daily confrontations of life. This goes for men, of course, as well as women. Thirty years in the same job atrophies a man, just as thirty years in the same house, doing the same tasks, atrophies a woman. I would also add that thirty years with the same man or woman can produce, except in the very rare marriage, the same results. Habit, since it means the end of curiosity, of adventure, of change, is a killer.

The tragedy is that the victim of habit is the victim of a society which imposes these patterns as the majority norm. And it is precisely this kind of social rigidity, this ceiling of limitations, which so many of the young are rejecting. They don't want to die young, either in the long death of social sterility or material goals or in wars which are imposed on them by rigid and outmoded patterns of power. They do not believe in the security of habit or the security of force.

Neither did I, from the age of eighteen onward. I was too fascinated by life to limit myself to one life. The result is that my biography would not make acceptable fare for the Ladies Home Journal or Good Housekeeping. The ladies would cluck at the many errors of judgement made by a woman committed to ideas as well as to love, to work as well as to home, and above all to new experiences in different places. The world was too big for me to restrict myself to any one corner of it.

Reading this, good women would say, with satisfaction and some justice, "Well, that's what comes of having a career." Maybe so. Maybe not. Not all women, any more than all men, function best in the categories allotted to them by virtue of their sex alone.

For myself, the price for freedom, for the integrity of choice, has been high—high in mistakes, high in pain, in insecurity, in torment, in disappointment. But the reward has been growth, another word for life.

Ten years ago, I would have said that the reward was youth, greatly aided and abetted by the biological and surgical advances made by scientific research and implemented by such corporations as the sponsor of this discussion.

But the irony now is this. Just as women have been given the capacity to live longer and look younger than ever before in their later years, this youth and sex-saturated society enshrines the sixteen-year old girl as female incarnate. The goddess is not Ceres, not even Aphrodite. The Goddess is now a teen-ager sprawled across the pages of magazines and the consciousness of millions in a leap of legs, hair and mini-fashions. With sullen lips and false eyelashes she consigns all women over thirty to the ash-heap and all over fifty to the morgue. Never in any age has any age been accorded this overwhelming idolatry, nor has age itself been accorded such contempt.

So what happens now to the woman over thirty, forty, fifty? She wears her skirts shorter than she thinks she should, if she can find the skirt in the first place. It is a fact that anybody over size twelve is the untouchable of the dress industry. She is given no choice between the infinitely dreary concoctions in the so-called Women's Section of the department stores, or the great expense of the private dressmaker. Nobody designs for us, nobody cares: it doesn't pay.

So again, what do we do? The last thing we should do is to compete. We should take enormous pride in being women—women of grace, of experience, of maturity. We should develop a healthy ego; an ego strong enough to applaud the color and dash the young bring into our lives, much of the music they make, and some of the sense. We should understand that much of their rebellion and disgust is justified, much of their torment inevitable. If they won't credit us with any sense, we must not make the same mistake in crediting them with none. The best of them may save this country yet, and we mustn't forget it.

But that doesn't mean that we should, God forbid, want to be their age—or like them. For one thing, we can't be and for another, who would want to be?

The only thing we ask is equality. As older men and women we ask only this: that we be judged not according to our years but according to our individual human worth. The fact of youth deserves no more respect than the fact of age, and there are just as many stupid and evil as intelligent and good in both generations.

To keep inwardly young, therefore, one must be secure in one's age, not in the sense of superiority, but, again, in the sense of equality.

This is, I admit, not easy to do. And here again, I am among the fortunate. As a woman living only the life of a woman, age could mean to me the end of many things: the end of active motherhood, the end of physical passion and reciprocal desire, and the choice between loneliness or a shared life that is little more than a repetition, however agreeable, of small habits.

But because I have also worked, as well as lived the life of a woman, the future still beckons. I am pulled along by the urge to write and to write better; to understand more, to encompass more, to express more clearly, this world we inhabit. I am lucky in that I still seem to have a market for what I write, although I am clearly and sometimes painfully aware that to an editor's ear the term "new talent" is automatically more desirable than the term, which is never used, "old talent." The two words are presumably incompatible.

Beyond this sad note, however, my work leaves me less time for the loneliness that is, inevitably, the common lot of age. For it opens doors to people and places and actions which are purely domestic, person-oriented life would never provide. I have never said or thought all women should have a life outside their home. But I will say that the woman who has never had a life outside her home has the most to fear from age. Perhaps that is why I fear it less. I am continually exhilarated by the prospect (if not always the fact) of new encounters, human as well as professional, of new assignments, of new environments.

Yet as time goes on, these can be very taxing, too, to a professional person. Because of this I have tried to devise certain measures of self-preservation which I have found essential.

At all times of my life I have always needed at least three or four hours a day alone—by choice. For a woman this is often difficult if not impossible to achieve—yet it is impossible to think, to breathe, to grow without this—let alone work. It is the only way towards an inward balance carved, very often, out of agonized doubt. Ideally, this balance should be the crown of age, the purpose of wisdom. It is also the companion of grace and dignity, a much ignored essential of life, especially in contemporary society. In truth, the three dirty words in our vocabulary now are grace, discipline, and dignity without which no civilization is worth saving, no life worth living.

A second essential to preservation is to jettison the irrelevant. A mind continually worried with small things, such as clothes, furniture, social involvements and above all, being "With It," destroys itself through fragmentation. Fussiness is an aging process. So is preoccupation with material possessions. The mind and body must be kept free for new sensations, open to change. More colloquially, you have to roll with the punches.

As for the body, it should be treated with the greatest respect, not by being afraid of using it but by using it as much as possible. Few of us, and certainly I am not one, can afford in money or time the kind of extensive care that famous actresses and society beauties indulge in to keep themselves young. But there is nothing to stop us from keeping our bodies as flexible and our tissues as resilient as exercise and air can make them. Swimming happens to be my passion and salvation, but since that is hard to come by in winter and in a city, I depend on a great deal of walking and one daily, very short, regime of exercises which leaves me limber and free from that stiffness and rigidity which are, as I have said, the mental as well as the physical harbingers of age. (Unfortunately, I can't give you a demonstration of these exercises since one of them closely resembles the routine of a strip-teaser!)

As for face and skin and general metabolism, the doctors and the cosmeticians are very much on our side, and we should use whatever they choose to give us. The only limit I would put upon their aid is simply this: beyond a certain point you can't fool anybody, nor should you want to. The woman who seems to be thirty-five but whom I know to be sixty is, to me, disquieting. A life should leave its traces, and the total lack of them is a negation of experience.

Finally, and by far the most important, the ennobling distinction of age is to give rather than to take. The capacity to love is timeless, and if anything, time should increase it rather than diminish it.

When you are young and expect to receive, you think it is your divine right. But the older you grow you learn that you get very little if you give very little.

As one who has always loved men, well if not too wisely, I have long been aware that the cards are stacked in our sociey, and particularly at this time, against the older woman. Men of sixty and even seventy find themselves much younger women to love and marry, but the opposite is clearly not the case.

I think I can speak for all women when I say that this is the hardest thing we have to bear in later life: the end of desirability as a woman—desirability, not capacity. This can happen as well in a long marriage as in a single state: the result of widowhood, divorce, or rejection by a particular man. And here the vicious circle begins. The feeling of undesirability actually produces it. if you no longer feel attractive you cannot attract. The aura of negation and indifference surrounds you and repels others. This is the time when so many women cease to hold themselves straight, to walk with grace, to emanate a sense of pleasure.

Other things begin to happen too, and I am sure the doctors in this audience must be aware of it. For it goes beyond the effects of menopause, now, thanks to them, so greatly relieved. The psychosomatic effects of sexual rejection, of the loss of love, can include a wide range of ailments from loss of teeth to the distortion of feet; from muscle spasms to tachycardia; from aches to pains of a wide variety. Some, of course, may be symptoms of far deeper trouble. But it has been my observation of others, as well as of myself, that many of them stem from the specific anguish of sexual neutralization, from the sudden withdrawal of the power and joy that has until now sustained them.

I would like to be a little more specific about this progressive aging of women by throwing out some observations which are purely speculative and, since I am not a doctor, clearly none of my business. Yet decades ago I could not help but see psychosomatic bases for so many afflictions that used to be considered purely physical. And when I spoke, as I just have, of stiffness in older women so frighteningly prevalent in the way they walk and sit and stand, I remain convinced that whether it is called arthritis or rheumatism it is the result of emotional resistance. They are actually set in their ways, stuck in their tracks, imprisoned in their mental and emotional rigidity. And the basis of this is fear: fear of loss, fear of change, fear of the dreadful inhumanity and insecurity accorded age now.

It is fear, too, that contracts the muscles of the feet and hands, so that the toes are distorted and the fingers misshapen.

It is resignation, the mark of defeat, that bows the back and raises the hump on the back of the neck.

As for cancer, still basically a mystery, I cannot help but feel that since it is a form of inverted life, of growth turned inward instead of outward, part of its origin in man or woman may lie in long term frustration of the creative impulse. More simply, what eats away the body is the denial of the dream. The life of the cancer victim may have been outwardly successful; inwardly it may have been stillborn.

But these, I know, are the speculations of an amateur, and I should return to time and the woman, and the loss of those functions that used to sustain us, the loss of those social forms that used to give us meaning and usefulness in the family structure.

Only in one area have we come out ahead. Largely thanks to hormone therapy, as I said, we remain female for a much longer span than before, endowed with the confidence and vitality which this implies. The irony here, again, is that the chances of literally enjoying our biological youth are slim. It is the rare man, young or old, who prefers the older to the younger woman, and we cannot delude ourselves otherwise.

Yet this by no means precludes the exchange of affection and mutual need without the bonds that so often constrict both. As one grows older, love must go wider rather than deeper. It must embrace friends as well as lovers, strangers as well as acquaintances, young as well as old. It must be, in essence, a love of life itself.

The transmutation here is from specific passion to general compassion. Compassion has no age. It is the immortal bond between time and man, time and the woman. It is the healing agent of humanity.

In these later years, the more we are able to feel and do for others in this world of torment and division, the less can we pity ourselves for the loss of youth.

Our time has not gone. Indeed, our time may have come.

The Loneliness of Old Age
by Mary Louise Conti, R.N., M.S.*

Loneliness and isolation sometimes form a vicious cycle in the life of the elderly, especially those living in large cities. Often it is difficult for the old person to admit his loneliness and ask for help from others. When companionship is offered, it may be rejected because the person doesn't know how to accept it. It takes the patience of a warm, friendly person to break the cycle and relieve in small ways the vast loneliness some of our elderly population feel.

In my work as a visiting nurse in San Francisco and later while trying to recruit the elderly to a Senior Citizen group during my clinical experience in the masters program, I encountered many examples and expressions of such loneliness. I found it difficult to be indifferent; yet I knew I could not be all things to these people. Avoiding them would compound their problems, but I knew that the constant frustration I felt at never being able to ease their loneliness might eventually cause me to avoid them altogether. Rather than shun the people who most needed care and attention, I decided to visit individuals and try to resolve their loneliness in small ways. The recognition of a person's needs seemed to be important in understanding the reasons for loneliness.

Why are old people lonely? Is loneliness to be expected with advanced age? As a person grows old, his circle of friends and family grows smaller with their death and as he himself loses mobility. This physical slowing down prevents easy replacement of friends. Eccentricities frequently found among the old, especially those living alone, also hamper the making of new friends. Keeping the family home often becomes impractical, and an elderly person or couple living on social security may have to move to an apartment in another part of town, away from familiar neighbors. Or urban redevelopment may force elderly residents to be relocated into low income housing. The new environment is not always easy to adjust to, without the familiar paper boy, druggist, and others who serve the community.

It is even more difficult to make new acquaintances when one has a hearing loss or visual impairment. The elderly person is more likely to withdraw when there is a decline in perceptual abilities. The new neighbors, too, feel frustrated when they try to communicate with "that deaf old lady." When urban redevol-

* *Nursing Outlook,* Vol. 18, No. 8 (August, 1970). Pp. 28-30.

opment housing contains a high proportion of elderly and infirm residents, there is a tendency toward depersonalization. References can be heard about "Gramps" in room 212 of the hotel or the "LOL" (Little Old Lady) in the lobby.

Difficult to Admit Loneliness

Many of the people I visited initially denied their loneliness. One such person was Mrs. M, who had moved to a downtown residential hotel after the death of her husband two years before. Mrs. M told me she had not been severely depressed after his death, as had many of her friends when their husbands died. She said her family and friends had kept her busy packing up the household furnishings and selling the home. She kept only the furniture suitable for a one-room hotel residence. Now she remained busy by attending Senior Citizen meetings at various church and social organizations about the city.

I saw Mrs. M on a regular basis as she had many questions about her health. She did not have "enough time," she said, to visit her doctor regularly. I felt that Mrs. M was looking for someone to talk to, and I readily agreed to see her. I had been visiting her for about two months when she first confessed to me how lonely she really felt. She cried for a long time and expressed many feelings that she had not been able to tell before. She had been very close to her husband, and her family had feared she would be severely depressed following his death. They had planned her activities for almost a year, and during the past year had checked regularly to make certain she continued them. She had not been able to sit and talk to them about her feelings since her husband's death. On later visits we discussed her feelings and fears.

Four months after our first visit, she was attending only one organized group activity a week and spending many enjoyable hours crocheting for her family. She explained to them that she enjoyed spending some of her time alone. I felt Mrs. M had been maintaining her feverish activity out of fear of loneliness and isolation. She had never been allowed to express the deep feelings she had and, in fact, had been afraid to do so. She told me of a close friend who had talked incessantly of her deceased husband. She was unable to adjust to solitary living, and was eventually placed in a nursing home, where she soon died. Mrs. M had dreaded the same thing occurring to her. When she was able to discuss with me that being alone at times was certainly acceptable, she gained the courage to approach her family with her own needs.

Some Adjust to Solitude

Not all old people need activity to avoid being lonely. Some people are quite well adjusted to solitude and are able to best enjoy themselves at those times. In a pamphlet entitled "Loneliness," by the National Council of Social Services in Great Britain, a story is told about an elderly woman living alone. She responded to an appeal for a donation to the National Old Peoples' Welfare Council, which made reference to another elderly woman who had died in London leaving behind a diary in which she had written on each day of the previous year, "No one came." The elderly lady responding presented her own point of view by writing, "From another old lady who writes in her diary: No one came—thank goodness!" [1]

Living alone does frequently encourage eccentricities that are sometimes unacceptable in our society and that can start a vicious cycle; for eccentricities keep people away, and isolation causes further eccentricities. An elderly man whom I visited weekly had been a widower for ten years. His doctor at a VA clinic had referred him to the nursing service and requested an assessment of Mr. H's home condition; for though he appeared for his clinic appointments regularly, he always wore ragged clothing and was frequently dirty. When I called on Mr. H to assess his living condition, he was friendly and seemed happy to have a visitor. I was somewhat taken aback at the appearance of his home. It resembled a large storage closet for electrical appliances, newspapers, and pieces of junk. His clothing could only be considered rags. His trousers were held up by a rope used as suspenders. He seemed unaware of the clutter and enjoyed relating tales of past experiences.

I made a telephone call to his relatives in town, which revealed they had been unable to make Mr. H conform and so had "washed their hands" of him. Mr. H's diet consisted mainly of toast soaked in milk and laced with a little whiskey. He said, "I've never enjoyed eating alone, and it's really too much trouble to cook for myself anyway." He readily accepted the help of a homemaker to help clean his home and prepare his meals. She was able to sit with him during mealtime, which he appreciated. After a trusting relationship developed between the two, he allowed some of his "precious articles" to be discarded. We were able to convince him that some things were unsafe and that modification would be necessary. For example, his habit in using the fireplace was to place the end of a board the length of the living room in the fireplace, ignite it, and simply push it farther into the fireplace as it burned while he remained in his chair.

He was receptive to our suggestions and followed them as long as we continued to visit. I eventually referred him to a Senior Citizen group in the neighborhood and he began to attend regularly, and he made new friends there. He began to take pride in his physical appearance and consented to wear some of his new clothing that he had been "saving." His family eventually began to accept him. Mr. H did not express loneliness; he had adapted to the isolation

---

[1] Cyril H. Powell. *The Lonely Heart.* New York: Abingdon Press, 1961. P. 19.

that had been imposed upon him. In this case the adaptation was not always safe. Lonely people like Mr. H frequently need to know they are still valued as human beings and accepted. Again, it took someone with an interest and much patience; the transition frequently takes a considerable amount of time.

Illnesses Exaggerated

Being isolated and lonely can cause an exaggeration of physical ills. The lonely elderly person expects to have some stiff joints or other aches and pains, but when there is no diversion they seem to become his only frame of reference. Sometimes one dreads to say, "How are you?" for it means hour after hour of complaints. This in turn increases the isolation as neighbors or friends avoid conversation. Such a situation could be extremely frustrating, but I found that being a patient listener and allowing the person to speak freely was beneficial. With time, I attempted to interject other topics of conversation and find out what interests the person had. If an interest can be developed, it will frequently help in removing many of the imaginary ills, or at least modify the existing ones.

The inability to communicate freely for the hard-of-hearing person is another cause of loneliness in the aged. They tire easily because they must listen carefully for every word, and many find it embarrassing to ask for constant repetition.

I met Mrs. S, an elderly resident of a mid-city hotel in San Francisco, while assessing the level of health of the tenants of the hotel. She had had a hearing impediment for 20 years. She was somewhat withdrawn and reluctant to talk, and she explained that she had a hearing loss and that I would have to speak loudly. We talked for a short time. I felt she would tire easily as she concentrated to understand me, and I discovered that speaking at loud volume tired me too. At the close of our conversation I was surprised that she warmly invited me to return.

From further visits I learned that she had isolated herself because she was reluctant to attempt conversation in her new environment. She had been a successful interior decorator, but after her husband's prolonged illness and eventual death, her money had been depleted, and she moved to a cheap apartment in the downtown area. She seemed to enjoy companionship and conversation if I spoke slowly. She told me of being very lonely at times and explained that before her retirement her life had been very active and productive. I suggested that she might enjoy attending the lip-reading class at the Senior Citizen center. She declined at first, saying, "I don't think they could really help me." But after a month of weekly conversations and with my encouragement, she attended the class. The group was informal and welcomed her readily, and it was not long before she began to take part in other activities at the senior center. She now actively participates in the painting class and occasionally serves on the noon soup committee. Mrs. S was able to find a way out of her loneliness by renewing her self-confidence through personal communications with others.

Language and Culture Differences

Loneliness caused by inability to communicate is also sometimes felt by new immigrants to this country. In large cities they are able to live in their own groups and maintain their own culture and language; but urban redevelopment or housing projects may cause the elderly immigrant to be isolated socially in a "foreign group" of people. Language is a frequent barrier and reminiscing is met with blank stares. Mrs. B, who immigrated from Russia to the United States when she was 30, had lived among others of her culture until her financial condition and the loss of her friends to care for her caused her to be moved to a housing project in downtown San Francisco.

Conversations with Mrs. B centered on the well-educated and cultural family and friends she had had. She did not have much tolerance for the "people who live here." She was "self-isolated" in this residential hotel—she rejected these "non-Russians" and consequently they rejected her. Mrs. B had refused several women sent to her by her social worker to assist her in the care of her room and meal preparation, with the complaints that, "They don't clean like I want it done. They are too sloppy," or "I can't eat my food that way." She had been labeled as "noncooperative and difficult."

Her accent was thick and her speech came rapidly. I interpreted her conversational overloading to be a sign of loneliness and a need to talk with someone. I spent long periods with her reminiscing about Russia, and she would maneuver in many ways to keep me from leaving. She would say, "My finger is swollen. Should I see the doctor?" or "Won't you have a cup of coffee?" I was able to control this problem with Mrs. B by telling her at the beginning of each visit how long I would remain and each time emphasizing the fact that I would return. We discussed some current events to help her relate to the present. Her conversations became less concentrated on her past, and she seemed anxious during each visit to tell me of recent events. Mrs. B is still lonely, but I hope she will one day be able to join a group of Senior Citizens and "accept them."

Loneliness can be caused by not knowing the environment and the fear of interacting with it, by isolation, as in the cases of Mrs. S and Mrs. B. Loneliness can also be unidentified, neither easy to understand or assuage. Examples of such lonely people are those who out of desperation resort to suicide. The elderly have many role losses. Children grow up and leave. There are deaths of those near to them. Retirement. Even the loss of well-loved pets. Many are isolated from family and friends by decreased mobility and moves to new environments. They need to feel valuable as human beings with something to contribute. And

I have found they do have something to contribute. The elderly person needs to exist for somebody and for something, and he wants his achievement to be accepted and acknowledged.

The old person living alone is sometimes afraid to admit loneliness or depression for fear of being sent to a nursing home, or worse, a mental institution. Sometimes it takes a long time for a person to reveal his feelings, even to a patient listener. Understanding the individual is an important aspect of helping diminish loneliness. Some people are happy and well-adjusted in solitude. A warm, receptive, understanding listener needs to assess the person and also determine whether he needs a one-to-one relationship or group interaction.

Inclusion in a group, I have found, is certainly not the answer to everyone's loneliness. Frequently making a person feel of value to others can be achieved only on a one-to-one basis. When the lonely individual begins to have a renewed interest in himself and his environment, he may be able to attempt involvement in an activity or interest group.

Old People Respond to Youth

Elderly people are very much interested in today's youth. They enjoy having a young person around to listen to their reminiscing and to discuss the events of the world. This was made evident to me when an elderly man who regularly attended the Senior Citizen group took me aside one day and said, "I really enjoy this group, but everyone here is old and we all have the same complaints. I have talked to some of the others and we would like to meet some young people. Since you are going to school, do you think you might be able to arrange a box lunch picnic with young people from the school and the Senior Citizens?" The influence of youth can sometimes make the elderly individual forget his loneliness and "oldness" too. The integration of generations has much to offer both in information exchange and as a challenge for both the young and the old.

chapter ten

DEATH, GRIEF, AND MOURNING

Death is sometimes the companion of nurses and physicians, and the nurse must know, both for her own sake and for the welfare of her patients and their families, how to function effectively in its presence. The nurse is sometimes placed under intense pressure as she attempts to focus on the patient who is dying and those who grieve for him, but although she must learn to accept death, she must also acknowledge that it should never be treated as commonplace.

In the past, death, as well as birth, was part of life within a home, but now hospitalization has changed all phases of human life. A person is born in a hospital and usually dies in one. Many critically ill persons are moved to a hospital, rather than remaining at home, to avoid the onus of a death in the family. Taken out of his familiar environment, the patient becomes dependent upon the hospital staff as well as his family for psychological support.

The nurse faces many additional responsibilities when her patient is dying. It is easy to forget the complexity of events as she tries to cope with the patient's critical condition, the responses of his relatives, and her own feelings. Observing the approach of death can cause even the most highly trained person deep distress and feelings of inadequacy. Effective performance in nursing care is usually oriented toward the patient's progress and health, but the dying patient makes nursing practice a very different matter. It is for this reason that nursing educators have begun to share this important responsibility and to provide better preparation of students for this part of their professional accountability.

Although research regarding death has greatly increased since Herman Feifel's book, *The Meaning of Death*, was written in 1959, and studies of death appear with much greater frequency in medical and social literature, society at large still restricts its emphasis to numbers and masses rather than the individual.[1] It is a truism that the more advancements we make in science, the greater we seem to fear and deny the reality of death.

This change of focus away from the individual follows such historic events as the bombing of Hiroshima and the mass murders of World War II. Numbed by the enormousness of the destruction of large numbers of individuals, we find ourselves accepting with relative calm the subsequent wars and riots, and the dying patient in a hospital too often fails to receive individual concern. As Kübler-Ross says:

> He may cry for rest, peace, and dignity, but he will get infusions, transfusions, a heart machine, or tracheotomy if necessary. He may want one single person to stop for one single minute so that he can ask one single question—but he will get a dozen people around the clock, all busily preoccupied with his heart rate, pulse, electrocardiogram or pulmonary function, his secretions or excretions, but not him as a human being.[2]

An important responsibility of both the nurse and physician is to mitigate and alter this mass-oriented response. The nurse as well as the physician should have an intelligent awareness of the problems of dying patients and should develop competence in dealing with them. She will, in her awareness, know that both her attitude toward death and that of the patient are influenced by many factors. Religion, culture, and education all greatly affect views on illness and health as well as on life and death.

The care of dying patients can be one of the most difficult and least gratifying tasks nurses have. Quint writes:

> The death of a patient is in conflict with the primary life-saving goals of the hospital. The responsibilities and decisions required of the nurse when the patient is dying are often difficult and tension-producing. The rules guiding her actions are not always clear-cut and simple. Rather, the choices available are determined by complex and sometimes conflicting pressures from many sources —the patient, the medical staff, the family, the hospital, and other nurses. These pressures on the nurse are not unique to assignments in which patients are dying, but they assume a special potency whenever primary occupational goals are threatened. . . .
>
> Whether he is recovering or dying, the hospitalized patient needs to be fed,

---

[1] Herman Feifel, ed. *The Meaning of Death.* New York: McGraw-Hill Book Company, 1959. Pp. 131–57.

[2] Elisabeth Kübler-Ross. *On Death and Dying.* New York: The Macmillan Company, 1970. P. 9.

bathed, and helped with many personal matters. He may require drugs and special treatments. He may be unable to do much for himself. The nurse's attitude toward performing these tasks for any given patient is greatly influenced by her perception of his future. In general, dying patients do not provide the same satisfactions as do patients who recover. The exceptions are those patients who come close to death and then are saved.[3]

Communicating with the Dying Patient

Eleanor Drummond writes:

It is agreed that the major responsibility of telling the patient he is dying belongs to the physician. The nurse must assume the responsibility of learning from the physician what he has said to the patient, and as much as possible, the patient's reaction to what was said. It is not easy for the physician to discuss death with the patient. The success of this communication is dependent on the type of relationship that exists between the patient and his physician. The nurse can help the physician in meeting his responsibility by encouragement and support at this time.[4]

Communicating with the dying patient and his family is not limited to words: the nurse's presence is frequently essential to both. Drummond notes:

The most important activity for the nurse is to simply be there. Reaching out with a hand can be the most important act of the nurse for the patient. It tells the patient, "I am here—you are not alone. I understand. I want to give you comfort." . . . If the pressures of our duties make it impossible for us to spend any amount of time in a block with the dying patient, then the nurse will be supportive of the patient by frequently looking into the room. The frequency is important, especially when it is not connected with the answering of the call light. By taking the initiative . . . the nurse is telling the patient she is there, she is concerned, and she is available.[5]

Impending Death

FATAL MALIGNANCIES

If a doctor speaks freely about a diagnosis of malignancy without equating it with impending death, he will do the patient a great service. He should

---

[3] Jeanne Quint. "The Dying Patient: A Difficult Nursing Problem." *Nursing Clinics of North America.* December, 1967. P. 73.
[4] Eleanor Drummond. "Communication and Comfort for the Dying Patient." *Nursing Clinics of North America.* March, 1970. P. 58.
[5] *Ibid.* Pp. 57–58.

leave the door open for new drugs, for treatment, and for new techniques and research. He should make it clear to the patient that all is not lost, that he is not giving up because of the diagnosis, that they are going to fight a battle together—the patient, his family, and the doctor—no matter what the result is. A patient approached in this manner will be less likely to fear isolation, deceit, and rejection, and will continue to have confidence in his physician.

The need for the physician to be straightforward with the patient is frequently discussed. Kübler-Ross notes that when a patient comes in with a lump in her breast, the considerate doctor will tell her about the possible malignancy and that a biopsy will clarify the situation. He will also tell her that if a malignancy is found, more extensive surgery may be required, so that she may have time to prepare herself if necessary.[6]

Nurses feel justifiable anger at a physician who does not properly prepare his patients for extensive surgery. In one instance, a patient was not clearly told that she might need a radical mastectomy if the biopsy showed a malignancy. The patient awakened after surgery extremely angry and distrustful of everyone. She especially blamed the nurse, saying, "Why didn't you tell me I might need this done? You knew and you refused to tell me." The patient's husband and her physician felt it best not to inform her regarding all the consequences that might follow a biopsy. The nurse was caught between the wishes of the doctor and the family and her natural desire to be honest with the patient.

OTHER FATAL ILLNESSES

When a patient is confronted truthfully regarding a serious illness, he may ask, "How much time do I have?" Kübler-Ross, with her extensive experience, suggests that it is the worst possible management of any patient to give him a time schedule on death, since such information is often wrong and exceptions in both directions frequently occur.[7] An example is a patient who developed severe diabetes in the early 1920s. This patient was given six months to live, but with the discovery of insulin, is still alive more than forty years later. Many factors influence the course of disease. The very ill patient needs the reassurance that everything possible will be done, that he will not be ignored, that treatments are available, and that there is always a glimmer of hope.

Sometimes the impact of painful information cannot be wholly accepted at the moment. Patients need to be told in a more intimate surrounding than the distracting hallway of a crowded clinic.

[6] Kübler-Ross. *On Death and Dying.* P. 26.
[7] *Ibid.* P. 26.

Almost every dying patient has some negative feelings toward his doctor, relatives, friends, and nurses. These negative feelings result in part from the anger and resentment he feels toward impending death. A nurse may see a patient near death still blame the doctor for an unavoidable mutilation from an operation. The woman who has had a radical mastectomy may feel intense anger at the surgeon for her disfigurement, despite its life-saving purpose. Both the doctor and nurse may suffer from the patient's projection of fears or his attribution to them of traits that he hated in his own parents. The regression so often present in illness means that the nurse or doctor may be transformed in a patient's mind to a figure, usually parental, that was invested with much emotion in his past.

Conversely, dying patients sometimes provoke negative attitudes in the nurse and the doctor. The dying patient not only is anxious himself, but can provoke anxiety in others.[8]

Support and Awareness: The Nurse's Role with Dying Patients

Because, unlike some other societies, ours does not simply leave the aged, the sick, and the infirm alone to die, the number of our aged is increasing, as is the number of people with malignancies and chronic diseases associated with old age. The nurse, therefore, has a greater proportion of her patients in the later stages of their lives, and must understand their needs and concerns. Much of their ability to carry out the terminal phase of life with dignity hinges on an empathetic and nonrejecting response from their environment. The nurse should be aware of the therapeutic aspects of memory and the helpfulness of the patient's reviewing of his life. Older patients, especially, like to talk about the past and enjoy discussing highlights of their experiences.

The nurse should not overlook the fact that a dying patient may also be grieving. Many people fall ill following a serious loss, and sometimes attention is directed toward the more obvious illness at the cost of failing to recognize the signs of grief. Such loss may be a part or a function of the body, for grief and mourning can follow a serious illness, an amputation, or loss of vision as well as the loss of a loved one.

This "awareness" of the nurse must include all participants in the events surrounding a death. She must recognize and respect a mother's need to minister to her dying child, yet sensitively perceive when she needs to be

---

[8] Janice Norton. "Treatment of a Dying Patient." In *Death Interpretations*, ed. Hendrik M. Ruitenbeek. New York: Dell Publishing Co., Inc., 1969. Pp. 19–38.

relieved, knowing, as we discussed earlier, that many mothers do best if they are involved in helping to care for their dying children. Studies have shown that they have less guilt to work through than mothers who are separated from their children at this critical time.

Regression plays an important part in the dying patient's adjustment and often affects one or more of the emotional stages he moves through. He often longs for protection and the security of infancy; he may express the wish to visit his childhood home. Close ties with the physician and friends are often strengthened in the final stages, particularly if they have been important earlier.

The fear of death is a common human experience, mainly because of death's mystery, but for other reasons as well. Impending death threatens one with abandonment, isolation, and loneliness, and the dying person often feels greatly the loss of familiar relationships. Levin, in the book *Psychodynamic Studies on Aging, Creativity, Reminiscing, and Dying,* notes that the fear of dying can be quite different from the dread of being dead.[9] Dying represents the ultimate, inevitable impairment of ego functions and the deprivation of human relationships.

Dying can be made easier for the patient by the provision of sufficient medication to relieve pain, and by the dignified ministrations of those people who tend him during the last stages of his life. Levin feels that the fear of dying is more pronounced among the relatively well than those who are critically ill, and he feels that ill patients are more concerned about the severance of relationships and the indignity of dependence than about survival for its own sake.[10]

When life is terminated at an early age, both the dying patient and those affected by the death are understandably more shaken than they would be if death came late in life. The death of a child is one of the most traumatic experiences possible for either parent or nurse. Death in the middle years is also difficult, because the person and his relatives may suffer from the feeling that he has failed to achieve cherished objectives. The elderly person seems best able to come to terms with death, perhaps because the physical ending of life correlates more closely in old age with diminished psychological functioning.

The dying person has a right to relief of somatic and psychological pain, but to avoid unnecessarily heavy sedation, he should be helped to use his own psychological resources. The nurse should also help the patient to fulfill his final wishes in the time remaining.

---

[9] Sidney Levin and Ralph Kahana. *Psychodynamic Studies on Aging, Creativity, Reminiscing, and Dying.* New York: International Universities Press, Inc., 1967.
[10] *Ibid.*

The Impact of Death on the Family

SOCIAL DEATH

Richard Kalish has discussed phenomenon of the acceptance of an individual's death by relatives before the biological event occurs. He uses the term "social death" to describe this condition, and writes:

> When is a person "dead"? When is he dead "for you"? . . . The subjectively perceived death of a person does not necessarily coincide with his biological death but may precede or antedate the latter.
> Social death occurs when an individual is thought of as dead and treated as dead, although he remains medically and legally alive. Any given person may be socially dead to one individual, to many individuals, or to virtually everyone, and perhaps to himself as well. . . .
> Social death can occur . . . at the time a person enters a nursing home or hospital, . . . at the time [of] a terminal diagnosis ("My mother died for me at the moment I heard the diagnosis—I didn't even shed a tear when she finally expired"). . . .
> Establishing a person as socially dead enables the survivors to attend to other matters with a minimum of interference and a reduction in affective involvement. . . . Family members may settle the "dead" person's affairs, give away his belongings, talk of him in hushed tones, refuse to "speak ill" of him, and think in terms of how they will take care of his body and spend his bequest. . . . If the biological death does not occur as anticipated, the family may become impatient . . . but other families can exist with these conditions for months or, I suspect, years.
> . . . It does not seem an exaggeration to state that social death may speed or even precipitate biological death.[11]

PREPARATION OF THE FAMILY

The news of death or of impending death is best communicated to a group in a private setting where the family can behave naturally. It is frequently emphasized that it is not only *what* we have to tell a family, but *how* we tell them that greatly influences how they can accept bad news. Unfortunately, in emergencies the nurse may not have time to prepare the family for news of a sudden death. Such a situation occurred in an emergency room of a hospital, where a man was brought in by a coronary care unit spon-

---

[11] Richard A. Kalish. Adapted from a presentation at a symposium. Death as a Research Problem in Social Gerontology, November 12, 1965, at the 18th annual meeting of the Gerontological Society, Los Angeles, Calif.

sored by the local fire department. The man died within moments, and it was necessary to tell his waiting wife. The shock for the nurse was great, since the patient was an apparently healthy 50-year-old who had never been ill before. Coming into the emergency room where the wife waited with other family members as well as others who were waiting to be treated, the nurse quietly walked over to Mrs. Jones and said, "I'm terribly sorry, Mrs. Jones, but your husband has just died." Mrs. Jones, already overwrought with the shock of her husband's sudden illness, screamed. The nurse was embarrassed, surprised, and upset. The survivors also felt humiliated that they were not better able to control their emotions under these extreme circumstances.

Proper preparation of the relatives by the nurse would have included the provision of a quiet place, away from others in the emergency room. When a death is expected, of course, it is much easier for the staff to prepare itself and the family for the information. The burden of emergency room work, which by definition calls for immediate response in the nurse and the physician, places the nurse in a doubly difficult role, as she must be responsible to both the dying patient and his family.

Nurses understandably avoid recognizing this task, for preparation of a family for an inevitable death is difficult. When the family is staying with the dying patient, it is helpful for the nurse to stop in intermittently and lend her presence and support. Sometimes her suggestion that they come outside and sit down for a few minutes, or offering them a cup of coffee, or just her brief presence gives the family the courage they need to stay with a patient during the last moments of life.

It is the wish of close relatives to stay until death occurs, for they are often reluctant to desert a loved one. Grinker and Spiegel note in *Men Under Stress* that this desire is shown in the extreme in combat, where men will stay with their fellow soldiers and will go down in a plane when it is not possible to save one of the crewmen.[12] The relinquishment of a loved one to death is one of the most difficult of all experiences, and it is the staff's responsibility to make the situation as bearable as possible.

The nurse may occasionally be aware that death is bringing a kind of relief to a family, particularly following a long, painful illness. If the family has mixed feelings regarding the death of a loved one, it is sometimes necessary for the survivors to discuss the negative feelings aroused by the long periods of stress with someone who can accept them.

The terminally ill patient cannot be helped in a meaningful way if his family is not included; their reactions contribute much to the patient's response to his illness. The loneliness anticipated by a person facing impending death often precipitates resentment; the inconvenience of doing without an important member can make the family angry in the awkwardness of dis-

[12] Roy Grinker and John Spiegel. *Men Under Stress.* Philadelphia: The Blakiston Co., 1945.

cussing the seriousness of an illness. The dying patient's problems come to an end; the family's problems go on. The tendency, unfortunately, is for the family to hide its feelings from the patient, to keep a smiling face and pretend cheerfulness. There often develops an ironic game of mutual deception.

If the dying patient can bear up well under some of his own grief and show by his example how one can die peacefully, they will remember his strength and bear their own sorrow with more dignity.

The good physician forms a therapeutic alliance with the dying person as well as with his survivors. The nurse can assist by understanding a range of customs and social values of the culture and of various religious beliefs. The more she knows about the religion of the patient and his family, the better she is prepared to contact ministers, rabbis, or priests when the family or patient wishes this to be done. The lack of religious beliefs should also be respected. If she is not up to this difficult task, she should recognize that fact honestly, accept it, and enlist the aid of someone else.

Nurses should anticipate that some survivors will behave in a very intense and disturbing manner at the time of death. Shock and disbelief are frequent first responses. Working with survivors requires tact, patience, and sympathy. Relatives should be allowed, even encouraged, to cry if they wish to do so. It is extremely important to give them time to regain their composure in a private place.

The nurse should not be surprised when confronted with angry, bitter, or accusatory relatives. She should keep in mind that, first of all, certain complaints can be justified. Increased sensitivity is one of the more prevalent reactions during periods of stress; little things bother seriously ill patients, and details often annoy the family of a dying patient.

Relatives may be attempting to come to terms with their own aggressive feelings and guilt. The nurse should try to concentrate her efforts on the provision of the best possible care to the dying person, and should avoid becoming involved in any disputes with relatives. It is not unusual for relatives to be in disagreement during the acute stressful period of staying with a dying patient.

The nurse should recognize that complaints of relatives are usually not directed to her as a person, but may serve to keep the complainants from falling apart psychologically. It is easier to blame someone else for one's own inadequacies. The helpless feelings relatives experience at the time of death are sometimes projected to the nurse and doctor.

The group support of the hospital staff in these situations is extremely important to the nurse who has to be with the family of a dying patient. Requests to see or to take leave of a dead or dying person should not be denied. Other people wish to remember a person alive and well, and avoid the hospital except to sign the necessary forms.

George L. Engel, in his article in the *American Journal of Nursing* on "Grief and Grieving," reminds us that we protect ourselves from death by developing a shell, assuming that if it does occur, it is not our concern. But it is too callous for a doctor or a nurse to deny the significance of death to the patient or its problems for the relatives.[13]

One of the most frequent responses of survivors on learning of death is, "It can't be." It is particularly difficult for the survivors to carry on as if nothing has happened, and news of death stuns many people into immobility. The nurse should be prepared for this response, and should allow time for relatives to be alone or, if they wish, to stay with them during this despairingly difficult state. Engel notes that this phase may last from a few minutes to hours, or even days, alternating "with flashes of despair and anguish." [14]

Sometimes a nurse will observe that relatives respond intellectually to the information they have been given and will not show immediate shock. In general, however, all responses are an attempt to deal with the overwhelming, intense emotions caused by news of death. The social and psychological functioning of a human being is based upon close personal ties, and when a human love object is lost, the relatives are faced with the psychological strain of trying to cope with and continue the demands of living.

Following a relative's death, the family often mentions somatic distress: tightness in the throat with shortness of breath and need for sighing, an empty feeling in the abdomen, lack of muscular power, weakness, and intense subjective distress. With the depression that comes in grief and mourning, the environment may seem frustrating and empty; a wish not to go on is common. This may be punctuated with feelings of anger toward persons or circumstances the relatives feel are responsible for the death. The family may blame the doctor, feeling that he didn't do enough or that he made a mistake.

Occasionally, survivors show aggression against themselves, beating the breast or pounding the head as an expression of the great anguish and despair. There are obvious cultural differences in the appropriateness of any response. In certain cultures, crying and loss of control are completely acceptable. Crying, either by the nurse herself or by the bereaved, is one of the most usual responses to death. Engel says:

> Some cultures demand loud and public lamentations, where others expect restraint. Familiarity with such cultural patterns is necessary in evaluating the appropriateness of the grief response.[15]

---

[13] George L. Engel. "Grief and Grieving." *American Journal of Nursing.* Vol. 64, No. 9 (September, 1964). P. 95. Also reproduced in this volume, pp. 376–87.
[14] *Ibid.* P. 95 (in this text).
[15] *Ibid.* P. 95 (in this text).

To maintain her own self-control, the nurse often may not show the depth of her feelings when she is attempting to support the family of a patient who has died. Louisa May Alcott, the author of *Little Women,* spoke of her despair at the death of a patient when she served as a volunteer nurse during the Civil War. She held on to one of the survivors and cried with him.[16] A nurse faced with the loss of her own self-control may be forced to leave the relatives alone with the dead, thereby avoiding her responsibility of comforting the family or being with them at this critical moment.

The nurse must recognize that a survivor's inability to cry may reflect an ambivalent relationship with the dead person for guilt, anger, and shame may overshadow feelings of grief. Inability to cry also may reflect an individual's difficulty in expressing feelings in general.

Grief and the Work of Mourning

Separation of any kind can cause a grief reaction. When divorce occurs, either spouse or both may experience symptoms of separation: depression, feelings of guilt, and isolation are not unusual. But the separation by death is irreversible and final.

The shock, sensitivity, and vulnerability of survivors following the death of a loved one remind the nurse of the same reactions in patients who have gone through a serious illness or major operation. Psychologically, the symptoms of serious illness and of mourning are quite similar, and the bereaved often compare their feelings to a kind of terrible wound.

In 1917, Freud defined mourning, in "Mourning and Melancholia":

... it is well worth notice that although mourning involves grave departures from the normal attitude of life, it never occurs to us to regard it as a pathological condition. . . . We rely on its being overcome after a certain lapse of time, and we look upon any interference with it as useless or even harmful.[17]

The nurse sees grief and mourning, then, in many forms, and death is but one precipitating circumstance. We rely heavily on time to heal wounds of all kinds, physical and emotional. It is obvious to the nurse in her daily work that serious trauma, physical or emotional, requires the passage of time as well as other help.

Freud, in "Creative Writers and Day-Dreaming," comments:

Whoever understands the human mind, knows that hardly anything is harder for a man to give up than a pleasure which he has once experienced.

---

[16] Louisa May Alcott. *Hospital Sketches.* Bessie Jones, ed. Cambridge, Mass.: Belknap Press of Harvard University Press, 1960.

[17] Sigmund Freud. "Mourning and Melancholia." *Complete Psychological Works of Sigmund Freud.* London: Hogarth Press, Ltd., 1917. Pp. 152–70.

Actually, we can never give anything up; we only exchange one thing for another. What appears to be a renunciation is really the formation of a substitute or surrogate.[18]

It is often very difficult to give up one love object for another. But, as Freud pointed out, this substitution is well within the human capacity, and often necessary for human survival. An example is the widow who is eventually able to love again and to remarry. It is particularly difficult for parents who have lost a child to turn their affection either to another child or to one born later, even though the latter may have been wished for as a kind of replacement. This process of healing that helps one to face and recover from the loss of a loved one Sigmund Freud called "grief work," and consists of gradually detaching one's emotional investment and reinvesting in other persons, things, or activities.

Normal Grief

Terminal illness often provides survivors with the opportunity to do some of their grieving ahead of time ("anticipatory grief"). It is not unusual for the wives of soldiers who have been reported missing in action to go through a grief experience. If a soldier has been mistakenly reported dead, his wife may have considerable difficulty accepting the returning husband, for she has already gone through the mourning process.

Normally, as we mentioned, the first response to news of death is a refusal to accept or comprehend it. It is not unusual for people to cry out, to try to find signs of life, or to try to bring the dead person back. Loved ones describe a stunned, numb feeling that allows no acknowledgment of reality. A relative may try to go about normal activities as if nothing had happened and find instead that he sits motionless and dazed for minutes, or even hours; his intellectual responses to the reality of the loss are overcome by his emotions.

Mourning often begins when increased requests are made by the patient. The sick and dying patient may become very demanding, and relatives or nurses caring for him may react with hostility. The helplessness medical people feel in the double demand of coping with a patient's fears and anxieties as well as combating his physical illness may cause them to turn away.

It is as appropriate for a nurse to feel saddened at the loss of a patient as it is for anyone to feel sad when someone loved dies. A sensitive supervisor will help her staff to express feelings—sadness, regret, helplessness, anger, or whatever—at the death of a patient, and nurses may assist in the surcease of sorrow by helping one another during critical times.

[18] Sigmund Freud. "Creative Writers and Day-Dreaming." *Complete Psychological Works of Sigmund Freud*. Vol. 4. London: Hogarth Press, Ltd., 1917. P. 173.

366 Death, Grief, and Mourning

In her concern with the relatives in the crisis following a death, the nurse should be aware of their occasional point of view that their grief may be interfered with by the unsound intervention of hospital personnel or that the hospital may fail to provide optimal conditions for "healing." The grieving process cannot be hurried or accelerated.

The nurse should know, too, that guilt frequently accompanies mourning. The survivors may feel that they have, in some way, failed to save the dying person; this is a feeling particularly prevalent in mothers who lose a child.

We have noted earlier that crying is one of the beginning ways, long before the human can speak, to express suffering and pain. This is the way the infant signals his distress to his mother, and this is the way that the grief-stricken person cries out for support from the people surrounding him. Grief is one situation in which the crying of an adult can be understood and accepted in most cultures, but some people find it difficult if not impossible to cry. They may have mixed feelings about the loss of the deceased; they may find it impossible to show emotions to anyone, and prefer to be completely alone before they are able to cry.

Engel notes that the work of mourning can be separated into stages, commenting that restitution is a third state of mourning. Frequently, when death of a loved one occurs, sharing grief with close friends and relatives can be one of the most helpful responses. Participating, these persons can give effective support to the survivors.

The rituals of the funeral ceremony, viewing the body, and burial all allow feelings to be shared and expressed. Occasionally, survivors reject the preliminary ceremonies, preferring cremation; there are many cultures, too, in which cremation is an important part of the funeral ritual. According to Engel:

In many cultures, the funeral ceremony includes a feast or some sort of wake in which is symbolically expressed a triumph over death, a denial of the fear of death or of the dead, or an attempt to return to life and living.[19]

Turning away from death is also a common response. It is for this reason that nurses need support of the group in caring for the dying patient and carrying out after-death procedures; it is also one of the reasons that hospital policy in most places requires more than one person to perform these duties.

Usefulness of Ritual

Each person reacts to dying and death in his own way, depending upon individual as well as cultural influences. We have previously noted that two

[19] Engel. "Grief and Grieving." Page 381 of this text.

patients can have exactly the same type of physical illness and respond in very different ways to that illness. American society has certain patterns for dealing with death, and the differences usually occur within that pattern. The contemporary American family (which consists of only the mother, father, and children) channels the child's love to a few people, thus allowing strong feelings of attachment, especially to the parents. This type of family structure means that death of a parent early in the child's life becomes overly significant, since the parent is normally the child's primary source of gratification and love. In societies where a child is reared in a larger group and does not have such intense involvement with the parents, a parent's death may be much easier.

Institutionalization of mourning in ritual helps the family to recover, and many cultures, recognizing this need, tend to emphasize and clarify the reality of death in their funeral procedures. The American culture, as well as our funeral industry, has come under sharp criticism in the past few years regarding the high cost of burial expenses and complicated funeral transactions. Jessica Mitford, in *The American Way of Death,* expresses deep concern and protest regarding "the burial business." [20] Individual religious and spiritual beliefs offer some families recourse and comfort they feel unable to achieve in any other way; it is a fortunate mourner who has private means to deal with the painful void that death can bring.

In attempting to recover from the loss of a loved one, a person may become exclusively occupied with thoughts of the deceased person, thoughts devoid of negative or undesirable features. Negative or hostile feelings often become diminished or repressed as the fact of death becomes a reality. The more dependent the relationship, the more difficult the resolution. An elderly, dedicated couple who have lost most of their friends through death or separation and who only had each other would find it very hard to adjust to loss. An aged parent who loses a child who provided emotional as well as financial support might also be especially hard-hit. Other factors that influence the response of a survivor include the degree of ambivalence toward the lost loved person; if a husband and wife have had many years of marital problems, for example, the survivor might well have mixed feelings about the loss.

The age of both the mourned and the mourners enters into the emotions engendered by death. An elderly person, as mentioned before, may be much less mourned than an infant or young child. On the other hand, an older person may find the death of a husband or wife an almost intolerable loss. Younger people who lose husbands or wives often find other partners and remarry. The young child who loses a parent is much more traumatized than the older person who loses a father or mother, partly because he does

---

[20] Jessica Mitford. *The American Way of Death.* New York: Simon and Schuster, Inc., 1963.

not fully understand death and it is fraught with fantasies and fears that make it especially difficult for him to deal with.

An additional factor is the number and nature of previous grief experiences. As life progresses and people have repeated losses, their ability to understand death and to cope with it may be increased. A degree of preparation for loss through death assists a mourner through the necessary psychological processes. The simple fact of good health has a similar effect. There is sound psychological sense in bringing soldiers to peak physical condition to be able to accommodate the great psychological stress of combat. The stress of losing a loved one also is met best by the healthy person.

Pathological Grief

The duration of normal mourning varies considerably, but the work of grieving ordinarily begins to subside in about six months and is largely completed within a year. When the feelings and outward signs of mourning persist for much longer than a year, pathological grief may be developing.

Difficulty in sleeping after the death of a loved person is not an unusual symptom, and like other symptoms in other relationships, pathology exists not so much in kind as in degree. Insomnia can be a symptom of pathological mourning when it continues for prolonged periods.

Denial is another mechanism for coping with death. It becomes pathological only in its degree. Introjection and identification are mechanisms that may be used to maintain an illusion that a person is not dead; if a survivor spends much time behaving as if the deceased is still living, he is displaying pathology.

A sudden and unexpected or a bizarre manner of death may contribute to pathological mourning (though death is almost always coupled with an element of shock and surprise). Death by sudden heart attack, stroke, or accident is especially hard to accept. Only terminal illnesses prepare a family in some measure for what follows. It is natural, then, that the family of a wartime soldier receives news of death better than the family of a man who dies in an automobile accident.

Mourning becomes more difficult, too, if a survivor has many mixed feelings about the person who has died. For example, when an elderly mother who had been highly controlling in the use of her large estate died, the entire family was unable to function. There was so much dissension and so many differences among the children by the time of her death that the death was seen as a mixed blessing; the children were happy, on one hand, to receive large quantities of money, but miserable and jealous of each other in the way the estate was divided. It was very difficult for this family to mourn the mother in a normal way.

The Bereaved Child

The first awareness of death usually develops between the ages of two and four; at that time, the child may ask the parents questions relating to life and death. Although death is usually associated with inanimate objects at this age, the child may make a consistent connection between death and absence or separation. It is for this reason that the child in the hospital feels especially frightened at being separated from his home and parents.

The child may begin to equate sleep with death, and for this reason it is very important that death should not be described as a kind of permanent sleep. Such a description can lead a child to be afraid to go to bed at night and sleep. Children have different concepts of death: up to the age of three, a child is concerned only about separation, followed by fears of mutilation; after the age of five, he often thinks of death as a bogey-man, who comes to take people away; around nine or ten, he begins to conceive of death realistically, as a permanent biological process.

Anna Freud considers that six months is too young for mourning to occur in the infant, and despite problems of separating from the mother, the experience of mourning is not the same for a very young child as it is for an older one or for an adult.[21] One of the reasons that the death of a parent is traumatic for a young child according, is that the ego of the child is not properly developed to bear the work and strain of mourning.[22] The consensus is that very young children are much more deeply affected than adults by the death of parents and loved ones. The child can remain attached to the fantasy of the dead person for many years, and can be frightened to love anyone but himself again, if he loses a parent very early in life. It is for this reason that the child who suffers such a loss should be encouraged to find another real person to love.

An accurate description of the cause of death should be given the child, and an explanation suitable for his age level. He needs to be reassured that he is in no danger of dying himself. The child is especially vulnerable if he loses a parent, for part of his development hinges on his feelings that his parents are all-powerful and can protect him; when they leave him and die, the loss can be irreparable.

Whenever possible, the child should be prepared for death, even for separation. In almost all situations, children react best to honesty, and they

[21] Anna Freud. "Discussion of 'Grief and Mourning in Infancy and Early Childhood' by Bowlby." *The Psychoanalytic Study of the Child*. Vol. 15 (1960). Pp. 53–94.

[22] John Bowlby. "Grief and Mourning in Infancy and Early Childhood." *The Psychoanalytic Study of the Child*. Vol. 15 (1960). Pp. 9–52.

sense dishonesty and deviousness when death is discussed. The child should be encouraged to express his feelings about death without being told what his feelings should be: allowing the child to play out his feelings can be much more beneficial than just listening to his speech about them. Play provides easier communication of feelings than speech, and a child often feels less vulnerable in expressing feelings by this means.

A small child may feel relieved when a sibling, especially a younger sibling or new baby, dies. He may consciously or unconsciously be relieved that he has no competitors for the love of his parents, and may later feel guilty because he feels so good to have lost the baby that he jealously resented. These feelings need to be accepted by the nurse and by the parents if the child is to later be able to tolerate and accept them.

The greatest help one can give to the child who survives a death in the family is to encourage the recognition and expression of grief. There are parents who feel that it is improper for even a young boy to cry if he is hurt or wounded, afraid or depressed. Johnny, who came into the hospital as a survivor of an automobile accident in which his older brother was killed, repressed his grief. He was in a leg cast and prided himself, as did his family, on the fact that he didn't cry; he was considered a "big boy." Johnny was seven years old. It was a long time before he could begin to express some of his feelings to the nurses about the automobile accident and what it meant to him to lose his older brother. He did this one day when he had two toy automobiles and crashed them together on the highway located on his bedcovers. The play allowed Johnny to express some of the feelings that he could not consciously discuss either with the nurse or his family.

Children are often the forgotten ones: not so much because nobody cares, but because at the time of death people are preoccupied with their own feelings and often are uncomfortable talking to a child about death.

Children will show different reactions to the death of a parent, from silent withdrawal and isolation to wild loud mourning, which attracts attention and is, thus, a means of "replacing" a loved and needed object. Since children cannot differentiate yet between the wish and the deed, they may feel a great deal of remorse and guilt for the death of a parent. Feeling responsible for the parent's death, they may fear a gruesome punishment in retribution. On the other hand, they may take separation relatively calmly and utter such statements as, "She will come back after spring vacation."

The child who angrily wishes his mother to drop dead for not having gratified his need will be traumatized greatly by her actual death, even if the event is not linked closely in time with his destructive wishes. He will always take partial or whole blame for the loss of his mother. It is well to remember the child will react in the same manner if he loses a parent by divorce, separation, or desertion.

Grief Reactions in Later Life

One of the ways of evaluating whether grief work has been done effectively is the capacity of the survivors to redirect their love and energies. Unexpressed grief that is not "worked through" often leaves survivors with symptoms of somatic illnesses and prolonged depressions. There may be also a tendency toward self-isolation and unreasonable hostility toward some living person.

In one sense, mourning is never really over. Many life experiences evoke memories of the loss. Lorraine Siggens notes:

> Anniversary reactions provide an interesting instance of identification with the lost person. These reactions take various forms such as the appearance of symptoms the lost person had during his illness, or a recurrence of a feeling the mourner himself was undergoing at the time of the loss.[23]

These reactions may occur at the anniversary of the loved one's death, or when the mourner attains the age of the lost person when he died.

Death of a loved one is the moment at which one comes closest to the confrontation of his own vulnerability. Frances Gunther in writing about her son's death expresses some of her thoughts about this experience.

"Death always brings one suddenly face to face with life. Nothing, not even the birth of one's child, brings one so close to life as his death. . . . It raises all the infinite questions, each answer ending in another question. What is the meaning of life? What are the relations between things: life and death? the individual and the family? the family and society? marriage and divorce? the individual and the state? medicine and research? science and politics and religion? man, men and God?" [24]

Suggested Readings

BOOKS

Anthony, Sylvia. *The Child's Discovery of Death.* New York: Harcourt, Brace & Jovanovich, 1940.

---

[23] Lorraine Siggins. "Mourning: A Critical Survey of the Literature." *International Journal of Psychoanalysis.* Vol. 47 (1966).

[24] John Gunther. *Death Be Not Proud: A Memoir.* New York: Harper and Row, Publisher, 1965. P. 155.

Brown, Norman O. *Life Against Death.* Middletown, Conn.: Wesleyan University Press, 1959.

Choron, Jacques. *Death and Western Thought.* New York: Crowell-Collier and Macmillan, 1963.

Draper, Edgar. *Psychiatry and Pastoral Care.* Englewood Cliffs, N.J.: Prentice-Hall, Inc., 1965.

Eissler, K. R. *The Psychiatrist and the Dying Patient.* New York: International Universities Press, 1955.

Engel, George L. *Psychological Development in Health and Disease.* Philadelphia: W. B. Saunders Company, 1962.

Feifel, Herman, ed. *The Meaning of Death.* New York: McGraw-Hill Book Company, 1959.

——— and R. Fulton, eds. *Death and Identity.* New York: John Wiley & Sons, Inc., 1965.

Freud, Sigmund. *The Child's Discovery of Death.* London: Routledge & Kegan Paul, Ltd., 1940.

———. *Complete Psychological Works of Sigmund Freud.* London: Hogarth Press, Ltd., 1917. Pp. 152–70.

Fulton, Robert, ed. *Death and Identity.* New York: John Wiley & Sons, Inc., 1966.

Glaser, Barney G. and Anselm L. Strauss. *Awareness of Dying.* Chicago: Aldine Publishing Co., 1965.

Gunther, John. *Death Be Not Proud.* A Memoir New York: Harper & Row, 1965.

de Hartog, Jan. *The Hospital.* New York: Atheneum Publishers, 1964.

Jackson, E. *Telling a Child about Death.* Des Moines, Ia.: Meredith Press, 1946.

Kastenbaum, Robert. "Time and Death in Adolescence." In *The Meaning of Death.* Ed. H. Feifel. New York: McGraw-Hill Book Company, 1959. Pp. 99–113.

Kutscher, Austin H., ed. *But Not to Lose.* New York: Frederick Fell, Inc., 1969.

———. *Death and Bereavement.* Springfield, Ill.: Charles C Thomas, Publisher, 1969.

Lindemann, Erich. *Stress and Psychiatric Disorder: Mental Health Research Fund Proceedings.* Oxford: Blackwell Scientific Publications, 1960.

Marris, P. *Widows and Their Families.* London: Routledge & Kegan Paul, Ltd., 1958.

Menninger, Karl. *Man Against Himself.* New York: Harcourt, Brace & Jovanovich, 1938.

Quint, Jeanne C. *The Nurse and the Dying Patient.* New York: The Macmillan Company, 1967.

Ruitenbeek, Hendrik M., ed. *Death: Interpretations.* New York: Dell Publ. Co., Inc., 1969.

Schoenberg, Bernard, Arthur C. Carr, David Peretz, and Austin H. Kutscher, eds. *Loss and Grief: Psychological Management in Medical Practice.* New York: Columbia University Press, 1970.

Sudnow, David. *Passing On.* Englewood Cliffs, N.J.: Prentice-Hall, Inc., 1967.

Tolstoy, Leo. "The Death of Ivan Illyich." *The World's Classics*, No. 432. Trans. Louise and Aylmer Maude. London: Oxford University Press, 1935.

Toynbee, Arnold, A. Keith Mant, Ninian Smart, John Hinton, Simon Yudkin, Eric Rhode, Rosalind Heywood, H. H. Price. *Man's Concern with Death.* London: Hodder and Stoughton Limited, 1968.

Wolf, Anna W. M. *Helping Your Child to Understand Death.* New York: Child Study Association of America, 1958.

Worchester, Alfred. *The Care of the Aged, the Dying and the Dead.* Springfield, Ill.: Charles C Thomas, Publisher, 1950.

ARTICLES

Aldrich, C. K. "The Dying Patient's Grief." *Journal of the American Medical Association.* Vol. 184 (1963). Pp. 311–29.

Baker, J. M. and K. C. Sorensen. "A Patient's Concern with Death." *American Journal of Nursing.* Vol. 63 (1963). Pp. 90–92.

Bergman, Abraham B. and Charles J. A. Schulte. "Conference on Care of the Child with Cancer." *Supplement to Pediatrics.* Vol. 40, No. 3 Part II. (September, 1967.)

Braverman, Shirley J. "Death of a Monster." *American Journal of Nursing.* Vol. 69 (1969). Pp. 1682–83.

Cappon, D. "The Dying." *Psychiatric Quarterly.* Vol. 33 (1959). Pp. 466–89.

Deutsch, Helene. "Absence of Grief." *Psychoanalytic Quarterly.* Vol. 6 (1937). Pp. 12–22.

———. "A Two-Year-Old Boy's First Love Comes to Grief." In *Dynamics of Psychopathology in Childhood.* Eds. L. Jessner and E. Pavenstedt. New York: Grune & Stratton, Inc., 1959.

Drummond, Eleanor E. "Communication and Comfort for the Dying Patient." *Nursing Clinics of North America.* Vol. 5, No. 1 (March, 1970). Pp. 55–63.

Encyclopaedia Britannica. "Dead," "Death," and "Death Rates." Vol. 7. Chicago: William Benton, 1961. Pp. 96–98, 108–14.

Encyclopaedia of Social Sciences. "Death Customs." Vol. 5. New York: The Macmillan Company, 1931. Pp. 21–27.

Engel, George L. "Is Grief a Disease?" *Psychosomatic Medicine.* Vol. 23 (1961). Pp. 18–22.

Feifel, Herman. "Death." In *The Encyclopaedia of Mental Health.* Vol. 2. Ed. A. Deutsch. New York: Franklin Watts, Inc., 1963. Pp. 427–50.

Folck, Marilyn Melcher and Phyllis J. Nie. "Nursing Students Learn to Face Death." *Nursing Outlook.* Vol. 7 (1959). Pp. 510–13.

Foster, L. E., Erich Lindemann, and Rollin J. Fairbanks. "Grief." *Pastoral Psychology.* No. 1 (1950). Pp. 28–30.

Freud, Sigmund. "Beyond the Pleasure Principle," Vol. 18. *The Standard Edition of the Complete Psychological Works of Sigmund Freud.* London: The Hogarth Press. 1955. Pp. 7–64.

———. "Inhibition, Symptoms and Anxiety." *Standard Edition.* Vol. 20. London: Hogarth Press, Ltd., 1959. Pp. 87–174.

Fulton, Robert. "Attitudes Toward Death: A Discussion." *Journal of Gerontology.* Vol. 16 (1961). Pp. 63–65.

——— and Phyllis Langton. "Attitudes Toward Death: an Emerging Mental Health Problem." *Nursing Forum.* Vol. 3 (1964). Pp. 104–12.

Glaser, Barney H. and A. L. Strauss. "The Social Loss of Dying Patients." *American Journal of Nursing,* Vol. 64 (1964). Pp. 119–21.

Green, M. and A. J. Solnit. "Psychologic Considerations in the Management of Deaths on Pediatric Hospital Services." Part I. "The Doctor and the Child's Family." *Pediatrics.* Vol. 24 (1959). Pp. 106–12.

Ingles, T. "Death on a Ward." *Nursing Outlook.* Vol. 12 (1964). P. 28.

Jackson, Edgar N. "Grief and Religion." In *The Meaning of Death.* Ed. H. Feifel. New York: McGraw-Hill Book Company, 1959. Pp. 218–33.

Lehrman, Samuel R. "Reactions to Untimely Death." *Psychiatric Quarterly.* Vol. 30 (1956). Pp. 564–78.

Leshan, L., E. Leshan, and R. E. Worthington. "Some Psychological Correlates of Neoplastic Disease: A Preliminary Report." *Journal of Clinical and Experimental Psycho-pathology and the Quarterly Review of Psychiatric Neurology.* Vol. 16 (1955). Pp. 281–88.

Lindemann, Erich. "Symptomatology and Management of Acute Grief." *American Journal of Psychiatry.* Vol. 101 (1944). Pp. 141–48.

Mahler, Margaret S. "Helping Children to Accept Death." *Child Study.* Vol. 27 (1950). Pp. 98–99, 119–20.

Mead, Margaret. "The Right to Die." *Nursing Outlook.* October, 1968. Pp. 20–21.

Menninger, E. "Death from Psychic Causes." *Bulletin of the Menninger Clinic.* Vol. 12 (1948). Pp. 31–36.

Monsour, Karem J. "Asthma and the Fear of Death." *Psychoanalytic Quarterly.* Vol. 29 (1960). Pp. 56–71.

Moellendorf, Fritz. "Ideas of Children About Death." *Bulletin of the Menninger Clinic.* Vol. 3, No. 148 (1939).

Quint, Jeanne C. "The Dying Patient: A Difficult Nursing Problem." *Nursing Clinics of North America.* Vol. 2, No. 4 (December, 1967). Pp. 763–73.

———— and Anselm L. Strauss. "Nursing Student, Assignments and Dying Patient." *Nursing Outlook.* Vol. 12 (1964). Pp. 24–27.

Rastus, Ruth. "The Loneliness of Death." *The American Journal of Nursing.* Vol. 58 (1958). Pp. 1283–84.

Schmale, A. H. "Relationship of Separation and Depression to Disease." *Psychosomatic Medicine.* Vol. 20 (1958). Pp. 259–77.

Wahl, Charles W. "The Fear of Death." *Bulletin of the Menninger Clinic.* Vol. 22 (1958). Pp. 214–23.

Zilboorg, Gregory. "Fear of Death." *Psychoanalytic Quarterly.* Vol. 12 (1943). Pp. 465–75.

DISCUSSION OF SELECTED ARTICLES

In the first article, "Grief and Grieving," by Dr. George Engel, the author reflects upon the theory and practical problems of the family as it must cope with the death of a loved one. The author discusses that there are many reactions to death, but the shock and disbelief often surround the event. Just as children cannot completely comprehend the totality and finality of death, so it often takes the adult time to react when confronted with this phenomenon.

In the second article, "A Time to Die," Wilma Lewis presents a study of the factors of nursing care which can be of help to the dying patient and his family. The essentials of necessary physical care are outlined.

The trauma of bereavement brings many responses, and the sensitive nurse needs a deep understanding of these reactions.

Grief and Grieving
by George L. Engel, M.D.*

Death is an intensely poignant event, one which touches the deepest sources of human anguish, one which each of us yearns to be spared. Yet as nurses and physicians, it is our constant companion. How can we protect ourselves from such repeated personal suffering? One way—and the easiest way—is to develop a shell, to insulate ourselves, to avoid engagement, to make out it does not occur or it is not our concern.

* *American Journal of Nursing.* Vol. 64, No. 9 (September, 1964). Pp. 93–98.

This is what all nurses and doctors do to some degree, a few to the point of callousness. But it is this very human need for self-protective measures that is responsible for the dearth of systematic knowledge, much less scientific study, of the processes of grief and mourning, for it takes courage to undergo the repeated and wrenching impact of the exposure to the grief-stricken that a scientific study of grief would demand (1–4). There are easier ways to win fame and fortune. Accumulated evidence suggests that the success of the grieving process may be a significant variable regulating the capacity to maintain health (5, 6).

Grief is so universal a phenomenon among human beings, if not among higher animals as well, that it hardly provokes wonder. It is taken for granted. For it seems only "natural" that one should feel badly upon suffering the loss of a loved one. But why? Why should it make any difference?

These are outrageous, almost insulting questions, yet the answers which they are likely to provoke are no more than restatements of the fact. "It's natural." "It's human." "Because the deceased is missed." "Because he was loved." "Because what we experienced together can never again be." "It is losing a part of one's self." And so on. All true, and yet somehow the essence of the experience is not captured in such phrases. Only the poets, through the ages, have come close to grasping the essential psychological varieties of this experience.

> Grief fills the room up of my absent child,
> Lies in his bed, walks up and down with me,
> Puts on his pretty looks, repeats his words,
> Remembers me of all his gracious parts,
> Stuffs out his vacant garments with his form.
> (Shakespeare, *King John* Act iii, Sc. 4)

> Give sorrow words; the grief that does not speak
> Whispers the o'er-fraught heart and bids it break.
> (Shakespeare, *Macbeth* Act iv, Sc. 3)

> Grief tears his heart, and drives him to and fro.
> In all the raging impotence of woe.
> (Pope, *The Iliad of Homer*, Book xxii)

> Home they brought her warrior dead;
>   She nor swoon'd nor utter'd cry.
> All her maidens, watching, said,
>   She must weep or she will die.
> Then they praised him, soft and low,
>   Call'd him worthy to be loved,
> Truest friend and noblest foe;
>   Yet she neither spoke nor moved.
> Stole a maiden from her place,
>   Lightly to the warrior stept,

> Took the face-cloth from the face;
>   Yet she neither moved nor wept.
> Rose a nurse of ninety years,
>   Set his child upon her knee—
> Like summer tempest came her tears—
>   'Sweet my child, I live for thee.'
>   (Tennyson, Songs of the Princess)

Study of even these few excerpts from literature shows how eloquently poets identify the characteristic features of grief.

1. The smooth, more or less automatic, taken-for-granted aspects of living are interrupted. The grieving person suddenly becomes aware of the innumerable ways in which he was dependent, often quite unconsciously, on the lost object (person) as a source of gratification and as an essential influence for his feeling of well-being and effective functioning, his sense of self, so to speak.

2. The grieving person attempts to refute, to deny, to dispute the reality of the event.

3. The grieving person, in the depth of his feeling of impotence, loss and helplessness, sends out various behavioral cries for help, to which his fellow men respond. Failure or inability to emit the cry or to elicit a response are fraught with dire implications for recovery.

4. The grieving person attempts to reconstitute in his mind a representation of the lost person to replace that which no longer exists in the real world. This is a difficult and painful process, in which the bitter and the sweet in the end are separated and the mourner ultimately comes to peace with himself and his new state.

5. Both the personal experience of grief and the institutionalized and social rituals of the mourning process serve ultimately to detach the grieving person from the dead and to restore him to his place as a member of the social community.

Further order may be brought into these poetical insights by using the analogy of wound healing. If we define grief as the typical reaction to the loss of a source of psychological gratification, we can compare the experience of the loss to the wound, while the subsequent psychological responses to the loss may be compared to the tissue reaction and the processes of healing.

Whatever one has become accustomed to as a natural and expected part of one's environment—whether it be the presence of a parent, a spouse, a child, a friend, a particular house, the scene of one's happy life experiences, a job, a pet, or even an old shoe—these come to constitute psychological sources of gratification and supply, and their absence is felt as a gap in one's sense of continuity and self-confidence. Functionally, the loss of such a source of gratification is truly a wound.

Successful grief and grieving follow certain more or less predictable steps which permit a judgment that healing is taking place. This healing process can be interfered with by unsound intervention, by failure to provide optimal conditions for healing, or because the individual's resources are not up to the task. But the normal healing processes of grieving cannot be accelerated.

A good grasp of the sequence of events characterizing normal grief and of the meaning of each is essential if one is to help wisely. Further, knowledge of what is normal enables one to identify the pathological.

Shock and Disbelief

The first response on learning of death is often one of shock and disbelief. The survivor may respond with a refusal to accept or comprehend the fact, often crying out, "No!" "It can't be!" Or he may throw himself on the body, attempting to find signs of life or to bring the dead back to life.

This reaction may then be followed by a stunned, numbed feeling in which the grief-stricken person does not permit himself any thoughts or feelings which acknowledge the reality of the death. He may try desperately, but in an automatic fashion, to carry on his ordinary activities, as if nothing had happened, or he may sit motionless and dazed, unable to move. At such times, the victim seems out of contact and it may be difficult to gain his attention. This phase may last a few minutes or hours or even days, alternating with flashes of despair and anguish as the reality of the loss briefly penetrates into consciousness.

Sometimes, the initial response is overtly an intellectual acceptance of the reality of the loss and an immediate initiation of apparently appropriate activity, such as making arrangements and comforting others. But it is only by not permitting access to consciousness of the full emotional impact of the loss that this can take place. In such an instance the loss is recognized, but its painful character is denied or at least muted.

In general, distinctive of this initial phase are the attempts to protect oneself against the effects of the overwhelming stress by raising the threshold against its recognition or against the painful feeling evoked thereby. Although such responses are more usual and more intense when the death is sudden and unexpected, they may also be observed even when the death has been anticipated.

Developing Awareness

Within minutes to hours the second stage begins. The reality of the death and its meaning as a loss begin more and more to penetrate consciousness in the form of an acute and increasing awareness of the anguish of the loss, the feeling of something lost, often felt as a painful emptiness in the chest or epigastrium. The environment seems frustrating and empty since it no longer includes the loved person.

Anger may erupt toward persons or circumstances held to be responsible for the death, as the doctor, nurse, hospital, or other family member. The mourner himself may feel he had in some way failed and may berate or even impulsively injure himself. Beating the breast, pounding the head, or thrusting the fist through glass are occasional impulsive, aggressive, and self-destructive acts on the part of the person who is suddenly overwhelmed with grief.

Crying, with tears, is typical of this phase. It is during this period that the greatest degree of anguish or despair, within the limits imposed by cultural patterns, is experienced and expressed. Some cultures demand loud and public lamentation, whereas others expect restraint. Familiarity with such cultural patterns is necessary in evaluating the appropriateness of a grief response. Regardless of such factors, the wish and need to cry is strong and crying seems to fulfill an important function in the work of mourning.

In general, crying seems to involve both an acknowledgment of the loss and the regression to a more helpless and childlike status. In the latter sense, crying is a communication. The grief-stricken person who cries is the recipient of certain kinds of support and help from the group, although this varies greatly in different cultures. Grief is one situation in which the tears of an adult are generally accepted and understood and the person who is able to cry still feels self-respect and worthfulness and that he is deserving of help.

Some persons suffering a loss want to cry or feel that they should cry, yet are unable to. This type of inhibition of crying must be distinguished from not crying simply because the person who died is not seriously missed, in which case there is no indication or need to cry, and from the voluntary suppression of crying because of an environmental or cultural demand, in which case the person either "cries inwardly" or waits until he is alone and unobserved before crying. Inability to cry, however, is a more serious matter. It is most likely to occur when the relationship with the dead person had been highly ambivalent and when the survivor is experiencing a good deal of guilt and shame.

Restitution

Restitution, the work of mourning, is the third stage. The institutionalization of the mourning experience in terms of the various rituals of the funeral help to initiate the recovery processes. First, it involves a gathering together of family and friends who mutually share the loss, although not all to the same degree. At the same time, there is acknowledgment of the need for support of the more stricken survivors whose regression is accepted. In this setting, overt or conscious expression of aggression is reduced to a minimum.

Many of the rituals of the funeral serve the important function of emphasizing clearly and unequivocally the reality of the death, the denial of which cannot be allowed to go on if recovery from the loss is to take place. The viewing of the body, the lowering of the casket, and the various rituals of different religious beliefs allow for no ambiguity. Further, this experience takes place in a group, permitting ordinarily guarded feelings to be shared and expressed more readily.

In addition, individual religious and spiritual beliefs offer recourse in various ways to the support of a more powerful, beneficent figure or provide the basis for the expectation of some kind of reunion after death and the expiation of guilt. The funeral ceremony also initiates the process of identification with the lost person through the various rituals which symbolize an identity between the mourner and the dead (for example sackcloth and ashes).

In primitive societies, this acting out of the identification is more vivid and literal. In many cultures, the funeral ceremony includes a feast or some sort of wake in which is symbolically expressed a triumph over death, a denial of the fear of death or of the dead, an attempt to return to life and living.

Resolving the Loss

For the mourner, however, the main work of grief goes on intrapsychically, the institutionalization mainly providing sustenance during the period of struggle to achieve this. As the reality of the death becomes accepted, the resolution of the loss involves a number of steps which proceed haltingly and interruptedly.

First, the mourner attempts to deal with the painful void, the awareness of the loss, which is felt also as a defect in the sense of intactness and wholeness of the self. He cannot yet accept a new love object to replace the lost person, although he may passively and transiently accept a more dependent relation with family members and old friends.

In this phase, he may be more aware of his own body, experiencing various bodily sensations or pains, in contrast to the earlier period when he may have been quite numb even to great physical hardship. Often such a pain or discomfort is identical with a symptom experienced in the past by the dead person, sometimes during the terminal illness. The mourner suffers in place of the dead person and by so doing not only maintains a tie with the deceased, but also appeases some of his own guilt for any aggressive impulses toward the dead. Normally, such symptoms are brief.

For some time, the mourner's thoughts are almost exclusively occupied with thoughts of the deceased, first with more emphasis on the personal experience of the loss, later with more emphasis on the person who died. He finds it necessary to bring up, to think over, and to talk about memories of the dead person, a process which goes on slowly and painfully, with great sadness, until there has been erected in the mind an image of the dead person almost devoid of negative or undesirable features.

Idealization

Such a process of idealization, however, requires that all negative and hostile feelings toward the deceased be repressed. Such repression may lead to fluctuating guilty, remorseful, and even fearful feelings, with regrets for past acts or fantasies of hostility, inconsiderateness, or unkindness, recollection of some of which may be exaggerated. Sometimes, there may be a haunting preoccupation with feelings of responsibility for the death. The various primitive concepts of the dead coming back to haunt or retaliate originate in such guilty feelings.

As the idealization of the dead person proceeds, though, two important changes are being achieved. The recurring thoughts and reminiscences about the deceased serve to establish in the mind a distinct image of the lost person, often buttressed by various external memorials and remembrances. The latter constitute tangible evidences of the more positive aspects of the lost relationship and permit one periodically to renew and relive the gratifications associated in the past with the deceased.

At the same time, the mourner consciously and unconsciously begins to take for himself certain admired qualities and attributes of the dead person through the mechanism of identification. This may appear in his adoption of certain mannerisms of and in his acknowledged wish to be like the lost person or to carry on his ideals and good deeds. When guilt is present there is a greater tendency for the mourner to take on undesirable traits or even symptoms of the deceased or to exaggerate the need to fulfill the wishes of the deceased.

Many months are required for this process and, as it is accomplished, the survivor's preoccupation with the dead person progressively lessens. Now, reminders of the dead person less often and less intently evoke feelings of sadness and more ambivalent memories can be tolerated with less guilt. As the ties are progressively loosened, the earlier yearnings to be with the dead person, even in death, begin more and more to be replaced by a turning to life. Now, the identification with the ideals, wishes, and aspirations of the lost person provide an impetus to continue in life. These are often expressed as a wish "to be what he would have wanted me to be" or "to carry on for him."

As the psychic dependence on the deceased diminishes, the mourner's interest in new relationships begins to return. Early in the mourning process, this may take the form of interest in and concern with other mourners who share the same loss. By so doing, the mourner is able temporarily to reduce his preoccupation with himself and the dead person and instead he feels sorry for and takes care of the other mourners. This allows him to reinvest feelings in his other love objects, his spouse, his children, as the case may be, and at the same time to gain some comfort by identifying with the person whom he now comforts and cares for. It also provides some respite from the painful, though necessary, task of dwelling on the loss and the lost object. In family units, different members may facilitate each other's work of mourning by alternating in such roles (7). Eventually, as the months pass by, the mourner renews his interest in persons and matters not so directly concerned with the loss and with the mourning.

The Outcome

The successful work of mourning takes a year or more. The clearest evidence of successful healing is the ability to remember comfortably and realistically both the pleasures and disappointments of the lost relationship. Many factors influence what the eventual outcome will be. A major determinant is the importance of the lost object as a source of support. The more dependent the relationship, the more difficult will be the task of resolving its loss. The degree of ambivalence toward the deceased is another. When there are persistent, unresolved, hostile feelings, guilt may interfere with the successful work of mourning. The age of the lost object is influential. The loss of a child generally has a more profound effect than the loss of an aged parent. The age of the mourner has its effect, too. The child has less capability of resolving a loss than does an adult. The number and nature of other relationships is still another factor. The person with few meaningful relationships has a more difficult time effecting the detachment from his dependence on the deceased. The mourner is affected by the number and nature of previous grief experiences. Losses tend to be cumulative in their effects. The most recent loss tends to revive that which was unsettled from earlier losses. The degree of preparation for the loss is a factor in that with the death of an aged or incurably sick person, some of the grief work may go on before the death. Finally, the physical and psychological health of the mourner at the time of the loss is important in determining his capacity to deal with the loss at the time it occurs.

Practical Considerations

Armed with such systematic knowledge of the grief process, the intuitive and empathic nurse is in a good position to help. While our present knowledge of grief is far too schematic and fragmentary to justify a how-to-do-it manual, clinical experience does provide a few guides useful to nurses. The rationale of these recommendations can be deduced from the preceding material.

First, news of death or impending death is best communicated to a family group rather than to an individual alone and should be done in a setting of privacy where the family can behave naturally without the restraints of public display. The perceptive nurse may well identify in advance the family member whose relation vis-à-vis the dying patient is such that he will be able to retain the composure and judgment necessary to help the more stricken survivors. She will alert the doctor of signs of impending death so as to give plenty of time to contact the family and prepare them for the inevitable.

When only one family member is available, the task may fall on the nurse to stay with and comfort the bereaved, at least until the clergyman or a friend can take over. Often, the nurse will be aware of the fact that she has been singled out for the role by the lone survivor of the dying patient. It will be well for her to consciously decide in advance whether she is willing and able to accept this responsibility and, if so, to plan how best she can discharge it.

The natural and understandable tendency is to run away from this painful task, to avoid recognizing that one is being singled out to play a crucial role in the unfolding tragedy. The prepared nurse will serve her patient and herself far better than the nurse who allows herself to be caught by surprise. And if she is not up to the task, for whatever reason—and there are many sound reasons why one may not be—her nursing responsibility is best discharged by recognizing the fact honestly and trying to enlist the aid of someone else.

Second, the request to see and take leave of the dying or dead patient should not be denied on the ground that it may be too upsetting or that it will disturb the floor routine. This need to take leave, to ask forgiveness, to touch, kiss, or caress the dying or dead loved one, to take a lock of hair, is of overwhelming importance to some and will not be requested by those for whom it will be disturbing. We forget that dying in the hospital rather than in the home is a recent social change.

Nor should the nurse be deterred in acquiescing to such a request by the fact that the body or death bed scene are not tidy (though certainly she should try to make them so), or by the anguished outcry that viewing of the deceased may evoke. The latter is part of a necessary psychological response, helpful in facing the reality of the death.

Third, when confronted by an angry, bitter, accusatory relative who berates the doctor, the hospital, the nurse, or other family members and accuses them of having neglected, mismanaged, or abused the dying or deceased patient, the nurse must keep two things in mind. Such a person could conceivably be justified in his complaint. But if not, he may be attempting to deal with his own aggression and guilt toward the dying person.

In either event, the nurse will do well to recognize that she serves best by redoubling her efforts to provide the best possible care to the dying person and by avoiding becoming involved in acrimonious dispute. By recognizing that the complaints are not directed to her as a person, that indeed they may be serving an important role in keeping the grieving relative from falling apart psychologically, she will almost certainly be able herself better to tolerate what appear to be entirely unjustified complaints and accusations. This is not the time or circumstance to expect thanks or gratitude, yet she can rest assured that such will be forthcoming later if she had been able to display the necessary tolerance and understanding of this distressing behavior.

Fourth, the nurse, knowing that shock and disbelief may be the first response to the news of death, should anticipate that some persons will behave in a grossly disturbed manner. She will require patience, tact, and warm sympathy for the person who refuses to acknowledge the truth of the news as well as for the person who literally collapses or loses control. Understanding that these are ways that people have to protect themselves from the overwhelming should provide her with the confidence that patient, gentle, and feeling reiteration of the reality coupled with the personal demonstration of a wish to help will go far in helping the grief-stricken over this difficult strait. Most important is encouraging the bereaved person to cry.

It is not sound to expect the suddenly bereaved person to maintain the social decorum demanded by a busy hospital floor. Rather than attempting to quiet the distraught relatives, out of consideration for other patients, the nurse should actively help the relatives to a place where they can grieve in private. Such behavior on the part of the nurse acknowledges the realistic needs of all and as such stamps her (the nurse) as a feeling as well as sensible person. These are qualities which can be a source of real strength to the bereaved.

Fifth, one cannot overemphasize the importance of knowing about and exercising the respect for the cultural, religious, and social customs of the mourners, no matter how strange or even abhorrent they may be to some of us. The institutionalized mourning rituals of peoples, sects, and cultures provide some of the most important external supports for the grief-stricken person, often essential to his ability to tolerate this first period of intense distress. The nurse must be familiar with the timing involved in the rites for the dying characteristic of different religions and see that the necessary steps are taken to assure that those responsible make the necessary provisions.

Grieving Patients

Sixth, a good nurse will not overlook the fact that a patient is grieving. Not infrequently people fall ill following a serious loss and because attention is directed toward the more obvious illness the attending physicians and nurses fail to recognize the signs of grief or to elicit the history of the loss (6). From time to time, one encounters a withdrawn, depressed, often tearful patient and nobody considers the obvious, that he has in the recent past suffered a grievous loss. Not to be overlooked is that the loss may be of a part or a function of the body, as after amputation or loss of vision, as well as after the loss of a loved one (8).

Even more tragic and less excusable are those instances where survivors of fatal accidents are afforded the best possible medical and surgical care but no one concerns himself with the grief. "Is my husband, my wife, my child alive or dead?" "Can I see him?" "Can I go to the funeral?" all too often are questions which not only are not responded to, are not even allowed to be asked. And all too often, physicians and nurses try to suppress by drugs or by avoidance the emerging reactions of grief under the misguided notion that such would interfere with the surgical or medical care. Here, perhaps, is one area most desperately calling for careful study and a more soundly based program of action.

Seventh, the grieving infant and child is commonplace. Especially for the child between six months and six years merely being separated from home and admitted to the hospital is in itself sufficient to elicit a primitive grief response (9). Consideration of grief in infancy and childhood is beyond the scope of this paper. Suffice it to say that attention to these children is a prime responsibility for the nurse. I have seen remarkable responses when a nurse simply on her own undertook to provide such an infant with the tender loving care so badly needed, even to the extent of carrying the baby about in her arms while performing her other duties.

The Dying Child

Finally, the grief of the parents of the dying child is peculiarly poignant and painful to witness. Here the nurse must exercise great wisdom and compassion if she is to be truly helpful and not get involved in a difficult competitive situation. She must recognize and respect the mother's need to minister to her own child, yet at the same time sensitively perceive when she needs to be relieved. She must be aware that the mother's attempt to cope may range from tender bedside care to frantic, inappropriate hospital room activity, from exaggerated praise and gratitude for the efforts of doctors and nurses to harsh criticism and complaint, from tearful sentimentality to philosophical resignation.

Because it is so inherent in her psychology as a woman, the nurse is likely to be more emotionally involved in the loss of a child than of an adult patient and she may be upset when the mother's reaction differs from her own or from her expectation of what it should be. An appreciation by the nurse that such behavior on the part of the mother reflects her attempts to cope with her own distress will be helpful in guiding the nurse in her responses. The mother who cannot bear to leave her child's bedside as well as the mother who cannot bear to enter her child's room each may be greatly assisted by the opportunity to share her feelings and thoughts with the nurse who is seen both as another woman and as a professional care-taking person. The assignment of little tasks on the hospital floor can serve the function of letting the mother know she is doing something for her child and at the same time keep her close to her child without being overexposed to the child's suffering (1, 2).

The nurse frequently is called on to minister to those experiencing grief. A clear understanding of the processes in grief will prove helpful in enabling the nurse to extend herself professionally beyond her status as a humane person.

References

1. Chodoff, Paul and others. Stress, defenses, and copying behavior; observations in parents of children with malignant disease. *Amer. J. Psychol.* **120**:748, Feb. 1964.
2. Friedman, S. B. and others. Behavioral observations on parents anticipating the death of a child. *Pediatrics* **32**:610, Oct. 1963.
3. Lindemann, Erich. Symptomatology and management of acute grief. *Amer. J. Psychol.* **101**:141, Sept. 1944.
4. Wretmark, G. A study of grief reactions. *Acta Psychiat. Scand.* **34**:Suppl. 292, 1959.
5. Engel, G. L. *Psychological Development in Health and Disease.* Philadelphia, W. B. Saunders Co., 1962, Chap. 26.
6. Schmale, A. H., Jr. Relationship of separation and depression to disease. *Psychosom. Med.* **20**:259, July–Aug. 1958.
7. Greene, W. A., Jr. Role of a vicarious object in the adaptation to loss. *Psychosom. Med.* **20**:344, Sept.–Oct. 1958.
8. Caplan, L. M. and Hackett, T. P. Emotional effects of lower-limb amputation in the aged. *New Eng. J. Med.* **269**:1166, Nov. 28, 1963.
9. Spitz, Rene. Anaclitic depression. *Psychoanal. Stud. Child.* **1**:53, 1945.

Bibliography

Bowlby, J. Grief and mourning in infancy and early childhood. *Psychoanal. Stud. Child.* **15**:9–52, 1960.

Engel, G. L. Is grief a disease? A challenge for medical research. *Psychosom. Med.* **23**:18–22, Jan.–Feb. 1961.

Freud, Sigmund. Mourning and Melancholia. In the author's *Complete Works.* London, Hogarth Press, 1957, Vol. 14, p. 237.

Marris, Peter. *Widows and Their Families.* London, Routledge and Kegan Paul, 1958.

Mead, Margaret. Nursing—primitive and civilized. *Amer. J. Nurs.* **56**:1001–1004, Aug. 1956.

Schaffer, H. R. Objective observations of personality development in early infancy. *Brit. J. Med. Psychol.* **31**:174–183, 1958.

A Time to Die*
by Wilma R. Lewis, R.N., M.S.

The rapid increase in scientific knowledge which began early in this century has brought about a dramatic change in medical and nursing practice. In many instances in which the care that could be given was once limited to comforting and sustaining the patient and refraining from giving medications or treatments which would cause further harm, it is now possible to effect a cure. Daring surgery, made safer by the use of antibiotics, is causing miracles. Pneumonia requires only a few shots of penicillin instead of the tense and wearing wait for the crisis which in years gone by meant life or death. A ruptured appendix has become a matter for routine treatment instead of an almost certain fatal illness. Mothers seldom die in childbirth or from its complications, and a woman now expects to raise all of her children to adulthood instead of feeling greatly blessed if half of them reach a marriageable age.

Great excitement has accompanied each new advance, and with it has come a growing feeling of power. The physician has truly become the healer, and the nurse his eager ally. This sense of power has made it difficult to consider the fact that there are illnesses which will not respond to any treatment—that even though our ability to cure may increase many times over, at the end of each life death is waiting.

Daniel Cappon has summed up the general attitude in this manner:

> Men of medicine have eschewed public utterances on the dying patient. The surgeon is superstitious. He needs to be optimistic and shut out twinges of professional guilt and worry. He turns away. The physician feels impotent. Though sympathetic, he turns away. The psychiatrist faces often the threat of man turned against himself; but if suicide is carried through, the psychiatrist also looks away, covered in guilt and shame. Even the priest absorbs his keenest feelings in ritual. The relatives and friends are immersed and blinded by grief; the nurses are busy; only the poet and the philosopher take a look from afar (1).

Gradually, however, the medical and nursing literature is beginning to give consideration to the needs of the dying patient. At first only occasionally and then in increasing numbers, there have been appearing articles that urgently

* Nursing Forum. Vol. 4, No. 1 (1965). Pp. 7–27.

ask, "Are we doing as much as we should for the patient who is facing death?" Other articles emphasize the need for studies to answer these questions. Cicely Saunders, a physician who has studied the care of the dying for many years, believes that one of the most rewarding services which can be performed is to help the patient "make a good end," and that this satisfactory closure to life should be given the same careful study and attention as are devoted to other phases of life (2).

Although according to the medical literature physicians are giving increased attention to the care of the dying patient, their primary emphasis must necessarily remain on the controlling and destroying of diseases! K. R. Eissler says that "the spirit (attained by medical training) of doing, controlling, combating, and destroying diseases is probably a great impediment to the understanding and study of death. . . . In view of death there is nothing to do, to control, to combat or to destroy, and I believe that most of those trained in medical schools feel out of place when they face the approach of death in their patients" (3).

Accordingly, as Morton J. Aronson has pointed out, the burden is thrust upon the nurse, for she is the only member of the medical team who is in any sustained contact with the patient. If she can conquer her inclination to withdraw into starchy, impersonal efficiency in the face of her own anxieties about death and meet the patient on a human level, she may render an immeasurable service (4). Margaret Mead believes that as nursing matures as a profession the nurse will find that she is in the best position to protect the vulnerable; she has a sensitive understanding of grief and, as a part of her art, knows the value of the compassionate service of her hands (5).

Two Case Studies

With this background in mind, a small study was undertaken to identify the factors in nursing care which contribute to the decrease of the dying patient's physical or emotional distress. Patients who were known to be suffering from terminal illness in the hospital were sought out, and various aspects of their nursing care were studied. The scope of the study was distinctly limited by the necessity of confining it to afternoon hours and to a short period of time, so that little nursing care could be given or observed. Indirect methods of investigation, such as talking with the patients and their families, consulting the nursing and medical personnel, and reading records, produced evidence of the care actually given. From the patients observed, two—Mrs. Allen and Miss Bane—were chosen for discussion because of the contrasting pictures they presented.

Mrs. Allen was in bed with her head elevated slightly when I first saw her. The side-rails were up and she was trying to reach a glass of orange juice on her bedside table. I held the glass for her while she took a small sip. "They told me to drink all the liquids that I could today," she said as she lay back.

I moved her table to a more convenient position and straightened the bedclothes, which had fallen to one side. "How are things going today?" I asked as I checked her pulse. "I feel better—and I hope I am better," she said with a sigh. As she spoke her eyelids drooped and she drifted off to sleep.

Mrs. Allen had been admitted four days earlier in a semi-comatose state. She was a 62-year-old woman who had undergone a radical left mastectomy two years previously. Three months prior to this admission she had developed a rapidly progressive weakness and malaise with jaundice, ascites, and pleural effusion. Sensitivity to a narcotic given prior to the ambulance trip had resulted in a comatose state which gradually cleared after her first few days of hospitalization. A thoracentesis was done to relieve the pressure that restricted lung function. Later a paracentesis removed fluid from the abdominal cavity. Diagnostic studies were under way. Metastatic carcinoma was suspected.

Special nurses had been with her until the coma cleared; now only the night nurse remained. A daughter, who had flown from California, was with her most of the time during the day.

Miss Bane, the other patient, was climbing laboriously into bed as I entered her room. She was small and thin but attractive, and appeared younger than her stated age of 47. Tears rolled down her cheeks as she lay back on her pillow, exhausted.

"Forgive me for crying," she said. "I don't want to cry, but I do anyway."

I handed her a tissue from the box, which was beyond her reach. "Sometimes it helps," I said.

"But crying is for babies, and I don't have anything more to cry about now than I've had for years. I just get so frustrated at being so weak." The tears flowed again.

"You've been fighting this for a long time," I said.

"Fourteen years . . . And now it looks like I am losing ground fast."

Miss Bane had been hospitalized for about a week. Pleural effusion had developed. She had been treated repeatedly in several other hospitals for a chronic lymphocytic lymphoma. A thoracentesis had been done, and bone marrow studies were under way to determine whether further treatment could be undertaken.

More tears rolled down her cheeks. I waited to see if she would go on.

"It's not that I mind dying. After all, everyone has to die some time. It's all this hell you have to go through first, being so weak and tired and having to depend on other people. Then I get cross and irritable and demanding, and I hate myself for being that way. Everyone is so busy. I hate to ask for things, but I just can't get them for myself."

Morton G. Aronson, in discussing the emotional aspects of nursing the cancer patient, says that the nurse, whether she wants to or not, stands in the same unique relationship to her patient that the mother does to her child. To the sick adult, the nurse, with her concern about food and pills, elimination, and baths, recalls the roll which mother fulfilled. She even threatens to report bad behavior to the doctor as mother threatened to tell father.

In response to the emotional stress of illness, patients adopt varying degrees of childlike behavior in relation to the nurse-mother. Because the patient is powerless to gratify his own needs and is dependent on another, he reverts to the techniques he used in childhood. These childhood dependency techniques and the conflicts that surround them now burst forth, colored by the adult personality structure and influenced by the behavior of the nurse. Thus the patient may attempt to curry favor by ingratiation or may demand it with the angry impatience so typical of children. When the demands for tender loving care are frustrated, the inevitable anger may erupt in hostile outbursts or critical attacks on the nurse; or it may be expressed in self-damaging defiance by refusal to eat or take medicine, or be projected onto the nurse in the form of paranoid accusations or delusions, or be turned violently against the self in the form of dangerous depression. Or, in the form of jealousy, anger may be diverted onto other patients who are rivals for the nurse's attention just as brothers and sisters were rivals for mother's love.

These behavior patterns, of course, represent everyday occurrences to the nurse. It is an unusually mature individual who does not demonstrate, to some degree, one or another of these patterns in the course of a major illness. The important thing to bear in mind is that such behavior is meaningful and purposeful. It is the perennial cry of the sick for succor (6)!

Miss Bane continued, "I've had so many friends who have died of cancer. In fact, one person said she didn't want to be a friend of mine because they all got cancer. It has been awful to watch them getting weaker and weaker and so thin. One girl had a full-length mirror in her bathroom. When she was so weak she could hardly walk she would drag herself into the bathroom by clawing at the wall and lean up against the mirror and stare at herself. She had been a pretty girl, but her face was so thin now that she looked like a skeleton—all eyes and teeth." She shuddered.

I felt that in her mind's eye she saw herself and not her friend. She, too, had obviously been a very pretty girl. She was thin now, but still attractive, and her frilly negligee and carefully manicured hands spoke of great pride in appearance.

Morton J. Aronson says that the cancer patient may be harassed much more by the fear of mutilation or deformity than by the fear of death. Broadly speaking, such fears are related to unconscious masculine-feminine conflicts deriving from childhood fears of genital mutilations as punishment for forbidden sexual thoughts. Beyond this, mutilation fears in cancer patients, although partly rooted in reality, are also partly rooted in the emotional significance of the specific areas involved. The loss of a breast in a lovely woman who admires this evidence of feminine beauty may provoke a mourning reaction as intense as if she had lost a loved relative (7).

Miss Bane, as learned from conversations with others, had been attractive and popular in her youth. She enjoyed relating to the younger nurses stories of her many conquests. Not only had she lost much of her beauty, but she had also gone through an early menopause due to X-ray therapy. These two factors alone could account for a considerable degree of her state of depression.

Miss Bane continued to talk, almost as though she were in a trance.

"Even before you begin to get weak you can't lead a normal life. It's sort of like a black cloud that follows you around everywhere you go. If you have a cold you can't take a day off from work because you know that sooner or later you are going to need that sick leave. If there is something that you would like very much to buy, you don't dare, because you know that you are going to need more money than you can possibly earn.

"I remember when this was first diagnosed, my parents and my husband—I was married at the time—really panicked. They wouldn't let me do anything!

"I think if I don't get out of here by next weekend, I'll go jump off the balcony."

As she said this she looked at me sharply to see what my reaction would be. I resisted the impulse to say, "Oh, no!" and looked at her for a moment longer. "You must get very discouraged," I said finally.

Tears welled up in her eyes again. "There ought to be an easier way out than this."

Morton J. Aronson compares a diagnosis of cancer to the death sentence which is imposed as punishment for crime. The knowledge of certain death in the near future, not death itself, is the punishment. Cancer is often seen as punishment, with the patient crying, "Why—what did I do to deserve this?" (8)

Mrs. Allen, the first patient, remained in fair condition for several days and then began to decline rapidly. Her daughter had to return home because of family responsibilities and her place was taken by one and then by another of her four sons and their wives. Each day one of the family members remained at the bedside or in the lobby. Special nurses were again engaged. The evening nurse stopped the hospital chaplain in the hall one day.

"Would you have time to step in and speak to Mrs. Allen? She seems to be comforted by having her pastor come, but he is too far away to come often. She is well aware of her condition and seems to accept it. The family has been very faithful. Someone is always here or within five minutes of the place. I told them this evening that I wasn't sure if she would last the night. She is quite weak, but doesn't seem to have any pain."

The chaplain spoke briefly with the patient and at her request offered a prayer. Mrs. Allen murmured her thanks.

J. M. Hinton, in his study of the physical and mental distress of the dying, found that the amount of distress suffered by those having ambivalent feelings toward religion was significantly higher than that felt by those with religious faith. He also found that patients under fifty suffered more than older patients, and, when contrasted with those in their sixties, had more than twice the incidence of anxiety and depression (9).

Miss Bane, during another visit, had spoken of a patient who had just left the floor for surgery during which a diagnosis of lung cancer was expected.

"She has the most wonderful attitude. You ought to meet her. She says if they can cure her that is wonderful, but if they can't and she dies, that is all right with her, too. Of course, she is very religious. I suppose that helps. . . ." And she added a bit wistfully, "I've never been very religious, myself."

The bone marrow studies which had been done showed adequate activity so that it was possible to treat Miss Bane with nitrogen mustard instilled into the pleural cavity. The day before she was discharged I visited her again. She was sitting up in bed looking very alert and almost happy.

"You are certainly looking much better today," I greeted her.

"Yes, indeed. They're finally letting me out of here. They'll never get me back either! Not unless it's on the locked ward. I just don't think it's right—all this suffering. They shouldn't allow it. I really think they should put people to sleep for good if they want to be.

"It's so horrible to watch yourself die by inches. The human body is pretty ugly, anyway.

"One of my friends who died of cancer—oh, I told you about her, the one that used to drag herself to the mirror—well, when she got so bad that she couldn't walk any more, she begged me to help her out to the railroad track. I said, no indeed, she wasn't putting me in the position of helping her. She should have done that while she was still able.

"I knew two doctors at home. Both of them found out they had cancer, and they shot themselves. It is funny they would do it that way when they could get all those drugs and things. It really is hard to understand. I was talking about it to a friend of mine at the office. He said that anyone who had been out with the coroner on as many suicides as he had wouldn't think that drugs were an especially easy way either. The body tries to throw off those things. . . . There really ought to be some better way. . . ."

Visitors interrupted our talk at this point, and I had to leave. The conversation left me feeling very uneasy. It sounded as though Miss Bane had carefully considered each method of committing suicide and rejected it as either too violent or too disfiguring. Her almost compulsive talk of death and suicide to me, a comparative stranger, made me feel certain that she had also talked as freely with the nurses who cared for her. But if she hadn't, and she was telling me of her desperate depression in hopes that I would prevent her self-destruction, it was my responsibility to be certain that those responsible for her care were aware of her feelings. (This despite the fact that the objective of the study was to observe and not to influence the care given.)

The conversations with her had been notable in that there had been no positive feelings expressed toward family, friends, or physicians who had cared for her in the past or for the care she was receiving at the present. She appeared to be lonely, bitter, and severely depressed.

Eissler, in his discussion of suicide, has made these observations:

> *Strange as it may sound, suicide is the result of a rebellion against death. For many—perhaps even most people—the idea of having to die is unbearable. Partly they respond to this necessity as if it made life senseless and meaningless. By committing suicide they believe they have cheated death as the condemned cheats the executioner and the populace when he kills himself. I believe that for most suicides the act does not mean really dying. Dying for them is something that is suffered and passively submitted to; when actively performed it becomes a triumph, as if the ego has proved itself to be almighty when it is strong enough to cast its own life aside. . . . Linguistic usage seems to share the conviction of the person who commits suicide. Language—it is my feeling—differentiates between dying and committing suicide. Logical analysis, of course, will see in this differentiation only a qualification of the form in which death took place. Nevertheless we have the vague feeling of being unprecise when saying of a person who committed suicide "he died" as if self-inflicted death were essentially different from biological death* (10).

Mrs. Allen died quietly in her sleep about a day after her nurse had asked the chaplain to visit. She had suffered very little physical pain. Intravenous fluids prevented excess thirst, a symptom which is frequently one of the most distressing during the terminal phases of an illness. Constant physical attention prevented the discomfort of skin irritation.

However, it is probable that other factors contributed much more heavily to her peaceful acceptance of death. Her strong religious faith undoubtedly gave her assurance that death did not mean the cessation of existence for her, but continuation in an altered form. Also, one must not also underestimate the part that having lived a rather useful and satisfactory life may have played. One of her daughters-in-law expressed this very well.

"She was such a wonderful person. All five of the children just adored her. She has really been about the only mother that I have ever had, too. There isn't anything that we wouldn't do for her, but there isn't much more that we can do now that she is so bad. The boys came into see her all the time even though I know that it hurts them terribly to see her so changed. But you couldn't keep them away. And Dad—I don't know how he will get along without her. He depended on her so!"

The end of Mrs. Allen's life could well be considered a "fitting closure." With the best in physical care, the support of a devoted family, and her complete faith in the goodness of God, she was able to make of it "not just a long defeat of living, but a positive achievement of dying. This, more than anything else, gives courage to their relations and leaves something to be remembered with pride" (11).

The complete unhappiness expressed by Miss Bane might lead one to believe that the nursing staff had responded to her demanding attitude with antagonism or withdrawal. This, however, had not been the case. Careful nursing care plans had been made and carried out. Her poor appetite resulted in this notation in the plan: "Be sure that food is hot. Make sure patient is awake before bringing tray." Another note stated "Patient likes backrubs. They have a soothing effect. Repeat as often as possible."

"She seemed to be very lonely and depressed," one nurse said. "She obviously wanted company very much. If we were busy, she would offer us a piece of candy and tell us to come back later when we had time to talk. I spent quite a bit of time in there. Mostly she talked about all the fun she had when she was younger. She wanted me to tell her all about my dates and parties that I went to. I think that she was very sad to think that these things were gone now. She spent a lot of time telling me how popular she had been and always added, 'I was real pretty, then.'"

At first there was notation of her hostile attitude, and then the nurses' notes lapsed into meaningless remarks about a "usual day" or a "fairly comfortable evening."

"At first she was very demanding. She would order me to see that someone came down and bathed her because she was too weak," another nurse said. "I thought that we were really in for trouble. Of course we all realized how sick she was and that she was probably real scared—I would have been. We did all that we could for her. You know, she turned out to be a really interesting person. She told me all about her work. She must be quite intelligent. She didn't talk much about her condition, but she sort of hung onto you when you had to leave. Once she said something about an event that was coming up in the future and sort of remarked aside that she might not be here then. She changed the subject in a hurry then and talked about something else."

"To me she talked mostly about all the things that she had missed," another nurse said. "She envied me because I am married and said that even that hadn't worked out for her. I got the idea that a lot of her depression was caused by the feeling that because she had missed out on so many things she had not really lived. You could understand why she was so unhappy. She said that she had wanted children so badly."

"She talked to me quite a lot about dying," one of the older nurses said. "Mostly about how awful it was to die by inches and to watch yourself grow ugly. She visited a lot in the other patients' rooms and seemed to be most interested in those who had unfavorable diagnoses. She never mentioned suicide—even indirectly."

Each conversation with a member of the nursing staff made it more apparent that death and suicide were not as freely spoken of as had at first seemed likely, and only to one of those interviewed, a middle-aged nurse who usually appeared to be serene and unhurried, had Miss Bane talked of dying. Perhaps it was only possible to mention suicide to one who was not a member of the regular staff. The physician who had cared for her was also queried.

"I could only tell her that I don't honestly know what the future holds for her," he said. "She is a very intelligent person and knows a lot about her disease. To be anything but honest and forthright with her would only have destroyed her faith in me. She would have seen right through any false encouragement.

"She had a lot of problems besides her illness. She has been able to accept the fact that some of the treatment that she had in the past was not the best that could have been done for her. We talked this over at great length, and I am satisfied that she is taking a pretty realistic view of it all. It can't be undone. We can just go on from here. She may have another recession of the disease and have several more good years, or she may not live another month.

"Yes, she talked about suicide. When she was feeling very low she would have liked to have given up the fight. But I don't believe that she will."

When discharged, Miss Bane had been given a return appointment at the outpatient department. I saw her after her examination as she waited for another appointment to be made.

"How pretty you look!" I exclaimed. Stylish clothes and carefully applied make-up made a great difference in her appearance, but the striking change was in her expression. She seemed really happy and pleased to see me.

"All the reports are good!" was her opening remark. "How nice that you came up to see me."

"You must be feeling better to be looking so good," I said.

"Make-up can cover up a lot. I'm still pretty weak, but I think I'll be able to go back to work part-time next week."

"Will your doctor at home be taking care of you now?"

"Indeed, he won't!" she said with considerable feeling. "He goofed once, and I'm staying as far away from him as I can. I'll come back here for anything I need—even if it is a two-hour drive. This is the first time since I have been sick that I have gotten really good care. The doctors, the nurses, everyone have been just wonderful to me—even when I must have been pretty unbearable. It is so nice to know that there is such a place that I can come to."

The expression that settled on her face as I left not only was one of hope, but contained an element of tranquility that I had never seen before.

Conclusions

What results were derived from the study of the factors in nursing care which help to alleviate the distress of a dying patient? What, specifically, can the nurse do?

In the realm of physical care little has been written. The care given to the seriously ill patient who may recover does not differ essentially from the care which a few writers have recommended for the dying. Cicely Saunders (12) and Alfred Worchester (13) are the writers most frequently quoted when this subject is discussed. Although the ordering of medication for pain is done by the physician, the giving of the medication is often left to the discretion of the nurse. Saunders stresses the importance of giving pain relief before the discomfort has become severe enough to generate tension and anxiety which will, in turn, contribute to the intensity of the pain.

Many patients hesitate to ask for medication until these interacting factors have produced a state of distress which is difficult to relieve. To ask for pain medication may seem to the patient to be an indication of weakness or immaturity, and, indeed, nurses have been known to refer to patients who complain by such terms as "that big baby in 310!" Would it be possible to become sensitive enough to the needs of the patient to know from observations of position, expression, and tone of voice when the end-point of tolerance is being reached? In many cases it would be. In other instances, an accepting attitude on the part of the nurse may be all that is necessary.

Meticulous cleanliness, mouth care, changes of position, and careful attention to potential pressure areas are doubly important in the care of the dying. Slowed circulation and increased susceptibility to infection predispose the patient to complications which would add misery to his already distressed state.

Not only do good grooming and attractive surroundings increase the patient's comfort, but they help perform the important function of maintaining as well as possible, his body image. Disease in itself is enough of a threat to this image, without the additional burden of unkempt hair and cluttered surroundings.

Good light and adequate ventilation are also important. The patient, whose vision may already be dimming, is not usually anxious to have the room shrouded in shadows. His bodily temperature control may become unstable as his other functions decrease through inactivity, and he may complain of feeling too warm or of the excessive weight of the covers.

Although the patient may not appear to be responding, he may still be able to hear quite acutely. Whispering may be annoying or frightening. The normal sounds of activity may be more reassuring than an unnatural hush of tiptoeing and stealthy movement.

Worchester adds to his recommendations for physical care that the most important thing of all is that the physician give *himself* with his pills.

The most difficult and complex aspect of the care of the dying is the relief of the emotional distress, although the two are essentially inseparable in practice. For the nurse to handle with sensitivity the problems which besiege the patient and his family, some understanding of the normal process of grief is essential. Erich Lindemann discusses the symptoms which may be expected (14). These symptoms often occur in acute forms in anticipation of the death of the loved one. If these are understood and their true source is recognized, the nurse will be better able to cope with hostility expressed by the family or with excessive protestations of guilt and may be able to help the relative to develop a more meaningful relationship to the patient. The patient is often as burdened with the grief of his family as he is with his own illness.

Edgar Jackson has written a book for the use of pastors which could be equally useful for nurses (15). He has discussed in considerable depth the understanding of the grief process and offers guidance in helping the grief-stricken work through their sorrow.

C. Knight Aldrich has discussed the dynamics of anticipatory grief on the part of the patient (16). Since the patient is facing the loss of his entire emotional investment in life, it is reasonable to expect a marked grief reaction in anticipation of this loss. This is quite graphically illustrated in the distress expressed by Miss Bane. Since she had lost a husband (the bitterness accompanying this loss can only be surmised by the fact that she resumed the use of her maiden name), a child (she did not discuss this loss but a therapeutic abortion was noted on the history), much of her prized beauty, her sexuality through radiation castration, and many of her friends, it is not surprising that the anticipation of further loss resulted in deep depression.

Gerald Aronson has these suggestions for helping the patient to retain his individuality to the end (17). The physician (or nurse) must be guided by the principle of permitting and helping the patient to keep up the role that is important to him to the extent that this is possible. Imparting information which will unduly distress the patient should be avoided. A sensitivity to the needs of the individual patient is necessary for making such a decision; the withholding of information may be as stressful in some cases as the imparting of the same information is in other cases. Hope must never die too far ahead of the patient— either hope of getting better or hope of enjoyment of conversation tomorrow —but the gravity of the situation should not be minimized. A too Pollyanna-ish manner will destroy trust; one too morbid will destroy hope. Most important of all is the gift of self. Unqualified interest in and personal respect for the patient are evidence of love which helps to hold back the loneliness.

The importance of religious belief as a factor in relieving distress has been pointed out in the case of Mrs. Allen. When religious ties already exist it is only necessary to encourage the patient to use this source of strength and to assist him through the early notification of a clergyman or the provision of any materials which might be requested. When the patient's feelings toward religion are ambivalent or antagonistic, the nurse can only offer her serene acceptance of any feelings that he may express. Proselytizing at this time, by either nurse or clergyman, would probably produce a negative reaction. However, adequate opportunity to express negative feelings may, in time, clear the way for more positive thinking on the part of the patient.

The need for the nurse to be a good listener cannot be overemphasized.

She needs to listen attentively to the patient to find out the extent of his awareness and acceptance of his condition. She needs to listen for the things which are of concern to the patient and his family—their interests, their fears, their hostility, and their sorrow.

To be sufficiently sensitive to be able to give this kind of care to the patient the nurse must have worked through her own anxieties about death. A security in her personal beliefs and philosophy will make it unnecessary for her to withdraw into starched efficiency to protect her feelings. She must be willing and able to invest the time and the emotion which will be required of her if she is to use the compassionate service of her hands and her heart to help hold back the loneliness, which can be as bad as the pain, when the time comes for her patient to die.

References

1. Daniel Cappon. "The Psychology of Dying." *Pastoral Psychology,* Vol. 12 (February, 1961). 35.
2. Cicely Saunders. "Care of the Dying." *Nursing Times.* Vol. 55 (October 9, 1959). 960.
3. K. R. Eissler. *The Psychiatrist and the Dying Patient.* New York: International Universities Press, Inc., 1955. P. 252.
4. Morton J. Aronson. "Emotional Aspects of Nursing the Cancer Patient." *Mental Hygiene.* Vol. 42 (April, 1958). 267–73.
5. Margaret Mead. "Nursing, Primitive and Civilized." *American Journal of Nursing.* Vol. 56 (August, 1956). 1001–1004.
6. Aronson. "Emotional Aspects of Nursing the Cancer Patient."
7. Ibid.
8. Ibid.
9. J. M. Hinton. "The Physical and Mental Distress of the Dying." *Quarterly Journal of Medicine,* Vol. 32 (January, 1963). 1–21.
10. Eissler. *The Psychiatrist and the Dying Patient.* Pp. 66–67.
11. C. Saunders. "Euthanasia." Letter to Editor. *Lancet.* Vol. 281 (1961). 548–49.
12. Cicely Saunders. "Care of the Dying." *Nursing Times.* Vol. 55 (October 9, 1959). 960.
13. Alfred Worchester. *The Care of the Aged, the Dying, and the Dead.* Springfield, Ill.: Charles C Thomas, Publisher, 1940.
14. Erich Lindemann. "Symptomatology and Management of Acute Grief." *American Journal of Psychiatry.* Vol. 101 (September, 1944). 141.
15. Edgar Jackson. *Understanding Grief.* New York: Abingdon Press, 1957.
16. C. Knight Aldrich. "The Dying Patient's Grief." *Journal of the American Medical Association.* Vol. 185 (May 4, 1963). 329–31.
17. Gerald J. Aronson. "Treatment of the Dying Person." In *The Meaning of Death.* Ed. H. Feifel. New York: McGraw-Hill Book Company, 1959.

EPILOGUE

The preceding chapters have introduced the reader to a view of the human personality in health and illness which reflects our psychoanalytic orientation with its emphasis on individual psychology. We have attempted to formulate and apply concepts which relate to the unconscious as well as the conscious mind; to the irrational as well as the rational; to the experiences of children as well as adults; to the needs of the very old as well as the very young; and to the emotional responses of nurses as well as their patients.

We have noted the fragmentation that seems to characterize so much of present-day medical, nursing, and hospital care. Technological advances have contributed a major share to the alienation of physicians and nurses from their patients. We have emphasized the environment as a crucial factor in an individual's well-being. The hospital, as the most frequent physical setting for health care, can be considered by the patient as either "good" or "bad" depending on the quality of the services received.

Health professionals too often overlook the close environmental association between physical illness and the psychosocial stresses of living. The influence of personality types or character traits on the development and the course of illness is a fascinating and still unfolding chapter in psychosomatic medicine which deserves far more attention than we have been able to give it.

Nurses are becoming increasingly aware of the socioeconomic factors in illness. For example, the poor suffer more illness and utilize fewer health services than do the nonpoor. Infant mortality, prematurity, and mental retardation are more common among the disadvantaged. Poverty is accompanied not only by poor nutrition, substandard housing, and inadequate sanitation, but by a variety of emotional stresses, feelings of hopelessness, and pervasive apathy. This deadly combination provides a breeding ground for physical and emotional ill health. The delivery of health services in the United States is undergoing revolutionary changes. One of the major problems is the provision of adequate medical and nursing care for the urban and rural poor.

As health care makes the transition from the hospital to the community, there will be greater emphasis on neighborhood health clinics, extended care facilities for convalescent and aging patients, as well as homemaker services. The nurse will then need an even more extensive knowledge of the psychosocial aspects of illness.

Curriculum reform and innovation will be necessary to broaden the nurse's understanding of these social and economic elements in illness. Sociology, political science, and psychology, as well as the various medical specialties, all have much to contribute to the education of the modern nurse and to the improvement and delivery of health services.

It is our conviction, however, that whatever directions are taken by the field of nursing in the years to come, the care of the individual patient will remain the primary concern and responsibility of most nurses. There should be no lessening of the need for a firm grounding in individual psychology as a "basic science" of human behavior. The nurse can also greatly benefit from knowledge about group psychology and the implications of group dynamics for patients, professional staff, and administrators. An awareness of group dynamics adds another dimension to understanding human behavior without lessening the need for individual psychology.

We have attempted to present a psychodynamic point of view that we feel is significant and useful. In addition, we have tried to point the way toward the implementation of these concepts within the nurse–patient relationship.

GLOSSARY

Abreaction: The process of bringing to consciousness and to adequate expression emotional feelings that have been unconscious.

Affect: The feeling-tone accompanying an idea or mental representation.

Aggression: In psychiatry, forceful attacking action (physical, verbal, or symbolic). May be realistic and self-protective, including healthful self-assertiveness; may be unrealistic and directed outwardly toward environment or inwardly toward self.

Ambivalence: The coexistence of two opposing drives, desires, feelings, or emotions (such as love and hate) toward the same person, object, or goal. These may be conscious or partly conscious; or one side of the feelings may be unconscious.

Anaclitic: Lit. "Leaning on." In psychoanalytic terminology, denotes dependence of the infant on the mother or mother substitute for his sense of well-being (for example, gratification through nursing). Normal in childhood; pathologic in later years if excessive.

Anaclitic depression: An acute and striking impairment of an infant's physical, social, and intellectual development which sometimes occurs following a sudden separation from the mothering person. (See also *Depression*).

Anxiety: Apprehension, tension, or uneasiness that stems from the anticipation of danger, the source of which is largely unknown or unrecognized. Primarily of intrapsychic origin, in distinction to fear, which is the emotional response to a consciously recognized and usually external threat or danger.

Autoerotism: Sensual self-gratification. Characteristic of, but not limited to, an early stage of emotional development. Includes satisfactions deriving from genital play; masturbation; oral, anal, and visual sources; and fantasy.

Body image: The conscious and unconscious picture a person has of his body at any moment. The conscious and unconscious images may differ from each other.

Castration: In psychiatry, usually the fantasied loss of the penis. In psychological terms also used figuratively to denote state of impotence, powerlessness, helplessness, or defeat.

Character: In psychiatry, the sum of the relatively fixed personality traits and habitual modes of response of an individual.

Child analysis: Application of modified psychoanalytic methods and goals to problems of children to remove impediments to normal personality development.

Climacteric: Menopausal period in women. Also used sometimes to refer to the corresponding age period in men.

Complex: A group of associated ideas that have a common, strong emotional tone. These are largely unconscious, and significantly influence attitudes and associations.

Conflict: The clash, largely determined by unconscious factors, between two opposing emotional forces. For example, an instinctual wish for gratification may conflict with restrictions of conscience (intrapsychic conflict), or with external social requirements. Conflict is basic in psychic life and fundamental in the etiology of psychological disorders.

Congenital: Present at birth.

Constitution: A person's intrinsic physical and psychological endowment; sometimes used more narrowly to indicate the physical inheritance or potential from birth.

Conversion: A mental mechanism, operating unconsciously, by which intrapsychic conflicts, which would otherwise give rise to anxiety, are instead given symbolic external expression. The repressed ideas or impulses, along with the psychologic defenses against them, are converted into a variety of somatic symptoms. Example: psychogenic paralysis of a limb, which prevents its use for aggressive purposes.

Defense mechanism: Specific intrapsychic defensive processes, operating unconsciously, which are employed for relief from emotional conflict and freedom from anxiety. Conscious efforts are frequently made for the same reasons, but true defense mechanisms are out of awareness (unconscious). Some common defense mechanisms: compensation, conversion, denial, displacement, rationalization, reaction formation, regression, repression, sublimation substitution, symbolization.

Denial: A defense mechanism, operating unconsciously, by which the person tries to resolve emotional conflict and allay anxiety by denying a thought, feeling, wish, need, or external reality factor that is consciously intolerable.

Dependency needs: Vital infantile needs for mothering, love, affection, shelter, protection, security, food, and warmth. May continue beyond infancy in overt or hidden forms, or may be increased in the adult as a regressive manifestation.

Depression: Psychiatrically, a morbid sadness, dejection, or melancholy; to be differentiated from grief, which is realistic and proportionate to what has been lost. A depression may be a symptom of any psychiatric disorder or may constitute its principal manifestation.

Deprivation, emotional: A lack of adequate and appropriate interpersonal or environmental experience, usually in the early developmental years.

Deprivation, sensory: Term for experience of being cut off from external sensory stimuli and the opportunity for perception. May occur accidentally (for example, in a marooned explorer) or experimentally. May lead to disorganized thinking, depression, panic, delusion formation, and hallucinations.

Depth psychology: The psychology of unconscious mental processes. Also a system of psychology in which the study of such processes plays a major role, as in psychoanalysis.

Descriptive psychiatry: A system of psychiatry based upon observation and study of readily observable external factors; to be differentiated from dynamic psychiatry.

Determinism: A doctrine common to all sciences. In psychiatry, it postulates that nothing in the individual's emotional or mental life results from chance alone, but rather results from specific causes or forces known or unknown.

Disorientation: Loss of awareness of the position of the self in relation to space, time, or other persons.

Displacement: A defense mechanism, operating unconsciously, in which an emotion is transferred from its original object to a more acceptable substitute.

Drive: Basic urge, instinct, motivation. In psychiatry, a term currently preferred to avoid confusion with the more purely biological concept of instinct.

Dynamic psychiatry: As distinguished from descriptive psychiatry, refers to the study of emotional processes, their origins, and the mental mechanisms. Implies the study of the active, energy-laden, and changing factors in human behavior and its motivation.

Dynamics: Refers to emotional forces that determine the pattern of feelings and behavior. These forces arise through the interaction of drives and defenses in growth and development.

Ego: In psychoanalytic theory, one of the three major divisions in the model of the psychic apparatus, the others being the id and superego.

Ego ideal: The part of the personality that comprises the ideal aims and goals of the self. Usually refers to the conscious or unconscious emulation of significant figures with whom the person has identified.

Emotion: A feeling such as fear, anger, grief, joy, or love. As used in psychiatry, the patient may not always be conscious of the feeling. Synonymous with affect.

Empathy: An objective and insightful awareness of the feelings, emotions, and behavior of another person, their meaning and significance. To be distinguished from sympathy, which is usually nonobjective and noncritical.

Enuresis: Bed-wetting.

Fantasy: An imagined sequence of events or mental images; for example, daydreams.

Fear: Normal emotional response to consciously recognized and external sources of danger; to be distinguished from anxiety. (See *Anxiety; Phobia.*)

Functional illness: An illness of emotional origin in which organic or structural changes are either absent or develop secondarily to prolonged emotional stress.

Grief: Normal, appropriate emotional response to an external and consciously recognized loss; self-limiting, and gradually subsiding within a reasonable time.

Homeostasis: The maintenance of self-regulating metabolic or psychologic processes that are optimal for comfort and survival.

Id: In Freudian theory, that part of the personality structure which harbors the unconscious instinctive desires and strivings of the individual. (See also *Ego; Superego.*)

Identification: A defense mechanism, operating unconsciously, by which an individual endeavors to pattern himself after another. Identification plays a major role in the development of one's personality.

Insight: Self-understanding. A major goal of psychotherapy. The extent of the individual's understanding of the origin, nature, and mechanisms of his attitudes and behavior.

Instinct: An inborn drive (q.v.). The human instincts include those of self-preservation, sexuality, and (for some authors), aggression, the ego instinct (q.v.), and the herd or social instincts.

Intellectualization: The defense mechanism that utilizes reasoning as a defense against conscious confrontation with the unconscious conflict and its stressful emotions.

Intelligence: The potential ability of an individual to understand what he needs to recall and to mobilize and integrate constructively previous learning and experience in meeting new situations. The ability to use intelligence is influenced by emotional factors.

Intrapsychic: That which takes place within the psyche or mind.

Introjection: A defense mechanism, operating unconsciously, whereby loved or hated external objects are taken within one's self symbolically. The converse of projection.

Involutional psychosis (involutional melancholia): A functional psychotic reaction occurring in late middle life. Formerly thought to be related to the menopause in the female and the climacteric in the male.

Isolation: An unconscious defense mechanism in which an unacceptable impulse, idea, or act is separated from its original memory source, thereby removing the emotional charge associated with the original memory.

Latency period: In psychoanalytic theory, the phase between the Oedipal period of psychosexual development (roughly 5–7 years) and the adolescent period.

Latent content: The hidden (unconscious) meaning of thoughts or actions (q.v.).

Libido: The energy arising from the sexual drive.

Magical thinking: A person's conviction that thinking about doing something is the same as doing it. Occurs in dreams in children and primitive peoples, and in patients under a variety of conditions. Characterized by lack of realistic relationship between cause and effect.

Menarche: The beginning of menstrual functioning in the female life cycle.

Mental hygiene: A term used to designate measures employed to reduce the incidence of mental illness through prevention and early treatment and to promote mental health.

Narcissism (narcism): Self-love, as opposed to object-love (love of another person).

Negativism: Perverse opposition and resistance to suggestions or advice.

Nervous breakdown: A nonmedical, nonspecific term for emotional illness; primarily, a euphemism for psychiatric illness or psychosis.

Object relationship: The emotional bonds that exist between an individual and another person as opposed to his interest in, and love for, himself.

Oedipus complex (Freud): Attachment of the child for the parent of the opposite sex. Accompanied by envious and aggressive feelings toward the parent of the same sex. These feelings are largely repressed (made unconscious) because of the fear of displeasure or punishment by the parent of the same sex. In its original use, the term applied only to the male child.

Oral stage: In psychoanalysis, the earliest of the stages of infantile psychosexual development, lasting from birth to 12 months or longer.

Overdetermination: In psychiatry, a term indicating the multiple causality of a single emotional reaction or symptom.

Personality: The sum total of the individual's internal and external patterns of adjustment to life.

Phallic stage: The period of psychosexual development, from about 2½ to 6, during which sexual interest, curiosity, and pleasurable experience center about the penis, and in girls, to a lesser extent, the clitoris. (See also *Oral stage* and *Latency period*.)

Play therapy: A treatment technique using the child's play as a medium for expression and communication between patient and therapist.

Pleasure principle: A regulatory mechanism of mental life, the function of which is to reduce psychic tension or disturbing stimuli, in a way that will most easily provide satisfaction or pleasure.

Preconscious: Referring to thoughts that are not in immediate awareness, but can be recalled by conscious effort.

Pregenital: In psychoanalysis, refers to the period of early childhood before the genitals have begun to exert the predominant influence in the organization or patterning of sexual behavior. Oral and anal influences predominate during this period.

Primary process: In psychoanalytic theory, the generally unorganized mental activity characteristic of unconscious mental life. Seen in less disguised form in infancy and in dreams.

Projection: A defense mechanism, operating unconsciously, whereby that which is emotionally unacceptable in the self is unconsciously rejected and attributed to (projected on to) others.

Psychiatrist: A doctor of medicine with postgraduate training and experience in diagnoses and treatment of mental and emotional disorders.

Psychiatry: The specialty of medical science that deals with the origin, diagnosis, prevention, and treatment of mental and emotional disorders.

Psychoanalysis: A psychologic theory of human development and behavior, a method of research, and a system of psychotherapy, originally described by Sigmund Freud.

Psychoanalyst: A psychiatrist with additional training in psychoanalysis, who employs the techniques of psychoanalytic therapy.

Psychodynamics: The systematized knowledge and theory of human behavior and its motivation.

Psychologist: One who specializes in psychology. Generally holds a Ph.D. or M.A. degree.

Psychologist, clinical: A psychologist with a graduate degree (usually Ph.D.) who specializes in research and/or diagnosis and psychotherapy in the field of mental and emotional disorders.

Psychology: An academic discipline, a profession, and a science dealing with the study of mental processes and behavior in man and animal.

Psychoneurosis (psychoneurotic disorders): Emotional maladaptations due to unresolved unconscious conflicts. One of the two major categories of emotional illness, the other being the psychoses. A neurosis is usually less severe than a psychosis, with minimal loss of contact with reality.

Psychosis: A major mental disorder of organic or emotional origin in which there is a significant departure from normal patterns of thinking, feeling, and acting. Commonly characterized by loss of contact with reality, distortion of perception, regressive behavior and attitudes, diminished control of elementary impulses and desires, and abnormal mental content including delusions and hallucinations.

Psychosomatic: Adjective to denote the constant and inseparable interaction of the psyche (mind) and the soma (body). Most commonly used to refer to illnesses in which the manifestations are primarily physical with at least a partial emotional etiology.

Rationalization: A defense mechanism, operating unconsciously, in which the individual attempts to justify or make consciously tolerable, by plausible means, feelings, behavior, and motives that would otherwise be intolerable. Not to be confused with conscious evasion or dissimulation. (See also *Projection*.)

Reaction formation: A defense mechanism, operating unconsciously, wherein attitudes and behavior are adopted that are the opposites of impulses the individual harbors either consciously or unconsciously. For example, excessive moral zeal may be a reaction to strong but repressed asocial impulses.

Reality-principle: In psychoanalytic theory, the concept that the pleasure principle (q.v.), which represents the claims of instinctual wishes, is normally modified by the inescapable demands and requirements of the external world.

Regression: The partial or symbolic return under conditions of relaxation or stress to more infantile patterns of reacting. Manifested in a wide variety of circumstances such as normal sleep, play, and severe physical illness, and in many psychiatric disorders.

Remission: Abatement of an illness, sometimes temporary.

Glossary

Repression: A defense mechanism, operating unconsciously, which banishes unacceptable ideas, affects, or impulses, from consciousness or which keeps out of consciousness what has never been conscious. Although not subject to voluntary recall, the repressed material may emerge in disguised form. Sometimes used as a generic term for all defense mechanisms. Often confused with the conscious mechanism of suppression.

Secondary process: In psychoanalytic theory, mental activity and thinking characteristic of the ego and influenced by the demands of the environment. Characterized by organization, systematization, intellectualization, and similar processes, leading to logical thought and action in adult life. (See also *Primary process*.)

Separation anxiety: The fear and apprehension noted in infants when removed from their mother (or surrogates) or in being approached by strangers. Most marked from the sixth to the tenth month. In later life, similar reaction may result from removal of significant persons or familiar surroundings.

Sibling: Term for a full brother or sister.

Sibling rivalry: The competition between siblings for the love of a parent or for other recognition or gain.

Subconscious: Obsolescent in psychiatry. Formerly used to include the preconscious (what can be recalled with effort) and the unconscious.

Sublimation: A mental mechanism, operating unconsciously, by which instinctual drives, consciously unacceptable, are diverted into socially acceptable channels.

Substitution: A defense mechanism, operating unconsciously, by which an unattainable or unacceptable goal, emotion, or object is replaced by one that is more attainable or acceptable.

Suggestion: In psychiatry, the process of influencing an individual to accept uncritically an idea, belief, or attitude induced by the therapist.

Superego: In psychoanalytic theory, that part of the personality associated with conscious ethics, standards, and self-criticism. (See also *Ego; Id*.)

Supportive psychotherapy: A technique of psychotherapy that aims to reinforce a patient's defenses and to help him suppress disturbing psychological material. Supportive psychotherapy utilizes such measures as inspiration, reassurance, suggestion, persuasion, counselling, and reeducation.

Suppression: The conscious effort to control and conceal unacceptable impulses, thoughts, feelings, or acts.

Surrogate: One who takes the place of another; a substitute person. In psychiatry, usually refers to an authority figure who replaces a parent in the emotional feelings of the patient (father-surrogate, mother-surrogate).

Symbiosis: In psychiatry, denotes an advantageous relationship of two disturbed persons who become dependent on each other.

Toilet training: The methods used by a child's parents, usually the mother, in teaching and encouraging control of bladder and bowel functions.

Transference: The unconscious displacement to others of feelings and attitudes that were originally associated with important figures (parents, siblings, etc.) in one's early life.

Unconscious: In Freudian theory, that part of the mind or mental functioning of which the content is only rarely accessible.

Withdrawal: In psychiatry, a pathological retreat from people or the world of reality, often seen in schizophrenics.

INDEX

A

Aasterud, Margaret, 255
  article by, 279–294
Acceptance, patient's need of, 30, 107, 240
Adaptation, defensive, 247, 320
Adolescence, 178, 196–225 *passim*, 227, 242, 305
Adult, reactions to illness, 226–304 (*see also* Middle age; Old age)
After-care, 40, 84, 109, 265, 401
Aggression, 112–113, 125, 129, 134, 175, 186 194–195, 283, 363
Aggrievement reaction, 285
Aging process, 306, 341–347 (*see also* Old age)
Alcohol, 81, 236, 332
Alexander, Franz, 245–247
Ambivalence, 113, 114, 128–129
Amnesia, 180, 181
Amputation, psychic impact of, 232, 385–386

Anal stage, 122, 125, 130, 140, 175, 178
Anesthesia, 236
Anger, 195, 357, 380
Anxiety, 7, 27, 51, 129, 189–192, 229–231, 235, 292, 301, 314, 331
  in adolescents, 196
  in children, 24, 140, 145, 198
  in nurses, 279–294
  in old age, 331, 332
  in parents, 128
  in patients, 29–30
Apathy, 401
Aronson, Gerald, 398
Aronson, Morton J., 389, 390–392
Auer, Edward, 19
  article by, 36–41
Authority figures, 217, 222, 286
Autoerotism (*see* Masturbation)
Autografts, in burn therapy, 188
Autonomy, psychic need for, 111, 122, 231
Avoidance, 278

B

Baby (*see* Infant)
Barbiturates, 332
Battered child, 82
Beam, Rebecca, 35
Beauvoir, Simone de, 309
Bedside manner, 33
Behavior, 7, 10, 16
 in adolescence, 196–198, 202–203, 205, 211–213
 in animals, 55
 in infants, 59–61, 63, 66–67, 77–78, 80–81, 90–93
 maternal, 56, 63, 66
 in middle childhood, 175–185
 in preschool children, 111–127, 129–131, 135–141, 146–148
Benedek, T., 103, 247, 306–307
Bereavement, 14, 354–371 *passim*, 376–387 *passim*, 397–398
Bergler, Edmund, 309
Bergman, Thesi, 179
Bernfeld, Siegfried, 59–60
Bettelheim, Bruno, 2, 7, 19
 article by, 20–29
Bibring, Grete, 239
Biestek, Felix, 33–34
Birth, 54, 58
 defects, 72–74
 premature, 74–75
Bladder control, 122
Blake, Florence, 131
Blos, Peter, 199, 202
Body image, 178, 181
Bowlby, John, 45, 61, 68, 148
Braceland, Francis, 311
 article by, 312–317
Brann, Beake, 236
Breuer, Joseph, 43–44
Brody, Sylvia, 45, 70–71
Bromides, 332
Burn injuries, 186, 187–195
Burns, Robert C., 116
Buxbaum, Edith, 115, 134
Byers, Mary Lou, 210
 article by, 213–218

C

Cancer, of breast, 232, 254, 256–266
 in elderly, 326
 emotional impact on nurse, 390–392
 frustration and, 347
 in hospitalized patients, 294–302
Cannon, W. B., 244
Caplan, Gerald, 73, 83, 103
Cappon, Daniel, 388
Cardiac cases, 277
Carey, William B., 76, 84
Casler, Lawrence, 70
Castration, fear of, 139–141 (*see also* Mutilation)
Charcot, Jean, 43
Child (*see also* Infant; Toddler stage; Adolescence)
 emotional and physical development, 7, 23, 45, 111–195 *passim*, 242, 283
 illness and hospitalization 27–28, 131–134, 139, 148–157, 159–171, 180–181, 283
 middle childhood, 175–195 *passim*
 play, 16, 135–136, 149, 152–153, 155
 preschool, 111–174 *passim*
 relations with family, 55, 119, 145
Child-rearing practices, 46, 112–113
Climacteric, 306–314
Cockerill, Eleanor, 204
Colitis, 124
Colostomy patient, 125, 232
Community health care (*see* Health care services)
Congenital defects, 71–76
Constipation, 124
Conti, Mary Louise, 271, 342
 article by, 348–352
Convalescent care, 401
Countertransference (*see* Transference)
Crises, developmental, 73, 74, 83, 305, 318

Crying:
  in adults, 366, 380
  in infants, 60
"Culture shock," 5

D

Day-care centers, 119, 126
Deafness, 327, 351–352
Death, 74, 354–399 passim (see also Bereavement)
  emotional impact of, 120, 156, 186, 260, 268, 293, 319, 355, 357, 358, 359, 394
  of infants, 76–77
  nurse's function in, 287, 288, 354–355, 357–358, 360–361, 376
Decompensation, 321
Defense mechanisms, 14, 50, 193, 228, 235–243, 283, 368 (see also Denial; Displacement; Identification; Isolation; Magical thinking; Projection; Rationalization; Reaction formation; Regression; Repression; Sublimation; Suppression; and Withdrawal)
  in nurse, 281–282
Defiance, 391
Dehumanization, 65, 349
Denial, as psychological reaction, 237, 238, 368
Dependency, 48, 55, 65–66, 83, 246, 382–383, 391
  in patient, 3, 132, 133, 221, 301
Depression, 69, 160, 186, 241, 261, 316–317, 363, 392
  in old age, 311, 314, 330–333
Deprivation, 162, 285
Detachment, 278
Diabetes, 248
Diarrhea, 124
Diet pills, 205
Di Leo, Joseph H., 116
Disorientation, 187, 277
Displacement, 238
Distortion, 11, 14

Dreams, 44–46
Drug abuse, 204–205, 236
Drummond, Eleanor, 356
Dunbar, W. F., 245

E

Eating (see Feeding)
Ego, 49–50, 50–51, 100, 123, 130, 140, 176, 204, 320, 344
Eissler, Kurt, 301, 389, 394
Elderly (see Old age)
Elmer, Elizabeth, 82
Empathy, nurse's, 28, 62–63
Enemas, 153, 284
Engel, George, 248, 254–255, 363, 366, 376
  articles by, 266–274, 376–387
Enuretic child, 122
Erickson, Florence, 133, 134, 145, 168
  article by, 148–157
Erikson, Erik, 46
  on adolescents, 204
  on adults, 226–227, 310
  on children, 45, 78–79, 137, 149, 177
  on "life-cycle concept," 46, 79, 122–123, 141
Escape, 320
Esterton, A., 31
Estrogen, 307
Exhibitionism, 138, 239, 330

F

"Failure to thrive" in infants, 69, 102, 104
Family, 50, 119, 159, 167, 201, 323–325 (see also Bereavement)
Fantasies, 13–14, 27–28, 44, 178–179, 283, 286, 319 (see also Fears)
Father's role, 57, 74, 104, 119
Fears, 8, 9, 132, 133, 139, 148, 189–193 (see also Fantasies)
Feeding, 80–81
  of infants, 63–65, 78, 81, 125, 130

Feifel, Herman, 355
Fenichel, Otto, 61
Ferrano, M. A., 64
Fiske, A., 145
Food (*see* Feeding)
Forgetting, 47
Fraiberg, Selma, 122, 127
Free association, 44
Freis, Margaret, 58–60
French, Thomas M., 245–246
Freud, Anna (daughter of Sigmund Freud):
  on adolescence, 197
  on anal sensitivity, 123–124
  on bereaved children, 369
  on children, 6, 45, 68, 124, 139, 148
  on defense mechanisms, 235–243
  on feeding problems, 125, 283
  on parental attitudes, 134
  on regression, 129–130
  on temper tantrums, 114
  on the "unwilling mother," 89
  work at the Hampstead Child Therapy Clinic, 114n, 117, 124, 125n, 130, 199
Freud, Sigmund, 42–44
  on anal phase, 122
  on authority figures, 286
  on death, 287
  on delayed reaction to trauma, 134–135
  on depression, 273
  on id and ego, 49–50
  on latency, 175
  on melancholia, 364–365
  on mind-body problem, 244
  on Oedipus complex, 137–141
  on play, 149
  on psychoanalytical method, 44–45
  on psychotherapy for the elderly, 335
  on repression, 180
  on theory of sexuality, 199
  on transference, 10–11
  on verbal slips, 47

Freund, Hedi, 2, 6, 9, 19
  article by, 29–36
Frustration, 66, 270

G

Gender, sense of, 140
Generativity, sense of, 227, 310
Genitals, infant's, 126, 138, 232
Gerontology, 338
"Giving-up–given-up syndrome," 248, 254–255, 266–274
Goffman, Irving, 232
"Good patient" stereotype, 8, 219
Grafting procedure, 192
Green, Morris, 76
Grief, 14, 73, 74, 354–371 *passim*, 376–387 *passim*, 397–398
Grinker, Roy, 361
Group for the Advancement of Psychiatry, 203, 205
Guilt, 51, 127, 132, 141, 159, 192
Gumpertz, Elizabeth, 72
Gunther, Frances, 371

H

Hall, G. Stanley, 51, 322
Hallucinogens, 205
Hampstead Child Therapy Clinic, London, 114n, 117, 124n, 125, 130, 139
Harlow, Harry F., 61
Health care services, 275, 400
  community nurse, 74–76, 82, 83, 109, 217–218, 327, 337
  community-sponsored, 40–41, 109, 275, 333, 400–401
  costs, 275
  mental health, 85
Helplessness, psychic impact of, 271
Hinkle, L. E., 248
Hinton, J. M., 392–393
Hiroshima, 355
Holmes, T. H., 247–248

Holt, Jacqueline, 134, 180–181
Holzman, Philip, 42
Homeostasis, 255
Homografts, 188
Homosexuality, 200–201, 330
Hopelessness, psychic impact of, 271, 401
Hormone changes, 196–197
Hospital:
    as community health center, 40–41
    cost of care, 39, 276
    new developments in, 38, 40, 41, 77, 169, 275, 401
    physical arrangements in, 158, 163–164, 276, 397
    social work in, 169
    staff, 40
    technology of, 4, 255, 276, 355
    visiting hours, 129, 145, 159, 162
    "ward culture," 163–164, 276, 397
Hospitalism, 69
Hospitalization, 4, 7, 400
    of adolescent, 161
    of adult, 226–321 *passim*
    care of body after death, 287
    of dying patient, 355–359
    of elderly, 334–335
    of infant and mother, 17, 105
    in middle childhood, 180–182
    of preschool child, 127–129
Hostility, 241–242
Hunger (*see* Feeding)
Hyperactivity, 134
Hypnosis, 43–44, 180
Hypochondria, 176, 310
Hypodermic needle, child's fear of, 283
Hypothalamus, 247
Hysterectomy, 10, 232
Hysteria, 43–44, 244, 332

I

Id, 47–51, 140–141, 235–236
Identification, 140, 242, 382
Identity, 47, 196, 207, 219, 224, 256

Illness:
    emotional impact of, 132, 139, 181–182, 227, 326, 389
    psychosocial aspects of, 243–244
Immobilization, 220
Indians, American, 322–323
Infant:
    amnesia, 181
    crying, 60
    development, 56–62, 67, 78, 81, 90–93, 102, 104, 122, 126, 140
    emotions of, 61, 67–70, 286
    growth rate, 102
    illness of, 68, 84, 99–101
    and mother, 58, 70, 74–77, 102, 140
    needs of, 16–62, 78
    newborn, 59–60
    premature, 58, 74
    treatment procedures, 284
"Infantilizing," 35
Ingles, Thelma, 89–90
    article by, 93–99
Initiative, 141
Insomnia, 331, 368
Instincts, 54–55
Integration of personality, 321
Intensive Care Unit, 233, 255, 275–278
Internalization, 140
Intimacy, 227
Intoxication, 236
Intrusive procedures, 148–150, 168, 284, 290
Isolation:
    as defense mechanism, 238–239
    as separation from other persons, 181, 227, 281, 351–353

J

Jackson, Edgar, 398
Janis, I. L., 285, 288
Johns Hopkins Hospital, 167
Johnson, Virginia E., 333
Josselyn, Irene M., 122

Jourard, Sidney, 30

K

Kalish, Richard A., 360
Kallaus, Jane, 72–73
Kaplan, David, 74–75
Kaufman, S. Harvard, 116
Kennedy Institute, Johns Hopkins Hospital, 167
Kerstenberg, Judith, 200
Ketosis, 248
Kimball, C. P., 245, 248, 249
Kindergarten, 136
Kinsey, Alfred, 201
Klagsbrun, Samuel C., 255–256
    article by, 294–302
Klein, Melanie, 117, 283
Kübler-Ross, Elisabeth, 355, 357
Kutner, Bernard, 231–232

L

Latency, 140–177
Lester, Jane, 67, 70, 87–90
    article by, 99–101
Levin, Sidney, 359
Levy, David, 45, 153
Lewis, Wilma, 376
    article by, 388–399
Libido, 203, 308
Life expectancy, 325
"Life islands," 297
Lindbergh, Anne Morrow, 309
Lindemann, Erich, 73, 397–398
Lindzey, Gardner, 41, 51
Lipton, Rose, 68–70
Loneliness, 30, 181, 342, 345, 348–353, 399
LSD, 205 (*see also* Drug abuse)

M

MacDonald, Betty, 8
Magical thinking, 180, 239
Malignancy, 356
Mannes, Marya, 341
    article by, 342–347
Marasmus, 69
Marijuana, 204–205
Marmor, Judd, 305–306, 311
    article by, 318–321
Mason, Edward A., 130, 145–146
    article by, 157–171
Mastectomy, 232, 254, 256–266
Masters, William H., 333
Masturbation, 126–127, 130, 138, 198–199
Maternal care (*see* Mother and child)
Mayo Clinic, 255
Mead, Margaret, 202–203, 389
Mediatrics, 308
Medicare, 319, 324–325, 328, 335
Megacolon, 121
Melancholia, 364 (*see also* Depression)
Menninger, Karl, 11, 14
Menninger, William, 266, 274
Menninger Clinic, 248n
Menopause, 306, 307, 312, 319–320, 346
Menstration, 199, 200, 205, 247
Mental mechanisms, 228, 235 (*see also* Defense mechanisms)
Menzies, Isabel E., 3, 281
Mescaline, 205
Metastasis, 261
Meyer, Herbert L., 210
    article by, 219–225
Middle age, emotional impact of, 227, 305–321
Mind, preconscious and unconscious, 44, 45, 47–48, 51, 283 (*see also* Id)
Mistrust, basic, according to Erikson, 78–79
Mitford, Jessica, 367
Money, patient's attitudes, 39
Mother and child, 58, 79, 102, 112, 115, 160, 171, 345
    deprivation of maternal care, 66–71
    nonthriving mothers, 102–107

Mother and child (*cont.*)
   substitute mothers, 57, 106, 115, 132, 166
Motivation, 236–237
Motor skills, 112–115
Mourning (*see* Grief)
Music and rhythm, 116
Mutilation, fear of, 140, 148, 283, 284, 391
Mutuality, 79–80

N

Narcissism, 136, 139, 233–234, 309, 319
Narcotic abuse, 205
Nasal reactions, 247–248
National Council on Aging, 328–329
National Health Survey (1960), 157
Negativism, 78, 112–113
Neurosis, 44, 45, 47, 235–236
Neylon, Margaret, 229–230
Nightingale, Florence, 1–2, 3
Nocturnal emissions, 198
Nurse, 4, 5, 8, 20, 100–101
   future of nursing, 31, 126, 275, 401
   personal and professional qualifications, 2, 4, 8–9, 15, 19, 28, 35, 56–57, 62–63, 100, 107, 228, 275, 278, 281–282, 389–391, 401
Nurse, relationships of:
   with accident survivors, 386
   with adolescent, 196–225 *passim*
   with adult patient, 125, 232
   with child in middle childhood, 175–195 *passim*
   with elderly patient, 335–337, 341
   with intensive care unit patient, 255, 275, 277–278
   with mother and new-born child, 54–110 *passim*, 118–119
   with patient's family, 81, 134
   with patients in general, 1–41 *passim*, 81, 84, 241–242, 255, 279–294

Nurse, relationships of (*cont.*)
   with physican, 5, 295–300, 303
   with preschool child, 111–174 *passim*
   with surgical patient, 25, 263–266, 295–298, 327
   with terminal patients, 298, 354–356, 358–359, 383–384, 389, 398–399
Nursery school, 113, 116, 119, 125–126, 136
Nursing homes, 326, 337
Nursing practice:
   community health, 74–76, 82, 83, 109, 217–218, 327, 337
   in hospitals, 4, 5, 15, 195, 237, 275, 295–297
   psychiatric, 47
   school nurse, 136–177
Nutrition, 74

O

Obesity, 306, 307, 315–316
Object loss, 229
Occupational therapy, 221
Oedipus complex, 136–141, 175, 178, 180, 198, 203–204, 305, 336
Old age, 227, 322–353 *passim* (*see also* Hospitalization; Death)
Oral phase, 59–60, 77–80, 130, 175, 178, 306
Orphans, 70–71, 99–100
Orthogenic School, Chicago, 19
Overcompensation, 320
Overprotection, 134
Ovulation, 307

P

Pain, 25, 189, 192, 291, 359
Paramedical personnel, 5
"Parapraxes of everyday life," 44
Parents, 128, 183, 219, 305

Participant observation, 257
Patient (*see also* Infant; Child; Adolescence; Adult; Old Age)
  needs of, 4–6, 19, 30–31, 240, 249, 285
  nurse's communication with, 11, 357–358
  nurse's reactions to, 14, 37, 395
  reactions to illness, 3, 6, 8, 29–30, 36–41, 219–221, 240, 255, 273, 302–303, 391
  reactions to nurse, 3, 4, 11, 13, 15, 213–218, 224, 243, 280, 284, 291–292, 351
  relationship with physician, 304
  self-care, 193, 221, 256, 298–301, 304
Pearlman, Helen Harris, 12
Pediatric units, 75, 131, 132
Peer group, 125, 136, 203, 224
Perception, 38, 78, 180
Personality development, 45–46, 54
Phallic–urethral stage, 130, 138, 141
Physician, 5, 13–14, 37, 186, 262, 294–301, 303, 304, 362, 397
Piaget, Jean, 149
Platt Report (1959), 170
Play:
  child's, 61, 115–117, 136, 156
  developmental, 56, 115–116, 135–136, 152, 155
  in hospital, 128, 145, 149, 151, 153
Poisons, 332
Positive intervention, 31
Preconscious mind, 47
Pregnancy, 55, 57, 73–75, 103
Prenatal care, 74
Prepubertal period, 197
Preschool child, 111–174 *passim*
Privacy, patient's, 277, 290
Projection, 241–242
Protest, 77
Provence, Sally, 68–70
Prugh, D. G., 129
Puberty, 178, 196–197
Punishment, illness seen as, 139, 186

Psychiatry, 9, 19, 31, 85–86, 295–298, 335–336 (*see also* Psychoanalytic treatment; Psychotherapy)
Psychic disequilibrium, 272
Psychoanalytic treatment:
  applicability to the elderly, 335–336
  impact of the movement for, 7
  orientation of the present study, 400
  origin and basic principles of, 42–51 *passim*
  techniques, 12, 117, 180
Psychobiologic state, 272
Psychodynamics, 181, 401
Psychoneurosis, 44, 47, 235–236
Psychophysiological theory, 247
Psychosexual development, 122, 140
Psychosis, 233, 236, 331
Psychosocial development, 81, 85, 249
Psychosomatic medicine, 22, 243–245, 347, 400
Psychotherapy:
  nurse's role in, 15–16
  transference in, 10–11
  unavailability to elderly, 336–337

Q

Quint, Jeanne, 254, 355–356
  article by, 256–266

R

Radiation therapy, 258
Rahe, R. H., 247
Rapoport, Lydia, 7, 8–9
Rationalization, 243
Reaction formation, 239
Regression, 8, 114, 118, 129–130, 132, 160, 178, 183, 186, 193–195, 219–221, 239–241, 295, 301, 359, 380
Repression, 44, 140, 180–182, 235–236, 291, 382

Index 421

Retardation, 58, 73–74
Retirement, 324–325
Rhymes, Julina, 81–82
   article by, 102–109
Ribble, Margaret, 63, 121
Rigidity, 343
Ritual, 118, 287, 366–367
Robertson, James, 127, 166, 170, 178
Roles, 204, 352 (*see also* Nurse, relationships of)
   of adolescent, 204
   of nurse, 5, 57, 282, 390–391
   of patient, 3, 5, 291
Rome, Howard P., 255
   article by, 275–278
Rubenstein, B. B., 247, 306–307
Rubin, Reva, 58–59, 63

S

Sadism, 128, 239, 289
Sandbox, 116
Saunders, Cicely, 389, 397
Schofield, William, 31
School, adjustment to, 136, 176
Schulman, Sam, 382
Sears, R. R., 122
Sedatives, 205
Selesnick, Sheldon T., 247
Self, concept of, 56, 111, 137–139, 204, 217, 232, 271, 281, 313
   origins of, 56
Self-awareness, 34, 225
Selling, L. S., 64
Selye, Hans, 245, 247
Senility, 329–330 (*see also* Old age)
Senn, Milton J., 62, 89, 145, 210
   developmental charts, 90–93; 146–148, 183–185, 211–213
Sensory deprivation, 220
Separation anxiety, 119–120, 129, 140, 145, 167, 176, 181, 193–194, 215–217, 283, 305, 319, 364 (*see also* Anxiety)
Sexuality, 75, 175, 198–201, 333

Sibling rivalry, 45, 48, 56, 153, 391
Siggens, Lorraine, 371
Simmons, Leo, 322–323
Sleep, 118
Smith, Dorothy W., 5
Social case work, 31–36, 74, 100–101, 169
Social Security, 325, 328
Socialization, 175, 329
Solnit, Albert J., 62, 73–74, 76, 84, 89, 145, 167, 210
   developmental charts, 90–93, 146–148, 183–185, 211–213
Spiegel, John, 361
Spitz, René, 33, 45, 66, 70, 90, 162
Stagnation, opposed to generativity, 227, 310
Starr, Paul, 327–328
Stoll, Carolyn P., 183
   article by, 186–195
Stress, 25, 40, 130, 186, 228, 245–247, 327–328, 401
Sublimation, 175, 242–243
Sucking reflex, 59
Suicide, 204, 316, 352, 393–394
Sullivan, Harry Stack, 11
Superego, 47–51, 140–141, 235–236
Suppression, 237, 291
Surgery, 25 232–233, 258, 278, 288–290
Symptom formation, 51, 297–298

T

Tavistock Child Development Research Unit, London, 3, 127n
Teething, 78
Temper tantrums, 114, 134
Thumb-sucking, 130–131
Tiza, Veronica B., 72
Toddler stage, 78, 111, 118, 140, 146–148
Toilet training, 116, 120–122, 125
Touch, sense of, 61, 62, 327

Index

Toxic agents and elderly, 332
Tranquilizers, 205
Transference, 8–16, 19, 281
 countertransference, 14–15
"Transitional objects," 117
Trauma, 134–135, 228
Treuting, T., 247–248
Trust, basic, according to Erikson, 78–79
Tsukisoi, 22
Tuberculosis, 8
Tufts–New England Medical Center, 167–168
Twins, 58

U

Unconscious mind, 44, 45, 47–48, 283
Unwed mother, 57
"Up-privileges," 216–217

V

Venereal disease, 204
Verbal development, 111, 115
Verbal slips, 44, 47
Verbalization, 180, 182
Violence, 154
Vision, impairment of, 326–327
Voluntary control, 111
"Vulnerable child" syndrome, 204

W

Weaning, 118
Winnicott, D. W., 117
Withdrawal, 241, 299, 330
Wolff, H. G., 248
Wolff, Sula, 133, 134, 248
Women's liberation, 311
Worchester, Alfred, 397